STARS IN THE SKY MORNING

STARS IN THE SKY
MORNING

Collective Plays of Newfoundland and Labrador

Edited

with an Introduction by

Helen Peters

Music prepared for publication by

Sandy Morris

kiLLick press
an imprint of Creative Publishers

St. John's, Newfoundland
1996

KILLICK PRESS, A CREATIVE PUBLISHERS IMPRINT
a division of 10366 Newfoundland Limited
a Robinson-Blackmore Printing & Publishing associated company
P.O. Box 8660, St. John's, Newfoundland A1B 3T7
Telephone (709) 722-8500   Fax (709) 722-2228

Cover painting, "The Play's the Thing" by Graham Howcroft, 1995, photographed by Ned Pratt.

Canadian Cataloguing in Publication Data
  Main entry under title:

  Stars in the sky morning

    ISBN 1-895387-74-4

  1. Canadian drama (English)—Newfoundland. *
  2. Canadian drama (English)—20th century. *
  I. Peters, Helen, 1942- II. Series.

  PS8315.5.N5S72 1995 C812'.5408'09718 C95-950099-5
  PR9198.2.N52S72 1995

PREFACE

The plays in this volume were created in the collective theatre movement which began in Newfoundland in 1973 with the Mummers Troupe and CODCO, and in Labrador in 1975 when the Creative Arts Festival was established. The collective play caught the imagination of Newfoundland and Labrador audiences and established norms that have characterised popular theatre in the province for over twenty years. It is tempting to dismiss these collectives simply as a popular form, but such dismissal would be misguided. The collectives have been popular because they dealt, in accomplished theatrical style, with social, political and historical issues that concerned the people of Canada's newest province. They put our culture on stage for us and restored the sense of pride we had lost when our parents, out of economic need, had voted away Newfoundland's independence.

While Newfoundland and Labrador's status as a province of Canada, since 1949, took away from our former sense of nationhood, it gave in return an increased ability for Newfoundlanders to leave the province in order to return home with new knowledge, skills and experience. Collective plays were a combination of the "matter" of our complex social, political and historical realities, and the "form," which arose out of the widespread Newfoundland and Labrador tradition of entertaining through concert, music, recitation, storytelling and dance, together with the techniques that young players brought home from professional theatre study and practical theatrical experience in Europe and North America.

Over the years, many collective groups formed in St. John's and performed one or several plays. Membership in these groups ranged from fleeting to stable and players frequently contributed to more than one group. The early to mid 1970s saw the beginning of indigenous professional Newfoundland theatre based in St. John's and led by the Newfoundland Travelling Theatre Company and the two collective groups—the Mummers Troupe and CODCO. The 1970s, the 1980s and the early 1990s saw the development of a flourishing professional theatre in St. John's in which collective creation played a key role. Among the collective groups which contributed to this renaissance of drama, along with the Mummers Troupe and

CODCO, are Rising Tide Theatre, Sheila's Brush Theatre Company, Resource Centre for the Arts (RCA) Theatre Company, Wonderbolt Circus Theatre and Corey and Wade's Playhouse. In Labrador, of the several groups performing in the annual Creative Arts Festival, Innuinuit Theatre Company, which has been comprised of various members of Innu Theatre Company of Davis Inlet, Nalujuk Players of Hopedale and Ulu Players of Nain, is the most widely known.

The plays in this volume are among the best known works produced by established collective groups or written by actor-play-wrights who learned their craft and produced their plays in the collective tradition. I regard each play in this volume as a star in the sky morning. Each has contributed particular light that has helped to establish the professional theatre which now exists in the province of Newfoundland and Labrador.

The title of this volume, *Stars in the Sky Morning: Collective Plays of Newfoundland and Labrador*, is borrowed, with permission, from one of the plays, *Stars in the Sky Morning*, written by Rhonda Payne with Jane Dingle and Jan Henderson. That title is itself taken from the quotation which forms the epilogue to the play that bears its name. The quotation deals with the attitude to work that characterises Newfoundlanders. I am quoting from the passage which, to me, summarizes the efforts and attitudes of the fifty-four playwrights who wrote and acted in the plays that constitute this volume, the musicians who helped them, the stage crews who enabled them to strut their stuff and the technicians and photographers who enhanced and recorded what they did.

> **PEG:** How hard did people work. My heavens, you couldn't believe it this day and age. If people today had to go back to what we did, it would kill them. Yes it would, it would kill them. Because, my dear, we didn't work we slaved. There was no such thing as any hours of the day's work, it was just from the stars in the sky morning 'til the stars in the sky night. And then you didn't have it all done. Wait for daylight to come, start all over again. But, my dear, 'twas only fun. We were really living then. Every day our work come to us and we done it and we wasn't tired or nothing.

Few collectives have been created by professional groups in Newfoundland during recent years although the will to create them still exists. The economic reality is that collectives, with their research and writing components done by casts which number up to eight, and with their frequent reliance on original music composition, are expensive to create and produce. Lack of funding, therefore, has influenced the movement in Newfoundland, as elsewhere, into scripted plays with small casts and single-author-acted performances.

ACKNOWLEDGEMENTS

The editor of a volume of collectively written plays owes many debts. There are the playwrights who created the works and agreed to their publication. In true collective spirit, they helped the publication process by reading my drafts of their scripts and mailing annotated copies to me, or, by sitting around my dining room table correcting faulty dialogue, restoring missing lines, providing stage directions and recreating something of the atmosphere of the play which has been of incalculable help in the editorial process. I therefore wish to acknowledge the assistance of the following: Pauline Angnatok, Kay Anonsen, Julius Barbour, Frank Barry, Mercedes Barry, Pierre Beaupre, Rick Boland, Chris Brookes, Donna Butt, Norma Denney, Mary Dicker, Jane Dingle, Philip Dinn, Brian Downey, Olivia Edmunds, Barbara Flowers, David Fox, Sheilagh Guy, Jan Henderson, Jenny Holwell, Flip Janes, Andy Jones, Andrew Karpik, John Koop, Bernice Lucy, Beni Malone, Rick Mercer, Catherine Mitsuk, Kevin Noble, Susan Nochasak, Mark Oakley, Dave Panting, Geoff Panting, Jim Payne, Rhonda Payne, Wayne Piercy, Connie Pijogge, Jeff Pitcher, Terry Rielly, David Ross, Val Ryan, Rick Salutin, Molly Shiwak, José E. Silva, Janis Spence, Paul Steffler, John Taylor, Greg Thomey, Glen Tilley, Beverly Tuglavina, Agnes Walsh, Mary Walsh, Bill Wheaton and Paulette Winters.

Other people involved in the production of these plays have helped too—Lois Brown retrieved the pre-production script of *On Edge* from her competent filing system. Andy Jones has allowed me to print a revised version of "Plays for Publishing," a talk he gave at the 1992 Workshop on Newfoundland Theatre Research held at Memorial University and published in *Proceedings from the Workshop on Newfoundland Theatre Research*, edited by Denyse Lynde, Helen Peters and Richard Buehler (St. John's: Memorial University, 1993) pp. 117-18. I wish to thank the following photographers for permission to include their photographs in this volume: Mary-Lynn Bernard, Mannie Buchheit, Dick Green, Janet Hannaford, Lynda Hendrickson, Peggy Hogan and Jim Winter. Two plays are illustrated by sketches: Julian Lawrence drew the sketches for *My Three Dads* and Bill Wheaton drew those for *Braindead*.

The preparation of musical scores was done by Sandy Morris who prepared camera-ready copy with the assistance of the musicians who had worked on the original shows: Geoff Panting, Jim Payne, Terry Rielly, Paul Steffler and Glen Tilley. They were assisted by musicians Charlie Barfoot and Wayne Warren. The cover is an acrylic painting on board measuring 24 by 36 inches by Graham Howcroft commissioned for this book and photographed by Ned Pratt. The production of camera-ready copy for this book has been the responsibility of Arlene Coffen. Production assistance was provided by Polaris Design.

Many members of the arts community have been of help in this venture. In addition to widespread support and interest among members of the community and the particular interest and timely assistance of those directly involved in the plays contained in this book, I have benefitted from the advice of several individual artists. These include members of the Advisory Board of the Theatre Anthologies Project: Rick Boland, Chris Brookes, Lois Brown, Andy Jones and Pete Soucy who gave support and advice on what plays should be included. Several playwrights gave generously of their time in order to ensure that introductory material and production histories are accurate; these include: Frank Barry, Rick Boland, Chris Brookes, Lois Brown, Donna Butt, Brian Downey, Flip Janes, Andy Jones, Beni Malone, Kevin Noble, Rhonda Payne, David Ross, John Taylor and Bill Wheaton. Greg Malone, White and Bob Joy of CODCO encouraged my efforts. Tom Cahill, Eric West, Bryan Hennessey, Dave Weiser, Dudley Cox, Paul O'Neill, Andrew Younghusband, John Moyes and Peter Gard gave me much necessary information and other assistance. Ann Anderson of the Canada/Newfoundland COOPERATION Agreement on Cultural Industries and Randy Follett and Reg Winsor of the Newfoundland and Labrador Arts Council provided practical assistance. Tim Borlase and Noreen Heighton of the Labrador Creative Arts Festival introduced me to the collective theatre of Labrador. My husband Henry Tremblay accompanied me to many theatrical events and encouraged my work in theatre research.

"A Sealer's Reply to His Wife" from *A Glimpse of Newfoundland in Poetry and Pictures* is printed with permission of J. Looker Ltd. "In Courtship There Lies Pleasure" and "The Ship That Never Came" from *Songs of the Newfoundland Outports* by Kenneth Peacock are reproduced with the permission of the Canadian Museum of Civilization. "The Praise of Christmas," from *The Oxford Book of Carols*, © 1964 Oxford University Press is reproduced with permission of the Press. "As Shepherds Watched Their Flocks by Night," from *Folksongs in a Trinity Bay Community*, is reproduced with the permission of Gordon Cox.

Memorial University has provided many services required in the completion of this book. The staff of the Centre for Newfoundland Studies (CNS) Archives, Bert Riggs, Gail Weir and Linda White, have cheerfully and efficiently provided me with play transcripts and other documents without which this volume could not have been produced. The CNS Archives also provided the photographs of *Terras de Bacalhau*. Linda Russell of University Relations gave assistance with graphics. Kathy Duarte of the Department of French and Spanish, together with José E. Silva, gave assistance with Portuguese in *Terras de Bacalhau*. Renée Husk, Bev Dalton and Sherry Baker from the Department of English Language and Literature keyed the existing play transcripts into computer format which allowed the editing process to begin. Doris Watts and Maxine Coates of Printing Services complied with my requests for the photocopies that posted to playwrights in St. John's and winged to those in Hopedale, Nain, Halifax, Montreal, Toronto, Peterborough, Thunder Bay, Edmonton, Vancouver, Kamloops and Surrey, BC.

The editing of this volume owes its initiative to the Workshop on Newfoundland Theatre Research at Memorial University in June 1992 which was attended by local theatre practitioners and theatre researchers from Canada and Germany. The participants, spurred on by Andy Jones' list of unpublished Newfoundland play scripts, encouraged the workshop co-organisers, Denyse Lynde and Helen Peters, to establish a Theatre Anthologies Project in order to publish two anthologies each of ten plays. This volume and *Voices from the Landwash*, an anthology of single-author scripted plays, edited by Denyse Lynde are the result. The preparation of both volumes has been financially assisted by the Canada/Newfoundland COOPERATION Agreement on Cultural Industries, the Newfoundland and Labrador Arts Council and the Social Sciences and Humanities Council of Canada (SSHRCC) funds internally administered by Memorial University. In addition, *Stars in the Sky Morning* benefitted from the student support financed by Challenge '94 and the Memorial Undergraduate Career Experience Program (MUCEP) programs. Preparation of the musical scores has been funded by the Canada/Newfoundland COOPERATION Agreement on Cultural Industries and the generosity of Rex Anthony. Costs of publication have been defrayed by a grant from the Publication Subvention Board of Memorial University.

I wish to thank graduate student Marc Otto for transcribing the text of *On Edge* from the single existing video tape of a performance, and undergraduate students: Charmaine Skinner for finding much of the material needed for the production histories and introduction, Gwen Thistle for skilled and tireless computer work to bring the play texts into a consistent format and for pains-taking proof reading, and Rhona Buchan for detailed proof reading and sound advice based on her professional theatre experience. Their work has been invaluable to me and has helped to make the text as accurate and reliable as possible; for the almost inevitable errors remaining, I am responsible.

CONTENTS

INTRODUCTION

Development

Collective theatre in Newfoundland began in 1973 and in Labrador in 1975 in response to internal and external influences. The external influences include the avant garde experimental theatre movements during the 1960s and 70s in western Europe and North America which saw theatre move away from the single-authorial controlling voice toward collective improvisation. Closer to home was the rise of alternative theatre in Canada during the 1970s, sometimes known as documentary drama and agit prop theatre. Much of this drama was collectively written. These movements have been well documented and need no further discussion here.[1]

Internal influences on the development of Newfoundland collective theatre have also been explored but these can stand further discussion. Chris Brookes and Alan Filewod have written on the influence of the old Newfoundland mummering tradition on the philosophy and practice of the Mummers Troupe in the development of the highly political collective theatre for which the troupe was known throughout Canada.[2] The Mummers Troupe was founded in 1972 by Chris Brookes and his partner Lynn Lunde. Brookes, a Newfoundlander, had studied at the Yale School of Drama and worked in both experimental theatre at Simon Fraser University in British Columbia and alternative theatre in Toronto before returning to Newfoundland in 1970. Touring a puppet show in rural Newfoundland with Lynn Lunde, he became convinced of the superiority of outport culture over the social pretension (as he regarded it) of St. John's society. He was intrigued by the remnants of the ancient mummers play which were performed in a few Newfoundland outports as "the rhymes" and by the nearly dormant tradition of mummering which had been banned by law in 1861. "The rhymes" contained elements of light overcoming darkness, surviving the winter solstice to herald in the new year, driving away the evil with good and restoring the sick to health. The tradition of mummering itself had elements of misrule—of workers confronting managers as equals on the managers' home ground, of workers intimidating managers and exercising control over their property and of the poor imposing their will on the rich—all temporarily, of course. Hence the Mummers Troupe was born in September 1972 as a left-wing, socially active, community oriented collective theatre group that aimed to stage events which would effect social change in Newfoundland. Its founding members were Chris Brookes, Lynn Lunde, John Doyle and Kevin Pittman. The troupe's first play was the *Traditional Newfoundland Mummers Play* (first performed 26 December 1972) and the first Mummers Troupe collectively-written play which was based on the cast's research was known variously as *Newfoundland Night, Cod on a Stick* and *Newfoundland Dressup*. Diane Olsen and Sandy Cantwell joined the group for this play which opened in St John's in May 1973. For the touring version of *Newfoundland Night*, the cast was Chris Brookes, Donna Butt, Christopher Knight, Paul Sametz, Andy Thompson and Mary Walsh, who toured the island by van and coastal boat from June to August in 1973. The Mummers Troupe had begun a life that would create and produce nineteen collective plays before folding in September 1982. They had also begun a tradition of fleeting, intermittent and long-term associations of individual actors with the group.

Although Brookes felt that the strength of Newfoundland lay in the outports rather than in the capital city, he recognised an urban influence in the development of socially aware popular theatre in Newfoundland. This influence was found in the ballads and satiric musicals of Johnny Burke, a well-known broadside balladeer who made his living selling song sheets of his original compositions on the streets of turn-of-the-century St. John's.[3] Burke assembled a loosely knit semi-professional group of performers who performed his parodies and burlesques which frequently mocked the legitimate theatre produced by the city's social élite. Burke restaged scenes in a local setting and used similar or identical music, substituting his own lyrics. Shortly after the performance of a British operetta, *The Geisha*, staged by Charles (later Sir Charles) Hutton around 1900, Burke opened his satiric *The Topsail Geisha* in which the original Japanese chorus was transformed into a chorus of Topsail (pronounced "tops'l") fishermen fanning themselves with dried salt fish. As Brookes remarks,

> John Burke was not what you'd call a political activist. But in the context of turn-of-the-century Newfoundland society his plays had an implicit political impact. He pricked the pretensions of the developing mercantile élite in its attempts to replace indigenous cultural expression with a highbrow 'official' art. His satire was an artistic response to the tide of his times, a caricature of social and economic imbalance. Audiences loved his loaded metaphors.

In 1977, the Mummers Troupe staged a play about Johnny Burke, who died in 1930, called *The Bard of Prescott Street*. The cast was Jane Dingle, Brian Hennessey, Ron Hynes, Bob Joy, Janet Michael, David Ross and Mary Walsh, with Chris Brookes as director.

In the days before Johnny Burke, St. John's boasted a regular supply of both imported and domestic drama. The city hosted plays performed by members of the Royal British Navy in colonial days, and in the nineteenth century the city was included on the route of American and Canadian professional actors who played the island while on tours of eastern Canada. In addition, early in the nineteenth century the very strong amateur theatre that Johnny Burke would satirize emerged. Outside St. John's, Newfoundlanders entertained themselves with shows and concerts held annually in church or school halls in the hundreds of outports scattered along six thousand miles of coastline. Ches Skinner, who has researched amateur theatre in Newfoundland, reports that community concerts, revue/variety shows, were common in every outport and town until as late as the 1960s. He writes,

> During the nineteenth century and up to the time when they began to die out, concerts were important theatrical events which were produced to raise money to support institutions such as church and school, and to provide social assistance, and in so doing contributed significantly to the character and development of the communities. It was the concert which provided a forum for people in the outports to get together once or twice a year to perform songs, dialogues, and recitations and, generally, to celebrate the holidays and to have a good time. Any comprehensive study of Newfoundland theatre must include extensive work on this particular folk activity, for, in many ways, it was the variety concert which helped establish attitudes towards theatre and therefore enabled groups such as CODCO and the Mummers to make in-roads during the 1970s; they were riding on a tradition of popular entertainment which had been around since the nineteenth century."[4]

These concerts or shows were significant "home-grown" entertainments which, while they may have included brief imported scripted sketches amongst their song, dance, recitation and story telling, basically arose from the capacity to invent and entertain within the community that produced them.

There is another important factor in the establishment of the collective play as a major force in the development of Newfoundland professional indigenous theatre. That factor was the coming together in the early 1970s of a number of the actors who would play major roles in the subsequent development of Newfoundland collective theatre. An initial meeting place was Eastport where a summer theatre festival took place between 1970 and 1972. A number of amateur theatre groups began to stage plays in the community which was a five-hour drive from St. John's and which boasted a fine beach. It attracted young actors many of whom went on to become professional. In 1971 Chris Brookes and Lynn Lunde, who were

touring rural Newfoundland with their puppet show, met up with
Dudley Cox at Eastport. That meeting was instrumental in leading
to the establishment of the Newfoundland Travelling Theatre Company (NTTC) which staged its first performance in July 1972 and
which offered most aspiring Newfoundland actors their first professional acting experience. The company was founded by Dudley Cox,
a Welshman who had moved to Newfoundland from Montreal, and
who—prior to establishing NTTC—had worked in St. John's amateur theatre and had initiated a strong development of theatre in
Newfoundland high schools. He collaborated with Dave Weiser, a
Montrealer who moved to Newfoundland and who continues to
make Newfoundland his home. With Dudley as director and Dave as
financial manager, NTTC toured Newfoundland communities from
1972 until 1976 when it folded because of financial difficulties. The
company employed overall more than two dozen Newfoundland
actors, various professional actors from the mainland and various
technical and stage crew. It toured during all seasons of the year
with each tour typically covering twenty to twenty-five communities. The company travelled with sets, which occasionally had to be
cut down to fit into the dimensions of the stages provided in the
variety of schools, town halls, church basements, etc. which were
the company's venue. Travel was by van (boat where necessary),
meals and accommodation were provided and the actors were paid.
Initially, the plays presented were from the international repertoire,
the 1972 season consisted of *See How They Run* and *The Wizard of
Oz*, but rapidly, NTTC interspersed such plays with a "Punch and
Judy" series and other plays written by Dudley Cox, plays from
Newfoundland playwrights such as Grace Butt, Michael Cook and
Tom Cahill. Grace Butt wrote *A Newfoundland Pageant*, which
NTTC toured to Labrador as well as across the island. Among the
actors who started with the Newfoundland Travelling Theatre Com-
pany are Rick Boland, Jane Dingle, Andy and Cathy Jones, Bob Joy,
Beni and Greg Malone, Kevin Noble, Diane Olsen, Rhonda Payne,
Paul Sametz, the late Tommy Sexton, Greg Thomey, Charlie Tomlin-
son and Mary Walsh.

Fans of CODCO will have realized that the six original members
of the group, as well as Andy Jones and Bob Joy who would later join
them, were all employed in the Newfoundland Travelling Theatre
Company. CODCO performed the group's first collective play, *Cod
on a Stick*, in Toronto in October 1973. In February 1974, CODCO
performed the play in St. John's and during April and May the group
toured twenty-three settlements in Newfoundland and Labrador.
Their success was phenomenal. The second play *Sickness, Death and
Beyond the Grave* (1974), followed by *Das Capital: Or What do You
Want to See the Harbour for Anyway?* (1975), *Do You Want to Smell
My ... Pocket Crumbs?* (1975) and *The Tale Ends* (1976) were im-
mensely popular in Newfoundland and on the Canadian mainland.
CODCO disbanded in 1976, but in late 1977 five members of the

group (Andy Jones and Bob Joy were not involved), got together to create the collective *Who Said Anything About Tea?* (1978). From the late 1970s to the mid 1980s CODCO Ltd. remained as a production company, producing individual and group works by CODCO members and other performers. CODCO reunited as a group, without Bob Joy and Diane Olsen, to perform on CBC Television in a weekly series that ran from 1988 to 1993.[5] In 1993, two CODCO members, Mary Walsh and Cathy Jones, teamed up with Rick Mercer and Greg Thomey, who are also contributing playwrights in this book, to write and perform the ongoing weekly CBC Television show "This Hour Has 22 Minutes."

If Chris Brookes intended to oust the Newfoundland establishment with the Mummers Troupe, CODCO, Newfoundland's leading edge collective comedy group, wanted to make audiences laugh at their pointed and typically dark humour. CODCO produced a black satire on a range of political and social issues in Newfoundland and in Newfoundlanders' relations among themselves with their fellow Canadians. The group always aimed to entertain as well as to satirize and many of the barbs of their political comment were ignored by audiences because of the laughter CODCO generated, especially outside Newfoundland. CODCO did not adopt the overtly political stance of the Mummers. The group's style was to snub the noses of those in authority and make audiences laugh. The point of their satire has not been missed in Newfoundland; noted humorist and playwright Ray Guy has called members of CODCO the children of Johnny Burke.

As important as the Mummers Troupe, Newfoundland Travelling Theatre Company and CODCO were in establishing an indigenous professional theatre in Newfoundland, there were other contributing factors that predated the founding of these groups and to some extent prepared the way for them. First of all, resident professional theatre began in St. John's in 1951, when Leslie Yeo, who had performed in St. John's as a member of Birmingham's Alexandra Players in 1947, and a group of fourteen actors migrated to Newfoundland and established themselves in St. John's as the London Players. From their first production in October 1951 to March 1957, when the company folded, the British troupe performed 107 productions of well-known British and American plays. In addition to the plays, the London Players staged an annual locally-written satiric review of the year's events in Newfoundland in which the company was joined by St. John's amateur actors.

The professionalization of indigenous Newfoundland theatre was also aided by the establishment in 1949 of the Provincial Drama Festival and its parent the Dominion Drama Festival. This development was of particular benefit to playwrights. The festivals gave Newfoundland amateur groups a venue in which to perform Newfoundland plays along with plays from other places, in annual competitions both provincially and nationally. The first year of competition was 1950. Although, over the years, the majority of plays performed were British, Irish or American (and latterly Canadian), within two years the first local play, Frederick R. Emerson's dramatization of Newfoundland outport life, *Proud Kate Sullivan*, was performed by Northcliffe Drama Club of Grand Falls (1952), and four years later Ted Russell's *The Holdin' Ground* (Grand Falls, 1956), won the provincial festival prize for best play. This success was followed by a series of Newfoundland plays performed by drama clubs throughout the province which include Ted Russell's *Groundswell* (Grand Falls, 1962), Tom Cahill's adaptation of Harold Horwood's novel *Tomorrow will be Sunday* (St. John's, 1967), Russell's *Holdin' Ground* again (Gander, 1967), an adaptation of Hammond Innes' novel, *The Land God Gave to Cain* (Labrador City, 1971), Michael Cook's *Colour the Flesh the Colour of Dust* (St. John's, 1971) and Tom Cahill's *Jody* (Gander, 1972). Tom Cahill also kept alive the London Players' tradition of an annual satiric revue for many years in Corner Brook with the annual Playmakers Company's production called "Home Brew" during the 1950s and early 1960s.

Between 1973 and 1994 around two-dozen plays written by Newfoundlanders were staged by participants in Provincial Drama Festivals. In addition to new plays by Ted Russell, Michael Cook and Tom Cahill, works by playwrights such as the non-resident but Newfoundland-born David French (*Leaving Home, 1949, Jitters* and *Of the Fields Lately*), Al Pittman (*A Rope Against the Sun, West Moon*), Katherine J. Pottle (*The Fishermen's Ordeal, Relocation*) and Grace Butt (*New Lands, Wheel in the Middle of a Wheel*) were performed. In the 1980s, Labrador groups produced Clar Doyle's *Not Recommended for Children* (Labrador City, 1981), Ian Strachan's *For You, Dear Hubbard* (Goose Bay, 1982), Leo Furey and D. Hickey's *Spirit of the Husk* (Nain, 1984) and in 1983 a collectively created play, *Sinnatomangnik R.E.M.*, by Nunaksoamiut Players of Nain, Labrador.

Newfoundland professional actors also gained early experience in the provincial Drama Festivals. Rick Boland, who had directed in high school drama festivals performed first with the Corner Brook Playmakers. At the 1974 Provincial Drama Festival in which the Playmakers were performing MacLeish's *J.B.*, he saw Michael Cook's play *Jacob's Wake*. He describes the experience as "mind blowing" and of great significance in developing his interest in becoming a professional performer in Newfoundland theatre.

On the island of Newfoundland the strong tradition of theatre ensured the successful birth of professional indigenous theatre in the form of the early collectives. In Labrador collective theatre got its start when the Creative Arts Festival was founded there in 1975. The Festival was initiated by Tim Borlase and Noreen Heighton, who still organize the event. Original plays, collectively written by students and directed by their teachers are performed during a week-long, non-competitive festival. The event draws together in Goose Bay, each November, groups of up to eight students accompanied by their teacher-directors from some sixteen schools in settlements scattered throughout coastal and central Labrador and the western border between Labrador and Quebec. Students from several of the schools in Goose Bay and the adjacent town of Happy Valley also participate so the total number of performers is close to two hundred. Two principles express the mandate of this Festival since its inception; these are: "That there is an expressed need for young people resident in Labrador—be they Innu, Inuit, Settler or Newcomer—to know their past, and their role in the developing Labrador community, to be active in the preservation of their heritage, and to be arbiters of their future" and "That there is a need to provide individuals with an opportunity to come together and share their creative experience. Through such a gathering, the geographical and social isolation of Labrador would be overcome, and the participants would become aware of the varied and composite lifestyles in Labrador."

The plays in the Creative Arts Festival are adjudicated by a professional animateur. In addition to the actors and their teacher-directors some fifteen to twenty professional people involved in the arts industry and cultural community—writers, publishers, visual artists, book illustrators, actors, dancers, story tellers, aboriginal drummers, etc.—from the island of Newfoundland and mainland Canadian cities attend the Festival and hold workshops in their disciplines and specialities. This Festival, because it provides diverse professional external influences and an ongoing opportunity for practice, has fostered the development of high quality drama among Labrador residents of all ages.

Collective Groups and Their Work

The Mummers Troupe (1972-1982)

The Mummers Troupe performed the first collectively-written Newfoundland play in 1973. Their first, and most frequently produced play, the *Traditional Newfoundland Mummers Play* (1972), contained many of the characteristics that defined the troupe's social and political philosophy. From the *Mummers Play*, which was first performed in private homes, the Mummers Troupe, in their ten-year span produced thirty-nine productions of twenty-two new plays, nineteen of which were collectively created. Often the collectives were created and performed right in the places where social and political unrest was occurring. Best known collectives include *Gros Mourn* (1973), a play about land expropriation to accommodate federal park construction in western Newfoundland; *Buchans a Mining Town/Company Town* (1974), a play about labour-management relations in a central Newfoundland mining town; *East End Story* (1975), on urban development in downtown St. John's;[6] *Dying Hard* (1975), on miners' lung diseases; *I.W.A. Newfoundland Loggers' Strike of 1959* (1975), co-written with Rick Salutin, on the bitter and violent International Wood Workers' Association strike in 1959; *What's that Got to do with the Price of Fish?* (1976), co-written with Susan Perly, on economic injustices in the east coast fishery; *Silakepat Kissinane: Weather Permitting* (1977), on social issues in Inuit-white settler communities on the northern Labrador coast; *They Club Seals, Don't They?* (1978), on the circus which international protest groups were making of the traditional Newfoundland seal hunt; *Some Slick* (1979), a cabaret on the social problems which proposed oil development could initiate; and *Makin' Time with the Yanks* (1981), on the influx of American servicemen in war-time St. John's. Several of these collectives toured Newfoundland and others toured the Canadian mainland.

Membership in the Mummers Troupe was both fluid and stable. Chris Brookes lists a total of 106 stars of the company.[7] CODCO's Tommy Sexton and Diane Olsen were present in the opening years, Bob Joy performed once and Mary Walsh appeared occasionally in Mummers Troupe productions. Co-founder Lynn Lunde who had moved into administration of the troupe left in 1976 and her place was taken by Ann Anderson. Donna Butt who had been with the troupe since 1973 and Rick Boland who had joined in 1974, together with Wayne McNiven and Madeline Williams left the Mummers Troupe after *The Price of Fish* to form the short-lived Community Stage. David Ross and Terry Rielly joined the troupe in 1976. They stayed for the 1978 production of *They Club Seals, Don't They?* a performance which saw Donna Butt lured back to perform with the troupe for the last time. Chris Brookes himself left his position as artistic director with the Mummers Troupe after the close of the *Some Slick* Canadian tour in 1980. His position was taken by Rhonda Payne, who had joined the troupe in 1974. Other performers who have contributed to the works in this book appeared at least occasionally with the Mummers Troupe; these include Kay Anonsen, Jane Dingle, Brian Downey, Sheilagh Guy, Jan Henderson, Beni Malone, Jim Payne, Jeff Pitcher, Janis Spence, Paul Steffler, and Greg Thomey. In the last years of the Mummers Troupe, the company moved away from creating collectives and of being a coherent theatre company. It became more of a production company producing scripted plays such as Al Pittman's *West Moon* (1980), Arvo MacMillan's *Billy Max in Progress* (1981) and Michael Cook's *Tiln* (1981) with a mixture of performers who had appeared previously with the Mummers Troupe, such as Rick Boland, and new Newfoundland-born performers in the city.

The Mummers Troupe gave St. John's what is still its newest theatre in 1976 when Chris Brookes and Lynn Lunde, purchased the Longshoremen's Protective Union Hall (LSPU Hall, now known simply as the Hall) and converted it into a two-hundred seat theatre. Initial plans to buy the Hall jointly with the Newfoundland Travelling Theatre Company and CODCO and subsequent plans to buy the building with the St. John's Community Planning Association as co-buyer fell through and in the fall of 1976, the newly renovated, under-financed and largely unsubsidised theatre opened. It was owned and operated by the non-profit organization, Resource Foundation for the Arts, which also owned and operated the Mummers Troupe. The aim of Resource Foundation for the Arts was to run the Hall as a community space, paying particular attention to the labour movement (the Longshoremen's Union maintained their office in the building until 1983), and to provide subsidised and unsubsidised theatre space (according to need) to local theatre and music groups. Running costs of the building were met mostly by the Mummers Troupe from their operating grants. Over time, things fell apart and in December 1979 after some five months of often acrimonious debate and uncertainty, operation of the Hall passed from Resource Foundation for the Arts to the Resource Centre for the Arts (RCA). RCA was also non-profit and it was a more widely based community group than Resource Foundation had been. Its mandate opened membership in the organization to any resident of the province with interest in the Centre's aims. A proviso of the transfer was that the Mummers Troupe should be the resident company of the theatre for a period of three years effective from 1 November 1979. The Hall was to be run by members of RCA's Board of Directors, members of Memorial University's Extension Services and volunteers. The first performance in the Hall under the new RCA management was the Sheila's Brush production, *Jaxxmas (Jack's Christmas)* which opened 28 December 1979.

They Club Seals, Don't They? (1978)

The large majority of Mummers Troupe productions bear the characteristic stamp of Chris Brookes in terms of their presentation as well as in terms of their political outlook. Brookes had grown up in Newfoundland, received his degree in theatre from Yale, experienced American alternative and popular theatre in Julian Beck and Judith Malina's Living Theater and the San Francisco Mime Troupe, and he had been involved in Canadian alternative theatre in British Columbia and Toronto. Through the duration of his tenure with the Mummers Troupe, Brookes hired both local and mainland actors. His productions are marked by the use of features such as rapid change, multi-media, dramatic sketch, monologue, song, dance, multiple role playing and mime that characterize alternative theatre, and to these features Brookes added puppetry and clowning. He also, as much as was possible, transformed the theatre into the milieu of the action of the play. The experience was less one of theatre goer in theatre than as (Brookes hoped) spectator-participant in an event in which change could occur or, at least, could begin to happen. Hence in *They Club Seals, Don't They?* the audience is the circus audience watching the traditional Newfoundland event that has become the annual sealing circus. By means of printed cards indicating the pros and cons of the seal hunt which each spectator finds on the seat, members of the audience are invited to become involved in the issues in the play and to debate them with the cast at the end of the show.

The action of the play comprises a short history of the settling and developing of Newfoundland which highlights how difficult the life of the little people—the fisherman-swiler (sealer) and his family—is. Juxtaposed are the contrasting lifestyles of a mainland factory employee and a Newfoundland fisherman; the machinations of scientists in their determination of seal populations and the approach of Mother Nature; and Greenpeace action as a clown show and the frightening reality of death on the ice. The play is rounded out and tempered by the songs written for it and performed live by musicians who also participate in the action. *They Club Seals, Don't They?* is representative of much of the political theatre collectively created by the Mummers Troupe under the direction of Chris Brookes. It is a poignant, funny and abrasive dramatic statement on the economically deprived state of the Newfoundland fishery and sealing industry, and on the plight of Newfoundlanders and Labradorians who try to make their living from the sea.

They Club Seals, Don't They drew large audiences on its Canadian tour and return to St. John's in 1978 and its controversial message attracted extensive positive and negative media attention across Canada.

Stars in the Sky Morning (1978)

Rhonda Payne, who had Newfoundland parents but who was raised on the Canadian mainland, came to Newfoundland with a degree in English and drama from York University and with theatre training from the Actors Studio in Drury Lane, London. In 1978 she studied clowning and mask work with Ian Wallace at the Theatre Resource Centre in Toronto. *Stars in the Sky Morning* is based, by and large, on Payne's research into the lives of her relatives living on Newfoundland's Great Northern Peninsula, whom she had met while touring the peninsula in 1975 with the Mummers Troupe production *Dying Hard. Stars in the Sky Morning* was co-written with Jane Dingle and Jan Henderson. The play is about the lives of young girls and women, growing up, living their lives, falling in love, marrying and having their children in pre- and post-Confederation Newfoundland. It is a series of monologues and dialogues quietly spoken by two actors who change both characters and ages as the play progresses; it presents the strong Newfoundland tradition of story telling. The play is nostalgic without being sentimental as highly contrasted characters deal matter-of-factly and humorously with their situations and expectations. It possesses great charm and arouses audience interest in lifestyles that are different. The language has a poetic quality in its candour and simplicity which is unusual in a collectively created work.

Stars in the Sky Morning (1978) was initially produced as a Molly Grub production; Molly Grub was a company Rhonda Payne formed in order to produce this play. Payne was a member of the Mummers Troupe and the play was held over a week after its opening run as a co-production of Molly Grub and the Mummers Troupe. It toured Newfoundland in 1978 and Nova Scotia in 1981 as a Mummers Troupe production.

Makin' Time with the Yanks (1981)

Makin' Time with the Yanks (1981) is a collective play produced by the Mummers Troupe when the company existed more as a highly polished professional production company than as a radical political theatre troupe. The original idea for the play was conceived in 1975 by Rhonda Payne when she was interviewing residents, businesses and retailers for the Mummers Troupe collective, *East End Story*. Many interviewees told wonderful stories of the war years which she felt would make a good play. Some of the incidents of the play are based on actual historical events such as the arrival on 29 January 1941 of the *Edmund B. Alexander*, a passenger liner turned troop ship, bringing American servicemen to Newfoundland and the tragic fire in the Knights of Columbus hostel during the broadcast of the weekly barn dance on 12 December 1942. The play, produced by Rhonda Payne, was researched and developed by the cast and director Mary Walsh who had studied theatre at Ryerson Tech before joining CODCO in 1973 and who had toured England and Wales in Theatre Passe Muraille's *The Farm Show* in 1979. Among the cast was Kay Anonsen, a Newfoundlander and theatre graduate of Case Western Reserve in Cleveland, Ohio (useful in staging a play featuring American characters) and the Nuffield Theatre School in Lancaster, England. These two working with Rick Boland, Jane Dingle, Brian Downey, Janis Spence and Paul Steffler created one of the high points of Newfoundland collective theatre. *Makin' Time with the Yanks* is considered to be perhaps the most popular play ever presented in St. John's, and it is estimated that 10% of the population of the city saw the show in 1981.

The play focusses on the relationships of three young women who fall in love with American servicemen and the different manners in which their relationships develop in the economic flush and social excitement of war-time St. John's. Within the overall sense of fun of the production, its music and its professionally choreographed dancing are the serious issues of religion and religious differences, the viewing of the Newfoundland self in relation to people who come from away and the ever-present feature of Newfoundland theatre— realistic, turbulent and sometimes dysfunctional family and family relations. The play makes no attempt to be political, it is rather a polished, stylish and funny theatrical dramatization of a unique social period in Newfoundland history which was perhaps a necessary step in the transition of the once independent country into a province of Canada.

Developed as a Mummers Troupe production, *Makin' Time with the Yanks* was taken on a Newfoundland tour in 1982 and remounted in St. John's in 1986 by essentially the same cast which had created the show. They were employed by a new production company, however, RCA Theatre Company, which by 1982 had replaced the Mummers Troupe as the new resident theatre company in the LSPU Hall.

Sheila's Brush Theatre Company (1977 to present)

Sheila's Brush Theatre Company was formed in 1977 by Philip Dinn and Valentine Ryan as a traditional Newfoundland musical group.[8] They were joined by musicians Dave and Geoff Panting and a group of dancers called the Wisht-to'Booneen Dancers who performed traditional Newfoundland set dances to the music. As a whole, the group drew upon the music, song, dance, stories and folklore of the Newfoundland outports and evolved into a distinctive theatre troupe with interests in traditions, music and dance of the province. The group's name suggests that its work deals primarily with Newfoundland life and traditions. "Sheila's Brush," a storm which typically occurs on March 18th, is named after St. Patrick's legendary sister, wife, housekeeper or acquaintance.

The Dream of the Hag, a Hallowe'en show first performed in 1979, was Sheila's Brush's first collective play. Centred on the traditional Newfoundland dream character, the old Hag is used as an oracle to prophesy humanity's doom as a result of its collective departure from spiritual values. In 1979, after *The Dream of the Hag*, Sheila's Brush was joined by Andy Jones who had the idea of turning the traditional Newfoundland Jack tales, which were first told to members of the group by Mr. Pius Power of South East Bight, into theatre shows which would incorporate song and dance. Sheila's Brush has had a reasonably stable membership. In addition to the performers named, the Brush includes among its writer-performers Bill Barry, Frank Barry, Mercedes Barry, Vicki Hammond, Cathy Jones, Flip Janes, and Agnes Walsh. The group has created and produced a series of Jack tales as well as many other diverse and original works; Sheila's Brush still creates and performs.

Two Sheila's Brush plays centre upon annual holidays: *The Dream of the Hag* and *Jaxxmas (Jack's Christmas)* (1979). *Jaxxmas*, a Christmas play, is a modern retelling of the Jack tale, in which Jack, a Newfoundlander, has lost his former magical powers and lives on the dole with his huge family. Sheila's Brush performed four Jack tales in addition to *Jaxxmas. Jack Meets the Cat* (1980), is the group's elaborate development from Pius Power's telling of the traditional "Jack Meets the Cat" story. In the play the poor boy Jack succeeds in the magical world of trolls, gypsies, evil leprechauns, dancing tornadoes, *et alia*, because of his kindness to a cat who ultimately reveals herself as a beautiful princess and the woman of Jack's dreams. This play, produced by Chris Brookes, has been broadcast by CBC Radio, and it won the silver medal at New York Radio and Television Festival's international radio programming in the children and young adults' category for 1993. *Jack Meets the Cat* exists as a commercially produced tape (released in 1994). *Jack Meets the Well-Pressed Well-Dressed Gentleman* (1982), presents Jack meeting the devil in the tiny village of Blackhead, Newfoundland where he is forced to play cards with him in order to save the princess from the arch antagonist's evil intentions. *The King of Ashes* (1984) tells the story of Jack's role in the fight between the church and the monarchy. In *The Magnafoot Mountain* (1988), Jack takes on the persona of Johnson, a poor orphaned boy, who becomes entangled with the cruel magnafoot who rules the kingdom with an iron fist and who must be conquered in order for peace to come to the land. An act of random kindness on Jack's part sees him through his dangerous ordeals and rids the land of a malicious tyrant.

Sheila's Brush has created and performed other collectives. *A Midsummer's Nightmare* (1980), is set in the early twenty-first century when the ocean is polluted by oil companies and the people of Newfoundland can no longer fish. The play tells the story of a band of revolutionaries who fight the government's plan to relocate the population to a Walt Disney-like mock up of Newfoundland located in the middle of the Arizona desert. *Last Chance to Dance— Pavement Pageant Profiles* (1982), is a piece of street theatre that looks at the role of urban developers and the trauma caused in the lives of downtown residents of St. John's when they are removed from their neighbourhoods.[9] *The History of a New Founde Lande* (1983), is the history of the island of Newfoundland from the Europeans' first meeting with the Beothuck Indians until the demise of the native aboriginal people at the hands of the European settlers, as told through the eyes of space travellers. *The Rise and Fall of Modern Campfire Songs* (1987), a series of sketches, round out the major collective creations of Sheila's Brush.

In addition to these plays, Sheila's Brush has performed plays such as Chekhov's *The Boor* (1984). The group has also done adaptations: a short story of Oscar Wilde's became the play *A Fisherman and His Soul* (1985). *Burbank and Volupine* (1986), is a play about love and revolution set in Nazi Germany, which involves a group of cabaret performers engaged in a plot to assassinate Hitler. The play incorporates works of Kafka, Camus, Baudelaire, Shakespeare, *et alia*. *A Gentle Creature* (1986), is based on a short story by Dostoevsky and *Crime and Punishment* (1989), adapted by Sheila's Brush member Frank Barry, is based on Dostoevsky's novel. Productions

by Sheila's Brush are identified by the group's distinctive characteristic traits: traditional music, folklore, whimsy, magic, colour,
noise and song.

Over the years Sheila's Brush have toured their plays to schools
located across Newfoundland. The group has toured Atlantic Canada and has been invited to perform in Edmonton and at the
National Arts Centre in Ottawa. In the nineties, Sheila's Brush
have remounted some of their earlier plays, performed scripted
plays such as Coburn's *The Gin Game* (1990), and three members of
the group, Mercedes Barry, Andy Jones and Agnes Walsh, have
collaboratively created *Time Before Thought* (1992), produced by
RCA Theatre, which is included in this book.

Jaxxmas (Jack's Christmas), 1979

Jaxxmas weaves together the story of how Jack meets the Cat and
an update on the tale in which Jack, having married the Princess,
lives in poverty in a squalid apartment with his wife and large
expanding family. Jack puts his soul in hock to a finance company,
dies, and is restored by a magical resolution. The play is typical of
Sheila's Brush productions in its use of magic, colour, traditional
music, songs and dance. It incorporates a political mummers play,
wild gypsies, a Newfoundland wake and it dramatises the stress that
economic hardship puts on the dysfunctional family. A version of
the original Jack tale in which Jack meets the Cat is interwoven into
the older Jack's story as part of the play. In keeping with Sheila's
Brush's own practice, the dramatized story of Jack and the Cat in the
play can be performed separately as well as being part of *Jaxxmas*.

Jaxxmas has been produced twice by Sheila's Brush, 1979 and
1986. A version of the play was scripted for television production,
but it has not been produced.

Rising Tide Theatre (1978 to present)

Shortly after the production of *They Club Seals, Don't They?* (1978),
Rising Tide Theatre was formed by Mummers Troupe members
Donna Butt, David Ross, Terry Rielly and Glen Tilley with Ann
Anderson as manager. Generally disgruntled by aspects of their
experience in the Mummers Troupe and eager to share in the direction of the company, they felt that they could make their own voice
heard only by forming their own company. The split occurred because of a disagreement between the actors and Chris Brookes over
a collective play which became Rising Tide Theatre's first show,
Daddy, What's a Train? (1978), a play about the rise and fall of the
Newfoundland passenger rail service. This show was performed at
the LSPU Hall, and together with the Newfoundland premiere of
Michael Cook's *Terese's Creed* (1979), it constituted Rising Tide's
first season. The "Train Show" was well received and met with

popular and critical acclaim. It established the style and direction of Rising Tide as a theatre company, a blend of humour and political satire grounded in the exploration of the character of the people of Newfoundland and Labrador informed by a sense of history and heritage.

The early years of the company were characterized by strong issue oriented productions and popular theatre. *Jelly Beans and Shattered Dreams* (1979), brought a company of young actors from around the province together to explore problems facing young people; *Filthy Rich and Easy* (1979), satirized the burgeoning oil industry; *Somewhere Over the Border* (1980), explored the stormy relationship between Newfoundland and Quebec with Labrador as the battleground; *I Was a Teenage Love Doll, 1* (1980) and *2* (1981) presented the beginnings of an introspective look at the baby boom generation; and *Joey* (1981), co-written with Rick Salutin, focussed on Smallwood's leading Newfoundland into Confederation with Canada and the resulting rise of a new generation of Canadian Newfoundlanders—or Newfoundland Canadians.

Joey represented not only a maturity in the collective process, it initiated a new working relationship for the company. Between 1981 and 1991 Rising Tide enjoyed a close working relationship with the provincial Division of Cultural Affairs and worked as the unofficial production company for the provincial government-run Arts and Culture Centre in St. John's. These years were characterized by an expanded season including a classic and Canadian repertoire including new works by Newfoundland playwrights Jeff Pitcher, *The Known Soldier* (1982); Tom Cahill, *So Oft It Chances* (1984); Michael Cook, *The Gayden Chronicles* (1985) and Donna Butt and Rick Boland, *Ocean Ranger* (1989). The collective roots were nourished by *It's a Big Fat Lie* (1983); *The Daily News* (1986); *Newfoundlanders Away* (1990) and the popular annual *Revues* which began in 1984 and which continue the tradition begun in the 1950s by the London Players and Corner Brook Playmakers Company's "Home Brew."

Rising Tide Theatre took stock in 1990 and in preparation for troubled economic times planned and instituted a number of diversifications. A "Young Company" was formed and began to perform strong collective work in high schools throughout Newfoundland and Labrador. *Falling Through the Cracks* (1989-90), *Nothing Else to Do* (1991) and *The Ones That Got Away*, (1992), under the direction of Donna Butt and Rick Boland explore the problems facing youth in rural areas of the province. A regular mix of collectively written and new scripted plays continued to be performed in St. John's. These include the collective *Gutted Head On* (1990), Pete Soucy's *Carolan: The Last of the Irish Bards* (1990), and Al Pittman's *Spring Awakening* (1991). Artistic Director Donna Butt initiated a new play development program, the "New Play Workshops" which led to the development of new works for the stage by Newfoundland and Canadian playwrights. Des Walsh's adaptation of Harold Horwood's *Tomorrow Will Be Sunday* (1992), Wayne MacPhail's *Abandon Hope, Mabel Dorothy* (1993), Berni Stapleton's *Woman in a Monkey Cage* (1993), and an adaptation of Kevin Major's novel, *Far from Shore* (1994) are a few of the works which have gone through the development process to production.

In 1990, Rising Tide Theatre initiated discussions with the Historic Resources Division of the provincial Department of Tourism and Culture and the Bonaventure-English Harbour Development Association concerning the implementation of a pageant in the town of Trinity. A monologue based on the life of Sir Richard Whitbourne, the Elizabethan navy admiral who established a Court of Admiralty, the first recorded law-court in Newfoundland, was performed by Rick Boland in Trinity in 1991 and 1992. In the summer of 1993 *The New Founde Lande*, a pageant on the history of Trinity, by Donna Butt and Rick Boland was performed by professional actors and local residents under their training. In 1994 a festival of Newfoundland works called "Summer in the Bight" was produced by Donna Butt in addition to *The New Founde Lande* pageant. The festival included David French's *Salt Water Moon*, Michael Cook's *Terese's Creed* and *Quiller*, Ken Murphy's *Black Stick Tales* and Rising Tide's first collective, *Daddy, What's a Train?* Both pageant and festival are ongoing events.

Rising Tide Theatre has produced a large body of work by and about Newfoundlanders and Labradorians and continues to reflect the lives and heritage of people of the province. It is one of the oldest surviving professional theatre companies in Newfoundland and it has demonstrated vision, tenacity and a willingness to change and restructure when change is necessary. Rising Tide has employed hundreds of Newfoundland artists and has participated in the development and growth of the vibrant provincial arts scene. The company remains firmly rooted in the province both as a respected theatre company and as a leader in theatrical historical interpretation and community economic development projects. Rising Tide has worked with some of the finest artists, administrators and technical crews available. It has been guided through turbulent and triumphant times by its sole Artistic and Executive Director Donna Butt (1984 to present) and by its Co-Artistic Directors Donna Butt and David Ross (1978-1984). Rick Boland is Rising Tide's Associate Artistic Director.

Joey (1981)

Joey is more than a dry history of "the only living father of Confederation," as Smallwood used to call himself. It is based on research and on extensive interviews with Smallwood conducted by Donna Butt. His speech in the play on empty victories and the laws of God (Act 2 Scene 10, repeated in Scene 19) consists of words which he actually spoke in conversation with her. Peter Cashin quoted from Sir Walter Scott's "Innominatus" at the National Convention, an incident which is dramatized in the play (Act 1 Scene 12). *Joey* was written in collaboration with Rick Salutin, who was known widely for his work with Theatre Passe Muraille on *1837: The Farmers' Revolt* and known in Newfoundland for his work in 1975 with the Mummers Troupe's play *I. W. A. Newfoundland Loggers' Strike of 1959*. *Joey* represents to the Rising Tide writers a passage from the Newfoundland of their fathers to a Newfoundland where they themselves were gaining the reins of power and their voices were being heard. For Rising Tide Theatre, *Joey* is a coming of age.

It is difficult for non-Newfoundland Canadians to appreciate fully the impact of *Joey* on Newfoundland audiences. The play juxtaposes Joey's ambitions, plans, successes and failures with the lives of the people who bore the brunt of the changes he inaugurated. There are music and slides which lend a sense of history and provide atmosphere; there are colour and variety of scenes. To Newfoundland audiences the play is ambivalent and expresses the mixed emotions that those Newfoundlanders who were born before Confederation and who grew up, or grew old, as first-generation Canadians feel. For them it causes laughter, scorn, sorrow, anger and pride—a shared awareness of gain and of loss. At the end of the play, Newfoundland audience members rise to sing "The Ode to Newfoundland," which had been the national anthem for those born before April 1949. The experience evokes within these people a sense of such wonderful sadness that they would not have to explain to each other and they could not or would not try to explain to anyone else. For younger generations of Newfoundlanders these complex feelings are weakening; however, for all Newfoundlanders this play records history that they need to know.

From 1981 to 1983 *Joey* was performed by Rising Tide Theatre in St. John's and on Newfoundland tours, it was nationally broadcast by CBC Television and it toured mainland Canada on three separate occasions.

RCA Theatre Company (1980 to present)

CODCO member Andy Jones became involved in the Resource Centre for the Arts (RCA) which took over the operation of the LSPU Hall at the end of 1979. In 1980 he became a director. He had formerly been an early member of the Newfoundland Travelling Theatre Company. Andy Jones's theatricality originated in the Newfoundland traditions of story telling, community concerts, oratorical contests and recitation of long poems. He remembers a seminal moment in his decision to become an actor as seeing a Theatre Passe Muraille production of Chekhov's *The Marriage Proposal* in Trinity Church (1969), in which the theatre was so filthy that the actor's white gloves were black with dirt; it convinced him that there was a place for him in theatre. His first acting job outside Newfoundland was a Passe Muraille production of Lope de Vega's *Dog in the Manger* directed by Louis del Grande. He subsequently worked at Passe Muraille with Ken Campbell in *Pilk's Madhouse* and went to London with the production where he became a member of the Madhouse Company of London to which Campbell acted as advisor. With this company he performed at the iconoclastic Up Stairs at the Royal Court Theatre on trendy Sloane Square and toured the Festival Europalia, playing Brussels, Oslo, Århus and Frankfurt before touring Campbell's show *An Evening with Hamlet* to New York and Philadelphia. After Philadelphia he returned to Newfoundland and joined CODCO in 1974.

Jones was in England during the early seventies where he espoused Peter Brook's idea of the sufficiency of the empty space for theatre. From Ken Campbell he caught the attitude that anything could be done and he developed a sense of irony and a way presenting theatre that could comment on itself. He observed that in the former bastion of colonialism the English were fighting against their own traditions and new English theatre was undermining what was already there. Jones learned that theatre did not have to conform to tradition and he decided that Newfoundlanders did not have to be actors who wore silk dressing gowns or velvet smoking jackets and spoke with British accents. He brought all this to CODCO and later to the management of the LSPU Hall where he was joined by Mary Walsh as artistic animateur and director of RCA Theatre in 1980. Jones and Walsh remained involved in the management and artistic development of RCA Theatre Company until they rejoined the reconstituted CODCO in the mid 1980s.

RCA Theatre Company has become one of the main professional theatre groups which has grown since the folding of the Newfoundland Travelling Theatre Company, CODCO and the Mummers Troupe. RCA Theatre, like Rising Tide, has carried on the tradition of collectively created plays such as *Terras de Bacalhau* (1980), on St. John's women and their Portuguese fishermen; *Between a Rock and a Hard Place* (1984), on the Newfoundland fishery; *High Steel* (1984), on Newfoundland high steel workers in the United States; *Nitassinan* (1987), on Innu-white settler relations in southern Labrador; and *No Pity* (1990), on Newfoundland urban youth. The company has also done adaptations such as *The Newfoundland Tempest* (1982). In addition, RCA Theatre has produced scripted plays by Newfoundland playwrights such as Ray Guy (*Young Triffie's Been Made Away With,* 1985; *Frog Pond,* 1988 and *The Swinton Massacre,* 1992); Greg Thomey (*The Best Man,* 1989 and *Hanlon House,* with Bryan Hennessey, 1991); Janis Spence (*Chickens,* 1989, *Cat Lover,* 1990, *Naked Bungalow,* with Jon Whalen and Elizabeth Pickard, 1991 and *Walking to Australia,* 1992); J. M. Sullivan (*Harpies,* 1992, *Wolf in the Fold,* 1993 and *Murder at the Royal Cafe,* with Bryan Hennessey, 1995); Ed Riche (*Possible Maps,* 1991 and *List of Lights* 1994) and Connie Hynes (*Later That Same Life,* 1994). One of

RCA Theatre's strong points has been the author-acted show. These have been created and performed by Mary Walsh (*Bloomsdays,* 1982), Andy Jones (*Out of the Bin,* 1983, and *Still Alive,* a co-production with Factory Lab Theatre, 1994), Rick Mercer *(Show Me the Button: I'll Push It (Or Charles Lynch Must Die),* 1990), John Taylor *(My Three Dads,* 1992), and Elizabeth Pickard (*The Alienation of Lizzie Dyke,* 1994).

RCA Theatre Company differs from both Rising Tide Theatre and Sheila's Brush in having developed over the years with a succession of artistic animateurs. When Mary Walsh left the position she was replaced by Rick Boland who served as animateur in an acting capacity (1986-7). During 1987 Boland was replaced by a stewardship committee which, later in 1987, was replaced by Charlie Tomlinson who was succeeded by Bryan Hennessey in 1990. Hennessey served until 1993. The current artistic amimateur of RCA Theatre is Lois Brown (1993-present) who is assisted by Jillian Keiley. The mandate of RCA Theatre Company is to perform original Canadian plays, most of which are written by Newfoundland residents. Currently, RCA Theatre stages three Mainstage plays every season. In recent years, because of budgetary constraints most of these plays have had small casts. The company also has a Second Space program which stages four to six experimental and developmental works each year. Works by new playwrights and groups and new directions by established writers are produced. A successful Second Space show is frequently repeated as a Mainstage production. Programming of RCA Theatre is planned by the artistic animateur and the Programming Committee which is generally comprised of members of the Board of Directors of Resource Centre for the Arts and performing artists all of whom are members of Resource Centre for the Arts. Resource Centre for the Arts operates the LSPU Hall, the resident RCA Theatre Company and an art gallery in the building, RCA Visual, which opened in 1981. The involvement of the Mummers Troupe and members of CODCO, in the history and development of the LSPU Hall, has stamped the Hall as an artist-run space based on principles of collectivism and it is run on these principles today.

The LSPU Hall has become synonymous with original Newfoundland theatre and has gained a reputation of being the home of the best original theatre produced in Newfoundland. The theatre is used not only by its resident company, RCA Theatre, but also by every professional and many amateur theatre groups in the province when they need a two-hundred seat theatre in St. John's. The LSPU Hall Theatre is technically far from ideal. It has no space behind the stage for set construction or storage and it suffers various other limitations as a theatre space. However, because of the resourcefulness and ability of the theatre groups who have used the building since its purchase and renovation in 1976, the Hall is the best known theatre in Newfoundland.

Terras de Bacalhau (Land of Cod) (1980)

This play was the first major production of RCA Theatre and it remains one of the company's best known collectives. Mary Walsh (director), Janis Spence, Kay Anonsen and Rick Boland were joined by Greg Thomey, José E. Silva, John Koop and musician-song writer Jim Payne to create this sad and funny drama on the relationships between St. John's women and visiting Portuguese fishermen. Like *Makin' Time with the Yanks* (roughly half the cast wrote both plays) *Terras de Bacalhau* does not set out to plumb psychological depths; it is instead, socially oriented, poignant, funny and extremely musical. The issues in the play are family relations, and self and other, both are viewed more realistically than romantically. There is pathos and humour in the contrast between the squalid conditions in which the women live and the air of confidence they convey in the company of their visiting men.

Terras de Bacalhau was produced by RCA Theatre Company four times in St. John's and toured the mainland twice between 1980 and 1986.

Time Before Thought (1991)

Time Before Thought is an RCA Theatre Company production of a play collaboratively written by cast members who work with both RCA Theatre and Sheila's Brush; they are Mercedes Barry, Andy Jones and Agnes Walsh. The play, directed by Jones, is based on the lives of two young women, Barry and Walsh, from Placentia Bay who marry American servicemen stationed in the U.S. naval base at Argentia. They accompany their husbands to the United States, the marriages fail and both women return to their Newfoundland roots. The action unfolds through the actors' dialogue which is interspersed with film sequences in which two romantic young princesses fall in love with and marry their fairy-tale princes—sailors from Neighbouring Kingdom. This play is imaginative and psychological in its approach. The language is beautiful and poetic. It would be interesting, perhaps, to consider *Time Before Thought* and *Stars in the Sky Morning* together as serious, imaginative and powerful dramatizations of the lives of Newfoundland women in a continuum of social change in Newfoundland.

Time Before Thought was performed in St. John's in 1991 and 1994 and in Ottawa in 1993. In 1996, with Glen Tilley as producer, it was broadcast nationally as a radio play by CBC Radio.

My Three Dads (1992)

This essentially one-person show started life as an RCA Theatre Second Space production acted by its writer John Taylor and directed by Andy Jones. There is an affinity between Jones and Taylor in that both are expert in the Newfoundland story-telling tradition. In addition, Taylor's earlier professional stage experience was in collective theatre—he participated in Rising Tide Theatre's *Nothing*

Else to Do (1991) and after *My Three Dads* he performed in Rising Tide's *The Ones That Got Away* (1992). *My Three Dads* tells another aspect of the story told by *Makin' Time with the Yanks* and, more particularly, *Time Before Thought* in presenting the auto-biographical account by the son of Newfoundland-American parents of his journey to discover his estranged father who lives in the United States.

My Three Dads played as an RCA Theatre Mainstage production a month after its Second Space opening (1992). It was recorded for broadcast on CBC Radio's "Morningside Drama" and was performed in Nova Scotia and Prince Edward Island. Since John Taylor moved to British Columbia in 1993 he has performed the play in various locations there. He has also appeared in other plays in British Columbia, including performances at the Vancouver Women's Festival with fellow Newfoundland actor, Christine Taylor, in 1994.

Wonderbolt Circus Theatre (1978 to present)

Wonderbolt Circus Theatre is the brain child of Beni Malone who founded the company and who is its mainstay. He began his acting career with the Newfoundland Travelling Theatre Company and the Mummers Troupe and has also performed with Mulgrave Road Theatre and RCA Theatre Company. Always a physical actor, Malone participated in clown workshops arranged by the Mummers Troupe in preparation for their production of *They Club Seals, Don't They?* Malone also studied the art of the clown in the theatre section of the Three Schools of Art in Toronto. When he went to Ringling Bros. Barnum and Bailey Clown College in Venice, Florida, he was the only Canadian in a class of sixty. Later Malone studied at L'Ecole Nationale du Cirque in Paris, France. In addition to contributing to collectives, he has successfully incorporated the art of the clown in many of his productions and he is the sole producer in Newfoundland of theatre in the *commedia dell'arte* tradition. As a practitioner of modern *commedia*, Wonderbolt Circus Theatre produces popular culture in which not-particularly identified—or stock—characters, such as "the gangster" or "the reviewer," etc., function in the manner of the old *commedia* stereotypes. To date, Wonderbolt has created and produced more than thirty shows.

Among Wonderbolt's clown-circus theatre performances created by Beni Malone are *Be Bop Deluxe* (1978), *Brainy and the Zanies* (1983), *Mixed Commotions*, a part-fairy tale part-pantomime performance (1984); *Der Cirk Bizzirk*, a new wave circus and *Skitz-o-Frantik* a play on the misadventures of Mister Mastermind, an eccentric scientist (1986); *Tyrannocircus Rex* co-written with L'Institut Jonglage de France (1988); *Both Ends Burning* (1988), part of which was *Cult of the Personality* by Lois Brown; *Clown Duet in Be Sharpe*, co-written with Cecile Truffault (1990); *Robotrix*

(1992) and *Ha-Ha-Holocaust* co-written with Lois Brown (1993), which has been revised and performed as *Laughtershock* (1994). This last play is a clown and puppet show set in a post-holocaust world. Wonderbolt has also produced Malone's adaptation of Goldoni's *Servant of Two Masters* with masked performers in colourful *commedia dell'arte* style (1985). In addition to Lois Brown who has frequently worked with Wonderbolt, Malone's early collaborators were Carol Wherry, Cathy Ferri and Marian White.

A strength of Wonderbolt Circus Theatre is its ability to produce various sizes of performances from one-person shows to plays with large casts. Beginning with the boat tour of *The Wonderbolt Circus Show* in 1982 along Newfoundland's south coast, the northern islands and coastal Labrador, the company began to tour, a practice which has seen it play in venues that range from private homes to bars to wharves to streets to community halls, indoor and outdoor festivals and Arts and Culture Centres throughout Newfoundland and Labrador. There are communities in Newfoundland and Labrador in which Wonderbolt's productions are the only professional theatre ever seen. In addition, Wonderbolt productions have played at Expo 86, the Canada Games and the bi-annual Multicultural Festival in Toronto. Wonderbolt has also performed in television series in both Newfoundland and New Brunswick. Currently, Wonderbolt is functioning as a theatre troupe and Malone is working with young upcoming actor-writers Chuck Herriott, Ruth Lawrence and Ken Murphy on shows such as *Out of Work* (1992), Wonderbolt's *Ha-Ha-Holocaust* (1993) and *Laughtershock* (1994). They were joined by Mark Critch in Rising Tide Theatre's *The Land That Clean Forgot* (1995).

Beni Malone is a longstanding contributor to the collective process; the first play he wrote was a collective called *Madman's Cabaret* with Kent Barrett and Jane Dingle which was performed at the Eastport Festival in 1971. He also worked on shows such as RCA Theatre's collectives *Sold Out* (1982) and *Twice Burned, Once Shy* (1987). Before they began to perform under the name Corey and Wade's Playhouse, Beni employed the four actors who went on to comprise that group both individually and together.

Corey and Wade's Playhouse (1987 to 1992)

Corey and Wade's Playhouse members are Ashley Billard, Rick Mercer, Christine Taylor and Andrew Younghusband. The four met in high school and began acting together under the unofficial leadership of Rick Mercer. Their aim was to perform stand-up comedy which they created collectively outside the perimeters of school. They first performed in the art gallery at the LSPU Hall. Early productions include programs of sketch comedy, accompanied by live music, called *Hardly a Sensible Evening* and *A Comedy Cabaret: Or*

Hardly a Sensible Evening 2 (both in 1987). The group's work was well received by members of the original Newfoundland comedy collectives; CODCO members such as Tommy Sexton and Andy Jones saw them as a second generation in the tradition they had begun.

Corey and Wade (the name is a variation on the names of a couple of hash dealers they'd met in Conception Bay), performed a show in Trinity, in the summer of 1987, called *Not your Average Night Out: Or Cold Snow on a Hot Day.* The venture was not a financial success and the group tried to recoup its losses with a benefit for Corey and Wade called *Too Big for our Breeches,* performed at the Hall. Corey and Wade moved into the theatre at the Hall in 1988 with a late night cabaret, *Slander, Libel and Three Months in Jewvy,* a co-production with RCA Theatre which was directed by Lois Brown. Brown, who had been their teacher in high school and who had directed them in high school drama festivals, became their director and more plays followed: *The Beatles Play Bishops Falls,* written by Rick Mercer and the cast, a co-production with RCA Theatre (1988); and the collective *Young, Stupid and Not All Together With It* (1989). Corey and Wade members were joined by Anne Evans and Elizabeth Pickard and the band Dead Reckoning in the creation of the collective *No Pity,* a play about urban youth living in downtown St. John's, which was produced by RCA Theatre (1990). *Man on the Moon, Woman on the Pill,* written by Christine Taylor was first performed as a Corey and Wade production and later presented by RCA Theatre Second Space (1990). *I've Killed Before and I'll Kill Again,* written and performed by Rick Mercer and produced and directed by Gerald Lunz, is the most recent project of Corey and Wade's Playhouse (1992).

In addition to their theatre work, Corey and Wade, who interspersed their comedy performances with live music, performed in bars. Their regular musicians were Sean Panting, Bob Earle, Ken Tizzard and Rod Wills. The serious and political side of Corey and Wade was manifested in *Father Loves Us,* a film on the Catholic Church and sexual abuse which featured Rick Mercer and which was made by Jamie Lewis in 1988—the film was part of *Slander, Libel and Three Months in Jewvy.* Members of Corey and Wade's Playhouse have gone separate ways in recent years which is a loss because their collective work created something of the excitement generated during the theatrical renaissance of the 1970s. Ashley Billard lives and performs in Toronto, Rick Mercer in Halifax and Christine Taylor and Andrew Younghusband in Vancouver.

On Edge (1989)

On Edge, produced by Wonderbolt, is the result of collaboration between Beni Malone of Wonderbolt Circus Theatre and Rick Mercer of Corey and Wade's Playhouse. Although the play was co-written and scripted, the original script was not retrieved until

late in the editing process, by which time the text had been transcribed from a video tape of the play. The script was dated a month
earlier than the play's production and there is evidence of collective
improvisation by members of the cast, under the direction of Lois
Brown, in several scenes in the play in order to bring it into its final
form. Randy Follett, Mary Lewis and Christine Taylor also appeared in *On Edge*.

The play is a tightly organized murder mystery based on the
American television and movie violence to which we are all now
routinely exposed as part of our cultural diet. It is set in an un-
named large eastern American city and St. John's appears as the
location of the orphanage, the purpose of which is veiled in mystery
until the end of the play. The production draws from the strengths of
the traditions which went into its creation—Beni Malone's drug
mobster Eddie displays the villainy of the *commedia dell'arte* zanni
characters Brighella and Pantalone, and the acrobatic ability of the
clown; Mary Lewis' Harlow/Monroe show the two sides of Colom-
bina; while Rick Mercer's fast-talking Tony is Harlequin and also
has something of the pugnacious but slick delivery Mercer went on
to develop in the protagonists in his one-man shows *Show Me the
Button: I'll Push It (Or Charles Lynch Must Die)*, 1990, and *I've
Killed Before and I'll Kill Again* (1992). The play's set and costumes
are extremely colourful.

On Edge played in St. John's in 1989.

Innuinuit Theatre Company and Nalujuk Players

Among the participants in the Creative Arts Festival, the Inuit,
Innu and mixed-parentage students living in communities along the
northern coast of Labrador have been prominent. Their works record, dramatize and protest the damage that has been inflicted upon
the native people since the settling of Labrador by Europeans. Such
early plays were performed at the Creative Arts Festival by students of Jens Haven School in Nain who created a play called *Okak
Spanish Flu, 1917* which tells the story of how the Inuit population
at the Okak mission was reduced from 263 to 59 within a week after
the supply ship *Harmony*, carrying sick crew members, made a
routine call. This play heralded a series of plays which attempted to
establish the Inuit and Innu perceptions of relations in northern
Labrador. These plays include: *Who Gets Labrador, Us or Them*
performed by students of Amos Comenius Memorial School in
Hopedale (1980), and Nain's play *Sons of Labrador* (1980) which
showed how the opening up of northern Labrador to outsiders re-
sulted in the uprooting of native cultures, loss of traditional life
skills, and breakdown of society through alcohol's destructive effect
on family life. In 1981, Hopedale's *Up the Base* showed further
deterioration of Inuit life and values, introduced the drunken native

girl as a play thing for the sexual pleasure of visiting airmen and showed the carefree withdrawal of the Americans leaving the Inuit unable to fend for themselves.

Subsequent plays from students of both Nain and Hopedale continued to dramatize the negative impact of white settlement on Inuit people in northern Labrador, but they also began to show attempts to bridge native and settler cultures (*All in the Family*, Nain, 1982; *Women of Labrador*, Hopedale, 1983). Typically, the plays were written and performed in English with the occasional word in Inuktitut. This situation changed with the Nain production *From Drums to Drums*, 1984, which focussed on music as a means of attempting to resolve cultural problems. The play opened with the missionaries' ban on Inuit drumming as heathen and their teaching the Inuit to play hymns on brass instruments in the Moravian Eskimo Band. However, the play continued to promote acceptance of cultural differences (seen in the juxtaposition of a traditional Inuit drum dance with a settlers' square dance and joint acceptance by all the young actors of popular music as universal). Productions continued to deal with inter-cultural problems: Nain, *Issumatsasiak* (1985), was based on the lure of a science fair versus caribou hunting with father.

In 1985, Bill Wheaton founded a young theatre company in Hopedale called Nalujuk Players. The group's first play, *Second Chance*, dramatized teenage suicide and won the Labrador High School Regional Drama Festival. The play was performed in Newfoundland and the Yukon. In 1987, students from Jens Haven School in Nain dramatized intercultural cooperation and used Inuktitut and Inuit drumming in *Kanitukuluk: Nah Far*. 1987 was also the year in which Nalujuk Players of Hopedale garnered awards at the Regional and Provincial High School Drama Festivals for *The Shaman: The New Dawn*, a play on the role of medicine men in Inuit culture.

In 1987, Innu students from the Nukum Mani Shan School in Davis Inlet performed their first play at the Creative Arts Festival in Goose Bay under the direction of Lou Byrne. The first play was *One Summer's Dream*, a humorous performance in which Winter aided by the spirits of the north, "Kamatshits" tries to kidnap Summer. Wheaton and Byrne believed that their drama groups could compliment each other and this belief led to collaboration between Innu students of Davis Inlet with Inuit students of Hopedale to found Innuinuit Theatre Company. The company's first jointly created production *Manitou: The People*, 1988, dramatized the powerful stories and mythologies of Innu and Inuit people's interrelationships with each other and with settlers on the northern Labrador. Innuinuit Theatre Company made a spring tour of Labrador with *The Shaman, One Summer's Dream* and the new play, *Manitou*. On Canada Day 1988, Innuinuit Theatre Company played at the LSPU Hall in St. John's. This and subsequent Innuinuit productions would use English, Inuktitut and Innuamaen. The actors, who ranged in age from 14 to 21, would wear costumes hand made from seal skin and caribou hide. In conjunction with the traditional aspects of Innuinuit's productions, which also include the use of traditional drums and masks, the troupe incorporates contemporary music, images and audio-visual effects to dramatize the conditions in which both groups of native people live today.

Innuinuit Theatre Company performed *Black/Brown* at the Regional High School festival in Happy Valley/Goose Bay in April, 1989 and in November of the same year they performed *My Blue Heaven* a play on the impact of low-level military flying on the animals and animal spirits in rural Labrador and of the airmen on the lives of the aboriginal people (particularly women) in settlements near the base.

1990 saw Nain and Hopedale represented separately at the Creative Arts Festival; Nain performing *Inuvia Viet Nainimi* a play on the establishment of social interrelationships between a settler girl and an Inuit boy. The Hopedale Nalujuk Players, now under the direction of David Nochasak, performed a play on the issues of heavy social drinking among the adults and gasoline sniffing among youngsters in *An Easy Way Out*. In the 1991 Festival, Hopedale presented, *Home Away from Home* on drinking, child abuse and young offenders. The actors from Nain were now under the direction of Bill Wheaton (who had left Hopedale for Manitoba but who returned to teach in Nain). The group began to perform under the name Ulu Players and produced *Our Land, Our People*, a symbolic play using music, dance and sound to represent a brief history of the Labrador coast. Innu Theatre Company from Davis Inlet presented *The Quest for Food*, a play based on the Innu's loss of their traditional hunting lifestyle and their growing dependence on the government store which they come to see as an evil villain producing negative changes in their traditions.

By 1992, Innuinuit Theatre Company was together again, now composed of the actors from Davis Inlet and Nain and co-directors Lou Byrne and Bill Wheaton. The next production was *The Boneman: Kaiashits* for the Provincial High School Drama Festival in May. This play, set in the 1920s, dramatized the conflict in which the spiritual values of the aboriginal people were defeated by the church, the law, the Hudson's Bay Company and the International Grenfell Association. In the play, the Boneman is crucified in a manner that invokes the power of the Christian passion narrative— the innocent prophet and visionary is destroyed by the more powerful forces in the clash of cultures.

Innuinuit toured *The Boneman: Kaiashits* together with *My Blue Heaven* in western Newfoundland after the drama festival and to the LSPU Hall in St. John's in November, 1992. In June, 1993, *The Boneman: Kaiashits* was performed twice in the Montreal based Festival de Theatre des Ameriques, both in the Laurentians on the banks of the River Rouge with torches for stage lights and accompanied by Micmac drums and at the Centaur Theatre in Montreal.

Braindead (1993)

The most recent joint production was performed in Nain, Hopedale and at the Creative Arts Festival in Goose Bay in November 1993. The play, *Braindead*, was performed under the Innuinuit Theatre banner, it was under the joint direction of Bill Wheaton and Norma Denney, director of Nalujuk Players, and acted by actors from Hopedale and Nain. The play, set in a native treatment centre, dramatizes how the young people came to be there. Since the actors were familiar with gasoline sniffing through living in their communities, the play was realistic, moving and powerful. *Braindead* is optimistic in that the characters, without exception, seize the opportunity to overcome their problems by facing them squarely and by using whatever facilities are available to them to beat addiction.

Note on the Texts

There appears to be widespread belief among theatre analysts that collective plays, created through research and improvisation, never really achieve a text that requires the same degree of diligence in its preservation and transmission as a text written by a single author. However, my experience in working with the established collective writing groups in Newfoundland indicates that such belief is wrong. In every collective play I have edited from every group, without exception, a text was developed during rehearsal and maybe even in early performance, but that text became established and served as the basis of performance, and it is the text that the writers want published. The text may exist only because the play was recorded or, more recently, video-taped, and that text may be a transcription of a single performance, but it is the text. Collective writers' interest in the accuracy of the finished text concerns ensuring that the atmosphere of the play is conveyed through set and costume descriptions and stage directions. Their interest also concerns minute details of language, pronunciation, punctuation and delivery of lines. The editor's responsibility is to present the play as its authors intended it in published form.

With the exception of John Taylor's *My Three Dads*, which he sent to me on a computer disk and which he unfailingly proofread and corrected in the draft edited versions that went back and forth between us, all the other plays in this volume are based on a transcription of a performance. Eight of the transcriptions are housed in the Centre for Newfoundland Studies (CNS) Archives at Memorial University. These transcriptions served as the basis on which the editorial work was carried out. Most of the plays were not recorded on video, but for those which were, *On Edge, Time Before*

Thought and *Braindead,* the videos provided information from which stage directions and set and costume descriptions could be developed.

The texts of *Joey* and *Time Before Thought* preserve the most recent versions of those plays. The transcription of *Jaxxmas* is the 1979 version of the play into which Sheila's Brush wanted three scenes from the 1986 version to be incorporated. There is no known transcription or usable tape of the 1986 version of the play. The text of *Braindead* is preserved in the version in which it was performed in Nain and Hopedale to which a scene which was performed in Goose Bay is added. The text for *On Edge* was transcribed from a video of a performance. In editing it was corrected from the pre-production script in cases where the dialogue was unclear or missing from the tape. For the remaining plays, *They Club Seals, Don't They? Stars in the Sky Morning, Terras de Bacalhau* and *Makin' Time with the Yanks,* which are all plays that were produced more than once in St. John's and on tour, exactly what performance was the basis for the transcription is hardly even a matter for conjecture. However, during the past year, the Newfoundland collective plays were read jointly by at least half of the writers who created them and the Labrador play was jointly read by the members of Nalujuk Players in Goose Bay in November 1994. The writers who could not be physically present for readings returned drafts of the text which contained their comments and corrections. The level of interest has been high, the response has been tremendous and I believe that the texts we have edited together present the plays as accurately as is possible.

Those who are familiar with Newfoundland and Labrador are aware of the large number of dialects and the variations in regional accents, individual pronunciation and punctuation in the language that is spoken. The plays, when they were created and performed, recorded that diversity. Since the written texts were transcribed from sound recordings of the plays, the spellings and punctuation used in transcriptions indicate, to a large extent, how words were pronounced and how lines were spoken. In editing, I have retained those distinctions and have attempted to make them consistent particularly in characters' individual speech and more generally within the play as a unit. I have not tried to force a consistency on language of the book overall because the plays and characters in them originated in different areas of Newfoundland and Labrador and the manner in which they speak should indicate the diversity of their origins.

Words and phrases used in Newfoundland are sufficient in number and in interest to have generated a *Dictionary of Newfoundland English,* edited by G. M. Story, W. J Kirwin, and J. D. A Widdowson (Toronto: University of Toronto Press, 1982). Unfamiliar words and phrases used in the Newfoundland and Labrador collective plays may be found in that work.

1. Changes in drama in various places have been explored in, for example: Theodore Shank, *American Alternative Theatre* (New York: St. Martin's Press, 1982); Dunbar H. Ogden, *Performance Dynamics and the Amsterdam Werkteater* (Berkeley: UCLA Press, 1987); Andrew Davies, *Other Theatres: The Development of Alternative and Experimental Theatre in Britain* (Totowa, NJ: Barnes and Noble, 1987); Alan Filewod, *Collective Encounters: Documentary Theatre in English Canada* (Toronto: Toronto University Press, 1987); Denis W. Johnston, *Up the Mainstream: The Rise of Toronto's Alternative Theatres* (Toronto: University of Toronto Press, 1991) and Diane Bessai, *The Canadian Dramatist, Volume II: Playwrights of Collective Creation* (Toronto: Simon and Pierre, 1992).

2. Chris Brookes, *A Public Nuisance: A History of the Mummers Troupe* (St. John's: ISER Books, Social and Economic Studies No. 36, 1988) and Alan Filewod, "The Political Documentary: *Buchans: A Mining Town*," *Collective Encounters: Documentary Theatre in English Canada* (Toronto: University of Toronto Press, 1987), pp. 112-51.

3. Brookes, pp. 32-3, 191-92. The couple of dozen of Johnny Burke's ballads that remain of the hundreds he wrote were collected by St. John's singer John White who published the collection as *Burke's Ballads* in 1960. Only one script of Burke's many plays is still extant.

4. Ches Skinner, "Newfoundland Amateur Drama—Historical Sources," *Proceedings of the Workshop on Newfoundland Theatre Research*, eds. Denyse Lynde, Helen Peters and Richard Buehler (St. John's: Memorial University, 1993), pp. 88-93.

5. The history of CODCO and the texts of five of the groups plays are found in *The Plays of CODCO*, ed. Helen Peters (New York: Peter Lang, 1992).

6. This play like the CODCO cabaret show, *What Do You Want to See the Harbour for Anyway?* which the group developed into *Das Capital* was commissioned by the St. John's branch of the Community Planning Association of Canada (CPAC). *East End Story* was the first Mummers Troupe production to play at the LSPU Hall.

7. Brookes, pp. xii-xiii.

8. Information on Sheila's Brush was written out for me by Frank Barry and Flip Janes, members of the group.

9. This play actually arose out of a chain of events orchestrated by the St. John's arts community to protest the demolition of significant buildings and residential areas in the city. One event was a death march which started at the LSPU Hall and went to the sites of buildings and neighbourhoods marked for destruction. A lasting result of this action is a Downtown Housing Cooperative which continues to act to ensure that older homes in the downtown are refurbished and occupied.

PLAYS FOR PUBLISHING

Andy Jones

In the fall of this year the following scripts will be published, thanks to a connection between the CODCO troupe and the academic community, specifically Helen Peters. The shows are: *Cod on a Stick, Sickness Death and Beyond the Grave, Would You Like to Smell My ... Pocket Crumbs? Das Capital* and *The Tale Ends.*

Whereas,

Sold Out, Gros Mourn, Once a Giant, Dancing on the Roof, Irregular Entertainment: The Bingo Show, Summer Festival (1881-82), Just a Postal, West Moon, A Midsummer's Nightmare, The Bard of Prescott Street, The 99 Cent King Lear, Six Gums Headed for Tulsa, The Boys Who Cried Wolf, Collette (The Captive), I.W.A. Newfoundland Loggers' Strike of 1959, Live Soap, Flux, Hold Fast, So Oft It Chances, Terras De Bacalhau, Makin' Time with the Yanks, Hanlon House, We're No Match for No One, Burbank and Volupine, The King of Ashes, We're S.A.V.E.D., Gutted Head On, Magnafoot Mountain, Be Bop Deluxe, Jack Meets the Cat, My Three Dads, Double or Nothing, Brainy and the Zanies, Wedding in Texas, Albert, Newfoundland Night, Gamblers Never Die, Cat Lover, Tomorrow Will Be Sunday, Chickens, Dave and Mona, Joey, Out of the Bin, After Joey, Trans Canada What? Bloomsdays, The History of a New Founde Lande, Ocean Ranger, Young Triffie's Been Made Away With, Last Dance at the Avalon, The Daily News, Harpies, John, The Rise and Fall of Modern Campfire Songs, Jelly Beans and Shattered Dreams, Last Chance to Dance: Pavement Pageant Profiles, Man on the Moon Woman on the Pill, The Known Soldier, A Fisherman and his Soul, A Gentle Creature, Stars in the Sky Morning, Walking to Australia, Filthy Rich and Easy, Possible Maps, Show me the Button: I'll Push It (Or Charles Lynch Must Die), Carolan: Last of the Irish Bards, The Beatles Play Bishop's Falls, Cult of the Personality, Dismus Sails the Seven Seas, Fish Wharf and Steamboat Men, The Ones That Got Away, Somewhere Over the Border, As Loved Our Fathers, East End Story, Dying Hard, High Steel, Only Living Father, It's a Big Fat Lie, Some Slick, I Was a Teenage Love Doll (1 and 2), What Does That Have to do with the Price of Fish? They Club Seals Don't

They? Daddy What's a Train? Silakepat Kissinane: Weather Permitting, The Ray Guy Revue and Caplin Supper, The Swinton Massacre, The Last Resort, Frog Pond, The Argentine Consul, The Trouter's Special, Both Ends Burning, Between a Rock and a Hard Place, Nitassinan, The Amazing X, The Fig Tree, The Best Man, Naked Bungalow, Ricardo's Palace, Who Said Anything About Tea? Wind and Water, An Evening with Dorothy and James, The Newfoundland Tempest, Newfoundlanders Away, Crime and Punishment, Barely Dead and Hardly Missed, Rigadoon, Billy Max in Progress, Cookstown Rag, Fantasy for Phylis, Jaxxmas, A History of Newfoundland, The Burying Ground, Hardly a Sensible Evening, Bilingual Readings, Mr. Master Minder, Cleaning up the House, Four Episodes X 16 Attitudes, Inside Stories, Wall of the Galaxies, Actordanz, Deviant Daisy and Strange Ray, Too Big for Our Britches, Slander Libel and Three Months in Jeuvy, Droppings From Heaven, Corey and Wade's Playhouse: Young Stupid and Not all Together With it, On Edge, I've Killed Before and I'll Kill Again, The Shaman, Manitou: The People, My Blue Heaven, Time Before Thought, No Pity, Town of Tiny Buckle Glen, Falling Through the Cracks, Nothing Else to Do, A Piece of Heaven, Rising Tide Revues, I Can't get No..., Der Cirk Bizzirk, Twice Burned Once Shy, Tyrannocircus Rex, Skitz-o-Frantik, The First Stone, The Dream of the Hag, The Well Pressed Well Dressed Gentleman, The Cask of Amontillado, Lost Island Oprey, Newfoundland Folk Opera, Mixed Commotions, Anatomical Energy, Wonderbolt Circus Show, Clown Duet in Be Sharpe, Robotrix, The Past Itch, The Hugh Moore Show and *Mr. Eddie's Travelling Apocalypse Show* are *some* of the locally written theatre pieces of the last twenty years in St. John's which have not been published. Few are available for production, some are probably lost, many are just in fragments and tapes in people's basements. Some of these tapes and fragments are, fortunately, in The Centre for Newfoundland Studies and the Folklore Archive.

Certainly, in terms of the practitioners and the academics cooperating together, the CODCO experience of getting the scripts published was an excellent experience for me, and I hope that the academic community will carry on and deal with some of these scripts. In the last twenty years, there has been a tremendous amount of activity here, and a tremendous number of the productions which have taken place in St. John's have been original pieces that were written here. I know that, in the Playwrights Union of Canada Catalogue about three or four years ago, Newfoundland had the highest percentage of Canadian plays being produced of any province in Canada. I think the figure was that ninety-two percent of the shows produced in that year in Newfoundland were Canadian, and probably one hundred percent of those were actually locally written plays.

So there is, for some reason or another---I don't know the macroscopic implications--- but for some reason or other we do produce our own theatre here, and there is a unique theatre tradition which I hope that the academic community will delve into and help the practitioners to preserve and disseminate.

It has been a very practical experience for us in CODCO. Because the university pushed us to do this we now have our scripts available. Hopefully, other people will be available to perform our scripts so that they will continue to live.

18 June 1992; revised April 1995.

ADDRESSES

Permission to perform the plays and music in this book must first be obtained from the authors who can be reached at the following addresses. For John Taylor, the Mummers Troupe, RCA Theatre Company, Wonderbolt Circus Theatre:

C/O Resource Centre for the Arts
LSPU Hall
3 Victoria Street
St. John's, Newfoundland   A1C 3V2
Tel. (709) 753-4531   Fax. (709) 753-5778.

Other addresses are as follows:

Innuinuit Theatre Company
C/O Jens Haven School
Nain, Labrador   A0P 1L0
Tel. (709) 922-2813   Fax. (709) 922-2119

Nalujuk Players
C/O Amos Comenius School
Hopedale, Labrador   A0P 1G0
Tel. (709) 933-3702   Fax. (709) 933-3805

Rhonda Payne
47 Parkhill Road West
Peterborough, Ontario   K9H 3G7

Rising Tide Theatre
P. O. Box 7371
St. John's, Newfoundland   A1E 3Y5
Tel. (709) 738-3256   Fax. (709) 738-0909

Sheila's Brush
P. O. Box 1561, Stn. C
St. John's, Newfoundland   A1C 5P3
Tel. (709) 722-3259   Fax. (709) 754-4849

The Mummers Troupe

They Club Seals, Don't They?

1978

Collectively written by
Chris Brookes
Donna Butt
Pierre Beaupre
Rhonda Payne
Jeff Pitcher
Terry Rielly
David Ross
Glen Tilley

Music created and/or arranged by
Glen Tilley and **Terry Rielly**

THEY CLUB SEALS, DON'T THEY?

They Club Seals, Don't They? was previewed by the Mummers Troupe at the LSPU Hall, 19 February 1978. During the following months the play toured Ontario, Newfoundland, British Columbia, Alberta, Saskatchewan and Nova Scotia before returning to Newfoundland; it played in Petrolia (24-5 February), Waterloo (27 February), Toronto (1-6 March), St. Anthony (9 March), Ottawa (13-18 March), Vancouver (21-6 March), Victoria (29 March to 1 April), Edmonton (4-8 April), Saskatoon (11-15 April), Halifax (18-22 April), Corner Brook (25-6 April), Stephenville (27 April), Grand Falls (29 April), and Gander (30 April 1978). *They Club Seals, Don't They?* played at the LSPU Hall in St. John's (4-14 May 1978).

Members of the Mummers Troupe who wrote, directed and acted in *They Club Seals, Don't They?* are the following:

Chris Brookes	Director.
Donna Butt	Maggie, Dr. Levigne, Mother Nature, Tom Hughes, Larry, George's Conscience, Female Customer, etc.
Pierre Beaupre	Louis XIV, Leander, Clown Two, Seal, Dr. Winter, Jim, Greenpeacer, Weber, Ottawa Reporter, etc.
Rhonda Payne	Clown One, Barbara, Stewardess, etc.
Jeff Pitcher	George, Kid, Orange, Sealer, etc.
Terry Rielly	Dr. Benjaminsen, Horatio, Sealer, etc.; music.
David Ross	Captain, King Charles, Ringmaster, Johnny Canuck, Brigette Bardot, Dr. Sargeant, Customer One/Manager, Brian Davis, Greenpeacer's Conscience, Bank Manager, Stan, Punk Singer, Sealer, etc.
Glen Tilley	Merchant, Dr. Capel, Customer Two, Sealer, etc.; music.

Additional Credits:

Stage management was by **Derek Butt**. Set design **Mavis Penney**. Set construction **Derek Butt**, **Jules Drake**, and **Jan Vannan**. Poster and program graphics **Aislin**. Photographs of the St. John's production are by **Manfred Buchheit**. Film sequences were assisted by **Newfoundland Independent Film Makers Cooperative (NIFCO)** and **Mike Jones**. Maggie's monologue (Act 1 Scene 2) was written by the late **Michael Cook**. "A Sealer's Reply to His Wife," was supplied by **Mrs. Dorothy Cook** to the Mummers Troupe. It is a variation on the version by **Solomon Sampson**, published in *A Glimpse of Newfoundland in Poetry and Pictures*, ed.

Robert Saunders (Poole: J. Looker, Ltd., 1963), p. 41 and reprinted in *Haulin' Rope and Gaff*, eds. **Shannon Ryan** and **Larry Short** (St. John's: Breakwater, 1978), p. 153.

Production of *They Club Seals, Don't They?* was assisted by the Government of Newfoundland Department of Rural Development. Tour costs were assisted by the Canadian Council Touring Office.

THEY CLUB SEALS, DON'T THEY?

ACT I

1. In the Beginning: The Five Minute History Lesson
2. The Call of the Ice-fields
3. Circus-Time
4. The Letter
5. The Other Letter
6. Clown Turn: Who Can You Believe?
7. Dual Statistics
8. Mother Nature's Store
9. Clown Turn: Tactics
10. It's All in the Image
11. A Scene for Leonard Tolstoy
12. Big Business
13. Comparisons

ACT 2

1. Happy Birthday / Moo
2. Meanwhile
3. We Cleaned All the Blood Off 'Em
4. A Night at the Opera
5. Luxury is Relative
6. Danger: Men at Work
7. What We Feel

CAST OF CHARACTERS
(In order of appearance.)

GEORGE	George Bugden a Newfoundland fisherman seen over three hundred years.
CAPTAIN	Captain of ship bringing Maggie to Newfoundland.
CREW	Crewman on ship bringing Maggie to Newfoundland.
MAGGIE	Maggie Bugden, George's wife.
KING CHARLES	King of England.*
LOUIS XIV	King of France.*
MERCHANT	The man who sets the price of supplies to fishermen; these are paid for with fish. The merchant also sets the price of fish.
LEANDER	A would-be successful Newfoundlander.
JOHNNY CANUCK	Spokesman for the Canadian way of life.
SEALERS	
CLOWN ONE	Female clown.
CLOWN TWO	Male clown.
RINGMASTER	
PAUL WATSON	Greenpeace activist.*
DR. PATRICK MOORE	Greenpeace statistician.*
BRIGETTE BARDOT	French film star and animal rights activist.*
JIM	Middle-class mainland Canadian.
BARBARA	Jim's wife, animal rights activist.
DR. SARGEANT	Scientist.
DR. CAPEL	Scientist from Denmark.
DR. BENJAMINSEN	Scientist from Norway.
DR. WINTER	Scientist from Canada.
DR. DAVID LEVIGNE	Scientist aligned with Greenpeace whose methodologies are even more experimental than those of the others.*
MOTHER NATURE	
CUSTOMER ONE	A shopper at Mother Nature's store; he becomes the;
MANAGER	
CUSTOMER TWO	Second shopper who deals with Mother Nature's replacement manager.

KID	Third shopper at Mother Nature's store.
BUYER	Fourth shopper at Mother Nature's store.
ORANGE	Greenpeacer in an orange nylon jacket who "protects" Mother Nature's wares. Greenpeace activists were known for wearing orange jackets during protests on the ice-fields.
REPORTER	Newfoundland reporter who covers Orange's action.
BRIAN DAVIES	Leader of the International Fund For Animal Welfare.*
TOM HUGHES	Representative of the Ontario Humane Society.*
SEAL	Talking baby seal.
LARRY	Sealer.
STEWARDESS	Woman involved in the anti-sealing campaign.
GREENPEACER	Member of the Greenpeace anti-sealing campaign.
GEORGE'S CONSCIENCE	
GREENPEACER'S CONSCIENCE	
MALE CUSTOMER	Man trying to buy seal flippers.
FEMALE CUSTOMER	Woman trying to buy seal flippers.
BANK MANAGER	Manager of George's bank.
PRIEST	
CHILD	George and Maggie's younger boy.
BOY	George and Maggie's older boy.
WILLIAM	Another son of George and Maggie.
HORATIO	Accountant who keeps track of sealers' earnings.
STAN	Stan Bassett, a visitor from British Columbia.
WEBER	Franz Weber, a Swiss industrialist, anti-sealing activist.*
REPORTER	John Wakefield, reporter from the *Ottawa Citizen*.

* Non fictional characters.

THEY CLUB SEALS, DON'T THEY?

ACT 1

In the Beginning: The Five Minute History Lesson
Scene 1

The play dramatises Greenpeace protests of the Newfoundland seal hunt in 1976 and 1977.

As the audience enters the theatre a tape is playing International Fund for Animal Welfare radio promotional ads featuring famous Hollywood stars, each reading the same ad-copy deploring the Newfoundland seal hunt, and asking listeners to write letters of support for the IFAW protest. It is the "every letter counts" campaign.

Sealed envelopes containing programs, listing various pros and cons of the seal hunt controversy, are on each spectator's seat.

The set represents a circus ring with ladders, aerial rigging and spotlights. The ring has a white canvas floor surrounded by a circle of moulded plastic sections which can be moved to represent tables, benches, etc. There is a band stand, as in the circus tradition, mounted over the entrance to the ring. Various large banners, bearing pictures, silhouettes and slogans, such as "Extinct," "Save the Seals," etc. are furled in the rigging like a ship's sails. They are unfurled in the course of the show to punctuate scenes.

The action begins in a barren setting in seventeenth-century Newfoundland. George is writing a letter.

GEORGE: May 25, 1640. Dear Maggie, I s'pose ya knows by now dat I jumped ship. It's a wonderful place here in the New Found Land. Dere's *lots* of fish an' *no one* ta bodder ya. I built a home for ya, Maggie, if ya has a mind to come over.
    (Meanwhile, at an English dockside.)
CAPTAIN: Now I wants to sail this tide. Is everything ready?
CREW: Everything ready, Captain.
CAPTAIN: All right, ya got da cattle on board?
CREW: Cattle on board, Captain.
CAPTAIN: Ya got feed for 'em?

CREW: Feed's dere, Captain.
CAPTAIN: Somethin' for 'em to drink?
CREW: Water's on board, Captain.
CAPTAIN: Very good. Cast off then.
(Enter Maggie.)
MAGGIE: Wait! Is this boat goin' to the New Found Land?
CREW: Yes it is, ma'am.
MAGGIE: Good. So am I. Here! *(She tosses her bag and herself on board.)*
CREW: Have a good trip.
CAPTAIN: All right, clear the anchor. Hoist the sails...away we go!
MAGGIE: It's a bit rough isn't it, sir? I got all I can do to hold on.
CAPTAIN: Never mind, missus, you go below and put on a cup of tea.
(Passage of time. The ship is docking in the New Found Land.)
CAPTAIN: *(Calling.)* Hello THIS island!
(Enter George.)
GEORGE: Who's dere?
CAPTAIN: Something for ya from the Mother Country.
GEORGE: What is it?
MAGGIE: GEORGE!
GEORGE: Maggie! What are ya doin' 'ere?
MAGGIE: I t'ought I'd surprise ya. *(She looks around in concern.)* *What* are we gonna do on dis desolate ol' spot?
GEORGE: Fish, Maggie, fish. We can make a *damn* good livin' off this fishery, Maggie.
MAGGIE: Are ya sure?
GEORGE: Positive.
MAGGIE: Well, den, we're not movin'. *(To Captain.)* Throw down me bags, sir.
GEORGE: Dat's the girl.
(They are left alone.)
GEORGE: Well, Maggie, it might be modest, but it's home.
(There's a cradle.)
MAGGIE: *(Coyly.)* GEORGE!
GEORGE: *(Coy.)* Built dat last winter...nothin' else to do, ya know.
(They're shy.)
MAGGIE: George, we're thousands of miles from anybody.
(They clinch.)
VOICES: *(Speaking from offstage.)* Dat got 'er goin'. She's really gettin' hot now.
GEORGE: Maggie, either we're gettin' pretty hot or...or dis house is on fire.
(He rushes out.)
GEORGE: Maggie, de're out dere burnin' my boat!
MAGGIE: Well, stop 'em, George.
GEORGE: All right! *(Shouting to invaders.)* What's goin' on out here?

VOICE: Just following orders.
GEORGE: Whose orders?
MAN: King's.

(Loud British anthem plays.)

KING CHARLES: In the year of Our Lord, 1675, by Royal Proclamation, "No person shall set up permanent habitation on the island known as the New Found Land." Burn them out!
MAGGIE: But we're just fishin'.
KING CHARLES: I'm sorry. *(Pause.)* Economic necessity.
MAGGIE: Well, ya got to reconsider.
KING CHARLES: Oh, well, can you grow tobacco here?
MAGGIE: No-o!
KING CHARLES: Well, that's it then.
MAGGIE: But we can fish. Dere's *t'ousands* a fish! Money...
KING CHARLES: Money!
MAGGIE: That's right, sir.
KING CHARLES: You said money.
MAGGIE: Yes, sir.
KING CHARLES: All right then. You take all the risks, supply all the labour, and sell only to my merchants at my price.
MAGGIE: Yis?
KING CHARLES: And you can stay. But if you sell to anyone else, especially those damned Frenchies, I shall burn you out.
MAGGIE: Okay den. But it won't always be like dis.
KING CHARLES: Wanna bet?

(King exits. George returns.)

MAGGIE: George, I just made a good deal wit' da King of England...
GEORGE: Maggie, I haven't got time for talkin'! I just got a berth on one of the schooners goin' up to the Labrador fishin'. So I'll see ya in about t'ree months. Bye.
MAGGIE: See ya, George.

(Loud French anthem plays.)

LOUIS XIV: Vive la Québec libre! Oop! Pardon me. It is only 1713. Vive la France! Hello, you little Anglais!
MAGGIE: We're not movin'!
LOUIS XIV: I'm not asking you to move, exactly...I'm just tellin' you to sell your fish to me.
MAGGIE: Oh, we can't do dat. We got to sell 'em to da English or de're gonna burn us out.
LOUIS XIV: C'est domage. You sell to me or I burn you out.
MAGGIE: I t'ought you guys were supposed to be different.
LOUIS XIV: Not different, separate!
MAGGIE: Well...well, all right, den. But George is gonna be really pissed off.

(George enters.)

George! I went an' made a bad deal with da King of France...
GEORGE: No time now, Maggie. I'm goin' sealin' off Labrador so

I'll see ya in about t'ree weeks.

(George exits.)

MAGGIE: George, don't you ever stay home? Blessed God, how am I supposed to make it atall?

(Enter Merchant.)

MERCHANT: Lovely day, missus!

MAGGIE: We're not a movin'. *(Sees Merchant.)* Oh, it's you. Now listen to me. I t'ink it's about time dat you merchant fellers started givin' us a bit a money fer our fish instead o' supplies. Seems to me dat me and George is takin' all da risks.

MERCHANT: Well now, dat's only as it should be, sure. Look, if you wanna do business with somebody *else*, you can sail down to St. John's or maybe Boston...

MAGGIE: You knows dat we can't sail nowhere, we're stuck out here in da middle o'...

(George returns.)

GEORGE: Maggie!

MAGGIE: What?

GEORGE: Come here.

MAGGIE: *(To Merchant.)* Don't go away.

GEORGE: Listen to me. You can't talk to a merchant like that, we depend on him...

MAGGIE: I can talk to anybody!

GEORGE: Don't answer back when I'm shoutin' at ya! Now watch this. *(To Merchant.)* Good day, sir! I just made some money out swilin', and I have ready cash to pay for all my debts. *(He pays Merchant and turns to Maggie.)* Dere! You see how it's done, Maggie?

MERCHANT: Well, that covers your debt for *two* years. Now ya only owes me for *last* year.

MAGGIE: Yeah, I see exactly how it's done.

(Enter Leander running.)

LEANDER: Maggie! George!

MAGGIE: Leander!

LEANDER: We heard there's a mine openin' up in Buchans...good steady employment, George...

GEORGE: Really?

LEANDER: Let's go, huh?

GEORGE: But we can make a damn good livin' off the fishery!

LEANDER: It's 1920, George, it's industry that's got the jobs now.

MAGGIE: We're not movin'.

LEANDER: Well, I'm goin'.

MAGGIE: Good luck to ya.

LEANDER: We'll see ya.

MAGGIE: Take care.

(Loud Canadian anthem plays.)

VOICE: *(Recorded.)* April Fool's Day, 1949.

MAGGIE: What a perfect day for Confederation!

VOICE: The official referendum vote...is fifty-one percent in favour.

GEORGE: Maggie, they can't push us into a country that only half of us voted for! (*Pause.*) Wait a minute, half of us...voted for (*Suspecting Maggie has voted yes.*) Maggie!

MAGGIE: (*Acting guilty.*) No, it wasn't me, George. Was it you?

GEORGE: No, it wasn't...(*He was right.*) MAGGIE!

MAGGIE: All right, all right, I t'ought dat maybe dey'd help our fishery like Joey Smallwood promised.

(*"As It Happens" theme plays. Enter Johnny Canuck.*)

JOHNNY CANUCK: And now from stations across central Canada by shortwave and Anik satellite, we bring you "As It Will Happen," featuring the baby bonus, transfer payments, welfare, the Canadian Postal Service, LIP, LEAP, Lester Pearson and Loto Canada!

MAGGIE: And what about a fisheries policy?

JOHNNY CANUCK: I'm sorry. We can't offend our trading partners.

MAGGIE: Oh, but sir. Dat's why I joined ya, 'cause I t'ought ya'd help us protect our fishery. See?

JOHNNY CANUCK: Ah, that's too bad.

MAGGIE: Well, you've got to reconsider.

JOHNNY CANUCK: Well, all right. Ah...can you grow any wheat here?

MAGGIE: No, but we can eat bread.

JOHNNY CANUCK: Good. We need more consumers.

(*Leander enters.*)

GEORGE: Leander!

MAGGIE: Welcome home, my darlin'.

LEANDER: They closed down the mine.

GEORGE: I guess you're comin' back fishin' again, huh?

LEANDER: Can't, I sold all my gear.

JOHNNY CANUCK: Well look. Never mind. It's the age of industrialism. We...we'll start a factory. How 'bout an oil refinery?

LEANDER: That only lasted five years.

JOHNNY CANUCK: ...linerboard mill?

LEANDER: They closed that down too.

JOHNNY CANUCK: What 'bout an orange juice factory?

LEANDER: That never even opened.

JOHNNY CANUCK: All right then, burn yer boats, leave the smaller communities, go to the larger growth centres, that's where the jobs are.

MAGGIE: We're *not* movin'.

JOHNNY CANUCK: Three hundred and ninety-nine other communities think you're wrong.

MAGGIE: WRONG?

JOHNNY CANUCK: They've already moved.

LEANDER: The Ryans and O'Reillys have already gone to Churchill Falls...

MAGGIE: They'll come back.

LEANDER: ...the Skinners are leavin' next week.

JOHNNY CANUCK: And there's fifteen hundred dollars cash for you if you move right now.

LEANDER: Well that settles it, I guess I'm goin'!

(Leander exits.)

GEORGE: Good luck to you, Leander.

MAGGIE: My God, George, I'm gettin' mighty tired of tryin' to make a livin' off a dis ol' rock.

GEORGE: I understand, Mag. But look, if Leander can go up to Churchill Falls and make fifteen hundred dollars just fer *goin'*, I can go up sealin', make two t'ousand dollars just fer *you!*

The Call of the Ice-fields
Scene 2

(George collects his gear, hauling rope, club, and duffle bag. Everyone else but Maggie is on the ice as sealers. Terry sings.)
>Now that March month has come
>And spring's in the air,
>The old seals are swimming
>Up north to their lair.
>And soon on the ice-fields
>Their young will be strown,
>So Maggie my darling
>I must leave you alone.

GEORGE: You take care a yerself, all right?

MAGGIE: George...have a *good* hunt.

GEORGE: Just for you.

(George leaves. Terry continues singing.)
>We will soon reach the ice
>And then hunt for the seals,
>I will jump from my ship
>As she shivers and reels,
>Copying the ice-pans
>With my comrades and so,
>But Maggie my darling
>I must leave you alone.

MAGGIE: *(Maggie is alone upstage holding a large lit candle.)* Oh, I worries about 'em. Ah, 'tis foolish, I know. T'ings ain't as dey used to be. But every year somebody gets caught out, ya know...de ice breakin' up, or it turnin' mild and da fog risin'. My mom was da same. I minds how me father used to bring in the gaff in February to rebind it. 'Twould be standin' dere in da corner o' da kitchen, all o' da houses in da community were da same...with da gaffs an' da men an' da women not sayin' a word.

But I minds now how me mom went at everything *hard*er. Sweepin' da floor, as if she wanted to wear da canvas out. An' dat look in da back o' her eyes...I never knowed what it was den. But I *knows* now...fear. And ya couldn't speak it, ya know. But dat's what it was. Fear...all o' da men sittin' around da kitchens a' night time an' talkin' o' dis an' dat, and always it come back to da disasters, an' who was lost, an' men seein' da' Angel o' Death on de ice...and dey not heedin', I s'pose, what went on in a woman's heart. Dat last year I was t'irteen an' we used to sing rhymes when we was skippin'...

(She recites.)
Me name is Maggie Torreville,
I come from Green's Pond Island,
An' Ma will get a brand new dress
When Pa comes home from swilin'.

We was out in da garden an' all of a sudden me mom turned on us an' said, "Get outta dat an' don't be tarmentin' me!" I was surprised, I never saw me mudder behave like dat before. But den, father was leavin' da next day to catch dat sealin' boat down at Lewisporte, an' so I put it down to dat. And my father said to me the mornin' dat he was leavin', he said, "What would you like most in all o' da world?" An' all dat I could t'ink about was dat barrel-o'-apples down at Mercer's store; we used to get one fer a treat when times was good. An' I said, "I'd like a whole barrel-o'-apples, please, sir." An' he said, "Dere'll be apples enough when I comes home!" An' he was gone. Da kitchen seemed empty den, with da men gone, an' da gaffs gone from da corner. An' he an' d'udders walkin' down da road wit' da gaffs in deir arms an' da ropes coiled over deir shoulders. Dat...was da last I seen of my father.

(As she speaks, the cast scatter sawdust and unroll bolts of white cloth to cover the stage with snow and ice.)

His back an' da rope coiled on his shoulder, and me an' me mom lookin' out de window...an' he never turned. It was bad luck to turn. When da storm come, da storm for da young swiles, my mom knew. She lit a candle an' she put it in da window an' she said, "Dat's fer yer father ..."

(The sealers are on the ice, lost, walking in circles in the blizzard trying unsuccessfully to find their ship.)

SEALER ONE: Me hands. I can't feel me hands.

SEALER TWO: Why don't she sound her whistle?

(The sealers slowly freeze to death on the ice pan, becoming rigid as they stand or kneel praying, like ice-covered statues, one by one they stop breathing. Sawdust covers them like snow.)

MAGGIE: Fer t'ree days and nights da wind come outta da east, an da snow...it was that strong it took all the noise out o' the world.

(The last breaths of the sealers stop. They are now

completely rigid.)

On da t'ird day me mom blew da candle out. (*She blows the candle out.*) She put her arms around me, an' she cried, an' I didn't know what to do, so I cried too. An' she said, "He's gone, Maggie. Your father is gone." An' dey thawed 'im out...in a swimmin' pool in St. John's an' dey sent 'im home in a box. We never opened it, it sat in the front room fer t'ree days an' nights, an' den we buried 'im. I don't believe my father was in it. I didn't den an' I don't now, not to dis day. Me mom didn't either. Everytime somebody'd walk t'rough da door she'd jump...an' her face...I'll never forget her face.

> *(Terry's singing continues.)*
> The call of the ice-fields
> Comes forceful and clear.
> It makes me feel restless
> At this time of year.
> And when I'm too old
> To the ice to be goin'
> Then Maggie my darling
> I'll not leave you alone.
> And when I'm too old
> To the ice to be goin'
> Then Maggie my darling
> I'll not leave you alone.

(Scene shifts back to the present and George enters.)

GEORGE: Maggie, I'm home.

MAGGIE: Oh, George, George...

GEORGE: How are ya?

MAGGIE: Oh, t'ank God, yer back home wit' me.

GEORGE: Maggie, I've only been gone six weeks, not six years.

MAGGIE: I must be gettin' foolish in me old age.

GEORGE: Yes, I'll go along wit' dat, my dear. Make me a cup a tea, will ya'?

MAGGIE: Well, how did it go?

GEORGE: Oh-h, lots o' swiles, Maggie, lots a money dis year.

MAGGIE: Good.

GEORGE: But it was like a bloody circus up dere dough.

MAGGIE: Ya had bad weather?

GEORGE: No, it wasn't da weather, it was dem protesters.

MAGGIE: Oh! What did ya say to 'em?

GEORGE: We had strict orders not to say a word back to 'em, but dat wasn't da worst of it...

Circus Time
Scene 3

(The sound of a circus calliope drowns out their conversation. Circus-time. The ice slowly becomes a sawdust-filled circus

ring, as two clowns enter and take pratfalls as they set up props. Ringmaster juggles oranges, etc. Terry sings.)

> Well step right up, everybody,
> It's that time again,
> It's the annual sealing circus,
> For seals and sealers' friends.
> It's sure to entertain you,
> It's the big event of the year,
> For urban dwellers, political fellas,
> Brings some of us to tears.
> It's quiet in St. Anthony,
> Most of the year 'round,
> But the place gets really hoppin',
> When the circus comes to town.
> Well there's blood-encrusted sealers,
> There's lovely movie stars,
> The aerial show's terrific,
> Helicopters fill the air.
> There's the Royal Canadian Mounted,
> And a millionaire named Franz,
> Lovely stewardesses,
> Looking for the Real Man.
> Here's lots of media people,
> Looking for a real sensation.
> The antics of the protest groups,
> And opportunistic politicians.
> So better grab your seats now,
> It will soon commence.
> It's the annual sealing circus,
> For seals...and...seal...ers'...friends!
> *(Bugle, drums, razzmatazz.)*

RINGMASTER: *(Speaking slowly and dramatically with frequent pauses for effect.)* Ladies and gentlemen, for the fifteenth consecutive year we are proud to present, at great expense to Newfoundland, a show that has captivated audiences around the world. You won't believe your ears. You won't believe your eyes. You won't be able to keep your dinner down. Put your flippers together now for the annual—SEALING CIRCUS.

(Cymbal crashes, etc.)

For our headliner this evening we bring you a man who knows no fear----that highwire daredevil, the greenest star of the Greenpeace tribe—Mr. Paul Watson! With his hands tightly bound to the winch cable of a Newfoundland sealing vessel, he'll attempt, while swinging high above the frozen Arctic waters, to create—headlines...

(Drums. Watson is revealed as a high-wire artist.)

This act will be performed *without* use of a net, with only the aid of his lawyer and a photographer, who will be there to help break

the news...I mean the fall.
(Watson swings from a cable, leaps down as the camera flashes.)
Can you *believe* it, ladies and gentlemen?

Photograph by Manfred Buchheit

(Canned applause and cheers. Drums.)
And now, ladies and gentlemen, this next act will require your
acute observation. A man who's been called everything----a
mentalist----an illusionist----a scientist----a liar----judge for
yourself, as he performs this mind-boggling feat. I give you
(Pausing dramatically between each part of the name.) Dr.
Patrick Moore...
  (Drums. Moore is revealed as a top-hatted magician.)
...taking a bona fide government estimate of the seal pup
population, he will place it *(Moore places a small stuffed seal on
a table.)* before your very eyes, in the forefront of public
attention, right off the top of his head. *(Moore removes his hat
and covers the stuffed seal with it.)* Dr. Moore will cover the seal
herd simply with his own imagination. *(Moore places hat over
statistic.)* Watch closely, as Dr. Moore subjects the seal herd to not
one----not two *(Moore gestures dramatically.)*----not three---not
four—but *five* consecutive years of wholesale slaughter...*(Moore
takes up his hat; the seal pup estimate has vanished. More
recorded cheers and applause.)*
  And now, ladies and gentlemen, our star headliner of this

evening—a woman whose name is synonymous with soft and cuddly, a woman who will come out here tonight in a attempt to tame the blood lust of a Newfoundland sealer. That great film star herself—BRIGETTE BARDOT!
(Recorded whistles and stomps as Bardot appears in a blonde wig with a whip.)

BRIGETTE BARDOT: Fermez la bouche! Eet is not humane to kill zee baby seals. Eet is not even masculine. I have been to zee ice, I know what it is like...*Eet was so cold there!* And all of a sudden I saw a baby seal, and I held him to me—he was so warm. All of a sudden I saw zee mama seal and she looked at me. Quizzically. "Oh, Mama Seal, do not be jealous of me—I will not harm your baby! I only want to have baby seals everywhere." Vive les bebes phoques libre!

RINGMASTER: BRIGETTE BARDOT, Ladies and gentlemen. *(More tinny recorded cheers. He continues weakly.)* Well, that's our show for this year, ladies and gents, but we'll stay in touch! *(The circus packs up and leaves. Two clowns linger for silent clown turn. Both blow up balloons with "Truth" written on them. Each tries to outdo the other. Finally one balloon explodes. They chase off.)*

The Letter
Scene 4

(The Bugden home.)

MAGGIE: Well, George, t'anks be to God I got ya home fer anudder four weeks, anyway.

GEORGE: Yeah, it's all right to be 'ere, too, my dear.

MAGGIE: It's all right to have ya. Wan' anudder cup o' tea? *(She is looking at the audience as she says this.)*

GEORGE: Yes, I was just gonna ask fer dat.

MAGGIE: Yes, I knows what yer gonna say. I've been wit' ya dat long.

GEORGE: *(Picking up the mail.)* Dere's a letter here from Leander, look.

MAGGIE: Ooh-h, dat's nice.

GEORGE: *(Reading from the letter.)* He says he might be laid off from dat factory next summer.

MAGGIE: Oh?

GEORGE: Yeah. Well looka dat. He wonders if he can come home an' work wit' me on da longliner if he gets laid off.

MAGGIE: Tell 'im to come back.

GEORGE: Yeah!

MAGGIE: Ya used to make wonderful partners, George.

GEORGE: Yes-s. *(Opening another letter.)*

MAGGIE: Do ya mind when ya brought in da boatloads o' fish.

GEORGE: Oh, I minds.

MAGGIE: And I used to be standing on da stage watchin' ya comin' in. Ya know somethin', George, if we gets a good enough price fer da fish dis year, I t'ink dat we should hire somebody to fix up da roof, ya know.

GEORGE: (*Reading the letter.*) "You dirty rotten son of a bitch. If I could get to you I'd beat you senseless and then I'd skin your hide like you do to the seals. You're a mean bastard; you'll pay for your sins. You're lucky I don't go up there now and do it. I hope you die. Don't be surprised if you hear or see me because I'd pay anything to have you for five minutes ..."

MAGGIE: What?

GEORGE: (*Still reading.*) "...your enemy forever, John Fulton."

MAGGIE: Who's that?

GEORGE: It's postmarked Florida.

The Other Letter
Scene 5

(*A middle-class apartment in a large Canadian city. Jim and Barbara enter with camping gear and fishing rods.*)

JIM: (*Entering.*) Christ, this apartment is stuffy!

BARBARA: It was so wonderful to feel fresh air instead of the city smell for a change.

JIM: Yeah, but it's good to be home.

BARBARA: You know, we should go camping more often, Jim.

JIM: Not for a while, I got a seven-day shift coming up.

BARBARA: Another one? (*She picks up their mail, and automatically hands him the bills.*)

JIM: What's this?

BARBARA: Just bills. You always say you want to know what's coming in and going out.

JIM: Well thank you so much. What did you get?

BARBARA: Oh, this is some stuff...I signed a petition last week at the PTA meeting.

JIM: Petition for what?

BARBARA: Greenpeace.

JIM: *Greenpeace.* What are they up to now?

BARBARA: They're saving the seals.

JIM: Saving the seals! From what?

BARBARA: Extinction.

JIM: I wish they'd save the *trout* from extinction! I remember fishing in that same lake with my old man twenty years ago. You'd throw in a fly and get a four or five pound trout. What did we get yesterday? A couple of minnows!

(*He settles in front of the TV.*)

BARBARA: You're not turning on the football game, are you?

JIM: Barbara, its the only chance I've got.

BARBARA: I thought we were going to have a quiet weekend.

JIM: I'll keep the sound down. (*Showing enthusiasm.*) Hey, it's the Redskins and the Oilers!

BARBARA: (*Reading.*) Jim...

JIM: Mmm?

BARBARA: (*Showing him a brochure.*) Look at this. Aren't they cute? Tracy would love one for them for her birthday.

JIM: What is it?

BARBARA: It says here that the purchase of every stuffed seal will help save the life of a real live baby seal.

JIM: How much?

BARBARA: It's for a good cause...

JIM: How much, Barbara?

BARBARA: Twenty dollars.

JIM: Twenty dollars! She's already got a teddy bear, what does she want with a stuffed seal?

BARBARA: Oh, Jim, I mean, that's not the same thing at all. This is for a good cause.

JIM: Twenty bucks is twenty bucks.

BARBARA: Well, you spend twenty bucks on beer in two weeks.

JIM: Twenty bucks for beer, yes; twenty bucks for a stuffed seal, no way.

(*He goes back to the game. She sidles over in front of the set.*)

BARBARA: Well then, ah...twenty bucks and you can watch your football game in peace.

JIM: Come on, I don't bug you when you're reading your "save the world" stuff.

BARBARA: But Jim, but this is really important, what these people are doing. I mean, listen to this: "Despite repeated warnings from the most respected scientists, despite mounting international criticism, and despite overwhelming public opposition, this ecologically barbaric industry continues to drive the harp seal closer to extinction." Jim?

JIM: (*Absorbed in the game.*) Mmmm.

BARBARA: Did you hear what I just read to you?

JIM: Oh, yeah, yeah.

BARBARA: Oh yeah, all you do is watch television, Jim. You never get *involved* in anything. You're just like everybody else—talk, talk, talk, talk, talk.

JIM: Listen to you, "talk-talk-talk-talk-talk." Don't get on *my* back.

BARBARA: You know it says here they're going to have a meeting next week. I think I might go and see what they're up to.

JIM: What night of the week is that?

BARBARA: Wednesday.

JIM: Great! There's a hockey game that night. You should go!

BARBARA: You'll never change, will you?

(*Jim and Barbara exit. Terry and Glen enter and sing*
"The Song of Statistics.")

The protest says the harp seal faces sure extinction,

If the killing isn't stopped today.
But the government keeps telling me the herd is on
     the increase,
Their management is stronger these days.
The protest says the government is trying to deceive us,
But the government says the protest groups mislead.
We can't seem to agree on a number,
Chorus: Who can I believe?

Clown Turn: Who Can You Believe?
Scene 6

(The two clowns enter with blackboards and chalk. They speak in gibberish but with the occasional word that can be distinguished as being meaningful---almost English. All clown turns are directly to the audience, trying to get a response. They laboriously count the audience, write down two dissenting totals on their boards. After a small squabble, they turn to a simpler task---counting their own feet. Again the two chalkboard results differ. A big squabble ensues. In desperation they count their fingers; again the results are totally different. They go off fighting and cursing.)

Dual Statistics
Scene 7

(Scientists enter with computer paper, muttering, a bit of slapstick with papers, etc.)

DR. SARGEANT: Here is the test computer printout from our population survey, doctor.

DR. CAPEL: Using the catch-and-effort-analysis method I came up with 220,000 pups at the front.

DR. SARGEANT: Oh, I see, yes. I used the survivorship-index method---came up with 228,000 pups.

(Dr. Benjaminsen enters with slide rule.)

DR. BENJAMINSEN: Good morning, doctor. By using the DeLume method, I calculated 209,000 seal pups.

DR. SARGEANT: 209? Right, there---there it is. *(Checks his papers.)*

(Enter Dr. Winter.)

DR. WINTER: Good morning.

DR. SARGEANT: Doctor Winter...

DR. WINTER: *(He consults a printout.)* The figures for the cohort-analysis system are in---235,000 pups.

DR. CAPEL: There it is.

DR. SARGEANT: So gentlemen, we have an average figure of 228,000 pups at the front. Are we agreed on a safe harvest?

SCIENTISTS: Yeah. *(Etc.)*

(They are interrupted by the helicopter arrival of Dr. Levigne swinging in from above in a bosun's chair.)

DR. LEVIGNE: Pictures, pups and population!

SCIENTISTS: *(Together.)* Are you selling something?

DR. LEVIGNE: Is this the 1976 meeting to set the sealing quota?

SCIENTISTS: *(Together.)* Yes, it is. Who are you?

DR. LEVIGNE: Well, gentlemen, last spring I flew over the herd and took pictures of all the pups at the front.

SCIENTISTS: *(Together.)* Doctor David Levigne!

DR. LEVIGNE: The same. *(He "lands" in the ring.)*

DR. SARGEANT: *(To audience.)* Allow me to introduce all of us. This is Dr. Winter from Canada, Dr. Benjaminsen from Norway, Dr. Capel from Denmark. My name's Sargeant.

DR. LEVIGNE: Gentlemen, I have some very good news for you. I have made all of your work of the last twenty years completely redundant.

SCIENTISTS: *(Together.)* Redundant?

DR. LEVIGNE: Redundant.

DR. SARGEANT: You realize, doctor, that we have spent years perfecting the science of population dynamics.

DR. CAPEL: And with the data we have on the harp seal, it's the most reliable for any marine resource.

DR. LEVIGNE: I do not question your methods, nor your ability, sirs. I merely say that in the age of photography, we no longer need computers.

(General kerfuffle.)

On what figures are you intending to base your 1976 quota?

DR. SARGEANT: On last year's pup population. We have an average figure of 228,000 pups at the front last spring.

DR. LEVIGNE: There were only 118,000 pups born last year!

(Embarrassed pause.)

DR. BENJAMINSEN: But...the sealers *killed* 132,000.

(Acutely embarrassed pause; Dr. Levigne is speechless.)

DR. SARGEANT: Doctor, what sort of ground-proofing did you use?

DR. BENJAMINSEN: Perhaps, doctor, you missed counting the seals hidden underneath the Arctic ice.

DR. CAPEL: I suggest you recheck your method, doctor.

DR. LEVIGNE: There may be some slight imperfections in my method. However, I do assure you, gentlemen, that my camera and I shall return.

(Dr. Levigne exits. General hubbub as scientists return to their charts. The lights dim and come up on the same scene twenty-four months later.)

DR. LEVIGNE: *(Entering.)* Pictures, pups and population...hello, boys.

DR. SARGEANT: Hello, Dr. Levigne.

DR. LEVIGNE: Is this the 1978 quota meeting?

DR. SARGEANT: Yes, yes it is.

DR. LEVIGNE: Well, how many did you get?

DR. BENJAMINSEN: I counted 208,000 seal pups at the front.

DR. CAPEL: 212,000.

DR. SARGEANT: 234,000.

DR. WINTER: 222,000.

(Pause.)

DR. LEVIGNE: 204,000.

SCIENTISTS: Oh, very good, very good, yes, same ball park.

DR. SARGEANT: Doctor, perhaps you'd like to come in and help us set the sealing quotas.

DR. LEVIGNE: No, there has to be a moratorium.

DR. SARGEANT: *Why?* Your figures agree with ours!

DR. LEVIGNE: Because, you have got to allow the seal herd to rise to a high enough maximum sustainable yield.

DR. SARGEANT: Doctor, the herd presently stands at 1.2 million. In six years it will reach 1.7 million—that *is* maximum yield.

DR. LEVIGNE: Do you not have a moratorium on whales?

DR. SARGEANT: Yes.

DR. LEVIGNE: Are not whales and seals marine mammals?

DR. SARGEANT: Yes, they are, but unfortunately there the similarity ends.

DR. LEVIGNE: It certainly does not.

DR. SARGEANT: Whales have a longer gestation period...

(Scientists exit; Drs. Levigne and Sargeant arguing.)

Mother Nature's Store
Scene 8

*(Old Mother Nature enters and tidies up, complaining.
Customer One enters.)*

CUSTOMER ONE: *(Entering.)* Hello, Mother Nature!

MOTHER NATURE: Oh, good morning. You didn't wipe your feet.

CUSTOMER ONE: Oh, look, I'm sorry. Hey, Mother Nature, I want all the plates you have in the store.

MOTHER NATURE: You can't have *all* the plates.

CUSTOMER ONE: Why not? I want them.

MOTHER NATURE: But we don't do it that way, I mean we need to keep some to regenerate...I probably, let me see, I can give you...

CUSTOMER ONE: Ah, look, Mother Nature...

MOTHER NATURE: ...four plates.

CUSTOMER ONE: Forget it, forget it. Come here. Hey, how have things been for you lately, huh?

MOTHER NATURE: Oh, it's so hard to keep up with it all, you know.

CUSTOMER ONE: Yes.

MOTHER NATURE: With the oil spilling everywhere.

CUSTOMER ONE: Tired eh, really tired? Imagine takin' a break, lyin' in the hot Florida sun, drinkin' tea all day. Wouldn't it be great, huh?

MOTHER NATURE: Uh.

CUSTOMER ONE: Eh? Yeah?

MOTHER NATURE: (*Tentatively.*) Ye-e-s-s-s.

CUSTOMER ONE: Okay! Okay!

MOTHER NATURE: But I have no one to look after the store.

CUSTOMER ONE: I'll manage it for you.

MOTHER NATURE: Huh-ho, you don't know anything about it.

CUSTOMER ONE: What's it matter? I'm young, innovative.

MOTHER NATURE: But...

CUSTOMER ONE: ...got fresh ideas. I can handle anything. See you. Bye-bye. (*He ushers Mother Nature out and becomes the Manager.*) Now I can set this place up to really move stock.

(*Knock on the door. Customer Two enters.*)

MANAGER: Yeah.

CUSTOMER TWO: Wh...where's Mother Nature?

MANAGER: She's on holiday. I'm runnin' the store.

CUSTOMER TWO: Well, look, I need all the knives you got.

MANAGER: Okay. Hey, it's gonna cost you a pretty penny.

CUSTOMER TWO: How much?

MANAGER: Three cents a piece.

CUSTOMER TWO: (*He mimes giving money.*) That's good.

MANAGER: Okay, here you are.

CUSTOMER TWO: Nice doin' business with you.

(*Customer Two exits; enter a kid.*)

KID: Yes, good evening, sir.

MANAGER: Yeah?

KID: I want ashtrays.

MANAGER: Ashtrays. How many?

KID: Fourteen.

MANAGER: Good for you. (*Mimes giving them to him.*) Okay, fourteen ashtrays.

KID: Great. Thank you. Really nice deal. (*He exits.*)

MANAGER: I know this is gonna work.

(*Knock. It is Customer Two again.*)

MANAGER: Yeah, come on in.

CUSTOMER TWO: I tripped goin' down the hill an' I lost some knives so now I need six more knives.

MANAGER: Hey, there's no more knives.

CUSTOMER TWO: No, you see I want to have a full set.

MANAGER: No, you see there's no more knives. Kaput, terminated, that's it forever for knives.

CUSTOMER TWO: What kind of a way is this to run a store? I mean, I need more knives.

MANAGER: Hold on, I'm gonna make a phone call. (*He dials.*) Hello, Mother Nature.

MOTHER NATURE'S VOICE: Hello.

MANAGER: Hi, how are ya? Look, say, a fella came in wanted all the knives, sold 'im all the knives, lost a few, wanted more, didn't have 'em, what am I gonna do?

MOTHER NATURE'S VOICE: I told you, you have to manage them properly.

MANAGER: Manage...manage!

MOTHER NATURE'S VOICE: Conservation.

MANAGER: Conservation. I understand.

MOTHER NATURE'S VOICE: You want me to come back?

MANAGER: No, no. Hey, have a good time, okay? Bye.

CUSTOMER TWO: What'd she say?

MANAGER: Wants me to manage the place.

CUSTOMER TWO: Do I get any knives?

MANAGER: No, you don't get any knives. I'm in a pickle.

CUSTOMER TWO: Who cares. I'm not looking for pickles.

MANAGER: Look, do you need a job?

CUSTOMER TWO: I do now.

MANAGER: Okay, look. Start countin' everything in the store. We'll keep a record. We'll *manage*, okay? Start with the cups.

CUSTOMER TWO: Cups!

MANAGER: How many?

CUSTOMER TWO: There's, ah...seven cups.

MANAGER: Seven cups. When the cups get down to four they need that many to regenerate. So we can only sell three. Okay? Three cups. Got it? How about blankets?

CUSTOMER TWO: There's, ah...seven blankets.

MANAGER: Uh-ho! Moratorium on blankets. They've got a long gestation period. (*Bulk buyer enters.*)

BUYER: Boys, boys, listen, I want some cups, seventeen cups.

CUSTOMER TWO: Seventeen cups? How about three cups and fourteen saucers?

BUYER: Come *on*. I'm havin' a party. Give me the cups.

CUSTOMER TWO: I'm sorry. You'll have to take the three cups and fourteen saucers.

BUYER: This is poor management on somebody's part.

MANAGER: You'll have to learn to change your ways, my friend.

CUSTOMER TWO: Right.

(Bulk buyer exits.)

MANAGER: Back to the stocktaking. How are the blankets doing? Oh, wait a minute. Before you check that, check those cups. How're they doin' now?

CUSTOMER TWO: They're back up to seven again.

MANAGER: It works! Management!

(Enter Dr. Levigne.)

DR. LEVIGNE: Cameras, cups and copulation! How many cups do you have on the shelf?

CUSTOMER TWO: We got seven.

DR. LEVIGNE: No you don't—you got two.

CUSTOMER TWO: I just counted them—there's seven cups up there.

DR. LEVIGNE: I took pictures.

MANAGER: Hey. Wait-wait-wait-wait, wait a minute. Where'd you take the pictures from?

DR. LEVIGNE: From the top, naturally.

MANAGER: Well that's it. You see, we stack the cups in columns of two, you only saw the two on the top.

DR. LEVIGNE: This is getting ridiculous. Well, then, what about your blankets?

CUSTOMER TWO: Blankets? Ah...seven.

DR. LEVIGNE: Are you selling any blankets?

CUSTOMER TWO: No.

DR. LEVIGNE: Then you can't sell cups either.

MANAGER: Blankets are *not* cups!

(Greenpeacer wearing an orange nylon jacket enters, stands in front of shelves.)

MANAGER: Who's this?

CUSTOMER TWO: Hey, wh...what are you doin', buddy? Come on you're not supposed to be behind the counter.

ORANGE: I am savin' the cups.

CUSTOMER TWO: From what?

ORANGE: Extinction!

CUSTOMER TWO: Why don't you save the boots? There's only three of them left!

ORANGE: Ah, come on. Ugly rubber boots? The public won't *care*! But they love pretty little china cups!

(Orange sprays the cups with a spray can.)

CUSTOMER TWO: Well now look what ya've done! Sprayed 'em all green. Now I can't sell 'em, they'll over-populate and...I'm gonna have to hire somebody once a week to come in and smash cups so we'll have room on the shelf.

(Reporter rushes in.)

REPORTER: Inhumanity to cups! The cup in danger of extinction! What a story!

(Glen and Terry sing "The Song of Statistics." Reprise.)
> I was reading in the paper this morning
> *Chorus:* Who do you believe?
> Ten years to extinction,
> Without a moratorium.
> *Chorus:* Who do you believe?
> They say there's scientific proof
> In the aerial photography,
> *Chorus:* Who do you believe?
> So join in the fight to save our ecology.
> *Chorus:* Who do you believe?
> But its proven by the catch and effort analysis,

Proven by the figures and
Proven by the graphs,
That there's no danger of extinction,
As those self-professed ecologists
Chorus: Would have you believe.
Would have you believe.

Clown Turn: Tactics
Scene 9

(By dint of true clown logic, Clown One "Tom Sawyers" Clown Two into believing that a pile of garbage is something much more important than it seems to be. It's a matter of publicity.)

It's All in the Image
Scene 10

(Enter Brian Davies and Tom Hughes, arguing.)

BRIAN: Tom, I think it's disgusting that you, as a representative of the Ontario Humane Society, should condone this senseless slaughter of helpless animals for nothing more than trinkets.

TOM: Brian, you seem to forget that I was the one that started the protest against this hunt back in the fifties, when it wasn't humane, when there was indiscriminate slaughter, when there *were* no controls. But today, Brian, it is the most humane animal harvest in the world.

BRIAN: Tom, I'm not saying you never did anything. You did, but somewhere along the line you got bought off.

TOM: Bought off? And what about you? Rewriting the Book of Genesis—Changing seal *pups* into seal *babies.* It's the worst kind of Walt Disney emotionalism.

BRIAN: It is not emotionalism to describe accurately what happens, when an unweaned baby seal...

TOM: *Unweaned* baby seal! There you go again.

BRIAN: ...an unweaned baby seal has its head smashed in, and I will do anything—*anything* to stop this hunt.

TOM: Hah! Then you, the highest paid sealer in the world, is out of work. Listen, Davies, I am damn glad I don't have your conscience.

BRIAN: The problem with you, Tom, is somewhere along the line you've lost your basic humanity. Normal people, with reasonable human responses walking out on the ice floes, looking into those large, tearful eyes, see their own humanity reflected there.
(He climbs to a spotlight and highlights the entrance of a giant whitecoat seal with a human head. It dances in to a Walt Disney-like theme and lies down in the ring. George enters.)

GEORGE: Okay, I'll take this pan.
(As he raises his club over Seal, it speaks to him.)

Photograph by Manfred Buchheit

SEAL: Hi, what's your name, sailor?

GEORGE: (*Spooked.*) Larry, you take this area, I'm movin' up west!

(George rushes off. Larry enters.)

LARRY: I'm comin'. (*He raises his club.*)

SEAL: Lovely day.

(Larry is not pleased. Shakes his head unbelieving,
and raises his club again.)

SEAL: Ya watch television?

(Pause as Larry tries to decide whether this is real.)

LARRY: Yeah, I watches it every now an' den, ya know, when I'm not too busy.

SEAL: I'm on TV on Sunday at seven o'clock—channel eight.

LARRY: Well maybe, if I'm not watchin' the Waltons, I'll...wait a minute, I'm talkin' to a goddamn seal!

GEORGE: (*Re-entering.*) How are you doing?

LARRY: You do it.

(George and Larry try to kill Seal, but it speaks again.)

SEAL: I want a glass of water.

GEORGE: Now *you* heard it.

SEAL: I want my mommy!

LARRY: If we gotta go back to the captain and tell 'im dat a seal was talkin' to us, we'll be da laughin' stock o' Newfoundland.

SEAL: I want my mommy!

GEORGE: All right, let's do it, together. Cover my eyes.

(They eventually steel themselves for the act, but as the club
comes down Seal sits up and begins to sing, with back-up
chorus of Brian Davies and Stewardess.)
Blood-thirsty Newfoundlanders,

Spit on them, curse and slander,
There's half of them not worth
To walk upon God's earth.
Ruthless, savage spoilers,
Barbaric heartless swilers,
The brunt of mainland humour,
Is all they're bloody worth.
(Glen and Terry respond singing.)
Now there's something to be said
For all those protests being led.
For a man speakin' out
What's on his mind.
But they try to rob the dignity
Of men who live and die upon the sea,
Trying to feed our families and our friends.
*(Grand finale as Stewardess carries Seal off, singing
as they exit.)*
Blood-thirsty Newfoundlanders,
Spit on them, curse and slander,
There's half of them not worth
To walk upon God's earth.
Ruthless, savage spoilers,
Barbaric, heartless swilers,
The brunt of mainland humour,
Is all they're bloody worth!
(Davies turns off the spotlight and climbs down.)

GEORGE & LARRY: Davies, you had somethin' to do wit' dis.

DAVIES: Oh, just a teeny, teeny bit.

GEORGE & LARRY: You're twistin' reality!

DAVIES: Not twisting, just orchestrating!
(Davies bows and exits.)

LARRY: I'm gonna get back to work, buddy, Davies or no Davies.

GEORGE: Gimme a smoke, will ya?

LARRY: Ya goddamn leach. *(He tosses cigarettes.)* S'pose ya wants
a bloody match now too, do ya?

GEORGE: Yeah.

LARRY: *(Tossing matches.)* Catch 'em.

GEORGE: Larry, my son, yer beginnin' to remind me more of my
wife Maggie every day. *(He lights up.)*

LARRY: She must be a little darlin' too, is she?
(Larry exits, leaving George alone on the ice.)

A Scene for Leonard Tolstoy
Scene 11

GREENPEACER: *(Entering.)* You from one of the Canadian
ships?

GEORGE: That's right...

(They are wary of each other.)

GREENPEACER: How many seals did you kill today?

GEORGE: About a dozen.

(Pause.)

GREENPEACER: I'm with Greenpeace.

GEORGE: Where ya from?

GREENPEACER: Vancouver.

(The consciences of the two men appear and coach from ringside.)

GREENPEACER'S CONSCIENCE: *(To Greenpeacer.)* Skip the pleasantries, get down to business.

GREENPEACER: *(To George.)* Look, the sealing industry is big business. We're on your side. We understand you're just workers trying to make a living...

GEORGE: How can ya understand when ya come from five t'ousand miles away?

GEORGE'S CONSCIENCE: *(To George.)* Don't provoke him. You can only lose in a confrontation.

GREENPEACER'S CONSCIENCE: Tell him it's mainly *because* you come from a long way away that you're able to see this question in a larger perspective, unlike those caught in the middle of it.

GREENPEACER: Look, man, we've been studying the figures now for two years. It's proof-positive the harp seal's going to be extinct.

GEORGE: I've been sealin' for ten years an' I can tell ya there's more seals out here today than I've ever seen before.

GREENPEACER: Come on, there are airplanes flying over here right now taking pictures of the whole herd. The population is going down.

GEORGE'S CONSCIENCE: Not even Levigne believes dat any more. Scientists are on *your* side.

GEORGE: I got a fisheries officer on my ship and he makes sure that I stay within the quotas. Listen, where were you guys ten years ago when we were fightin' for the cod stocks, tryin' to bring in the two-hundred mile limit? I didn't see ya down here fightin' for our fishery den, did I?

GREENPEACER'S CONSCIENCE: Change the issue. Tackle him on cruelty.

GREENPEACER: I suppose you get off on clubbing little baby seals, eh?

GEORGE: Oh, dat's bull!

GEORGE'S CONSCIENCE: No! Put it back on *him*. Ask him about where *he* comes from. Ask him about industrial pollution, an' mines, an' slaughter houses, an' how *he* lives with nature.

GEORGE: Why don't ya go back to your own back yard?

GREENPEACER: The world's my back yard. Why don't you do like Mother Nature does and take the old ones instead of the

young ones? What you're doing is completely against nature.
(George seethes.)

GEORGE'S CONSCIENCE: Careful, don't touch him.

GREENPEACER: I suppose when you're finished wiping out the harp seal you'll find some other species and wipe them out too, eh?
(George starts to grab him.)

GEORGE'S CONSCIENCE: *(Stopping George's fist and almost shouting.)* No! Hold it!!

GREENPEACER'S CONSCIENCE: See! He's going to hit you, he *is* a barbarian!

GREENPEACER: *(To his conscience.)* I didn't come here to insult people!

GREENPEACER'S CONSCIENCE: You came here to save seals. This is how you save seals.

GREENPEACER: This is not the way to do it.

GREENPEACER'S CONSCIENCE: Are you telling me you're not willing to take a few stitches to your head to save 180,000 seals?

GEORGE'S CONSCIENCE: *(To George.)* Ignore him. Go back about your business.

GREENPEACER'S CONSCIENCE: All we need is *one* picture of him hitting you and we've won.
(George approaches a seal.)

GREENPEACER'S CONSCIENCE: Look, he's going to kill a seal!
(Greenpeacer rushes George, winding up on his back as he wrestles with him for the club. George and Greenpeacer stagger as they struggle.)

GEORGE'S CONSCIENCE: *(Arguing.)* You can't isolate the seal hunt from every other issue in this society.

GREENPEACER'S CONSCIENCE: We have to start somewhere. We have nothing against you people.

GEORGE'S CONSCIENCE: Then get off our backs!
(George, with the Greenpeacer on his back, topples over as he is wrestled to the ice. Blackout. In the darkness the taped Hollywood voices of the "every letter counts" radio promotional campaign tumble across the stage.)

VOICES: *(Tape of the stars' actual voices in anti-sealing campaign.)* This is Zsa Zsa Gabor...Hi, I'm Donny Osmond...Hello, this is Anne Baxter...Hi, this is Hugh O'Brien for the International Fund for Animal Welfare...Please, the letters must continue. Every letter counts...

Big Business
Scene 12

(George with his income tax return.)

GEORGE: George Bugden. Address—Change Islands, Newfoundland. Occupation—Fisherman. Income for 1977—seventy-eight-hundred dollars.

MAGGIE: My God, das not all we made, George?

GEORGE: Dat's it!

MAGGIE: An' we t'ought we was gonna win da world last year.

GEORGE: I t'ink we lost it instead.

MAGGIE: Well now, we're gonna get enough back from de income tax to go to our son's graduation in St. John's, aren't we?

GEORGE: Now, Maggie. You knows as well as I do dat we're not gonna have da money to be goin' to St. John's. Plain as dat.

MAGGIE: You'll change yer mind, George, because I *wants* to go.

GEORGE: Maggie, I am tellin' ya, I didn't even make enough money to give Pierre Trudeau here what *he* wants! You're *not* goin' to St. John's.

MAGGIE: George, I t'ought dat I might buy ya a nice new suit for de occasion.

GEORGE: Sure, I'd look pretty good in rubber boots and a new suit, wouldn't I?

MAGGIE: You'd look smarter than Robert Redford. (*Pause.*) I'd get ya a pair o' shoes, too.

GEORGE: I'd get you a new pair o' black, high-heeled shoes.

MAGGIE: An' maybe one o' dem dresses wit' da low necks so I'd look sexy.

GEORGE: And a diamond necklace right dere. (*He points.*)

MAGGIE: An we could hire a limousine an' drive up to our son's graduation.

GEORGE: I can see it now. Premier Frank Moores drivin' us.

MAGGIE: Ha-ha-ha.

GEORGE: hm-mmm.

MAGGIE: Whatta ya say?

GEORGE: Impossible.

MAGGIE: George. *Come on!*

GEORGE: Mag, look. Can you remember last spring when I had da lobster traps out.

MAGGIE: Yeah.

GEORGE: An' de ice come in an' how much I lost along with dem traps.

MAGGIE: I knows.

GEORGE: Then during da summer I had da nets out an' dem two storms we had...the money I lost dere. Maggie, I am fifteen-t'ousand dollars in debt an' every time I turn around somebody has got deir hand out for more money. The answer is *no*.

MAGGIE: I under*stand*. 'Tis not as funny as I makes it all out to be, is it, George?

(They get coy with each other.)

GEORGE: You, ah...really want to see city lights?

MAGGIE: I wants to see my boy graduate.

GEORGE: How about (*Pause.*) Toronto city lights?

MAGGIE: No, t'ank you very much.

GEORGE: Now, Maggie.

MAGGIE: Now, George. Ya knows dat we was up dere fer two weeks visitin' me brudder an' you never went outside da door da whole time.

GEORGE: Dat was different, it was a holiday.

MAGGIE: George, give you t'ree weeks away from de ocean an' you'd be too cantankerous to live wit'—I'd have to find myself a new man.

GEORGE: Maggie, listen. I am t'inkin' in terms of dis family...bread 'n butter on da table. We gotta go.

MAGGIE: What are you gonna do in Toronto? I'm damn well sure you can't go fishin' in Lake Ontario.

GEORGE: Have you got a brudder up dere?

MAGGIE: Yes. An' my brudder works in a factory, an' a factory is no place fer George Bugden. You belongs out dere on dat ocean.

GEORGE: George Bugden belongs where he can make money to support his family!

MAGGIE: Well, I'm not goin'.

GEORGE: We're goin' to Toronto. So ya better learn to like it, Maggie.

MAGGIE: Dis is *one* time in my whole life dat I'm goin' against ya. I'm *not* goin' to Toronto. I'd shrivel up an' die. *Dis* is our *home.*

GEORGE: Maggie, dis will always be our home. We can always come back to dis place.

MAGGIE: Yes, just like Leander come back...when da boat's gone, da fishin's gone. Don't you remember da night dat we joined Confederation, an' dey announced it over da radio. An' your father was sittin' dere in dat chair...an' he made you swear on da Bible, George Bugden, dat you would never leave dis place. Well, he'd turn over in his grave if he heard you talkin' now.

GEORGE: Turn over in his grave? With the rocks dat's piled on his back around dis place I doubt if he'd be able to move down dere.

(Maggie laughs.)

GEORGE: It's not funny, Maggie.

MAGGIE: No, but it's true. Dis is hard place to be turnin' over, eh George? My, what a character he was, George.

GEORGE: I did promise 'im.

MAGGIE: He loved dis place.

GEORGE: All right, one more try, Mag, and dat's it...just once more.

(Maggie embraces him.)

GEORGE: Now, I didn't ask for any o' dat. Just make me a cuppa tea. An' yer *not* goin' to St. John's.

MAGGIE: No-o-o, sir!

(George concentrates on the income tax forms again.)

Comparisons
Scene 13

(Glen and Terry sing "That's What He Does.")
There's a man on the west coast,
He takes his harvest from the forest,
He takes responsibility for what he's done,
And he believes the trees will grow again,
He's a logger, that's what he does.
　　There's a man on the prairie,
He takes his harvest from the wheat fields,
With luck he'll reap the seed he's sown,
And he believes the wheat will grow again,
He's a farmer, that's what he does.
　　There's a man in north Ontario,
He takes his harvest from the trap line,
A native skill he learned when he was young,
And he believes the animals will come again,
He's a trapper, that's what he does.
　　There's a man living by the sea,
He takes his harvest from the ice-fields,
He takes responsibility for what he's done,
And he believes the swiles will come again,
He's a sealer, that's what he does.
*(George, the Newfoundlander, and Jim, the Ontarian, move
around the circus ring like a huge sundial. They
speak in short bursts.)*
JIM: I live for the weekends. Watch the game. Spend time with the
wife. It's the only thing *(Pause.)* keeps me going.
GEORGE: Seems like the winter is *(Pause.)* the only time a fisher-
man can rest. Time to fix up my nets and lobster pots. Time to
spend with the family.
(Glen sings "The Seasons Song.")
Late in the spring when the ice-flows are melting,　·
The fishermen head out from the coast,
Setting their nets and their traps for the summer,
Living a life of hope.
　　Some years are good ones when fish they are running,
Bad years can break a man's soul,
Some boats come back with fish to the gunwales,
Some boats never come home.
JIM: I don't mind Mondays myself. A lot of the other fellas at work
hate 'em. But the factory seems cleaner at *(Pause.)* the start of
the week.
GEORGE: Come March and I'm really lookin' forward to the start
of the fishin' season. Money's gettin' scarce so I go after seals. It's
good money, two-t'ousand-four-hundred dollars last year.
JIM: Mid-week is a bore. You get into a kind of work rhythm

though. Seven bucks an hour. Seven bucks an hour.

GEORGE: Summertime I got the nets out. If it's a good year there'll be lots of fish in June. But by August I'm jiggin' and handlinin'. Slow work for eight cents a pound. But I made almost seven t'ousand dollars.

(Glen sings.)
> Late in the fall when the season is over,
> What money is left is his own,
> He wonders if it will last him till swiling,
> When it's time to go out on the flows.
>> Some years are good ones,
> Some years are bad ones,
> No matter which way it goes,
> They'll see it through this one,
> With hopes for the next one,
> For this is his life and his home.

JIM: Fridays never end. At least it's pay day. I been making pay-ments out of my cheque for the past couple of months to buy a real nice birthday present for the wife. Today I pick it up.

GEORGE: The fall was the worst time last year. I lost over a t'ousand dollars worth of gear in a storm. Oh well!

ACT 2

Happy Birthday / Moo
Scene 1

(Jim and Barbara's apartment. Barbara is talking on the phone.)

BARBARA: Listen, Mona. They can't...they can't sell the furs. Nobody wants to buy recognizable seal skins.
(Jim enters.)
JIM: I'm home, Barbara.
(She doesn't hear. He unwraps the box he is carrying. It is a fur coat. He hides it behind his back.)
BARBARA: They're stockpiling them on the European markets. France has banned the importation. Oh, it's so exciting! You know, they won't be able to withstand another year of bad public-ity. That's right, the markets will fold and...and the hunt'll be finished. That's why this meeting next week is really important. So we're all going to meet at Carol's house and then we'll go down together, Okay?...Right...Right...See you then. Bye, bye. *(She sees Jim.)* Oh! Jim.
JIM: Hi, how are you?
BARBARA: Oh, I just spent the whole afternoon on the telephone; I feel like I'm attached to it.
JIM: Right...Right...Ah...

BARBARA: I'm sorry, dinner's not ready. I'll go get it right now.

JIM: No-no, wait-wait-wait. Just a minute. Stand over there and turn around and...

BARBARA: Why?

JIM: ...and close your eyes.

BARBARA: For God's sake, don't be silly.

JIM: Sh-h! Be quiet.

BARBARA: Jim, I've got a lot of things to do.

JIM: Sh-h! (*He places the fur coat on her shoulders.*) HAPPY BIRTHDAY! Don't worry about the money—it's all paid for.

BARBARA: Oh-h!

JIM: Your mom helped me pick it out, too. Come on, let's see you walk around in it.

BARBARA: It's beautiful...and it's really sweet of you, but I can't wear this coat, Jim.

JIM: What?

BARBARA: If I wore this into a meeting, they'd throw me out. I just spent the whole afternoon on the telephone...

JIM: It's not seal, it's muskrat.

BARBARA: Oh, I know, Jim, but it's the same sort of thing. I mean, they're helpless little animals that are slaughtered so we can decorate our backs.

JIM: Look, they're on your feet! Moo! Moo!

(*Barbara stares at her shoes.*)

BARBARA: That's not the same thing. I mean, calves are slaughtered for the meat anyway.

JIM: So you don't want the coat.

BARBARA: Oh, I'm sorry. Look, we'll take it back, and...and we can take a trip together instead.

JIM: Take it back! The guy went to a lot of trouble, you know, payments on it...

BARBARA: Jim, he'll take it back. Look, I'll go down with you and I'll have a talk with him; he'll take it back, believe me. See, it's a matter of hitting the markets...

Meanwhile
Scene 2

(*Dockside in St. John's. The sealing ships are in.*
There is a series of vignettes.)

SEALER: Seal flippers for sale! Greenpeace special only two dollars. Pass 'em down, boys.

MALE CUSTOMER: How much for a dozen?

SEALER ONE: Twenty-four dollars a dozen for you.

(*They haggle.*)

SEALER TWO: Flippers...FLIPPERS!

FEMALE CUSTOMER: Good morning.

SEALER TWO: Morning, ma'am. Would ya like some flippers?

FEMALE CUSTOMER: Yes, I...I'd like a dozen, please.
SEALER TWO: A dozen flippers. Here you are.
FEMALE CUSTOMER: And I wants a carcass too.
SEALER TWO: A carcass.
FEMALE CUSTOMER: Yes, a nice young tender one now.
SEALER TWO: Oh yes, this is the best ya can get.
FEMALE CUSTOMER: Oh, dat's *lovely!*
SEALER TWO: That'll be twenty-eight dollars, ma'am.
FEMALE CUSTOMER: (*She digs into her purse.*) Twenty-eight
    dollars, yes.
SEALER TWO: It's goin' to a good cause.
FEMALE CUSTOMER: Yes, I'm sure it is.
SEALER TWO: You wouldn't happen to be goin' to da Stardust
    later, would ya?
FEMALE CUSTOMER: I don't know. I might.
SEALER TWO: Maybe if I see ya dere I can buy you a drink.
MALE CUSTOMER: (*Still haggling.*) Twenty-two dollars!
SEALER ONE: All right, okay, twenty-two dollars.
            (*Terry sings to the tune of "Mussels in the Corner."*)
            When the boats come back to St. John's town,
            All the folks they gather 'round,
            Grab yer partner, spin her round,
            Flippers in the harbour.
BANK MANAGER: Now, Mr. Bugden, what can I do for you?
GEORGE: I'd like a loan, sir.
BANK MANAGER: What do ya want the money for?
GEORGE: Well, I'd like to fix up my wharf.
BANK MANAGER: And, how much is that gonna cost?
GEORGE: It's gonna cost me t'ree-t'ousand dollars.
BANK MANAGER: How much d'ya want from me?
GEORGE: A t'ousand.
BANK MANAGER: Good. Where are you getting the other two-
    t'ousand?
GEORGE: Sure, I just got back from sealin'!
BANK MANAGER: No problem, Mr. Bugden, sign here.
GEORGE: (*Excitedly to Maggie.*) Maggie, I got the loan!
                    (*Terry sings.*)
            A dollar for the grocery man,
            Two for the mortgage on his land,
            Three for to give the church a hand,
            When the boys come home from swilin'.
GEORGE: Good day, Fadder.
PRIEST: Good day, my son. It's (*Hesitating.*) Michael, isn't it?
GEORGE: It's George.
PRIEST: George...George, yes.
GEORGE: Well, just got back from swilin'.
PRIEST: Swilin', boy. Ye got something for the church then?
GEORGE: Forty-dollar donation, Fadder!

PRIEST: Bless you, my child, bless you.

GEORGE: Maggie blesses you, too.

CHILD: Daddy, daddy, daddy, please, can I get a new bike. All da kids got one, but I haven't got one.

GEORGE: Mag?

MAGGIE: What odds, sure. It's only a couple dozen flippers worth.

GEORGE: Well, all right den, but just one!

CHILD: Oh-hoo!

(Terry sings.)
>The store-fronts they are all dressed up,
>To try to woo their hard-earned bucks,
>With aftershave and a new dress shirt,
>When the boys come home from swilin'.

BOY: Now Ma, am I old enough to go swilin' or what?

MAGGIE: You certainly are not.

BOY: Why not?

MAGGIE: You're too young.

GEORGE: Now, Maggie, remember when young Harry went swilin', we were able to tar da roof dat year.

WILLIAM: Yes and I...I put da foundation in da house.

GEORGE: Yes, an' young Jim went an' we got da new shed out back.

MAGGIE: And, when Georgie went I did get me floor canvassed, didn't I? *(To boy.)* Yes, my son, go with yer mudder's blessin'.

BOY: If ye keep breedin' like dat, Pa, you'll soon have a palace!

GEORGE: *(Calling up to the bandstand.)* Now, listen now, Horatio, can you gimme a breakdown of dat money I made at da hunt dis spring?

HORATIO: Yes sir, Mr. Bugden. You made one-thousand-three-hundred-and-fifteen-dollars-and-seventy-four cents for the pelts you brought in...

MAGGIE: Oo-h!

HORATIO: ...one-hundred-and-fifty-one-dollars-and-twenty-six cents for the oil products. Which brings to mind that's a lovely perfume you have on, Mrs. Bugden...

GEORGE: Now, Horatio, watch it.

HORATIO: Yes, George, certainly. Ah...nine-hundred-and-thirty-three-dollars-and-ninety-eight cents you made from the meat products. Two-thousand-four-hundred-dollars-and-ninety-eight cents altogether.

GEORGE: That's great!

HORATIO: Well it's all relative, George. Your total income is still below the Canadian poverty level, you know.

We Cleaned All the Blood Off 'Em
Scene 3

(The Bugden kitchen.)

MAGGIE: George, in—hale!

GEORGE: *(Inhaling.)* Seal flippers!

MAGGIE: *(Speaking excitedly.)* Oh, my son, I got flipper pie in de oven tonight. I tell ya we're gonna have some f-e-e-d!

GEORGE: I'm starved, Mag.

MAGGIE: All right den, I'll take up da vegetables.

(Dum de de dum dum knock on the door.)

GEORGE: I'll get dat.

MAGGIE: Dat's a good idea.

GEORGE: *(Answering the door.)* Oh, come in, come in, Stan.

STAN: Hi. I hope I'm not late.

GEORGE: Maggie.

MAGGIE: What?

GEORGE: Come out. I want ya to meet somebody.

MAGGIE: Hello.

GEORGE: This is Stan Bassett from British Columbia.

MAGGIE: My, right over on de udder end of 'er.

STAN: Yeah, right.

GEORGE: I met him over at Pat's place and invited 'im up to supper so ya might as well get out anudder plate, all right?

MAGGIE: *(Surprised.)* Supper?

GEORGE: And Stan, you...

MAGGIE: *(To Stan.)* You go in dere an' sit down an don't move, sir. *(He goes into the room.)* George! Do you know who else comes from Vancouver? Das where all da Greenpeace crowd comes from, George. Dey t'inks we're all savage an' barbarian, and *(Speaking in a loud whisper.)* here I am makin' a meal o' *flippers*! What's he gonna t'ink? *(She rushes to Stan.)* Sir, sir. You don't smell nutting, do ya?

STAN: Now that you mention it, there is kind of a strange smell in here.

MAGGIE: It's the garbage. I forgot to put it out.

GEORGE: Maggie, get out here!

(Maggie's distress shows as she rushes back and forth. She rushes to George.)

MAGGIE: George, you go down to dat takeout down the road an' you get him some takeout chicken. Dey eats chicken. *(Rushing back to Stan.)* Now sir, how do you like Newfoundland? Aren't we a lovely, gentle race o' people?

GEORGE: Maggie, get out here. *(She rushes to George again.)* Now you can't...It's Sunday an' da takeout is closed, an' I am gonna tell dis man what's goin' on.

MAGGIE: No! *(She rushes back to Stan.)* Sir! You can just eat da vegetables!

GEORGE: Stan, there's something you should know.

MAGGIE: No!

GEORGE: We are havin' seal flippers fer supper an' you are quite welcome to stay if you like.

Photograph by Manfred Buchheit

MAGGIE: I cleaned all da blood off 'em.

GEORGE: Maggie!

STAN: I've never had them before, but I'm willing to give them a try.

MAGGIE: But I thought you came from Vancouver?

STAN: Well, ah...actually I come from a little place up the coast called Quadiaski Cove.

MAGGIE: An' ya eats animals? Well, my son, das a blessed relief to me.

STAN: I'm a logger. My brother-in-law and I have got a small sawmill operation.

GEORGE: Ya see, Maggie? He's one of us.

MAGGIE: Ya saved me from a heart attack, sir.

(They serve up the meal, and tuck in as the music begins. Glen and Terry sing "Blood-thirsty Newfoundlanders.")

Now in our home of fish and seals,
From Cape Chidley to Cape Freels,
In every bay and harbour on our shore,
It's a tougher life than nine-to-five,
And every woman, man and child,
Provides the strength to live there and survive.
　　Blood-thirsty Newfoundlanders,
Spit on them curse and slander,
There's half of them not fit

To walk upon God's earth,
Ruthless, savage spoilers,
Barbaric heartless swilers,
The brunt of mainland humour,
Is all they're bloody worth.
      (Maggie, George and Stan sing.)
Well, it takes a special breed
To make a livin' off the sea,
And brave the frozen vastness
Of Greenland's southern floes,
To put a meal upon the table,
As long as they are able,
It's a way of life,
That they can call their own.

A Night at the Opera
Scene 4

(A Swiss gentlemen with a hundred-dollar bill in his mountaineer's cap enters.)

WEBER: Have I got a deal for you!

GEORGE: An' who might you be?

WEBER: I'm Franz Weber and I'm here to build up a fake seal fur factory. All you have to do is sign this contract and you can stop clubbing real seals and manufacture polyesters instead!

MAGGIE: But we're fishermen, not factory workers.

GEORGE: Where do ya plan on buildin' dis factory to? See, us fishermen live all along a two-t'ousand-mile coastline. How are we supposed to commute to wherever ya build this factory?

WEBER: Let's not quibble over minor details. We'll just take that out of the contract. *(He tears off the bottom two inches.)* There. Now there's a second clause *(He points.)* here. It's the raw materials. We're going to ship them in from Europe.

MAGGIE: What are ya gonna do wit' the finished ones?

WEBER: Good question, madam. We're gonna ship them back to Europe again.

MAGGIE: I see, like the orange juice factory. We're the cheap labour.

GEORGE: Wouldn't it seem reasonable for some fella in Germany somewhere, who's closer to both the raw materials and to the markets, to start a similar factory and run you out of business?

WEBER: Look, I didn't come here to argue with you, I came here to make a deal. *(He tears off another two inches from the contract.)*

MAGGIE: What's left?

WEBER: About three inches. Look, here's the promissory clause. Promise never ever to kill a seal again.

MAGGIE: Oh, no-no-no. I'm not givin' up my seal flipper dinner for nobody, sir.

(Weber tears another inch off.)

GEORGE: What's next?

WEBER: The, ah, sanity clause.

GEORGE: My son, if you'd been livin' in Newfoundland since Confederation you'd *know* there was no Santy Claus!

(Weber tosses away the last contract scrap.)

MAGGIE: I'm gonna tell you something, sir. Your fake fur factory is a luxury us people cannot afford.

WEBER: But, madam, the seal hunt is a luxury the seal can't afford.

MAGGIE: What about dat coat you got on?

WEBER: What about this coat? It's nylon. Nothing had to die for this.

MAGGIE: How much money did ya pay for it?

WEBER: A hundred dollars.

MAGGIE: Well, on George's salary dat would be some luxury t'buy a skinny little coat like dat for a hundred dollars, I can tell you. I don't know where you fellas got yer ideas about luxury, but it certainly wasn't growin' up in Newfoundland.

Luxury is Relative
Scene 5

(David, accompanied by Glen and Terry, sings a punk rock number.)

Fish eggs is luxury, chicken eggs is scum
Chorus: How come?
You got all the bread
I ain't got none.
Chorus: How come?
You are takin' Valium
I am suckin' Tums.
Chorus: How come?
We got Aubrey Mac
You got Barbara Frum.
Chorus: How come?
Kids are starvin'
Dogs are eatin'
Filet mignon.
Chorus: How Come?
The System...SUCKS!
The System...SUCKS!
You got your touch-tone telephone
(Touch-tone, touch-tone)
Quadraphonic stereo, (ster..e..o)
Channel Commander, colour TV (T...V)
And your refrigerator, baby,
Is frost-free...

Synthetics may be cheap (Ba-ba-ba-ba-day)
But in another sense (Ba-ba-ba-ba-dooh)
The cost to the environment (Ba-ba-day)
Comes as a great, great, great expense.
Yeah—Nature has its cycles
Things return from whence they came,
It's luxury to take from the earth
That which will not come again.
But those synthetic fibres—RAYON
They may wash and dry with ease—DACRON
But they do not rot or decompose—ORLON
They will always hold their crease—NYLON
Now that's luxury.
You s'pose your pantyhose will decompose?
Chorus: NO WAY!
Do you think we'll take the guilt
For your non-renewable ways?
Chorus: NO WAY!
Look to your own lifestyle
Before you try to change our ways
Chorus: OKAY?
You want green plastic garbage bags
The rest of your days?
Chorus: NO WAY!
Luxury is relative
So's my Uncle Ray—OKAY?
OKAY!
NO WAY!
OKAY!
HOOOOWWW COOOMMME!
*(Grand dirty punk finale destroys instruments, beats up
musicians, kicks in lights, etc.)*

Danger: Men at Work
Scene 6

*(A silent clown turn performed in the circus ring. Clown One
strokes a small white seal glove-puppet. Clown Two rushes out
with a large bag labelled "Sealers Kit." He unpacks an instruction sheet excitedly and reads it as Clown One cuddles the seal.*

*Clown Two unpacks various props from the kit, including a
sign reading "Danger: Men at Work" which he arranges artisti-
cally for Clown One to hold up.*

*Clown Two reads instructions again and unpacks a huge
blunderbuss. He takes aim at Seal and fires, a sign flops out the
muzzle reading "OOPS!" as Clown One is hit in the rear end by
the shot, and begins to cry. Clown Two cheers Clown One up
and arranges his shot again.*

There is a second shot. The muzzle flag reads "Bang!" and the seal puppet gasps and flops over apparently dead. With great glee Clown Two "skins" the puppet by pulling the fur glove off. This reveals a red glove which flops around to the great horror of both clowns. Clown Two quickly puts the "skin" back on the puppet, thus restoring it to cute and cuddly life.

Clown Two reads instruction sheet again. "Aha!" He produces a huge clown club. Sneaks up on Clown One and her seal, winds up and clobbers the puppet. It dies immediately. Clown Two pulls off the "skin"---this time no red quivering mass appears. He is triumphant. Clown One demands her toy back and they both chase off.

A white-smocked scientist comes on to pick up the props.)

SCIENTIST: And so, animals die for our needs. Our responsibility is to make sure that death meets two requirements. First of all that there is as little psychological stress as possible prior to death and secondly, that in the act of death itself there be as little pain as possible. Now in the last twenty years we have experimented with a number of methods to kill seals, some of those commonly used in our slaughter houses. The rifle is *not* efficient on the ice because of ricocheting bullets. Other methods have been used---impact shock bolts, electrical shock, acoustic shock, but they all involve sophisticated technology and when you introduce such technology in the death of an animal, psychological stress goes up because the animal has to be prepared and the technology itself has to be set up. So, curiously enough, the instrument that the Newfoundland sealer has used for one-hundred-and-fifty years, his gaff, this hardwood bat, and the Norwegian hakapik, provide the least psychological stress and the most painless death.

What We Feel
Scene 7

(The Bugden home.)

MAGGIE: I'll get you a cuppa tea, George.

GEORGE: All right, den. Make it a good *strong* cup.

MAGGIE: Ya know somethin', George?

GEORGE: What now?

MAGGIE: I spend half my life gettin' you cups o' tea. I'm just beginnin' to see me situation now...I think it'll soon be time fer me to leave you an' join the "women's liberals," whatta ya say, huh?

GEORGE: *(Still waiting for his cup of tea.)* Yes, my dear.

MAGGIE: Ya t'ink ya could learn to cook fer yerself?

(There is a knock at the door.)

MAGGIE: I'll get da door, you stay at what you're doin'. *(She answers the door.)* Oh my, come on in outta da cold, my son.

(Enter a reporter.)

REPORTER: I didn't really dress for winter. Is this the house of Mr. George Bugden?

MAGGIE: Dat's right. Sit down dere by da stove till you gets warm.

REPORTER: Thanks very much.

MAGGIE: You're not from around here, are ya?

REPORTER: No, ah, I'm a reporter. John Wakefield.

MAGGIE: O-oh!

REPORTER: I'm writing a series of articles for the *Ottawa Citizen* on the seal hunt.

MAGGIE: Oh yes.

REPORTER: Yeah, yeah.

MAGGIE: Well, dat must be nice.

REPORTER: Oh it's...it's good...good fun.

MAGGIE: What are ya doin' down here?

REPORTER: Well, ah, their idea was to do this special article, see, from the "little man's" point of view. Pardon me! Ah, from...your common working man's point of view.

GEORGE: Oh yeah.

MAGGIE: Well, how come ya came to us?

REPORTER: Well, I stopped into the store down in Twillingate...

MAGGIE: Oh yes.

REPORTER: ...and I told buddy what I was after, and he said, "My son, you wants to talk to George Bugden up in Change Islands."

MAGGIE: Now ya knows who he was talkin' to, George, he was talkin' to Harry, 'cause Harry's been tellin' everybody to come down here and talk to George fer as long as I can remember.

REPORTER: Oh!

MAGGIE: Oh, George is a wonderful talker, ya know? My son, he'll talk da leg right off o' ya! You go ahead now. You ask 'im any questions dat you wants.

REPORTER: All right. Ah, I'll start with your name...

MAGGIE: Why do ya want to put his *name* in the paper?

REPORTER: That's so when I quote something that he said, like, you put his name underneath, see?

MAGGIE: But den, everyone will know 'twas George who said it!

REPORTER: That's the idea.

MAGGIE: Be careful of what ya says to 'em, George.

GEORGE: Yes, Mag.

REPORTER: Well now, how much money did you make at the hunt last year?

GEORGE: Well, dat's a mighty personal question to be askin' right off the bat.

REPORTER: *(Writing away.)* No, it's only so I can set it in context for mainland readers, you see.

GEORGE: Two-t'ousand-four-hundred dollars I made last year.

REPORTER: And ah...what was your income then from *all* sources last year?

GEORGE: Seven-t'ousand-eight-hundred dollars.

REPORTER: Seven-thousand-eight-hundred dollars. So that means the seal hunt, then, provided about one-third of your annual income.

GEORGE: Smart fella.

REPORTER: The next question is, ah, you know how seal pelts...now they're not processed here in Newfoundland, right? They actually go over to Norway and most of the money is made over there. Now I wonder whether you folks ever feel...exploited by the process? You see, exploitation is when you're taken advantage of...

GEORGE: We knows what exploitation is around dese parts.

MAGGIE: You see, me an' George been livin' in Newfoundland for all our lives.

REPORTER: Ah, yes. Now, ah, the next question then is, ah, you know how some scientists say there's so many seals out there, somebody else says there's so many. Now, *you're* out there. Ah, with your own eyes now, how many seals do *you* think are out there?

GEORGE: To tell ya da truth, I never counted 'em. But I can tell ya how many families dere are in Change Islands dat depends on dem seals, an' dat's sixty-six.

MAGGIE: Sixty-seven at da last church women's meetin', all of 'em tryin' to stay off a da welfare. Now put dat in your story.

REPORTER: Yes, yes I will. All right, the next question is a bit different. Ah, what do you actually *feel* when you kill a seal?

GEORGE: (*Thoughtfully.*) Nuttin' really.

REPORTER: Nuttin'? Well I can't say nothing, now see, I'm writing this for mainlanders, to explain how you feel.

GEORGE: It's a job, ya see, a job dat got to be done and I...I...I do it.

REPORTER: Y-yes, b-but you must've felt something somewhere along the line. I can't say "nothing."

GEORGE: When I was a young fella, eh? Sixteen years old...first time I ever went to de ice...went up wit' me older brudders...felt a little something den, the first time, I guess.

REPORTER: And you mean now after you've been at it for twenty years that you've become a killing machine?

GEORGE: We're not machines, sir, but we don't feel nuttin'. It's the same as fishin', killin' fish. It's my job...

REPORTER: (*Really pushing now.*) Well now, what I want to know is—when you bring that club down and you smash that seal's head, and there's blood on the ice, what...

MAGGIE: (*Speaking angrily.*) Sir, yer not puttin' dat in da paper!

REPORTER: Mrs. Bugden, please! (*To George.*) What do ya feel when that *happens* now?

MAGGIE: You want him to say that he feels like a murderer and that he kills dem little seals because he hates 'em! Well, you're like all da rest a da crowd. You might be savin' da seals, young man, but you are killin' George Bugden...an' he does not deserve it. An' I am tired of watchin' my husband hurtin' an' sufferin' because o' da likes o' ye. Now if you don't mind I would like you to leave my home until you have some respect for a decent workin' man...NOW!

REPORTER: I'm sorry, I just wanted to find out what he felt.

MAGGIE: Now you know what we all feel.

REPORTER: Yes, I suppose I do.

(Reporter leaves.)

GEORGE: Well, Maggie, you've gone an' outdid yerself dis time.

MAGGIE: George, I never shoulda been so rude to da young man. I s'pose 'tis not really his fault, is it? But, I gits tired of everybody puttin' you down all da time.

GEORGE: Ya don't have to explain dat.

MAGGIE: You're not mad at me?

GEORGE: No.

MAGGIE: George, you don't t'ink he's gonna write all dat stuff up in da newspapers, do ya?

GEORGE: No, but I'd say he'll remember it for a while. Ya know somet'ing, Maggie? See, dat's what I wanted to talk about—right out the window by da wharf there—young Jimmy Evans, seventeen years old he is. You remember last year, he was talkin' about how he was gonna go into da university. Look where he is now out fishin' wit' his old man. For so long the young people was *afraid* o' being a fisherman, because it was such a poor livin'. Now that's changin'. If dey'd just leave us *alone* for a while, we could *do* it. Wit' the young fellas gettin' into it, and finally some protection for the fish stocks, and a decent price for my fish...

MAGGIE: We're not movin', George Bugden.

GEORGE: We can make a damn good livin' off dis fishery *yet*, Maggie!

(A ninety second film of pork being "processed" from pit to hot dog in a commercial slaughterhouse is screened while Glen and Terry sing the "Standard of Living Song.")

> To see animals killed,
> You say you can't stand,
> But you're eatin' your porkchop,
> With your other hand.
> It's easy to judge,
> When you're one step removed,
> And you don't have to walk,
> In another man's shoes.
>   Who pays the price?
> Do you know who pays
> For your comfortable cushions

And affluent ways?
Who pays the piper?
Who's singing your song?
Who owns the hog
That you're living high on?
*(The chorus is repeated. As the final chorus finishes, the fading
stage lights linger on a backdrop portrait of a fisherman and
family.*
*Note: It can be useful to follow the performance with a discus-
sion.)*

THE END.

Rhonda Payne

Stars in the Sky Morning

1978

Created with
JANE DINGLE and **JAN HENDERSON**

STARS IN THE SKY MORNING

Stars in the Sky Morning was first produced by Molly Grub Production Company at the LSPU Hall, 21-24 September 1978. It was held over a week later (2-6 October), as a co-production between Molly Grub and the Mummers Troupe, and it toured Port Saunders (10 November), Hawke's Bay (11 November), Daniel's Harbour (12-13 November), Cow Head (14 November), St. Paul's (16 November), Norris Point (17-18 November), Baie Verte (19-20 November), Springdale (22 November), Roberts Arm (23 November), Corner Brook (24-25 November) and Buchans (26 November 1978) as a Mummers Troupe production. It was restaged by the Mummers Troupe at the Hall (14-25 October, 1981), and it toured Nova Scotia, playing in Chester (6 November), Halifax (8-9 and 14 November) and Wolfville (12 November, 1981). *Stars in the Sky Morning* has also been produced by Kam Theatre at Thunder Bay in 1981 and again in 1985 (23 October to 10 November), when it went on to tour northern Ontario playing in Kapuskasing, Cochrane and Kirkland Lake.

Stars in the Sky Morning was created by **Rhonda Payne** with the assistance of **Jan Henderson** who directed the 1978, 1979 and 1981 productions of the play and **Jane Dingle** who co-starred in the 1978 and 1979 productions. The original cast was as follows:

Rhonda Payne	Lilly, Rach, Peg, a gossip.
Jane Dingle	Sus, Nora, Mary, Ruby, a gossip; music.

Additional credits:

In 1978, music was by **Jane Dingle**; lighting **Derek Butt**; set **Derek Butt** and **Terry Ridings**; and poster and program **Carol Wherry**. In the 1979 and 1981 productions set design, lighting design and stage management were by **Derek Butt** and costumes were by **Debbie Clark-Penton**. In 1981 music was by **Stephanie Squires** and the poster and program design were by **Mavis Penney**. Photographs of 1978 St. John's productions are by **Lynda Hendrickson**. In the 1981 production, **Jane Dingle's** roles were played by **Michele Flieger**.

Songs were provided by the following: "Lullaby," **Forward Ayre**, Hawkes Bay; "The Ship that Never Came," **Mrs. Charlotte Decker**, Parsons Pond (Kenneth Peacock, *Songs of the Newfoundland Outports,* 3 vols, 1965, PEA 109 No. 816, vol. 3, pp. 795-6) and "In Courtship There Lies Pleasure," **Becky Bennett**, St. Paul's (Peacock, PEA 95 No. 756, vol. 2, pp. 465-6).

Research for *Stars in the Sky Morning* was funded by an Explorations Grant from the Canada Council. The script development workshop was funded by the Government of Newfoundland Cultural Affairs Division, the Mummers Troupe and financial assistance provided by the Canada Council administered in Newfoundland under a temporary and one-time seed funding program called Funds to Initiate Stage Happenings (FISH Fund).

AUTHOR'S STATEMENT

Summer 1975, Parsons Pond, the Great Northern Peninsula, Newfoundland. I am on tour with the Mummers Troupe performing *Dying Hard*, a play about the dying men and the widows of St. Lawrence, a community devastated by the silicosis deaths of miners in their midst. We are setting up to perform this evening in Edgar Payne's bar. I am intrigued by the predominance of the Payne family name on signs all along this part of the coast. I introduce myself to Edgar as "Vig Payne's granddaughter," and he greets me enthusiastically, "My dear, your grandfather and I were just like that," crossing his fingers. It is a declaration I will hear repeated warmly by many along this coastline in the coming years.

In the darkened bar the performance is intense. Most of the adult population of this community of two hundred has turned out to see us. All along the route with this play we have been reminded time and again that our audiences really seem to believe we are the characters we play. They listen intently to our stories. After the show when they share their concerns for their personal safety in the mines in which they work, they speak to me as Julia, the widow I have played, not to Rhonda the actor. It is an experience rarely offered to one as a performer, eerie and humbling in its power. After the performance I am swarmed. "I'm your cousin Doug Payne...I'm Aunt Sue Payne's daughter...I'm your Uncle Sam Payne's nephew...your grandfather and I..." warm hands eagerly clasping mine...their lineage and mine flaunted proudly...generations in living memory...bright eyes beaming in recognition and welcome. The next night the scene is repeated in Daniel's Harbour. For me it was overwhelming.

I grew up the daughter of divorced Newfoundland ex-patriates, isolated from the island after the death of my maternal grandfather. In small-town southern Ontario I felt awkwardly out of place, unconnected, lonely for a family and a place to belong to. Fifteen years later, on the Northern Peninsula in Newfoundland, I was engulfed in a family network scattered along a hundred miles of coastline, over two thousand descendants spawned by English and French settlers seven generations back. And here they could still name every generation. That experience lit a spark that led to the creation of *Stars in the Sky Morning*.

In 1976-77 I moved for a year to the Northern Peninsula, into the household world of women. I learned to bake bread, to bottle salmon and how to knit socks. Mostly, I listened. Newfoundland is a nation of story tellers and raconteurs. Our personal histories weave a colourful fabric of fact and fancy. My return to the Northern Peninsula meant rekindling connections with the traditions of story telling and music in my own family. My rediscovery of family meant being welcomed into homes of near strangers, consuming excessive amounts of tea and food, sharing stories and, in time, opening up confidences and setting memories free.

Eventually I brought out my tape recorder and collected stories from a dozen individuals, most family members, related to me by birth and marriage. In 1978 I transcribed the tapes, raised a little money and hired Jane Dingle and Jan Henderson to collaborate with me on the material. Using the transcripts as text, Jane and I memorized certain stories and improvised our way into scenes and story lines. The challenge with this project was to transfer the magic of the story telling art into living characters on stage and to reproduce, as nearly as possible, the authentic voices that inspired the work. I aimed to create a lyrical and evocative study of character and language. It was my first independent project and rooted as it was in my personal exploration of family and ancestral myths it is one that still holds deep meaning for me. That it strikes strong chords in a wider audience is for me a great gift.

The characters and situations in this play are fictional, but they are composites of women that I came to know. The only real names that are used are in stories of certain characters whose exploits are immortalized in the folklore of the coast. The women that this play is based on are my family, literally. With few exceptions they are related to me by birth or marriage. I lived with them as they spun their wonderful tales and I grew to respect and love them. This play is based on their words, our improvisation, my editing and a few theatrical tricks. Like most plays created by the collective creation process in which I have worked for so long, the play belongs, not to the writers and performers who brought it to the stage, but to the real life characters who lived the stories and found joy in the telling of the tale. This play is dedicated to that indomitable spirit that ensures that people survive, if only through sheer bloody minded-ness and for the fun of telling the story.

I want to thank Carrie and Rufus Guichard for giving me a home in Hawkes Bay; Mildred and Trevor Bennett and their family for welcoming me at any hour of the day or night as I rambled up and down the coast; my maternal grandmother Eliza Pretty who inspired my love of story telling; Floss Noble, Bernice Prince, Jane Hutchings, Maud and Forward Ayre, Charlotte Caines, Tress Patey, Dora Sinnicks, Nurse Myra and Angus Bennett, Alec and Jane Bennett, Margaret and Charles Moss and the countless others who welcomed me into their homes and their memories.

RHONDA PAYNE

CAST OF CHARACTERS
(In order of appearance.)

LILLY

Former inhabitant of the now abandoned King's Cove; she appears as both an adult and child.

SUS

Lilly's older sister who appears in the play only as a young girl.

NORA

Aged nineteen, married with two children, in her first appearance; she is older in subsequent scenes.

RACH

Nora's sister, fourteen when the play opens, working for Nora; she also ages in the play.

AUNT MARY

Aged eighty-one; she also appears as a young woman.

PEG

Mary's mid-sixty-year-old niece, visiting her aunt.

RUBY

A young girl, a friend of Lilly's in King's Cove.

GOSSIPS

Two women at a wedding in King's Cove.

STARS IN THE SKY MORNING

Scene 1

The set consists of a floor cloth painted to represent a white pine floor and a hooked rug, a rocking chair, a straight backed wooden chair and a small table. The upper rear portion of the stage is a neutral change zone, fully visible to the audience. It contains a set of hooks to hold costume changes: two aprons, two sweaters, a coat and a headscarf, which the actors use to portray different characters and different periods in the same character's life. There is also a folded quilt and a kerosene lamp.

At the end of a scene each actor turns back on to the audience, freezes, "drops" out of character into neutral, changes costume pieces and assumes the new character as she rearranges the furniture for the next scene. Frequently both actors remain onstage while one delivers her monologue. The setting for each scene is changed through lighting and character focus.

The lights come up as the actors enter, one from either side. They cross to the costume rack. Each takes down an apron, Sus exits with hers, Lilly crosses to the table carrying her apron and sits on the edge of it.

LILLY: Does the sound of a brook make you lonely? I remember when I was at home, after everyone was in bed, I used to rise up my window on a moonlit summer's night, and I'd sit and I'd listen...and the only sound you could hear was the sound of the brook...and the air would be right perfumy with the smell of clover and daisies from the meadow.

We were living in King's Cove and there was only five families there...and when I think back to it now, to the way I was reared, I'm glad I was reared like that, in a sense of speaking, because I know I have experiences you could never have. I've experienced...loneliness...and, like, the stillness of the evening...so much time to watch a plant grow, or so much time to watch a little animal grow. And I think that's good for you. But that and that alone, that's all you learn. You learn no evil, but

you learn no good either.
(She starts to put on her apron.)
It was lovely when I was small. When I was really, really small, you know, four, five, six, back as far as I can remember. It seemed like there was more sunshiny days than rainy days. That was all a child of that age could ask for—space, a lot of trees and grass and beach and rocks. I used to go round the shore. I wasn't s'posed to go, but I used to go round the shore and I'd pray I'd pick up a doll's head...

Scene 2

(Sus enters wearing her apron. She mimes dusting the bedroom. She moves the chair downstage centre, climbs up on it and mimes dusting a box on the wall, notices that something is loose and starts picking at it.)

LILLY: Sus?

SUS: I'm up here, Lilly, in Mom's room. *(Gets down from the chair hurriedly and resumes her "dusting." Lilly approaches her. She is wearing her apron.)* Where were you to?

LILLY: Down the shore.

SUS: What were you doing down there?

LILLY: Nothing. *(She sits on the chair Sus was standing on.)*

SUS: Nothing?

LILLY: Reg says he wants some more hot water for his bath.

SUS: He knows I'm busy. It's heating.

LILLY: He won't let me get it for him.

SUS: You're too little.

LILLY: Sus, do you think I might find a doll's head down on the shore? I was hoping one might wash up. I could make a body for it.

SUS: No, maid, I don't think you'll find a doll's head down on the shore.

LILLY: I wish I had a doll.

SUS: What do you want a doll for?

LILLY: To play with.

SUS: There's lots of youngsters to play with. Go out to play with them.

LILLY: No, they're too rough.

SUS: So that's where you were all morning, down by the shore looking for a doll's head.

LILLY: Oh, Sus, don't tell Mom!

SUS: No, I won't tell Mom.

LILLY: *(Looking up at "wall" above her.)* Sus, where'd Mom get that doll to?

SUS: That doll? She won that. She come first in something in school

LILLY: Never takes it out of the box, does she?

SUS: No.

LILLY: Some pretty, isn't it?

SUS: Yeh, she's some sweet. Wanna see her? Get outta the way.
*(Sus climbs up on the chair and mimes gingerly removing the
"box" from the wall and setting it on the floor.)*

LILLY: Oh, Sus, what're you doing? Sus, you can't do that! Mom'll
kill you!

SUS: Mom's down packing lobster. She won't be back before dinner.
And Reg is busy. He won't bother us.

LILLY: Sus, she'll give you a trimming!

SUS: Don't be so foolish.

LILLY: Yes she will, she'll hammer you.

SUS: She won't know. Look the glue's come out from the sides of
the case. I noticed it while I was cleaning it. All we gotta do is
take the nails out.

LILLY: Look at her.

SUS: She's some pretty. Look at her ribbon. *(She mimes touching
it.)* Oh my! It's gone! The ribbon went all to dust! Look, it's all in
little bits.

LILLY: Mom'll kill us. You took it down.

SUS: She won't notice that...her eyes is too bad. Look at her. *(She
takes the "doll" out of the case.)* Look, Lilly, her eyes opens and
closes. Here. Careful now.

Photograph by Lynda Hendrickson

LILLY: *(Hugging the doll.)* Isn't she pretty. Look at her little shoes.

SUS: You wants a doll, don't you?

LILLY: Yes.

SUS: I'll make you one.

LILLY: Will you?

SUS: Don't drop her! If you're a good girl and goes to bed right after supper, I'll make you a doll.

LILLY: Can you make a doll, Sus?

SUS: Yes.

LILLY: What'll it look like?

SUS: Well, I'll give it hair and booties.

LILLY: And eyes?

SUS: Yeh, I've got a couple of buttons.

LILLY: And a dress?

SUS: Lilly, I'll see what I've got in my scrap bag. But you gotta go to bed right after supper, now.

LILLY: I'll go to bed right now.

SUS: Don't be silly, you don't have to go to bed right now.

LILLY: *(Sus starts to put doll back in its case and return it to its position on the wall.)* Let me hold her again, Sus.

SUS: Lilly, I can't take her out again.

LILLY: Oh, please, Sus.

SUS: Now Reg is calling me. I'll be down in a minute. Watch the door will you.

LILLY: Mom'll see the ribbon's gone. She'll give us a trimming.

SUS: She won't notice that, Lilly, you can't see where the glue's gone from there can you?

LILLY: Yeh.

SUS: Oh, Mom won't notice that. She can't see that far. *(She calls offstage.)* I'm comin', Reg, I'm comin'. *(Speaking to herself.)* He's some crooked.

> *(She moves off to "see" to Reg. She freezes. Lilly removes her apron and becomes her adult self reminiscing.)*

LILLY: And when I come down in the morning, Sus had made me a doll. It was only small, but it was just beautiful. And I don't know what happened to me when I saw that doll, I just started crying to break my heart. And I took her and I went into the little room off the kitchen and I hugged her to me...and now I wonder why my heart didn't split in two.

> *(Lilly freezes. Both actors simultaneously cross to the back of the stage, hang up their aprons and put on their respective sweaters to become Nora, aged nineteen, and Rach, aged fourteen, Nora's sister.)*

Scene 3

> *(Nora's kitchen. Nora picks up the quilt from the chair and folds it to resemble a baby. She sits in the rocking chair*

holding the "baby." Rach is "scrubbing" the floor.)
NORA: *(Sings.)* Hushaby, my little piccaninny,
                 The black fox'll get you if you don't.
                 Hushaby, rockaby, mama's little babe,
                 Dadda's little anna banna coo.
Rach, haven't you got that floor scrubbed yet? Soon be time to put supper on. 'Course I don't know if I'll be able to eat any. Me stomach's still qualmy after that boat trip up the coast.
RACH: That was three days ago, Nora.
NORA: Hangs on, girl. Least it does with me. I hates them damn boats.
RACH: I'd love to go for a trip on one of them.
NORA: What's that you're scrubbing the floor with?
RACH: That's just an old rag I found in the pantry.
NORA: Rach! That's me dish cloth! *(Rach giggles.)* Rach, you got a brush for scrubbing the floor with, not the dish cloth. You're foolish you are. You're not foolish, you're wasteful. You needs your head read, my girl.
RACH: Nora, did you hear what the boys did last night?
NORA: No, and I don't want to hear. That crowd of hooligans.

Photograph by Lynda Hendrickson

RACH: Well, you know how Uncle Jim is so frightened of the Germans coming over here? Well last night, Ron and Will and Henry and a whole crowd of 'em went up around the point and they sounded off the foghorn and they shot off the guns and they frightened the life out of the poor old fella.

NORA: That's a sin tormentin' that poor old man.

RACH: And he took runnin' and he run up to Mrs. Payne's and he burst in over her door, and he said, "They're yer, Mrs., they're yer!" And she said, "Who's here?" "The Germans is yer, Mrs., didn't you yer 'em?" And Ron says he didn't even stop to put his pants on. He just slung his bracers over his shoulder and he took runnin'. I wish I'd seen him.

NORA: That's enough about Ron Payne. Now get back to that floor. I'm not paying you two-fifty a month so's you can carry on when you're s'posed to be working. And you needn't take advantage of me either just 'cause I'm your sister. You think I'm hard on you, don't you? Well I'm not. My dear, you don't know what hard work is. When I was your age *(Rach begins aping her)*. I went out to work for Rose and Sted Brophy up the way, and I can tell you I worked. Not just hauling the water and tending the cows and the gardens. But Sted had nineteen men working up in the woods for him. And we had to cook for them. Bake thirty loaves of bread at a time, as many cakes and cookies as we could manage, and mind the youngsters. *(She notices Rach aping her.)* What're you doing? Come here, Rach. I s'pose I gotta get down on my hands and knees and show you how it's done.

RACH: No.

NORA: *(Handing her the baby.)* Hold Freddy. *(Rach coos at the baby.)* Pay attention! I'm not doing this for the good of my health. Now, when you scrubs a floor, you don't flop the brush around like this. You puts a little elbow grease into it like this. *(She demonstrates.)*

RACH: That's what I was doin'.

NORA: You were not.

RACH: Yes I was.

NORA: Rach! I don't want another word out of you 'til you gets it done. Now give Freddy to me.

(Rach returns to scrubbing her portion of the floor. She emits three horrendous groans as she does her exaggerated imitation of Nora's scrubbing.)

NORA: What's the matter with you?

RACH: I'm just doin' it like you told me to.

NORA: *(Laughing.)* You're a trial for me, Rach. I tell you I can hardly wait for Fred to come home. You're drivin' me cracked.

RACH: There, it's all done.

NORA: *(Pointing to the area she has scrubbed.)* This is whiter.

RACH: Looks the same to me.

NORA: No. This is definitely whiter.

RACH: Nora, how come you're so fussy? Mom was never fussy like that.

NORA: Mom was a dirty worker. Now you know yourself, if you got up and washed the dishes in the scrubbin' bucket Mom didn't care. Now you got to learn to do it right. You'll have to manage a home of your own one of these days. It's for your own good.

RACH: I'm never getting married if it means doing all of this.

NORA: What're you going to do? Work out to service all your life? Minding other people's homes?

RACH: No! Me and Ron Payne is gonna run off to the South Sea islands and look at the naked dancing girls. Alec was telling us when he come back from off the boats...

NORA: Rach! I don't want to hear any more stories.

RACH: Well he said they didn't have no clothes on.

NORA: Go on now, clear that away and get supper started.

RACH: Nora, is it always like this to be married?

NORA: You'll find out soon enough if you keeps going out to the dances and not coming in 'til daylight in the sky. I heard you.

RACH: Well I had to walk home, didn't I? It's nine miles.

NORA: If you don't watch yourself, my girl, you'll end up like me, nineteen years old, and married with two youngsters.

RACH: It was only a bit of fun, Nora. I was tellin' Diane about that time when Jimmy Field told you that story about when he first started courtin'.

NORA: *(Screeching with laughter.)* No! You didn't tell her that did you?

RACH: Remember, Nora, that was the time when all the lumber vessels was in the harbour?

NORA: There must a been thirty of them.

RACH: And you were all dressed up, Nora, up on the dance floor goin' right to her, and fallin' down right black in the face over Jimmy's stories?

NORA: We never had a grain did we?

RACH: And then when you was walkin' home, Nora, right proper like, and you fell down over that stump and had like to kill yourself. You were some funny.

NORA: How foolish were we? *(She gives a start.)* Oh, now the baby's awake.

RACH: I didn't do it.

NORA: Just get supper on, Rach.

RACH: We need some water, Nora.

NORA: Well go get some.

(Rach goes to get water; freezes. Nora gets up to walk the baby.)

NORA: *(Calling after Rachel.)* And come right back, Rach. *(Speaking to herself.)* I hope he doesn't keep me up all night again.

Scene 4

(Nora replaces the quilt on the back of the rocking chair, and goes to the rack where she takes off Nora's sweater, picks up Aunt Mary's sweater and sings the following song as young Mary.)

MARY: *(Sings.)* In courtship there lies pleasure,
　　　　Between my love and I.
　　　　I'll go down to yonder valley,
　　　　For to meet my love on high.
　　　　I'll go down to yonder valley,
　　　　For to meet my heart's delight.
　　　　I'll sit and sing for Mary,
　　　　From morning until night.
(The lights dim. Mary, wearing the sweater, sits in the rocking chair and puts the quilt on her lap to become Aunt Mary, aged eighty-one. Her niece Peg, mid-sixtyish, enters and sits. The lights come up to find them in mid visit.)

PEG: Poor old Aunt Mary, no one comes in to see her in the daytime any more? They leaves you all alone, do they?

MARY: No, Peg. There's me next door neighbour, she comes in for tea. And last week me granddaughter brought her new baby in to see me. He's some sweet. I got a snap of him here somewhere.

PEG: You got lots of snaps around here, Aunt Mary. Cute little place you got for yourself. You know I never thought I'd see you again. All these years and I never knowed if you was dead or alive. Now here we are, the two of us, two old chickens.

MARY: *(She mimes finding a photograph which she passes to Peg.)* Here he is.

PEG: My, isn't he sweet? Just look at the wrinkles. He looks just like you.

MARY: I s'pose I must be going to die, all me people coming to see me.

PEG: No, you're not going to die, Aunt Mary.

MARY: I might see another Christmas.

PEG: How old are you now, Aunt Mary?

MARY: Eighty-one.

PEG: No, you're not!

MARY: Yes I am.

PEG: Sure you don't look a day over sixty.

MARY: Go on with you, I married and buried three husbands.

PEG: That's what kept you young.

MARY: And I reared up eight youngsters, three of me own and five of Eli's after he died.

PEG: Eli...that was your second husband, was it?

MARY: Yes. Now when I married me third husband Jack I thought he'd look after me in my old age. He was ten years younger than me. We did have twenty one good years together but I had to bury him too.

PEG: And my Uncle Jim was your first, wasn't he? You know I remembers when you got married. I was only 'bout this high, but I remembers I danced at your wedding. You were some pretty, and my, wasn't he handsome.

MARY: I was five years waiting for him. Five years courting.

PEG: Five years! You weren't, were you?

MARY: Well, I was only fourteen when I met him.

PEG: Sure, I was married at fifteen.

MARY: Fifteen! Well, I had to wait. See, he was sailor and he was gone away to sea most of the time. But, my dear, the times we used to have. It wasn't like it is now, you know. Youngsters today knows too much of the ways of the world.

PEG: Yes, and they knows it in the filthy way.

MARY: You know, I don't understand them hanging around on the street corners like they do. We weren't allowed that.

PEG: They only does that for badness, you know.

MARY: We had better times than they do now.

PEG: I s'pose you did.

MARY: We used to have singsongs and make candy—molasses candy—go on picnics or go rowing in the boat, go swimming or trouting. Jim used to come up and get me. I always used to know when he come, 'cause our outside porch had a latch on it. Soon as ever he touched that latch, I knew it was him.

PEG: Just imagine.

MARY: Funny thing, wasn't it? We used to go to the theatre in Petries, or to the dances, or to the pie socials.

PEG: What was that?

MARY: Oh, they used to have them to raise money for the old people, you know, who was real poor off. The girls used to bake a pie and the men would bid on the girls' pies.

PEG: Pay money for 'em?

MARY: Yeah. Now, Uncle George, he was the auctioneer, he used to figure out who was going out with who, and he would bid against them to drive up the price. "What am I bid for this pie? Dollar fifty? I make it two dollars." Up she goes. The old devil, I got to say it. You know one time, Jim had to pay twenty-two dollars for my pie?

PEG: Twenty-two dollars! My, he must a had some lot of money, Aunt Mary.

MARY: Took every cent he had. And you know the funny thing about that? I didn't even bake that pie. Me sister baked it. It was awful.

PEG: Oh my, he must have loved you some lot, Aunt Mary.

MARY: I s'pose he did, maid, I s'pose he did.

PEG: My dear, you went out with him for five years, did you? Now tell me, Aunt Mary, you mean to say you was going together for five years and you never even gave him one little snick?

MARY: Oh my, Peg, you're some hard case, aren't you?

PEG: I only says it for badness, Aunt Mary. I don't mean no harm by it. But didn't you?

MARY: No. And do you know that there was eight of us in the same class and not one of us had to be married. And we had a wonderful time too. You know it's wonderful when you got your memories, good times to remember. Nothing stays the same. Everything changes. Oh my, I'm getting tired.

PEG: Well, you go on and have a little nap now.

MARY: No, I don't want to sleep while you're here.

PEG: Sure I'm gonna stay with you for a few days now.

MARY: Oh that's wonderful.

PEG: Yes, indeed I am. Now, you go on and have a little nap and I'll make myself a cup of tea.

(Peg goes to make tea. She freezes, then she puts on Lilly's apron and sits on the table in darkness, hugging her knees to her chest throughout Mary's speech. Aunt Mary falls asleep.)

Scene 5

MARY: *(Awakening as her younger self.)* Mom, it's some hot. Oh, me feet are burning! Out in that hot sun all morning in the garden. I think I got a blister. Well, it feels like one. No, I don't have to get dressed yet, Jim won't be here for another hour. Should I wear me red dress or me blue one? Think I'll wear me blue one. That way I can wear me new bow in me hair, if I ever gets this dirt off me feet. Who's that at the door, Mom? That's not Jim is it? Mom! Don't go letting him in, me in me slip! Mom!...Jim! Don't look at me. No, Jim! *(She runs across the stage, up the stairs and slams the "door." The following takes place from behind the door.)* Go 'way. Go 'way. I knows you're out there. You did not see me bare feet. Go 'way! Go downstairs and get yourself a cup of tea. Well, I can't get dressed with your ear to the door. Jim? Jim, you still there? *(She hesitates, then slowly opens the door, peeks around it, screams and slams it again.)* Mom! Jim's tormenting me. Make him go away. *(Crosses to sit in her chair, catches sight of herself in a mirror.)* Oh, no. I would have to have on me old slip and not me pretty new one.

(She falls asleep. The lights go down on Mary and come up on Lilly who is sitting on the table.)

Scene 6

(Lilly is in the milkhouse.)

LILLY: I remember when I was at home, I used to go out to the milkhouse. You know what the milkhouse is, don't you? The little place out back where you keep your milk for scalding it. Well, I used to go out there. There was a big crowd of us living at home then, and it was only a little tiny house we were in, so I used to go out to the milkhouse. And you know they used to time me. They had nothing else to do only get to the window and watch out for me. I'd be out there maybe forty minutes, or an hour and a half, or what have you, and you know they used to time me. They'd be wondering what I was doing out there. Well, I know what I used to do out there. It was nothing only be alone. I always had to be alone so much every day for a while. I don't know what it was for...to empt out or to clear my head or...to daydream. Yeah, I think probably most of what I did out there was daydream. 'Cause, you know, the sun used to shine in there. The window was to the west and you'd get all the evening sun in there. I used to coil up, feet and all by the window. On that side the wall was covered in old newspapers, and there'd be just a little bit of this story, or the start of something or the finish of something else. You know, I read every bit of that umpteen times. King's Cove was an awfully lonely place, after I got up in my teens. The games of childhood didn't satisfy you then, and...well, there was no one my own age...and the loneliness...it was more than loneliness. It was mental torture. And, you know, some evenings we used to go across to Port Saunders in the boat.

(The scene change begins as Mary begins to move the chairs out of the way.)

We'd only just go across for a few minutes and come right back again. But you know, there was a whole crowd of young people over there, or I thought there was. They'd be all bunched up together and they'd be laughing and talking and carrying on. I'd be watching them and I'd be thinking, "How can they be doing all that laughing? What can they be talking about? How can they find so much to laugh at?" And oh, they all seemed to be so pleasant and I was so alone. But I couldn't go over and speak to them, 'cause I didn't know them.

(During this last segment about Port Saunders, Mary goes upstage, freezes, then removes her sweater to become Ruby. She begins a mimed carrying on with the young crowd, enacting the scene which Lilly is watching.)

Scene 7

(The wedding. At the end of Lilly's monologue Ruby begins to sing the tune of "Mussels in the Corner" and dances as if she were taking part in an old-fashioned set dance. Lilly, now as a young girl, is standing off to the side by herself watching the dancing and trying to shoo away her little brother. The dance ends and Ruby crosses over to join Lilly.)

RUBY: *(Thanking her imaginary dancing partner.)* Thanks, Lige. Hi, Lilly.

LILLY: Hi, Ruby, some nice wedding, isn't it? You know when I grows up I'd like to have a wedding just like this. My, you got on some lot of bows.

RUBY: How come you only got one?

LILLY: That's the one they give me when I come in the door.

RUBY: *(Displaying "bows.")* That's the one they give me when I come in. Lige give me the blue one, Peter give me the red one and

Jack give me the green one. Oh! Hi, Jack. Hi, Lige. What? Dance? Oh, don't mind her, she's shy. That's Lilly. Lilly's shy, ain't you, Lilly? She won't say nothing. Lilly, come on and dance. Lilly!

LILLY: No, I can't dance. No. No, Ruby, I can't.

(Lilly is finally dragged onto the floor and they dance, again as if they were taking part in an old fashioned set dance. The "set" ends with a spin around and the actors transform themselves from girls into two old gossips.)

Photograph by Lynda Hendrickson

GOSSIP 1: Some crowd here tonight, isn't it?

GOSSIP 2: Mmm. Just imagine marrying the two of them off at once. I'm glad it's not coming out of my pocket.

GOSSIP 1: Some spread they got over there.

GOSSIP 2: You know, my dear, I don't know half what they got on that table. Never laid eyes on it before.

GOSSIP 1: Oh, that was Lot's job, maid, when she was down in Boston. She worked with some fancy people. Worked with food.

GOSSIP 2: Look at the two brides out there. Aren't they sweet? Sin for that little one though. She's only fifteen years old.

GOSSIP 1: Some skinny, isn't she?

GOSSIP 2: Yeah. She's got a pretty face though. Prettier than Patsy.

GOSSIP 1: Well Patsy's got a nice figure though.

GOSSIP 2: Yes, she's nice and fat.

GOSSIP 1: You know she's got four petticoats on under that? He's

gonna get some shock when he takes off her gear. What? No
indeed, I don't want a drink. No! Trying to get me drunk, see.
He'd love that.

GOSSIP 2: My dear, that thing of mine's been asleep in the corner
this last hour. I s'pose there's not a chance of a scuff.

GOSSIP 1: I s'pose we're gonna have to dance with each other.

GOSSIP 2: Yes, girl.

*(They dance together and spin back around as Lilly and Ruby
shrieking with giggles.)*

LILLY: You didn't!

RUBY: Yes, I did.

LILLY: No, you did not.

RUBY: See, I was walkin' down by the post office, Shirl and me,
see, and we saw Mr. House comin'. He was comin' down the path.
And I says to Shirl, "Now, when he comes handy don't say a
word." You know what he's like. He's always so proper. So when
he comes alongside of us, he lifts his cap and he says, "Good
evening, girls." and I let go the biggest fart you ever heard.

LILLY: Oh no! Did it smell?

RUBY: It was awful.

*(They dance through another set after which they face
their "parents.")*

LILLY: Oh hello, Mom.

RUBY: Hi, Dad.

LILLY: I don't know where he is, Mom.

RUBY: I wasn't drinking!

LILLY: Well I s'pose he's with the other youngsters.

RUBY: Uncle Joe gave me a sip, that's all.

LILLY: Well, Mom, it's not my fault if he peed his pants.

RUBY: I never did eat too much.

LILLY: Well, Mom, I didn't come here to spend all night looking out
to the youngsters.

RUBY: I only had two pieces of cake.

LILLY: I'll go find him then.

RUBY: All right, I'll put it back.

*(They edge away backwards from their parents, bump into
each other and burst out laughing, becoming their
carefree selves again.)*

LILLY: Come on, let's go outside.

RUBY: What for?

LILLY: Nancy's got cigarettes.

RUBY: Sure I never smoked before.

LILLY: Haven't you? Oh my, it's the easiest thing in the world. I'll
show you how.

RUBY: All right. Come on.

BOTH: Oh! Hi, Jack. Hi, Lige. Dance?

(They look at each other.)

LILLY: Nancy'll wait.

RUBY: Okay.

(They dance off with their "partners" to their respective sides of the stage. They cross to the rack to change characters.)

Scene 8

(Aunt Mary's sitting room. Mary is in her rocker, Peg on the other chair.)

MARY: And I would have had the biggest kind of a family if Jim had lived, 'cause every time he come home from sea he made another youngster and then he was gone again.

PEG: He was that kind of a man, was he? My dear, they're all alike, all those men. My husband was the same.

MARY: Well at least he was there with you.

PEG: No indeed, he was not. He was gone in the woods all the time hunting, trapping, logging. Come out long enough to make another youngster and then gone again. My dear, I was years and years and years in the loose dresses. Make no wonder I lost me figure. 'Course I never did have much of one to start with.

MARY: I did one time, you know. 'Course it's all falling down around me now. But you know, even after I had me youngsters it fell back into place again. And I had some hard time with them, you know. Especially the first.

PEG: Yeah, the first is always the hardest.

MARY: Jim was never there when I needed him. I wish he hadda been there when I was having Kate.

PEG: No! You don't need a man with you then. No, my dear, there's nothing more squeamish than a man when a woman's gonna have a baby. They run screaming from the house. Yes, indeed, that's it now, woman takes sick, man gets gone. They're only under foot if they're around anyway. My dear, what you need with you is women. You needs a good midwife. Now we had a good midwife down the coast. She borned hundreds and hundreds of youngsters. She borned all of mine.

MARY: You had yours at home, did you?

PEG: Yes indeed, all eleven of 'em. And Nurse Bennett borned everyone of 'em. She was good, maid, she was some good.

MARY: I had a doctor for mine.

PEG: Doctor! I wouldn't be going to no doctor for having a youngster. No.

MARY: Well if it hadn't been for that doctor I wouldn't be here today. He done all he could for me. Well, he had to. He promised Jim he wouldn't let me die. I haemorrhaged. I lost every drop of blood was in me. Well anyway, he got the baby, and he said, "This baby is dead," and he christened it. Nurse threw it down on a trunk of clothes. See, they never had time to fool with it, 'cause he had to see to me. My dear, he had some fight. Well I stayed alive, but just barely. I was semi-unconscious and I didn't know anything about it, but the Nurse told me about it afterwards. She went over and she said, "Doctor, this baby's not dead. This baby's alive." And they went to work on her and brought her to. But I couldn't feed her. I had no milk, no blood, no nothing. They had to feed me with a spoon for a week. I was a whole month in bed. I couldn't get up. I was just like marble they said. Someone had to watch me all the time in case I might slip away. But gradually I got better. Well, you know I did.

PEG: Well now, Aunt Mary, that doctor done good for you, but my dear, what we had down the coast there...when a woman took sick she was better off sending for Nurse Bennett. She knew what she was doing.

MARY: Well certainly, she's a woman herself. She understands what's going on.

PEG: She knew better than some of the nurses we got down there now. Because, my dear, I tell you, we have some...well there's this one in particular...she does not know a thing and she's not prepared to admit she does not know a thing. There was one woman there, my cousin she was, well, my husband's cousin she was. Four days she was in labour. And finally in exasperation I went in and I looked at her and I said, "My dear, there's no way that woman is going to have that baby. That baby is gonna have to be took from her." And I told the nurse, I said, "You put her on that boat and you send her up to the doctor in Bonne Bay." But she would not do it. No. She went in there and she took that baby on her own...forceps, you know...and that woman have never been the same since. Thirty-six operations she've a had in her lifetime. Shocking, you know, what some of 'em do! Butchers they are, and it's only foolishness. Stupidness. Won't admit they don't know what they're doing.

MARY: Now, Peg, you can't blame 'em all. Some of 'em are very good. They save some women a lot of suffering.

PEG: I s'pose you're right, Aunt Mary. There's some good ones. They saves a lot of women from dying.

MARY: Some people got a gift for it. Others can't stand the sight of it. You know, I always loved seeing a baby being borned.

PEG: Well, you borned a few didn't you, Aunt Mary?

MARY: Yes. Seemed it come natural to me. When I was young, doctor said I shoulda trained as a nurse, but of course, I never had the chance. Seemed I was always nursing somebody though. After I got my family raised up, I finally did take a course as a midwife.

PEG: Aunt Mary, I wish now that you had gone and trained as a doctor and come down the coast with we people. That woulda been some nice. 'Cause my dear, we was years and years with no doctors and no nurses. And when they did start sending them out what did they send? The puniest little things...just out of college...still wet behind the ears. From England and Japan.

MARY: Foreigners?

PEG: Yes they sends 'em to us from all over. And they don't know nothing. I mean how can you trust someone like that? I don't know how the young ones does it now. When they're expecting their babies now...they got to go in there once a month. I heard them talk about it. They got that big table in there. Climb up onto that big table, strap their legs...my dear! You wouldn't get me in there. No way would they get me up there.

MARY: No I don't s'pose they would. Speaking of the young ones today...I don't know what the world is coming to...the other day I was out doing some shopping and I saw this young girl, she was expecting a baby. She had a tee-shirt on with "BABY" written across the front and an arrow point down.

PEG: No! You're joking.

MARY: She did so. They flaunts it now, you know.

PEG: Yes, indeed they do.

MARY: Sure, in my day you hid yourself away.

PEG: Yes, that's right.

MARY: You didn't go out of the house and you didn't let no one see you either. I remember one time when I was carrying Kate, I was staying with Gram, and this woman came to the house and Gram said to me, "You go and hide yourself away in the back room and don't be showing yourself." And you'd go and hide yourself away, and you never said nothing to no one about it, did you?

PEG: Some didn't even tell their husbands. I don't understand 'em now at all, Aunt Mary. I sees 'em down at the club, you know, nine, eight months pregnant, up on the dance floor. I think that's right ugly, you know. They say a woman looks beautiful when she's like that, but I don't think so. I thinks it's right ugly. Great big belly on her, up on the dance floor, going right to her. They got no shame. I think you gotta have a bit of shame.

MARY: They don't seem to mind, do they?

PEG: No indeed, they do not.

MARY: Things are different now. They got a choice now. They don't have to have youngsters now if they don't want to. They got the prevention.

PEG: Aunt Mary, if they'd a had that in our day, would you have used it?

MARY: Me? I don't know. It's hard to say. I s'pose it's sensible, you know, to plan out your family. But for me? No. I wanted Jim's youngsters. I wanted part of him with me in case something happened to him.

PEG: You know, Aunt Mary, sometimes I sits down and I thinks how wonderful would it a been if I'd a had that pill! No youngsters. No responsibilities. Oh my, wouldn't I 'ave had fun. But then again I thinks about it and I thinks, "Well, it's God's will." You know there is some gets married and never haves a youngster and that's God's will too. No, I think I was meant to have all them youngsters.

(Actor playing Peg rises and moves upstage to become Rach.
Actor playing Mary removes her sweater, puts on coat
and scarf and moves offstage.)

Scene 9

(Nora's kitchen. Rach is onstage alone, humming to herself,
"tidying," folding the quilt, etc. Nora, bundled up in coat
and scarf, enters silently from offstage.)

NORA: Rach, Rach, I'm home!

RACH: *(She starts as if she has seen a ghost.)* Nora.

NORA: I can't believe I'm finally here. My, oh my, oh my, Rach, I'm home again.

RACH: My God, Nora, you give me some fright.

NORA: Oh Rach, just look at you, maid. I can't believe I finally made it through.

RACH: Nora, where did you come from?

NORA: I come from St. Anthony, girl. Where'd you think I come from?

RACH: But how did you get here?

NORA: You won't believe it, maid, 'cause I can scarcely believe it myself. I come all the way on an open komatik.

RACH: Oh Nora! My heavens! Here, take this coat off you and sit down by the fire.

NORA: Rach, where's me old sweater? You know, I even missed that old thing. *(She sees it and puts it on.)* Where's the youngsters?

RACH: They're up at Mrs. Payne's.

NORA: Fred in the woods?

RACH: Yes, he should be out tonight though. My Nora, it's hard to believe you're really here.

NORA: Well now, Rach, I tell you it's some good to be sittin' in me own kitchen, and after all I've gone through, I can tell you there were times I thought I'd never see this place again.

RACH: But, my God, Nora, how did you ever get here?

NORA: I told you, maid, I come on an open komatik.

RACH: You never did, Nora!

NORA: Indeed I did. All the way from St. Anthony. See, the doctor said if I could find a way home, I could come on. So soon's ever I got the chance, off I went.

RACH: What's he? A come-from-away? Don't he know the boats can't run through the ice?

NORA: No, Rach, he knew how anxious I was to come. See, when that last boat didn't get through 'cause of the ice I thought I'd die. Five months in that place was long enough. So by and by, this fellow, a Mr. Decker, he come up for his daughter from Cook's Harbour, so I ask him could I go as far as Cook's Harbour with him and he said yes.

RACH: Cook's Harbour is a long way from here, Nora.

NORA: Yes, but I figured I'd meet someone, or perhaps I'd just get so far as Reet's in Barr'd Harbour. I didn't know, maid. I tell you I didn't know when I'd get another chance to try it. And see, he had a coach box, quilts up to me neck, and it was very good. But still, I tell you, maid, I had to rest for three days when I got there. It was so cold down there, it hurted me lungs to breathe, I almost lost me courage there, I wasn't too strong I can tell you.

RACH: You want some tea, Nora?

NORA: Yes, maid, I'd love a cup. You know, Rach, I never even had a pair of socks to put inside me skin boots. I went looking to buy a pair of socks and I couldn't even get a sock. They had to give me some rabbit skins to put inside me boots to keep me feet from freezing. No scarf. No mits. My gollys, maid, the people down there is some poor off. Worse off than we.

RACH: Just imagine.

NORA: So then I didn't know what I was gonna do. But then when Arthur Fields left to take the mail up to Eddy's Cove I thought I'd go along with him.

RACH: Yes, Nora, I know you made some small parcel now.

NORA: I tell you, maid, that was your trip. Thirty miles on an open komatik and the day was never colder out of the heavens than it was on that thirty-mile drive. I thought I was done for. 'Twas just like flakes of lye coming down. It wasn't snowing. It was frost, fair falling down from the sky. 'Twas too cold for the dogs to run. And not a shelter of a tree nor a stick nor a stump so far as your eye could see.

RACH: So you mean to say if it come on a storm there'd be nothing in the world to shelter you?

NORA: Not a thing. So anyway, I was three nights in Eddy's Cove waiting. And then Lot Mitchmore come along. He takes the mail to Flowers Cove. No, I'm wrong, he takes it back to Green Island Brook, so I come up with him and I was three nights there. Then I come up to Flowers Cove to meet the mail and I was three nights there. And then I was one night in Brig Bay. And then Uncle Joe Gaslard brought me up to Barr'd harbour. Now that was your bad day comin' across St. John's Bay. Slob ice up to your knees and poor old Joe had to walk all the way and let me ride on his dog team. And poor Reet! You shoulda seen the look of fright on her face when I walked in her door. Almost so bad as you. You looked like you didn't know me.

RACH: Well Nora, I wasn't expecting you. My gosh, maid, it's still snowing out and it's only the second of April. The boats isn't through yet.

NORA: Is that what it is now, Rach? So I've been three weeks travelling. My gosh, maid, If I'da known what I was up against I never woulda tried it.

RACH: I tell you, Nora, you got more courage than me.

NORA: Courage! Rach, I'd say I need more brains, 'cause I tell you, Rach, when I got to Reet's I didn't have the strength to make another attempt. I was that sick I stayed in the bed for five days. Me feet swolled up. I was really sick, sicker than I was in the hospital. But see, when Bob come up for me on his horse, I thought, "Well, maid, you come this far, it's only a little bit further now."

RACH: You could almost see the lights of home then, Nora.

NORA: But Rach, when we left Reet's it come to snow. I swear a bigger batch of snow never fell out of the heavens as fell Monday last.

RACH: My God, Nora, you weren't out in that!

NORA: Yes indeed. Up on the horse. Snow right up over the horse's back, and I thought, "This is it. I come all this way to die five miles from me own doorstep." (*She looks around in alarm.*) What's that I smell burning?

RACH: Oh, me cake! Oh my God, Nora, I forgot all about the time. (*She looks at her burnt "cake."*) Oh, look at it! Freddy'll kill me. He pleaded and begged me to bake a boiled raisin cake and now it's burned.

NORA: Naw, maid, he won't notice that. Oh, how I missed me youngsters.

RACH: And they sure missed you. Poor little Milly'd sit down in the middle of the floor and bawl her eyes out. And I'd say to her, "What're you crying for your mam for? She's not crying for you."

NORA: Rach, you didn't!

RACH: No, I didn't. You know, it's funny, Nora, but you been on my mind an awful lot lately. I don't know if it's being stuck up here in this lonely place. Way away from everybody else.

NORA: Lonely! You don't know what lonely is, Rach, 'til you spend five-and-a-half months in a hospital bed.

RACH: Yes...well, I saw something the other day and it made me kinda fidgety...well I didn't exactly see something...too foolish to talk about now.

NORA: What?

RACH: No, it was nothing...

NORA: Now, Rach, don't go starting a story and not tell me the end.

RACH: Well, I come out of Uncle Jimmy's house the other night, and I was coming along by the back of his house, you know. There wasn't a soul around, Nora, only me...it was right quiet, just dark in the evening...I come along by the back of the house and when I got to the corner, Nora, it was just like something went by me with a squall of wind, grabbed ahold of me by the arm and swung me right around. Almost knocked me off my feet.

NORA: There was no one there?

RACH: There wasn't a soul only me. There wasn't even a footstep in the snow. Well I lagged meself and I took running, and I run up to Aunt Min's house. Oh my, what a fright! Well then she asked me what happened and I told her, but she didn't know what to make of it. You know, Nora, I could feel the hand right there. *(She puts her fingers around her wrist.)* It was a woman's hand. I could feel the small neat hand and the long bony fingers. Well then, after that I started thinking about you being in the hospital...and I didn't...I was kind of worried about you...

NORA: *(Interrupting.)* Thought I was dead, did you?

RACH: No!

NORA: You did so. You thought I was dead!

RACH: No! I did not. Indeed I didn't...Well, you're home safe now. I'll go get the youngsters.

NORA: Oh, Rach, turn on the radio 'fore you goes, will you?

RACH: No, I don't like to fool with it, you turn it on.

(Rach goes to fetch youngsters. She freezes and stands in darkness.)

Scene 10

(Nora's kitchen. Continuation.)

NORA: That was Fred, see. No one would touch the radio where he was to. We had the second radio on the coast. Angus Bennett brought it up on the horse and sleigh and we had it for eighteen years. Now, I was sick in bed with Freddy, was it Freddy? Or was it Milly? Yes, it was Freddy. Now when they went to get the midwife they brought it in and they put it in the kitchen. You know I could hear it, but I didn't dare get up. But I can remember the first song ever I heard on her. That evening I got up and I come out, but I didn't know how to turn her on. My dear, you wouldn't dare look at her. Youngsters wouldn't dare to touch her, not where he was to. Now then, the first song ever I heard was "You are my Sunshine." Yeah, I can remember that. But after a while we got used to her. She used to run on these two big batteries. She was some sweet she was. She was furniture. 'Bout this high. Mahogany. With a little red thing across her face. She was all dials, one for the loud, one for the low, one for tuning the stations, one for the power, one for everything. She had an antenna. We used to get the broadcasts from Antigonish and Charlottetown. When we got her, we put the clock on Canadian time. Now, when we took her down we put the clock back. But for eighteen years, we had Canadian time. Half an hour slower than Newfoundland!

(She freezes and sits in darkness.)

Scene 11

(Lights up on Lilly.)

LILLY: You know, I always wanted my youngsters to get better than what I got. Get out in the world and make something of themselves. You know...get an education. Well, if I'da had grade eleven and a course or something...When I was growing up, you learned to read and write, but only just...not to be any big reader or any great writer...and college! That was out. That was way up the mountain that was. You have to have someone to pattern your life after. Because, growing up in a little community like that, you can't think because you have no experiences. Well, I thought the only thing in life was to be married. And I thought, my goodness, everyone should be married by the time they was seventeen or eighteen years old. I thought that would be a very wise and sensible thing to do. There was no such thing as a job. The only thing one could do was teach school or have a post office. And I thought, well, only one could have a post office, 'cause I thought there was only one post office in any little place all over the world. And only one worked in that. And all a man ever done was saw lumber or fish. There was no other jobs, clear of teach school or be a minister. And not we kind of people could be ministers. Oh no. You had to be from England to be a Church of England minister. We thought that was the way it had to be. The way it should be. There was no jobs. That didn't belong to our world. That belonged to people of a different world that I would never know about or could never know about. And you know, people thought things would never change. They thought we would always live in King's Cove and nothing would ever be any different.

Scene 12

(Nora's new shop. Rachel is visiting.)

NORA: What do you think of the new shop, Rach?

RACH: You got a lot of room here, Nora. What are you going to do with the extra rooms out back?

NORA: Oh, I'm gonna use them as store rooms. Except for one, I'm keeping that for Millie when she comes home with her youngsters.

RACH: I s'pose she'll be expecting you to look out for her youngsters now, will she?

NORA: I won't be looking out to them. I did me stint with youngsters.

RACH: You must have just about the biggest business in the bay now, Nora.

NORA: Yes, girl, it's growing. I'm run off me feet though.

RACH: You're lucky to have all of this.

NORA: Had to work for it. It didn't come easy.

RACH: I can't even get a house for meself.

NORA: How's that coming?

RACH: It's not.

NORA: That's two winters now, isn't it?

RACH: Yes.

NORA: Takes a lot of work to build a house, Rach.

RACH: I know. If I could get him to do any work on it. My dear, if he'd stop running around at night, playing cards with this one, or drinking and dancing with that one, staying out 'til all hours of the night. And that little shack I'm living in up there. It's not fit for a dog.

NORA: It's not that bad, Rach.

RACH: You know, yesterday I went out of doors and when I come back in...the youngsters! They had the curtains tore down off the windows, they had every bit of bed clothes hauled off the bed and stuffed in the corner, and everything in the pantry was out on the floor.

NORA: What were they doing?

RACH: Playing! I was so discouraged I sat down and cried. I barred them out of doors then. Didn't even have the strength to put it all back together again. And then he come home late for his supper again.

NORA: Where was he to? Up to the dance?

RACH: I don't know. Didn't bother to ask him. No point in asking. You'll only get a lie from him. Say to him, "Who was at the dance?" Oh no, he was never near the place, never laid eyes on it. Perhaps Mary was just after telling me how he was carrying on and making the fool of himself down there. I can't stand someone who lies to me like that.

NORA: Well you married him.

RACH: I wish I hadn't.

NORA: That's a sin for you, Rach.

RACH: I know it's a sin for me, Nora, but I wish I had never married him.

NORA: Well, if you hadn't married him, you woulda married someone else.

RACH: No I wouldn't, Nora. No. I know that now. I shoulda never gotten married. How foolish was I, Nora. I had me whole life. All those years I swore I'd never get married. I said I didn't want to settle down. Wanted to wait 'til I was old enough. I wasn't young and foolish. I was old and foolish.

NORA: I don't know what to be saying to you, Rach. You got your youngsters.

RACH: Yes and I loves me youngsters.

NORA: And they'll be gone before you know it and you'll be wishing they were home again. You'll be stuck with the old man then.

RACH: Just me and him? Perhaps then I will run off to the South

Sea islands, eh, Nora, you and me?

NORA: Oh my, the stories you used to come up with.

RACH: I wish I had me life to live again. Out to the dances all the time. Carrying on. Oh my, Nora, what a clown I was. You know, I can't even go to a dance with that fool thing anymore. We were up to the wedding last week and I was dancing with Jack and Lige, all the fellers I grew up with. And you know, ten o'clock in the evening he comes up and marches me home.

NORA: Jealous was he?

RACH: Yes, he can't stand to see me have a bit of fun. Sure yesterday he got right upset just 'cause I was talking to John Benoit...oh my, Nora, have you seen that new snow machine he's got?

NORA: No, but I heard it. Some racket.

RACH: He's got it parked out there on the bank. Come over here, Nora, and look at it. Some nice, isn't it?

NORA: It's all right I s'pose. What's that where the wheels are s'posed to be.

RACH: Some sort of chains it runs on. It can go over anything. I had a ride in it yesterday.

NORA: You didn't.

RACH: Yes, indeed I did. He come into Annie's for something and I was carrying on with him, like I do. And so I said to him, "Come on now give us a ride in your new machine." And by jingo he did. Me and Annie and the youngsters. Oh my, Nora, we went right out around the bay and back in again. It's some fast I tell you. Oh, and, Nora, she bouncing and jouncing all over the place. You woulda been right sick. Worse than any boat. Becky was right frightened. Mikey loved it though.

NORA: He's just as bad as you. How many people can he fit in it?

RACH: Well you climb in through that little door and perhaps seven, eight, ten people could get in her. And you'll never believe it, Nora, he's going to make a trip clear down to St. Anthony in her.

NORA: He's not!

RACH: Yes, indeed. Now then, Nora, you wouldn't a had to hitchhike with the mailman if he'd a had that a few years back. Oh my, I've got to get going. I've got the youngsters barred outdoors.

NORA: You've got lots of time, maid. You don't have to go yet.

RACH: They'll be sitting on the step, screeching for me. See ya.

NORA: See ya.

(Nora and Rach walk to change area. The actors change to become Aunt Mary and Peg, taking their places in their chairs.)

Scene 13

(Aunt Mary's sitting room. Lights come up to find them in mid-visit.)

MARY: I often wondered what happened to your mother after your father died and she went down the coast again.

PEG: She got married again.

MARY: Did she? Good for her.

PEG: And she had more youngsters too. And you'll never believe what happened.

MARY: What?

PEG: She and me married two brothers.

MARY: Two brothers?

PEG: Now there's no relation there, you know.

MARY: No.

PEG: But you'll never figure it out. You know that song, "I married me own Grandma?" Well that's how we are. Minister come to the house one time and he was wanting to know who was what to whom. So anyway, now I says to him, I says, me and Mom married two brothers. So I says, you'll never figure it out, you know. I said now, that makes him me stepfather and...what...me uncle...no he's not me uncle...me brother-in-law, that's it. And now to me youngsters, he's their grandfather and their uncle. That's it. And then Mom, now Mom, she's me sister-in-law and me mother. And now her youngsters to my youngsters, well now they're...and so I said to him, "You can try so hard as you like, but you'll never figure it out." "Well now, missus," he says, "I'll take it all away with me and when I gets it figured out, I'll bring it back." Never saw him again.

MARY: You know you was always my favourite, Peg. I can remember when your mother went down the coast and took you youngsters with her, the two youngest ones stayed with Gram. And I said to her, "Why don't you leave Peg with me?" And she says, "No. She's coming with me." I even wrote letters on down after you. She wouldn't part with you.

PEG: I wanted to come too.

MARY: Did you?

PEG: Indeed I did. I used to sit down and cry. Oh, usen't I cry. But then you know, you got to live out your life in the present. I settled down and I got married, had me own youngsters. But it was hard you know, Aunt Mary, being taken down the coast. Leaving behind the whole crowd that you knew, the ones you grew up with, the uncles and grandfather.

MARY: Your grandfather missed you, you know. Wasn't a day went by, he didn't talk about you.

PEG: You know it was twenty-five years before I saw me own sister again? I come up to Corner Brook on business one time. I had me oldest son with me then, well he was a grown man by then. So I says to meself, "Well now, I'm going to go up to Curling and see is any of the old crowd leaved behind." So I went up and I found Uncle John's house. Knew it soon's ever I saw it. So I went up and I knocked on the door. And when he saw who 'twas, oh my dear, he mopped and kissed me—time was on. So I stayed with him

then. Now one morning, I was sitting out on his bridge and there
was this feller going up along by the fence, and he sung out to
me, you know, he said, "Is that you, Peg?" I didn't know who it
was. "Yeah," I said, "that's me." My dear, he jumped over that
fence and he was no small man, he jumped over that fence and he
run up and he hugged right into me. Come down to it, this was
me cousin Cyril. Oh my, I woulda never known him, but he'd
heard I was staying there now, see. Well, by and by, I got up me
courage and I says, "Now, I'm going up to see me sister Kath-
leen." So I got on the bus, and I said to the driver, I said, "Do you
know..." and I give him her husband's name and I said, "Do you
know where he lives to?" And he said, "Yes, I knows where he
lives to." So I said, "Now you put me off to his house." So he did.
I went up and I knocked on her door. She come out. So I said,
"Well now, maid, you probably don't know who I am." "No, maid,"
she said, "I don't." So I said, "I'm your sister Peg." Well now, she
took me in, and I started to cry, and then she started to cry, and
we cried and we laughed and we talked and we done it all. And
you know now she comes in to see me every time she comes down
the coast.

MARY: That's wonderful. See, you don't know who you are 'til you
knows your relations.

PEG: You think you're all alone in the world and when it comes
right down to it, there's a whole crowd of them all around you.

MARY: Your family's always there when you needs 'em.

PEG: You people were good to us, you know, after father died.
Grandfather always looking out to us. And you, you were like a
second mother to me.

MARY: You got to look out to your own, don't you? The way I
figures it, we're all born and we're not buried. We don't know
what's gonna happen. We haves our children and we don't know
the future.

> *(Lights change to spot on Mary who sings the following*
> *song a cappella.)*
>
> As I roved out one evening I sat down to take rest,
> I saw a boy scarce four years old, close to his mother's
> breast,
> Saying, "Once I had a father dear, who did me kind
> embrace,
> If he was here he would wipe the tears
> Roll down my mother's face.
>   Oh Mother, oh Mother, come tell to me,
> Oh Mother, tell me why
> Why don't my father's ship come home,
> Why do you sob and cry?
> All other ships are coming home,
> Leaving the white waves foam,
> But my father's ship is not come yet,

What makes her tarry long?"
"Oh, the ocean is wide and fathoms deep,
As the earth is from the sky,
There's a heaven above, my darling child,
There's home for you and I.
You're the only one that's leaved to me
And I press you to my side."
Where they both lay down together,
The son and mother died.
(Peg goes to change area and freezes.)

Scene 14

(Aunt Mary's sitting room. She sits in her rocking chair alone.)
MARY: Jim and I were married eleven years and then he gave up
going to sea and I had him home with me. Then he took sick and
he was in bed for a year. He took a turn for the worse just before
Christmas. I sat with him for seven days and seven nights, and I
had seven cups of tea and seven sips from one cup. My head
never touched the pillow. No one else would sit with him only his
brother John. They were all too frightened, you know. He had
TB. Even his own mother used to hold a handkerchief over her
mouth when she come in the room. That hurt him, you know, his
own mother. He used to say to me sometimes, "Aren't you afraid,
Mary?" and I'd say, "If God means me to have TB, I'll take it, I'll
take it." Sometimes John would push me out of the room and he
would say, "Get some rest, Mary, I'll sit with him." But he'd call
for me, "Mary, Mary," and John would come out and he'd say,
"You'd better go back in, maid, he won't get no rest without you."
That last day we carried him out to the living room. He wanted
to face the west. He watched the sun set and his last words were,
"What will tomorrow bring?" That was the twenty-seventh of
December and I've always hated Christmas ever since. He was
the only man I ever loved.
(Full blackout. Mary exits.)

Scene 15

(Spotlight on Lilly.)
LILLY: Did it ever happen to you? Did ever you go out and look out
at the stars, and did ever a special sort of feeling come over you?
Like a joy that you couldn't explain? The night before my father
died, I went outdoors to take in the clothes. I was tired that
night, really tired. And when I went out the cold air was really
refreshing. I took in a deep breath and this special sort of feeling
come over me. It was kind of like an excitement. I was sort of
shocked and I thought, "Why did I feel like this?" And I thought
it was just such a wonderful feeling if only it didn't leave me. So

I took down the clothes and I went back inside, and the youngsters was there and they said to me, you know, "Who was I
talking to?" "I wasn't talking to nobody." "Yes Mom, you were. You
were talking to Shirl. She told you something." "No, nobody
didn't tell me anything." "We can tell it," they said, "'cause when
you went out, you were right ugly and now you're right pretty."
And you know I was just beaming. And then Shirl come in and
they questioned her up on it and she said no, she hadn't seen me.
And I was talking to Shirl later on and I was telling her how sick
Pop was, and you know, that's what it was. My brother come in
and said, you know, "If you wants to see Pop alive, you better
come now." I don't know why that happened. I don't believe in
ghostes. (*Two syllables.*) I think most of it is imagination and
nerves and illusions, but you know, that was something I could
never explain.

Scene 16

(*King's Cove. Nora and Rach have just walked in the three-mile
road to King's Cove. The set is in semi-darkness. Nora lights
the kerosene lamp.*)

NORA: Oh, me feet are killing me.

RACH: Well we got a nice lot of berries, Nora.

NORA: Where's the lamp?

RACH: Over here by the table. How's your back?

NORA: It hurts. That's how it is. Them damn rocks, walking over
that beach.

RACH: Well, you didn't want to come in through the woods. You
said there was too many flies.

NORA: It was your idea in the first place. Imagine. Going camping
at our age!

RACH: Well, Nora, I've been wanting to come back and spend a
night at King's Cove for a nice few years. I always liked it out
here.

NORA: You didn't have to live out here, only a short time when you
was out here with me. After I got married, I lived here twenty-
one years. Served a jail sentence. That's what it was.

RACH: Some quiet out here, Nora.

NORA: Too quiet. Always was.

RACH: I love it when it's right still like this. I wonder, Nora, would
we hear anything out here tonight?

NORA: There's nothing to be heard.

RACH: Remember you always used to tell me you felt uncomfort-
able in that little house of yours up in back of here?

NORA: Yes, but I never heard nothing. It was just a feeling.

RACH: What kind of a feeling?

NORA: Like I wasn't s'posed to be here. I was frightened in the
noon day in that house. It was a constant fear.

RACH: I never felt that when I was up there.

NORA: You know them two rooms on the back of the house? I could never go in them two rooms. I always felt like someone was watching me through the window.

RACH: No! Did you ever see anything?

NORA: No, but one time when Aunt Reet stayed with us she seen something funny. She used to sleep in that back room. One night she come out to my room and she said, "Can I get in bed with you?" So I said yes. I thought maybe she was nervous, where she was an old lady. She says, "Was you up?" I says, "No", I says, "'cause when you come in you woke me." I says, "Why?" "'Cause," she says, "I thought you come in my room." So anyway we went on to sleep, and next morning I asked her what happened. She said it was like someone come in her room and hauled the bed clothes off her. Like she seen 'em, or something, and rattled a pan at her.

RACH: Was it a woman?

NORA: Musta been. She thought it was me. And do you know we shifted out of that house and built another one not twenty yards away? I was fine there. So happy as a lark. You know I don't believe in ghostes, but I do believe that house was haunted. Now, I don't know what it was haunted by.

RACH: Oh my, Nora, I'd love to see a ghost out here tonight.

NORA: There's no such thing as ghostes. I long to see three dead people, then I might believe it.

RACH: You might get your wish out here tonight then, Nora. You know, Nora, the way I figures it, some people can see 'em and some people can't.

NORA: Dogs can.

RACH: Yeah, my dog Spot could. One time she was at home with me. I was home alone, like I always was. She was laid down on the floor beside me. I was just sitting there in the dark, and she started to growl. So I said, "Shut up." But she wouldn't shut up. No, she jumped up and she run over to that door and, my dear, every hair on her back was stood right up on end. And she growled and then she started barking, the fiercest kind of bark. And then, my dear, the noise outside me house...it was just like a thousand pound horse running up and down me bridge. The whole house shook with it. Well then, I jumped up and I run over and I looked out the window. There was nothing there. By and by the noise stopped, dog stopped barking, come back, laid down by me chair again and went back to sleep...That was a token. Exactly one week later, that exact same hour, Ned's sister died. Yes indeed. But that was only a token. That wasn't a ghost.

NORA: No.

RACH: But I have seen a ghost.

NORA: Oh, Rach.

RACH: Well now I don't know if it was a ghost, but it was something I couldn't explain. You remember how I used to stay up with Bett? Well, one night, I was staying up to Bett's, and now, I slept in the bed with Harley, her youngest son, on one side of the room, and the other two youngsters slept in a bed on the other side of the room. So Bett says to me before she goes to bed, she says, "You know, maid, I often gets up in the middle of the night, and I comes in to cover up the youngsters." So I said to her, "Well, maid, if I wakes in the middle of the night and I sees they got the bedclothes thrown off them, I'll cover 'em up again." So she says fine, and goes on to bed. So I fell asleep and by and by, I woke up and I heard her coming, or so I thought. Well now, see, our bedroom was on this side and she had a big long kitchen and her bedroom was over there, and she always kept a light on the kitchen table where the youngsters was small. I heard her, like she got out of bed and come across the kitchen and she stood up in the door. It was a woman, same shape of woman as Bett. She had nice wavy hair, like Bett had. She had on her night-gown, bare feet, bare legs. My dear, she come and she stood up, right at the end of my bed, and she looked at me. And then she started, like she was spinning, turning around and around, all the while she was looking at me, her eyes right bright. And she...like, she lowered right down, right down, 'til she disappeared. And then I jumped out of the bed. And I said, "You son of a bitch, you're not going to trick me like that." And I looked up in under the bed...there was nothing there. And then I went and looked up in under the other bed and there was nothing there either. So I went out in the kitchen and I looked around...there wasn't a soul. So then I creeped over to her bedroom door, right quiet like, and I peeked in...there was the two of them in the bed snoring like the pigs. So I went back to my bed then, but you know, I lay there and I thought about it and I thought about it. And then in the morning when I got up I asked her, "Bett," I said, "did you come in my room last night and cover up the youngsters?" "No, maid," she said, "I never even woke." So then I told her what happened. "You know, Rach," she said, "you are the second person, have a slept in that bed, that exact same woman have a come in, exact same thing have a happened." "Is that right?" I said, "Well, maid, I won't be sleeping in that bed again." And you know I never could, not from that day to this. But now, I wasn't frightened, you know. No. Nothing could frighten me. There's nothing any uglier than meself. But it's a funny thing, maid.

NORA: Funny.

RACH: What's the matter, Nora, you're not frightened, are you?

NORA: No. I'm just cold, that's all.

RACH: You know how Pop always used to say that ghostes is better than people? When there's too many people in one place, the ghostes shifts out of it. I believe that. You know, Nora, there's not a soul living out here any more. This place is probably a mast of ghostes.

NORA: That's foolishness that is. I'm going to bed out of it. You know I thinks we should bunk up together in that bed in there. Warmer that way.

RACH: That's fine with me.

NORA: You coming to bed now?

RACH: No, you go on.

NORA: What are you going to do?

RACH: Nothing.

NORA: Nothing?

RACH: I likes to sit here in the dark by meself for a while. Listen to the ocean. You knows how I am. You go on though.

NORA: I'm going. *(She takes the lamp off the table and moves gingerly away. After a suitable pause, Rach suddenly raps sharply on the table.)* Oh, my God! What was that?

RACH: What was that, Nora?

(Rach raps on the table again.)

NORA: Rach! You almost frightened the life out of me.

RACH: That's a ghost, Nora, go let him in.

NORA: Rach, stop it!

RACH: That's a sin for you, Nora, go let the poor old feller in.

NORA: Rach, you coming to bed or what?

RACH: Yes, maid, I'll go to bed with you.

(Blackout.)

Epilogue

PEG: We're living in a different world now. I don't think it, I knows
it. Things are easier now, but people aren't happier. There's too
much now to be happy. To think back, now, to the way we lived, I
s'pose you could say people was poor off. But people didn't know
they were poor off. I mean everyone was living on the one standard. Everybody had something to eat. They didn't have no
canned goods or luxuries like they got now, but they roughed it
you know. People on this coast had good homes, 'cause they built
them theirselves and they had good food, 'cause they grew their
own gardens. People had to work for theirselves or do without.
'Cause no one was gonna give it to them. It was all hard work
just to survive. How hard did people work. My heavens, you
couldn't believe it this day and age. If people today had to go back
to what we did, it would kill them. Yes it would, it would kill
them. Because, my dear, we didn't work we slaved. There was no
such thing as any hours of the day's work, it was just from the
stars in the sky morning 'til the stars in the sky night. And then
you didn't have it all done. Wait for daylight to come, start all
over again. But, my dear, 'twas only fun. We were really living
then. Every day our work come to us and we done it and we
wasn't tired or nothing. You don't know how good your life is.

THE END.

Sheila's Brush Theatre Company

Jaxxmas

(Jack's Christmas)

1979

Collectively written by

Frank Barry	Mercedes Barry
Philip Dinn	Flip Janes
Andy Jones	Mark Oakley
Dave Panting	Geoff Panting
Valentine Ryan	Agnes Walsh

Using a free adaptation of a traditional tale told by
Mr. Pius Power

and with the assistance of
**Della Cohen, François Cambron,
Val Ekdahl** and **Joy Skanes**

Music composed and/or arranged by
Philip Dinn, Mark Oakley, Dave and **Geoff Panting**
and **Valentine Ryan**

JAXXMAS

Jaxxmas was first presented at the LSPU Hall in St. John's, Newfoundland by the Sheila's Brush Theatre Company as a Christmas entertainment 28-30 December 1979 and 2-6 January 1980. It was revised in 1986 and played at the Hall (10-21 December 1986), as part of the tenth anniversary of the LSPU Hall as a theatre. The text presented here is the play as it was presented in 1979 with the following three variations: "The Jack Tale," adapted from the story by Pius Power, which originally was narrated totally by Uncle Val, is updated to the version of the tale that was performed in 1986 in which the actors perform actions synchronized with the narration and participate in the dialogue; the opening scene of Act 2, which was underdeveloped in the 1979 version, is given in the completed form written for the 1986 production of the play; the combined roles of Reverend Freep and Father Dinn which had been played by the actor who played Jack in 1979 are re-assigned.

The members of Sheila's Brush who wrote, arranged the music for and performed the play are as follows:

Andy Jones	Uncle Val, Jack, Household Finance Company (HFC) Man, Willy Nilly, Reverend Freep, Father Dinn, etc.
Mercedes Barry	Rose (wife to Jack), Mudder, Catcha, etc.
Agnes Walsh	Cat, Vi, Princess Freckelonia Rose, Pope Jacqueline Paulette, etc.
Frank Barry	Young Jack, Jack, Jr., the Doctor, etc.
Philip Dinn	Dickie Dinn, Cedrico (King of the Gypsies), Stick Man, Mr. Wilmot/Gilmor Albummus, etc.; music.
Flip Janes	Cyril, King Peck, King Bolognia of Muldonia, Reverend Freep, Father Dinn, etc.
Dave Panting	Quigley Dinn, Joey, etc.; music.
Geoff Panting	Nelson, Accordiono, Merchant, etc.; music.
Valentine Ryan	Tom, Hobby Horse, etc.; music.
Della Cohen	Mona, etc.
Joy Skanes	Joy, etc.
Francois Cambron	Henri Lafayette, etc.
Mark Oakley	Bas, Friend of Family, etc.; music.
Val Ekdahl	Gran.

Additional Credits:

The East End Boys and Girls Club Dancers danced as Gypsies in the 1979 play. In the 1986 revision version, **Agnes Walsh**'s roles were played by **Paula Nolan, Mark Oakley**'s by **Paddy Mackey**, Rev. Freep and Fr. Dinn were played by **Flip Janes**; other small roles were written out. In 1979 lighting was by **Boo Noseworthy** and the rest of the backstage and technical work was shared by members of the cast. In 1986 sets were by **Elly Cohen** and **Vicki Hammond**, lighting **Harold Hiscock**, production **Ann Anderson**. Photographs of the 1986 production of *Jaxxmas* are by **Janet Hannaford**.

Except for "The Buckeroo Song," which was written by Sheila's Brush, the songs sung in *Jaxxmas* are traditional. Words and music for "The Praise of Christmas" come from *The Oxford Book of Carols*, 1928 (rpt. 1964), pp. 16-17; and "While Shepherds Watched Their Flocks" is the version sung in Green's Harbour, Trinity Bay collected by **Gordon S. A. Cox** in *Some Aspects of the Folk Music Complex of a Newfoundland Outport*, Memorial University, M.A Thesis, 1976, pp. 101-2. The "Portuguese Waltz" was taught to the musicians of Sheila's Brush by **Art Stoyles**.

Jaxxmas was developed with financial assistance provided by the Canada Council, administered in Newfoundland, under a temporary and one-time seed funding program called Funds to Initiate Stage Happenings (FISH Fund).

Jaxxmas is a modern adaptation of the ancient story of poor Jack, as told originally, by Mr. Pius Power of the settlement of South East Bight in Placentia Bay, Newfoundland; In which "The Jack Tale" is brought up to date, and Jack and the Princess Rose are long married; Jack has lost his magical powers and is now living with his many children in a basement apartment on Hamilton Avenue Extension; In which the traditional Mummers Play of long ago, is presented in a new form, as well as songs of the Christmas season, dances of the Isle of Newfoundland and the telling of the story of "Jack Meets the Cat" by Uncle Valentine.

SHEILA'S BRUSH

CAST OF CHARACTERS
(In order of appearance.)

DICKIE DINN Live-in, eat-in neighbour (musician).

UNCLE VAL Uncle Valentine Nugent, story teller of the old tradition, chronicler of Jack's life "The Jack Tale" (retired).

TOM Brother to Young Jack in "The Jack Tale," son to Jack in the play, a fiddler and a dandy (unemployed).

BILL Brother to Young Jack in "The Jack Tale," now Mona, daughter to Jack in the play (unemployed), aged thirty-four.

MUDDER Mother of Tom, Bill and Young Jack in "The Jack Tale."

YOUNG JACK Hero of "The Jack Tale."

CAT Principal puss in "The Jack Tale."

HOBBY HORSE Horse in the mummers tradition.

PRINCESS Princess Freckelonia Rose, known as the Princess, Princess Freckelonia, Princess Rose and Princess Freckelonia Rose; heroine of "The Jack Tale."

JACK Jack, poor Jack, jack-a-tar, Ivan Ivanovich, Hanswurst, just Jack, our man Jack, a plain fellow with magical powers, late of "Avon Calling," Father of six children and husband of Rose.

ROSE Formerly princess from the story, now wife of Jack and mother of six children, no longer in possession of the crown jewels, recently laid off from Merrymeeting Laundromat.

JACK, JR. Son to Jack and Rose, suffers the ennui of the unemployed.

CYRIL Sensitive younger brother of Rose (unemployed), aged thirty-four.

GRAN Silent matriarch (pensioner), aged ninety-two; she sits motionless, except for one twitch, throughout the play.

JOY Disco daughter to Jack and Rose, aged fourteen.

MONA Daughter to Jack, formerly Bill in "The Jack Tale," (unemployed), aged thirty-four.

HENRI LAFAYETTE Frenchman, boyfriend to Mona, aged seventeen.

BAS Son to Jack and Rose (musician), aged sixteen.

QUIGLEY DINN Illegitimate son to Dickie Dinn and Miss Mystery (an exotic dancer), aged fifteen.

NELSON Son to Jack and Rose (a musician), aged eighteen.

VI Girlfriend to Jack, Jr., pregnant (unemployed).

REV. FREEP Sanctimonious Protestant minister.

FR. DINN Loud, booming Roman Catholic priest.

WILMOT/GILMOR ALBUMMUS Giver of both doom and life.

VARIOUS GYPSIES, DANCERS, MUMMERS, SINGERS AND OTHER CHARACTERS

JAXXMAS

ACT 1

BAGMAN: (*Sings.*)

> All hail to the days that merit more praise
> Than all the rest of the year,
> And welcome the nights that double delights
> As well for the poor as the peer!
> Good fortune attend each merry man's friend
> That does but the best that he may,
> Forgetting old wrongs with carols and songs,
> To drive the cold winter away.
>   'Tis ill for a mind to anger inclined
> To think of small injuries now;
> If wrath be to seek, do not lend her thy cheek,
> Nor let her inhabit thy brow.
> Cross out of thy books malevolent looks,
> Both beauty and youth's decay,
> And wholly consort with mirth and with sport,
> To drive the cold winter away.
>   This time of the year is spent in good cheer,
> And neighbours together do meet,
> To sit by the fire, with friendly desire,
> Each other in love to greet.
> Old grudges forgot are put in the pot,
> All sorrows aside they lay;
> The old and the young doth carol this song,
> To drive the cold winter away.
>   When Christmas's tide comes in like a bride,
> With holly and ivy clad,
> Twelve days in the year much mirth and good cheer
> In every household is had.
> The country guise is then to devise
> Some gambols of Christmas play,
> Whereat the young men do best that they can
> To drive the cold winter away.

Scene 1

The setting is the living room of a hideously seedy basement apartment on Hamilton Avenue Extension. The furniture is shabby: there is a chrome kitchen set with six battered chairs (none of which match) at stage right; an old black-and-white floor model TV back-on to the audience and facing two decrepit over-stuffed chairs at centre stage; an old radio on a table; an orange imitation-leather hide-a-bed couch and a sparsely decorated scrawny Christmas tree at stage left. The room is littered with newspapers and comic books. Three mannequins, dressed as angels hover above the set. Behind the chairs at centre stage are drums, amplifiers, microphones and other musical equipment. Scene opens with various family members watching TV.

Enter Uncle Val, wearing a shiny-arsed suit and a salt'n'pepper cap. He begins his narration. During Uncle Val's narration of "The Jack Tale," the actors who play the roles in his story perform the actions he describes, synchronized to the narrative.

UNCLE VAL: It was the Christmas to end all Christmases. It was the apex of Yuletides. It was the Rolls Royce of Bon Noëls. I'm talkin' about many, many years ago, way back in the year nineteen and seventy nine. The central event of that year, is generally referred to, in the ancient books, as Jack's Christmas. I'm not goin' to go tellin' you all about Jack, 'cause I knows you knows all about Jack. In fact, the last thing Allie said to me before I left the house was, "Don't go goin' on about Jack, 'cause they knows all about Jack."

Allie, by the way, is my sister. Let me see if I can do Allie for ya—"Now you listen to me, Val, don't you go goin' on about Jack now, 'cause they knows all about Jack, yes they do, they knows all about Jack. There's no sense goin' on about Jack now, 'cause they knows all about Jack, yes they does, all about Jack, yes Jack, yes Jack, yes Jack, Jack, Jack." That's Allie.

I will take Allie's advice and I won't go goin' on about Jack, 'cause I knows you knows all about the time that Jack married the Princess, and how he flew across the ocean in a flying dory; how he beat the devil at a game of Chinese Checkers; how he used his magic powers to make the world stand still, then got off and changed a tire; how one time he had over a thousand women in love with him for a forty-eight hour period; how he wrestled an elephant; how he belly-danced with a frog; how one time he swallowed the entire provincial cabinet; how he was discovered to be a woman; how the woman-Jack was discovered to be a man again; how he was swallowed by a whale; how he never climbed the beanstalk at all; how, dressed as Jupiter, he attended the planet's annual soup supper and dance...'cause I know ya knows all about that.

Besides, I'm talkin' about Christmas of nineteen seventy nine, when Jack's magic powers had more or less faded away, when he and the Princess had settled down to this little apartment, here on Hamilton Avenue Extension, long after Jack had walked off in a huff from his job in the men's department at the Big Six and the Princess's periods of employment at Merrymeeting Laundromat and the Pop Shoppe, were as much a memory as the crown jewels that she let slip through her fingers the day she married Jack. Not that the Princess regretted marrying Jack, she knew what she was gettin' herself into.

(As Uncle Val describes Young Jack, he appears looking ragged and dirty with a swag bag on a stick.)

She'd heard about Jack; how all he'd ever done when he was young was to sit around in the coal box all day long; how he never combed his hair; how he never cut his toenails and never washed his face and never shaved till he was twenty-one years of age; how all he ever done was take a potato, stick it on his big toe, stick it in the fire, roast it, and eat it. And that's how young Jack spent his time.

Now Jack had two brothers, Bill and Tom. Now Bill and Tom, they were kind of handy, they were actually able to do something. But Jack, well, Jack was another story altogether.

(Enter Bill and Tom and Mudder. She is a tough washer woman type.)

Now one day, Jack's two brothers, Bill and Tom, they come into the kitchen, and they said to their mudder, "Mudder," they said:

BILL: Mudder, bake us a cake and roast us a hen...

TOM: For we're off to seek our fortune.

UNCLE VAL: Well, their mudder was broken hearted, she was smitten at the thought of her two bouncing baby boys goin' down the road to seek their fortune.

(There are tears and wailing. Bill and Tom exit.)

But the next day, when Jack said to his mudder:

JACK: Mudder, bake me a cake and roast me a hen, for I'm off to seek me fortune.

UNCLE VAL: All the mudder said was:

MUDDER: Wisht-to'booneen, Jack, me prayers have been answered, 'tis not for your goin' I'm sorry, 'tis only afraid you might come back. Now go on. Be off with ya.

JACK: And that's the right way too, Mudder.

(Mudder exits.)

UNCLE VAL: You see, Jack and his mudder, they never got along all that well, and so Jack headed down the road to seek his fortune. *(Jack strides jauntily.)* "Now," said Jack to himself, "on my first day seeking my fortune I'm gonna walk for a hundred miles."

So he walked and he walked and he kept on walkin', and he didn't stop walking and he walked some more. He did walk. He did walk. He didn't not walk. He didn't not walk and he walked and he walked till he stopped. He couldn't go another step further. His legs were swollen up like balloons and his feet were falling off the bottom of his legs. So he said to himself, "I think I'll go into the woods and take a little rest."

But the trees in the woods were very, very tall and it was very, very dark in the woods and Jack was very, very frightened, when all of a sudden he heard a very strange noise.

(Sound of a horse whinnying.)

"Sounds like a horse," said Jack. And it was a horse.

(Horse whinnies again.)

The strangest horse Jack had ever seen in his life.

(Hobby Horse comes out and begins to sniff about Jack.)

A brown and green horse comes through the woods towards him. Now Jack was scared to death, and so he stretched his arms out at bizarre angles and pretended to be a stunted tree so the horse wouldn't eat 'im.

(Jack pretends to be a tree. Hobby Horse snaps at him a few times, forcing him to assume more and more bizarre positions.)

Oh no! Now the horse is coming over to me!

(Hobby Horse advances on Uncle Val threateningly.)

I'd better pretend to be a tree too.

(He does so. Hobby Horse takes a couple of snaps at him and suddenly takes off into the audience, snapping and behaving outrageously. Uncle Val addresses the audience.)

Now all of you better pretend to be a tree too. *(He calls to Jack.)* Jack! Jack! Save us from the horse. Jack, for God's sake, tame that horse!

(Jack runs into the audience, jumps on Hobby Horse's back and an improvised bronco busting scene ensues. Jack finally gets him under control.)

Oh, thank you, thank you, Jack. Jack is after taming the horse. Go on now, Jack, bring him round and show him to the audience. Give him a little pat there, boys and girls. *(Ad lib.)*

(Jack does so.)

Yes, formerly a bad horse, now a good horse. Ladies and gentlemen, boys and girls, it gives us hope for change in our own lives here today.

"Well, well, well," said Jack to himself, "I'm a very lucky boy. Now I won't have to walk to seek me fortune no more. I got a horse and I can ride."

(Jack leads Hobby Horse offstage.)

Here I am, inadvertently, tellin' the story of how Jack married the princess. If Allie were here, she'd brain me. Allie, actually, has got quite a powerful left hook. I believe, if I'm not mistaken, it was Allie that was responsible for that dent in the Coca-Cola sign, down at Croak's Snack Bar. I remember one time, during the war, we had to keep Allie down in the basement for a couple of weeks. She wanted to go over to Germany and hit Hitler, or was it pummel Rommel; or maybe it was rommel Pummel. Sounds like a German open-line show host; Rom Pummel. "Hello, Rom." Well, anyway, where was I—oh, yes.

What Jack did not realize was that this was not a wild horse at all; that this horse, in fact, belonged to somebody. It belonged to a very strange group of people. It belonged, in fact, to a wild and crazy band of Gypsies!

(A band of Gypsies spring onto the stage with malicious glee, shouting and screaming.)

CEDRICO: Hey, who stole our horse?

GYPSIES: *(Together to audience.)* Did you steal our horse? How about you? *(Etc.)*

CATCHA: Ya know what we're gonna do with that horse thief when we catch 'im?

ACCORDIONO: What are we gonna do?

CATCHA: Tell 'im, Cedrico!

CEDRICO: We're gonna build a big fire. We're gonna put a stick in 'im. We're gonna put a bit of salt and pepper, garlic, put a bit of marjoram and basil, baste 'im up in tamarind, roast 'im up and eat 'im for our supper.

(Gypsies cheer at the prospect of a spicy tasty bit of Jack for their tea. They hear Hobby Horse whinny and shush each other.)

UNCLE VAL: And so the Gypsies hid.

(They all hide.)

And Jack, innocent as an uncarved pumpkin, comes riding through the woods.

(Jack comes riding along on Hobby Horse's back singing "Happy Trails." The Gypsies leap out insanely.)

Photograph by Janet Hannaford

GYPSIES: Get 'im!

(*They seize Jack.*)

CATCHA: What have we here? A scrawny little horse thief! What are we gonna do with 'im, Cedrico?

CEDRICO: We'll roast 'im up and eat 'im for our supper!

GYPSIES: YAH!!

ACCORDIONO: Wait a second! Wait a second! Wait a second!

GYPSIES: What? What? What? What? What? What?

ACCORDIONO: Maybe he can be of some use to us.

CATCHA: Yeah? Like how?

ACCORDIONO: I don't know, maybe he can sing.

CEDRICO: Can you sing?

JACK: (*Singing.*) "The hills are alive with the sound of music!"

GYPSIES: (*Holding their ears.*) No, he can't sing.

CATCHA: What are we gonna do with 'im?

CEDRICO: Roast 'im up and eat 'im for our supper!

GYPSIES: YAH!!

ACCORDIONO: Wait a second! Wait a second! Wait a second! Maybe he can still be of some use to us.

CATCHA: Yeah? Like how?

ACCORDIONO: Maybe he can play a musical instrument.

(*Jack takes the accordion from Accordiono and produces a cacophony of bum notes.*)

GYPSIES: (*Holding their ears.*) No, he can't play.

CATCHA: What are we gonna do with 'im?

CEDRICO: Roast 'im up and eat 'im for our supper!

GYPSIES: YAH!!

(*They go to take him off to the bonfire.*)

JACK: W-A-A-I-I-I-T!!

GYPSIES: W-H-A-A-A-T??

JACK: I can be of some use to ye!

GYPSIES: Yeah? Like how?

JACK: Like, I can dance how.

CATCHA: Well, we need a dancer. Somebody ate our last one!

CEDRICO: Yeah! We did! (*They all laugh wildly. Jack quakes with fear.*) But if you fail, we'll eat your lips, we'll eat your elbows, we'll eat your knuckles, we'll eat your kneecaps, we'll even eat your socks!

CATCHA: (*Sniffing at Jack's boots.*) Cedrico, not the socks.

(*Jack starts to step dance to the tune of Accordiono's accordion accordingly. The Gypsies begin to clap along and make gestures and noises of approval. Jack finishes with a flourish.*)

CEDRICO: Fine step on ya, my lad. Come along, Jack.

We'll steal the world together.
(With much cheering and hullabaloo the Gypsies
exit with Jack.)

UNCLE VAL: And so, because he could dance, Jack was allowed to join the wild and crazy Gypsy band.

Now, in the meantime, in the neighbouring kingdom of Muldonia, King Bolognia was having a birthday party for his beautiful daughter, the Princess Freckelonia. And who was entertaining the King and the Princess that night? Anyone know? Yes, it was Jack and the Gypsies.

(The King and Princess enter to processional music and three
rousing cheers of "All hail the King!")

And then the King calls for the entertainment for that night. He calls, "Clap, clap, Gypsies!"

KING BOLOGNIA: Clap, clap, Gypsies!
(Cedrico enters, wearing colourful Gypsy regalia and
jingling bells.)

CEDRICO: Your Majesties! Lords and ladies! Dukes and earls likewise! Make room! Make room! Make gallant room for us Gypsies we have arrived! We've come to entertain you all dressed up in greens and blues and reds...

KING BOLOGNIA: And do it well, for if you fail me, you'll surely lose your heads.

CEDRICO: Oooooh, oooh, Gypsies, Gypsies!
(Gypsies and Jack enter with a lot of hullabalooing and
jumping about.)

CEDRICO: *(Struggling to get their attention.)* Gypsies! Gypsies!

GYPSIES: What? What? What? *(Etc.)*

CEDRICO: Gypsies, our heads are at stake, Gypsies!

GYPSIES: Oooh, ooh, our heads. *(Etc.)*

CEDRICO: Gypsies! Gypsies! Gypsies!

GYPSIES: What? What? What? *(Etc.)*

CEDRICO: Gypsies, are we to let the sly surly slippery blade of monarchy come down and sever our heads from our bodies?

GYPSIES: No! No! *(Etc.)*

OLD PERLICAN: *(Gypsy dotard.)* Well ah, well ah, what ah what ah, what ah, *(He slaps himself on the face.)* what shall we do then?

CEDRICO: We'll sing our way out!

OLD PERLICAN: But, Cedrico, ah, what ah, what ah, what ah, *(He slaps himself on the face again.)* what shall we sing?

CEDRICO: We'll sing our greatest hit!

OLD PERLICAN: Ah, what ah, what ah, what ah, what is our greatest hit?

CEDRICO: "The Buckaroo Song."

GYPSIES: (*Sing.*) How many "roos" would a buckaroo
   buck,
    If a buckaroo could buckaroo?
    If we had a clue we'd have a buck or two,
    But we haven't got a buck, boo hoo,
    Boo hoo, boo hoo, boo hoo, boo hoo,
    No, we haven't got a buck, boo hoo,
    No, we haven't got a buck...

KING: 'Cause they haven't got a clue!

GYPSIES: No, we haven't got a buck, boo hoo.
    When we first started to buccaneer,
    Three long months ago,
    We thought we'd go to London town,
    To rob ourselves some dough,
    Some dough, some dough...

KING: To rob?

GYPSIES: Some dough! A great big lump of dough!
    We ran into a captain bold,
    Who offered us some gold,
    Now here we are without a ship,
    And we can't even get the dole,
    The dole, the dole...No dole!

KING: What dole!

GYPSIES: We can't get the dole.
    How many "eers" could a buccaneer buck
    If a buccaneer could buccaneer?
    We should have picked a better career,
    For it's woe to the buccaneer,
    Oh woe, oh woe, oh woe, oh woe,
    It's woe to the buccaneer.
                (They all cheer.)

KING BOLOGNIA: That was terrible! Guards, guards,
   off with their heads!
         (Gypsies plead for their lives.)

BASIL PESTO: (*Shady Gypsy lawyer/agent type guy.*)
   Your Majesty, please, please, I understand your rea-
   sons for wanting to cut off our heads. I would like to
   cut off the heads of the singers here tonight too, but
   Your Majesty, I think we have a little treat for you.
   Something that will make you not want to cut off our
   heads, it is a dancer! A boy dancer! The boy's name is
   Jack. (*Speaking to Jack.*) Quick Jack! Dance, dance
   and save our lives!

PRINCESS: (*Looking long and hard at Jack.*) Aw, come
   on, Dad, give 'em another chance.

KING BOLOGNIA: Oh...all right then.

(Jack dances to accordion music. They all cheer when he

finishes and it's obvious that the king is pleased.)

UNCLE VAL: And then all of a sudden a great hush fell over the grand ballroom.

(Gypsies exit quietly as the focus shifts to the Princess.)

And the Princess stepped down from her throne and she walked over to Jack and she said:

PRINCESS: Who are you?

JACK: I'm Jack.

PRINCESS: Are you that Jack that I've heard so much about? The Jack who's every inch a sailor? The one who climbed the beanstalk and jumped over the candlestick?

JACK: No, I'm the other Jack.

PRINCESS: Dance with me anyway, Jack.

(Jack and the Princess start to dance a waltz to the "Portuguese Waltz.")

UNCLE VAL: And so Jack and the Princess began to dance, and the Princess, why she fell madly in love with Jack, and Jack, well Jack fell madly in love with the Princess. But alas their love could never be.

(They stop dancing and gaze wistfully at each other.)

For she was a high and mighty Princess and Jack—why Jack was nothing but a poor and lowly beggar boy. So sadly, the Princess had to say goodbye to Jack, and Jack had to say goodbye to the Princess. Forever.

(Exit Princess, waving sadly to Jack.)

And so with a heavy heart, Jack headed down the road to seek his fortune. He walked along for a couple of miles till he came to the side of a river, and he sat down. *(Jack mimes actions, using his swag bag as prop.)* He opened up his swag bag and took out a little bit of the cake his mudder had baked for him, and a little bit of the hen she had roasted, and a hard-boiled egg. He put a bit of salt and a bit of pepper onto the egg, and to tell you the truth, a tear come to Jack's eye, rolled down his cheek, and fell into the salt on top of his egg. Poor Jack, he was feeling pretty low, when all of a sudden he seen the strangest thing he ever seen in his whole life. He seen a cat rowin' down the river in a canoe.

(A cat comes onto the stage, miming rowing a canoe.)

CAT: Hello, Jack.

JACK: Hello, Puss.

CAT: What are ya doin', Jack?

JACK: Well, I'm off seekin' me fortune. Actually, I'm lookin' for a master.

CAT: Well met, Jack, 'cause I'm lookin' for a man. Will ya ship to me?

JACK: Sure I might as well ship to you sure, as ship to anyone else sure.

UNCLE VAL: And so Jack got aboard the canoe and he shipped to the cat for a year and a day. And every morning Jack got up and he scrubbed the canoe from stem to stern, and every day he brought the cat breakfast in bed. (*Jack and Cat mime actions.*) But, when the year and a day was almost over, Jack and the cat were sittin' in the canoe one day, when who should they see goin' home through the woods, but Jack's two brothers, Bill and Tom, with great big bags of money on their backs.

(*Bill and Tom cross the stage carrying large bags of loot. They walk using the alternating piston method.*)

"Well, well, well, well, well, well, well, well," says the cat.

CAT: Well, well, well, well, well, well, well, well, they done good. Didn't they, Jack?

JACK: Yes, they done very good, indeed.

CAT: Well, today is the twelvemonth, and tomorrow is the day, so I reckon I'd better pay you your wages.

UNCLE VAL: And the cat went over and she got a great big bag of money, and she gave it to Jack. (*She does so.*) Well, Jack was delighted. He said goodbye to the cat, and the cat said goodbye to Jack, and Jack headed home. Over field, down dale, up hill, over meadow, under overpass, over underpass, bottom line, ball park figure, rattle me cage, let's do lunch, check the mail, up the garden path, in through the kitchen door, and who do you think was there waitin' for him? It was Mudder.

(*Mudder enters.*)

Well, she didn't see Jack. No, she didn't see Jack at all. All she seen was the bag of money. And the eyes was bulgin' out of her head. And Jack takes the bag of money and slaps it down on the floor. (*He does.*) And the old woman goes nuts, tryin' to get the money out of the bag, tryin' to get the money out of the bag, tryin' to get the money out of the bag. (*She does.*) Till Jack comes along and gives her a puck of his knee and drives her under the table. (*He does. She did.*) Oh, she didn't mind that. She kept on tryin' to get the money out of the bag, tryin' to get the money out of the bag, tryin' to get the money out of the bag. Till Jack comes along and gives her another puck of his knee. (*He does.*) But this time she struck her head on the hob of the fireplace. And with that the racket riz. "I'll bet," says Jack's father from the other room, "Jack is home."

(*Jack and Mudder get into a big wrestling match, with Uncle Val as ad lib commentator. Jack succumbs to ignominious defeat and Mudder emerges as household champion.*)

It was Mom all the way, and Jack was banished back to the coal box once again. So Mudder took the three bags of money and they had a great big Christmas party that lasted for a whole year.

Now, this wasn't the Christmas of nineteen seventy nine, that was referred to in the ancient books, but still, the rafters was shakin', and the floor was creakin' with an excess of merriment that eventually drove the family dog to takin' over the day-to-day running of household affairs. I'm tellin' you, that was some time!

(Uncle Val exits. Rock music plays. Members of the family dance. Uncle Val removes his hat and returns as the middle-aged Jack. Jack interrupts the family dance by turning on a light as he enters. The musicians stop playing suddenly.)

JACK: Dickie, Dickie, Dickie, Dickie, Dickie!

ROSE: C'mon, Jack, it's just a bit of fun.

DICKIE: We were just gettin' goin'.

JACK: I told the boys they could rehearse, but I didn't expect them to have all this electronic equipment out here.

(General protests throughout from members of family and Dickie Dinn's band.)

DICKIE: Jesus, Jack, you told us we could come into the house and practise, and here we are.

JACK: Jesus, Dickie boy, ah, you said practise *music*. I pictured someone with a guitar, or some folk singers, or somethin'.

DICKIE: That's old fashioned, boy, you're in the dark ages.

JACK: C'mon now, Tom, you give us a song, something you can dance to. *(He speaks to family.)* Now, you fellows, you'll hear some real music.

DICKIE: All right, boy, all right.

(General murmurs of, "All right, boy, all right, etc." as the family urges Tom to play. Tom takes his position to play his fiddle and they line up to dance.

Photograph by Janet Hannaford

As they take their positions, they snigger at Jack making comments such as, "Watch your heart, now Jack, watch your heart." They dance the "Lancers" (in 1986 they danced "Running the Goat," a dance from Harbour Deep), after which they collapse

around the living room. Everyone asks Tom to sing a song and
after coaxing he sings the traditional song, "A Keg of Brandy.")

    Love is pleasing, love is teasing,
Love is a pleasure when it is new,
But as love grows older it grows quite colder,
And fades away like the morning dew.
    I placed my head on a keg of brandy,
It was my fancy I do declare,
For when I am drinking I'm always thinking,
How can I win that lady fair.
    I am in love and I can't conceal it,
For all the pain is in my breast,
It was never known in this wide world,
That a troubled mind it knows no rest.
    I am always drunk, I am seldom sober,
I am always roaming from town to town,
But when I am dead and my frolic is over,
It is you, my fair one, come lay me down.
    The ocean is wide and I can't wade over,
Neither have I got wings to fly,
But I wish I had some jolly boatsman,
To ferry over my love and I.
    I am always drunk, I am seldom sober,
I am always roaming from town to town,
But when I am dead and my frolic is over,
It is you, my fair one, come lay me down.
    It was often said in Castle Koover,
Where rolling stones were as black as ink,
I would pledge my coat for the want of money,
And I'll sing no more till I get a drink.

(Jack, Jr. and Vi start to leave after the song, but Jack stops
them with a request.)

JACK: How about a little Christmas carol before you go?
ROSE: Yeah, give us a song before we go to bed.

(General murmurs of protest and consent from the family who
agree that there should be a carol before they go. This results in
the singing of "While Shepherds Watched Their Flocks by
Night.")

    While shepherds watched their flocks by night
All seated on the ground,
The angel of the Lord came down,
The angel of the Lord came down,
And glory shone around.
    "Fear not," said he, for mighty dread
Had seized their troubled mind.
"Glad tidings of great joy I bring,
Glad tidings of great joy I bring
To you and all mankind."

"To you in David's town this day
Is born of David's line,
A saviour who is Christ the Lord,
A saviour who is Christ the Lord,
And this shall be the sign."
  "The heavenly babe you there shall find
To human view displayed,
All meanly wrapped in swaddling bands,
All meanly wrapped in swaddling bands,
And in the manger laid."
  Up spake the Seraph and forthwith
Appeared a shining throng
Of angels praising God who thus,
Of angels praising God who thus,
Addressed their joyful song.
  "All glory be to God on high
And to the earth be peace,
Goodwill henceforth from heaven to men,
Goodwill henceforth from heaven to men,
Begin and never cease."
(Jack and Rose go to bed; the rest go out. Blackout.)

Scene 2

(It's Christmas Eve at Jack's apartment. Gran is sitting in the rocking chair in which she sits motionless throughout the play. Jack, Jr. is lying on the couch reading comic books. Jack enters through the door wearing a wig and a dress and carrying an Avon lady's suitcase. He walks across the living room, taking off the wig and dress and putting on his trousers. He looks toward Jack, Jr. lying on the sofa watching him, apprehensively.)

JACK: *(Looking at Jack, Jr.)* Wha'?

JACK, JR.: *(The ennui is great.)* Nothin'.

JACK: Wha'?

JACK, JR.: Nothin'.

JACK: It's all right for you, I'm out sellin' goddamn Avon products all day.

(Long pause, shuffling feet; tension. Jack goes over to Jack, Jr., picks his feet up off the couch and puts them on the floor. Jack, Jr. puts his feet back up as soon as Jack's back is turned.)

JACK: *(Without looking.)* Get your feet off the couch.

(Jack goes over and turns on the TV. The TV doesn't work. He bangs it with his hand. It still doesn't work. He goes to the table and turns on the radio. The radio doesn't work. He bangs it with his hand. It still doesn't work. He takes out a cigarette, tries to light it. The lighter doesn't work. He throws the lighter down on the table. Jack, Jr. continues to read his comic book.

Jack sits down and picks up a newspaper. He looks over at Jack, Jr. who is hiding behind his comic book. When Jack looks away, Jack, Jr. looks up over the top of the comic book. Jack looks and tries to catch him looking, but he's hidden behind the comic book. They keep this up until finally they see each other. Jack, Jr. gets up and tries to sneak out.)

JACK: Where're you goin'?

JACK, JR.: Out.

JACK: Out where?

JACK, JR.: Out around.

JACK: Out around where?

JACK, JR.: Out around nowhere.

JACK: You're not goin' anywhere. You're stayin' home and helpin' your mother get ready for Christmas. Now sit down and shut up.

(Long pause.)

JACK, JR.: Mom said she was goin' down to the store. She'll be back in about ten minutes.

(Pause.)

JACK: Where's your mother?

JACK, JR.: I just told ya, she's gone down to the store. She'll be back in about ten minutes.

JACK: Don't talk to me in that tone of voice, will ya?

JACK, JR.: I'm not talkin' to ya in any tone of voice.

JACK: You're talkin' to me in that tone of voice right now.

JACK, JR.: But you asked me...

JACK: Don't talk to me in that tone of voice, I said.

JACK, JR.: But you asked me...

JACK: My son, don't think I won't give it to you across the face, because I will.

JACK & JACK, JR.: *(Together. Screaming.)* Don't talk to me in that tone of voice—You told me—Don't talk to me in that tone of voice—I'm not talking to you in any tone of voice. *(Etc.)*

(Enter Rose as the argument almost comes to a fight. Screaming as loudly as Jack and Jack, Jr., she breaks them up.)

ROSE: *(Screaming.)* Are ye at it again?

(Silence as they all glare at one another.)

ROSE: Ya have it on ya tonight, Jack. As far as you're concerned he can't do anything right.

JACK: As far as I'm concerned, he can't do anything.

(Jack goes back to the table, picks up the newspaper and Jack, Jr. goes back to the couch and sits down. Rose goes over to where Jack left his dress and wig. She picks them up.)

ROSE: Pick up your dress when ya come in, will ya?

(Jack, Jr. sniggers. Jack stares him down.)

ROSE: How d'ya do today, anyway?

JACK: Great.

ROSE: Did ya sell anything?

JACK: Yeah, I sold five thousand dollars worth of stuff.

ROSE: (*Amazed.*) Ya never?

JACK: You're goddamn right, I never! I sold five dollars worth of stuff, which is five dollars more than I'm sellin' tomorrow, 'cause I'm quittin'! I'm finished—finished with it—over with—quit—no more Bird of Paradise cream sachet—no more "Ding dong, Avon calling." (*As he throws down newspaper.*) I'm sick of it—I'm finished with it!

(He notices Jack, Jr. trying to sneak out the door again.)

JACK: Where're you goin'?

JACK, JR.: Out.

JACK: Out! Out! Not out—in! The opposite of out—in. Do you hear me? Not out—in! In! In! In! In! (*Etc.*)

ROSE: Jack, can ya leave him alone for five minutes?

JACK JR: I can see what kinda Christmas this is goin' to be, right now.

JACK: What do you know about it?

JACK, JR.: I know lots about it.

JACK: What do you know about what kinda Christmas we're gonna have?

JACK, JR.: Lots about it.

JACK: What do you know about it?

JACK, JR.: Lots.

JACK: Tell me what ya know about it.

JACK, JR.: Lots.

JACK: Tell me what you know about it.

JACK, JR.: Lots about it! Lots! (*Etc.*)

(They begin screaming at one another.)

JACK: Ya don't know nothin' about it.

JACK, JR.: I know lots about it.

JACK: You don't know goddamn nothin' about it.

JACK, JR.: I know lots about it.

JACK: Ya don't know goddamn nothin' about it.

JACK, JR.: I know lots about it.

JACK: Ya don't know goddamn nothin' about it.

(Building to a crescendo of screams.)

JACK: (*Insisting.*) Tell me what ya know about it—tell me what ya know about it!

JACK, JR.: Lots about it—Lots about it!

(They reach another crescendo. Jack grabs Jack, Jr. by the front of his shirt and Rose hauls them apart.)

ROSE: (*Screaming.*) Stop it! Stop it!

(Enter Cyril. He walks between the two Jacks.)

CYRIL: Christ almighty! You're at it again, Jesus!

(Cyril goes over to TV and tries to turn it on. It doesn't work. He bangs it.)

JACK: (*Ironically.*) It's not workin', is it?

CYRIL: No, it's not.

JACK: The TV's not workin', is it?

CYRIL: No.

JACK: You're not workin' either, are ya?

CYRIL: No.

JACK: (*He carries on, not listening to anybody. Pointing to Jack, Jr.*) And you're not workin'! (*Pointing to Rose.*) And she's not workin'! (*Pointing to Gran.*) And you're not workin'! And guess what? I'm not workin'! (*Pointing and rushing around to people and objects as he speaks.*) I'm not workin'; she's not workin'; you're not workin'; you're not workin'; you're not workin'; the TV's not workin'; the radio's not workin'; the lighter's not workin'; nothin's workin' and nobody's workin'.

(Jack goes over to his chair and plunks himself down in a huff. He picks up the newspaper and buries his head in it. There is a long pause while Jack looks at the newspaper. The rest of the family stands about looking sheepish. Jack slowly brings down the paper from his face and becomes a character from a Household Finance Company ad on TV.)

HFC MAN: Let's face it, folks, in these troubled economic times, financial ups and downs are pretty much part of day-to-day life. I know this year, when Santa Claus's reindeers were gearing up for the big trip south, and visions of sugar plums were preparing to enter the collective consciousness, I threw open the shutters of my bank account to find...Well, let me put it this way, we're pretty much a typical Canadian family, although we are caught out here in the wilds of New*found*land. Take, for example, little Ricky here; (*Jack, Jr. gives appropriate little Ricky smile.*) Well, come January first, Ricky starts his first semester at college. Not a cheap proposition. Right, Ricky?

JACK, JR.: Right, Pop.

HFC MAN: And Billy, here (*Cyril.*)...well, let's face it. Billy here, can't go through another football season without a helmet. Right, Bill? Billy? (*Cyril stares vacantly.*) And little Valda here (*Joy.*)...well, Valda's on enough medication to kill a horse. Paranoid schizophrenia with complications is not a cheap disease. And, well, a little bird told me that Sue here (*Rose.*), is expecting to find a new sewing machine underneath the Christmas tree. This year I decided not to be a turkey. I decided to borrow confidently from the folks I trust. So I won't have to blow my brains out on Christmas Eve. Borrow confidently from HFC.

ROSE: (*Playing along.*) Brad, dear, isn't it time to trim the hedge?

(Jack puts the newspaper in front of his face and turns back into Jack. He throws the paper down on the table.)

JACK: All right, do it! Go ahead and do it. Get that goddamn HFC loan—go on, call him up.

ROSE: (*To Jack, Jr.*) Jack, do it. Go on, call him up. But I'm telling you we're gettin' together next year and we're payin' it off—every bloody cent of it. Now go on—call him up.

(There is a pause. Jack, Jr. doesn't move.)

JACK: I notice you're not goin' to the phone, Jack, and I think I know why. 'Cause you know that if you go to that phone and call up the HFC, I'll break both your arms and both your legs. Now listen, I don't want to hear anything else about HFC this Christmas! Not one word! Not one syllable, do you hear me? Not another word, and that's the last I'll say about it; the last I want to hear about it.

(The family stands sullenly around not knowing what to do. Jack goes back to his newspaper. There is a long pause. Jack picks up Uncle Val's hat, puts it on and becomes Uncle Val. The family exit and the band sets up in black as Uncle Val speaks.)

Scene 3

UNCLE VAL: It was HFC that was the cause of all the problems that merry little Christmas of nineteen and seventy nine, and it was the arduous nagging by the Princess Rose and Jack, Jr. that eventually led the very proud Jack to take on the job with Avon Calling. As you will see later on, as our story unfolds, HFC also turned out to be the solution to quite a few of the problems, and it was years later, that they would look back and laugh at Jack's brief flirtation with the oleo-eccentric world of cosmetics and body-odour suppressants. So hang on to your hats, folks, the story continues. *(He exits.)*

(The band breaks into two Newfoundland tunes, "Pussy Cat Up the Plum Tree" (traditional) and "Diane's Happiness" (Emile Benoit.) When the music is finished, Uncle Val enters. Meanwhile, all members of the family have filtered back on stage as the band played and are lounging about the living room.)

No doubt you are all wondering why, with such a strapping great family as Jack has here, why there is no inward cash flow, so to speak. So I thought what I'd do is give you a little biographical run-down on some of the members of the family, or as they call them in the show-biz world 'Bios.' I'll start off first of all over here with Jack, Jr.. Now here he is over here with his girlfriend, Vi, I think that's Vi. *(Jack separates Jack, Jr. from Vi with whom he is in a passionate clinch.)* Yeah, that's Vi.

Now, Jack, Jr. and I, we don't communicate all that well. A few weeks ago, I decided to take the plunge, so to speak, and I said to him, "Jack, Jr.," I said, "what do you be doing all the time?"

He replied, "Knocking around with the girls. The odd toke." Now what do that mean?

But anyway, now drunk with curiosity, I decided to press on further, and I said, "Be more specific, Jack. What do you intend to do tonight?"

He said, "Nothing."

I said, "How about tomorrow night, then?"

Once again, he replied, "Nothing." When I questioned Vi on her activities, she had quite a similar scenario. So I can only conclude from this, that "knocking around with the girls, the odd toke" involves male and female youths hanging around together, doing nothing. Which totally fails to explain the alarming rate of pregnancy among today's youth; and specifically, fails to explain...Vi's pregnancy—which little hand grenade has yet to be lobbed at this merry little Christmas ensemble. I happen to know that, because I'm the narrator.

It's quite a burden, really, being the narrator—you can't go to narrator school or get a grant from the narration section of the Canada Council.

Over here is Gran. Gran's ninety-two years old and she hasn't spoken since Confederation. I don't know if it was due to a deterioration of the brain cells or the lightning ascendency of Mr. Smallwood, but Gran only pulls her marbles together once a month, and that's when the pension cheque comes in, and she goes down and deposits it in the Bank of Commerce, where it stays; and she probably has all her money left to the Church. (*Gran twitches.*) So for all intents and purposes, Gran is not a breadwinner.

Now, over here, in the blue shirt playing cards, is Cyril. Now Cyril is Rose's younger brother. I guess he's Prince Cyril, in that sense. Cyril is thirty-four years old. Now, what they usually say about Cyril, is that he's as useless as the pontifical testicles. You know what I mean—the papal pips. (*Addressing Cyril.*) Cyril, if you were to say what was your one aim in life, how would you describe it?

CYRIL: Colour TV.

UNCLE VAL: You're aiming high, Cy. And next to Cyril, here, is Joy. Joy is fourteen years old, and although you can't expect her to bring any money into the family, nevertheless, she's a considerable drain on the family exchequer, most of her purchases being along the disco attire line, long-playing records and the gum that goes squirt in your mouth. (*Addressing Joy.*) What's that gum called, anyway, Joy?

JOY: Well, it's called Bubblicious, but I call it the gum that comes.

UNCLE VAL: She got a dirty mouth on her, too. Next to her, here, is Rose, the Princess Rose from the story. And although every bit as royal, her income level contrasts sharply with that of, say, Princess Anne or Princess Margaret. Rose was laid off from the Merrymeeting Laundromat about two months ago.

And next to Rose is Tom. Remember Tom from the story—Tom, Bill and Jack? Tom is handsome; he's charming; he's a very talented fiddle player, all of which brings in zero dollars and zero cents per month, in fact, when you consider the cost of violin strings, rosin and Brylcreem, he's a bit of a liability really.

Now, here is Mona. Now, Mona used to be Bill, and that's all
I'm going to say about that. Mona is thirty-four years old, and
next to her is her seventeen-year-old boyfriend, Henri. Henri
Lafayette—he's a Frenchman. A very good choice of boyfriend for
Mona. He's young enough not to know exactly what to look for,
and he's French enough not to be able to ask any questions. (*He
addresses Henri.*) You know what I mean by that, do you, Henri?
You understand me?

HENRI: Non, je ne vous comprend pas.

UNCLE VAL: Yeah, well, ooga-booga to you too. And now in the
middle here, on the drums, is Dickie Dinn. Dickie is one of them
live-in, eat-in next door neighbours. Usually described as a dilly-
dallier in rubber. Sometimes he's known as Dickie Dinn;
sometimes Philip Dinn; sometimes George Dinn; sometimes Soc-
rates Dinn, depending on which name he's signed to the last
cheque he forged. He is a musician, and next to him is Jack's son,
Bas. Bas is sixteen years old, and for some strange reason or
other, Bas looks up to Cyril here. Amazing! I don't know why he
tries to emulate him in every way. (*He addresses Bas.*) Why is
that, Bas? Can you explain that to me?

(Bas does not answer.)

UNCLE VAL: Now that's one of the wittier things he's said in the
last year. Next to Dickie, this young fella with the black hat on
here, is Quigley Dinn. He's Dickie's illegitimate son. In fact,
Quigley just came back last week. He was up in Toronto for a
couple of months. (*Addressing Quigley.*) How was the trip up in
Toronto, Quigley?

QUIGLEY: Well, yeah, ya know, it's Toronto, right?

UNCLE VAL: Yeah? Toronto, yeah?

*(Uncle Val waits for more comment from Quigley. No comment
comes. Pause.)*

UNCLE VAL: Well, ooga-booga to you too. And last but not least,
here is Nelson. Now for some reason or other they say that
Nelson takes after me. I don't know why. (*He addresses Nelson.*)
Why is that, Nelson?

NELSON: (*Speaking in imitation of Uncle Val.*) I don't know why,
Uncle Val, why is that?

UNCLE VAL: I don't know, I really don't. Now Nelson, actually, is
a bit of an anomaly in the family, because Nelson is the only male
member of the family, other than Jack, to have worked in the last
two years. Nelson had a job for two days as a type-setter down at
the *Evening Telegram*. Picture, if you will, thousands of Newfoundland families sitting around the fire of a Friday evening
trying to read *Pravda*, and you have some idea why he lost his
job. Now, I myself, am totally unemployable due to the fact that I
am a victim of a life-time of cigarette smoking, and my fingers
stayed like this. (*He holds his fingers in a cigarette-holding pose.*)
I've lost the use of that hand.

So that's a little run-down on the family. Any questions? Speak now, or forever hold your peace. No questions? Are you sure now? You can pass it from me to them now if you want to. (*Addressing family.*) Uh, everybody!

EVERYBODY: Yeah, wha'? (*Etc.*)

UNCLE VAL: Fire!!! (*Family runs offstage.*) They may seem like a hard crowd, but they're very gullible when it comes right down to it. Now where was I in my story? Oh yes, Jack was back in the coal box once again. There was a Christmas party that went on for a whole year. And when the party was over all three fortunes had been pissed away. There wasn't a cent left in the house, not a penny, not a farthing, not a kopeck, not a sou. not a zee, not a quu. Nudding.

(*Enter Bill and Tom and Mudder.*)

So once again, Jack's two brothers, Bill and Tom, they came into the kitchen and said to their mudder, "Mudder," they said:

BILL: Mudder, bake us a cake and roast us a hen...

TOM: For we're off to seek our fortune.

(*Tears and wailing from all. Bill and Tom exit.*)

UNCLE VAL: Well, their mudder was shockin' broken up at the thought of her two bouncing baby boys goin' down the road to seek their fortune.

(*Enter Jack.*)

But the next day when Jack said:

JACK: Mudder, bake me a cake and roast me a hen, for I'm off to seek my fortune.

UNCLE VAL: All the mudder said was:

MUDDER: Wisht-to'booneen, Jack, me prayers have been answered, 'tis not for your goin' I'm sorry, 'tis only afraid you might come back. Now go on and be off with you.

JACK: And that's the right way too, Mudder.

(*Mudder exits and Jack strides off jauntily again.*)

UNCLE VAL: And so Jack headed down the road once again to seek his fortune. He was walkin' along with a spring in his step, and a song in his heart, and a twinkle in his eye, until he found himself by the side of a great big huge ocean. Jack looked around for a ferry boat, but there was no ferry boat. He looked around for a fishin' boat, but, of course, there was no fishin' boats any more. "Oh no," says Jack, "now I'm goin' to have to go home to me mudder, and I wont be able to seek me fortune at all!" And Jack was just about to burst into tears, when all of a sudden he heard a very strange noise.

(*Sound of a tornado in the distance, but getting closer.*)

"Sounds like wind," said Jack. And it was a wind. All of a sudden, out of the east come a wild and woolly, diaphanous but deadly, great white tornado.

(*Tornado dressed in crinolines and women's lacy under-things*

comes onstage, spiralling around like a tornado.)
And the tornado picked Jack up *(It does.)* and it swung him around and around and around and around *(Jack bellowing all the while.)* and when it set Jack down *(It does.)* what do you know? He was on the other side of the ocean. He'd made it across in two minutes and thirty-four seconds—a new world record. Jack was so happy that he and the tornado did a little dance together.
(They dance a can-can, accompanying themselves with a little chin music.)
So Jack says goodbye to the tornado and the tornado says goodbye to Jack.
(They wave goodbye to each other and Tornado exits.)
"Now," Jack said to himself, "on this, the first day of me second year seekin' me fortune, I'm gonna walk for two hundred miles." So he walked and he walked and he kept on walkin', and he didn't stop walkin' and he walked some more. He did walk. He did walk. He didn't not walk. He didn't not walk and he walked and he walked till he stopped, dead in his tracks. One-hundred-and-ninety-nine-point-nine miles. He couldn't go another step further. His legs were swollen up like balloons and his feet were falling off the bottom of his legs. So he said to himself, "I think I'll go into the woods and take a little rest." And it was very dark in the woods and Jack was very, very frightened, when all of a sudden a huge troll jumped out from behind a juniper tree.
(Troll comes onstage brandishing a club, looking ferocious, and dressed like the marked-down fruit bin at the supermarket.)
The troll come over to Jack, and he raised his huge hand high in the air, and he brought it down, and *(Pause.)* patted Jack on the head. He was a friendly troll. Thank goodness for that.
(Jack and Troll stand around getting friendly.)
But what Jack did not realize was that this part of the woods was inhabited by a crazy, evil creature.
(Evil Leprechaun enters and starts creeping up behind Jack and Troll, looking crazy and evil.)
It was a leprechaun!
(Leprechaun goes mad, grabbing Uncle Val's hat and going wild in the audience. Troll chases him, and after much excitement, they find their way back onstage. Leprechaun points to a place in the heavens, and when Troll is looking to see what it is, he kicks Troll in the arse and runs off, much to the delight of the audience. Troll follows after.)
Well, Jack was so delighted that he wrote the troll a little note of thanks and pinned it to a tree. *(Jack does so.)* Well, Jack only took five more steps—one, two, three, four, five...*(Jack takes six steps.)* Oh yes, well, maybe it was six steps. Anyway, he finds himself right down by the river, where he was the year before.

*(Uncle Val takes off his Uncle Val hat and becomes Jack. He
sits at the table. Lights fade as Rose enters.)*

Scene 4

ROSE: Jack, do you think we'll make it through another year?
JACK: Yeah, I guess so.
ROSE: Yeah, I guess you're right. We always manage to make it
through somehow.
JACK: Not always, though.
ROSE: Most times, though.
JACK: Not always, though.
ROSE: Most times, though.
JACK: Not always, though.
ROSE: Oh, shut up! *(Pause.)* Oh, my...
  (Rose joins Jack at the table. He stares at her shoulder.)
JACK: Do you know you have dandruff? You didn't have dandruff
when I first met you.
ROSE: I didn't have a lot of things when you first met me.
JACK: Like what?
ROSE: Seven kids, poverty, stretch marks and thou; all two-hun-
dred-and-fifty pounds of thou.
  *(Rose laughs as lights go down on Jack and Rose and they
begin to waltz. "Portuguese Waltz" fades in. Enter the young
Jack and the Princess waltzing. Rose and Jack pause and
watch their reflections. Young Jack and the Princess stop danc-
ing, the Princess moves away from Jack and they wave sadly to
each other. Rose and the Princess exit together. Jack goes to his
spot to become Uncle Val and continues his narration.)*
UNCLE VAL: I believe the last time we left Jack, he was down by
the side of the river. And who should be comin' down that river in
a canoe, but his old friend the cat.
  (Cat paddles over to Jack.)
CAT: Hello, Jack.
JACK: Hello, Puss.
CAT: What are ya doin', Jack?
JACK: Well, I'm off seekin' me fortune again. Actually,
I'm lookin' for another master.
CAT: Well met, Jack, 'cause I'm lookin' for another man.
Will ya ship to me?
JACK: Well, ah...ah...ah ha...
CAT: What's the matter, Jack, wasn't I good to ya?
JACK: Oh yes, Puss, you were good to me. Very good
indeed.
CAT: And didn't I give you enough money?
JACK: Oh yes, maid, enough money. No problem with
the money.
CAT: Well, what seems to be the obstacle, Jack?

UNCLE VAL: Well now, between you and me, Jack wasn't all that delighted about the idea of spendin' another whole year and a day with a cat. But Jack was an easy goin' fella', and what with bein' a Newfoundlander, and what with conflict avoidance, and one thing and another, Jack shipped to the cat for a second year and a day. And Jack and the cat had a wonderful year and a day together. And every morning Jack got up and he scrubbed the canoe from stem to stern, and every day he brought the cat breakfast in bed.

But, when the year and a day was almost over, Jack and the cat were sittin' in the canoe one day, when who should they see goin' home through the woods, but Jack's two brothers, Bill and Tom, with great big bags of money on their backs. But this year, each of them also had a beautiful woman by the hand.

(Bill and Tom march across the stage, loot and "beautiful" women in tow.)

Well, when Jack seen that, he was vicious. He says to himself, "Look at that, there's Bill and Tom gone home with beautiful women by the hand, and what have I got? Nothin' but an old cat." And after awhile, Jack got himself into an awful bad mood, and every time the cat would speak to him Jack would only grumble.

And after awhile, the cat said to Jack, "Jack, you seem to be in an awfully bad mood."

"No," says Jack, "I'm not in a bad mood."

"Yes," says the cat, "you are in a bad mood."

"No," says Jack, "I'm not in a bad mood."

"Yes," says the cat, "you are in a bad mood."

"No," said Jack, "I'm not."

"Yes, you are."

"No," said Jack, "I'm not."

"Yes you are."

"No, I'm not."

"Yes, you are."

"No, I'm not."

"Yes, you are."

"No, I'm not."

"Are."

"Not."

"Are."

"Not."

Finally Jack breaks down and tells the cat what's on his mind.

"Well," says the cat, "is that all you wanted, Jack? A beautiful woman to take home by the hand?"

"Well, yes," says Jack.

"Well, no problem," says the cat, and she reaches into her pocket and she takes out the one half of a ring, and she gives it to Jack. "Now, Jack, when you meet the woman with the other half of that ring, she will be the woman of your dreams."

"Thank you, very much," says Jack.

"Now," says the cat, "before you go, Jack, I want you to do three things for me."

"What's that?" says Jack.

"Number one, I want you to go out into the woods and bring me a great big pile of dry wood." Jack goes out in the woods and he brings in a great big pile of dry wood. "Number two," says the cat, "I want you to take that wood, and build me a great big fire." Jack takes the wood and builds a great big roarin' fire. "And now," says the cat, "number three. I want you, Jack, to take me and throw me in that fire."

"No," says Jack, "I could never do that."

"Yes," says the cat, "you got to do that."

"No," says Jack, "I'll never do that."

"Yes," says the cat, "I am your master and you are my man. Now, you do as I say. Throw me in that fire."

"No," says Jack, "I'll never do that."

"Yes," said the cat, "you got to do that."

"No," says Jack, "I'll never do that."

"Yes," said the cat, "you got to do that."

"No," says Jack, "I'll never do that."

"Yes," said the cat, "you got to do that."

"No, I won't."

"Yes, you will."

"No, I won't."

"Yes, you will."

"No, I won't."

"Yes, you will."

"Won't."

"Will."

"Won't."

"Will."

"Won't."

"Will."

Finally Jack loses his temper, picks up the cat and throws her in the fire. (*Cat exits screaming as if burned.*) The cat bursts into flames, shoots up through the chimney and disappears. Well, Jack was sorry the moment he done it. After all, the cat was his best friend in the whole world. And then Jack says to himself, "Oh no! What am I after doin'? I'm after killin' the cat. Now I'm goin' to go to jail for the rest of my life and be hung for murder." And so Jack was feelin' pretty bad, when all of a sudden a knock comes onto the door. (*Three knocks. He speaks to the children in the audience, ad libbing, "Do you think Jack should answer the door? Yes? etc.*") Jack says to himself, "It's better to know than not to know." So he goes over and opens the door, and standin' there in the doorway is the most beautiful woman that water ever wet or the sun ever shined on. It was the Princess.

(Enter Princess.)

"Princess, what are you doin' here?" asks Jack.

"I come to see you, Jack," says the Princess.

"Well," says Jack, "you couldn't have come at a worse time."

"Why is that?" says the Princess.

And Jack tells the Princess the story of how he killed the cat.

"Well, after all, Jack," says the Princess, "the cat *did ask* you to throw her in the fire."

"I know," says Jack, "but that's no excuse for killin' a cat."

Then the Princess says, "Jack, did, by any chance, the cat give you anything before she burst into flames?"

"No," says Jack, "I don't think so."

(Uncle Val addresses the audience directly.)

Ladies and gentlemen, boys and girls, did the cat give anything to Jack before she burst into flames?

(Hopefully the audience responds with "Half a ring.")

Well, tell Jack, "the half a ring."

(They tell Jack.)

So Jack reached into his pocket and pulled out the one half of a ring. And what do you know? The Princess reached into her pocket and took out the other half. And the two halves fit tight together.

"Princess," says Jack, "you are the woman of my dreams."

"Jack," says the Princess, "you are the man of mine."

"Now we can get married," says Jack.

"Yes, yes, yes," says the Princess, "and live happily ever after."

"Yes, yes, yes," says Jack. "No, no, no," says Jack, "I'm after killin' the cat and I'm goin' to go to jail for the rest of my life and be hung for murder."

When all of a sudden the Princess says, "Jack, don't worry about the cat."

"Don't worry about the cat?" says Jack.

"No," says the Princess, "the cat is not dead."

"The cat is not dead?" says Jack.

"No," says the Princess, "I am the cat."

"You are the cat?" says Jack.

"Yes," says the Princess, "I was turned into a cat by an evil wizard, who told me that unless I could get a man to serve me, as a cat, aboard a canoe for two years and two days I would remain a cat forever, But you done it, Jack. You saved me from eternal catdom."

"Well, come on home and meet the mudder," says Jack. He takes the Princess by the hand, takes the big bag of money and headed home. Over field, down dale, up hill, over meadow, under overpass, over underpass, bottom line, ball park figure, rattle me cage, let's do lunch, check the mail, up the garden path, in through the kitchen door, and who do you think was standin'

there waitin' for him? It was Mudder.
(Enter Mudder, greedy as usual.)
She didn't see Jack. She didn't even see the Princess. All she seen
was the big bag of money. The eyes were bulgin' out of her head.
Jack takes the bag of money and slaps it on the floor and the old
woman goes nuts tryin' to get the money out of the bag, tryin' to
get the money out of the bag, tryin' to get the money out of the
bag. Till Jack comes along and he's just about to give her a puck
of his knee, but he decides against it *(Jack stops himself in mid
kick.)* because after all, the princess is there and he wants to
make a good impression. So after a while they tell the mudder
the story of how the Princess was turned into a cat, and what do
you know? It turns out that the two women, who went home with
Bill and Tom, they were the Princess's two younger sisters.

ACT 2
Scene 1

*(Vi is opening Christmas cards and handing them to Rose, who
is hanging them on a string over the mantle. Gran is asleep in
her chair by the stove.)*
VI: Here's one from 13 Oceanview, Palm Beach, Florida.
ROSE: That's from Verne and Edna. What are they saying?
VI: *(Reads.)* Christmas time has come again;
That cheery time of year;
You're probably freezing your asses off;
But it's warm as hell down here!
Here's a picture of them; look, they have the palm tree decorated.
ROSE: Look at the face on Verne. Even with the tan it looks like a
hen's hole.
(Pause.)
VI: Mrs. Rose, what would you think if Jacky and I got married
after Christmas? I mean...I'm here all the time anyway.
ROSE: What do I think? I think you're sixteen years old. My God,
Vi, there's plenty of time for all that. Have a bit of fun while you
can. You'll have all of this soon enough—the bills, cooking, clean-
ing—running around after a bunch of snotty-nosed youngsters.
*(Vi looks sheepishly at Rose and finally it dawns on Rose that
Vi is pregnant.)*
ROSE: You're not! Sweet Christmas-face Christ! Jack is gonna
have a conniption. *(Suddenly there is a loud banging on the door.
Rose hugs Vi as she goes to the door to see what the noise is.)* It's
okay. We'll look after it. Don't you go saying anything to Jack
until after Christmas.
*(There are cries of "The mummers! The mummers! Let the
mummers in! Let the mummers in! Will you let the mummers
in? etc." Members of the family and Dickie Dinn have dressed*

up in costumes to perform a mummers play they have written. Stick Man is played by Dickie Dinn, Willy Nilly by Jack, Doctor by Jack, Jr., King Peck by Cyril, Joey by Quigley Dinn, Merchant by Nelson and Hobby Horse by Tom. They rush through the door and the mummers play begins. Vi and Rose go and sit in the audience to watch the play.)

STICK MAN: Good evening, ladies and gentlemen,
And all the rest of ye.
We've come to show our ragged play,
As soon you are to see.
Our players be a mangy crew,
Being fed on naught but old fish stew,
And now and then a bean or two.

ONE PLAYER: But not often.

STICK MAN: Their parts are well rehearsed, they say,
For they seem to know the score.
Such clamour, fuss and frolic, folks,
Must surely never bore.
(Shouts and cheers from the mummers.)
Just to be on the safe side
We've thrown in murder, too.
Plus a scattered few drops of politics
            (Mummers cheer.)
For such a perjurious lot as you.
First we'll bring in King Joe...

(Cheers from mummers. Enter Joey Smallwood wearing horn rimmed glasses and a bow tie. Also enter Hobby Horse——a diabolical looking wooden horse's head with glaring red eyes operated by Tom who is covered in a bright green blanket. During this scene, Hobby Horse runs around the stage causing mayhem.)

            Whom I'm sure some of you may know.
Then we'll bring in Willy Nilly...
    (Enter Willy Nilly, dressed in oil skins and sou'wester.)
And he's certainly a dilly.
Then there's good King Peck of Oilford...
*(Enter Brian Peckford in an oil sheik's costume and wearing
            sunglasses.)*
A big stuffed shirt, not much of a reward.
Then there's our noble Merchant...
        (Enter Merchant, with big head.)
Who stole from the fishermen, the dirty sea urchin.
Last but not least, our noble and esteemed Doctor.
With his phony dress from Gamble and Proctor.
(At this point Hobby Horse who has been charging around really gets out of control and begins to attack Rose, Vi and the audience. He has to be held back by the actors who rush forward toward him. Hobby Horse turns and attacks other

*members of the family onstage. He is subdued to sounds such as
"Hiya hup! Hiya hup!" and "Boona goona! Joona Loona!" and
other oriental sounds. However, Hobby Horse rises once again
and attacks the mummer who is making the oriental sounds,
the mummer then changes into making karate type sounds. A
mummer tries to subdue Hobby Horse with words such as,
"Hiya hup! Get along! Whoa!" Suddenly the magic words,
"Glue factory! Glue factory!" subdue him and the narrative
continues.)*

So settle in your seats and stop your jaws a clappin'.
Let our spectacle begin before my jargon sets you
all a nappin'.
(Cheers from mummers. Stick Man shouts.)
Bring on King Joe.
(Joey steps forward. Willy Nilly goes crazy at the sight of him.)

WILLY:　　Joe, Joe, Joe, Joey, Joe, Joe.
Speak, oh, toothless gob.
We await your sacred spittle, oh Joey.
We attend your magic mucous.
Speak, speak, speak, speak, speak.

JOEY:　　Here I am, King Joe.
My crown 'tis broke,
And my throne, it's gone.
So, now, around this dreary land, I go.
Hobnobbing with this lowly throng.
　　(Murmurs of protest from mummers.)
Now, this burden on my back,
As surely all can see,
Are great big books,
Writ by me.
Not one, not two, but three.
First is pure rubbish,
And the second perjury.
The third explains the former two.
Just a little bit of trash,
No apologies from me.
Not one, not two, not three.
(Mummers protest but Joey shrugs it off and continues.)
For a quarter of a century,
This land was mine to bleed,
So I lived just like a god.
Served bold, it did, my greed.
And I travelled the whole world over,
Just like the eagle free.
And round and round and round, I'd go,
Not one, not two, but three.
*(All mummers join in chorus of the words, "but three." They are
getting angry at Joey's repetition.)*

Up jumps Master Moores,
Damnation on his head.
Oh, he learned his lessons well, from dad,
On the way that fishermen are bled.
And he told them, I said, "Burn your boats."
Oh, what a dirty liar.
How was I to know that gasoline
Was sure fuel for a fire?

(Willy Nilly interrupts Joey.)

WILLY NILLY: Sure, Joey, you never said, "Burn your boats," you said, "Fry your dories."

JOEY: What!

WILLY NILLY: No, no, no, no, no, no, no, it was, "Poach your punts."

JOEY: What!

WILLY NILLY: No, no, no, I got it now. It was, "Teriyaki your trap skiffs."

(Joey starts hitting Willy.)

JOEY: Ah, it was people like you who ruined my rubber boot factory!

WILLY: No! No! No! Joe.

JOEY: But don't blame that on me.
I told you all more than once,
Not once, not twice but thrunce.
You may as well forget it, boys,
'Cause there'll be no apologies from me.
But, Willy, the streets can still be paved with gold,
So come along with me.
So come along, dear boy,
Come along with me.

(He grabs Willy by the lapels.)

WILLY: Joey, of course I'll go with you, Joey, for God's sake. Joey boy, it was you who took the poor little Newfoundlanders in your warm sweaty little hand and shoved them up...the bosom of Confederation. Oh Joe! For God's sake, Joe. Sure, everybody loves you, Joe.

(Suddenly, Willy freaks out, saying, "Everybody loves you, you goddamn bastard! Tear the face off ya! Etc." He starts beating up on Joey but is hauled off by Merchant. He ends up sobbing over the betrayals that Joey has laid on him in years gone by. He turns to Merchant.)

WILLY: Who the hell are you, anyway?

MERCHANT: I am the big fat merchant.
My stomach's always full,
My head is like a puncheon,
And I'm built just like the bull.

WILLY: So you are, too. Look at the size of ya. Next to you, I'm only a fart in a mitt.

MERCHANT: My cellar's full to burstin',
                 And you'd never break the lock.
                 For the magistrate, my cousin's
                 In his seat above the dock.
WILLY: (*Who has now been subdued to the floor by Merchant who
     is standing over him.*) Mercy! Mercy! Mercy!
MERCHANT: (*With his hands around Willy's throat.*)
                 Bring on your fish now, laddie,
                 There's room enough for all.
                 I'll call it all West Indy,
                 And I'll sell it in the fall.
                 I'll keep you through the winter,
                 But don't you linger in the spring.
                 Don't let the cold thaw hinder,
                 For empty stomachs sing.
WILLY: I know, boy, I know. Sometimes, mine sounds like the
     Mormon Tabernacle Choir. (*Sings.*) "My guts are alive with the
     sound of music..."
MERCHANT: (*Angry at Willy's interruption.*)
                 On with it, on with it.
                 But hard times have befallen.
WILLY: Oh, my God! What, what, what, what?
MERCHANT: The price of fish has dropped.
WILLY: Not again!
MERCHANT: Yes, again.
                 So, pull harder on the lines, boys,
                 Or your wages I will chop.
                 Now, don't ask to see your money.
WILLY: Money! Jesus, sure, I never seen money in me life, sure.
MERCHANT: You have no use for it.
                 I'll give you flour,
                 Lassie, baccie, and that's an end to it.
                 Times, they say, have changed,
                 But I'm laughing up my sleeve.
                 This fisherman can still be hanged.
                 For him I'll never grieve.
WILLY: Where do I sign? Where do I sign?
     (*Willy is about to go off arm-in-arm with Merchant when he is
                 pulled back by King Peck of Oilford.*)
KING PECK: (*To Willy.*) Boy, boys, boys,
                 Now, stop this talk of merchants
                 And all their dirty tricks.
                 There's gold beneath the seabed,
                 And we'll have it pretty quick.
MERCHANT: Bullshit!
KING PECK: I've spoken to the Arabs,
                 And I've spoken to the Yanks.
                 They're goin' to buy our oil, me boys,

And store it in big tanks.
And when the oil comes gushin',
You can lie down on your backs,
There'll be allowances to buy it
Tacked on to your welfare cheques.
Now, you say you've never seen an oil rig?

WILLY: No.

KING PECK: And there's no work for you?

WILLY: No.

KING PECK: Well, listen to me, laddie,
and I'll tell ya what we'll do,
We're gonna build an institute,
And give you all a course,
There'll be jobs cleaning oil spills
That will cover all our shores.

JOEY: Don't listen to him, Willy.

KING PECK: So, don't burn your boats now, laddies,
You'll need 'em soon enough,
You can load 'em to the gunwales,
With the oily slimy stuff.
Now, you'll get three bucks an hour,
We can't afford no more.
And it's like we often told you,
It's an honour to be poor.

Willy: This is true.

KING PECK: And when the oil's all gone,
Don't worry, we'll be rich,
And we'll start a brand new industry
To manufacture fish.

WILLY: Sounds reasonable. (*He begins to scream.*) I'm with you, Peck! I'm with you, Peck!
(*Willy jumps up into Peck's arms and throws his arms around Peck's neck. Peck starts to carry him off, but then in great confusion, Joey and Merchant get a hold of Willy and a tug-of-war ensues in which Willy is pulled by his arms and legs back and forth across the stage. Willy cries out, "Help me, Peck! Help me! I'm with you, Peck! Help me!" Willy is finally knocked down unconscious on the floor. Stick Man disentangles the combatants.*)

STICK MAN: Hold off, hold off, hold off, I say. (*He goes over to inspect the prostrate form of Willy. He looks at the audience.*) Why, this man is dead. Is there a doctor in the house? This man is dead. Is there a doctor in the house? Doctor! Doctor! Doctor!

DOCTOR: (*Replying from the audience.*) Of course, there's a doctor in the house. Someday, I hope to see a doctor in every house. We own half the houses around here, anyway.

JOEY: Someday I hope there'll be not one, not two, but three doctors in every house.

DOCTOR: (*Coming over and mistaking Stick Man for patient.*)
Was it a long illness? (*He touches various parts of Stick Man's body.*) Where does it hurt? Where does it hurt? In the head?
(*Doctor suddenly starts to go insane. Stick Man grabs him.*)
STICK MAN: Come back to your senses, Doctor. Come back to
your senses!
DOCTOR: Dum de dee. Why, my good man...
(*Doctor comes to his senses, calms down and begins to examine
an audience member.*)
His cranium-full to bursting, in fact it's full of shit!
(*Doctor goes insane again. Stick Man brings him back to his
senses.*)
STICK MAN: Doctor, come to your senses, boy. You'll have us all in
the mental, boy. Doctor, Doctor, calm yourself down, man.
DOCTOR: Sorry.
(*He goes back to Stick Man. Hobby Horse walks over to inspect
him too, he gives a few claps of his wooden jaws and looks at
Stick Man.*)
DOCTOR: (*Addressing Willy.*) Why, my good fellow, I've just the
place for you. You and your family can move in immediately. A
little hovel down on Gower Street. Picture it, if you will? Up-
down window ventilation, cold and cold running water, wall to
wall running rats. I can give you anything. (*He begins to sing to
the tune of "The Kelligrews Soiree."*) I own hotels, motels, broth-
els, oil wells, drug stores, liquor stores...
STICK MAN: (*Calming Doctor down from his role as real estate
agent.*) We need you in your role as a doctor, Doctor.
DOCTOR: Why didn't you say so? (*Doctor slips into the tune of
"The Kelligrews Soiree," as he goes over the edge once again.*) I
have Librium, Valium, benzedrine, aspirin, morphine, codeine
and even vitamin C...
STICK MAN: Jesus, Doctor, you seem to be suffering from a vita-
min deficiency of some sort.
MERCHANT: We need a cure, Doctor, a cure.
DOCTOR: I can cure anything. (*Once again "The Kelligrews Soi-
ree" as Doctor freaks out once more.*) I've cured leprosy, pleurisy,
juvenile delinquency, boils, blood clots, and water on the knee...
STICK MAN: (*Calming him again.*) Doctor, we need you here as a
healer of this here mortal man.
DOCTOR: (*Pointing at Willy.*) You mean healer of the sick?
STICK MAN: Yes.
DOCTOR: Hippocratic Oath?
STICK MAN: Yes.
DOCTOR: Et cetera? Et cetera?
STICK MAN: Yes.
DOCTOR: (*Flustered.*) It's a busy time. I'm so busy with my prop-
erties. (*He digs into his doctor's bag and takes out a stethoscope.
Then he takes out a human skull. He holds it up.*) Alas, poor

Yorick. I knew him well. Yorick Delaney. Not one of my more successful operations. And the bastard owed me two months rent. Pay me! Pay me! Pay me! (*Doctor freaks out at the memory of his failed operation and starts screaming, "Yorick! Yorick! Yorick!" and freaking out. The other mummers try to calm him down as Doctor carries on with his examination of Willy and makes his final pronouncement.*) This man is suffering from a case of terminal death.

> How this man died is plain to see,
> He died of simple poverty.
> Add to that, such misery,
> And, bingo! Dead for all to see.
> Now, Merchant, don't look so sad,
> You robbed him blind, you drove him mad.
> > (*At the word "mad" he goes mad once again. He addresses Peck.*)
> And you, young rogue, dry up your tears,
> > (*He freaks out for one tiny second.*)
> For soon enough they'll turn to sneers.
> I tell you this man may be cured,
> By something you simply all ignored.
> > (*He takes out three gold coins.*)
> A pure soul shines with light so bright,
> Naught but gold, may serve it right.
> No base coins these, but purest gold,
> Mined by Solomon long ago.
> Down through countless ages, they have shone,
> Countless good and harm they have done.
> Stand back, make room,
> For magic medicine soon shall loom.
> Choke in fire! Choke in fume.
> Abbra Cadabra! Abbra Cadab!
> Call this man a Burgess cab!
> > (*He freaks.*)

ALL: (*Shouting.*) Doctor, Doctor, Doctor!!
DOCTOR: Gold with wisdom, shall fly far,
Through bursting light, the newest star.
Rise, Willy son of Nilly, and act your deed.
> (*Willy does not rise.*)
MERCHANT: Quack! Quack! Quack!
DOCTOR: Arise, Willy, son of Nilly, and act your deed. Ah, well, some of those old spells, don't work on new people. I'll have to go to modern science. Ayatollah Pepsi Cola! Come alive, you're in the Pepsi generation. Sparkle, bubble, fizz! Sparkle, bubble, fizz!
> (*Now all the mummers become angry at the fact that Willy, played by Jack, seems to be dead drunk and not responding to the play.*)
DICKIE DINN: Every year, it's the same story.

JACK, JR.: Well, you're the one who gave him the London Dock. (*Strong dark rum.*)

DICKIE DINN: Sure, what can you do? Even when you hide it in people's flush boxes, he finds it.

JACK, JR.: Well, you were supposed to be taking care of him. The same Jesus thing happens every year.

(*Rose enters.*)

ROSE: Well, it wouldn't be Christmas if Jack wasn't drunk.

JACK, JR.: C'mon now, Dad boy, get up on the couch. C'mon now, c'mon, Dad, c'mon now, Dad, c'mon now, Dad, c'mon, Dad. (*He starts shaking Jack. Jack doesn't move. Jack, Jr. starts to scream.*) Dad! Dad! Jesus, boys, I think he's dead.

(*Rose comes over to take a look.*)

ROSE: Go on, boy, he's drunk. Get up, Jack! (*Her tone of voice becomes vicious.*) Get up, and stop makin' a fool of yourself. Get up, get up! Jack, Jack! (*Her tone changes as she realizes he's dead.*) My God, he's dead. My God, you've killed Jack.

Scene 2

(*The lighting changes suddenly to back light. An air of tragedy bathes the stage. The mummers gather around Jack, pick up his body and ceremoniously remove his mummering costume as if preparing and washing a corpse. The coffin is brought in slowly. Jack is placed in the coffin and the lights come up again to reveal a Christmas wake scene in Jack's living room. The whole family is gathered around and there is much crying. Great sadness. Music in the background is a combination of "Dies Ires" and "Hark the Herald Angels Sing." The family stand about looking at the coffin. Tom is asked to say a few words about Jack. He does. He improvises tall tales, such as, for example, about the time that he and Jack were out fishing, and Jack stood up to climb up the wharf and put his foot through the boat, and actually dragged the boat up the wharf with him, he was that strong. Etc. More sad talk from Tom. Jack, Jr. asks Tom to sing Jack's favourite song. Tom breaks into the traditional song, "The Champion of Coat Hill."*)

TOM: (*Sings.*)
>In smiling June, when roses bloom,
>The warbler cheers the grove;
>'Twas by a babbling brook,
>My way I took, quite carelessly to roam.
>And I met with White, my heart's delight,
>On my returning home.
>Oh, he smiled and said,
>"My blue-eyed maid, why is it you're alone?
>The day, being fine, if you're inclined,
>Along with me to roam.

We'll sit awhile, we will walk and talk,
Convenient to Coat Hill."
"I'm sorry, but, I can't accept your invitation now,
For my ma, she will be harshed at me,
No pastime she'll allow."
"Your ma won't know where we shall go,
So let us try our skill,
We will sit awhile,
We will walk and talk convenient to Coat Hill."
I gave consent and 'twas off we went
On our discourse along.
'Twas many the time he said to me,
"No one I love, but thee."
But now he's gone and wed to one
By the name of Belle Madelle,
And left his poor Kate in that sad state,
heart-broken on Coat Hill.
Oh, ye ladies all, both great and small,
A warning take by me
Don't ever depend on any young man
uuntil the knot is tied;
For if you do, you will surely rue,
Like me you'll cry your fill,
For I am ruined right by Willy White,
The Champion of Coat Hill...

(Tom breaks down and starts to cry. So does Rose, Mona, Vi,
Bas, Nelson and the other characters. It is a very sad
moment. Jack, Jr. turns to Tom.)

JACK, JR.: This was Dad's favourite time of year, Tom. He used to come right alive.

VI: That's the way of it though, I suppose.
(There is a chorus of "Yep, yep, yep. That's right. Yeah. Etc."
"Yep" is spoken on an in-breath, a common practice among
mummers in an attempt to disguise their voices.)

NELSON: Well, there's people dyin' now, that never died before.
(A friend of the family rushes in through the door.)

FRIEND: Merry Christmas, everyone, Merry Christmas. Look, I've got some presents here for ya, but I haven't got time to stay. See ya all tomorrow now. Merry Christmas, everyone. Merry Christmas, Rose. *(To Jack in coffin.)* Merry Christmas, Jack.
(He rushes out through the door. There is a sad pause. Rose
breaks down again and crying resumes.)

JACK, JR.: *(Suddenly asks.)* How are we gonna bury him, Mom?

ROSE: I don't know. We can't let him rot, I suppose.

JACK, JR.: Well, we can't let Welfare bury him. You know how he felt about the dole. We'll have to get the loan.

ROSE: No, we're not gettin' the loan.

JACK, JR.: Well, what are we gonna do, we have to get the loan.

ROSE: No, not the loan. It'd kill your father.

JACK, JR.:   Not much he can say about it now, is there?
> *(Rose nods to agree that they have to get a loan.)*

JACK, JR.:   Are you sure, Mom?

ROSE: Yes, go on, go ahead. Call HFC for the loan.
> *(Jack, Jr. goes over, picks up the telephone to call HFC. There is*
> *a knock at the door. It is Reverend Freep, a sanctimonious,*
> *Protestant minister. Rose bursts into tears when she sees him.)*

ROSE: Reverend Freep!
> *(Reverend Freep shakes various hands. He goes to Jack, Jr.*
> *who refuses to shake hands.)*

REV. FREEP: I'd like to say how very sorry I am to hear about Jack...Jack...ah...joining the ranks of the horizontal. Though Jack and I were of different religious stripes, I think I can truly say, Jack has been a friend. (*Jack, Jr. sneers at these words and leaves.*) I've written a short poem which, with your permission, I would like to read. (*He recites.*)

> The hungry bum upon the street would say,
> As his frame grew thinner and thinner,
> Dear Lord, send down Your love,
> In the form of a complete chicken dinner,
> But what of us, who've lost our dear one?
> Will we turn our heads from God's huge eye
> Scream and bawl and kick the house down?
> Nay, nay, we'll humbly pray for a piece of comfort pie.

NELSON: (*Knowingly.*) I understand, Father Dinn is coming here.

REV. FREEP: (*Shocked.*) What, Father Dinn, coming here? I must be on my way, Rose. Goodbye.

REV. FREEP: (*Shaking hands all around.*) Father Dinn and I served on an ecumenical advisory council together and we didn't exactly see eye to eye.
> *(He rushes out. Instantly there is a knock on the door. It is*
> *Father Dinn who is played by the actor who just played*
> *Reverend Freep. Dinn has a loud, booming voice.)*

FATHER DINN: Rose!
> *(He goes to various members of the family offering condolences.)*

FATHER DINN: I think we should kneel down and say the rosary. We'll say the shortened Vatican II Council version of the rosary. In the name of the Father and of the Son and of the Holy Spirit, amen. The five sorrowful mysteries all at once. Hail Mary, humpin' humpin' humpin' humpin' Jesus.

FAMILY: Amen.

FATHER DINN: Hail Mary, humpin' humpin' humpin' humpin' Jesus.

FAMILY: Amen.

FATHER DINN: Hail Mary, humpin' humpin' humpin' humpin' Jesus.

FAMILY: Amen.

FATHER DINN: Hail Mary, humpin' humpin' humpin' humpin' Jesus.

FAMILY: Amen.

FATHER DINN: In the name of the Father and the Son and the Holy Spirit, amen.

(Father Dinn offers condolences once again and leaves. He and Jack, Jr. meet in the doorway.)

JACK, JR.: *(To Rose.)* Dad'd turn over in his grave, if he knew that bunch was hangin' around here.

ROSE: Now, Jack, they mean well.

(Jack turns into Uncle Val who rises up in the coffin wearing his hat.)

UNCLE VAL: Well, Jack is dead. The family mourns. HFC is on the way. Denouement is just around the corner. Can our story possibly have a happy ending? Things look pretty grim, but then again, so they did for Tiny Tim. But that's another Christmas story, and I don't want to get involved in that. Yes, it seems, like now our only chance would be divine intervention, or on the other hand, we could use a very, very, bold stroke on the part of the playwright. Let's wait and see.

(Uncle Val lies back in the coffin. A knock comes at the door and all the actors begin to make a weird humming sound. A strange looking character wearing a cape and a top hat enters. Humming stops.)

ROSE: *(Speaking in a stagy manner.)* You must be Mr. Wilmot, from the HFC.

(Actors start humming again. They stop.)

MR. WILMOT: Yes, I am, madam. I have here in my pocket the benevolence for the bereaved. Would you care to sign now?

(Actors start humming again. They stop.)

ROSE: Yes.

(Humming begins again, as Rose goes over, picks up a pen and signs the loan application. The humming grows weirder and weirder and builds to a wild crescendo as she signs. Lights flash in strobe light effect. The music resumes while Mr. Wilmot undergoes a strange transformation. He announces to all.)

MR. WILMOT: I am Gilmor Albummus of Atlantis, late of Avalon. Four thousand years I have nurtured the kings of Atlantis deep in my bosom. Waiting, waiting for the new king to appear. For it was prophesied in the great book of Plunge, the chapter of Glad, book one, verse one, "When the two-hundred-thousandth Newfoundlander was dispossessed by Household Finance, life would pass from him into me, until my tale was revealed, and then the life would pass from me back to him *(He approaches the coffin to begin the exchange with Jack.)* and he would be crowned King of Newfoundland and Labrador—a new Atlantis; and it would be a happy province, and a joyous occasion, glorious for all to see." *(As he begins to die he sings the following. He ends very slowly.)*

Never borrow money, needlessly, but when you must, borrow from the oldest company, from folks you trust. Borrow confidently—from—H—F—C.

Photograph by Janet Hannaford

(As Gilmor Albummus slowly dies and sinks into the coffin, Jack slowly begins to rise out of it. They help each other change places. There is beautiful organ accompaniment, "Crown of Roses," as Jack rises from the coffin, walks over to Rose and takes her hand. They walk together down centre stage and kneel down. The first female pope, Pope Jacqueline Paulette the First walks up the centre isle of the theatre, flanked by monks bearing candles. Jack is crowned King of Newfoundland and Labrador and Rose is crowned Queen. Jack rises up from his place as the music fades. He assumes his Uncle Val role once more.)

UNCLE VAL: So, later that year the old King, King Bolognia, he retired and Jack and the Princess were crowned King and Queen of Newfoundland and Labrador by the first female pope, Pope Jacqueline Paulette the first. And when the ceremony was over, they all sat down to a big meal at a tin table. But the tin table bended, so our story's ended. If the table had been stronger, our story would have been longer; and if they don't have good luck, then may all of ye.

    (The company rise to sing "God Rest Ye Merry Gentlemen.")
God rest ye merry, gentlemen, let nothing you dismay,
Remember Christ our saviour was born upon this day,
To save our souls from Satan's fold which long had gone astray.
(Chorus.)   And 'tis tidings of comfort and joy, comfort and joy,
           And 'tis tidings of comfort and joy.

We do not come to your house to beg or to borrow,
But we do come to your house to sing away all sorrow,
The merry time of Christmas is drawing very near.
(Chorus.)
We do not come to your house to beg for bread and cheese,
But we do come to your house so give us what you please,
The merry time of Christmas is drawing very near.
(Chorus.)
God bless the master of this house, the mistress also,
And all the little children that round the table go,
And all their kith and kindred that travel far and near,
And we wish you a merry Christmas, merry Christmas,
And we wish you a happy new year.

THE END.

Resource Centre for the Arts
(RCA) Theatre Company

Terras de Bacalhau
(Land of Cod)

1980

Collectively Written By
**Kay Anonsen
Rick Boland
José E. Silva
John Koop
Jim Payne
Janis Spence
Greg Thomey
Mary Walsh**

Music created and/or arranged by
Jim Payne

TERRAS DE BACALHAU

Terras de Bacalhau was first produced by Resource Centre for the Arts (RCA) Theatre Company at the LSPU Hall during the Portuguese Festival, 19-31 August and 4-7 September 1980. In 1981 the play toured Ontario; it played in Toronto (18-24 April), Thunder Bay (28 April) and Toronto again (18-24 May, held over 2-7 June). On returning to Newfoundland, it played at the St. John's Arts and Culture Centre (10-11 June 1981). In 1982, RCA Theatre Company toured *Terras de Bacalhau* to Vancouver (20 April to 1 May), Edmonton (7-9 May), Saskatoon (10-15 May), Toronto (17 May to 6 June), and Ottawa (7 June). On returning home it played at the Hall (10 to 13 June 1982). The most recent staging of the play was by RCA Theatre Company at the Hall (3-15 June 1986) to celebrate the tenth anniversary of the LSPU Hall as a theatre. The text presented here is the play as it was originally performed in 1980 which was also the touring version.

Members of the cast who wrote, directed and acted in *Terras de Bacalhau* are the following:

Kay Anonsen	Ros, Kay, Coccyx.
Rick Boland	Joaquim, Cecil, Mr. Ford, Rickie Ricketts, Albertino.
José E. Silva	João.
John Koop	Captain, Pedro, Mike, Uncle Vanya.
Jim Payne	Manuel, Ambrose, Frank, pilot; music.
Janis Spence	Rosa, Doreen, Agnes, Rita, Marge.
Greg Thomey	Toninio, Rickey Dunn, Ronny, Carlos, Cyril, Lackey.
Mary Walsh	Director.

Additional credits:

The musical director was **Jim Payne**. In 1980, 1981, 1982 and 1986, the set was designed by **Michael Kearney**, lighting design and technical coordination **Boo Noseworthy** and producer **Ann Anderson**. Publicity photographs of the play (1980), are by **Jim Winter**. In 1986 costumes were by **Kerry Cornell**. In the 1986 production, **John Koop** did not participate and his lines were assigned to other characters. Assistance with Portuguese for this edition was given by **José E. Silva** and **Kathy Duarte**.

The production of *Terras de Bacalhau* was assisted by Canada Council Explorations, the Newfoundland and Labrador Arts Council, the Government of Newfoundland Cultural Affairs Division and the Canada Council. The play was sponsored by Mobil Oil.

CAST OF CHARACTERS
(In order of appearance.)

JOÃO	Young Portuguese fisherman on his first visit to Newfoundland, Kay's lover.
ROSA	João's mother in Portugal.
JOAQUIM	João's father, who fishes off Newfoundland, Doreen's lover.
TONINIO	João's younger brother in Portugal.
ROS	Rosalynn Dunn, Newfoundland woman, friend of Doreen.
DOREEN	Newfoundland woman, friend of Ros.
RICKEY	Rickey Dunn, Ros's son.
MR. FORD	Social worker.
CAPTAIN	Captain of the *Manuelá*.
CARLOS	Radio operator on the *Manuelá*.
PILOT	St. John's harbour pilot.
COCCYX	Friend of Doreen and Ros.
PEDRO	Portuguese fisherman.
MANUEL	Portuguese fisherman.
RITA	Employee at the Arcade Store.
KAY	Kay Halloran, young woman who falls in love with João.
AGNES	Agnes Halloran, Kay's mother.
CECIL	Cecil Halloran, Kay's father.
RONNY	Ronny Halloran, Kay's younger brother.
UNCLE VANYA	Kay's uncle.
AMBROSE	Ambrose Lewis, friend of Cecil Halloran.
ALBERTINO	Portuguese fisherman.
MARGE	Cocktail waitress at Mike's Bar.
RICKIE	Rickie Ricketts, piano player and singer at Mike's Bar.
CYRIL	Kay's former boyfriend.
FRANK	Patron at Mike's Bar.
MIKE	Bar owner, friend of Cyril.
LACKEY	Bar patron, a flunky friend of Doreen.

TERRAS DE BACALHAU

ACT 1
Scene 1

A mandolin plays two Portuguese waltzes in the dark, over which a taxi horn is heard. Music fades. Lights up. The play opens in a kitchen in Portugal, as Joaquim and his son João are leaving for the Newfoundland Grand Banks. Rosa is wearing a black wig and a black shapeless dress.

JOÃO: O taxi deve estar a chegar.

ROSA: Credo homem nem me fales nisso, que me aperta o coração.

JOAQUIM: Mulher, a vida é assim.

ROSA: Why don't you get a job inland?

JOAQUIM: The earnings are small here. The way of living is always going up. It is starving to death.

ROSA: There are many people here. They take care of themselves.

JOAQUIM: Yes, I know, but I don't think it is this time that I stay.

ROSA: No, I think not now or ever, and this time you take the boy.

JOAQUIM: He has to learn to make a man out of himself, and even though his makings will be small, it will be good for all of us. *(To João.)* Where were you earlier, João? I was worried about you.

JOÃO: I said good-bye to Maria. She was sad.

JOAQUIM: No time to think about that now. You have everything packed? Gillette, blades, soap. There is no store out there where you can buy those things; and you pack a tie. I want you to look good in St. John's. And Antonio, what you want me to bring you back this time?

TONINIO: Uma tenda.

JOAQUIM: Well, I'll see what we can do. It's between your brother and I what we can do. You be good, eh! Get good marks in school, then when you come out maybe you'll be an officer, eh.

ROSA: No, no, no, Joaquim, the sea will not have this boy.
(Taxi horn sounds.)

JOÃO: The taxi is here.

ROSA: You take care, you take care of the boy.

JOAQUIM: Be good. You, boy, take care of Momma, eh!
ROSA: You write. Okay.
TONINIO: Boa pesca.
(They leave and walk across stage to the ship.)
JOAQUIM: Ah, como está, Capitaõ.
CAPTAIN: Ah, Joaquim. Como estás.
JOAQUIM: Estou bem. Este é o meu filho, João.
CAPTAIN: You'll be bunking together in cabin thirteen.
MANUEL: *(Singing.)* "Only a Fisherman."

I'm only a fisherman, and I do whatever I can,
I don't like to take from my brothers and sisters,
Who are just as poor as I am.
When Mother Portugal was a great power,
We left our homeland to die by the hour,
In some foreign land, we'd take what we can,
And leave nothing for the people.
We incurred the wrath of Jah,
When we plundered Ethiopia,
Bullets flew against the wall,
We marched in and took it all,
But Jah said colonialism must fall.
I'm only a fisherman, and I do whatever I can,
I don't like to take from my brothers and sisters,
Who are just as poor as I am.
Yes, I'm only a fisherman I take my living from the sea,
We catch the fish, one man chop the head off,
Then it's out with the guts, split the backbone,
Salt 'em down in the hold.
In India, in Guinea and Cabo Verde,
We were masters there and we were feared,
Everywhere the war plan was tried,
But like Mozambique, the people's spirit never died,
'Cause they cried out,
"No, no, no, no, to your prisons.
No, no, no, no, to exploitation.
No more I'll be your slave,
No more go to early grave.
No, no, no to oppression."
We finally left Angola alone.
Now they are masters of their own home.
Much to the dictator's dismay,
The people's revolution had its day.
There's still bad blood in Brazil.
People there have had their fill.
Still many tears, still much pain,
People there are still in chains.
Workin', workin', workin' for the rich man.
Portugal was fascisto for years,

People shed their tears for freedom,
For a better way, they had their say,
Like Mozambique, like Angola, they cried out.
They said, "No, no, no, no, to your prisons."
They said, "No, no, no, no, to exploitation."
They said, "No more I'll be your black slave.
No more go to early grave."
They said, "No, no, no, to oppression."
    Yes, I'm only a fisherman, and I do whatever I can,
I don't like to take from my brothers and sisters,
Who are just as poor as I am.

Photograph by Jim Winter

Scene 2

(Rosalynn Dunn's kitchen in St. John's, Ros is mopping the floor frantically while she talks on the telephone. She is incredibly pregnant and wearing Woolco maternity clothes. Her hair is teased but not back-combed and she looks frazzled. Doreen sits comfortably at Ros's chrome set. She is dressed to the nines, ready for the club. She is painting her fingernails hot pink and smoking a cigarette.)

ROS: *(She speaks to her son who is offstage.)* Pedro Manuel, get out of the fridge and shut up! I'm on the phone. *(Speaking into* *telephone.*) Oh, they're comin' in tonight. I thought they weren't comin' in until next week. (*To Doreen.*) Oh, they're comin' in tonight to get their license. (*To telephone.*) All right. (*She hangs up and shouts at Pedro.*) Will you get out of that goddamn fridge!

DOREEN: Oh, they're comin' for their license, are they?

ROS: Isn't that what I just said?

RICKEY: Mom.

ROS: Look! Don't go callin' me Mom, I'm after changin' me name.

RICKEY: Mom-Mom-Mom-Mom-Mom-Mom-Mom.

ROS: You dirty little bastard. God, I was out all last night and now I'm goin' to have to go out again tonight.

DOREEN: What about your Spaniard?

ROS: Ah! Let Donna have him. I'm after takin' so many of her buddies, time I threw her a bone.

DOREEN: Not that he got much. I seen night worms crawl bigger than that.

ROS: How would you know?

DOREEN: I knows what I knows! God, girl, I don't want to go out tonight either. I feels like a bloody leopard. I got hickeys all over me body. Thank God they left this morning.

(Telephone rings.)

ROS: Hello! What? Yes, they're comin' in tonight. (*To Doreen.*) Christ, what do they think I am, a bloody answering service?

DOREEN: God, Ros, I got some head on me. Gotta a cuppa tea?

ROS: No, Got no tea. Wanna Coke?

DOREEN: Gotta Pepsi?

ROS: Oh? (*Looking in fridge.*) Yeah.

DOREEN: T'anks.

ROS: God, what am I gonna wear tonight when Manuel comes in?

DOREEN: Wear that white dress.

ROS: God, I can't wear that. I looks like a great white whale in that. Whore for the killing. Ha, ha, ha.

DOREEN: Yeah, you're after puttin' on some old weight, Ros.

ROS: I know, my dear, I wish they'd hurry up and haul this t'ing outta me.

RICKEY: (*Wheedling.*) Mom, gimme a quarter.

ROS: No!

RICKEY: Pedro Manuel gotta quarter.

ROS: Whatta ya think this is? An endless supply of quarters? Go on. Get outta my sight. Gimme, gimme, gimme...

DOREEN: Here, honey. I'll give you a quarter. Look, here. My God, are you after pissin' yourself again? Ros, he's after pissin' himself again.

ROS: My dear, that's the second pair I'm after puttin' on him today. (*She searches and mimes passing pants to Doreen.*) There's a clean pair of pants around somewhere. Here take these. (*To Rickey.*) That's the last pair. If you wets dem, you'll go out wit' nudding on.

DOREEN: Sure they're not clean.

ROS: They're not wet, are they? Good enough for him. He'll only be after pissin' in them in another couple of minutes. Listen, Doreen, lend me a dollar, will ya?

DOREEN: Yeah, here ya go.

ROS: Rickey, go up to the store and get me a large tin of meatballs and gravy.

DOREEN: My God, Ros, you're not givin' the youngsters meatballs and gravy, are ya? What's-her-name up the street opened up a tin and there was this one meatball bigger than all the udders. She put it on the plate and dere was a tail on to it. She sent it back to Canada Packers and they sent her a whole case, but she wouldn't have nuttin' to do with it; she t'rew dem all out.

RICKEY: Sure, Mom, I'd rather have mice den Kraft dinner anyway.

ROS: Look. Shut up, will ya? Go on up to the store. Go on! Well, I'm goin' to have to wear that white dress 'cause I got nudding else decent, and I wants to look right nice for when Manuel comes in too. I really missed him, you know. My God you spends nineteen or twenty days with 'em den dey're gone, right? You know, I think he's the only one I've ever had any real feeling for lately.

RICKEY: Sure, Mom, you said dat about your German.

ROS: Look, shut up, will ya, and go on. Get out, get out.

DOREEN: Ros, what are Germans like?

ROS: My dear, they'd teach the Portuguese a few t'ings.

RICKEY: (Under the table.) Like what, Mom, like what?

ROS: Where are ya, you dirty little pervert? Get out!

DOREEN: He can't even hold his water and he's there lookin' up me skirt. (To Ros.) Listen, why don't you wear that black suit? Black is really slimmin'.

ROS: My dear, it'd take more than a black suit to slim me down. That's not fit to wear anyway. Weren't you down to the Stardust the night I got into that racket with Phyllis.

DOREEN: (Speaking very flat.) No.

ROS: She t'rew a drink at me. D'ya know what I did? She'll never call me a slut again. I backed her into the bathroom, right? (She demonstrates on Doreen.) I grabbed her by the hair of the head, right, and rammed her down the toilet, right, hauled her up and said, "Are you ever goin' to call me a slut again? Friggin' right you won't." And I pushed her back down in the toilet again, left her down there for about fifteen minutes. I thought she was gone there for a minute. (Pause.) She's some hard case.

DOREEN: Imagine her doin' dat to you, and you after taking her in so many times when she was squattin' down to Cross's. My God. She's had a hard life dough.

ROS: Yeah, she's had a hard life, yeah. Imagine her bein' married to that Trinity Bay bastard and him t'reat'nin' to do a homicide-suicide on her. Imagine that bastard from Trinity

Bayt'reat'nin' to do that on ya. She had to call the cops and get him pounded.

DOREEN: Pounded?

ROS: Yeah, pounded.

DOREEN: Not pounded—impounded.

ROS: Yeah, I knew that.

DOREEN: Dat's when she started getting deep down into the Portuguese.

ROS: Sure, she went out with dem before dat.

DOREEN: Yeah, only one or two.

ROS: Proper t'ing. At least they don't go t'reat'nin' to do a homicide-suicide on ya every time ya looks at 'em sideways.

DOREEN: Treats ya like a queen. Dey're de best kind.

(Knock at the door.)

ROS: Who in the name of God is that?

RICKEY: Mom, man out on de steps, Mom.

ROS: Doreen, get that for me, will ya?

(Enter Mr. Ford.)

MR. FORD: How do you do? My name is Ford. I'm with the Department of Social Services and Rehabilitation.

DOREEN: Ros, the man from Welfare's here.

MR. FORD: *(To Doreen.)* We prefer Social Services. *(To Ros.)* Mrs. Dinn?

ROS: Dunn, and it's not Mrs.

MR. FORD: May I come in?

ROS: You're in, aren't ya? Listen here, did Phyllis call you? Now look, I got no men here; I got no boarders; I'm not babysittin' and someone else bet that window out, none of my crowd...so blah blah; woof woof!

MR. FORD: I beg your pardon?

ROS: Oh, nudding.

MR. FORD: I have a form here that states your mother Anastasia, who is sixty-seven, I believe...

DOREEN: Seventy-two.

ROS: Sixty-six.

DOREEN: Yeah, but she's that sick she looks seventy-two. *(To Mr. Ford.)* She should get more money for her.

MR. FORD: Well, yes. It says here that your mother is now domiciled at 27 Commonwealth Avenue. Is that correct?

ROS: That's a dirty lie, and listen, I wouldn't put my mother in a home. "M" is for the many things she did for me. "O" is for she's only gettin' older. "T" is for the tears...

MR. FORD: I'm not suggesting that you put your mother in a home. I'm merely asking has she taken up residence elsewhere?

ROS: *(Flat.)* No.

MR. FORD: May I speak with her then?

ROS: No. She's sick.

MR. FORD: Well, maybe you could tell me your mother's income at this time.

ROS: One-hundred-and-fifty-six dollars a month.

DOREEN: Yeah, that's her pension cheque. He wants to know how much you're getting off the Welfare for her.

ROS: Shut up out of it, will ya? I'm not gettin' anything off the Welfare for her.

DOREEN: Only trying to help ya, girl.

MR. FORD: Exactly how many dependants are in the house at this time?

ROS: Well, let's see, there's Pedro Manuel, there's Rickey, there's Charlene, Marlene, Arlene and the baby. Not really Arlene 'cause she's up in the girls' home, so, that don't count. Then there's the mystery guest I got under wraps in here. I gets more money for him in a couple of weeks. Don't forget to mark that down. Ya get that?

DOREEN: (*Watching over Mr. Ford's shoulder.*) Yeah, he's got that marked down.

MR. FORD: Ros, have you ever had, ah, birth control counselling?

ROS: Yeah, I was on that old pill once.

MR. FORD: And why did you stop using the oral contraceptive?

ROS: The kids got at 'em, right? You can't keep nudding around here, and then little Rickey started growin' these little breasts, right, so I had to throw 'em out.

DOREEN: Yeah, I had one of them loop things, y'know, the new kind, y'know, the copper T's? It got imbedded right in me uterus! You don't know pain 'til you've got a piece of copper drove up your uterus.

ROS: (*To Doreen.*) You shut your mouth. Nobody's asking you. He don't care what you got drove up your uterus.

MR. FORD: Rosalynn, don't you think that having all these children is making your life increasingly more difficult?

ROS: Yeah, it's terrible! But what can ya do, right? You got to take the good with the bad.

MR. FORD: Well, had you considered marrying the father of the child?

ROS: No, he's already married, b'y, and living in Portugal.

MR. FORD: You're having a baby for a married man?

ROS: Yeah, shockin' what? (*Speaking to herself.*) What am I gonna get dem youngsters for supper tonight?

RICKEY: (*Rooting in Mr. Ford's brief case.*) Mom, can I have dis piece of paper here?

ROS: Look, get out of Mr. Ford's brief case, will ya. For the love of God I just mopped that. Get up or I'm goin' to give you away, my child. What's wrong with ya? I'm givin' you away.

MR. FORD: Pass me that brief case, please. Thank you, and that's my calculator. That's an expensive calculator. Ah, Rosalynn, I have a pamphlet here on family planning. I wonder if you might be able to read it? I had it here somewhere.

RICKEY: Dis it?

MR. FORD: Yes, thank you.

RICKEY: Got any more of dem birth control pills? Dat's the ones I used to take. I loves the taste of dem.

MR. FORD: Rosalynn, if you get a chance could you read this?

ROS: Oh, no, I'm not gettin' me tubes tied. Time enough for the change of life later on.

MR. FORD: There are other methods of birth control, Rosalynn. There's just one other thing I wanted to talk to you about.

ROS: Yeah, go on, don't let me interrupt you. (*She picks up her mop and mops the area under his feet.*) I just got this little bit left to do, luh.

MR. FORD: Well, we're instituting a new program of home-care. What we do is we get a community worker to come in once a week, and ah, help you take care of your mother. I know it must be very difficult for you and that would give you a chance to, say, go out, and ah, and ah, go...shopping?

ROS: Yeah, right. And is she gonna look after the youngsters too? And is she gonna know how to stick the tube down Mom's throat to get the phlegm out? And she's gonna have to change him every half hour, he's got no muscles down dere. And how in the hell am I supposed to go waltzin' up and down Water Street with diabetes on me water?

MR. FORD: I don't know. I really don't know. This is my first day in the field. And I realize that Social Services is merely a band-aid for the ills of society, but I didn't realize the wound was so open and festering.

DOREEN: You'd go through some lot of old band-aids around here.

ROS: Rickey, would you leave Mr. Ford's face alone? For the love of God, Rickey!

(Rickey is crawling all over Ford trying to pull his nose back over his head and stick cigarettes in his ears. Ford tries to remove him. Rickey screeches. Ros and Doreen are talking at once in an improvised "wall of sound" as Ford backs off. They say things such as, "I'll see you in court." "People think you can come waltzin' in..." "My son, I could have you up in court." "Who do you think you are?")

ROS: My God, you're not allowed to do dat. You can't go hittin' my youngsters.

MR. FORD: I didn't hit him. Honestly, I love children.

DOREEN: My son, you could go to jail for dat. You can't go beatin' up her youngsters.

MR. FORD: I didn't hit him. I love children. I have two children of my own. I just thought I'd lose my nose.

(Ford leaves, having backed himself offstage. Rickey is bawling.)

ROS: Ah, shut up, look, or I'll give you something to cry about. (*He stops.*) Now, get out, go on! (*He leaves.*) Well, I'll have to wear dat white dress after all 'cause I got nudding else decent.

DOREEN: I sure hope that *Navaganté* and the *Manuelá* don't come in at the same time, we're gonna be screwed.

ROS: Yes, my dear, we'll be screwed silly!

Scene 3

(At sea aboard a Portuguese fishing boat during a storm. Joaquim is at the wheel. They are swaying as if in a boat being tossed by a storm. They speak English with fake Portuguese accents.)

CAPTAIN: Quite a swell we got going here, Joaquim.

JOAQUIM: Aye, sir.

CAPTAIN: A little bit over to port now, please. We must be getting near the centre of the storm, the wind is shifting about every two minutes now.

JOAQUIM: If this weather continues we won't have enough time on the Banks to fill our quotas, as small as they are.

CAPTAIN: A few buckets would fill that quota.

JOAQUIM: I think that soon it won't be worth our while to go to the Banks at all.

CAPTAIN: I think that in a few years you may be right.

JOAQUIM: The company is sending more ships to Africa each year.

CAPTAIN: Bring her a little over to port, the wind seems to be shifting again.

(Enter João carrying coffee.)

JOÃO: Sir, your coffee.

CAPTAIN: Ah, João, how are you enjoying your first North Atlantic storm?

JOÃO: *(Trying to be brave.)* It's very nice.

CARLOS: *(Looking up from his radio.)* The *Santo Spirito* is taking on water, sir. They asked that we would follow them into St. John's.

CAPTAIN: Ah, what's their location?

CARLOS: About three-and-a-half kilometres east-south-east, sir.

CAPTAIN: Joaquim, take her around. Hard to port. We'll have to circle round and come up behind them.

JOAQUIM: Aye, sir.

JOÃO: I bet Toninio would be frightened if he were here, wouldn't he, Dad? But there's nothing to be frightened of, is there?

JOAQUIM: Not as long as we stay on top of water.

CAPTAIN: Carlos, radio the *Spirito* we'll be swinging around behind them.

CARLOS: Aye, sir.

JOAQUIM: Sir, ah, the wheel is sticking. I think we might be losing the hydraulics, sir.

CAPTAIN: Losing hydraulics?

JOAQUIM: Aye.

CAPTAIN: (*Talking to the engine room.*) Chief, switch over to the auxiliary hydraulics. We've got trouble.

JOAQUIM: She won't budge.

CAPTAIN: She won't budge at all? Okay, back to the manual wheel, and get me on the walkie-talkie when you get there.

JOAQUIM: Aye, aye. (*He exits to the manual wheel outside the bridge.*)

CAPTAIN: (*Talking to the engine room.*) Chief, back down to four knots. How long do you think before we get that leak repaired? (*Pause.*) All right, keep me posted.

CARLOS: Radio negative...

JOAQUIM: (*His voice coming from the captain's walkie-talkie.*) Reached manual wheel, sir.

CAPTAIN: (*Into his walkie-talkie.*) Excellent, now hard back over to starboard and see if you can hold her steady into the storm.

JOAQUIM: (*Through walkie-talkie.*) Aye, aye.

JOÃO: How far to land, sir?

CAPTAIN: It's over two hundred miles yet, João.

JOÃO: There aren't any rocks around here, are there?

CAPTAIN: No, No, the nearest rocks are seventy fathoms down. But we're not going to hit those. (*Listening to the walkie-talkie.*) Yes...excellent! Take the wheel, João.

JOÃO: Me?

CAPTAIN: Yes, you! Carlos, we've got control on the bridge now.

CARLOS: Aye, aye.

CAPTAIN: Okay, over to port now.

JOÃO: Port?

CAPTAIN: Into the red on the indicators. There, hold it there. (*To engine room.*) Chief, back up to eight knots.
    (*Joaquim re-enters and approaches João who is beginning to feel seasick.*)

JOAQUIM: Ah, you got to take the wheel, ah. You did well.

JOÃO: I think I'm going to be sick.

JOAQUIM: No, no, don't be sick here now. Wait 'til you go below, eh? (*To Captain.*) Ah, sir, do I have permission to take him below?

CAPTAIN: Oh, all right then. Carlos, take the wheel.
    (*Carlos takes the wheel from João.*)

JOAQUIM: Ah, come on now, João.

JOÃO: Where are we going?

JOAQUIM: We go outside.

JOÃO: I don't want to go outside, there's water out there!

JOAQUIM: The fresh air will do you good. Come on, it will be good for you. The air is good, really.

JOÃO: (*He resists.*) I can't move.

JOAQUIM: Come on. Eh, you know I was in a storm so bad once, we didn't have to fish. The bow of the boat would go down, right, when she came up she'd be full of fish.

JOÃO: Dad, stop it. I'm going to be sick.

JOAQUIM: All you'd have to do is go get 'em.

JOÃO: I want to go home, can we go home?

JOAQUIM: I thought you wanted to see St. John's.

JOÃO: I want to go home, or die.

JOAQUIM: No, you're not going to die.

JOÃO: I want to die.

JOAQUIM: You can't die. If you die your momma will kill you.

JOÃO: Dad, that's not funny.

JOÃO: Don't let them bury me at sea if I die, Dad. Take me home.

JOAQUIM: Yes, yes, we'll bring you home.

JOÃO: Momma is going to cry a lot at my funeral, isn't she?

JOAQUIM: Yes, she's going to cry a lot. (*Gives him a couple of pills.*) Here, you take these.

JOÃO: (*Moaning.*) What are they?

JOAQUIM: For your stomach. Sleep now, before you know it we'll be in St. John's and everything will be all right.

MANUEL: (*Singing.*) "Go to Sea No More"
>
> We shipped aboard of a fishin' barque
> Bound for North Atlantic seas,
> Where cold winds blow through ice and snow
> And Jamaican rum would freeze,
> And worse to tell we'd a hard weather spell
> And wished we was back on shore,
> Oh, a man must be blind to make up his mind
> To go to sea once more.
> *Chorus:*   Once more, once more, go to sea once more,
>   A man must be blind to make up his mind
>   To go to sea once more.
> Some days, boys, we got lots of fish,
> More days, boys, we got none.
> With haulin' nets and settin' trawls
> From four o' clock in the morn,
> And then you see the night come on,
> And your back is gettin' sore,
> 'Tis then you wish that you were dead
> And could go to sea no more.
> *Chorus:*   No more, me boys, no more, go to sea no more,
>   'Tis then you wish that you were dead
>   And could go to sea no more.
> So come all you hard-living sailor men
> And listen to me song,
> When you come off of that long sea trip,
> I'll have you not go wrong.
> Take my advice drink no strong drink,
> Don't go sleeping with no whore,
> Get married instead, spend all night in bed,
> And go to sea no more.

Chorus: No more, no more, go to sea no more,
Get married instead, spend all night in bed,
And go to sea no more.

Scene 4

(Below deck on the Manuelá. *Two bunks flip down from the wall; there is a porthole and a ladder leading up to the deck. The boat is entering St. John's harbour.)*

JOÃO: Hey, Dad, is this St. John's? Can we go up on deck?

JOAQUIM: *(Lying down and trying to sleep.)* Não, I'm going to go to sleep. I'm tired.

JOÃO: Yeah, I'm tired too. *(He's too excited to be tired and is trying unsuccessfully to be nonchalant.)* Hey look, there's a little hut on top of the mountain up there, what is it?

JOAQUIM: That's Cabot Tower.

JOÃO: Oh yeah, right. Hey look, there's cars and buses just like Portugal.

JOAQUIM: Yeah, and girls and stores...

JOÃO: We'll need some sleep for tonight, hey Dad?

JOAQUIM: Yeah, goodnight.

(João is keen and pacing.)

JOAQUIM: Why don't you go up and help the pilot aboard?

JOÃO: What happens if he speaks to me in English?

JOAQUIM: Oh, don't worry, just give him a hand.

(João climbs the ladder to greet the pilot.)

JOÃO: Hello! How are you? I am fine! Nice country!

PILOT: Well, all right I s'pose. Yeah, I'd rather be in Newfoundland, ya know. *(Pilot switches to Portuguese.)* Leva-me ao teu chefe.

(Enter Captain.)

PILOT: *(To Captain.)* Como está, capitaõ.

CAPTAIN: *(To Pilot.)* Take her round to pier thirty-five will you. *(He repeats in Portuguese to Carlos.)* Carlos, doca número trinta e cinco. Oh, I almost forgot, this is for you. *(Gives a bottle of brandy to Pilot and addresses him.)* Let's go and have a drink.

(Doreen and Coccyx are on the pier waving as the ship is docking. They improvise excited conversation.)

COCCYX: Look, dere dey are!

DOREEN: *(Waving.)* They're over here!

COCCYX: No, dat's not dem.

DOREEN: Yes, it is! *(Calling.)* Joaquim! Joaquim! *(She sees João.)* Joaquim, Who's he?

JOAQUIM: Meu filho.

COCCYX: Oh, it's his filho—his son.

DOREEN: You look just like your daddy. *(He throws her the rope from the ship.)* Oh. *(She misses the rope.)* Come on, do it again. Okay, what do I do with it now?

JOAQUIM: Pull it in, pull it in.

DOREEN: Okay, now what?

JOAQUIM: Around the grump.

DOREEN: Around me rump? I know it's big, b'y, but it's not that big.

JOAQUIM: (*Laughing.*) No, no, not your rump, the grump.

DOREEN: Oh, the grump, okay, okay.

> (*Everyone is happy and excited.*)

DOREEN: Come on down, we've been waitin' for you.

JOAQUIM: One minute.

> (*Manuel accompanies the singing on an acoustic guitar. Coccyx plays a pretend guitar. As they sing the song, "Blood is Thicker than Water," the gangplank is quietly lowered and ship's lights are silently strung in semi-darkness.*)

Momma said Daddy was a sailor,
From somewhere across the deep blue sea.
I always longed to see my Daddy,
I wonder if Daddy longed for me.
Chorus: "Blood is thicker than water,"
          That's what my momma said to me,
          And I know that it's true after all I been through,
          'Cause Momma never lied to me.
At fifteen I was hitting all the nightspots,
Looking for a daddy in each man,
And then one night alone down at the Stardust,
A young boy gently offered me his hand.
"Pareces uma flora de Portugal,"
His big brown eyes begged me to understand,
And when he asked to sit down at my table,
I knew I'd met a different kind of man.
We strolled down the steps to the Concorde,
And danced 'til 'bout a quarter after three,
He said I'm leavin' in the morning,
So won't you please spend the night with me.
Chorus: "Blood is thicker than water,"
          That's what my momma said to me,
          And I know that it's true after all I been through,
          'Cause Momma never lied to me.
We took a taxi to the south side,
I could see the tears in his eyes,
And as that ship sailed slowly through the Narrows,
I knew our love would never die.
For fifty days and fifty lonely nights,
I dreamed about my dark-haired sailor boy,
Then one sunny day in mid-October,
The sea returned to me my only joy.
I couldn't wait to take him home to Momma,
Up over Barter's Hill we both ran,

Momma stood there speechless staring at him,
She wanted me to name that sailor man.
"Miguel Manuel Aveiro is his name, Mom."
A troubled look crept into her bright eyes,
"Daughter there is something I must tell you,
That you should know about your sailor boy."
Chorus: "Blood is thicker than water,"
       That's what my momma said to me,
       And I know that it's true after all I been through,
       'Cause Momma never lied to me.
"That boy is your own half-brother,"
Were the very words my momma spoke to me,
No wonder that you both love each other,
But married you and he can never be.
Momma said Daddy was a sailor,
From somewhere across the deep blue sea,
I never knew a thing about my daddy,
But now I know he was a Portugee.
Chorus: "Blood is thicker than water,"
       That's what my momma said to me,
       And I know that it's true after all I been through,
       'Cause Momma never lied to me.
       And I know that it's true after all I been through,
       'Cause Momma never lied to me.

(On gangplank. Carlos is trying to get Coccyx on board.)

DOREEN: Hey Carlos, ya must be some happy. It's your first time back in St. John's this year, eh? Carlos, you gustas me?

CARLOS: *(He is interested only in Coccyx.)* No.

DOREEN: My God, Carlos, yer after gettin' some saucy this year.

COCCYX: I don't wanna go! *(Carlos is pulling her up the gangplank.)*

DOREEN: Well, what's wrong with you now?

COCCYX: Remember the last time I was on a boat? All I said was this guy said that all the women in Newfoundland are like men, right. And all I said was you could find women like men anywhere, even in Portugal. And then bang, bang, right over the side of the boat and I broke me coccyx.

DOREEN: Are you still goin' on about that old tail bone?

COCCYX: Well, I couldn't sit down for six weeks. I can still hardly sit down, luh. *(She tries to sit down to show that she can't.)* Ohhh!

DOREEN: Get up off the gangplank. We're gonna have a ball.

COCCYX: That's what I'm afraid of.

(Carlos pulls her up.)

DOREEN: Joaquim!

(As Doreen and Joaquim embrace, Pedro grabs Coccyx's arm. She backs away and stands against the wall frightened.)

COCCYX: No, no, I'll just stand here.

(Doreen and Joaquim kiss. João stares at his father in disbelief.)

JOAQUIM: *(Awkward pause. He says to João.)* Hey, why don't you go below and get us some bread, cheese, wine, olives, eh? *(Pause. João exits.)* Ah, ah, some music. *(To Doreen.)* You remember?

DOREEN: I remember.

(Girls greet Pedro——reprise of the Portugeuse waltzes which opened the play. Joaquim and Doreen start a folk dance.)

COCCYX: Oh, look at them, they're dancing.

JOAQUIM: Eh, ah, you want to learn. *(He dances again.)*

COCCYX: I know how to do that. *(She dances stiffly, in a dorky manner.)*

JOAQUIM: No, not like that. I'll show you. *(He moves with full body movements.)*

CARLOS: This is my little Coccyx. Reminds me of my first voyage. When I had to kiss the codfish. *(Coccyx appears confused.)*

(Enter João carrying food.)

JOAQUIM: Hey, food——the food.

DOREEN: Oh, it's great. It looks wonderful. My God, it musta cost a fortune.

(Doreen and João look each other over.)

CARLOS: *(To Coccyx, putting olives in his eyes.)* Olive eyes.

JOAQUIM: *(To João.)* Why don't you get us some more olives, eh?

JOÃO: *(He is drunk.)* Olives there!

JOAQUIM: No, you get some more olives, eh.

(João exits. Pedro comes in wearing a crinoline and a wig. He carries a broom for a partner. The men perform a dance; the women talk.)

PEDRO: *(Singing. He is joined by men.)* "San João."

Foi no porto de St. John's,
Que conheci uma menina,
Que se chamava Andreia,
Que se tornava coisa fina.
Então eu disse Andreia querida,
Eu te quero amar a car,
Teis qui dizer a verdade,
Porque me andas a enganar.
Eu sou San João, eu sou santo,
É só com dois ou tres,
Eu sou San João, eu sou santo,
São os mesmos da outra vez,
São os mesmos da outra vez.

COCCYX: *(Speaking during the song.)* What are they saying?

DOREEN: Well, see, this girl in St. John's takes this sailor home to meet her mother, right, and her mother says, "You're the first Portuguese sailor who's come in this house——today." Get it? *(Coccyx shakes her head.)* And then she says, "I'm a St. John, I'm a saint. Take me." Get it? Take me, a sa-a-i-i-nt!

COCCYX: I don't get it.

(Doreen lifts her hands in exasperation and turns back to the music.)

JOAQUIM: *(Singing.)* Rosa!

(Men start another song, accompanying themselves with heavy sniffing sounds and stomping feet.)

MEN: Sniff, ah, ah. *(Stomp. Stomp.)*

DOREEN: No, no, no! No dirty songs, no way.

JOAQUIM: Hey, you used to like that one.

(Chatter. Re-enter João, he's quite drunk now and staggering.)

JOÃO: *(To Joaquim, laughing.)* Here's your olives, dogface.

JOAQUIM: I think he has been drinking. No more drinking for you. Hey, now you play the accordion.

COCCYX: Oh, the accordion. Oh, I loves the accordion. *(She mimes playing an accordion and sings in the tune of "Mussels in the Corner.")* Ni, ni, ni, ni, ni, ni, ni...

JOAQUIM: No, no, we don't play the accordion like that in Portugal. Doka. Mi tango.

(Accordion music----they dance.)

COCCYX: Oh God, I got ashes in me drink.

PEDRO: I take care of that. *(He tosses it overboard.)*

COCCYX: Oh my drink! Oh my drink!

(She reaches for it and puts her back out.)

DOREEN: No, no, it's all right, girl. They'll give you another one.

COCCYX: *(Bent over and holding her back.)* Oh me back, me back!

DOREEN: What's wrong with you now? You got a drink. What more do you want?

COCCYX: My back, I put me back out, God.

DOREEN: *(Demonstrating.)* Carlos, put your hand on her shoulders, put your foot in her back and snap her back up. *(He does it; he whips her back up and Coccyx cries out in agony.)*

(Music goes off key and João passes out.)

PEDRO: Hey! He's drunk, he's drunk.

JOAQUIM: Está bebido, he's drunk. Pedro, call the priest, baptisimo.

COCCYX: What are they doin' now?

DOREEN: It's his very first drunk. They're gonna baptize him as junior drunk and then he can start the steady climb to his daddy's level, to senior drunk.

JOAQUIM: Me innocente.

DOREEN: Innocent! My God, I'd be in a convent today if you hadn't got your hands on me.

(Champagne pops.)

PEDRO: In nome de pai...In nome de filho, in nome de espirito santo. Amen. I baptize you in the name of the vino, the porto, the brandy and the champagne. *(Douses João with the champagne. Everyone cheers.)*

JOÃO: Hey.

DOREEN: Don't worry, honey, I'll take you below. I'll change those wet pants for you.

JOAQUIM: Oh no, little brown eyes, I think that João can change his own pants, eh.

JOÃO: (*Very drunk.*) I want to dance.

JOAQUIM: No, no, you don't dance. You go below and you go to sleep.

JOÃO: No.

JOAQUIM: Yes, I think so. Now is the time for the old folks.

DOREEN: You speak for yourself. Goodnight, honey.

(João exits.)

JOAQUIM: Manuel, cante um fado.

DOREEN: Fado, my God, I love fado.

COCCYX: What's fado?

DOREEN: It's Portuguese love music and it's so sad.

COCCYX: Oh God, I hate sad songs.

(The couples get amorous and go off during the fado.)

PEDRO: (*Sings.*) "Quando os Outros te Batem."

> Se bem que não me vista e fostembora
> É tudo que en intersante me es que coeu
> Com muito eo meo grito e deste agora
> Quandos os outros te batem beijo tão.
> Se bem que as minhas modicoes fugiste
> Por ti hei-de dar tudo que ile moeu
> Com muito eo meo grito de agora deste
> Quandos os outros te batem beijo tão.
> Mas ha de viro dia que eu saudada
> Que lembra que em porti je se perdeu
> O fado quando triste qui averdada
> Quandos os outros te batem beijo tão.

Scene 5

(The fishermen are playing soccer on the dockside; the scene is improvised. General shouts that accompany a soccer game. The ball goes into the audience, etc. Coccyx and a girlfriend enter with Manuel's baby whom he has never seen. They chatter.)

COCCYX: Hi, Carlos.

CARLOS: Hello.

(Carlos walks over to the girls; he's carrying the ball. All the men shout, "Hey! The ball! The ball!" Coccyx points and tells Carlos that the baby belongs to Manuel and Manuel walks over to see his baby.)

CARLOS: My God, who's that? Who's that? Who's that!

MANUEL: My filho.

(Laughter. Men walk over and coo over the baby.)

CARLOS: (*Pretending to bounce the ball off the baby's head.*) Péle!

(The men return to soccer. Carlos and Manuel walk off with the

*girls. João and Joaquim continue to play on until Joaquim
says it's time to go. They exit.)*

Scene 6

*(Ladies department in the Arcade. Rita pushes in a large bin
on wheels; it is full of ladies lingerie.)*

VOICEOVER: In our Arcade shoe department, downstairs, brand-name sneakers. Out they go, while they last, at the incredibly low price of three for a dollar. That's right, shoppers, brand-name sneakers, out they go, while they last, at the low, low price of three for a dollar. *(Muzak plays.)*

RITA: My God, girl, I don't know why we stays open on Thursday night. We're never busy. All we got to do is tidy up the bins.

KAY: I know, girl. Just as ya tidy 'em up someone comes along and messes 'em up again, right, Rita?

RITA: *(Folding clothing busily as she speaks.)* I know, Kay, I'm bet out from tidying up these bins.

KAY: Oh well, it's nine o'clock. We'll be off in half an hour.

RITA: I know, Kay, but half an hour here is like two days any place else. And then, all I got to do is go home. I got nothing to do at home. I might as well be here tidying up the bins. Oh no, here come the gees.

KAY: What's the gees?

RITA: The Portuguese. There's a whole flock of 'em on their way in. *(Carlos, Pedro, Joaquim and João enter. Rita rushes to prevent the men from messing up the bins.)* No, no, no, no, no! I'll get it for you. What size do you want?

CARLOS: Size?

RITA: What size do you want? 34, 36, 38, 40? What size?

CARLOS: Wife size.

RITA: Is your wife a big woman or is she small like you?

CARLOS: Sim, sim, 93-56-93!

RITA: She must be deformed. You're gonna have to go into yardgoods to get something to fit her.

CARLOS: Não, não, não, 93-56-93, like you, smaller. Like you.

RITA: Like me! Smaller! I don't have to take that from you. *(Calling out to manager.)* Mr. Baird, Mr. Baird! And me after starving meself all day. Do you know what I had to eat all day? A piece of dry toast and a cup of weak tea, that's all.

KAY: Rita, I think he's talkin' in kilometres or something! *(Kay mimes using cash register. Pedro is buying a bra. She asks Rita.)* Is this a dollar-sixty-nine or sixty-nine cents?

RITA: No, it's marked down, Kay honey. It's got no hooks on it.

PEDRO: *(Turning to Rita.)* What is the name for you?

RITA: My name?

PEDRO: Sim.

RITA: Rita.

PEDRO: Rita? They call me Pedro. Pedro.

RITA: Good, very good...

KAY: That's sixty-nine cents plus tax is a dollar-forty-three.

JOAQUIM: No, no, no—no tax.

KAY: Rita, do the Portuguese pay tax?

RITA: No girl, the Portuguese don't pay tax.

KAY: Now, what am I gonna do? I've already got it rung in.

RITA: Well, I'll fix it after. I've only got one pair of hands.

KAY: Okay. (*She puts the bra into a bag for Pedro.*)

JOAQUIM: Obrigado. Até logo.

RITA: (*To Carlos who has found a bra.*) Did you find one in kilometres? Take it to the cash.

CARLOS: (*Puzzled.*) The cash?

KAY: (*To Carlos.*) I can't ring anything in 'til I get this straightened out.

RITA: Look, I'll straighten that out and you come and serve him, okay?

(*Rita gestures to João. She comes over to the "cash register" and Kay moves to help João who is holding a pair of trousers.*)

KAY: Do you wanna try them on? (*She points. He doesn't understand.*) You have to go in the dressing room. I'll take you to the dressing room. (*She uses hand gestures.*) Me—you—dressing room. Okay, you can take those off to try these on. (*João puts an arm around her, suggestively.*) No, no, no, no! Rita! Rita, he thinks I'm gonna go in the dressing room with him.

RITA: My God, girl, ya gotta be careful. They're out to sea for eighty days. Men got nee's, Kay.

KAY: (*Laughing, unafraid. To João.*) Just you in the dressing room.

RITA: (*To Carlos.*) What do you want now? It's twenty-five after nine. You're not gonna have time to buy anything else. You already got a bra.

(*Carlos demonstrates slip by moving his hands voluptuously down his body. Shaking his hands he cries "Woo, woo!"*)

RITA: Oh, you want a slip? Here. Now this is the same size as the bra.

CARLOS: Wife size. Like you.

RITA: Yeah, wife size.

CARLOS: Like you.

KAY: (*To João.*) Oh, no, no, no, you want...you want this? Oh yeah, they're nice. You might have to shorten them a little bit. Are you goin' to take them?

(*Kay moves to the cash register.*)

JOÃO: Sim. You finish?

KAY: What?

JOÃO: You finish?

KAY: Oh yes, we're closing soon. That will be twelve dollars and eighty-seven cents.

(*João pays.*)

PEDRO: Rita. (*Trying to give her a note.*) For you.

RITA: (*Speaking slowly and distinctly.*) Take it to the cash.

PEDRO: (*To Kay, pointing at Rita.*) You give this Rita? Goodbye, cash.

(Pedro exits.)

KAY: Yes. Okay. (*To Rita about João.*) He was kind of cute.

RITA: My God, Kay, you wouldn't go out with a Portuguese, would ya?

KAY: I never said anything about goin' out with him.

RITA: Sure, Kay, you're goin' to university in the fall, you don't have to go out with Portuguese.

KAY: (*She mimes trying to enter tax at cash register.*) Rita, I don't know how to fix this.

RITA: Oh, don't worry about that, Kay girl. You go on home now, I'll fix that later.

KAY: Gee, thanks, Rita. I'll see you tomorrow. Oh, someone left a note for you, it's on the cash. (*She exits.*)

RITA: (*Finds note.*) Oh, no. "You—me—movies—'Herbie Goes Bananas.' Love Pedro." What am I goin' to do now? He's probably on the street waiting for me. I'm gonna have to spend the whole night in the store. I'm gonna have to sleep in me bins.

(On sidewalk outside store.)

KAY: (*Surprised to see João there.*) Oh! I kinda thought you'd be here. (*He smiles charmingly, but he looks forlorn.*) You don't understand, do you? Well, I have to go now.

JOÃO: A onde está Basilica?

KAY: The what?

JOÃO: The Basilica? Where is Basilica?

KAY: Oh, the Basilica; oh yeah, it's up, just up there on top of the block to the right. (*João looks confused.*) Oh right, I'm sorry, look. (*She gestures.*) Well, you go down this street and when you get to the Courthouse then you go up the steps and it's to the right.

JOÃO: This my first viagem a St. John's.

KAY: What?

JOÃO: First voyage to St. John's.

KAY: Oh, your first voyage to St. John's. Oh, I see. Well, that's nice. Listen, I have to go to my house. My house.

JOÃO: Your casa. You—me—your casa?

KAY: No, no, I'll take you to the Basilica, okay?

JOÃO: Me—you—Basilica.

KAY: Yeah. (*They exit.*)

Scene 7

(Kay's house. Her mother, father, brother, Uncle Vanya and her father's friend Ambrose Lewis, have gathered to play cards.)

AGNES: You got the cards, Dad?

CECIL: Yeah, I got the cards.

AGNES: All right.

(More chatter.)

AGNES: Okay, cast jacks for partners.

VANYA: *(Grabbing cards.)* Right, you deal that, Cec.

RONNY: We can't have partners, there's only five.

AGNES: No. There's me and Dad, there's Uncle Vanya, there's Ambrose, there's Ronny and Kay...my God, where's Kay?

RONNY: I saw her hangin' down around the store with some big ugly fella on a motorcycle.

AGNES: No, you did not see her hangin' around the store with some fella on a motorcycle. She's workin' tonight.

RONNY: Ah, must have been a dream den.

VANYA: Are we gonna play or what?

AGNES: Dad, it's ten-thirty and the store is shut at nine-thirty.

AMBROSE: A-hundred-and-twenties is a lousy game anyway.

RONNY: It's not a lousy game if you know how to play.

AMBROSE: I'll go twenty-five, I suppose.

AGNES: Yeah, pass me.

RONNY: Pass.

VANYA: Yeah, me too.

CECIL: You're gone twenty-five, are ya?

AMBROSE: Twenty-five, yeah.

CECIL: Well I'll take yer twenty-five.

AMBROSE: What are ya goin' on?

CECIL: Yer givin' it to me, are ya?

AMBROSE: Yes b'y, I s'pose it's just as well for you to take it.

CECIL: Clubs.

AGNES: Clubs, yer goin' on clubs are ya? Oh God.

CECIL: Um, hum.

AMBROSE: Give us a full hand will ya, Cec?

RONNY: Yeah, gimme three, Dad, will ya?

(Everyone tells Cec how many cards they want.)

AMBROSE: Now look at this, luh. Here's August come and gone and not a trump in sight, luh.

RONNY: Mom, Mom, I'm starvin'.

AGNES: You got a stomach on ya like a long boot. Go in the kitchen and fill up on bread.

AMBROSE: What did you take my ace with that time, Cec?

CECIL: The five.

AMBROSE: Well, I never seen ya puttin' ne'er five on it.

CECIL: Well, if you'd been lookin' at the board, ya would have seen I put the five on it.

AMBROSE: I was lookin' at the board, b'y, but I never seen you put ne'er five on it though. If I hadda known you had the five there I wouldna put my ace on it.

CECIL: A card laid is a card played.

(Kay and João enter. Whenever any of the people address João they speak slowly and loudly, especially Mom.)

RONNY: Will somebody play.

VANYA: We'll never get a game out of it at this rate.

KAY: Sorry I'm late, Mom. I brought someone home I'd like you to meet.

AGNES: Oh, hello.

RONNY: (*Wanting his mother to play a card, pointing at the table.*) Mom, Mom?

AGNES: What?

RONNY: Mom?

AGNES: (*She plays a card.*) Oh here, luh!

KAY: Mom, this is João. João, this is my mother.

AGNES: Joan?

KAY: No, Mom—João!

AGNES: Joan?

KAY: And this is my father and my brother Ronny.

RONNY: Hi! You're not from here, are ya?

KAY: And my Uncle Vanya and a friend of my father's, Ambrose Lewis.

CECIL: How are ya, João? Listen, we'll call ya Joe for short, okay?

AGNES: Anything's better than Joan, God.

RONNY: Will you play, Ambrose? It's your lay.

AMBROSE: I already played, b'y, look at that.

RONNY: What did ya play that for? There was no trump called to the board. (*He urges his mother to play a card.*) Mom! Mom! Mom!

AGNES: (*Playing a card.*) Oh here, look. (*To João.*) Joe, why don't you pull up a chair and sit down?

CECIL: Oh yes, that's a good idea. We can have a game of railroad auction, eh?

JOÃO: Chair? I'm fine.

CECIL: Yeah, come on. Pull up a chair, luh. Sit down.

AGNES: Yeah, well, you might as well sit down.

CECIL: Now, ya know how to play cards, don't ya?

JOÃO: No comprendo!

KAY: Dad, he doesn't speak any English; he's from Portugal.

AGNES: Portugal? He's from Portugal!

CECIL: Well, I suppose in Portugal they must play cards.

AGNES: Yes Joe, you sit in and have a game of cards. (*Questioningly.*) Cards?

RONNY: I wouldn't mind having a game of cards. (*Sarcastically.*) Cards.

AGNES: (*To Kay.*) He's at the university, is he?

(*João sits next to Cecil. Kay sits at the opposite end of the table.*)

CECIL: It's no sweat, it's a simple game. I'll teach it to him.

AGNES: I asked you, is he at the University?

KAY: No, Mom, he's not at the University.

RONNY: Joe, Joe, is it cold in Portugal like it is here? Brrrrr!

JOÃO: No, muito sol.

EVERYONE: (*Puzzled.*) Sol?

(*They chatter.*)

AGNES: Soul, he's talking about his immortal soul!

EVERYONE: Sol? (*They see the light.*) Oh, souls! Soul!

AMBROSE: (*Disproving their theory.*) Oh, sol; he's saying it's sunny in Portugal.

AGNES: Oh, sunny, yes, yes. Kay, where did you meet him?

CECIL: That's all right, I'll explain it to him.

RONNY: Dad, sure she just said he don't speak any English.

VANYA: What difference is it, b'y? Sure, cards are a universal language.

CECIL: Sure, he just said it was sunny in Portugal, didn't he?

RONNY: Yeah.

CECIL: Now, you deal out five cards to everybody, right? That's five! Now you deal three cards into the kit, the kit. Do you understand the kit?

KAY: Dad, he doesn't speak any English!

CECIL: The kit, kit, kitty, meow. (*They all mime a cat.*) Now, after you got them all dealt out, right, you can figure out what you got in your hand. Now the five is the highest trump.

AGNES: (*Speaking above Dad.*) Kay, where did you meet him?

KAY: At the Basilica.

AMBROSE: They goes up there all the time.

AGNES: The Basilica, the Basilica?

RONNY: Dad, he don't know what you're saying. Dad, Dad? He don't speak English.

CECIL: If you'd shut up, I can explain it to him.

AGNES: Dad, she met him at the Basilica.

CECIL: God, it's a simple enough game, but you'd never know it the way you play it.

KAY: Well, actually, I was walking down Water Street and he asked me directions.

AGNES: He picked you up off the street. My God, Kay, he's off the Portuguese boats.

AMBROSE: Ah, go away, Agnes, she did the right thing bringing him home to meet the family too, maid. Sure, look at him over there, he's a nice enough young fella.

CECIL: Now after the five comes the jack.

RONNY: Dad, Dad, you never dealt me in. (*He tugs at Cecil's card.*) I'll take your cards while you explain it to him.

CECIL: You will not take my cards. (*Cecil and Ronny wrestle over the cards.*) Now, give me, give me them cards.

AGNES: Will somebody just give him some cards and shut him up?

VANYA: Here's five cards. There b'y, now play, b'y, play.

RONNY: (*Whining.*) Look at the cards I got.

VANYA: For God's sake, what kinda game is this at all?

AMBROSE: B'y, it's ne'er kinda game at all if you ask me. You might as well have gave him all the cards. My God, b'y, you can't go dealin' someone five cards off the bottom of the deck like that, can ya?

AGNES: Ambrose, he's only a youngster.

VANYA: Well shag it then, mis-deal.

AMBROSE: (*Discovering that he has a good hand.*) No, no, never mind. Come on, we'll wrap it up in this hand. Come on, will ya?

RONNY: Wrap it up! Wrap it up! Hard to wrap it up with you crowd.

CECIL: Now it's highest in red and it's lowest in black. Understand that? Like how do you say highest in Portuguese? Grande. The presidente. The highest. Ya got that? (*He motions high with his hand.*)

AMBROSE: (*Slamming table.*) Sixty for a-hundred-and-twenty on clubs.

EVERYONE: What?

AGNES: Sixty for a-hundred-and-twenty. You better have some good cards in your hand, Ambrose my son. My God, what's the sense of playin' cards with someone foolish enough to go sixty for a-hundred-and-twenty.

CECIL: I forgot to tell ya about the ace of hearts. Now, the ace of hearts is trump, no matter what's trumps.

AGNES: Kay, you know they're all married.

KAY: Mom, he's not married. He's only eighteen years old.

AGNES: They get married very young over there, Kay. Their ways are not our ways. (*To João.*) Your wife must miss you when you're gone, does she...your wife?

KAY: Mom, he's not married.

CECIL: Oh, yer not married.

AGNES: Are you married?

KAY: Married? Ring?

JOÃO: No, no, no...

AGNES: Oh, yes.

CECIL: Fine, now he's not married. Can we get on with the game. Now, like I was sayin', it's highest in red and lowest in black. Now, we're playin' black, right? That means the highest is the lowest. Like the presidente is the pig. The presidente. That's the way ya look at it.

RONNY: What are you talking about?

CECIL: (*Gesturing to indicate height again.*) Now, like, the ten is lower than the nine. The eight is higher than both of them, and so on. You got that, haven't ya? Now, what do you call these? Clubs.

JOÃO: Paus!

CECIL: Pows?

JOÃO: Paus.

(*Laughter.*)

CECIL: Did you hear that, Ambrose, yer gone sixty for a-hundred-and-twenty on pows. Oh my, you know I was over in Portugal once.

AGNES: Dad, you were never in Portugal.

AMBROSE: Sure he was.

CECIL: Sure, I was so in Portugal in the war. Yeah, I was over in Portugal durin' the war.

AMBROSE: I was over there wid him.

CECIL: Yes, durin' the war we were over in Portugal.

AGNES: Dad, there was no war in Portugal.

CECIL: That's because we were there, ha.

VANYA: That's right. It was a good place to be during the war. That Balboa.

CECIL: That's right, Balboa. Yeah, Balboa. *(To João.)* You've been to Balboa?

JOÃO: Balboa? Lisboa.

CECIL: Lisboa, Lisboa.

AMBROSE: That's right, Lisboa, that's it, Lisboa. 'Course, it was nothin' like Italy though, Cec.

VANYA: Ah, you're right there, my son, Ambrose.

AMBROSE: You've been to Italy have you? Italia.

JOÃO: Ah Roma, Roma.

CECIL: Rome, yeah.

AMBROSE: Ah, the aroma of fresh Italians, what Cec?

(Laughter.)

CECIL: Do ya get that? The aroma of fresh Italians.

RONNY: He thinks you're laughin' at him.

AGNES: No, we're not laughin' at you, honey, we're laughin' with you. It's just a little fun. *(To rest of table.)* He doesn't understand, does he? No.

CECIL: The aroma of fresh Italians.

RONNY: Sure he understands, with you laughin' at him and pokin' at him all the time.

AGNES: Who asked you? What do you know about it?

RONNY: He doesn't know whether you're laughin' at him or not. Look at him.

(They all peer intently at João.)

AGNES: Never mind.

CECIL: You know, Mom, we should go to Portugal for a vacation. Yeah, and go down to that place in the south. What's it called? Torremolinos?

VANYA: No, no, Cec, that's in friggin' Spain, b'y.

CECIL: *(To João.)* Oh, that's in Spain.

(General agreement.)

AMBROSE: Sure, Cec, what do you want to throw away all that money on air fare for, old man, when you can take her down to Portugal Cove? Same thing ain't it?

CECIL: *(To João.)* You've been down to Portugal Cove, have ya?

JOÃO: Portugal Cove? *(He pronounces the word "port-de-gal," which the family seizes upon.)*

CECIL: Portoogal Cove, yeah, that's it, just about eight miles outside of town. Pretty place.

RONNY: Dad, Dad, why don't ya ask him something sensible?

CECIL: Well, why don't you ask him something sensible, smart aleck?

EVERYONE: Go, go, yeah ask him.

AMBROSE: Shut up now, he's gonna ask him a question.

CECIL: Well, come on.

RONNY: I can ask him by meself. (*Pause.*)

AGNES & CECIL: Well come on, come on.

RONNY: Give me a chance.

AMBROSE: He don't know what to say now.

AGNES: Well, come on.

RONNY: How long are you stayin' in St. John's?

AGNES: Oh, that's a good question.

(General agreement.)

RONNY: (*Shouting at João.*) How long are you stayin' in St. John's?

VANYA: Here dagos, dagos?

KAY: (*Gesturing as she speaks.*) João, you in St. John's how many days—one, two, three, four...

JOÃO: Oh, sim, now stay here three days in St. John's.

CECIL: Oh yeah, three days, three days.

JOÃO: Stay three days. Metore not very well.

CECIL: Oh, his mother's not very well.

AGNES: Oh, I'm sorry, that's too bad.

JOÃO: No, no, no mother.

CECIL: He doesn't have...his mother is dead.

AGNES: His mother is dead.

JOÃO: Não, não. Metore, metore—brooom, brooom.

AMBROSE: Oh, yer broke down.

(Everyone talking.)

CECIL: (*Speaking over everyone else.*) Oh, the motor, the motor is dead, his mother is alive.

JOÃO: E.F. Barnes.

AGNES: Oh yes, E.F. Barnes, yes.

CECIL: A lot of them come over here to get repaired at E.F. Barnes.

AGNES: (*Amazed.*) My God, all the way from Portugal just to get fixed up at E.F. Barnes.

CECIL: Yeah, yeah, they got Portuguese working down at E.F. Barnes, ya know.

AGNES: I don't think so, Dad, they got no Portuguese down to E.F. Barnes.

AMBROSE: Sure, how do you know, Agnes, you been down to get your engine overhauled lately or what?

JOÃO: Amigos at E.F. Barnes.

(Everyone chattering.)

AGNES: Oh, I see, I see. (*To João.*) And your mother? Your mother's in Portugal is she?

JOÃO: Sim.

AGNES: Oh yes, and your father also.

JOÃO: Father here.

RONNY: Have you got any brothers like me?

KAY: (*Gesturing in her magical way; true love breaks all language barriers.*) Like, he is my brother. Do you have any brothers?

JOÃO: Ah, sim, um.

CECIL: Well, if he's anything like him ya must be crucified.

AGNES: So your father is a fisherman, is he ? A fisherman?

KAY: (*Gesturing.*) Like fishing, fishing.

JOÃO: Ah, sim, father, father fisherman.

AGNES: (*Speaking with slight disapproval.*) Oh, I see, yes, yes.

CECIL: And what, ya got something against fishermen, have ya Agnes?

AGNES: Well Cec, there's a very big difference between bein' a fisherman here in Newfoundland and bein' a fisherman in Portugal.

AMBROSE: No Agnes, my dear, that's what there's not.

AGNES: Portugal is a very poor country, Ambrose.

AMBROSE: Yeah, and Newfoundland is a very poor country too, my dear.

CECIL: And I suppose ya got something against blacks too, have ya?

AGNES: Dad, we got no blacks in Newfoundland. (*To João.*) We got no blacks in Newfoundland.

CECIL: And what about Globy Collins? He played centre for the Corner Brook Royals for years. He was black.

JOÃO: Black?

CECIL: Uh, huh.

AGNES: Oh no, honey, we're not talking about you. We're talking about blacks—blacks. (*To rest of table.*) He doesn't understand.

AMBROSE: You know, Agnes, them Portuguese is pretty dark theirselves sometimes. I must say he's not very dark though, is he?

AGNES: No, he's not very dark, is he? (*To João.*) No, we're saying you're not a very brown person. You're not one of the darker Portuguese. You're more white, like we are.

KAY: Mom, please!

AGNES: Yeah, would you like something to eat? You must be starved. He must be starved. They don't feed them on the boats you know, Kay.

KAY: Oh Mom, they eat better on those boats than we do.

AGNES: Why, Kay, I don't believe they've even got meat in Portugal.

KAY: Mom, you don't know anything about Portugal. Dad, please!

CECIL: All right then, we'll ask him, won't we?

AGNES: Yes, ah, do you have meat in Portugal? Have you got any pork—beef—have you got any chickens in Portugal? Chickens?

EVERYONE: Chickens...(*They make noises like a chicken.*)

JOÃO: Sim, galinhas.

(General agreement.)

CECIL: Now, see, we know they got chickens in Portugal and we know they got beef in Portugal, right? Because of the bull fights, right?

AGNES: Now that's not right. You know that's not right.

AMBROSE: Yeah that's right, Agnes my dear, 'tis awful the way they treats them bulls over there. (*To João.*) Have you got anything like Greenpeace in Portugal? You know, "Save the Bulls," or something like that. Bulls.

VANYA: Bulls, yeah, like torros you know, they go...(*Mimes a bull and charges at João. The family is horrified.*)

AGNES: What are you doing? Don't go running at the boy, you'll scare him half to death. For God's sake, sit down, will ya.

CECIL: Well, he's not my brother.

AGNES: Well, he's not my brother.

CECIL: Where the hell did he come from, then?

RONNY: Well, ever since Joe came in you've been laughin' at him, and pokin' at him, and then everybody started doin' chickens in his face.

AMBROSE: What are you grumblin' for, what? Luh, he's got a family hisself, b'y.

(Everyone talking and arguing.)

CECIL: Will you give it up? Can't we have a decent game of cards in this house without general pandemonium breakin' out?

KAY: Mom, I'm taking João down to the boat. He has to leave in the morning.

(Kay and João stand.)

AGNES: Oh, Dad will give him a run down to the boat, Kay.

KAY: Oh, no, no, no, I've got the keys right here. I'll see you later. Bye-bye.

(They exit.)

AMBROSE: Oh let 'em go, Agnes maid. Couple of young people out havin' a good time. Nothin' wrong with that.

RONNY: (*After a pause.*) You know what they're doin' on the boats.

ACT II
Scene 1

(On the deck. There is a foghorn in the background. The Portuguese fishermen sing, "Soup of Sorrow")

I'm a lost man, I'm a dead man, drifting in the fog
With the soup of sorrow coursing through my veins,
I'm bound to the Banks, I'm bound to the sea,

I'm bound to this cold and misery.
I'm a lean man, I'm a strongman, I'm hauling in the nets
With the soup of sorrow coursing through my veins,
Fish mouths gaping, blind eyes staring,
The virgin rocks are singing in my brains.
All night long, I dream about pretty girls,
Missy, missy, you like me? I love you!
I'm a ladies' man, a gentleman, I want my share of loving
With the soup of sorrow coursing through my veins,
But my hands are rough, skin cracked and raw,
It's freezing and my hands will never thaw.
I'm a killer, I'm a hunter, like my father long ago
With the soup of sorrow coursing through his veins,
The codfish moan, down in the hold,
My father's sins are floating in my soup bowl.
All night long, I dream about pretty girls,
Missy, missy, you like me? I love you!
I'm a worker, I'm a doer, I'm filling up the hold,
With the soup of sorrow coursing through my veins,
Day in, day out, it never fills,
Split me, gut me, 'fore I go insane.
All night long, All night long,
All night long, all night long,
All night long I dream about pretty girls,
All night long I dream about pretty girls,
All night long I dream about pretty girls,
Missy, missy, You like me? I love you!
I'm a dead man, I'm a lost man, I'll never make it home
'Cause the soup of sorrow is a curse from God,
We eat it now, they ate it then,
We'll never end the search for this goddamn cod.
All night long, I dream about pretty girls,
Missy, missy, you like me? I love you.

Scene 2

(At the Stardust Lounge. A mirrored disco ball descends from the ceiling. The song "One Way or Another" is playing on jukebox as the women talk.)

DOREEN: My God, what are we doin' here tonight?

ROS: I couldn't stay home another night, my dear. Mom got me drove cracked.

DOREEN: Oh yes, I suppose when ya gets that old there's nothin' else to do.

ROS: *(Looking offstage.)* Oh, who's that?

DOREEN: Oh, that's Marion. *(Marion's presence is pretended.)* Hi, Marion. How are ya? Yeah, grand girl, thanks, yeah. No, no boats in tonight, girl, no.

ROS: My God, that's not Marion! That's not Marion Evans! She's after losin' some lot of weight!

DOREEN: Yeah, looks terrible on her too, don't it?

ROS: What's that hangin' down off her chin?

DOREEN: That's her skin. Sure, she got them old diet pills. My God, how crooked is she at all.

(Ros gestures Marion to come over.)

DOREEN: Don't go callin' her over. (*She hits Ros's arm.*) I can't talk to her since she went on them old pills, my dear.

ROS: I can't look at her, she turns me stomach. God she's like a big old frog, ain't she? Just like Don Jamison.

DOREEN: Want a 7-Up?

ROS: No, I'm plimmed up on 7-Up. My God, there's nudding in the harbour.

DOREEN: Yeah, there's a Japanese boat in.

ROS: My God, ya wouldn't go with a Japanese, would ya?

DOREEN: Yeah, I went with a Japanese once.

ROS: Yeah?

DOREEN: Yeah, after he gave me eighty dollars. I said, "I'm not in the business, b'y," and he wouldn't take it back, he wouldn't crack a smile. I said, "Shag ya," and went out and bought meself a new sweater. The one with the fur around the collar.

ROS: Sure, I heard that the Japanese wouldn't go with ya unless they paid ya first.

DOREEN: Ever go with a Polish?

ROS: Yeah. My God, it's like sittin' down with a dummy all night. Dead, dead, dead. Did ya ever meet anybody who went with a Russian?

DOREEN: Not a soul, girl. They must be neutered, are they?

(The girls sip their drinks.)

ROS: No, they're communists. They got to be back in the boat by ten-thirty. Ah, what odds about 'em.

DOREEN: Yeah, tonight I'd love to see me Spaniard. Have a few drinks. Do up the town, you know.

ROS: Nah, they're too pushy for me. One dance and they thinks they owns ya.

DOREEN: They knows how to spend their money, honey. I mean they knows how to have a good time, right?

ROS: You went with a Cuban didn't ya?

DOREEN: Yeah.

ROS: What was it like?

DOREEN: Ever been through World War II? Better than the twins.

ROS: Oh go on, there's nudding better than that twin.

DOREEN: Yeah, I thought me back was gonna break on that old box spring.

ROS: You weren't on the box spring, you were on the mattress on the floor.

DOREEN: No, I was on the box spring, you were on the mattress on the floor with Juan, or Carlos, or whatever his name was. Never could tell them apart.

ROS: God! Remember Manuel. He was some sweet, wasn't he?

DOREEN: Yeah, really sweet.

ROS: Yeah, he was some sweet.

DOREEN: Yeah, sweet, God.

ROS: You know I must say the Portuguese are still my favourite.

DOREEN: Nah, I'd rather have a Spaniard any day.

ROS: Nah, I knows them too well, right? Like I was goin' out with them since I was fifteen. That was ten years ago, my dear. That's a long time.

DOREEN: Yeah, I been goin' with 'em longer than that. Ever since I moved in to town. Remember I used to babysit for Miz Monroe? She's dead now, she died in that car accident. She used to bring them home all the time. I remembers the first time I saw one, I was scared shitless, you know. Then she started bringin' 'em home all the time. That's when I started gettin' really deep down into the Portuguese, but now I think I'd rather have a Spaniard.

ROS: Ah, go on, you're sayin' that now 'cause you're broke up with Ricardo.

DOREEN: Ten years I was goin' out with him, ten years. Missed one night down here and he was gone off with Diane. Yeah, I saw him the next night and I wouldn't even speak to him.

ROS: You know, I was thinkin' about goin' up to Catalina. Georgina was up there and said that the *Navaganté* was up there.

DOREEN: You wouldn't go chase 'em around up there, would ya?

ROS: Sure, why not, there's nudding around here to do.

DOREEN: What are the Portuguese doing up in Catalina?

ROS: I don't know, something about the fish, I suppose.

DOREEN: God, girl, I'm gutfounded.

ROS: Go away, sure, you just finished a big supper.

DOREEN: Sure love a big pizza now wid everything on.

ROS: Nah, I hates mushrooms.

DOREEN: God, yer gainin' a lot of weight, Ros.

ROS: Sure, what odds! No one around here to notice. Oh, come on, let's get a pizza. I'll starve meself tomorrow, come on.

(Ros gets up to leave.)

DOREEN: Yeah, all right, let's get fat.

ROS: Yeah, maybe there'll be a new boat in tomorrow.

DOREEN: Maybe we'll all fall in love. Who knows?

(They exit.)

Scene 3

MANUEL: *(Singing.)* "Salt Water Charly"
    She was only a Salt Water Charly,
    But a queen to the Portuguese,

In a dress of chiffon and a glass of John Barley,
She dreamt of a life of ease.
 In the warmth of her bed, in the dark of night,
She'd hold them, and kiss them, and cry,
"Carlos, Manuel, Francisco, Miguel,
I love you, don't leave me, I'll die."
 I'll marry Miguel, oh, the lies he would tell,
As he held me and called me his own,
He kissed my soft cheek, sweet words he would speak,
"Mi amore, mi amore," he'd moan.
 She was only a finger pier girl,
But a lady to the boys at the bar,
With a twirl and a turn, she'd dance and she'd yearn,
For her sailor to take her afar.
 I'll marry Luis, oh, the sweet dreams of peace,
As he gently caressed my brown hair,
My gown is all ready, is your arm steady?
His answer dispelled my despair.
 When the piers of the harbour are empty,
No velvet-eyed boys at the Dust,
She'd squat down to Cross's, forgetting her losses
With men who knew nothing but lust.
 I'll marry José, he'll take me away,
To Coimbra, Lisboa, Oporto,
And the scent of red roses, sand warm 'neath my feet,
We'll drift 'til the red sun sinks low.
 She was only a Salt Water Charly,
But a queen to the Portuguese,
In a dress of chiffon and a glass of John Barley,
She dreamt of a life of ease.
   (The ship, the crew's quarters.)

JOÃO: Albertino, como está?

ALBERTINO: Ah, como está, João? Uma cerveija?

JOÃO: Manuel told me you write in English? Do you write English?

ALBERTINO: Yes, sure I do.

JOÃO: I was wondering if you could write a letter for me?

ALBERTINO: Yeah yeah, I can write a letter for you, yeah.

JOÃO: Ah, well, it's to a girl.

ALBERTINO: A girl, eh?

JOÃO: From St. John's.

ALBERTINO: Las mulheres de St. John's são muito bonitas.

JOÃO: She's a good girl though, I know.

ALBERTINO: Ah, yes, they're all good girls, João.

JOÃO: She's going to be a nurse.

ALBERTINO: Yeah, well what do you want to say to her?

JOÃO: I don't know. Make it good, make it good.

ALBERTINO: Well, I don't know what to say. Did you say goodbye to her when you left St. John's?

JOÃO: Yes, we stayed up all night, we talked.

ALBERTINO: Oh, you talked, eh. All night?

JOÃO: I met her family. It reminded me of home. I miss home.

ALBERTINO: Well, don't get too serious.

JOÃO: Yeah, well, I know what I'm doing.

ALBERTINO: Hey, what about your girl in Portugal.

JOÃO: Ela é muito nova e inocente.

ALBERTINO: Ah, leave the girls for the boys, eh. Men want women. So, ah, tell me about your—what's her name?

JOÃO: Kay. Querida Kay.

ALBERTINO: Kay, querida Kay, that's a good start. Now tell me about your Kay.

JOÃO: Ela tem cabelo da cor de areia ao pôr do sol e olhos como o mar de Aveiro.

ALBERTINO: Sounds like you know what you want to say. Let's go write your letter.

(They exit. João speaking in Portuguese to Albertino telling him what to write while Kay, at home, reads the letter.)

JOÃO: Querida Kay, Desejo que ao receberes está carta te encontras bem de saude em companhia dos teus pais...

KAY: Querida Kay, I wish you happiness and good health in the company of your family. I am fine. We just stopped in Greenland for half a day which gave me some time to quickly write a letter to my favorite girl. The days out here at sea pass extremely slowly, and I long for the day when I will see you again standing by my side. My father thinks you are very pretty and is anxious to meet you the next time we are in St. John's. How are you doing in your studies? Are you still working at the Arcade? I hope you are enjoying yourself. I am not very happy. For one, you are very far from me and also I do not like this life. I have been thinking that maybe in the future, I can get a job in St. John's and migrate there, like some of my friends who work at E.F. Barnes. Then we can be together making a life for ourselves. I'll have to go now, my love. Say hello to your parents for me, your uncle and your little brother. Hopefully we'll go to St. John's in exactly three weeks. *(She looks up and exclaims.)* Oh, that's tomorrow! I miss you very much. Goodbye, my love. João.

Scene 4

(Mike's Bar, a more upscale establishment than the Stardust. A green plant descends as the lights come up. Rickie Rickets is at the piano, he can't play or sing. Kay and João are sitting at a table.)

RICKIE: *(Singing.)* Blue eyes, you got pretty blue eyes, blue, blue eyes, etc.

MARGE: Rickie! Rickie! Rickie, cut it. Why don't you take a break for a while. Relax. Come up and have a drink.

RICKIE: Yeah, yeah, I think I will. Can't have a drink though—too nervous. I'll have a cup of coffee.

MARGE: Oh, yeah.

RICKIE: Yeah, I'm a cuttin' a record in the morning.

MARGE: Oh yeah, goin' up to Toronto, are ya?

RICKIE: No, no, just goin' down to Echo Studios, right. Yeah, hey, ah, you think Mike'd let me sell it over the bar?

MARGE: Yeah, sure, as long as you don't play.

RICKIE: Yeah, right, right, yeah. Well maybe not, right, maybe not, maybe not. I mean if, ah, if they got the album, right, they don't need me, right? Yeah, give us a coffee, will ya?

KAY: João, what time is your boat leaving on Monday?

JOÃO: Ah maybe two, three, four...

KAY: Can I come home to the boat to say good-bye to you?

JOÃO: Oh, yeah, good, that's good.

KAY: I suppose you'll be glad to go back to Portugal.
(João sees Frank and Cyril enter.)

JOÃO: Oh no.

FRANK: How's it goin', Cyril b'y?

CYRIL: How ya doin'? Nothin' much, nothin' much.

FRANK: Where you comin' from?

CYRIL: From Rob Roy's.

FRANK: Any tail down to Rob Roy's tonight or what?

CYRIL: No b'y, just a bit of pig, a few dogs. *(He passes Kay and João's table.)* Hello, Kay.

KAY: Hello, Cyril.

CYRIL: Didn't take you long, did it?

FRANK: Ah, leave them alone, Cyril b'y. You know what it's like, they comes, they goes, right. Who needs 'em, right?

CYRIL: Who's the bozo hangin' off ya, Kay?

JOÃO: He's speakin' to me?

KAY: Just ignore him. Don't pay any attention to him at all.

CYRIL: Just asked who yer buddy was, that's all.

KAY: Cyril, this is João. João, this is Cyril. Okay?

JOÃO: Hello, How are you?

CYRIL: What are you—Portuguese? What's the place turning into, Mike, the new Stardust...wall to wall gees?

MIKE: *(He is working with his pocket calculator.)* Take it easy, Cyril. Don't you go startin' either racket. *(To Ricketts.)* What have ya got there, Rick?

RICKIE: *(He has one maraca.)* Oh, ah, I'm learning how to play it. Listen to this, listen to this now. *(He shakes the maraca once.)*

MARGE: That's amazing.

RICKIE: See, there's eighteen tracks on the album, right. Gotta put something on every track, right.

JOÃO: Do you fish?

CYRIL: What?

KAY: He's just asking you if you fish. He's a fisherman off the *Manuelá.*

CYRIL: No, I'm not a friggin' fisherman. I'm an artist. I draws unemployment. (*He laughs. João does not.*) Over your head, was it?

JOÃO: (*To Kay.*) You like a brandy?

KAY: Oh, sure, I'd love a brandy, sure.

JOÃO: Oh good.

RICKIE: Oh, excuse me, you're Portuguese, are ya.

JOÃO: Portuguese.

RICKIE: Yeah.

JOÃO: Sim.

RICKIE: My name is Rickie Ricketts. You might have heard of me.

JOÃO: João Manuel.

RICKIE: João Manuel, you mean Juan Manuel don't you.

JOÃO: João.

RICKIE: No b'y, your name is Juan, b'y. Juan, you know, like Don Juan, Juan Carlos, all them Juans, right.

FRANK: That's over in Spain, b'y.

RICKIE: Oh yeah, Spain, yeah right. Hey ah, there's one other thing I wanted to ask you there, you know? You know that song "Blue Spanish Eyes" (*Sings "Blue Spanish eyes, prettiest eyes in all of Mexico..."*) You know that one? Listen, there's one thing I could never figure out, right. I mean the only Spanish eyes I ever saw were brown. Why would they say *blue* Spanish eyes?

JOÃO: Ah, two, two Spanish eyes.

RICKIE: Oh, *two* Spanish eyes. Oh. I get it now. See, ah, I can't read music, right.

(*João stands up and goes to get Kay a brandy. Cyril takes his seat.*)

CYRIL: Where'd you pick him up? Hangin' around the pier? Boardin' at the Welcome? Got your name on a room yet, Kay?

KAY: Cyril, why don't you go back and sit with your buddies.

CYRIL: Don't know what happened to you, that's all. You're gone down hill all the way since you left me, girl.

KAY: Cyril, I can take care of myself. Look, I'll talk to you about it later, all right. Would you please just leave us alone?

CYRIL: All right, I'll leave you alone.

JOÃO: (*Returning.*) Ah, your brandy.

KAY: Look, would you please get up and let João have his chair back.

JOÃO: May I sit please?

KAY: Look, why don't you just go away and leave us alone. Give me a break.

CYRIL: Why should I give you a break, Kay?

KAY: Well, then I'll have to call the manager.

CYRIL: Oh, you're gonna call the manager, are ya? Well I'll call him for ya. Mike.

MIKE: Yeah?

CYRIL: Somebody wants to talk to the manager.

MIKE: (*Coming over.*) Yeah, what can I do for you?

KAY: Would you please ask him to get up so my friend can have his chair back?

MIKE: Got nothin' to do with me, has it? I don't know whose chair that is. And over there look, they're all my chairs. What's wrong with that one?

RICKIE: Hey Mike, is this a musical calculator?

MIKE: No Rick, no, it's not.

RICKIE: Ah, that's too bad, b'y, I could have put it on one of the tracks on me album, right?

KAY: Oh Cyril, would you please just sit over there and leave us alone?

JOÃO: Yes please.

CYRIL: Aw, shut up.

JOÃO: Hey, you don't say my namorada to shut up.

CYRIL: I'm not telling your namorada to shut up. I'm telling you to shut up.

JOÃO: Me shut up?

CYRIL: (*Pushing João.*) Yeah.

(They fight, Kay screams, everyone is yelling. The following dialogue is being shouted virtually at the same time, until Kay and João leave.)

MIKE: (*Grabbing João.*) All right, break it up, break it up.

FRANK: (*Grabbing Cyril.*) Take it easy, Cyril boy.

JOÃO: No problems, eh, no problems.

KAY: He didn't start it.

MIKE: (*Pushing João out.*) I don't care, just leave.

JOÃO: No problems.

(João and Kay exit.)

MIKE: Goddamn Portuguese. Everytime you let them in there's trouble.

RICKIE: Well I guess it's time for me to start another set. (*He sings.*) "Blue Spanish Eyes...oh, two Spanish eyes..."

Scene 5

(The Halloran home. Kay is sneaking in.)

CECIL: And where do you think you're goin', young lady? Do you realize what time it is? It's five...it's six o'clock in the mornin'! And what do you mean by comin' in here at this hour?

KAY: Well, I live here.

CECIL: Don't get saucy with me, little miss, "Well, I live here." What do you think I'm runnin' here, a hotel? Listen, when you get a place of your own, then you can come waltzin' in at six o'clock in the mornin'! But as long as you're livin' under my roof you'll do as you're told.

KAY: Dad, I'm sorry I didn't realize how late it was.

CECIL: Oh, you didn't realize how late it was! The fact that the sun was out and that the birds were singin' didn't give you a clue!

KAY: Dad, João is leaving the day after tomorrow.

CECIL: As far as *you're* concerned, young lady, he has already left!

KAY: Oh, Dad, will you just stop treating me like a child?

CECIL: Oh, like a child. You're not actin' like a child, are you? You're actin' like an adult, are you? Do you see your mother and I waltzin' in here at six o'clock in the mornin'!

KAY: Dad, I'm really sorry I've upset you, but I'm not sorry I stayed out late and I'll probably be out late again tomorrow night.

CECIL: You're going nowhere, young lady! You're going to march up over those stairs and into the bed, and you're goin' to stay there until I tell you to move! What do you think I'm runnin' here? A flop house for common whores who run around with Portuguese sailors?

KAY: (*Angry.*) I am not a common whore and I don't run around with Portuguese sailors! I just happen to be going out with a guy from Portugal and (*Emotional.*) I, I think that I'm in love with him!

CECIL: Oh, wonderful! That makes everything all right. I suppose you got the wedding date set, have ya? I can see the invitations now. "Mr. and Mrs. Halloran are pleased to announce the wedding of their daughter Kay, to the gee who picked her up on Water Street!"

KAY: (*Angry.*) Don't call him a gee! His name is João. If you want to talk about him, call him João!

CECIL: Don't you ever speak to me in that tone of voice! (*Pause. His voice softens.*) Kay, what's become of you? I mean you used to be a nice, sensible, decent, reliable girl and you get picked up by a Portuguese sailor and you go nuts. And your mopin' around the house for a month, and now you're out until six o'clock in the morning.

KAY: Dad, if you'll just give me a chance I'll explain it to you. I'll tell you what's been happening.

CECIL: (*Frustrated.*) I'd love it. I'd love an explanation. I've been waitin' for an explanation. I've been waitin' for an explanation since twelve-thirty! That was when the little hand was on the top and the big hand was on the bottom! Now the little hand is on the bottom and the big hand is on the top!

KAY: Dad, does this make any sense to you? Cyril and I went out together for six months and we couldn't communicate. We couldn't talk to each other, and yet in the little time I've know João he's become the best friend I've ever had. We can talk about anything.

CECIL: And what are you supposed to do now? Run off to Portugal and get married?

KAY: Oh Dad, I'm not talking about getting married.

AGNES: (*Offstage.*) Dad, is that Kay? Did she finally come home? What does she think this is—a hotel that she can come traipsing in at any hour of the day or night?

CECIL: (*Whispering to Kay.*) Now go to bed. (*To Agnes.*) She fell asleep over to Vicky's.

(She exits.)

AGNES: Oh, I see. Of course Vicky doesn't have a telephone, I suppose, us home all night worrying about her. She could have called home...

CECIL: Mom, will you shut up and go to bed out of it?

(He exits.)

Scene 6

(The Stardust Lounge, with the disco ball. The boats are in. "Fernando" is playing on the jukebox. Ros is sitting at a table linked arm-in-arm with Albertino who is Doreen's current boyfriend. Enter Doreen and her lackey.)

LACKEY: (*He points at Ros and Albertino.*) Doreen, Doreen? At the table, luh.

DOREEN: Shut up, will ya?

ROS: Onde Carlos?

ALBERTINO: Yes, Carlos está na Norvega.

ROS: Não, nasia Carlos há dois anos.

ALBERTINO: Forget about Carlos. I'm here now. We go to your casa.

ROS: No.

ALBERTINO: Yes, yes.

ROS: No, we have one more drink and then we go.

ALBERTINO: No. I don't want no more to drink.

ROS: Come on, one more drink.

ALBERTINO: No more.

ROS: One more rum and Coke.

ALBERTINO: Okay. One rum coca for you, no for me.

(He leaves for the bar.)

LACKEY: Doreen, go over now, luh. Go over and get her while he's gone, luh, I'll back you up.

DOREEN: You go over there and you tell her that's my buddy and she better keep her hands off him, or else.

LACKEY: (*Going over to Ros. He speaks with false bravado.*) It's like this, Ros, Doreen says that he's her buddy, right? And you better keep your hands off of him or...

ROS: (*Grabbing his collar.*) Or what?

LACKEY: Ah, it's not me, Ros, I'm not sayin' nothin'. Doreen said she's gonna rearrange your face with the heal of her shoe. Something like that.

ROS: Look, you tell Doreen if she got something to say to me to come over here and say it herself!

LACKEY: (*Mumbles to Doreen.*) Did you get that?
(Albertino returns from the bar and Ros drapes herself over him.)
DOREEN: Do you want to go outside and talk about it?
ROS: Oh, I'd love to, honey, but I'm busy right now. (*She fondles Albertino.*) I don't have time.
DOREEN: (*To Albertino.*) You, you filho de puta. You said you'd meet me here tonight, tu falas mentira.
ALBERTINO: No, no, I meet her tonight. I say that. No problems, no problems, please.
DOREEN: You know that's my buddy.
ROS: I don't see your name written on him anywhere.
DOREEN: He's wearing my collar. (*A neckerchief that the girls often gave their men when they went out.*)
ROS: Oh that, I thought that was just a bit of old rag wrapped round his throat.
(Ros tears off Albertino's neckerchief and throws it on the floor.)
LACKEY: What do that mean?
ROS: (*To Albertino.*) Come on, let's dance.
ALBERTINO: I love to dance.
(They dance.)
DOREEN: (*To lackey.*) Come on, let's dance.
LACKEY: I can't dance, b'y.
DOREEN: Yes, you can. Get down here.
(They dance.)
ROS: (*Indicating Doreen.*) My God, there's some lot of old flies buzzin' around here tonight.
DOREEN: Well you should be used to that, Ros. There's some hum comin' off you. Talk about the hum on the Humber.
ROS: My God, look at her she's like an old stray dog following us around. Luh.
DOREEN: Listen to who's talking—last of the elephant people.
(Ros bumps Doreen intentionally.)
DOREEN: Sure, I don't believe he's a Portuguese. He must be Dutch, dey always had a t'ing for dykes.
ROS: Oh yeah, look at who's talkin'—Queen of the leather grannies.
(Dancing stops and they lineup for the fight.)
DOREEN: You come over here and say that!
(Ros walks slowly over to Doreen and positions herself nose-to-nose. She speaks slowly and menacingly.)
ROS: Look at who's talkin'—Queen of the leather grannies!
DOREEN: You get out of my face.
(Doreen puts her hand over Ros's face and pushes her away.)
ALBERTINO: No, no, don't fight, don't fight over me.
DOREEN & ROS: (*To Albertino as they shove him aside.*) You shut up.
(Ros frees herself; she lunges at Doreen who gets her in a

headlock and punches her pregnant belly. Doreen looks straight at the audience.)

DOREEN: *(To audience.)* What are you lookin' at?

(Fight. Albertino finds lady in the audience to dance with.)

LACKEY: Doreen, Ros, look at Albertino, look. Doreen, Ros, look, look, look.

(They stop fighting.)

DOREEN: Oh, my God, he'd go with anything, luh.

ROS: Don't you ever go at me like that again.

DOREEN: Well you keep your hands off my buddy, okay? Jesus, you bit me. There's nothing dirtier than the human bite.

(They exit, muttering and arguing, improvised conversation, "Look, you broke my nail, etc.")

ALBERTINO: *(Leading his partner from the audience off toward ship.)* Oh, you're such a good dancer. You come back to the ship with me. I have some brandy.

Scene 7

(On the dockside, near the gangplank.)

JOÃO: You call the *Blue Peter* in Mars. *(March.)*

KAY: Okay, but write to me and tell me when you're leaving Portugal, okay?

JOÃO: You no forget me? You forget me.

KAY: No, I won't forget you. Time will go fast. We'll write letters. I no forget you. Why am I talking like I don't speak English? I speak English.

JOÃO: *(He is unhappy, confused and thinking the worst.)* I don't speak English. You don't speak Portuguese. I no come to St. John's. I no see you no more, I finish. No more fishing.

KAY: *(Consolingly.)* Oh, you know I'll be here.

JOÃO: *(She gives him a photograph.)* Picture for me?

KAY: Oh, yeah. Ronny took it with his Polaroid. It's terrible. I had to pay him two dollars.

JOÃO: Estás muita linda.

KAY: Oh, your address. You never gave me you address.

JOÃO: Number, number for me?

KAY: Number?

JOÃO: I telephone for you Christmas.

KAY: Oh, great. Oh, I'd love it. I can't wait to talk to you on the phone. *(João looks perplexed.)* Oh nothing, it's not important.

(Ship's whistle blows.)

KAY: God, you've got to go. I don't want you to get in trouble with your captain.

JOÃO: No problem. Captain good man.

KAY: I love you.

JOÃO: I love you too.

(They kiss. The ship's whistle blows.)

KAY: João, go on, go on, you have to go. João. (*She runs up gang-plank for a last embrace, then exits.*)

(*From the deck of the ship.*)

CARLOS: Hey, João, you come back to St. John's, hey?

PEDRO: Ela é uma muito linda menina, João. Very nice girl. Fine, very fine.

DOREEN: (*From the wharf.*) Come on you guys. This is the last time in six months. Bebida, bebida. (*Pedro gives her a drink. She toasts.*) To Joaquim, to Manuel, to Carlos, to Pedro, to Alberto, to Albertino, to the whole friggin' bunch of ye—to Portoogal!!!

EVERYONE: Portoogal!!!

(*Enter Ros.*)

DOREEN: Oh my, God. There's Ros. My God, look at the size of her. You won't need a pilot boat. She'll float you right out t'rough the Narrows. Hey Ros, how are ya?

ROS: (*Coming up over the gangplank.*) Where the hell were you? I had to get a taxi out here. I haven't got three dollars to throw away on no taxi. Where the hell were you?

DOREEN: I'm sorry, girl. I forgot. I never got home.

(*Ros shouts to the men.*)

ROS: Any brandy left here or has she drunk it all? Oh look, all me buddies goin' again. What am I gonna do without ye?

(*Pedro gives stuffed toy to Ros.*)

PEDRO: Ros, for the baby. From Carlos, Joaquim, Juan, Manuel, from all of us.

ROS: (*As she kisses them all.*) Oh, isn't that sweet. I adores each and every goddamn one of ye.

(*Doreen and Joaquim stand together. Their goodbye is a separate scene, played simultaneously with Ros's farewells.*)

DOREEN: You never got that bit of carpet laid.

JOAQUIM: No, next year I guess.

DOREEN: Next year, next year. I'm sick to death of hearing about next year.

JOAQUIM: You have my heart now, what more do you want?

DOREEN: (*Lustfully, as she grinds her pelvis into his.*) Do you want me to answer that?

JOAQUIM: We go down below and you could answer that.

DOREEN: Jesus b'y, that's the only answer you ever gave me.

CARLOS: Where's my Coccyx, my little Coccyx?

ROS: She's over in the hospital, b'y, up in traction.

CARLOS: Traction?

ROS: Yeah, she was doin' the bump down to the Stardust, right, b'y? Bump she did and bump she went.

CARLOS: Is she dying?

ROS: No, b'y, she's not dying. She may as well be dying though. She'll be no good to you for a while.

PEDRO: Poor João. Why the long face? Look, we're going home to Portugal. You'll be able to see your mother, and your baby brother, and your girlfriend over there.

ROS: Oh, he's not homesick, luh, and he's not seasick either. He's lovesick and that's the worst of the lot.

JOAQUIM: I have a present for you so you won't forget me.

DOREEN: Jesus, b'y, I wish I could forget you. But what's eight months after eighteen years?

JOAQUIM: Eighteen years?

DOREEN: Yeah, eighteen years.

JOAQUIM: No.

DOREEN: What do you mean, no?

JOAQUIM: No. I'm not coming back. I'm going to retire. I'm not going fishing anymore. The young João take over the fishing now.

DOREEN: That's a lie. You couldn't give this up.

JOAQUIM: Yes, I have to. Rosa wants me home. And next year we act like a family and go on summer holidays.

DOREEN: No kidding? I was thinking about taking a cruise around the world meself.

JOAQUIM: *(Offering money to Doreen.)* Here you take this, hey?

DOREEN: What's this? For services rendered? I'm not a whore.

JOAQUIM: No. Don't you ever, ever say you're a whore. It is for the babies.

(She does not take the money and he sticks it down her bra. They embrace.)

ROS: *(To Pedro who tries to hug her.)* Go away, b'y. Sure, I wouldn't have anything to do with you even if you had a brown paper bag pulled up over your head and were disguised as the unknown turnip. *(To Doreen.)* What's wrong with you, my dear? Look at the face on ya. Christ, you're not at a wake, you're at a party. What's wrong with ya?

DOREEN: Nothin', nothin' a bottle of brandy won't fix.

JOAQUIM: Hey come on, João. Don't be so sad, eh. You're coming back next year. Play a song, eh, to say goodbye to St. John's.

(During the song the final whistle blows, everyone says their last good-byes and Ros and Doreen walk down the gangplank. They turn to wave from the wharf as the men sing "O Mar Enrola na Areia")

> O mar enrola na areia
> Ninguém sabe o que ele diz
> Bate na areia e desmaia
> Porque se sente feliz.
> O mar também é casado, ai,
> O mar também tem filhinhos
> É casado com a areia, ai,
> Os filhos são os peixinhos,
> O mar também é casado, ai,
> O mar também tem mulher
> É casado com a areia, ai
> Bate nela quando quere.

O mar enrola na areia
Ninguém sabe o que ele diz
Bate na areia e desmaia
Porque se sente feliz.

THE END.

Photograph by Jim Winter

The Mummers Troupe

Makin' Time with the Yanks

1981

Collectively written by
Kay Anonsen
Rick Boland
Jane Dingle
Brian Downey
Janis Spence
Paul Steffler
Mary Walsh

Music created and/or arranged by
Paul Steffler

MAKIN' TIME WITH THE YANKS

Makin' Time with the Yanks was first produced by the Mummers Troupe at the LSPU Hall, 10-21 March 1981. Ten days later it was repeated at the St. John's Arts and Culture Centre (31 March to 1 April). Resource Centre for the Arts (RCA) Theatre Company toured the play to the Newfoundland Arts and Culture Centres in 1982; it played in Stephenville (25 January), Corner Brook (26-7 January), Grand Falls (28 January), Gander (29-30 January) and St. John's (4-6 February, 1982). RCA Theatre restaged *Makin' Time with the Yanks* again at the Hall (21 January to 2 February and 5-7 February, 1986) to celebrate the tenth anniversary of the LSPU Hall as a theatre.

Members of the cast who wrote, directed and acted in *Makin' Time with the Yanks* are the following:

Kay Anonsen	May, Vivian, Shirley, Theresa, NCO's date, Operator 1.
Rick Boland	Leo, Stretch, Eddie Lacey, Barry.
Jane Dingle	Laura, Bride, Nellie, Shirley's mother, Operator 2.
Brian Downey	Michael, Tiny, Eddy Reardon, Newfoundlander.
Janis Spence	Agnes, Miss Kent, Irene, Biddy, Loretta.
Paul Steffler	Tom, NCO; music.
Mary Walsh	Director.

Additional credits:

The musical director was **Paul Steffler**. In the 1981 and 1982 productions, the producer was **Rhonda Payne**, lighting design **Derek Butt**, set design **Philip Craig**, and choreography **Cathy Ferri**. In 1986, **Philip Craig**'s set design was redone by **Peter Walker** and **Steve Woodcock**, lighting and technical support **Boo Noseworthy**, choreography **Sandi Blackmore** and costumes **Costume Workshop**. Photographs of the 1981 production are by **Manfred Buchheit**. In the 1982 production **Mary Walsh** replaced **Kay Anonsen** and **Greg Thomey** replaced **Brian Downey**. **Elizabeth Pickard** replaced **Jane Dingle** in the 1986 production.

Production of *Makin' Time with the Yanks* was assisted by the Canada Council, the Newfoundland and Labrador Arts Council and the Government of Newfoundland Cultural Affairs Division. The play was sponsored by Mobil Oil and Abitibi-Price Ltd.

CAST OF CHARACTERS
(In order of appearance.)

AGNES	Agnes Lacey, Laura's mother.
LEO	Leo Lacey, Laura's father.
EDDY	Eddy Lacey, Laura's brother.
MAY	May Lacey, Laura's sister.
LAURA	Laura Lacey (Lol, Lolly), in love with Stretch.
TINY	Stan or Stanley, American soldier in love with Vivian.
STRETCH	Chester or Chet Kowalski, American sailor in love with Laura.
MISS KENT	Supervisor at the Caribou Hut.
VIVIAN	Vivian Doyle, in love with Tiny.
TOM	Lemondrop, American airman in love with Irene.
IRENE	Irene Reardon, cautious girl in love with Tom.
EDDIE	Eddie Reardon, Irene's brother.
BRIDE	Bride Reardon, Irene's mother.
MICHAEL	Michael Reardon, Irene's father.
THERESA	Theresa Oakly, Bride's friend.
BARRY	Barry Hope, host of barn dance.*
TIM	Tim Collins, star of barn dance.*
NELLIE	Nellie Ludlow, torch singer.*
SHIRLEY	Shirley Saunders, child singer.*
SHIRLEY'S MOTHER	A stage mother.
BIDDY	Biddy O'Toole, entertainer.*
OPERATOR 1	Senior Newfoundland Telephone Company operator.
OPERATOR 2	Newfoundland Telephone Company operator.
LORETTA	Friend of Laura.
NEWFOUNDLANDER	Newfoundland movie goer.
NCO	NCO movie goer.
NCO's DATE	Newfoundland woman.

* Non-fictional characters.

MAKIN' TIME WITH THE YANKS

ACT 1

Full cast sing opening number, "Makin' Time with the Yanks."
Makin' time with the Yanks,
On a Saturday night,
Makin' time with the Yanks,
Romance takes flight.
Makin' time with the Yanks,
Down in Bannerman Park.
Is he tall? Is he short?
I can't tell, it's too dark!
    Holy Mother Church says
"Don't dance in Lent."
That's the kind of rule
That's meant to be bent.
The Yanks got the moolah
That's got to be spent,
Stateside is gone
But this berg is sent,
Makin' time with the Yanks
Is great in a tent! Great in a tent!
    Blackouts, blackouts all across the town,
But that won't stop us gettin' around,
Jump in a cab and we're Pepperell bound.
The new USO show and the big band sound,
Makin' time with the Yanks gets my feet off the ground,
Feet off the ground.
    Makin' time with the Yanks,
Dinner at home.
Makin' time with the Yanks,
Watch his hands don't roam.
Makin' time with the Yanks,
Movies down on the base.
What's he bring?
Real French wine, and his cute Yankee face.

Those boys are here making this a safe place,
Camouflage trucks, it's a real arms race,
The Nazis and the Japs will never stand the pace,
And Dad'll get a job working down on the base.
Makin' time with the Yanks,
Puts a smile on my face,
Smile on my face.
Makin' time with the Yanks,
I'm glad they're here.
Makin' time with the Yanks,
Year after year.
Makin' time with the Yanks,
A ninety-nine year lease.
Are there more? Will they come?
Will their jeeps need more grease?
Makin' time with the Yanks,
Shoo doo shoobie doo.
Makin' time with the Yanks,
Shoo doo shoobie doo.
Makin' time with the Yanks,
Shoo doo shoobie doo.
LOVE THOSE YANKS!
(Blackout.)

Scene 1

It is winter 1941 in St. John's Newfoundland. The United States has not entered World War II but has signed a ninety-nine year lease to construct military bases in Newfoundland. On 29 January 1941 the Edmund B. Alexander *landed a large contingent of American servicemen in St. John's. The Lacey living room in St. John's. There is a couch and one chair; there is also a piano facing the wall in a neutral area at downstage right.*

AGNES: Why the hell aren't you overseas, Leo?

LEO: I'm not overseas, Agnes, because the army wouldn't take me. God knows, I went to them on my hands and knees. They wouldn't take me because I broke my back trying to keep your big maw mouth full during the depression.

AGNES: That surprises me, Leo. I would have thought that you would have been recruited with the first wave. I would have thought the Allies would use you now as their secret weapon.

LEO: Agnes, why should I go overseas? Sure, I'm right here in no-man's land now. The Maginot Line goes right down through the living room. *(Pause.)* Where's May?

AGNES: She's out looking for a job.

LEO: My God, she's got two commercial courses. You'd think she could find one job. *(Pause. He burps.)* I'm thinking of leaving Harvey's.

AGNES: My God, Leo, you didn't get fired?

LEO: No, I didn't get fired. I'm just thinking of bettering myself, that's all. Dirty work, coal. I don't see why I should be breaking my back for forty dollars a month. I hear tell when the Yanks get here they're going to be paying big money.

AGNES: Leo, my son, you're a dreamer. You should get down on your hands and knees everyday and thank God and Mr. Harvey that we're not on relief.

LEO: (Sniffing.) What's that you're burning for supper, Agnes? My God, the stomach's burnt off me from breakfast.

AGNES: I'm glad you didn't like it, Leo. The way you shovelled it down you, I thought we'd have to get out the coal chute next.

LEO: I'll tell you what, Agnes. You be Hitler, I'll be Churchill, and we'll call a truce, okay? (Enter Eddy. He clambers all over his mother.) Oh, my God, here comes Mussolini!

EDDY: Mom. Mom. Me old mom...Mom, Mom.

AGNES: Get him off me, Leo! Will you get him off me?

LEO: He's your creation, my darling Agnes, Hitler. Besides, it'll keep you in shape for when the Huns come.

EDDY: It's not the Huns coming, Dad, it's the Y-Y-Y-Yanks!

LEO: What's that, a new trick is it? Stuttering? Listen, we got it made. You got stuttering, your sister got commercial. We got it made. Why don't you go out and get a job? That'd be a good trick. There's your secret weapon for you, Agnes. They'll never be able to break his code!

AGNES: Well, the Yanks won't be getting in the harbour tonight with this storm going on.

LEO: They'll never get in the harbour anyway. Sure, that *Edmund B. Alexander* is as big across the beam as the Newfoundland Hotel.

EDDY: (Beginning to maul his mother again.) Not as big across the beam as me old mom.

AGNES: Leo, get him off me!

(Enter May.)

LEO: (To May.) Close the door. (To Agnes, Eddy and May in turn.) Now you shut up and you shut up and don't you start.

EDDY: Well, did you get your big job today, May? Princess May Lacey, private secretary to nobody.

MAY: What business is it of yours if I get a job or not, you old slacker.

EDDY: I am not a slacker.

LEO: Then why the hell aren't you overseas?

EDDY: Because I got a speech sediment.

MAY: Impediment!

EDDY: But sure, that's half the problem, I can't even say it.

LEO: Well, I suppose it's better than last week when he was going on with his asthmatic attacks. (Eddy wheezes.)

MAY: Well, maybe if you gave your tongue a rest your brain might catch up with it.

EDDY: Look, b'y, you gotta be able to warn the soldiers that the Germans are coming. You know, "Here come the G-G-G-G-Germans." Sure, it'd be all over before I got it out.

MAY: Yah, you'd definitely screw up the war.

(May exits in a flurry.)

LEO: *(Burping which shows severe indigestion.)* My God, what was that we had for breakfast, Agnes? Listen, go get me a little bread soda, will ya?

AGNES: *(To Eddy.)* Will you go and get your father the bread soda? *(He doesn't move.)* What's wrong with you—can't you walk?

(Enter May followed by Laura.)

MAY: *(To Laura.)* No, no, no, no, no, no, no.

LAURA: Please, May, please.

AGNES: What is it now?

LEO: Look, I told you not to start, now didn't I?

AGNES: What is it?

LAURA: I just wants to borrow her coat. I only wants to borrow it just for tonight.

LEO: *(To May.)* Look, you give your sister the coat *(To Laura.)* you shut up *(To Eddy.)* and you stay right where you are because I'm coming over in a minute to give you a bat.

AGNES: Besides which, nobody's getting any coat because nobody's going out over the door.

LEO: Where were you going, anyway?

LAURA: I'm going to the Caribou Hut.

LEO: You're going nowhere, my darling. If you were going anywhere, it would be right through that window now, blackout shutters and all.

(May snickers.)

EDDY: *(To Laura.)* Where you going? Sneaking off to see the soldiers, were ya? And Frank over there getting killed for you.

MAY: Yes, that's a sin for you, my dear.

LAURA: Over in Scotland they treat Frank like they owneded *(Two syllables.)* him and it's a good thing all Newfoundlanders aren't as mealy-mouthed as you, my son. It's a good thing some of us are doing our bit for the war.

EDDY: Oh yah, that's a real sacrifice for you, isn't it wha'? I mean, the way you been looking forward to it all week. You're a real friggin' martyr, aren't ya?

LAURA: You're just jealous because you can't get yourself a girlfriend. At least the soldiers have got a bit of manners.

(Exit Laura.)

EDDY: Yah, and that's more than you've got, s-s-s-sardine breath!

AGNES: Where's May gone now?

MAY: I'm May. Laura's gone out to the kitchen probably trying to think up a new plan to get my coat.

LEO: Agnes, why don't you put on your glasses. You know you're

half blind.
(May snickers.)

AGNES: Well, I must have been half blind to have married you, Leo.
(Enter Laura.)

LAURA: Where's puss? *(To Eddy.)* Did you kill puss?

MAY: No, he didn't kill puss.

EDDY: I never killed puss, Laura.

AGNES: He's bad enough but he's not a cat killer.

LAURA: *(Crying.)* Oh, Dad.
(Family argument ensues. Everyone talks at once for twenty seconds.)

AGNES: I don't know what we got the blackout for, the goddamn Germans can hear us!

LEO: Agnes, can't you talk low and sensible? *(He burps.)* My God, what was that we had for dinner last Sunday? Keeps coming back on me but I can't quite identify it anymore.

AGNES: *(To Eddy.)* Will you go and get your father the bread soda. What are you, a cripple?

MAY: No, he's saving that one for next week.

EDDY: I'm too c-c-c-c-comfortable.

MAY: Oh, I got to get out of here. This place is driving me cracked. I'm going up to Carol-Anne's. She's giving me a home permanent. *(Speaking to Laura as she passes a letter back and forth between her hands.)* Guess what I picked up at the post office today, Lolly-anne?

LAURA: *(Struggling with May over the letter.)* A letter from Frank. Give it to me, May. Give it to me.

LEO: I didn't know that the great shuffling fighter could write.

LAURA: Dad! *(To May.)* Give it to me.

AGNES: Well, we never did see his face, Lol. All he did was shuffle around out back mumbling your name.

EDDY: *(As he exits.)* Yah, he's probably over in Paris right now parlez-vousing with some gorgeous French frail.

LAURA: He's over in Scotland, dolt head.

AGNES: Lolly darling, did he ever say what his intentions were?

LAURA: Mom, if I told you once, I told you a thousand times, we were just keeping company, that's all.

MAY: Oh, I got to go.
(She exits.)

LAURA: Look, I'm going to be late for my first night at the Caribou Hut.

LEO: Didn't I tell you that nobody was going over the doorstep tonight?
(Argument flares up again. Leo points at the girls, then gives up.)

LEO: Oh, sweet sacred heart of...go on, get out. Take your brother with ya.

LAURA: What? I'm going to work. I can't take me brother with me.
(She exits, leaving Leo and Agnes alone on stage.)
AGNES: Leo, why don't the two of us build a house out back where you and I can get a bit of peace and quiet.
LEO: Agnes, the only way that you and I can get a bit of peace and quiet is if we built two houses out back and mine'd have to be in Topsail.

(Blackout.)

Scene 2

(On board the Edmund B. Alexander. Tiny is polishing his shoes and whistling a tune. Stretch enters out of breath.)
TINY: Hey, Chester, where you been? Boy, we got an inspection at sixteen hundred hours. You better get your boots all shined up, or you gonna be on KP for about a month.
STRETCH: Yeah, well, I'll shine my shoes now as soon as they thaw out. I been up on deck unloading supplies while you been all cosy down here in the stateroom.
TINY: Yeah, boy, I don't care if we ever get off this boat. I could stay here forever. It's about as close to heaven as I'm ever goin' to get.
STRETCH: Well, I'd rather be back in Fort Snelling, I tell ya.
TINY: Hey, boy, you never had it so good.
STRETCH: Hey listen, are you going to that dance?
TINY: Stretch, see these feet?
STRETCH: Yeah.
TINY: These feet got wings! These feet almost got drafted into the thirty-second airborne division. *(Snicker.)* Am I goin' to the dance!
STRETCH: Well, I sure am disappointed in this place.
TINY: Is that right. Why's that?
STRETCH: Well, I don't know. I was hoping to get to see a little bit of, ahhh...Eskimo life!
TINY: Boy, I think about the only way you're goin' to get a woman to go with you to that dance is if somebody gives you one.
STRETCH: Why? I mean, I got everything. I got two eyes, two nostrils, two ears, two arms, two hands, two legs and two feet...
(Stretch takes off one shoe and passes it to Tiny.)
TINY: You got it all, Stretch, you got it all. Trouble is, you just don't have enough of it.
STRETCH: *(Speaking sadly.)* Yeah, I know.
(Tiny spit shines Stretch's shoe.)
TINY: Ah, come on now. Stick up for yourself. Look, I'll tell you what I'll do...you give me them three Glen Miller discs you picked up in New York before we shipped out and I'll line you up with the cutest little filly that you ever saw.
STRETCH: I don't want a horse.
TINY: Come on now, Stretch, I know that even a dumb plough jockey from Wagner, South Dakota, cannot be that naive. Don't

insult my intelligence, boy.

STRETCH: Well, I don't know. She'd have to be as cute as a cupie doll for three Glen Miller discs. Those discs mean more to me than just about anything. I got those discs with the five dollars that my daddy put in my pocket when I got on the troop train. I'll tell you what, I'll let you listen to them any time you want.

TINY: No sir, you want to hold the girl of your dreams, I'm goin' to have to hold those records.

STRETCH: Well, I'd like to at least meet her first.

TINY: Nope.

STRETCH: Get to see her anyway?

TINY: Look, boy, I'm goin' to have to put myself out an awful lot, you know. I'll tell you what I'll do. You give me two now and one later. How's that?

STRETCH: One now and two later.

TINY: Boy, for a dumb rube you sure drive a hard bargain.

STRETCH: Tiny.

TINY: Yeah?

STRETCH: (*Pause.*) Do you ever get...

TINY: Ever get what?

STRETCH: Well, you know...scared.

TINY: Scared? Scared of what?

STRETCH: Well, women, girls, frails, you know.

TINY: Hell, no. They're just little gals. What have you got to be scared of?

STRETCH: Well, they're women.

TINY: They're women, that's very good. Yeah, they're women.

STRETCH: But they're different, you know.

TINY: Like the Frenchmen say, vive la difference.

STRETCH: Yeah, I don't know. I'd just like to go up to one and say, "Hi, pretty lady, my name is Stretch, and I sure would like to take you out." How do you do that?

(*He gives Tiny the other shoe.*)

TINY: Well sir. One thing you always got to remember—that's that she's the gal and you're the man, right?

STRETCH: She's the gal and I'm the man! Yeah.

TINY: You *are* the *man*. Say that like that. I *am* the *man*!

STRETCH: I *am* the *man*.

TINY: That's right, that's right. I'm in control.

STRETCH: I'm in control.

TINY: I'm in the driver's seat.

STRETCH: I'm in the driver's seat.

TINY: I'm the man.

STRETCH: I'm the man.

TINY: And she's just a little gal.

STRETCH: And she's just a little gal.

TINY: And her soft white flesh is just all a quiverin' waitin' for me!

STRETCH: What?

Photograph by Manfred Buchheit

TINY: I said, she's just goes nuts at the thought of meetin' you.

STRETCH: Yeah, right.

TINY: Damn right. Yeah! And is she beautiful!

STRETCH: Yeah.

TINY: (*Drawing the mental picture for Stretch.*) She got glistenin' hair.

STRETCH: Yeah.

TINY: Pearly white teeth.

STRETCH: Yeah.

TINY: She got lily white hands.

STRETCH: Yeah, yeah.

TINY: Shapely gams.

STRETCH: Yeah...and little tiny feet?

TINY: And little tiny feet!

STRETCH: Oh, I can't wait. I'm in love. I just love her, Tiny.

TINY: Oh, you lucky dog.

(Tiny gives the shoe back to Stretch.)

STRETCH: (*Looking at his shoes which Tiny has polished.*) Hey, one of them is shinier than the other. That won't do.

TINY: Yeah.

(Blackout.)

Scene 3

(At the Caribou Hut, a social centre for visiting servicemen. There is a table and two chairs. Laura is being sworn in for the first time by the very British Miss Kent. Vivian, an old hand, stands beside Laura and repeats the oath with her.)

MISS KENT: I pledge to work in the Caribou Hut...

LAURA & VIVIAN: I pledge to work in the Caribou Hut...
MISS KENT: Between the hours of six to ten.
LAURA & VIVIAN: Between the hours of six to ten.
MISS KENT: To be on time.
LAURA & VIVIAN: To be on time.
MISS KENT: Wear the uniform.
LAURA & VIVIAN: Wear the uniform.
MISS KENT: And obey my supervisor at all times.
LAURA & VIVIAN: And obey my supervisor at all times.
MISS KENT: Only if I am sick...
LAURA & VIVIAN: Only if I am sick...
MISS KENT: Shall I be absent.
LAURA & VIVIAN: Shall I be absent.
MISS KENT: And then I shall let my supervisor know...
LAURA & VIVIAN: And then I shall let my supervisor know...
MISS KENT: In time to get relief.
LAURA & VIVIAN: In time to get relief.
MISS KENT: Thank you, gels, thank you very much. Now, Viv
here has been with us for over a month and knows the ropes and
she will tell you, Laura, how we women of Newfoundland, in our
own small way, have become a very important part of the war
effort. Laura dear, that's a very nice smock.
LAURA: Oh, thank you, Miss Kent.
MISS KENT: But it's a little loud for in here. We only wear white.
Now, the menu for every meal every day is posted up here, and as
Vivian will tell you, no matter what service the boys are in, they
all get the same portions. That includes the merchant marines.
Now, the menu for today is as follows (*Indicating a "menu
board."*) three sausages...
LAURA & VIVIAN: (*Mimicking her accent.*) Three sausages...
MISS KENT: Two potatoes...
LAURA & VIVIAN: Two potatoes...
MISS KENT: And one egg.
LAURA & VIVIAN: And one egg.
MISS KENT: Thank you, gels. (*Looking away from them.*) Now,
I'm sure that as hostesses of the Caribou Hut you will conduct
yourselves with the utmost propriety.
LAURA: Oh yes, Miss Kent.
MISS KENT: Good. Now carry on, gels, and I do spot checks.
                              (*Exit Miss Kent.*)
VIVIAN: We call her SS Kent. Newfoundland womanhood, ha! We
works down here like Torbay ponies. Look at that, (*She shows
"scars" and "burns" on her arms and legs.*) that was the Jig's
Dinner day. And look at that one, (*Pointing at a burn mark.*) that
was pea soup and cabbage night. And look at these hands. (*Showing her injured hands.*) How are you supposed to sooth the
fevered brows with these hands? We wash the dishes here in lye.
LAURA: In lye?

VIVIAN: And I got no feet left. Sometimes I think I'm just walking around on me ankle bones. Get the bread out of the oven for me, would ya? And mind the cockroaches.

(Laura mimes removing bread. She screams.)

VIVIAN: *(Stomping.)* My dear, you can't kill them. It's just as well to feed them.

LAURA: I really admire you, I want to be just like you...do my best for the boys here.

VIVIAN: Oh, you will, duckie, you will. Oh, wait till you see them. They're really sweet and most of them are perfect gentlemen.

LAURA: Oh, good.

(Enter Tiny and Tom.)

VIVIAN: *(Gasps.)* Yanks! Oh, my God, they're brand new. They're just off the *Edmund B.* Oh, look at the teeth on them!

LAURA: Look at their uniforms!

VIVIAN: Oh, it really makes you feel sorry for the poor old Brits, doesn't it?

LAURA: Do I look okay?

TINY: Boy, I tell ya. I sure am hungry. I could eat myself about a dozen eggs all smothered in chili...

TOM: Well, just hang on there, Stanley. *(Indicating the menu board.)* How about three sausages smothered with one egg?

TINY: *(Seeing the board.)* Oh, damn!

VIVIAN: There's the menu. Three sausages, two potatoes and one egg. *(Pause. She speaks to Tiny who is staring at her.)* Ah, perhaps you'd like something cold—a ham sandwich, maybe?

TOM: *(To Laura.)* I'll have some.

LAURA: *(She starts serving, staring at Tom.)* Okay.

TINY: *(Breaking his fixation.)* Gosh, Ma'am. I'm sorry, I just never expected to see Carol Lombard workin' down here at the Caribou Hut.

VIVIAN: I'm not Carol Lombard.

TINY: You're not?

VIVIAN: No.

TINY: Who are ya?

VIVIAN: Vivian Doyle.

TINY: Vivian Doyle.

(Laura mimes putting sausages on Tom's outstretched plate as she gapes open-mouthed at the Yanks and forgets to stop dishing up sausages until Tom says:)

TOM: Hang on, I can't eat two dozen sausages.

LAURA: Oh, I'm sorry, it's my first night here and everything.

TOM: No, it's okay. You're doing a real fine job and we appreciate it.

LAURA: Here.

TOM: Thank you.

LAURA: Thank you.

TINY: *(Apparently smitten, saying to himself as he and Tom go to* *sit.*) Vivian Doyle. Vivian Doyle. (*He shovels his food onto Tom's plate.*) Here.

TOM: (*To Tiny.*) I can't eat this, come on.

(*Tiny rushes back to Vivian with his tray.*)

TINY: (*Presenting his tray to Vivian for more.*) Gosh, Ma'am. I don't know what's wrong with me—I must have hollow legs. Ah, you workin' right through the night, Ma'am?

VIVIAN: No, our shift finishes at eight.

TINY: Oh, at eight. Yeah, good. Eight o'clock. (*He rushes back to Tom and dumps his food onto Tom's tray again.*) Here.

TOM: Dessert?

VIVIAN: (*To Tiny who is back for food again.*) Hollow arms?

TINY: Ma'am, my name is Stanley, but the boys call me Tiny, and I sure would like to take you out.

VIVIAN: Well, I don't know.

TINY: It's a big formal dance, Ma'am, on board the *Edmund B. Alexander*. Goin' to be chaperons and everything. (*Overly sincere.*) You see, Ma'am, we're here to defend the women of Newfoundland!

VIVIAN: Well, okay.

TINY: Oh, great! Say, you know, if you feel more comfortable bringin' along a friend, by all means do so.

VIVIAN: Okay, I'll see what I can do.

TINY: Ah, yeah...well you see, Ma'am, I sort of have to have a definite answer.

VIVIAN: (*To Laura.*) Do you want to go?

LAURA: Me? Oh, I'd love to go if my mom lets me.

VIVIAN: Okay.

TINY: Great, great. Well, thanks for the three sausages and the two potatoes.

EVERYONE: (*Speaking together.*) And one egg!

Scene 4

(*The Reardon home. Couch and chair. Irene is brushing Vivian's hair. The girls are applying powder and nail polish during this scene.*)

IRENE: Well, I'm not going.

VIVIAN: Well, if you won't go, then she can't go, and if she can't go, then I can't go, and I'm going. (*As Irene pulls her hair.*) Owwww!

IRENE: If you would just sit still for a minute.

VIVIAN: (*Wildly excited.*) Oh, I can't, I can't, I can't, I can't, I can't...He is so divine.

LAURA: What's mine like? What's mine like?

VIVIAN: I don't know, I haven't met him.

LAURA: Oh, wonderful! He's probably the only ugly American on the entire *Edmund B. Alexander*.

VIVIAN: No, I made mine promise yours wouldn't be ugly.

LAURA: Oh, good.

IRENE: Well, I wouldn't go out with a Yank no matter what he looked like. I'd go out with a British officer or a Canadian...

VIVIAN: Oh, I wouldn't go out with a Canadian. They make you feel like you're worth two cents.

LAURA: Yah, they make you feel right inferior.

VIVIAN: Sure, the crowd from Vancouver Island lie like rugs.

IRENE: But sure, at least they got manners. And the British officers are real gentlemen, not like the Yanks.

VIVIAN: Sure, the Yanks are real gentlemen. What do you know about the Yanks anyway?

IRENE: I see them all over town walking around like they own everything. Like they own the whole town.

LAURA: Oh, go away. They're gorgeous!

IRENE: Well, I don't care how gorgeous they are. I got too much integrity to go out with that type.

LAURA: You got to go. Mom says I can only go if you go. I did lend you my dress.

VIVIAN: My dear, this is making history, the *Edmund B.* The least we can do is go and see. We owe it to ourselves, to our grandchildren, to Newfoundland. Oh, I'm going to dance, dance, dance, dance till my feet fall off.

(Vivian dances.)

IRENE: My dear, you're half hysterical. I wouldn't be caught dead on the street with you even, let alone a Yank. Now, do you want me to fix your hair?

VIVIAN: (*Sitting down.*) Oh, yes, fit it, fix it, fix it, fix it. (*Flinging herself back on the couch.*) Do you think I look like Carol Lombard?

IRENE: Yah, sort of a cross between Carol Lombard and the hunchback of Notre Dame. Say now, if the hunchback of Notre Dame and Carol Lombard got married and had a child, you could be that child.

VIVIAN: You know, you can say whatever you like to me tonight, Irene. It rolls right off me because I don't care.

IRENE: My dear, you're cheapening yourself.

LAURA: Oh, take a powder.

VIVIAN: Look they're absolutely gorgeous and that's my final word on it. Those great big shoulders...ohhhh!

IRENE: My dear, that's only padding. Some of them are broader in the shoulders than they are long in the arms.

LAURA: They're elegant. They're more elegant than anything you've ever seen. They're like Greek gods.

IRENE: Elegant! Elegant! With them fur parkas they look like Eskimos, and cigarettes dangling out of the corner of their mouths, and them big old galoshes hanging off them. My dear, it turns my stomach just to look at them.

LAURA: You're boring, Irene.

IRENE: Sticks and stones, Lol. You may call it boring. I just don't want to get into trouble.

LAURA: I don't know where your mind is; thinking you're going to get into trouble when all you're going to do is go to a cotillion on a gorgeous luxury liner—dancing with people who know President Roosevelt.

VIVIAN: Oh, they don't know Roosevelt.

LAURA: Well, that's besides the point. Anyway, they're giving up their lives for God and country.

IRENE: They're not even in the war. That's another reason I wouldn't be caught dead with a Yank.

VIVIAN: Oh, lend me your nail polish, will ya?

VIVIAN & LAURA: (*They sing.*) Somewhere over the rainbow, way up high...

IRENE: I just don't understand you. I don't mind her, but you with Frank over there fighting in them rabbit holes over in France...

VIVIAN: Fox holes!

IRENE: What odds. (*Irene gives Laura a hard look.*) And the first chance you get you runs off with that dough-boy, and Frank really loves you too.

LAURA: Frank wouldn't mind. He'd want me to go. I mean, I'm only going to see the boat. It's a chance of a lifetime. It's, ah, it's ah...

VIVIAN: Historic!

LAURA: Historic.

VIVIAN: (*Falling to the floor.*) What time is it? What time is it? What time is it?

LAURA: Seven-thirty, seven-thirty.

IRENE: Get up, look at ya. You're full of dust. Your seams are all crooked now.

VIVIAN: (*Rising and peering behind her.*) Ahhh, that's not my seam. I don't have any stockings on. It took me three quarters of an hour to draw that on. It's ruined, it's all ruined. I feel so bad I could turn my face to the wall and die.

LAURA: Hold on, I'll get a pencil and fix it. (*She uses an eyebrow pencil to fix Vivian's seam.*)

IRENE: Sure, the Yanks will go out with any old dog.

(*Knocking at door.*)

I'm not going, I'm not going.

VIVIAN: What do you mean—you're all dressed up and you're going. Now come on.

LAURA: Your coat, Irene.

(*Vivian lets Tom in.*)

VIVIAN: Hi.

TOM: Hi. I've come to take you down to the boat.

VIVIAN: Oh! Where's Tiny?

TOM: Oh, he's on board.

(*Tom turns and leads the way off. The girls follow.*)

LAURA: (*Whispering.*) Is he mine? Is he mine?

VIVIAN: (*Whispering.*) I don't know, I haven't met him.

IRENE: Okay, okay. I'm ready.

VIVIAN: Now remember...be interesting!

Scene 5

(*On board the* Edmund B. Alexander. *The stage is cleared for dancing. Tiny leads the girls, who appear to feel out of place, onto the stage.*)

TINY: Well, here we are. Can I take your wraps?

VIVIAN: Oh, yes, thank you. (*Irene clings to her coat.*) Take your coat off, Irene.

(*Irene takes her coat off reluctantly.*)

TINY: My, oh my! What charmin' outfits.

VIVIAN: Thank you.

TINY: Now I know you're Carol Lombard. (*To Laura.*) Stretch has been lookin' forward all week to meetin' you. Sure is a lucky man. Well, can I offer you ladies any manner of refreshment?

LAURA: Well, what have you got?

TINY: Well, for the ladies we got Hawaiian fruit punch, we got Gingerale, we got all manner of fruit juices, we got Coca-Cola...

IRENE: (*Speaking breathlessly.*) Hawaiian fruit punch.

LAURA: Yah, I'll try that too.

VIVIAN: I'll have Gingerale.

TINY: (*Turning to go.*) Gingerale. Okay.

VIVIAN: (*To Tiny. Anxiously.*) Where you going?

TINY: I'm just goin' to look after your wraps and I'll get your refreshments for ya and I'll let the rest of the boys know you're here.

VIVIAN: (*To Tiny.*) Listen, I'll just come with you. (*To Laura and Irene.*) You guys, wait right here for me and I'll be right back. (*To Tiny.*) Listen, Stan, you don't mind if I brought my friend along, do ya? She's a really good sport.

TINY: Oh, no.

(*Tiny and Vivian exit.*)

IRENE: I could just kill Viv for leaving us standing here like this. I knew this dress wasn't going to be good enough.

LAURA: I don't believe this. I couldn't have dreamed it better. You know, the biggest ship I was ever on could fit in this room.

IRENE: I wonder who I'm going to get stuck with.

LAURA: Oh, my God, I'm so nervous. Irene, look at their uniforms.

IRENE: (*Desperation in her voice.*) I don't care. I just want to go home.

LAURA: What? How would you get home? I'm not going home with ya. (*She is enthralled with the table groaning with food.*) Oh, look at the food! Look at that table! It looks like it's gonna bend under the strain. Look.

IRENE: There's enough food on that table to feed all of St. John's. Do you want to eat?

LAURA: No, I'm too nervous.

IRENE: Yah, you know what you're like. You'd get food all over your new dress.

(Tiny and Vivian and Stretch and Tom re-enter.)

LAURA: Oh, Irene, here they come. I wonder which one's mine.

IRENE: *(Still afraid.)* I don't want either one of them. I just want to go home.

LAURA: How would you like it if your brother Kevin was being treated like that over in Scotland? Now straighten up, my dear, and do your bit.

TINY: Well, ah...Laura. I'd like you to meet Chester "Stretch" Kowalski. Stretch here, he's just about the finest man afloat.

LAURA: Hello.

(Stretch nods to Laura; he's too choked up to speak.)

TINY: Yeah! And Irene. I'd like you to meet Tom "Lemondrop" Jefferson.

TOM: Hi, Irene. *(He offers a pack of lemondrop candies.)* Want a lemondrop?

IRENE: What?

TINY: Tom here, he can take off and land faster than an American eagle.

IRENE: *(Baffled.)* What?

TOM: Oh, I'm in the air force.

TINY: *(Not understanding Irene's confusion.)* Air force, yeah.

STRETCH: *(Speaking to Laura in a rush.)* Hi pretty lady my name is Stretch and I sure would like to take you out.

LAURA: Out? Out where? Sure, we just got in.

STRETCH: *(Lost for words. He speaks to Tiny and they confer under the girls' exchange.)* Uh, what do I say now?

IRENE: *(Knowingly, to girls as she moves to leave.)* I knew it. They're fast. My worst fears are confirmed. I'm leaving right now very quickly and very quietly.

VIVIAN: *(Pulling her back.)* No, you're not. We're all in this to-gether.

STRETCH: Why, out on the dance floor, Ma'am. I'd like to take you out on the dance floor. As soon as the band starts.

VIVIAN: Oh my, I'm just having too good a time. I have to warn you though, Stan. Once you get me out on that dance floor, you might not get me off.

TOM: You know, I think we'll have some pretty lively music here tonight. We got a twenty-five piece band on board. You know this is great. We never expected to be on a luxury liner when we reported to New York City. You know, it's too bad they don't let us show you around the rest of the boat, but this is the best part right here.

LAURA: When is the band gonna start?

TINY: The band starts at twenty hundred hours sharp, Ma'am. Would you ladies like to sit down now?

VIVIAN: Oh, no. I simply couldn't possibly sit down. I'd crumple my dress and everything.

LAURA: I'd like to sit down, please.

IRENE: I'd just like to go home.

("Band" enters. It is cardboard cut-outs flown in.
Dance music starts.)

VIVIAN: *(To Tiny.)* Oh, the rumba! I just love the rumba!

TINY: And I love you.

LAURA: *(To Stretch.)* Do you rumba?

STRETCH: Yeah, a little.

LAURA: Either you rumba or you don't, I guess.

TINY: *(To Vivian.)* Well, come on, let's go first anyway.

(Tiny and Vivian start to dance.)

TOM: Can I ask you for this first dance, Irene?

IRENE: Okay.

(Tom and Irene start to dance.)

STRETCH: Well, Laura, would you care to take a turn on the floor?

LAURA: Yes please. *(Stretch and Laura start to dance. The three couples dance positioned as in a triangle. The couple at front and centre speaks, then moves to the next position. Stretch and Laura are currently at front. Laura pauses before speaking.)* Where you from, Stretch?

STRETCH: Wagner.

LAURA: Oh.

STRETCH: That's in South Dakota.

(Laura and Stretch start to dance. Tom and Irene mis-step.)

LAURA: Oh. *(To Irene.)* Step, step, slide.

IRENE: *(To Laura.)* You're mixing me up.

(Tom and Irene.)

IRENE: Let's start again.

TOM: Yeah, okay. My sister taught me to dance.

IRENE: I haven't got any sisters. *(Pause.)* I got brothers. They can't dance. Laura taught me to dance.

TOM: Yeah, well, she done a real find job.

IRENE: Thank you.

(Tiny and Vivian.)

VIVIAN: Oh, dancing, dancing, dancing, dancing, dancing. I could just dance till my feet were bloody stumps.

TINY: *(Taken aback.)* Well, Ma'am. I admire your spirit. I admire you too.

VIVIAN: Oh, Stan, this is my first dance and already I'm having the time of my life.

(Stretch and Laura.)

STRETCH: I'm an able seaman. I mean, I hope to do better, rise up the ladder.

LAURA: You're a good dancer.

STRETCH: Oh, thanks.

LAURA: I like the way you dance.

STRETCH: You're good too.

> *(Vivian laughs with pleasure. Tom and Irene.)*

TOM: Your friend Viv sure is having a good time, eh?

IRENE: Oh yes, she always does. She's a lot of fun.

> *(First dance ends; couples applaud. Jitterbug music starts.*
> *Tiny and Vivian.)*

VIVIAN: Oh, the jitterbug. I just love the jitterbug.

TINY: And I love you.

> *(Tom and Irene.)*

TOM: I'm not very good at this, Irene, but I'm willing to have a try.

> *(Stretch and Laura.)*

STRETCH: Hey, I got this disc in New York (*He looks down, still dancing and thinking that Laura is great.*)...I don't know what I ever saw in tiny feet.

LAURA: What?

STRETCH: Oh, nothin', nothin'.

> *(The three couples jitterbug madly for about three minutes,*
> *doing twirls, jumps, etc. The music ends; the dance stops;*
> *there is silence. Tiny and Vivian are at front.)*

TINY: Havin' fun, Viv?

VIVIAN: Oh, am I ever! I wish Mom was here, she'd really have a ball.

IRENE: (*She is out of breath.*) Tom, Tom the piper's son. (*This is the first spontaneous phrase ever bleated from Irene's mouth. Kay and Laura respond, "Why did she say that? Etc."*)

TOM: What?

IRENE: (*Embarrassed.*) I'm sorry, it doesn't matter.

LAURA: (*To Tom.*) I can't get my breath. I need some fresh air.

> *(Waltz music starts.)*

STRETCH: Do you want to go outside for a little while on deck?

LAURA: (*As she leaves.*) Okay, come on, everyone, let's go up on deck.

> *(Stretch and Laura cross to far stage right. Tiny and Vivian*
> *move centre stage to dance. Light cross fades and the stage*
> *accommodates two separate scenes.)*

VIVIAN: Oh no, they're playing the waltz and I just love the waltz.

TINY: And I love you.

LAURA: I hate the blackout. It makes everything so dismal. So sad and cold.

STRETCH: Well, there's always the moon, Laura. You can't black-out the moon.

> *(They recognize a shared favourite song, "You Can't Blackout*
> *the Moon.")*

LAURA: Do you know that one? I love it, it's one of my favourites.

STRETCH: Hey, you know, this is a lot easier than I thought it was going to be.

LAURA: (*Speaking suspiciously.*) What do you mean by that?

STRETCH: (*Embarrassed and nervous.*) Well, I mean, we just met and we like the same music, and we dance well together, and I just think it's wonderful, and well, I, I was just wondering if you would like to go out with me tomorrow night?

LAURA: Oh Chet, I don't know.

STRETCH: Oh, I didn't mean to be forward or nothing.

LAURA: Oh, you're not being forward, it's just that I'm sort of spoken for. We never really said anything, but Frank went overseas last year to join the Fifty Seventh Regiment, Royal Army. He's over in Sussex right now and...well...I'm kind of waiting for him.

STRETCH: I understand. Well, he's a lucky man, Laura. Well, ah, well, I'd be honoured if we could just be friends.

LAURA: Oh, I'd like that.

(*The couples are walking to indicate the passage of time to the end of the evening. Light cross fades to Tiny and Vivian dancing.*)

TINY: Gosh, Viv. You been so popular all evening. Count myself lucky to have you back in my arms again.

VIVIAN: Well sure, you know I been saving the last waltz for you, Stan.

(*Light cross fades to Tom and Irene dancing.*)

TOM: Sure glad you didn't go home, Irene.

IRENE: I am too, I suppose.

TOM: Maybe you can come down for the next dance we have on board.

IRENE: Maybe. Is Jefferson a Catholic name? (*Tom stops dancing; he looks puzzled.*) It's not your fault. Thomas is a Catholic name.

(*Tiny and Vivian dancing.*)

TINY: So, ah, you're goin' to go down to the personnel office first thing in the morning?

VIVIAN: Yep.

TINY: Well, Jim Grimes is going to be expectin' you. I mentioned your name to him. I'm sure he feels just like I do. You'd be a marvellous addition to the staff down at headquarters.

VIVIAN: Oh, I'd give anything for a job. Oh, Stan, sometimes I feel so lucky to be me, *here, now.*

(*Tom and Irene dancing.*)

TOM: Well, ah, are you a working girl, Irene?

IRENE: No, but I'd like to be though. I have my name in at several places. I want to be a telephone operator.

TOM: Your voice is much too pretty for that.

IRENE: Thanks.

(*The dance comes to an end.*)

IRENE: I have to go home now. Could you get my wrap, please?

TOM: Yes, certainly and I'll call a cab if you're in a hurry.

IRENE: Yes, please.

(The boys exit to fetch wraps and Irene and Vivian wait.)

VIVIAN: Oh, Irene, didn't you just have a ball?

IRENE: Yes, but we have to go home now. Where's Lol? Lol!

*(Laura joins Irene and Vivian, the girls move off and
the boys gather.)*

TINY: Well, Stretch?

STRETCH: Well, I don't know. She's a great dancer, likes the same
kind of music I like. She's already spoken for, but I don't care. I
like her anyway.

TOM: *(To Tiny.)* Well, you looked like you were having a lot of fun
going across the dance floor.

TINY: Oh, she's a lot of fun. What about you?

TOM: Oh, I really like Irene. She's a nice, quiet, home-loving girl
but I never danced with anyone else all night long.

TINY: *(To Stretch.)* Now, don't forget those three records now.

(The boys move off.)

VIVIAN: Oh, I simply cannot possibly believe what a wonderful
time I had this evening. I think I danced with all one thousand of
them.

IRENE: You know, Tom was a real gentleman.

LAURA: Chet is sweet. He calls me Laura. You know, I told him
about Frank and everything, and he doesn't care. He just wants
to be my friend.

IRENE: Oh, that's nice!

*(Irene and Vivian exit. The lights change and Laura moves
nearer the piano to sing. The lights fade to a single spot.)*

LAURA: *(Sings.)*

> You never said, "Wait for me,"
> But I knew by the tear in your eye,
> That a picture of me would be next to your heart,
> And our love would never die.
> The clock in the hall would tick off the hours,
> Till you're safe in my arms again.
> But, darling, a letter, just a word from your heart
> Will keep our love strong till then.
>   You never said, "Wait for me,"
> As you climbed on that midnight train.
> How I hoped, how I prayed, that you'd come home to me
> To a cottage in a country lane.
> Oh, darling, it's hard to stay home alone,
> Waiting till God knows when,
> So write me a letter and send all your love,
> 'Cause this town is crawling with men.

(Light fades.)

Scene 6

(The Reardon home. Couch and chair. The family is on their knees saying the rosary using rosary beads.)

EDDIE: *(Reciting as fast as possible.)*
    Hail, Mary, full of grace,
    The Lord is with thee.
    Blessed art thou amongst women,
    And blessed is the fruit of thy womb, Jesus.

FAMILY: *(Family responds.)*
    Holy Mary, mother of God,
    Pray for us sinners,
    Now and at the hour of our death. Amen.

EDDIE: Hail, Mary, full of grace,
    The Lord is with thee.
    Blessed art thou amongst women,
    And blessed is the fruit of thy womb, Jesus.

FAMILY: *(Family responds.)*
    Holy Mary, mother of God,
    Pray for us sinners,
    Now and at the hour of our death. Amen.

EDDIE: Glory be to the Father,
    And to the Son,
    And to the Holy Ghost.
                 (Enter Bride.)

FAMILY: As it was in the beginning
    Is now and ever shall be,
    World without end. Amen.

IRENE: Hail, Holy Queen, Mother of Mercy, hail our life...

BRIDE: Irene, Irene! If you're going to hail the Holy Queen, darling, I'd suggest we crucify our Lord first. The fifth sorrowful mystery...

                  (Pause.)

MICHAEL: Edward, come on.

EDDIE: The fifth sorrowful mystery, the crucifixion and death of our Lord.

FAMILY: Our Father, who art in heaven, hallowed be Thy name,
    Thy kingdom come, Thy will be done...

(There is a knock at the door which Irene rises to answer. Eddie stops. It is Tom and Vivian.)

BRIDE: Irene, get back here! *(Trying to get Eddie to resume.)* Edward.

EDDIE: I'm not saying anymore till she comes back.

BRIDE: Edward!

          (Eddie resumes "Our Father...".)

IRENE: *(Whispering to Tom.)* They don't know about the dance. Don't say a word. *(Tom nods in agreement.)* Come on.

(Vivian kneels and beckons Tom to follow; as a non-Catholic,

he's confused.)

EDDIE: Hail, Mary...(*He sees Tom.*) Yanks!

VIVIAN: Tom, this is Mr. and Mrs. Reardon.

IRENE: (*To Tom.*) This is Eddie, my brother. (*To her parents.*) And this is Tom off the *Edmund B.*

EDDIE: (*To Tom.*) The *Edmund B. Alexander?*

TOM: Yeah, that's right.

BRIDE: (*With a stern look.*) Edward, come on. Edward!

EDDIE: I'm finished. (*Bride gives him a stern look.*)

> Hail, Mary, full of grace,
> The Lord is with thee.
> Blessed art thou amongst women,
> And blessed is the fruit of thy womb, Jesus.

FAMILY: (*Family responds.*)

> Holy Mary, mother of God,
> Pray for us sinners,
> Now and at the hour of our death. Amen.

EDDIE:
> As it was in the beginning,
> Is now and ever shall be,
> World without end. Amen.

BRIDE: Hail, Holy Queen, Mother of Mercy...

IRENE: Mom, please...

BRIDE: (*Angry.*) In the name of the Father,
> The Son and the Holy Ghost. Amen.
> *(They all rise from their knees.)*

EDDIE: Look, me knees are all bent up. I can't get up.
> *(He does a Groucho Marx imitation.)*

BRIDE: (*To Eddie.*) You'll be laughing on the other side of your face if the wind changes.

MICHAEL: Well, ah, Tom is it? Have a seat, Tom.

TOM: Thank you.

BRIDE: Where are you from, Tom?

TOM: I'm from Pennsylvania, Ma'am.

BRIDE: Oh, Pennsylvania, that's nice for you. You know, my cousin's first wife was from Pennsylvania. Yah, that was a long time ago now. What was her name? She had the most peculiar name.

EDDIE: She's some big, isn't she?

BRIDE: No, she was a surprisingly small woman as I remember. She was almost a midget.

EDDIE: No, Mom. The *Edmund B. Alexander.* (*To Tom.*) She got guns on her, hasn't she?

TOM: Yep, that's right, sonny.

EDDIE: She's not a warship though, is she?

TOM: No she's a troop ship.

EDDIE: I knew dat. I got a brother in the war. Yah. He's in the army—that's the Royal Air Force. He's overseas now. Probably bombing Germany right now.

TOM: Well, you must be real proud of him.

EDDIE: Yah.

MICHAEL: (*Trying to get it right.*) Tom—is it Tom? Tom...Tom. *Is* it Tom?...

TOM: Yes, sir.

MICHAEL: Tom, I, I, I was reading the other day where the Huns are driving right into Egypt now.

TOM: That's right, sir.

MICHAEL: Yah, yah, yah. Tom, you know, I was wondering when are you boys going to be joining our fellas in the defence of the free world?

TOM: Well, you see, ah...any time they give us the word, we'd be in there. You know, we're just following orders.

MICHAEL: Ah yes, I understand, sure. You know, I don't understand your President's reluctance in joining his allies, you know.

TOM: Well, sir, you got to understand our country's isolation policy. It seems that the American people aren't interested in joining a bloody conflict in Europe at this present time.

BRIDE: You know, I'm sure our Kevin didn't have a burning desire to join in the conflict, but he knew where his duty lay.

MICHAEL: Now, Bride, now, Bride. I'm sure this young fella enlisted just like our young Kevin, you know.

TOM: That's right.

BRIDE: (*To Irene.*) Where are you going, dressed like that?

IRENE: Ah, we're just going out for a walk and then we're going up to Imelda's.

BRIDE: What's that you've got on your mouth, young lady?
  (*Bride starts to scrub off Irene's lipstick. Everyone stands.*)

IRENE: Oh! Now, Mom, please! Ah, Mom, don't. Oh, Mom, please.

BRIDE: Why have you got your lips painted up if you're just going for a walk?

EDDIE: (*Speaking loudly in a background voice, trying to crucify Irene to their parents.*) She's going to the dance on the *Edmund B. Alexander*.

IRENE: I was only trying it on. You got most of it rubbed off now anyway.

BRIDE: Look at me. Where are you going?

EDDIE: (*Speaking as background voice.*) She's going to the dance on the *Edmund B. Alexander*.

IRENE: We're just going out for a walk. I told you.

EDDIE: (*Background voice.*) She's going to the dance on the *Edmund B. Alexander*.

BRIDE: You're not going to that dance on that American troop ship, are you?

IRENE: No, Mom.

BRIDE: If I thought a daughter of mine was going to a dance in the holy season of Lent I don't know what I would do.

MICHAEL: Bride, Bride. Now there's no need to go on. Now, young lady, where are you going?

EDDIE: (*Background voice chanting.*) I know where they're going, I know where they're going.

IRENE: We're just going for a walk, I told ya. Tom is thousands of miles away from home and he just needs someone to show him around.

MICHAEL & BRIDE: (*To Eddie's voice.*) Well, where are they going?

EDDIE: (*Taken aback by the attention.*) Wherever they said they're going, I guess.

BRIDE: Well, it's on your immortal soul, Irene. If you're lying to me you're just compounding the sin.

IRENE: I'm not lying. Come on, Tom, come on, Viv. Let's go.

TOM: (*Rising to leave.*) Okay.

BRIDE: What time will you be home?

TOM: What time would you like us to be home. Is there a Lenten curfew imposed?

BRIDE: Of course not. Ten o'clock will be fine.

TOM: Yep, we'll be back at ten. Yep, okay.

VIVIAN: Come on, let's go. Goodnight, Mr. and Mrs. Reardon.
                    (Michael exits.)

IRENE: Yah, goodnight.

EDDIE: (*Speaking slyly to Irene.*) Have a good time at the dance.
          (Bride and Eddie exit. Irene, Vivian and Tom start to leave.)

IRENE: It's no good. I just can't go. I feel too bad.

VIVIAN: Why?

IRENE: I can see my milk bottle turning black right now.

TOM: What does that mean?

IRENE: It's a mortal sin to dance in Lent.

VIVIAN: But we're doing it for them, when it comes right down to it. It's sort of like one of them corporal acts of mercy, right?

IRENE: Oh, it's no good. I just feel too bad. I just can't go.

VIVIAN: All right. If we just go and we don't dance and we don't eat anything, we'll just be there, right?

IRENE: What's the sense of going if you can't dance?

TOM: Well, maybe if you go and you dance but you don't enjoy it, God would be more lenient.

IRENE: It doesn't work that way, Tom.

VIVIAN: Well sure, look. You don't know what God is thinking. I mean, if He doesn't mind 'em dying in Lent, why would He mind us dancing with 'em in Lent?

IRENE: (*As she, Tom and Vivian exit.*) You're gonna be struck down dead talking like that, my dear. I got fourteen more novenas under my belt.

Scene 7

(Night-time in a tent in the military camp a couple of months later. The boys are in sleeping bags. Tiny has a bottle of Jack Daniels bourbon.)

BOYS: *(Singing.)* "From the halls of Montezuma, to the shores of Tripoli..."

STRETCH: Boy, you ain't ever gonna make it as a leatherneck.

TINY: *(Laughing.)* I don't think we're ever goin' to make it to the marine choir.

TOM: *(Entering.)* Whoo, it's cold out there.

STRETCH: Well, why don't you close the flap then and don't let the cold air in here.

TOM: You'd say it was the end of January, not the end of May. This camp's no Garden of Eden.

TINY: Yeah. You know the last two weeks have been the coldest, I said the coldest and the worst two weeks of my entire life.

STRETCH: I swear there were tears in my eyes when I saw that *Edmund B. Alexander* pulling out of the Narrows leaving us here in tent city.

TOM: Yeah, yeah.

STRETCH: Hey listen, you got any more of that sour mash left?

TINY: Yeah, I got a bit.

STRETCH: Well, could you just pour a little bit down my throat?

TINY: What the hell is wrong with you? Here, take it.
(Passes around the bottle of Jack Daniels.)

STRETCH: Well, I just didn't want to take my hand out of the sleeping bag.

TOM: Yeah, pass that thing around.

TINY: You know, we oughta to get ourselves paralysed drunk and forget about this post.

STRETCH: Yeah. *(He takes a drink.)* I can feel it now. Creeping down my hands into my fingertips.

TOM: Say, did you hear "Fireside Chat" Sunday on the radio? Sounds like we're getting mighty close to war, don't it?

TINY: Well, there ain't gonna be too many people very happy about that, I'll tell ya. Now, I for one don't wanna get my head blown off in some European country for a bunch of people...why, they haven't even paid America back for the last war.

TOM: Yeah, but there's no sense talking isolation anymore. I mean Roosevelt's got Churchill on his back. We've had a peace time draft for six months. Let's face it, boys. It's only a matter of time and we're gonna be in there.

TINY: Well, hell, it's not us being attacked.

STRETCH: I don't see where the war's apt to getting better. It's only getting worse. We're in no better position for waiting.

TOM: I say stop them now while they're over there before they get over here.

(Pause.)

STRETCH: You know what I miss the most?

TINY: What do you miss the most?

STRETCH: A real bed.

TINY: A real bed, yeah.

STRETCH: Yeah, you know, feather mattress, feather pillow.

TINY: Yeah.

TOM: I miss the Fridgidaire.

TINY: Frigid air? Hell, look around you. You're sittin' right inside it.

TOM: I'm talking about the contents.

TINY: Oh yeah, you like real food.

STRETCH: What was that they served us up for dinner tonight— chipped beef on toast?

ALL: *(In unison.)* Shit on a shingle!

TOM: Yeah, well, I like home, I like being at home.

TINY: Now don't get talkin' like that. You're just gonna go get everybody depressed. Only thing I really miss is the warm weather.

STRETCH: Yeah. Back home they got all the planting done now. Skies right big and bright...

TINY: And warm. Playin' baseball...short sleeves...swimmin'. All them pretty city girls sashayin' up and down the street in them thin summer dresses.

TOM: Yeah, you know the peach blossoms will be all gone by now...I wonder who the peach blossom queen was this year?

(Pause.)

STRETCH: *(Resolved.)* Well, lights out, boys!

TOM: Yep.

(The lights go out.)

TINY: Yeah! We better turn in or we'll never get up for reveille.

TOM: Hey, who's gonna win the pennant this year, boys? The Dodgers?

TINY: The Yankies.

STRETCH: I'll put money on that.

TINY: Well, I'll take it.

STRETCH: Well, you ain't gonna get it.

Scene 8

(The Reardon home.)

EDDIE: *(Imitating an airplane followed by machine gun fire.)* Yeeooww yeeooww rat-tat-tat-tat...

(Enter Bride.)

BRIDE: What in the name of God are you doing, Eddie?

EDDIE: Formation hands, Mom. Watch, I'm Kevin, right? I'm taking off on the coast of Britain. Going out over the Channel protecting Britain, Mom. Yeeooww. Then I sees three Messerschmidts...Yeeooww, rat-tat-tat-tat...yeeooww, rat-tat-tat-tat...yeeooww, rat-tat-tat-tat. They got him, Mom. Put-put-put...flying home on a wing and a prayer.

BRIDE: (*Worried about Kevin's safety she smacks Eddie.*) Eddie! Oh, Eddie, I'm sorry.

EDDIE: Mom!

BRIDE: Mom's little pet rabbit. I'm sorry.

(Enter Michael.)

MICHAEL: What is going on in here? I don't get home from work until six, I got a civil defence meeting at eight o'clock. All I need is a little peace and quiet. Is that too much to ask for?

BRIDE: It's nothing, Michael. I'm just trying to finish the band on Kevin's sweater so I can get it sent off in me Christmas parcel.

(Bride has a big basket with knitting needles and lots of wool.)

MICHAEL: Yah, well, it doesn't look like it's going to be much of a Christmas for anybody, the way things are going.

EDDIE: Kevin might be home for Christmas, sure.

BRIDE: All we can do is hope and pray.

(Enter Irene.)

IRENE: Oh, Eddie, you know Kevin's not coming home for Christmas. Mom, the dishes are done. Tom's coming over.

BRIDE: Oh, good. Therese is coming over and we're going to finish off the Women's Patriotic Association knitting. It should be a nice evening, just the five of us.

EDDIE: I hope you're not including me in that five. I got work to do. I got an ARP meeting tonight.

MICHAEL: Yah, and if you're going to continue being an Air Raid Patrol messenger, then you're going to have to start being a little more punctual, my son.

EDDIE: I am not a messenger boy. I am an Air Raid Patrol dispatcher.

MICHAEL: (*Putting on his overcoat.*) All right, Mr. Dispatcher. Go get your coat and get mine too. And get your history books, you got an exam coming up.

(Eddie fetches his books and coat.)

IRENE: Mom, Tom and I are going out tonight.

MICHAEL: Well, you don't stay home much anymore, do you, Irene?

IRENE: I was home last night.

BRIDE: You're going out too much, my dear, it's starting to tell on you. Where are you going tonight?

IRENE: We're going up to the K of C to see the barn dance. Tom has been here for a year and a half now and he still thinks it's broadcast out of a barn.

BRIDE: You won't be late now, will you?

IRENE: No, I won't be late.

MICHAEL: Come on, Edward.

(As Michael and Eddie exit, they meet Theresa entering.)

THERESA: Oh hello, Michael. Lovely evening, isn't it? It's right Christmassy, but, you know, I miss the lights.

MICHAEL: Yes Theresa, yes, yes indeed.

EDDIE: (*Speaking importantly.*) Mrs. Oakly, could I have a word with you?

THERESA: Oh certainly, Eddie.

MICHAEL: Come on, Eddie, come on.

EDDIE: In a minute, Dad.

MICHAEL: Well, don't dilly-dally. Good evening, Theresa.

THERESA: Good evening.

(Michael exits.)

EDDIE: Mrs. Oakly, you're gonna have to be more careful.

THERESA: More careful, Eddie?

EDDIE: Yes, Mrs. Oakly. The other night when I was walking by your place, I noticed a crack of light coming out of your attic window. You're gonna have to get that barred up or I'm gonna have to tell Dad to get the Air Raid warden.

THERESA: (*Speaking icily.*) You're certainly doing your part, aren't you Eddie? Don't wear yourself out now.

EDDIE: Thank you, Mrs. Oakly. (*Pause.*) Carry on.

THERESA: Thank you, Eddie!

(Eddie exits. Theresa continues into the living room.)

IRENE: Hello, Mrs. Oakly.

BRIDE: (*To Theresa.*) Look, I'm trying to finish the band on Kevin's sweater, girl, but look, the wool's a different dye lot.

THERESA: Oh, that's too bad, Bride, but you know, you won't notice that.

BRIDE: No, I suppose.

THERESA: Hello, Irene, how are you?

IRENE: Fine thank you, Mrs. Oakly.

THERESA: Have you got yourself that permanent job yet?

IRENE: No, but the Royal Stores is taking me on part time for Christmas and I still got my name in to the Telephone Company.

THERESA: Oh, that's grand for you.

(Knocking at door.)

IRENE: Oh, that's Tom.

BRIDE: You haven't met Tom yet, have you, Therese?

THERESA: No.

BRIDE: No? He's an American, you know. But he's very nice. Irene's been keeping time with him for almost over a year now.

IRENE: (*Whispering to Tom.*) Listen, don't tell her we're going out to the Bucket of Blood, okay?

TOM: What?

IRENE: She'd never let me got to a place like the Bella Vista. I told her we were going to the K of C, okay? (*Tom nods his agreement.*)

BRIDE: Tom, Tom, come in and meet Mrs. Oakly.

THERESA: How do you do, Tom.

TOM: How do you do, Mrs. Oakly. Hi, Mom, where's Pop?

BRIDE: Oh, Mike and Eddie are up to an Air Raid Patrol meeting.

TOM: I brought something for you. Look, dark chocolate—your favourite.

(He gives her a box of dark chocolates.)

BRIDE: Oh my, how sweet.

TOM: It's nothing.

IRENE: Come on, Tom. Let's go.

BRIDE: You won't be late, Irene?

IRENE: No, I won't. Goodnight, Mom. Goodnight, Mrs. Oakly.

THERESA: Goodnight, Irene, goodnight, Tom.

TOM: Goodnight, Mrs. Oakly, have a nice night.

(Tom and Irene exit.)

THERESA: Calls you Mom and Pop? Isn't that a bit forward, Bride?

BRIDE: Therese girl, it took me almost a year to get used to it but you know, I don't care anymore.

THERESA: What are you doing?

BRIDE: Oh, my socks. I'm hoping when this war is over I never have to see another sock.

THERESA: How many is that now?

BRIDE: This is my one-hundred-and-fifty-third bundle for Britain!

(Blackout.)

Scene 9

(Barn dance at the Knights of Columbus hostel. 12 December 1942. There are microphones for Barry Hope and Tim Collins. They are wearing straw cowboy hats. Barry is working the audience.)

BARRY: *(Speaking in an ad lib fashion.)* Good evening, ladies and gentlemen. Now, we'll be starting our show very soon but first I'd like to have a couple of words with you. Lloyd, could you bring up the house lights just a little here?

(House lights come up.)

Now, I want you all to remember that you are a very important part of the barn dance. Now, by your applause and by your laughter, you become as important a part as anyone up here on stage. If you want to laugh at any jokes, if you find them funny, well, just go ahead and laugh. *(Laughter.)* There you go. Yes, just like that. And if you want to sing along with any of the songs we sing, if you know any of them, you just sing loud and hearty and they'll hear you all over St. John's because we broadcast all over St. John's, right around Conception Bay South and all the way down the southern shore, right from Pouch Cove right down to Trepassey.

Now, ah, we have a big crowd here tonight at the K of C hostel, don't we? We call this the "Hayloft" in our barn dance. Is there anybody here in the audience tonight from out of town? Anybody? (*Pause.*) What? no baymen in the audience! Perhaps there are some but they're pretending to be townies. I hate them when they do that, don't you? But I can't really imagine why a bayman would pretend he was being a townie. Nobody from out of town? Nobody. (*Appearing to single out an individual.*) Now don't tell me you're not a bayman? You are a bayman, aren't ya? You're a Doyle. King's Cove. (*To audience.*) I knows him.

Anyway now, we'll be starting very soon and we'll be starting our broadcast in about fifteen seconds. I want you to count down with me, if you could, from ten on down to one. That's ten, nine, eight, seven, six, five, four, three, two, one...like that, and then when we get to one I want a big applause because then we'll start our broadcast, okay? Here we go now...ten...

AUDIENCE: Nine, eight...

BARRY: I can't hear ya!

AUDIENCE: Seven, six, five...

BARRY: I can't hear ya at all!

AUDIENCE: Four, three, two, one.

(Applause. House lights fade. Barry, Tim, and audience sing the barn dance theme song, "If You're Irish Come into the Parlour."

BARRY: (*Speaking in his radio voice.*) Good evening, ladies and gentlemen. This is your host, Barry Hope, bringing you another barn dance from the old Hayloft at the K of C hostel. We have a galaxy of stars for you, and here to tell you all about them is himself, the star of the barn dance—Uncle Tim Collins.

(Applause.)

TIM: Thank you, thank you, thank you, Barry. Thank you, ladies and gentlemen. Thank you, thank you, thank you. Wonderful, wonderful. Yes, push the old stove back in the corner, roll up the carpet and get ready for the barn dance, and we do have a galaxy of stars for you tonight. They're so bright that the Air Raid wardens are worried for the blackout. Yes, we've got the vivacious, and exciting, Nellie Ludlow right here tonight. Yes, indeed we do. We've got with us little Shirley Saunders, the belle of Bannerman Park. And, of course, your favourite, my favourite too, Miss Biddy O'Toole. Wonderful, wonderful, wonderful. And later on in the evening, as a special treat we're going to have the country and western stylings of Hayford Fong, the Singing Chinee. And not to forget our own barn dance crowd, let's have a big hand for the band, ladies and gentlemen. Come on!

(Tim sings "I've Got Spurs That Jingle Jangle Jingle" as he and Barry mime riding horses around the stage. Barry exits.)

Thank you, thank you, thank you. The barn dance is brought to you tonight by our consolidated sponsors, Chalker's Meats and Hams and Henley's Mattresses. Awake when you buy them, asleep when you try them! And now, ladies and gentlemen, I

want you to give our warm welcome to the barn dance microphone, the vivacious, the exciting Miss Nellie Ludlow.
(Enter Nellie. Applause. She sings in a very robust voice, à la Sophie Tucker, "It's a Sin to Tell a Lie.")

TIM: Wonderful, Nellie, wonderful. Wasn't that wonderful? Yes, indeed it was. And now, a song from the barn dance crowd.

(Barry enters carrying Carmen Miranda fruit hats for the men. They sing to the tune of "Rum and Coca-Cola" by the McGuire Sisters.)

If you ever go down to Newfoundland,
We make you feel so very grand.
If you ever go trouting on Salmonier Line,
Guarantee you one real good fine time.
Drinking Screech and Coca-Cola,
Gonna make you holla.
Both sister and brother,
Working for the Yankee dollar.

In Newfoundland, I make it clear
The situation is mighty queer,
Package from the PX up your sleeve,
Make every day like Christmas Eve.
Drinking Screech and Coca-Cola,
Gonna make you holla.
Both sister and brother,
Working for the Yankee dollar.
Working for the Yankee dollar.

(Applause. The men put on straw cowboy hats again.)

TIM: Wonderful, wonderful. Thank you, ladies and gentlemen. God love you, God love you. And now, a very special treat, and here to tell you all about it is your host, Barry Hope.

BARRY: Ladies and gentlemen. She is as cute as a button. She has a voice like a bird, she's the darling of the forces, a big welcome for little Sheila Saunders...*(Her mother's voice yells "Shirley" from the wings.)*

BARRY: ...little Shirley Saunders, I'm sorry!

(Enter Shirley. She is played by an adult crouching down, wearing a full crinoline dress.)

BARRY: Now Shirley, you're such a little girl. Tell me, how many years have you been singing?

SHIRLEY: Four years.

BARRY: About four years. And what's your favourite song?

SHIRLEY: "Cow Town Boogie."

BARRY: And what song are you going to sing for us tonight?

SHIRLEY: My mother's favourite song, "The White Cliffs of Dover."

BARRY: Okay. Here she is, little Shirley Saunders.

SHIRLEY: I'm singing this song...*(She looks at her mother who stands exposed in the wings and prompts her.)*...because it reminds me of all the boys fighting in the war.

(Shirley sings "The White Cliffs of Dover." Throughout the song, which she mangles, she is coached by her mother who calls from the wings, instructions such as "Heart, Shirley, heart." "Hands, Shirley, hands." "Smile, Shirley, smile." "Heart, smile.")

BARRY: Thank you very much, Shirley. Wasn't that amazing, ladies and gentlemen, wasn't that amazing? And now, some even bigger things in store for you, and here he is to tell you about them, Uncle Tim.

TIM: Thank you very much, Barry. Now, ladies and gentlemen. If I was to say to ya, that we're gonna be bringing on your very favourite right now, who would ya think of? You're right, Biddy O'Toole, and here she is, Biddy O'Toole.

(Piano vamp music begins and plays softly as background to Biddy who runs on stage.)

BIDDY: Good evening, ladies and gentlemen. It's wonderful to see your lovely smiling faces here tonight, especially the boys in uniform. My boys. Are ya my boys? *(She milks the audience.)*

(Yeeahh!)

I can't hear that. Are ya my boys?

(Yyyeeeahhh!!)

That's right, of course you're my boys. And who have we got here tonight? Hello, darlin', and what's your name, my honey? Don't be shy. What's that? Don Jones. My God, Corporal Don Jones. Well darlin', I'll be waitin' for ya when ya come home. And I bet he's somethin' worth waitin' for too, isn't he, missus? And who have we got over here? Let's have a look. Let's find someone big enough for me to sit on. There you go. Get your hand out of there, you old frigger. Now, let me tell you somethin' that happened to me the other day.

(Sings.)   The landlord came along the other day for his rent,
    And I gave him the penny I had.
    And how could he ever expect me to pay,
    When the times they were so very bad?
    But he wasn't content without getting his rent,
    He shook his old head with a frown.
    Said he, "I take ha'pence and put up the rent."
    Do you want your old lobby washed down?
    Do you want your old lobby washed down, landlord?
    Do you want your old lobby washed down?
    Said he, "I'll take ha'pence and put up your rent."
    Do you want your old lobby washed down?

(The lights cross fade. In the Reardon home, Bride and Theresa are listening to the radio program from the K of C hostel. Biddy's song is coming through on the radio.)

BRIDE: She's a grand woman, isn't she?

THERESA: Oh, she's a grand old girl. Now what was it she was saying last week? Now, oh my, I had to laugh. Oh, I can't remember now, but I had to laugh.

(Biddy's voice continues singing, "Do you want your old lobby washed down? Do you want your old lobby washed down?" Suddenly loud crackling noises are heard.)

BARRY: *(His voice coming through the radio.)* Fire! Fire! Please, everybody, don't panic. Please remain calm. Fire! Keep quiet, for God's sake. Keep quiet!

(The radio crackles and goes dead.)

BRIDE: What's going on, Therese?

THERESA: Oh, it must be the radio, Bride.

BRIDE: No, no, it's not the radio.

THERESA: It must be the radio, Bride. The lines must be down.

BRIDE: Oh, Sacred Heart of Jesus, Irene and Tom are down at the K of C hall!

THERESA: Now Bride, there's no sense gettin' worried till we know what's going on.

BRIDE: Oh, God forgive me, Therese. I couldn't stand it now if anything happened, what with Kevin overseas, it would just be too much. Me nerves just couldn't take it. *(Irene and Tom enter.)* Oh, thank God, Irene!

(They all freeze.)

RADIO ANNOUNCER: *(Recorded voice.)* A few minutes after eleven o'clock on Saturday night, the blackout of St. John's was suddenly and startlingly dispelled by an immense column of flames shooting skywards from the Knights of Columbus hostel on Harvey Road. It was not seen by many, since those in their houses were sitting behind windows screened to prevent a glimmer of light from escaping, while a few were attempting to grope their way through the blackened city over streets covered with ice, and with the thermometer registering twenty degrees of frost.

The work of searching the ruins of the K of C for victims, which began almost before the fire was quenched on Saturday night, was continued until this afternoon when it was certain that no more bodies were to be found. It is estimated that at least five hundred persons were in the building at the time of the outbreak, most of them in the auditorium. Even now, the total death toll cannot be given exactly; but, including four who succumbed in hospital, the known dead now total ninety-nine. The survivors reached safety by bursting down the doors and smashing through the blackened out windows. The heaped up masses of charred remains by the exits are the only too grim and conclusive truth that, as the result of a mass panic, the unfortunate people died in their rush to safety...

ACT 2
Scene 1

*(Telephone Company switchboard. Operator 1 and Irene are
seated facing the audience, miming switchboard.)*

Photograph by Manfred Buchheit

IRENE: Number please.

OPERATOR 1: Number please.

IRENE: I'm sorry, sir, that line is busy. Would you care to hold for
a minute?

OPERATOR 1: Number please.

*(Enter Operator 2. She dons her headset and takes her place at
the keyboard.)*

OPERATOR 2: Oh, my God. It's a wonder I made it in tonight! I
was ice dancing up at the Prince's rink. Mom made me this
luscious little rust and green velveteen costume: but, my dear,
the legs nearly froze off me!

OPERATOR 1: What were you doing, a Nellie Ludlow?

OPERATOR 2: No, I was just sick to death of wearing them itchy
old lisle stockings.

OPERATOR 1 *(To Operator 2.)* My goodness, your tongue goes a
mile a minute. *(To Irene.)* What's the matter with you? Cat got
your tongue?

IRENE: Where's the supervisor?

OPRATOR 1: Oh, I'm the senior operator. I take over for the
supervisor on the night shift.

IRENE: I'm sorry, I didn't mean to say anything.

OPERATOR 2: My, I got vinegar burps. Them chips I had up to the rink are comin' back on me.

OPERATOR 1: My dear, just relax. Sure, I don't care as long as you do your job and nobody complains. You can talk your head off!

IRENE: Oh, I was trying really hard to be careful. I've wanted this job for over a year now. All I ever wanted to be was a telephone operator but I have no prior experience and Dad didn't know anybody.

OPERATOR 2: Well, we're really short staffed down here now. Violet and Joan and Loretta left just last week and fled down to the base. 'Course, the old faithfuls...

OPERATOR 1: If you stay loyal to the Telephone Company, the Telephone Company will stay loyal to you.

IRENE: Oh, I'm sure I'm really going to like it here. Oh. (*Speaks into mouthpiece.*) Number please...five-three-three-seven-four...Hollywood! I'm going to have to connect you to the overseas operator, sir. May I have your name? (*Speaks to girls.*) It's Victor Mature. He's callin' from the Newfoundland Hotel!

OPERATOR 1: Victor Mature? My most favourite actor. Oh, he's such a devil.

IRENE: Oh, he's gorgeous. He was some good in *Geronimo*!

OPERATOR 1: (*Pulling rank.*) Listen, I'm the senior operator. I better take over for this call.

IRENE: (*Getting vicious.*) No, no, you're the senior operator, you give the orders. We're the workers, we'll do the work.

OPERATOR 1: Come on, I work here too. I can do it.

(Operator 1 grabs at Irene's headphones.)

IRENE: Don't touch that. (*Speaking into mouthpiece.*) Yes sir, I'm still here. May I have the name of the party you wish to contact in Hollywood...(*To girls.*) Rita Hayworth! I bet they're in love. (*Speaking into mouthpiece.*) Yes sir, do you want to hold the line or shall I call you back? (*To girls.*) He's going to hold the line. His voice is heavenly. (*Inserts plug.*) Oh, I almost cut him off. No, I didn't...(*All girls rush to listen in. Irene screams.*) Don't touch that. (*Speaking into mouthpiece.*) Yes sir, I'm still here. I just have to connect the overseas operator. Just one moment. Hello, Montreal, Hello, Montreal, I have a party that wishes to be...

OPERATOR 1: Number please.

IRENE: ...connected to Hollywood.

OPERATOR 2: Number please.

IRENE: Yes, would you hold the line, please. Yes sir, Mr. Mature, your call is through, sir. You can go ahead now. (*She takes plug out.*)

OPERATOR 2: (*To Irene.*) Well, what did he say?

IRENE: Oh, not much.

OPERATOR 1: Would you please hold the line, sir. (*To Irene.*) Well, what's he saying? Aren't you listening in?

IRENE: Oh no, I couldn't do that.

OPERATOR 2: (*Lunging forward.*) Well, I could.

IRENE: All right, I will.

OPERATOR 2: Number please.

IRENE: He's talking to her.

OPERATOR 1: Oh, I'm afraid I'm going to have to cut you off, sir.

OPERATOR 2: Number please.

IRENE: He misses her.

OPERATOR 2: I'm sorry, we're very, very busy. Would you hold the line please?

IRENE: She doesn't love him, I can tell.

OPERATOR 1: It's eleven o'clock, sir. (*To Irene.*) What's he saying now?

IRENE: I can't tell you, I can't repeat it.

OPERATOR 2: What! Oh no, ma'am. No, I don't know...I, oh, they're no longer at that address. No, I'm sorry, I don't know where they've moved. (*She removes plug and speaks to girls.*) Honestly! Did I miss anything?

IRENE: She's two-timing him.

OPERATOR 2: Did she say that.

IRENE: No, but I strongly suspect it.

OPERATOR 1: No, I'm afraid I'm busy tonight. Yes, and tomorrow night, yes, and Saturday night, and yes, I think for the rest of the year. (*She pulls plug and says to girls.*) Stunned as a quilt!

IRENE: They're saying goodbye. He's worried about the charges and him with all that money!

OPERATOR 2: That's how he keeps it.

IRENE: Oh, I knew this job was going to be like this!

OPERATOR 1: (*Covering mouthpiece.*) Goodbye, Victor. Goodbye, Victor. Goodbye, Victor.

OPERATOR 2: What's he like?

IRENE: Well, he's nothing like he is on the screen. He sounds short.

OPERATOR 1: Another dream shattered. Number please. Yes, I like your voice too, sir. Married, sir? We've only been on the line four seconds. Yes, I'll certainly take that into consideration. (*She pulls plug and says to girls.*) Another proposal!

(*The boys enter and mime making a phone call.*)

GIRLS: (*Sing.*) The lines are busy, the wires are crossed,
    All the lights are flashing and my memory is lost,
    The calls just keep on coming and my arms are getting weak,
    I've said so many "Busy, sir" that I can hardly speak.
    It's a battle that is never won,
    I'll be so happy when the shift is done.

BOYS: (*Leaning on piano, they sing.*)
    Operator, please hang on,
    I know you must be lonely working midnight to dawn,
    Your "Number please" is charming,
    And I love your sweet "Hello,"

But I've had enough long distance, let's get on with the
show.
Operator, put me on your line,
And we could have a real fine time.

GIRLS: (*Sing.*) Sorry, soldier, I can't quite hear,
My supervisor's standing with her face in my ear,
I know you need assistance but you'll just have to wait,
So call again tomorrow and we'll fix up a date,
Sorry, soldier, gotta end this call,
But tomorrow night we'll have a ball.

GIRLS: (*Ad lib.*) Number please. I'm sorry, sir, that line is busy.
(*Etc.*)

(Blackout.)

Scene 2

*(A social evening. Tom starts to play the piano in darkness. As
the lights come up the boys start to sing. The girls join the boys
singing, "It's a Long Way to Tipperary.")*

LAURA: Oh, that's a great song.

IRENE: Oh, don't stop playing. Don't stop, Tom, please.

TINY: Can I get you somethin'?

VIVIAN: A Gingerale.

IRENE: Oh, I'd love an orange beer.

LAURA: Get me a Coca-Cola.

VIVIAN: Oh, you're gonna turn into a Coca-Cola.

IRENE: (*She strikes two notes on the piano.*) Oh, I wish I hadn't
given up my piano lessons.

*(Irene, Vivian and Tom mime chatter around the piano. Stretch
and Laura move off. Laura seems down.)*

STRETCH: What's the matter, Laura?

LAURA: That song just reminds me of absent friends.

STRETCH: Well, it must be nice to know you got a girlfriend
waiting at home for ya. I'm shipping out...gonna look for a bit of
action.

LAURA: Where will you be going?

STRETCH: I don't know. North Africa, I guess. I don't really know.
I don't care.

LAURA: Do you have to go? Can't you stay here?

STRETCH: Well, I could ask for an extension of my tour of duty.
Like the man said, you can always ask.

LAURA: You don't want to stay here anymore, do you?

STRETCH: Lol, if I had something to stay for...Look, I like it here
and I like you an awful lot. But, well, look...I know we said we'd
be friends and all that, but I just can't get in any deeper now.
And, well, if you're still thinking about Frank, then I think I
might as well bow out.

LAURA: Well, I'm keeping it going mostly for him. I haven't seen him in three years.

STRETCH: That's not fair, Laura. It's not fair to you, it's not fair to me, it's not fair to Frank in the end.

LAURA: Oh, I don't know what I feel. I feel guilty. I feel like I owe it to him to keep it going. How can I tell him now?

(Tiny re-enters with drinks.)

TINY: Hey, you guys, what's goin' on over there?

VIVIAN: How come so glum, chum?

STRETCH: Oh, just a little chit chat.

TINY: Oh, a little Chet chat, eh?

VIVIAN: Oh, a little Chet chat. *(She laughs.)*

TOM: Hey, come on, Laura. Play us a little tune on the piano.

IRENE: Oh, yeah, come on, Lol.

LAURA: I don't want to.

VIVIAN: All right, Tom, you play us something. Play us something bright and brave.

TINY: That would be nice, yeah, sure.

(They sing "Keep the Home Fires Burning." Laura starts a new song. The light focuses on her.)

Photograph by Manfred Buchheit

LAURA: *(Sings.)*   Ohhhhh, temptation
   Is tearing at this heart of mine,
   Is tearing me from you,
   It's the new arms around me
   It's the new voice saying, "I love you."
   Can't you hear the crying,
   In the endless nights I'm calling you.
   How can it be heartbreak, when I'm yours and yours alone?
   How can I keep on waiting, when I long to have you home?
   Oh, to see your face, to feel your touch again,

Babe, it's temptation will I find my way back to you.
Ohhhhh, temptation, ohhhh, temptation.
(Blackout.)

Scene 3

(The Lacey home, a few days after the previous scene.)

IRENE: Hi, Lol.

LAURA: Oh, Irene. I'm some glad you came over. *(She holds up a piece of paper.)* I've been trying to write this letter to Frank since I got off work. It's been on my mind all day. *(Pause.)* All day? All day, all week, all month, all year! I feel so bad. I feel like a real heel writing this to Frank now, but it's better to tell him the truth than to have him think I'm still here waiting for him.

IRENE: Are you sure you're doing the right thing?

LAURA: I don't know what else to do. I feel like I'm being dishonest to the both of them. I think I'm in love with Chet. Listen to this, okay? *(Reads.)* "Dear Frank, it's been a long time between letters. I hope you're keeping well. I've been over to see your mom almost every day. She looks forward to your letters and hopes and prays for you to return home soon. I am keeping very busy what with my volunteer work at the Caribou Hut and my job down on the base. Dad's working there too. I have always had the greatest respect and affection for you. You know that and it was not my intention to hurt you in any way, but I feel I must tell you that I've been seeing someone else. I couldn't, in all honesty, let you go on thinking that things would still be the same between us. You know, Frank, that it is not the sort of thing I ever dreamed of happening..." *(She stops abruptly seeing that Irene is crying.)* Irene. What's the matter? It's not that bad, is it?

IRENE: Lol, it's Kevin. We got the letter today. He was shot down over Holland. They say he's missing in action. I just had to get out of the house. Mom's heart is broken. She's just beside herself.

LAURA: Oh, I'm so sorry, Irene.

IRENE: Right from the very beginning of all this, you never think it's gonna happen to you. I know everybody thinks that, but he's been over there four years now, Lol. Why now?

LAURA: Look, you've gotta keep hoping that...there's still hope that he's alive. They say just presumed dead...there's still hope.

IRENE: Lol, he was so slight you wouldn't know but he was only a little boy.

LAURA: Look, you remember Harry Fitzgerald? You remember he was missing for over a year, and then one night he turned up on Aunt Gert's doorstep. Remember that? He said, "Got a room for a sailor?" He had his sailor's hat in his hand. Sure, Aunt Gert nearly died. Remember?

IRENE: Oh, I hope so, Lol, I hope so.

Scene 4

(At a movie. The chairs are in two rows. Laura, Stretch, and Laura's friend, Loretta, are lined up for admission. A Newfoundlander is already in place in the second row as is an NCO and his date. A light flickers on the actors making them look as if they were watching a film.)

MOVIE ANNOUNCER: *(Recorded.)* Your commentator is Robert Stevenson. "America Goes to War." Men of the army, navy and marines reinforce the battlefront...

LORETTA: Are we going down to the base after?

LAURA: I don't know. I can get Chet to take us down to the NCO Club after.

LORETTA: Is he mad because I came along?

LAURA: Oh, I don't think so, Loretta. He's good like that.

LORETTA: I thought he was really upset because I came along. I think he wants to be alone with you, Lol.

LAURA: I don't think so.

STRETCH: *(At the wicket.)* Can I have three, please?

LORETTA: Oh, look. he's paying for me. Isn't that sweet?

LAURA: Yah, it is.

LORETTA: Course, they're made of money, why shouldn't they spread it around?

STRETCH: So where would you girls like to sit?

LAURA: Let's sit down at the back.

STRETCH: Okay.

LORETTA: Oh, no. I got to sit down up the front. I'm far sighted.

STRETCH: Well, you sit up the front and we'll sit down the back.

LORETTA: I can't go sitting by meself. What's the sense of going to the movies if you got to sit by yourself?

STRETCH: Well, sit down in the back with us.

LORETTA: Well sure, I might just as well have stayed home. I won't be able to see nothing!

LAURA: Chet, let's sit up at the front, okay?

STRETCH: Okay.

(They move to take seats in front of the Newfoundland man and the NCO who is necking with his date.)

LORETTA: Um, I wants to sit on the outside. It makes it easier for me to get up.

STRETCH: Yeah, good idea. *(Speaking as he moves to his seat.)* Excuse me, excuse me.

LORETTA: Is he going up to the canteen to get a bar?

LAURA: I don't know. Chet, Chet, are you going up to the canteen to get a bar?

STRETCH: Do you want a bar?

LAURA: No, I had a big supper. I'm not hungry.

STRETCH: Well, why don't you go up and get yourself a bar, Loretta?

LORETTA: Oh no, I don't think so. Crowds make me really nervous.

STRETCH: All right. (*He goes to get Loretta her bar.*) Excuse me.

LORETTA: (*Taking Stretch's seat beside Laura.*) He's really sweet. he's gorgeous.

LAURA: Yes, I know. You know, he's not tall but he is dark and handsome.

LORETTA: There's a big crowd here...Oh look, there's Gert.

LAURA: Hi, Gert.

LORETTA: Who's she with?

LAURA: He's an American from the base.

LORETTA: I heard tell he was married. But you know what they say. If you can't get a man, get a Yank.

LAURA: Does she know?

LORETTA: No.

    (*Stretch returns. He gives Loretta a chocolate bar.*)

STRETCH: Here you go.

LORETTA: Oh, thank you. Am I the only one having a bar? Hope you don't mind? This is really cosy, isn't it? I've having a really good time, aren't you?

STRETCH: Oh, I think I dropped my wallet. Oh, there it is just behind you. Would you excuse me for just a second?

    (*He gets Loretta to stand up from her seat beside Laura.*)

LAURA: (*Staring intently at the movie.*) You got it?

STRETCH: Oh, ha, well I might as well sit here now. Well, there you go now. (*He takes the seat next to Laura which Loretta had been in, forcing Loretta to sit on his other side.*) Look at me...a thorn between two roses. Got a pretty girl on each side of me.

LAURA: (*Looking at the screen.*) Oh look, she's fabulous looking. Do you think that hair style would suit me?

LORETTA: Yeah, if you could get your face to look like that. But it would take a lot of work, girl. Oh look, see buddy...he's in love with her and so is Gary Cooper but she chooses Gary Cooper.

LAURA: Don't go telling us the whole movie.

LORETTA: Oh no, that's not the whole movie. He's in love with her and so is Gary Cooper, so buddy gets Gary Cooper sent off into the desert, and just before he sends him off into the desert he asks her to marry him. He says it's him or me and she takes off her shoes and then...

STRETCH: (*Looking at the screen.*) What's her shoes got to do with it?

LORETTA: It's the last scene in the movie. It's the big scene. She's going for a walk in the desert. You can't go for a walk in the desert with four-inch heels on.

LAURA: Well, we might as well go home now we knows the whole movie.

LORETTA: No, that's not the whole movie. I don't remember the end.

STRETCH: Good, we got something to look forward to.
(*Pause.*)

LORETTA: I think he dies. Or maybe they both die. (*She is ssshhhed.*) All I can remember is the shoes.

LAURA: Oh, shut up about the shoes.

STRETCH: (*To Laura.*) I got a present for ya.

LAURA: What? A present for me.

STRETCH: Yeah, but I'm not gonna give it to you until after the movie, okay?

LAURA: Oh, can't I see it?

STRETCH: No, you gotta wait. You gotta be patient.

LAURA: Okay.
(*Pause.*)

LORETTA: Oh, come on, give it to her now.

LAURA: Oh, come on, Chet, please. Please give it to me now.

STRETCH: Well, okay, okay. But you're not allowed to open it now till after the movie, okay? (*He gives her a ring box.*)

LAURA: Okay. I wonder what it is?

LORETTA: I know what it is. Congratulations. (*She looks at the screen.*) Oh look, this is her big scene, she got a tuxedo on.

STRETCH: You know I'm shipping out?

LAURA: I know.

STRETCH: I got that for you so you can remember me.

LAURA: Can I look at it?

STRETCH: Yeah, sure.

LAURA: (*She screams with delight as she sees an engagement ring.*) Oh, it's beautiful. Chet, I'm so...

STRETCH: Hi, Mrs. Chet Kowalski.

LORETTA: (*Over her shoulder to the second row.*) They're getting married! Oh, can I see? Can I see it? Let me see it, let me see it! Oh, it's gorgeous. Is there a diamond?

LAURA: It's a solitaire, look.

LORETTA: Oh, when I get engaged I want a star burst...that's a whole one with little chips like that all the way around it.

LAURA: I love it. I think it's perfect.

LORETTA: What's your mother gonna say? He's not Catholic.

LAURA: He can always take instructions.

LORETTA: (*To the other movie goers.*) They're not gonna get married in the Church.

LAURA: Are we gonna get married here?

STRETCH: Well, I don't know, ah...

LORETTA: Are you moving to the States? (*She announces to the other movie goers.*) They're moving to the States.

NEWFOUNDLANDER: (*Speaking from his seat in the second row of chairs.*) I don't care...Look, I came here to watch the movie, do you mind?

LORETTA: What difference does it make? They're gonna go and live in the United States.

NEWFOUNDLANDER: I don't care. I paid good money to come in here, you know, not to listen to you.

LORETTA: Are you saying we got in for free? Chet paid for me, didn't ya, Chet? Go on, tell him!

NEWFOUNDLANDER: (*To Stretch.*) Can you do something with her?

STRETCH: No, I can't do anything with her.

LORETTA: You better watch your mouth because I'm sitting here with a United States naval officer.

STRETCH: I'm an able seaman.

NEWFOUNDLANDER: Do something with her.

NCO: (*He stops necking with his date.*) Hey listen, I don't see what all the fuss is about, if the little lady has something to say let her say it!

NEWFOUNDLANDER: Oh, yah?

NCO: Yeah! What are you—a Canuck or something. What's this "N-F-L-D" on your shoulder?

NEWFOUNDLANDER: It means, "Not Found Lying Down," like the Yanks were at Pearl Harbor.

USO: Hey!

(*Fight breaks out. NCO's date breaks it up.*)

STRETCH: (*To Laura.*) Listen, why don't you pretend you're going to the washroom and I'll meet you in the lobby in a couple of minutes.

LAURA: Okay.

LORETTA: Where you going?

LAURA: To the washroom.

LORETTA: I'll go with you.

NEWFOUNDLANDER: Sit down.

LAURA: No! You stay here and tell me what happens in the movie.

(*Laura leaves.*)

LORETTA: Okay. (*Pause.*) I'm sure glad you're going to marry Lol.

STRETCH: Why.

LORETTA: Well before you guys came along no one would take her out. I mean, she can't do very much but I think she's got a lot to offer. (*She looks at him closely.*) You know what? You got gorgeous eyes. I always thought they were blue but they're not, they're brown, aren't they? A sort of blue-brown.

STRETCH: Excuse me, will ya?

(*Stretch escapes.*)

LORETTA: (*Getting herself between NCO and his date.*) Excuse me. Can I sit in there? I say, what's the sense of going to the movies if you got to sit by yourself? Have you two been going together very long?

(*Blackout.*)

Scene 5

(The Lacey home on VE day. 8 May 1945. Couch and chair. "Remember Pearl Harbor" is played on piano. There are fireworks in the background. Family members enter the house into the living room which appears to be unoccupied. Eddy is singing "Deutschland über Alles" and Leo gives him a bat on the head to shut him up.)

LEO: Agnes! Agnes, we're home.

MAY: *(Holding out her hand to Laura for her coat.)* All right, now take it off.

LAURA: No, you said I could wear it for the celebration.

MAY: Yah, well the celebrations are over. Now take it off.

LAURA: No.

EDDY: Where's me mom? Where's me old mother? *(He peers behind the couch and giggles.)* Not behind the couch, is she? Come out, come out, wherever ya are.

LEO: Agnes, for God's sake, it's VE day. The Germans have surrendered. People are out in the streets celebrating.

AGNES: *(Emerging from behind the couch with a paper bag on her head.)* It could be a trick.

LEO: Agnes, they never bombed us before. I seriously doubt that they're gonna start now.

AGNES: Well, I heard explosions. *(She pulls the bag further down over her head.)*

LAURA: Those were the fireworks, Mom.

AGNES: Well, we're still at war with Japan. One of those little Japs could fly over here on a suicide mission at any time.

EDDY: Me poor old crazy mom. Look, me mom's gone nuts. Look.

AGNES: If I'm nuts, it's you got me driven nuts.

(Eddy exits.)

LEO: Agnes, for God sake. Can't we be normal just for VE day?

AGNES: Well, I guess it's all over now. Wave goodbye to the good times. The Yanks will be pulling out. We'll be on the dole before you know it. There goes your big job on the base, Mr. Electrician. I told you not to leave Harvey's. But, oh no, you wouldn't listen to me, no.

LEO: Agnes, take the bag off your head.

AGNES: I just don't want to see it when the bombs hit.

(Agnes removes the paper bag.)

MAY: Oh, Dad. Please make her take off my coat.

LEO: For God's sake, will you give up about that? I'm after giving you more coats now that Hitler's got enemies. What are you worried about that old piece of rag for? Give it to your sister, go on, give it to her.

MAY: Why does she have to get everything? You got her into the Frank Sinatra concert that time when you knew he was my fantasy of love, my favourite singer in the whole world. And then she got to go back into the apartment and everything. It's easy to see who's the favourite around this place.

AGNES: May, that was in 1943. Let it drop.

LAURA: You know, I don't remember much about that. Wasn't he the short, stocky one with the blond hair?

(May commences to scream and cry.)

AGNES: The more you get the more you complain about what you haven't got. May God strike me dead if I didn't wish the Yanks hadn't come here with all their big money.

LEO: Big money? Big money? Sure, you wouldn't know what big money was. Big money is what they paid the Canadians and the American civilians. Small money is what they paid us.

AGNES: Leo, my darling, when you first started getting that forty cents an hour, you were like a youngster with a new toy. You didn't know what to be doing with yourself or the money. I'll never forget when I got the shock of me life—I put me hand up in the kitchen cupboard and down came floating twenty dollar bills on top of me head.

(Eddy re-enters.)

LEO: That was me pin money.

AGNES: Well, all that money ever did for me was to get me new instruments of work.

EDDY: *(Putting on his jacket.)* Listen, Dad, before we goes on the dole, now what about gettin' me that new Harley Tri-Star down at E. K. Motors?

LEO: Number one. We're not going on the dole. Number two. The Americans aren't leaving, they got a ninety-nine year lease down on the base. And number three. You're stupid looking enough without hanging off a motorcycle.

EDDY: Okay. We'll compromise, Dad. What do you say you get me a new four cylinder?

LEO: No, no, no, no, no, no. *(To May.)* Now, you give your sister the coat. *(To Agnes.)* You shut up...and *(To Eddy.)* where are you going?

EDDY: Going out to get me girl.

AGNES: Oh, Leo, he's all grown up and he had to do all his formative growing under the shadow of a world at war.

EDDY: Yah.

LEO: Agnes, face it, he was eighteen in 1939. He had all his forming done.

AGNES: You've always resented him haven't you, Leo? It takes a small man to resent his own son.

EDDY: Yah, I know. Marked me for life. Well, see ya.

(He leaves.)

LAURA: Oh, why, why, why, do I ever have to have holidays? I hate having a day off 'cause I got to stick around here listening to you fellas go on and on.

AGNES: What are you? Chained to the floor? Go off on out of it, my dear.

LAURA: No, I'm waiting for Chet to pick me up. We're going to the Victory Day dance at the Hotel.

LEO: (*Growing angry.*) Well, why don't you wait up in your room? With your nice little frilly curtains and your mat on the floor and your fifteen-dollar bedspread across the bed. I'm surprised that a couple of princesses like ye would lower yourselves to wait down here with the likes of your mother and me.

LAURA: Dad, why can't you act like a human being?

LEO: Why can't you act like...listen to the twang on her. My God, she hasn't been out of the country, she's got a smell of the States and now she's talking right grand.

AGNES: Ya can't think very much of yourself if you don't like the way you talk.

LAURA: Oh, Mom, don't start with that we-might-not-have-had-very-much-but-we-were-a-proud-family bit, please.

LEO: Now don't you go getting saucy with your mother.

LAURA: Oh, I got to get out of here.

MAY: I'm going too. Now you take off my coat.

LAURA: Dad said I could have it.

(*Laura and May exit still quarrelling over May's coat.*)

LEO: Well, Agnes, VE day. It's hard to believe it's all over, isn't it?

AGNES: Yes Leo, we did it. We fought the good fight.

LEO: Yah, that's two world wars for us now, Agnes. (*Looking at her.*) What's it gonna take to put us down, eh?

Scene 6

(*Later in the Lacey house. Laura's wedding gifts are around.*)

IRENE: Oh, Lol, you've got so much wonderful stuff. How you gonna get it all back to Wagner?

LAURA: Oh, I'm just gonna pack it all up in the trunk and get it sent on later. You know, Chet and I are leaving straight from the reception to go to Wagner. He got it all arranged.

VIVIAN: You know, I could never live in the States. I could never live any place but here.

LAURA: How would you know? You've never been any other place but here.

VIVIAN: I don't know, I'd be afraid. Away from everyone and everything that you know. Sure, look what happened to Carol-Anne. Buddy got shipped overseas, got a leave. She was supposed to meet him in New York at his mother's place, they were gonna get married. Sure, he gave her the address and everything. And when she got there, there was no such place. And neither a hide nor hair of him. She's still up there, she hasn't got the face to come home.

IRENE: Sure, look what happened to my cousin Ruth. She married a guy from Argentia and when she was on her first baby he was shipped overseas. So he sent her down to stay with his family in Florida. My dear, he gave her the impression she was gonna live in a mansion. When she got down there, there was nothing. It wasn't fit for a dog to live in. It was only an old shack and they treated her like a slave. She wasn't allowed out over the door...My God, this is scary, isn't it?

LAURA: I'm some glad Chet's not like that.

VIVIAN: Oh no, we all know Chet's not like that. Sure, we all know you're gonna go and live on a farm.

IRENE: Well, I wish I was gonna go live on a farm, or an igloo, or a dog house. Any place but here.

LAURA: What's the matter with you, my dear? You've got a face on you like a plate of mortal sins.

IRENE: Nothing's wrong with me. What could possibly be wrong with me? I'm just three months pregnant, that's all.

LAURA: Irene, are you sure?

IRENE: Yes, I'm sure.

VIVIAN: But what did Tom say?

IRENE: Tom didn't say anything.

VIVIAN: Well, haven't you told him? He's the father, isn't he?

IRENE: Yes, he's the father and I don't have to do anything.

VIVIAN: Well, you're gonna have to. You're gonna have to get married before you start to show.

IRENE: What odds. Everyone can count. And besides, he hasn't asked me to marry him.

VIVIAN: Oh, you know he's gonna ask you now that you're pregnant.

IRENE: But I don't want him to marry me because he has to. I can't figure out why he hasn't asked me before. We've been going out together ever since he got here and now he's being shipped overseas with the occupational forces.

VIVIAN: Oh, he's probably going over to Germany with Stan.

IRENE: Do you think he's married already?

VIVIAN: Oh, don't be so foolish, Irene.

IRENE: Well, sure look at Pearl Downy. She got married up at the Cathedral. The works and everything. Everything was going along just grand. She had one youngster, and then one day right out of the blue, there was a knock on the door and there was this well-dressed American woman standing there...his wife.

VIVIAN: No, I can't see Tom...No, no.

IRENE: Well, I don't want to marry anyone who doesn't want to marry me. I don't see any shotgun weddings in my future.

VIVIAN: Well, what are you gonna do?

IRENE: I'll manage, I suppose. (*Pause. She's trying to be cheerful. To Laura.*) Lol, who gave you that? My dear, there's no card attached. I told you to keep the cards for thank you notes.

Scene 7

(Still later. Reception after Laura and Stretch's wedding. The servicemen are waiting for the girls.)

TINY: Boy, I don't know. Sendin' women off to the washroom. They're there all day, aren't they? What d' they do in there, anyway?

TOM: I don't know either but it takes three of them to do it.

(Enter Irene and Vivian. They join Tiny and Tom, waiting for the bride and groom.)

IRENE: Sorry we're late, you guys.

TOM: Oh, hi.

IRENE: Oh look, here they come.

VIVIAN: No, that's not them. Oh, where are they?

IRENE: They were still signing the register when we left.

VIVIAN: Oh, didn't she look beautiful? I've never seen her look so good.

IRENE: Well, I did.

VIVIAN: Irene, it's her wedding day.

IRENE: Well, suit just doesn't say wedding to me.

VIVIAN: Look, I'm not going to fight with you today, of all days. Stan, have you got the rice?

TINY: Oh yeah, I got the rice. *(He shows her a bag of rice.)* Everything's fine.

VIVIAN: *(Aside to Tiny.)* I can't talk to her today.

TOM: Is everything all right, Irene?

IRENE: Yes.

TOM: They're shipping us out in three days.

IRENE: I know.

TOM: Well, I been thinking. And, ah...I really like it here, and it's more like home to me than any place else and, ah...I'd like to settle here. You and me. Would you like that, Irene?

IRENE: I suppose so...*(Turns to Viv.)* Viv, Viv, I think I'm engaged.

VIVIAN: Oh Irene, you couldn't have found a better man if he was carved out for ya.

TINY: Are you two jokin'? *(He slaps Tom on the back in congratulation.)* Congratulations, old Lemondrop, you finally did it. Irene, you couldn't have found a better man than old Tom.

(He gives her a longer-than-necessary kiss.)

VIVIAN: Stan, Stan.

TINY: *(To Vivian.)* I'm just jokin'. *(To Tom.)* Have you set the date yet?

TOM: Well, I got permission from my CO, so any time.

IRENE: As soon as they publish the banns.

TOM: Well, how about you, Stan? Have you got the peacetime discharge yet? Boy, I can't wait for the air force to see the last of me.

TINY: Well, I'll tell ya now. I got another two-and-a-half years to go. I don't mind spendin' my time in this man's army. 'Sides, me and Viv been havin' a good time, haven't we?

TOM: Boy, Ziggy's starting to look impatient. He's got a great spread laid out over there.

IRENE: Oh, you know what? I'd just like to go home and put my feet up. That'd be a real celebration to me.

VIVIAN: Irene. This is the celebration to end all celebrations. Lol is married, you're engaged. It's the week of the end of the whole war.

TOM: That's right.

TINY: Yeah, Ziggy's got a great cake baked up, all baked and iced...

TOM: Yeah, you should see that cake.

IRENE: You're not gonna have a girl coming out of Lol's cake on her wedding day, are ya?

TOM: No, it's done up brown, you're gonna love it.

IRENE: Brown?

TINY: Yeah, brown. It means real fancy like. Oh, you're gonna love it.

VIVIAN: Oh, what a day! It feels like everything's just beginning and yet everything's ending at the same time. Oh, thank God, but still I feel kind of sad about it, after all.

IRENE: Viv, what are you saying? This is the beginning of a new world of peace. You don't think they're ever gonna let anything like this ever happen again, do you?

TINY: Hey, here they come.

(Celebration with glasses of champagne.)

STRETCH: Hey, you're never gonna believe this, but, ah, we have a flat tire.

TINY: Well, Viv, think you're ever gonna settle down?

VIVIAN: Well, I don't know, if I ever find the right man, I suppose.

TINY: Do you think you're gonna find the right man around here?

VIVIAN: Well, I sure hope so 'cause I have no intention of leaving.

TINY: Well, ah, too bad. *(Pause.)* Ladies, soldiers, sailors. I'd like to propose a toast. Here's to Laura, on the day of her weddin', the most beautiful flower in the garden of Newfoundland womanhood.

LAURA: Thank you.

TOM: I'd like to propose a toast to Chet. A good sailor, a good buddy, a good laugh and I'm sure, an excellent husband.

STRETCH: And here's to Wagner. I hope we get there soon.

LAURA: What do you mean by that?

(They toast and move around the piano to sing the last song.)

> Oh yes, those were the good days,
> The very best of times,
> When pop was beer,
> And stockings only pencilled lines
> On shapely legs of working girls,
> Who glide to rumba rhymes.

The future didn't worry us,
We lived on borrowed time,
We loved, we laughed, we paid the price,
But dancing soothed the pain of wondering
If those boys of ours had died in vain.
Those days are only memories,
Sad sweet strains of song.
Sisters married Stateside, we didn't hear 'fore long
From Pennsylvania, Akron, Dallas or Tucson.
Those faces now are fading,
Only snapshots to recall
Those boys and girls whose bright brave smiles
Said live and fight, no backward glance,
They'll say we had a ball.
We'll never see those times again,
When strangers kissed and cried,
The echoes of their footsteps,
As they swing and swagger by,
A Yankee flag unfurled,
Oh yes, weren't we the luckiest people
In all the whole wide world?
(The last stanza is repeated and the last line is sung twice at the end.)

THE END.

Rising Tide Theatre

Joey

1981

Collectively written by
Donna Butt
Brian Downey
David Fox
Sheilagh Guy
Kevin Noble
Jeff Pitcher
David Ross

In collaboration with
Rick Salutin

Music created and/or arranged by
Rick Hollett and **Don Wherry**

JOEY

Joey was produced by Rising Tide Theatre Company at the Arts and Culture Centre in St. John's, 16-18 September 1981. The play toured the Arts and Culture Centres in Gander (22 September), Grand Falls (23 September), Corner Brook (24 September) and Stephenville (25 September 1981). In 1982, Rising Tide performed the play as a co-production with Toronto Workshop Productions in Kitchener (8-9 January) and Toronto (12-31 January). A production of *Joey* in St. John's (28-29 June 1982) was nationally televised by CBC Television. Rising Tide remounted the play in St. John's (23-25 September 1982) and subsequently toured Vancouver (7-30 October) and Ottawa (2-20 November 1982). In 1983, there was a tour of Quebec, New Brunswick and Nova Scotia; *Joey* played in Lennoxville (23-24 September), Pictou (27 September), Antigonish (28 September), Saint John (30 September to 1 October), Annapolis Royal (5 October), Yarmouth (8 October), Halifax (11-13 October) and Glace Bay (16 October 1983). In the course of its twenty-five months existence, *Joey* was revised and developed. The text presented here is the final touring version.

Joey was written by the original cast and director in collaboration with **Rick Salutin**. The writer/performers of Rising Tide Theatre are:

Donna Butt	Director.
Brian Downey	Wise Man, Voice, Singer, Announcer, Worker, Captain Joe, Jack Pickersgill, Logger, Whiffen, Bill, Valdmanis, Mr. O'Brien, Rossi, etc.
David Fox	God, Old Socialist, Newsboy, Greg Power, Worker, Merchant, Dave, Murray Lander, Census Taker, etc.
Sheilagh Guy	Lillian, Mary, Sheilagh, etc.
Kevin Noble	Joey (in present-day and in history).
Jeff Pitcher	Wise Man, Newsboy, Anti-Communist Worker, Dickey, Priest, Fisherman, Jeff, Teddy, Pat, etc.
David Ross	Wise Man, Landon Ladd, Speaker, David, Eli, St. Laurent, Peter Cashin, David, Les, John Crosbie, etc.

Additional credits:

Music was arranged and/or composed by **Rick Hollett** and **Don Wherry**. In 1981, lights were by **Rick Burt** and **Peter Conway**, visual design **Bob Petrie**, stage management **Derek Butt**, sound **John Coombs**, set construction **Rick Barela, Bob Stamp, Bob**

Sharpe and **Mike Manning**, properties **Brenda Carroll**, costumes **Marie Sharpe** and **Deborah Clarke Penton**. Photographs are by **Dick Green**. The mainland touring set design was by **Phillip Craig**, lighting **Ross Nicole**. Slide collection and preparation **Richard Stoker** and costumes **Peggy Hogan**. From the 1982 tour on, **Boyd Norman** replaced **David Fox**. Musicians **Mack Furlong** and **Paul Steffler** replaced **Don Wherry** and **Rick Hollett** as of September 1982.

The words of "We'll Rant and We'll Roar" in the play are a modification by **Tom Cahill** of a song called "The Baby Bonus Song" by **Ed Learning**.

The production of *Joey* was assisted by the Office of the Secretary of State, the Canada Council, the Canada Council Touring Office, the Newfoundland and Labrador Arts Council and the Government of Newfoundland Cultural Affairs Division.

Joseph R. Smallwood
Premier of Newfoundland and Labrador
1949-1972

When Joey Smallwood was born in Gambo, Newfoundland, 24 December 1900, Newfoundland had been an independent country governed by a House of Assembly and a Legislative Council (Upper House) since 1855. On 16 February 1934, the country, financially battered, in part by effects of the Great Depression, voluntarily relinquished Responsible Government. Newfoundland was subsequently ruled by a Commission of Government appointed by the British government — a commission consisting of three appointed members from Britain and three appointed from Newfoundland under the chairmanship of an appointed British governor. In 1945, Newfoundland's financial affairs had recovered as a result of stringent management and wartime development and the country had, at that time, a surplus of more than twenty-eight million dollars. On 11 December 1945, the British government announced that a National Convention of forty-five delegates would be elected by full adult suffrage in Newfoundland to examine the country's condition and to make recommendations on possible forms of future government to be voted upon in a national referendum. Members of the National Convention were elected 26 June 1946 and the Convention opened 11 September of the same year.

Joey Smallwood, socialist, journalist, union organizer, broadcaster and pig farmer, who had worked in Halifax, Boston, New York and Newfoundland, saw Confederation with Canada as the only possible future for Newfoundland. As a proponent of Confederation, Smallwood had as his chief rivals Major Peter J. Cashin leader of the movement for a return to Responsible Government and Chesley Crosbie who favoured return to Responsible Government as a means by which to form an economic union with the United States. The powerful St. John's merchants solidly opposed Confederation and Smallwood focused his campaign on the people throughout Newfoundland. He used the petitions they had signed to push for the inclusion of Confederation on the referendum ballot. As Smallwood himself describes the campaign, "Feelings ran deep and bitter. Churches were split wide open, societies, trade unions, families. Friendships were shattered. Each side accused the other of unspeakable crimes, and the accusations continued to be made long after the issue was settled. I was, of course, the villain, the 'Judas Iscariot' the 'Quisling,' the 'traitor.'"

Debate at the National Convention continued through the fall and winter of 1946, throughout 1947 and into 1948 and the various options were investigated by delegations both to and from Newfoundland. The Convention determined the referendum slate in February 1948. A referendum was held 3 June 1948 with three possibilities: Responsible Government, Confederation and Commission of Government with the following results: 44.55%, 41.13% and 14.32% respectively. A second referendum followed 22 July which dropped Commission of Government as an option. The results were 52.34% for Confederation and 47.66% for Responsible Government. The Terms of Union between Newfoundland and Canada were signed in the Canadian Senate, 11 December 1948, and passed in subsequent months by various levels of government in Newfoundland, Canada and Britain. Just before the stroke of midnight on 31 March 1949, Newfoundland became a province of Canada.

Joey Smallwood became the first premier of Newfoundland and leader of the provincial Liberal party, a position he maintained for twenty-three years, winning six elections and a leadership convention in 1969 when John C. Crosbie ran against him. Smallwood demonstrated little belief in the fishery as a viable source of income for Newfoundland. Through the federally and provincially funded Resettlement Program in the mid-to late-sixties, he relocated residents of hundreds of coastal communities to designated "growth centres." Throughout his premiership he launched a seemingly endless series of efforts to establish foreign industry to Newfoundland. He initiated large-scale developments which failed to live up to the expectations they raised. His government's image was frequently tainted with rumours of corruption and Smallwood himself ultimately lost his touch with the people. He lived for nineteen years after his retirement from politics working towards the completion of his massive *Encyclopedia of Newfoundland and Labrador*. He suffered a stroke in September 1984 and died 17 December 1991, a week short of his ninety-first birthday. Joey left the residents of the province he forged to wonder at his creations and to ponder his influence on our lives.

HELEN PETERS

JOEY

ACT 1

1. Introduction
2. God and the Wise Men
3. Socialist and Logger
4. New York
5. Captain Joe and Eli
6. The Sanitorium
7. The Barrelman
8. The Opportunity
9. Joey in Ottawa
10. St. Laurent's Office
11. Joey Meets Greg
12. The National Convention
13. Joey Visits Eli and Mary
14. The Arguers
15. Eli and Mary: Will We Join?
16. Greg and Joey: Orangemen's Meeting
17. Cashin and the Outporters
18. Eli and Mary on the Day of Confederation
19. Captain Joe and Dickey on the Day of Confederation
20. Joey and Greg

ACT 2

1. After Confederation
2. Jack Pickersgill and Joey Campaign
3. Murray Coming into Harbour
4. Joey and Valdmanis Meet
5. The Census Taker
6. End of Valdmanis
7. IWA Strike
8. Greg Power Quits
9. Resettlement
10. Empty Victory
11. Joey Visits Greg
12. Eli and Pat
13. Rossi
14. Come Home Year
15. Churchill Falls Deal
16. Eli and Mary Leave
17. Joey and John Crosbie
18. Pat at the District Meeting
19. Liberal Leadership Convention
20. Captain Joe and Pat

CAST OF CHARACTERS
(In order of appearance.)

JOEY — Joseph R. Smallwood, Newfoundland Premier.*

GOD

THREE WISE MEN

OLD SOCIALIST

BRIAN

LANDON LADD — Union leader during the IWA strike.*

DAVID

GREG — Greg Power, Joey's friend and political colleague.*

VOICE

NEWSBOY

SINGER

ANNOUNCER

WORKER 1

SPEAKER

ANTI-COMMUNIST WORKER

WORKER 2

LILLIAN — Lillian Zahn, woman Joey loved in New York.*

CAPTAIN JOE

ELI — Eli Morgan, fisherman.

MARY — Mary Morgan, Eli's wife.

DICKEY — Dick Elijah Byrd.

PICKERSGILL — Jack Pickersgill, Federal Member of Parliament.*

ST. LAURENT — Louis St. Laurent, Prime Minister of Canada.*

WHIFFEN — Pro-Confederate.

MERCHANT

CASHIN — Peter Cashin, anti-Confederate politician.*

PRIEST

BILL

FISHERMAN

JEFF — Newfoundlander.

BRIAN — Newfoundlander.

DAVID — Newfoundlander.

DAVE	Newfoundlander.
SHEILAGH	Newfoundlander.
MURRAY	Murray Lander, Department of Human Resources employee.
VALDMANIS	Alfred Valdmanis, Joey's economic advisor.*
LES	Cabinet Minister
TEDDY	Minister of Finance.
MR. O'BRIEN	Earl O'Brien, fish plant owner.
PAT	Pat Morgan, son of Eli and Mary.
ROSSI	Ross Barbour, Cabinet Minister.*
CROSBIE	John C. Crosbie, politician who lost Liberal leadership convention to Joey.*

* Non-fictional characters.

JOEY

ACT 1
Introduction
Scene 1

St. John's, Newfoundland, 1981. The stage is configured into five playing areas through which actors move or on which coordinated action takes place. These areas represent an outport home at stage right, an office upstage, a general playing area at centre stage, a wharf at stage left to which is attached a "boat" which juts out into the audience. Behind is a screen from behind which God speaks and onto which slides are projected during the play to provide a sense of history and to create atmosphere. The two main characters, Joey and his pal Greg, age as the action of the play develops.

Musicians play "Badger Drive." An elderly Joey (Joey in present-day) enters from audience and goes to centre stage taking in the set as he goes and disrupting the action of the play. The musicians sputter to a stop surprised by his presence and make appropriate comments such as "It's Joey! Look! It's Joey! Etc." until he stops them. When Joey speaks it is directly to the audience. He remains on the stage observing and commenting until the end of scene three.

JOEY: Good evening, ladies and gentlemen. I can't say I'm surprised to see you all here this evening. I'm delighted, I'm glad. I'm very, very pleased indeed, overjoyed. I would be a lot happier if I knew what was in store for you tonight, what was in store for me. I can't imagine how it could be too mean. I met the young man who is going to try to play me tonight. He's going to try, he'll attempt it, he'll make an effort, he'll try, I've met the man. I can't say that I was too impressed. He doesn't talk like me, he doesn't look like me, maybe he can act like me, maybe he can. I don't know, I wouldn't know. I'm not an actor. A politician yes, a statesman yes, a propagandist yes, but not an actor. It would be nice to be an actor in this great Arts and Culture Centre, one of the five great Arts and Culture Centres. They wouldn't have this great Arts and Culture Centre if it wasn't for me. I put it here, there was no building here, I had it built, I built it. But I'm not here to give a speech. If I wanted to give a speech, I could give a speech. If you wanted me to give a speech, I could give a speech. I'm a bit of an orator, you know, I attend hundreds of speaking engagements every year, giving speeches at every one of them. I could give a speech about anything, but I'm not here to give a speech. Now, those young people backstage. (*Turning to back stage.*) You young thespians back there, I'm adlibbing for you out here, you know. The show was supposed to start seven-and-one-half minutes ago. (*Turning back to the audience.*) Well, I suppose when they're ready to begin they'll begin at the beginning, they should start at the beginning, they must begin at the beginning you see, I was born on Christmas Eve in 1900. Now a lot of famous people were born on Christmas Eve.

God and the Wise Men
Scene 2

(Gambo, Newfoundland, 24 December 1900. The backlight behind the scrim creates a large silhouette of God dressed as a fisherman. The speech is a voice-over and has a booming resonance. Music plays.)

GOD: Joey, Joey, I found you. And that's as true as the light. Listen, me son, I was mad when I built the rock, so riled up I could eat ya, the grey and purple rock, the barrens, the scrub trees, and everlasting water. And that made me so mad I went out and wrecked Labrador. Even then, fools come to live on her, they gotta be looked after, Joey. I've given them over to men like Carson, Alderdice, Carter, Coaker, and even Commission of Government. It's all come up to nothing. I'm at the end of my hawser. You got to take her, Joey...

(The Three Wise Men, also dressed as fishermen, peer skyward and point.)

WISE MAN 1: Luh!
WISE MAN 2: Luh!
WISE MAN 3: Luh!
WISE MAN 1: Looks like a lighthouse.
WISE MAN 3: No, b'y, that's a big moose eye.
WISE MAN 2: It's a star.
WISE MAN 1: It's a blue star.
WISE MAN 3: That's the biggest one I ever saw.
WISE MAN 2: It must mean something, b'y.
WISE MAN 1: Let's go see where she's shinin' to.
WISE MAN 3: That's over Red Indian Lake, b'y.
WISE MAN 1: No, b'y. That's over the Port au Port Peninsula.
WISE MAN 2: Go way, that's Twillingate, b'y.

WISE MAN 3: Luh!

WISE MAN 1: Luh!

WISE MAN 2: Luh!

GOD: (*From offstage. His voice booms making the Wise Men jump.*) Luh!

WISE MAN 3: Here we are.

WISE MAN 2: Where are we to?

WISE MAN 1: (*All pointing to Joey on stage.*) It's...Gambo.

WISE MAN 2: There's a little baby, luh...

ALL: Ahh...

WISE MAN 1: I think we're supposed to give him a present or something, b'ys.

WISE MAN 3: Here you are, little fella, I don't know what it means, but, the "Terms of Union."

WISE MAN 2: Here you are, little fella, I give you an iron will and boundless energy.

WISE MAN 1: Here you are, little fella, the gift of gab.

WISE MAN 3: Now, little fella, get yourself a bow tie and big black glasses.

WISE MAN 1: Now you use the gift of gab wisely.

WISE MAN 2: And for God's sake, don't forget the fishery.

(*A star shines over Joey as the Wise Men exit singing "Star of Wonder Star of Light."*)

JOEY: (*Still in present-day.*) That's not exactly what I had in mind, but I suppose it's one way of looking at it.

(*Joey begins to exit.*)

Socialist and Logger
Scene 3

OLD SOCIALIST: I first met Splits Smallwood when he was a student at Bishop Feild College. He would venture into my shop on Water Street. We would discuss socialism.

JOEY: (*Still in the present he addresses the audience and tries to take control of the play.*) That's good. Yes, yes. They should have something in the play about my socialism. I always have been a socialist, you know, still am to this very day. (*To the actor.*) Carry on.

OLD SOCIALIST: I said Bishop Feild is a strange breeding ground for socialism.

JOEY: (*Interrupts, again addressing the audience.*) Not at all, I was the poorest boy from the poorest family, and there I was mixing with the mercantile aristocracy, the young mucky mucks, the young punks of the Water Street merchants. And they spat on me because I was poor. But I didn't feel inferior, not for one minute. I learned at a very early age, that you can be born into a rich family and still be as stupid as an ox.

OLD SOCIALIST: (*Bangs his cane against the desk in agitation.*)

And I said, young man, I said, if you want to learn about social-ism you'll have to go to its centre, New York...

JOEY: I did, I did go to New York.

OLD SOCIALIST: *(Dropping out of character and addressing Joey while looking for the stage manager in the wings.)* How long is this going to go on. The play has begun. Are you going to let me...

BRIAN: *(The actor and not the character.)* What's going on?

DAVID FOX: He is. On, and on...

(He exits.)

JOEY: *(To the audience.)* I did go to New York, and I did learn about socialism. You know, I've always remained true to those goals, to serve the toiling masses of Newfoundland, her miners, her log-gers, her mill workers, and, of course, her fishermen.

BRIAN: Excuse me, Mr. Smallwood, sir. You see the play has already started.

JOEY: Yes.

BRIAN: Well...we have a seat for you, sir...we'd like to get on with it.

JOEY: Good, good, yes. I'd like to know what's next. What's next?

BRIAN: Well, right here we're going to have a scene about when you turned your back on the workers and on socialism in 1959; we'll have the IWA union, with Landon Ladd and the loggers freezing on the picket line.

JOEY: Stop! Stop! They always drag up the IWA strike business. Now, I don't mind criticism, never have, but if you're going to do a play about me, then at least have the courtesy to do it in the right order.

BRIAN: The right order?

(Lights come up on Landon Ladd the union leader during the 1950s IWA strike.)

LANDON LADD: The premier of this province is smashing our union for the simple reason that it's strong and free. Well, we'll run a logger against him.

BRIAN: *(Interrupting Ladd's speech.)* Dave, Dave, we can't do this bit right here.

DAVID ROSS: *(The actor.)* Brian, there is an audience out there.

BRIAN: We're going to do the New York bit.

DAVID ROSS: Cute, Brian, I'm not in that scene.

JOEY: Stop! Stop! Go out, go out and start again. And see if you can get it in the right order.

DAVID ROSS: *(To Brian as they exit.)* Who is that old fart?

JOEY: And tell your friends, tell your friends. Make sure they know.

GREG: *(Also in present-day, he calls from audience.)* Joe, I warned you, Joe.

JOEY: Greg, Greg, come up, come up. *(To audience.)* This is my oldest and dearest friend, Gregory Power.

GREG: *(He comes on stage.)* I warned you. I was suspicious of this project from the very beginning.

JOEY: There's no need to be frightened, Greg. It's only a play, about me.

GREG: But what about that racket? Aren't you frightened of the questions they'll ask?

JOEY: Well, if it's all going to be that unkind, that miserable, we'll just stand up and do what that man on "All in the Family" always does.

GREG: Archie Bunker?

JOEY: Yes, that's the man.

(Raspberry. Present-day Greg and Joey exit laughing.)

New York
Scene 4

(New York, 1920-24. Musicians play.)

VOICE: New York! New York!

NEWSBOY: Extra, extra, read all about it, "Communist Corners in New York."

VOICE: Peanuts, peanuts, get your red hots...

(Newsboy moves across the stage.)

NEWSBOY: Extra, extra, read all about it, "FBI Infiltrates Union."

SINGER: Five foot two, eyes of blue...

(Dancers and watch seller cross the stage.)

VOICE: Watches, watches, genuine Swiss movements...

NEWSBOY: Extra, extra, read all about it, "Scab Labour Breaks Picket Line."

ANNOUNCER: It's the bottom of the ninth with two out and Babe Ruth comes to bat.

NEWSBOY: Tonight, socialist meeting, right here in Cooper Hall, 8:00 tonight, Cooper Hall, socialist meeting, be there.

WORKER 1: New York is one hell of a town.

SPEAKER: Labour is wealth. Wealth only exists because it was created by labour. Mr. Vanderbilt cannot say to you, "Accept the wages I offer you or get out of my factory."

ANTI-COMMUNIST WORKER: Go home, you Bolshevik pig.

SPEAKER: You tell Mr. Vanderbilt, "You pay us what we need, sir, or we will close your factory, and your wealth will dry up."

ANTI-COMMUNIST WORKER: The Reds are destroying America.

WORKER 1: Capitalism is anarchy. Socialism is not.

WORKER 2: Let the man speak. This is a democratic meeting.

ANTI-COMMUNIST WORKER: It's you, the union leaders, who are the Lenins, the Trotskys, the real enemies of America.

SPEAKER: We are not anti-American. The workers of America are the only true patriots.

WORKER 1: Workers of the world unite...

ANTI-COMMUNIST WORKER: You'll spill the workers' blood in the streets.

WORKER 2: A fair day's pay for a fair day's work.

JOEY: (*As a young man.*) I have a question.

WORKER 2: We have a new brother in our midst. Let the man speak.

JOEY: Can socialism become dominant when every community, when the entire economy, is set up on a credit system, and the working man never has cash in hand?

SPEAKER: The credit system must be broken. Whenever a man must buy his goods from the same man who pays him his wages he will always be exploited.

JOEY: Are fishermen workers? Are they the toiling masses?

SPEAKER: Fishermen are some of the most important workers because their labour creates food.

JOEY: How can you organize people when they are spread over six thousand miles of coastline?

SPEAKER: If you have the strength, the will, and the determination, socialism can free the worker no matter what the obstacles. Where are you speaking of, sir?

JOEY: Newfoundland.

ANTI-COMMUNIST WORKER: God save America.

(He sings the American national anthem. General shouting from Anti-Communist Worker and Speaker. Musicians play and Workers shout. Both Anti-Communist Worker and Speaker exit. Joey crosses the stage. Music plays loudly.)

JOEY: Ladies and gentlemen, brothers and sisters, members of the toiling masses, how can you expect to smash the establishment if you can't even run a meeting? (*Silence.*) Now that I have your attention, and I'm very pleased to have your attention, I'd, ah, I'd like to say that we workers of Newfoundland believe that if we work together, and if we unite, we can build a better world for all the nations of the earth.

(Applause.)

LILLIAN: Our brother from Newfoundland has shown us that we are not alone, even in the country of Newfoundland there are workers struggling like us. I want to thank our brother from Newfoundland.

(Musicians play "Let Me Call You Sweetheart." Joey and Lillian waltz. Then he spreads out his coat, removes his hat, and they sit.)

JOEY: I don't know what came over me tonight, but I felt I could talk to those people, and make them hear. You have beautiful eyes.

LILLIAN: They heard you, ah...?

JOEY: Joseph. Joe.

LILLIAN: My name is Lillian, Lillian Zahn.

JOEY: Zahn, what kind of name is that?

LILLIAN: It's Jewish.

JOEY: Jewish, you're a Jew. The Jews have been around a long time, longer than we have.

LILLIAN: But we have been homeless.

JOEY: Our people have been homeless too. Our people are travelling far and wide just to escape their poverty.

LILLIAN: We have been homeless for over two thousand years.

JOEY: That is longer than us. You know, I've always admired the Jewish people. Such strong people. Perhaps the strongest people in the world today. Perhaps even stronger than Newfoundlanders.

LILLIAN: We have suffered.

JOEY: Well, our people are suffering right now, at this moment.

LILLIAN: You should be proud of that.

JOEY: Proud?

LILLIAN: Yes. Only a noble, courageous people could suffer so much.

JOEY: Yes, you're right, we must be proud.

LILLIAN: I can see it in you. Even when you were speaking tonight, how much you care about your people.

JOEY: You can see it in me?

LILLIAN: I can see it in you now. You know what it's like to be poor and oppressed. There's a fire in your eyes when you're talking about them, Joe. I could see it tonight when you were talking and everyone was listening to you.

JOEY: Do you know that you're the first person that ever talked to me like that?

LILLIAN: You've got it in you, Joe.

JOEY: I know I do. But no one else ever saw it before. God, it's good not being alone.

LILLIAN: I can see you back there in Newfoundland, going from cove to cove in the rain, the fog, the wind; and going into their houses, looking into the sunken eyes of the fishermen, them worshipping you, adoring you, letting you into their hearts.

JOEY: (*He kisses her and rises----uncertain.*) Well, if I do as you say, as we both say...

LILLIAN: (*Standing.*) You will, Joe, I know it.

JOEY: Not here. (*He picks up his jacket and holds it.*) It won't be here in New York. It'll have to be in Newfoundland, where the people are, where my people are. And I think I know that your place is here, where your people are.

LILLIAN: Yes...

(Joey starts to leave but stops.)

JOEY: Lillian, will I see you again?

LILLIAN: Yes, of course.

(Joey clicks his heels and exits. Lights cross fade to wharf.
Sound of foghorn.)

Captain Joe and Eli
Scene 5

(Captain Joe and Eli are on boat. Captain Joe is at the wheel.)

CAPTAIN JOE: Throw off the line, take her slow. Bit foggy. It'll clear up though. I got a new wireless down below...why don't you go down and listen to it?

ELI: No. I wish we coulda taken Father in in the spring when we first found the TB.

CAPTAIN JOE: No beds?

ELI: Hundreds on the waitin' list. Father waited eight months for a place in that sanitorium.

CAPTAIN JOE: It's all God's will.

ELI: Your father died on the water, didn't he?

CAPTAIN JOE: Hangin' onto the wheel. Sent all of us down below. Sea was poundin' over the boat...poundin'. Just...swept him off, never found him.

ELI: An empty coffin.

CAPTAIN JOE: Not even his hat in it.

ELI: God's will. Where would we be if we couldn't say God's will? I wish I could see through this.

The Sanitorium
Scene 6

(Newfoundland, 1930-31)

GREG: I saw your father die. He coughed himself awake. He spit up blood. They say there's no pain. They say it's like freezing.

ELI: Who are you?

GREG: I'm scared, boy. Tubercular, like him. My name is Gregory Power.

ELI: Where do you belong?

GREG: Dunville, Placentia Bay. Don't come too close, you might get it.

ELI: I held my father many times. If I'm gonna get it, I got it. My father was a master mariner. Had a hand in the buildin' of every boat come out of Round Harbour these fifty years. All the lads used to follow him fishin'. They said father must talk to the fish, 'cause he always knew where they were. Kind of man everyone in the cove could depend on.

GREG: I just came back from the British Empire Games in Ontario. I set two Games records, the high hurdles and the hop, step and jump.

ELI: They got the hop and the skip for fellas your size, have they?

GREG: The hop, and the skip, and the jump. Stand back, I'll show you. Take a long run at the pit, then a hop and a skip *(He tries but can't make it.)* I can't breathe.

ELI: Take care of yourself, b'y. You're here now. They can help you.

GREG: Help? Here? You know the only help they gave your father was to pull the curtains around his bed. When they first found the tuberculosis in me there was five-hundred-and-seventy-one wanted to get in the sanitorium. Sir John Crosbie got me in before the lot of them.

ELI: How?

GREG: I was somebody. International athlete. Sir John was my patron. Men like him own the island. Yes, sir. What money wants, money gets.

ELI: Is this my father's reward? For a lifetime of work and work and work? Why? To come in here and die alone? God's will?

GREG: God's will my arse.

ELI: If you believe that, if you believe you can change things, you should be runnin' as hard as you can from this death house. Get out, b'y! Change things! Get out!

(Music ends scene. Lights cross fade to house area.)

The Barrelman
Scene 7

(Newfoundland, 1937-43. Eli and Mary are in the kitchen of their house while Captain Joe and Dickey are near the wharf.)

ELI: Hey, b'ys, it's time for "The Barrelman!"

(They all gather in the kitchen to listen to Joey over the radio.)

JOEY: *(In the office area with an old fashioned microphone. He rings the bell six times.)* F. M. O'Leary presents, the Barrelman. Our first story comes from Mr. Fred Stuckless of Englee. Mr. Stuckless found entangled in his net the biggest shark ever found in Newfoundland waters. Thirty-seven feet long and the liver filled six pork barrels.

CROWD: My God, that's some size. *(Etc.)*

JOEY: You wouldn't want to be swimming with that around now, would you?

CROWD: No, b'y. *(Etc.)*

(Ding sound.)

JOEY: Then there was Francis Lewis of Fleur de Lys who fired his double barrel shotgun at a thick flock of ducks. Nothing happened until they'd flown on some distance. Then fifty of them dropped from the sky. They had been so tightly packed that the dead ducks couldn't fall through.

CROWD: Go on, b'y. *(Etc.)*

JOEY: Proving once again that Newfoundlanders have what it takes every time they get the chance. Thank you for your stories and please, please, keep sending them in.

ELI: Dickey, b'y, you should send in the story of your wooden leg, b'y.

MARY: Yes, Dickey.

DICKEY: No b'ys, I'd be too embarrassed, eh.

CROWD: Come on, b'y. (*Etc.*)

DICKEY: No b'y, sure I already told you the story anyway.

CROWD: (*As they get an idea of their own.*) Oh, yeah.

(Amused, Joe silently reads the letters. Music sounds.)

ELI: Dear Mr. Barrelman, I got a story for ya now you might want to use it on the radio. It concerns my friend Dick who was down in St. John's and went up to Signal Hill to have a bit of fun. All of a sudden he sees this canon, and bein' in a playful mood he sticks his leg in it. Little does he know it was twelve o'clock and he was inhabitin' the noon-day gun. Needless to say my friend and his leg were soon separated. But with the help of a bit of plankin' from his schooner, he was right as rain, and to this day he is one of the better step dancers in the cove.

MARY: Dear Mr. Barrelman, we got a young fella here who only got one leg. The other bein' wooden. Now he lost his leg sealin' on the Labrador one year. He was only fourteen at the time. One night him and his friend was lost on the ice all night long. He fell asleep, but his friend was a brave man. He dragged him body and soul all the way back to the ship. And when he came to sometime the next day, his leg was gone. You see it was froze and had to be cut right off. I always uses the molasses from F. M. O'Leary.

CAPTAIN JOE: Dear Mr. Barrelman, I got one for you all about my mate, one legged Dick. On a fishin' trip about six year ago, Dick made a leap at a net that was slippin' over the side. And as a consequence he wounded himself up in the water, where upon a passing shark made a snap at him, but luckily got just his wooden leg off at the ankle. Well, such a fright it was that he got, that he propelled himself out of the water and onto the deck of a boat with such force that the splinters from his chopped off leg stuck into the deck like nails, and I said to him, "Stay there, you stunned bugger!" And he did until we got to Burgeo. Some folks around here says that Dick got more wood between his ears than he have into his legs.

MARY: The Barrelman.

(Six dongs.)

JOEY: F. M. O'Leary presents the Barrelman. One of the hazards of the rugged Newfoundland way of life is a loss of limbs, and one of the commonest sights is the wooden leg. This weekend I received several stories. There was the man who playfully stuck his leg in the noon-day gun. When the clock struck twelve he darn well knew what time it was. Two friends went sealing on the ice one day. Four legs went out, but only three came back. And last, a man whose leg was snapped off by a shark. And do you know that all these stories came to me from the same community.

CROWD: (*Realizing Dickey has told them all a different story.*) Dickey!

BRIAN: All right now, how did you really lose your leg?

DICKEY: Well, b'ys, one time I was up loggin' at the North Pole, eh...

CROWD: Go 'way. (*Etc.*)

JOEY: And finally, finally, think of Skipper Jonas Pratt of Fogo who cornered the island's only rat, grabbed it with his bare hands and bit the rat's head off. Proving once again that Newfoundlanders got what it takes every time they get the chance.

ELI: My God, we Newfoundlanders got a lot to be proud of.

The Opportunity
Scene 8

(Montreal, Quebec, 12 December 1945. Musicians play Newfoundland tune.)

JOEY: Twenty years. Ever since New York I've been a union organizer, a broadcaster, a journalist, and now a pig farmer. God, the socialist rallies...I walked right across the island organizing the railway. My Barrelman days, all those people, all those people, and what's it all been for?

(A slide of the Canadian Parliament buildings appears on the screen.)

My God, this is it. The moment I've been waiting for. This is our chance. My chance. Commission of Government is doomed. No more tyranny rule. We're going to get a chance to choose for ourselves who will lead, and who else is so prepared to guide—to lead? But who will follow? Not the merchants, not the money bags. The people. The people. What can I offer the people? Money. More than anything else they need money? Who has money? Who can give us what we need?

(Musicians begin playing "O Canada.")

Joey in Ottawa
Scene 9

(August 1946.)

JOEY: Good day, sir. My name is Joseph R. Smallwood. Newfoundland and Canada together will make a great nation, Mr. Prime Minister.

PICKERSGILL: I'm the executive assistant to the prime minister, Mr. Jack Pickersgill.

JOEY: Oh...

(Joey begins to walk away.)

PICKERSGILL: But I absolutely agree with you.

JOEY: (*Stopping.*) You do. Well. We must get in to see the prime minister, Mr. Pickersgill.

PICKERSGILL: Well, it's always been a dream of mine, Mr. Smallwood, to get out of the backrooms of politics and into an elected seat in the house.

JOEY: I see.

PICKERSGILL: And I know the Ottawa political machine like I know the back of my hand.

JOEY: Well, I need to know Ottawa, Mr. Pickersgill. And I have just the district for you.

PICKERSGILL: But you don't have a government, Mr. Smallwood.

JOEY: I will, Jack.

PICKERSGILL: Well Joe, you can find the acting prime minister in a small office off the house every afternoon at two thirty.

JOEY: I see. Well, Jack?

PICKERSGILL: I'm behind you, Joe.

St. Laurent's Office
Scene 10

(Joey is sitting at St. Laurent's desk snooping. Louis St. Laurent enters.)

JOEY: Mr. St. Laurent is out at the moment. I'm just taking care of a few things for him.

ST. LAURENT: I am Louis St. Laurent.

JOEY: *(Jumping up and pushing St. Laurent into the chair.)* Well, sit down, Mr. St. Laurent. Newfoundland and Canada will make a great nation, Mr. St. Laurent. Is it true the baby bonuses will be raised and the old age pensions? They are important to our people, you know.

ST. LAURENT: I was just about to have some lunch. Would you care to join me?

JOEY: Yes, yes. I'll have some salmon, some Newfoundland salmon. I'll bet you don't have any of that, do you? You may have the other salmon, the chum, the pink, the coho, the sockeye, the chinook, but I bet you don't have any Newfoundland salmon. You could have, you know. If Newfoundland joined Canada, you could have hundreds of tons of Newfoundland salmon dumped on your doorstep every morning.

PICKERSGILL: Sea to sea.

JOEY: Think of it, Mr. St. Laurent, one great nation from sea to sea. One total, complete, great nation.

ST. LAURENT: It would be a nice idea.

PICKERSGILL: You could be prime minister.

JOEY: Our people are saying that they will vote for Confederation the day you become prime minister. They are just waiting for you to become prime minister. They're calling out for you, sir, and they're calling out for me. They are singing your praises and they are singing mine as they prong the fish out of their boats. They are calling out for me. *(He calls out of the door.)* I'm coming! *(Joey begins to move across the stage as if he were returning to Newfoundland.)* They're waiting for me now, sir, I have to go.

(*Calling.*) I'm coming. (*To St. Laurent.*) But, I'll be back, you haven't heard the last of me. (*Calling.*) Wait, I'm coming, don't despair Newfoundland, I'm coming.

(Joey exits.)

ST. LAURENT: Jack, what was all that about?

PICKERSGILL: The Terms of Union.

Joey Meets Greg Power
Scene 11

(The lights come up on Joey reading.)

GREG: (*Sneaking up from behind.*) Honk once if you believe in Confederation.

JOEY: Honk.

GREG: Honk. Mr. Smallwood, I am the man writing letters in support of you in the newspaper.

JOEY: Mr. Power. Mr. Gregory Power. We meet at last.

GREG: It's a pleasure, sir.

JOEY: Mr. Power, I have the Terms of Union right here in my breast pocket.

GREG: You do not.

JOEY: Well, they don't know that.

GREG: (*They stand back to back.*) Mr. Smallwood, here we stand, the terrible two. Up with the people.

JOEY: Down with the merchants.

GREG: God, how I do detest them.

JOEY: Detest, detest, I detest shining my shoes. I detest brushing my teeth. Detest.

GREG: All right, I have contempt for them.

JOEY: I hate them.

GREG: I hate them more than you do.

JOEY: No you don't.

GREG: Yes I do.

JOEY: No you don't.

GREG: How much do you hate them?

JOEY: I hate them more than sculpins.

GREG: I hate them more than a squid's squirt.

JOEY: I hate them more than water pups.

GREG: What?

JOEY: Sores, Greg, sores.

GREG: Good, but do you know how to fight? I do. I can make them look foolish. The pen is mightier than the sword. Listen to this. (*They laugh.*) This is a little something I wrote about the Responsible League and Peter Cashin:

> The Responsible rule of Peter Cashin,
> Appears today to be the fashion,
> Merchants to maintain the status quo,
> They wear the top hat, we get the toe.

(They laugh again.)

JOEY: That's good, Greg, That's good, that's good, that's good. But you see I speak right into the people's heart. I tell them what they want to hear. I tell them you can't eat Responsible Government.

(Greg snores.)

JOEY: Greg...

GREG: We'll make a wonderful team. We must circulate a newspaper, a Confederate newspaper to every outport in the country. Here's another one. This one is a limerick. Listen to this:

> He swallowed some sacred tradition,
> Prescribed by the merchant's dietician,
> Then he said to his missus,
> "Have some, it's delicious."
> They died of acute malnutrition.

JOEY: *(They laugh.)* That's good, Greg, good, but I think we should leave out the contractions. I think you should stick to the King's own good English.

(Greg slaps the book closed and begins to leave.)

JOEY: My God, man, keep your contractions.

GREG: After working for only a few minutes with you I can only marvel at the humility of a man like Archbishop Roach.

JOEY: Honk.

GREG: Honk.

JOEY: Well, come on, man. We have the fight of our lives on our hands.

(They exit saying "Honk, honk, honk.")

The National Convention
Scene 12

(St. John's, Newfoundland. The Colonial Building. 11 September 1946 to 30 January 1948. The scene opens in chaos. "Lukey's Boat" is playing.)

WHIFFEN: Now, look, right now in Canada you got nine provinces and we should be number ten because ten is a good number. You got ten fingers, you got ten toes, there's ten numbers in a deck of cards, and there's ten commandments in the Bible and 'tis a sin to go against the Bible, brother.

MERCHANT: Confederates are quislings. Confederates are traitors. We who favour independent Responsible Government put before the people a broader, more articulate choice than the shrill hysteria of Mr. Smallwood. We say an independent Newfoundland, "Where once our fathers stood we stand."

WHIFFEN: Now, look, there's them that are accusin' Mr. Smallwood of playin' like the devil, and there's them that are accusin' Mr. Smallwood of playin' like God. Seems to me that you don't know which end of the gun you are shooting from.

MERCHANT: The opponents of Responsible Government have raised the spectre of the Water Street bully boys heaping their feudal injustices on the toiling masses.

(Music plays. Whiffen feigns a stroke and falls on the floor. Merchant rushes to aid him and Whiffen springs up.)

WHIFFEN: Huffin' and puffin' like an old locomotive, aren't ya? Well, it don't matter how much ya toot you are still on the wrong track.

JOEY: Mr. Chairman, this is my last chance to speak to the people of Newfoundland and I say to the people...

CASHIN: Never mind the people, speak to the chair...

JOEY: I have never opened my mouth without speaking to the people, my masters who sent me here.

CASHIN: Well, at least speak to the point.

JOEY: I speak to the people through you; therefore, you are the most honoured men in this country today. Now, Mr. Claude Hicks of Fogo wrote to me, he has a house, a barn and five acres of land. And he wants to know how much tax he'll have to pay under Confederation. I cannot answer Mr. Hicks until I know if Fogo will decide to have a town council or not. Now the council may collect a small sum, perhaps five dollars. Now Mr. Hicks may be on the council, and decide his own tax, and what I say to the people of Fogo, I say to all the people of Newfoundland, to every Newfoundland outport. The people need not worry about taxes.

CASHIN: Whenever Mr. Smallwood is faced with an issue with which he cannot deal, he evades, he dodges, and finally he sends up a smoke screen.

JOEY: Sir, our country is fast becoming a land of festering monopolies.

CASHIN: There he goes, he's doing it again.

MERCHANT: Bolshevism. Centuries of energy, vision, breeding and education have guided us. My great-great-great-grandfather arrived in Conception Bay in 1759. He saw his opportunity and he took it.

WHIFFEN: I'll give you opportunity.

(He attacks Merchant, grabbing him by the lapels.)

CASHIN: What does this have to do with Confederation? You are a British plot.

JOEY: I'll tell you what it has to do with Confederation. The twenty-one millionaires are anti-Confederate. The twenty-nine dictators are anti-Confederate. They sit and shiver in their stylish offices for fear Confederation will come along and sweep them into the ashcan of history.

WHIFFEN: Now Mr. Smallwood has called them what they are, the twenty-nine dictators. And instead of them havin' jobs as dictators we should kick them into the potato patch and give them jobs as tater diggers.

JOEY: Whiffen, I'll do the talking.

WHIFFEN: Suit yourself, sir.

CASHIN: If you're going to do the talking, at least have the courtesy to have something to say.

JOEY: The lid is coming off, it's coming off. You take it now. You take it. Our people will no longer be held back by men like Mr. Cashin. We will no longer be bullied by the Water Street merchants.

CASHIN: This man wants to lead our country. Well, who is he? Is he an experienced politician? No. A leader of the Church? No. A businessman? No. What is he? He's a failure. He couldn't even run a pig farm.

JOEY: I've learned a great deal about pigs, Mr. Cashin. There are two kinds of pigs, Mr. Cashin. Those with four legs and those with two.

CASHIN: He writes books, no one buys his books. He hasn't even paid back the money he borrowed to write the books. And this man wants to lead our country. He's a lunatic, a lunatic.

MERCHANT: Bolsheviks, Trotskyites.

(Whiffen attacks Merchant. Joey and Cashin tell them both to sit down. Music.)

JOEY: If I weighed fifty pounds more I'd throw Mr. Cashin through the window.

WHIFFEN: I'd help you.

CASHIN: And where were you in 1914?

JOEY: At Bishop Feild College, Mr. Cashin. I was thirteen years old.

MERCHANT: What's past is past. We are at the edge of a new beginning.

JOEY: Ladies and gentlemen.

CASHIN: There are no ladies in this Convention.

JOEY: Ladies and gentlemen. I was never so close to our people as in those days of the dole. And as long as I live I'll remember those friends of mine, toilers—struck down by beri-beri, children who felt the pinch of hunger, patient mothers with heartbreak in their eyes, the baffled sullen rage of fishermen whose greatest toil and endurance could not provide enough for their families. The unemployed of St. John's waiting around street corners in their despairing hundreds for jobs that never turned up. I saw them and I swore an oath that, as long as I lived, I would never become party to letting such things come back to our people again. That is why I became a Confederate. We don't want to be millionaires, Mr. Cashin. We're just aching for a common justice in our own land. And I'll see to it that we get it.

CASHIN: There is a plot at this moment in Newfoundland. A plot to sell this country to the Dominion of Canada. To sell us right up the St. Lawrence River for thirty pieces of silver. Listen to what Mr. Smallwood is saying. He's telling us that we Newfoundlanders are a lost people, that our only hope, our only salvation, is to follow this new Moses across the Cabot Strait into the Promised Land. Well, I for one do not believe that this good ship of state is all that leaky, and I am not prepared to send out an SOS for a Canadian rescue tug. If Mr. Smallwood had his way, we would cease to exist as an independent country. There would no longer be such a thing on God's green earth as a Newfoundlander. And to that I say, Mr. Smallwood, at least Judas Iscariot had the decency to hang himself.

(As they begin to move downstage the lights fade on Convention and two spots come up on Joey and Cashin.)

JOEY: Our people will have a chance to vote for Confederation. There is no doubt about that. Our people are on the march in their tens of thousands. A great crusade has arisen. The people will not be denied. The people, the people...when wilt thou save the people? Oh God of mercy when? The people, Lord, the people. Not thrones or crowns or merchants, but men.

CASHIN: *(Reads from "Innominatus" by Sir Walter Scott.)*
    Breathes there a man with soul so dead,
    Who never to himself hath said,
    This is my own, my native land.
    Whose heart hath not within him burned,
    As home his footsteps he hath turned,
    From wandering on a foreign strand.

JOEY:
    God save the people,
    Thine they are, thy children and thine angels fair,
    Save them from bondage and despair,
    God save the people.

CASHIN:
    If such there breathe, go mark him well,
    For him no minstrel raptures swell.
    The wretch shall forfeit fair renown,
    And double dying shall go down,
    To the vile dust from whence he sprung,
    Unwept, unhonoured and unsung.

(Music plays. Light out on Cashin who exits.)

JOEY: I haven't missed one minute of the National Convention; not one minute did I miss in two years. I'm no merchant. For me this is no sideline. I'm not running a business during the day and then grudgingly coming up to sit in the Convention afterward. To me this is the greatest thing that has happened in Newfoundland history in the last five hundred years. And God, the contempt I feel for those who don't realize that they are historic figures. They stand on the stage of history...oblivious...oblivious.

Joey Visits Eli and Mary
Scene 13

(Eli and Mary's house. Music plays.)

MARY: Where's that water I sent you for?

ELI: The well's gone dry.

MARY: Well, go out and dig another one.

ELI: I'm after diggin' up half the cove as it is. And another boat went to the bottom.

MARY: What, another one?

ELI: That's three in a row. I launches them down the slip, straight to the bottom. I don't know what the hell I'm doin' wrong.

MARY: And maggots in the damn flour again.

ELI: There you go, no flour, no boat, no water, no fish. Thank God we're independent, best kind of life.

(Joey enters.)

JOEY: Good day, sir, madam. I was talking to your energetic son down on the wharf and he told me where you lived. My name is Joseph R. Smallwood.

MARY: Yes sir, I been listening to you on the radio with the Convention, and when you were the Barrelman.

ELI: Oh, the Barrelman. How are ya gettin' on? I got one for you. It's all about the time I took Aunt Mary out in the boat, see. We were going out past the point when all of a sudden she sees a bobber in the water. She reaches over the side to get it, weddin' ring falls off the finger, straight to the bottom. Aunt Mary, over the side, straight to the bottom, forty fathoms down, gets the ring, and back. And when she come to, b'y, she was number one.

(Joey sits. When Eli and Mary sit, Joey jumps back up.)

JOEY: Sir, madam, I'm sick...and do you know what I'm sick of? I'm sick of poverty, I'm sick of disease. And do you know the one way out of it? Sir, how many children do you have? Five, five times seven is thirty-five times twelve is four-hundred-and-twenty. How much did you make fishing last year? Fifty dollars? Sir, your children could bring you in four-hundred-and-twenty-dollars a year. And, of course, if there are any old people around, there is the old age pension, and if you can't find work, if there's no work to be had, there's the Unemployment Insurance.

ELI: How soon can I get some of this money?

JOEY: You have to vote for Confederation first. Could you tell me who lives in that buff house next door?

ELI: The widow Bragg.

JOEY: A widow. Oh good, there's the widow's pensions too.

(Joey exits. Lights cross fade to wharf.)

The Arguers
Scene 14

DICKEY: Eli, you down there on the wharf?

ELI: I'm not here...

DICKEY: *(As he enters.)* You are so here 'cause I can hear you're here.

ELI: I'm here, but I'm not here to you.

DICKEY: You are so here to me, because I'm here to you. So there! Lovely day, Eli.

ELI: Go 'way, b'y, not a cloud in the sky.

DICKEY: You're lookin' miserable, Eli.

ELI: I'm feelin' wonderful.

DICKEY: You're lookin' miserable, Eli.

ELI: I'm feelin' wonderful.

DICKEY: Feelin' wonderful. I hear Cashin is at it again.

DICKEY: Only one I heard was Smallwood.

ELI: That Cashin is a wonderful speaker.

DICKEY: Can't speak for brewis. Smallwood now, talk like the fish.

ELI: All lies.

DICKEY: All truth. Cashin is all lies.

ELI: No b'y, Cashin's all truth. Smallwood's all lies.

DICKEY: Smallwood can speak though.

ELI: Yes, but Cashin is a better speaker. Smallwood would do well to listen to him.

DICKEY: He would listen if he couldn't speak, but he can speak so he's not gonna listen, is he?

ELI: Who?

DICKEY: Cashin.

ELI: Guaranteed. If you put the two of them in one room, one is doin' all the talkin', the other is doin' all the listenin'. The one doin' the listenin' should be doin' the talkin' 'cause he's the only one got something to say.

DICKEY: Who are you votin' for?

ELI: Undecided.

DICKEY: Yeah, well you should go on home out of it now then, Eli b'y.

ELI: No b'y. You go on home out of it.

DICKEY: No, I'm not goin' home out of it, you go on home out of it.

ELI: Well b'y, you better go home out of it, 'cause I'm not goin' home out of it.

DICKEY: Well, I'm not goin' home out of it, you're gonna have to go home out of it.

ELI: All right then, all right, I'll go on home out of it...Wait a minute, this is my bloody wharf.

DICKEY: Well if you're stayin', I'm goin' home out of it.

ELI: Go then.

DICKEY: Gone, b'y.

(Eli and Dickey exit arguing. Musicians play Light cross fades to house.)

Eli and Mary: Will We Join?
Scene 15

MARY: My God, Eli, things are going to be some grand after Confederation.

ELI: Yes girl, guaranteed.

MARY: Well, what's the matter with you? You're after sourin' on the idea are ya?

ELI: Well, I've been thinkin', girl. God's eyes shine on this little corner of the earth. We got a lot to be proud of.

MARY: Eli, I don't know how I could have thought of votin' for Confederation and the future of our youngsters with your pride at stake.

ELI: I hears that tone in your voice. That's Tilt Cove talkin' now. Tilt Cove. No proud independent woman from Round Harbour ever said a thing like that. And to think this humble little cove produced three eligible young women that I could have had my pick of. But as luck would have it they was all travellin' on to LaScie on the schooner one day. Lightnin' struck and they fell over the side.

MARY: Jumped over is more like it.

ELI: Tilt Cove, Tilt Cove talkin'.

MARY: Well anyway, they died like true independent Newfoundlanders, didn't they?

ELI: Yes, and I had three brothers drowned too, and as soon as it pleases God to call me, I'd be proud to join them.

MARY: Were they with the three going to LaScie or was that another time?

ELI: You can be as smart as you like, but the truth is I'd just as soon go right to the bottom as become a foreigner in me own country.

MARY: But Eli, if you goes and drowns yourself I won't have any pride to cook for supper. But, never mind, I could take the starving youngsters down to the wharf every Sunday and I could point you out. Look, there he is, there's your father, proud independent Newfoundlander that he was.

ELI: Yes, and our bloated rotting bodies would float to the surface and give you a chorus of "When sun rays crown thy pine clad hills, And summer..."

MARY: Turn on the radio, luh, they're gonna talk about the referendum and where we gotta vote.

ELI: That's not Smallwood talkin', is it?

MARY: No, it's not, but I wish it was. I'd like to find out more about those baby bonuses. (*While Mary is talking Priest enters unobserved.*)

ELI: Smallwood, Smallwood, Smallwood.

PRIEST: Eli, Eli, Eli, I've been hearing that you're been having political meetings around your radio.

ELI: No, Father b'y. There's not a bit of truth in that. No, b'y, no, no.

PRIEST: Eli, what's Mary listening to?

ELI: She's just waitin' now to find out where she can vote for Cashin.

PRIEST: Eli, we must continue to live decently, and honestly, and soberly, recognising that there has grown up with us for the past four-and-one-half centuries a decent God fearing way of life that we must pass on untarnished to posterity. And I feel that the placing of the Confederation issue on the ballot at this time is nothing short of a political crime against the freedom loving people of this small island of ours.

ELI: Heave it out of you, Father b'y, heave it out of you.

(Enter Bill. He doesn't see Priest.)

BILL: Hey Eli, we're havin' a Confederation party down at my place and we needs another bottle of rum, Eli. I bet the whole cove is votin' for Smallwood.

PRIEST: Rum, Bill?

BILL: *(Caught off guard.)* Father. Well...Eli...I was just out for a bit of a run, you know, to get ready for Sports Day...and ah...I picked up that small wood that you ordered, the chunks and the splits. No big wood among it. I'll see ya later, Eli...Father.

PRIEST: Well, my flock, I have to be going now. I expect to see you all in the confession booth Saturday afternoon. And, Eli, no doubt you'll be heading up the line.

ELI: Guaranteed, Father brother b'y, guaranteed. *(Priest exits.)* Mary, you could have shown a little respect talking about the baby bonus when he came in here.

MARY: And how, in the name of God, did I know the man was coming in the door?

ELI: Couldn't you smell him comin'? I could.

Greg and Joey: Orangemen's Meeting
Scene 16

GREG: Look here, Joe. I've got the results of the first referendum, Joe. No one got a majority.

JOE: I know the results, Greg. I know the percentages. I know the outcome. Now, no one got a majority. There'll have to be a second referendum. There'll have to be a run-off. So come on, man...

GREG: Joe, Joe, Joe, look at this, front page story in today's paper. For the first time in Newfoundland history nuns and priests flock to the polls to defeat Confederation.

JOEY: My God, man, they've started a holy war.

GREG: Now, who has been at the centre of the worst of the holy wars in the history of mankind.

JOEY: The Jews.

GREG: The Battle of the Boyne, Joe.

JOEY: The Jews weren't at the Battle of the Boyne, Greg.

GREG: Joe, William of Orange, crossing the English Channel.

JOEY: The Orangemen. We'll talk to every Orange Lodge in Newfoundland. No, no it's against my morals. It's against my political principles.

GREG: Joe, this is the biggest fight of our lives.

JOEY: A holy war it is.

Cashin and the Outporter
Scene 17

(On the wharf.)

CAPTAIN: Now, Mr. Cashin, there's forty-two of us here in this cove fishin', sir, and we got no choice but to go out there every day, no matter what kind of sea is on, sir. Now all we wants is the right to be able to say, "No, I don't have to go out there if there is a storm on." Smallwood told us we'd have a choice, sir.

CASHIN: Do you really believe that Smallwood and his ragtag band of Confederates are going to give you something for nothing? Nothing comes from nothing. You'll be paying Canadian taxes on everything, your boat, your house, your fish, your barn.

MARY: Mr. Cashin sir, you got some fine words, Mr. Cashin, and you got some grand ideas. But I had a little girl, Mr. Cashin, seven years old she'd be, but she died because I didn't have enough food to give her. Now, Mr. Cashin, can you bring her back to me?

CASHIN: Madam, I lay the responsibility for your daughter's death at the foot of the Commission of Government. I wish they'd taken my life, I'd have given it to help another Newfoundlander. This is our heritage, Newfoundlander helping Newfoundlander against the foreign forces arrayed around us.

FISHERMAN: You're the foreign force, Cashin. I knows you, you're a merchant from St. John's down here to get our vote and then you'll be gone and we'll never hear tell of you again.

CASHIN: And would you rather have the immorality of the Canadian baby bonus? Does your pride have a price?

FISHERMAN: Don't you talk pride to us. Talk food in the stomach and maybe then we'll listen.

(Lights out on wharf. Slide comes up of Fisherman at his father's grave.)

FISHERMAN: Dad, wish you were here now. You had twelve youngsters and I can never remember goin' hungry. I got five and it kills me to see them without enough food in their stomachs. I know it's our birthright. There was your grandfather and your father and you. I don't want to be the first to say that I'm not a Newfoundlander, but I can't see my youngsters go hungry. I pray to God and I pray to you that I make the right decision.

(Sound tape plays announcing Confederation while slides

*appear of the Confederation meetings, ending with the
Canadian flag.)*

TAPED VOICE: At one minute before midnight last night, Newfoundland, the oldest colony of the British Empire, relinquished
forever her cherished sovereignty as a free and independent
country. With one final stroke of a pen she became the tenth
province of the Dominion of Canada. After a long and hard fought
battle, the referendum campaign ended at the ballot box. Fifty-
one percent voted in favour of Confederation, Forty-nine percent
voted in favour of Responsible Government. Today we are Canadians.

Photograph by Dick Green

Eli and Mary on the Day of Confederation
Scene 18

(Newfoundland, 1 April 1949. Eli and Mary's house.)

MARY: Well now, this is something, you downstairs and me not
even out of bed. What are you doing, your drawers?

ELI: Go way, girl, I've done this a hundred times.

MARY: What's got you moving this morning?

ELI: Nothin'.

MARY: You're all stormed up now 'cause we won last night.

ELI: We lost.

MARY: Well, win or lose, Confederation has made a changed man
out of you. I haven't seen you move this fast in thirty years.

ELI: I don't s'pose now Confederation will have any effect on me at
all.

MARY: Oh, how is that?

ELI: I figures if I keeps myself busy enough I'll be able to ignore it.

MARY: Well, you can ignore it but I been thinking about the baby bonus.

ELI: What about it?

MARY: Well, Eli, you're not going out hauling traps on a day like this are you?

ELI: Mary. You...ooo. Oh...ooo...

(He playfully chases her offstage.)

Captain Joe and Dickey on the Day of Confederation
Scene 19

(On the boat.)

CAPTAIN JOE: Signed 'er over to Canada. Nothing we can do about it now, I suppose. I guess it's for the best.

DICKEY: But it's not Newfoundland anymore.

CAPTAIN JOE: He was the only one worth votin' for. Smallwood got more gumption than the rest of them put together. Father would have liked him.

DICKEY: Yer father was a sensible man. He wouldn't sign himself over to no one.

CAPTAIN JOE: *(Addressing his father.)* Oh, Father...you woulda had it easy with all the new money coming our way. I suppose Joey'll do right by us. But they better keep calling us Newfoundlanders. That's what we are—what you were, old man.

DICKEY: Yer old man was a Newfoundlander, we're not. We're flyin' a new flag now.

CAPTAIN JOE: I can hear you now. "Don't turn your back on your decisions." *(He pauses.)* Smallwood it is then. I'll still put flowers on your grave, Father.

DICKEY: Yer father is dead, Captain Joe.

CAPTAIN JOE: Take the wheel, Dickey.

DICKEY: *(He peers into the darkness and shakes his head.)* Anybody out there? Cracked.

Joey and Greg
Scene 20

(Joey and Greg enter and embrace.)

JOEY & GREG: Honk, honk, honk, honk.

JOEY: By God, Greg, I did it. I did it. I did it. I did it.

GREG: Joe, Joe, Joe...we did it.

(They laugh.)

JOEY: We did it, we did it, we did it, we did it.

GREG: *(Exiting.)* Honk, honk, ho-o-n-n-nk

JOEY: Honk.

(Greg exits.)

JOEY: Yes, we did it. You know there have been nineteen prime ministers of this country, only nineteen. And now me. Of course we're not a country now. We're a province. But it's our province. And I created it. I'm the only person alive in the world today who can say that. I created a province. (*He checks around for Greg.*) I did it. I did it!

(*Blackout.*)

ACT 2
After Confederation
Scene 1

(*Musicians play. A group of outport Newfoundlanders in the early days after Confederation enter in the dark; they sing and mime drinking.*)

EVERYBODY: (*Singing.*) "We'll Rant and We'll Roar"
We'll rant and we'll roar like true Newfoundlanders,
Shout out like hell for Premier Joe.
He thought he'd hightone us,
With the big baby bonus,
And it's back to our bedrooms, us Newfies go.

JEFF: The old hearty with the smooth flavour. Drink Molson Canadian, brewed right here in Canada. Well, b'ys, how does it feel to be Canadians?

BRIAN: Don't feel like nothin', b'y.

JEFF: What are we going to talk about?

DAVID: Well, I used to like to sit around the bar and bitch about the hard times. But ever since Confederation I wakes up with a smile on my face. I walk in front of that bathroom mirror, and, my son, I'd like to smack the face right off you.

BRIAN: I used to like goin' down to the ice, you know, smack a few seals, lose a leg every now and then, but, b'y, that never mattered.

DAVE: I used to like runnin' down the caribou, smackin' them into the cliff side, lose a finger every now and then, but shag it.

JEFF: I used to like goin' up into the woods loggin', hey. Smack down a few cords of wood, lose your head every now and then, but what odds about it.

DAVID: I used to enjoy gettin' into a racket with the Catholics and gettin' me face smacked off.

JEFF: Hey b'ys, remember what it was like going to school before Confederation?

(*They form a line as if in school. They look and act dumb.*)

DAVE: There goes me *Royal Reader* into the stove. I'm goin' fishin' with me father.

DAVID: You got your three R's, have ya?

DAVE: No, but I've resigned meself to a life of ignorance.

DAVID: Good enough, b'y.

JEFF: Door is off to the outhouse, Miss.

BRIAN: Yes, the snow all over the toilet seat, Miss.

JEFF: Had to do it with my pants on, Miss.

DAVID: Miss, my sister won't be in this morning. She went to God last night.

BRIAN: Apple, Miss? A-P-E-L, Miss?

DAVID: What's a happle, Miss?

DAVE: It's awful cold in here. There's no wood left.

JEFF: We're going to have to burn you, Miss. (*They mime grabbing teacher and throwing her into the fire. They laugh.*) Hey b'ys, remember what it was like goin' to school after Confederation?

    (*They reform the line, bright-eyed and alert.*)

EVERYBODY: (*Singing.*) "O Canada."

DAVE: Miss, may I go to the new learning resource centre to devour the last three books on advanced calculus?

JEFF: Miss, may I go to the four-hundred-and-seventy-seventh indoor toilet in Newfoundland?

BRIAN: Don't forget the Florient.

DAVE: Miss, my brother won't be in today. He's on an exchange trip to Quebec.

BRIAN: Apple: A-P-P-L-E, Miss.

DAVE: I have one in my lunch.

EVERYBODY: We all do.

DAVE: Miss, what's hunger?

BRIAN: What are maggots?

JEFF: Miss, what's death?

DAVID: Liberalism is enthusiasm.

EVERYBODY: Yeah.

BRIAN: Hey b'ys, I got one!

    (*Musicians play. Jeff and Brian sit and mime driving a car.*)

JEFF: Lovely bit of pavement.

BRIAN: Beautiful Liberal Confederation pavement.

    (*Boys mime driving on a dirt road.*)

JEFF: Must have been a PC town.

    (*Music.*)

DAVID: I got one.

    (*He mimes flushing a toilet as the others look down the bowl.*)

DAVE: It's got a leak in it. Look at the water.

DAVID: No b'y, water's supposed to be there.

JEFF: Hey Aloysius, mind if I tries it?

DAVID: Go on.

    (*Jeff spits his gum into the toilet and flushes it.*)

DAVID: Amazing! Excuse me now, b'ys, I got to use the outhouse!

DAVE: Here, b'ys. I got one.

    (*Dave mimes going to the dentist.*)

DAVID: (*As dentist.*) Half of them are in sideways anyway. Take them out. (*He removes Dave's teeth.*) Wonderful grand, b'y.

JEFF: Loves it, b'y.

BRIAN:　Me teeth are dirty. Take 'em out. (*David removes Brian's teeth.*)

　　　　　　　(They reform in the centre.)

SHEILAGH:　(*Singing.*)　We'll rant and we'll roar like true Newfoundlanders,

　　　　Back to the bedrooms in droves we all go,

　　　　Well, our backs may be achin', but the money we're makin',

　　　　We'll all be a credit to Premier Joe.

Pickersgill and Joey Campaign
Scene 2

(On the deck. Joey and Pickersgill are approaching the wharf.)

JOEY:　There it is. There it is, Mr. Pickersgill, your district.

PICKERSGILL:　You're sure this is the district for me, Joe?

JOEY:　You'll love them and they'll love you, Jack. Look, Jack, look, they're coming in droves, and why, why to see you, Jack. (*David and Sheilagh move toward wharf.*) There is not one single person who has not benefitted from Confederation. Not one. It's like the gentle dew of heaven falling on the just and unjust alike, the Protestant and the Catholic, the Confederate and the anti-Confederate. All, everyone benefits. (*To David and Sheilagh.*) I want you to meet one of those blessings now. Your right hand in Ottawa when you elect him, Mr. Jack Pickersgill. Now, I want you all to say his name. Say, "Pickersgill."

Photograph by Dick Green

DAVID & SHEILAGH:　(*They mangle the name.*) Piggergill.

JOEY:　No, that's not right. You, sir.

DAVID: Picker. Picker. Pickergill.

JOEY: That's not right. Now, you, madam.

SHEILAGH: Pickengill.

JOEY: That's not right either. Now, what do you do with berries in the fall of the year? You go out and you...(*He pauses expectantly.*)

DAVID: Pick them.

JOEY: Now, if you want your shipmate to slip you lines? You say, "Let 'er go," don't you? Now, forget the "let" and forget the "go," and what have you got?

DAVID & SHEILAGH: Er, er.

JOEY: Now, what do fish have? Not fins but gills, that's more than one. If it was only one, there would be just one...

DAVID & SHEILAGH: Gill, gill.

JOEY: Right, gill, gill. Now put it all together and what do you have?

DAVID & SHEILAGH: Pickersgill.

JOEY: Say it again.

DAVID & SHEILAGH: Pickersgill.

JOEY: Let me hear it again.

DAVID & SHEILAGH: Pickersgill. Pickersgill.

JOEY: Who is it?

DAVID & SHEILAGH: Pickersgill.

JOEY: Who are you voting for?

DAVID & SHEILAGH: Pickersgill.

JOEY: Whose your man in Ottawa?

DAVID & SHEILAH: Pickersgill.

JOEY: Jack, you tell 'em how to vote.

PICKERSGILL: Vote Gillerspick.

JOEY: Just call him Jack.

Murray Coming into Harbour
Scene 3

(On the boat.)

MURRAY: Not every mainlander has rape and pillage on his mind, you know.

CAPTAIN JOE: Oh, that's marvellous, Mr. Lander. Me missus is gonna sleep a lot easier now...Fish, that's why I voted for Confederation, fish. How much fish you got down in the United States? (*Before Murray can answer.*) A lot. How much fish you got down in the West Indies? A lot. How much fish you got over in Europe? A hell of a lot. How much fish you got into Canada?

MURRAY: A lot.

CAPTAIN JOE: Hardly any! They barely gets enough for theirselves. They wouldn't ship it through the Frenchmen anyway. So the rest of the country what don't get theirs, wants ours.

MURRAY: I never looked at it that way.

DICKEY: Don't get onto him about fish, or you'll be here all day.

MURRAY: It's too late. This is a great day for New-*found*-land.

DICKEY: Newf'n'land

CAPTAIN JOE: Why's that? 'Cause you're gettin' here. Thinks a lot of yourself, don't ya?

MURRAY: (*Pointing.*) Look, there it is.

CAPTAIN JOE: What?

MURRAY: New-*found*-land.

DICKEY: Newf'n'land.

MURRAY: Beneath the fog.

CAPTAIN JOE: Yes, b'y. Sometimes I thinks there's nothin' out there except the fog.

MURRAY: It looks like a whale surfacing. Beautiful. Rugged beauty. Blue green and purple rock. Look at the houses, stuck to the cliff side as if they don't belong.

CAPTAIN JOE: Well, b'y, we tried buildin' 'em right on the water but they kept floatin' away.

MURRAY: This place is like a new frontier. The blank space of Canada.

CAPTAIN JOE: That's because of the fog.

MURRAY: Have we got plans for this place. 1949—year one for New-*found*-land.

DICKEY: Newf'n'land!

CAPTAIN JOE: And Canada is changin' our dirty diaper.

MURRAY: I feel like John Cabot.

CAPTAIN JOE: Funny, you don't look like him. He was short, fat, and Italian.

(Crash sound as they lurch.)

CAPTAIN JOE: (*Yelling.*) Dickey, get back at the wheel. You almost runned us onto the rocks. You're gonna have us all killed.

DICKEY: Welcome to New-*found*-land.

Joey and Valdmanis Meet
Scene 4

(St. John's, Newfoundland, 1950. Joey's office.)

JOEY: (*Joey is pacing.*) Confederation was fun. It was the best time of my life. I enjoyed every minute of it. But now comes the hard part. We must develop, develop or perish. We can't go on being a glorified poorhouse. All the young people will leave. We need jobs, industry. But where to go?

(Valdmanis enters.)

JOEY: What to do? Who can help?

VALDMANIS: (*He kneels.*) Mr. Smallwood.

JOEY: Mr. Valdmanis, I presume.

VALDMANIS: Forgive me for barging in like this, but I simply had to meet the only man alive who has created a province of Canada.

JOEY: Yes, yes. I can understand that. They tell me that you were the Latvian finance minister at the age of twenty-nine.

VALDMANIS: Yes, I have made finance and economic planning the study of a lifetime. (*Showing false modesty.*) I have had some success.

JOEY: I have forty million dollars, Mr. Valdmanis. Left over from the Commission of Government. Not ten, not twenty, twice twenty, forty million dollars, to change the face of Newfoundland.

VALDMANIS: Yes, yes, I do understand your desire to quench your country's economic depression. Perhaps some concentrated investment in the development of new industries.

JOEY: Develop or perish is what I said.

VALDMANIS: What a unique way to put it. You know, there have been many men of genius who have recognized that the socio-economic ambiance contingent upon primary resource materials has a low percentile average and that industrialization only is the answer.

JOEY: That has been my dream. My vision. My hope. To bring prosperity and to provide jobs for my people.

VALDMANIS: Perhaps, I am out of place. But you realize Germans have been the greatest industrialists. I could offer my services, I have had experience.

JOEY: We must tread carefully. We must spend our money wisely.

VALDMANIS: And we must remember that it is *your* vision that is important. When we discuss my salary remember that it is my reward to follow behind in your footsteps.

JOEY: You may follow, Alfred.

VALDMANIS: (*He gives Nazi salute.*) My Premier.

JOEY: Alfred, Alfred, don't get carried away. People might take it wrong...they might get the wrong idea.

VALDMANIS: (*He gives American salute.*) My Premier. My Premier.

(Valdmanis exits. Greg and Les enter.)

JOEY: Now, who's in the Cabinet? Greg, Les, get in here. Pack your bags, boys, we're leaving for Europe. I'm going to tackle the businessmen, the hard hardened businessmen. It's either them or communism. (*Greg tries to interrupt.*) Men who have money don't part with it easily, they wouldn't have it if they did. Now why would they come to Newfoundland? Why not Bermuda? Why not Louisiana, why Newfoundland? Now, I'm taking Mr. Valdmanis as a great advisor and translator. It's the toughest selling job of my life. But I'm going to crack it.

GREG: Joe, how much do we know about Valdmanis? We know this much, he's acted as advisor to Latvia, and the Third Reich— two outstanding successes there.

JOEY: We're taking Valdmanis, Greg.

LES: I don't like that sleeveen, Joe.

JOEY: Now, Les, he's not better than you. He's different. Now, what's the difference between you, Les, and Dr. Valdmanis?

LES: He's from away.

JOEY: He has ideas, Les. Ideas for bringing German industry to Newfoundland.

LES: I got an idea, Joe. I got an idea for a cabbage industry.

GREG: I think you mean cottage industry, Les.

LES: Yeah, right, I think that we should make something that every Newfoundlander needs. Right, I think that we should make brooms. See, we can get the stick part from the wood on Labrador and we can get the brush part from the long grass on the barrens.

JOEY: That's a good idea, Les. Good. We'll send one out with Liberal paper.

GREG: You always get my day off to a good start, Les.

LES: Go 'way, luh.

JOEY: Now, Les, we only have two choices. (*Les holds up two fingers.*) One is Newfoundland industrialists (*Les puts one finger down.*) two is German industrialists. (*Les puts his second finger down.*) But there are no Newfoundland industrialists, Les. (*Les puts one finger back up.*)

GREG: What have you got left, Les?

LES: One finger.

GREG: Joe, even the German carpenter fixing my house warned me——look out for Valdmanis, Valdmanis is at it, Valdmanis has sticky fingers.

JOEY: He's an honourable man. He has great respect for me and I for him.

GREG: Drive on, oh truck of state.

JOEY: I have great love for Newfoundland, Greg.

GREG: Then don't let it be raped, Joe.

JOEY: Valdmanis would shine my shoes.

LES: He's a suck, Joe.

JOEY: Now, Les, I want you to be at the airport by five o'clock. I'm counting on you, Les. Don't let me down. Now you go on out Portugal Cove Road past the Pioneer Restaurant until you come to a sign marked "Airport." That's the road to take, Les. If you come to Windsor Lake you're gone too far. You have to turn around and come back. I'm counting on you, Les, don't let me down.

LES: I'm really looking forward to this trip, Joe.

(Les exits.)

JOEY: By God, Greg, I can see it now, the factories in their hundreds, the workers in their thousands streaming through the gates. The fishermen will come to work in the factories. They'll haul their boats up on the beaches and leave them there to rot. The day will come when we will have to import fishermen.

GREG: That's horseshit and dandelions, Joe, and you know it.

JOEY: Five o'clock, Greg.

(Greg exits. Teddy enters.)

JOEY: All right, Teddy, I can see you're sobbing. What is it, Teddy?

TEDDY: Sir, I need an adding machine.

JOEY: I can understand that, you are Finance Minister.

TEDDY: Sir, where will I get one?

JOEY: You go down town and you buy one, Teddy.

TEDDY: Sir, I'm broke.

JOEY: Well, you know that cash fund the secretaries let you dip into—petty cash.

(Teddy starts to cry.)

JOEY: All right, Teddy, I can tell you've done something wrong. What is it, Teddy? Own up.

TEDDY: Well, sir, you know the contract for the Harbour Breton road, you told me to give the construction company $300,000, they told me to give them $500,000, so I added it up and gave them $800,000.

JOEY: Teddy. Teddy. Teddy.

(Mr. O'Brien enters.)

MR. O'BRIEN: Mr. Smallwood, you in there, sir?

JOEY: Yes, who is it?

MR. O'BRIEN: Earl O'Brien, sir, Chapel Arm.

JOEY: Mr. O'Brien, I'm pleased to meet you. Chapel Arm. I know your father, good Confederate. Marvellous Confederate. Now sir, what's on your mind?

MR. O'BRIEN: Guts.

JOEY: Guts?

MR. O'BRIEN: Well, ah, fish guts, sir. See, I owns the plant in Chapel Arm, owns it outright. I'm me own man. Well, sir, I been dumpin' me guts in the harbour there for years. Now the Environment people they come along and they told me I got to stop, that fish guts along the shore was stinkin' up the whole town.

JOEY: I certainly never thought it would come to this, Mr. O'Brien. Newfoundlanders complaining about the smell of fish.

MR. O'BRIEN: They made me put guts in me trucks and take them to the dump.

JOEY: Yes, one of two-hundred-and-fifty-five municipal dump sites since Confederation.

MR. O'BRIEN: The guts broke the road.

JOEY: The highway?

MR. O'BRIEN: Guts are heavy, sir. Now, the highway people they're on me back. The whole lot of 'em, they're makin' me feel like a criminal, b'y. I wants that environment law changed, sir.

TEDDY: *(He sneezes.)* Guts, sir, I'm allergic to them.

(Teddy starts to sneeze again.)

JOEY: Teddy, don't butt in.

(Whenever Teddy starts to sneeze Joey stops him by pointing his finger at him.)

TEDDY: Ah...Ah...

JOEY: I don't think there'll be any problem, Mr. O'Brien.

(Teddy sneezes over Joey and O'Brien.)

The Census Taker
Scene 5

(Newfoundland, 1951. The men are on the wharf mending a net. Eli is talking incomprehensibly about his car. Brian enters also talking incomprehensibly. They are joined by Dickey who is also talking incomprehensibly. Murray enters.)

MURRAY: Mind if I join you?
> *(There is a moment of silence.)*

DAVID: No b'y, go ahead.

MURRAY: Nothing so powerful as the sea, eh?

DAVID: Yeah. Get a bit of a blow on, she'll be powerful.

BRIAN: Yeah. I'll tell you something powerful. I got a giant squid in the net the other day. When I tried to pull it over the side of the boat, that was powerful, wha'?

JEFF: Not as powerful as Mary Bugden, that's some powerful, wha'?
> *(They all laugh.)*

MURRAY: Fishing good?
> *(Another puzzled silence.)*

DAVID: Gettin' lump fish, caplin, herring. Nuttin' else.

MURRAY: What's that?

BRIAN: *(Holding up the net.)* Luh.

JEFF: *(Pointing to the net.)* Luh.

DAVID: *(Pointing to the net.)* Luh.

MURRAY: Did you tear it?

DAVID: Friggin' shark went right through that.

JEFF: *(Gesturing.)* Teeth on it that big.
> *(An argument erupts and they all talk at once until Murray interrupts.)*

BRIAN: Gonna take us a week to fix that, b'y.

MURRAY: See that rock out here on the point...do you get by that on the right or the left?
> *(Short puzzled silence.)*

DAVID: Depends on where you wants to get to.

DICKEY: *(Speaking very rapidly.)* What are you doin' down here anyway buddy?

MURRAY: I beg your pardon?

DICKEY: *(Speaking very slowly.)* I said what are you doin' down here anyway buddy.

MURRAY: I'm working for inter-governmental affairs. Human resources development division.

BRIAN: Oh yeah.

DICKEY: What did he say?

BRIAN: I don't know.

MURRAY: I'd like you to take a look at these census forms.
> *(He hands out the forms.)*

BRIAN: Nice colour.

MURRAY: The information we need is in this column: family name, size of family, ages of all its members, the number involved in the fishery, your religious affiliations, income over the years, taxes paid. Beneath that we have index of amenities: common household conveniences, car, TV, refrigerator, hot and cold...

BRIAN: I got a well that's as cold as a refrigerator.

ELI: You could have had a refrigerator too. I offered ya one...

(Argument erupts and they all talk at once until Murray
interrupts.)

MURRAY: If you have a refrigerator, just check the box beside the word.

ELI: You said taxes.

MURRAY: What I mean by that is...

ELI: We don't pay taxes, see. We made a deal with Joey years ago. We don't pay no taxes.

BRIAN: And don't bring religion into it. That's no good.

ELI: This cove is split right down the middle, the Catholics on the east, the Protestants on the west, in the middle there's a bridge. Every Saturday night we meets on the bridge and beats the shit out of each other. That's our only recreation; don't take that away from us.

MURRAY: All the forms are completely confidential. You simply fill them out in the privacy of your own home and seal them and mail them to Ottawa.

ALL: Post office, post office.

DICKEY: Mary Bugden works in the post office and she got her nose into every envelope goes through and she got a mouth on her like a miller's clapdish, attached in the middle and danglin' on both ends.

BRIAN: She steams 'em open.

DAVID: Anything you wants everybody in the cove to know, put it in a letter, mail it to Mary, everybody'll know.

(They all start to talk again.)

MURRAY: All right can we just look at a sample form here? Dick, what's your full name?

DICKEY: Dick Elijah Byrd.

MURRAY: All right, we just need a middle initial so we put down Dick E. Byrd. How big's your family?

DICKEY: How big is me what?

MURRAY: Your family.

DICKEY: Well, it begins with me great-great-grandfather. He come over from Ireland in 1592. (*Etc.*)

BRIAN: I got brothers,

(They all start talking again until Murray interrupts.)

DAVID: Boys, there's the mail truck, let's get there before Mary does.

End of Valdmanis
Scene 6

(St. John's, Newfoundland, 1954. Joey's office.)

VALDMANIS: My Premier, I have read your statement to the press about the failure of the battery plant and the rubber shoe factory. It was brilliant! I think that now we will not have to justify our support of the chocolate industry quite so much. And I see 1954 as the greatest year...

JOEY: *(Stopping him coldly.)* I don't know who's the bigger fool, you or me. I trusted you, I believed you, I even believed that you were my friend.

(Joey hands Valdmanis a document.)

VALDMANIS: My Premier, this is a mistake.

JOEY: We have the evidence. It's not just me you betrayed. It's the people. It was their money.

VALDMANIS: I will repay it, my Premier.

JOE: It's too late. Because of you I have betrayed my promise to my people. My dream for Newfoundland.

VALDMANIS: We could tell them something. We could make them believe that it was for the Liberal Party. My Premier, I will...

(Joey takes the document back.)

JOEY: Not another word. Not another word. Your corruption has become my corruption. You have stained me. You have dirtied my hands. I will make it up to the people. But there is only one place for you.

VALDMANIS: I will leave Newfoundland.

JOEY: Prison. Prison is the place for you. It's finished.

VALDMANIS: Why should you punish me? You are surrounded by embezzlers...in your cabinet...kissing your feet while they line their pockets. Prison! I will be ruined. Please, my Premier, please, not prison.

(Absolutely no response from Joey. Valdmanis exits in defeat.)

IWA Strike
Scene 7

(Newfoundland, 12 February 1959. Eli and Mary's house.)

DAVID: *(Entering.)* He's coming on the radio tonight at eight o'clock.

DAVE: He'll come out on the side of the union, sure.

DAVID: My son, Joey's gonna put the boots to the company to-night.

DAVE: Hey, who's gonna tend the picket line?

DAVID: If Joey's on our side, b'y, we don't need a picket line do we, eh?

DICKEY: Lovely day, Mrs. Eli.

MARY: Now, Dick, keep quiet because he's coming on the radio.

DICKEY: Who? The Barrelman?

MARY: He's the Premier of the province now.

DICKEY: Well, he's the same old Joey Smallwood isn't he?

    (The music intensifies. Lights come up on Joey in his office
    about to make his speech.)

JOEY: The IWA strike is a failure. The IWA is a failure. The IWA has failed the loggers of Newfoundland. In my opinion the IWA never can and never will win. The IWA are the greatest danger that has ever struck Newfoundland. It is not a strike they have started, but a civil war. There is more lawlessness, more violence, more cheating, more lies, in the last four weeks than we have ever seen in Newfoundland before. How dare those outsiders come into our decent, Christian province spreading their black poison of class hatred and bitter bigoted prejudice. How dare they come amongst God fearing people and let loose their dirt, and filth and poison. For forty-eight days I said nothing. But now I'm going to free the loggers of Newfoundland from this foreign union tyranny. I am going to give the loggers a union of their own and it will be a union free of rats and crooks and criminals and scoundrels and panderers and white slavers, the greatest collection since Hitler. A plague creeping into our decent island home.

BRIAN: *(Crying.)* If I was God, I'd...

    (Brian makes a fist and shakes it.)

DICKEY: From the moment he walked into this cove twelve years ago I knew this day would come.

MARY: And I thought the man cared about us.

DAVID: *(Burying his axe in a block of wood.)* Ahhhhh!

Greg Power Quits
Scene 8

(Joey's office.)

GREG: You didn't tell me you were going on the radio last night.

JOEY: The IWA speech. You heard.

GREG: It was remarkable.

JOEY: Well, what else could I do?

GREG: Just like old times, one man fighting the many.

JOEY: I can't abide lawlessness, Greg.

GREG: In honour of the old times. I have here a broadside, hot from the press. Want to hear it?

    There was a not-so-young ruler from Gambo,
    With a kingdom from Badger to Fogo,
    He forced beans and molasses on his loyal toiling masses,
    Is he now taking advice from the dodo?

JOEY: This is a joke, isn't it, Greg?

GREG: Here, I have another good one for you. You read it aloud to me.

JOEY: (*Reads.*) Years ago as a prince he got bunions,
    While he walked, organising the unions,
    But since coronation he's contracted inflation,
    When he breaks wind his gas will kill youngin's.
(*Angry.*) This better be a joke, Greg.

GREG: It's not just the strike, Joe. The whole thing has gone sour. Years ago, I nearly died. I did not beat tuberculosis in order to help yes-men and half-witted cabinet ministers, and fly-by-night promoters, looking for hand outs. Taste it, Joe, it's sour. Don't you remember "The people, Lord, the people." Honk. Let's get it all back, Joe. Go on the radio tonight. Tell them you made a mistake. Give them one week to ratify a contract. If they can't reach an agreement then bring the government in to arbitrate.

JOEY: That strike had to be stopped. It's like a new religion, IWAism. They come out of their midnight camp meeting with their eyes shining for Landon Ladd, the way they shine for me, Greg.

GREG: Well you said it, Joe. You care more for yourself than you do for them, but they are the ones who elected you, Joe, because you did care for them. And the truth is the more you glorify yourself, the faster they'll sprint to the Landon Ladds or anyone else who puts their interests foremost.

JOEY: To hell with Landon Ladd, I am the captain. And every captain needs a good first mate. And you are, Greg. You're a good first mate, but I'm captain.

GREG: That's it then.

JOEY: I did what I thought was best.

GREG: (*Recites.*)   I was once a young lad from Placentia,
    And I once said, "Thank the Lord who has sent ya,"
    But the fun and fight soured
    So here is one Power'd
    Be damned if you held him, I betcha.
    (*Greg exits leaving Joey alone.*)

JOEY: You'll be back. You'll be back. You've nowhere else to go.
    (*Music.*)

Resettlement
Scene 9

(*Newfoundland, 1960s. Eli and Mary's house.*)

MURRAY: These designated growth centres give us the opportunity to grab progress before it destroys us.

PAT: Dad, I agree with him, you know...

ELI: (*Cutting him off.*) Well, thank you, Mr. Lander, for coming by and explainin' all about this resettlement to us, but the fact of the matter is...

MARY: Me and Eli, we likes it here just fine and we don't want to move, sir.

MURRAY: You don't understand, Mr. Morgan, the fishing industry as it exists is dead. Newfoundland cannot support services like education and health and welfare to one-thousand-three-hundred settlements over a coastline of six-thousand miles. Those fishermen we cannot support must relocate. If you'll pardon me for saying so, you are like a drowning man grabbing at straws.

ELI: I am not drownin', all right. Not that there aren't hundreds who haven't up and down this coast over the years. But I'm not drownin', not yet.

MURRAY: How long are you going to lean, Mr. Morgan? You're only here now because Ottawa pays you during the winter what you can't earn fishing in the summer.

ELI: Joe Smallwood begged me to take that money.

MURRAY: You have depended upon the British Government for four-hundred years, you have depended on a merchant class who treated you like children, the whole time they bled you white. You have depended upon a relieving officer who alone decided if you were worth six cents a day dole. Christ, you were even persuaded to give up your own government.

ELI: My son, you got a pretty queer idea of history, but I'm gonna set you straight right now. England did not give to us for four-hundred years. She came here to get our fish and nothin' else. You could say that we gave to her; and as for givin' up our own government, you're too young to remember the hard times, but I'm not. And I'll tell you about them. Newfoundland wasn't the only place in trouble them times. The entire world was in trouble. Don't tell me it was only us who failed.

MURRAY: Centralization will happen. There are economic forces at work that you cannot stop, that I cannot stop.

ELI: I may not be able to stop it, but I don't have to be a part of it, we don't have to be part of it.

(Pat leaves angrily.)

MURRAY: This is the twentieth century. Your own Premier Smallwood, your own neighbours, are marching down a road they don't want to go back.

ELI: That's my road right out there, the water, and that's my car at the head of the wharf.

MURRAY: It's not your son's.

(Murray exits.)

MARY: Well, he's right there, Eli. This place is all right for the likes of you and me. Marg's gone off, Pat's almost reared, but what about a man like Bill Billard with five youngsters on the floor? They're not going to have a teacher here after June, b'y. You can't send youngsters out into the world today without an education.

ELI: Joey don't know about this! I'll guarantee you that. He would never walk into this house, and tell me to me face, "Eli, you leave your home now, and move to one of me growth centres, 'cause if you don't, b'y, I'll cut you off. There'll be no schools, no doctors, no mail, no nothing." He wouldn't do it. This Confederation now is really something, isn't it? More money than we ever dreamed of, but we're too poor to stay where we are.

Empty Victory
Scene 10

(Joey alone.)

JOEY: Why would anyone want to go on living there? Why ought they live there? They must disappear. Will they blame me? Will they think that I have failed them? Some will stay. Some will fight to stay, for them it will be a great victory, yet it may be an empty victory. If all the laws of God and nature and economics and social existence point to the disappearance of something, and something comes along and delays that, isn't that an empty victory? Greg?

(He realizes that Greg is gone.)

Joey Visits Greg
Scene 11

(It is a cold, wet, night. Joey is standing outside Greg's house. Greg is watching through the window.)

JOEY: *(Knocks.)* Greg, I don't need you. I *want* you to come back. Greg, there's no first mate. *(He bangs on the door.)* Greg, you're the greatest poet Newfoundland has ever seen, you make E. J. Pratt look like a clumsy ox. *(He knocks on the door again.)* Greg...

(Joey exits.)

GREG: You son of a...If I'd opened that door one crack you'd have had me. We're both gonna be lonely now, Joe.

Eli and Pat
Scene 12

(On the wharf. Pat has no shirt on.)

ELI: Cover yourself for God's sake. You know the sun is bad for your skin...what are ya at?

PAT: Fillin' out my unemployment card.

ELI: You got a job. You're fishin' with me.

PAT: Well Dad, I been meanin' to tell you, seein' as how I got enough stamps to collect my unemployment. I got a little bit of money poked away, and Joey is gonna pay me tuition into university when I goes anyway. I was thinking I'd take a few months off and go for a holiday up to Huntsville. Lie in the sun, nice little holiday. What do you say?

ELI: It is the middle of July. One of the best summers for fishin' we have had on this coast. You don't leave until the job is done.

PAT: Dad, you know you don't really need me. You and Bill can manage. The only reason you hired me on was so I could make some pocket money.

ELI: That's not so. I wanted you to learn about fishin'. You never know when the hard times might come again and the only place you'll get a meal is on the water.

PAT: Dad, I needs a holiday. I been fishin' every summer since I been thirteen years old.

ELI: You're only fifteen now. I been fishin' forty-three summers without a holiday.

PAT: And I don't want to end up looking like you. You're gone, b'y, hook, line and jigger. No, b'y. It's the new Newfoundland. We can afford to take time off. Huntsville, here I come. Movin' on, you know.

ELI: Well, I wouldn't want to get in the way of you movin' on!
(Pushes him off the wharf.)

Rossi
Scene 13

(Joey enters his office to find Rossi snooping around his desk. Rossi quickly straightens up and speaks after a pause.)

JOEY: *(Sniffing the air as he sits.)* My God, Rossi, did you fart?

ROSSI: No, sir. *(Short pause.)* Do you want me to? *(Joey gives him a "look.")* Sir, I got a constituent. He got a boat...

JOEY: I've got my problems too, Rossi. I have my constituents and you have your constituents.

ROSSI: Can I go, home now, sir?

JOEY: Yes, Rossi, go home.

ROSSI: Are you coming, sir?

JOEY: No, Rossi, I'm not coming home.

ROSSI: You should come home, sir.
(Rossi exits.)

JOEY: All Newfoundlanders should come home. Revisit their island home. See everything we've accomplished. I'll put aside a year, reserve a year, when all Newfoundlanders can come home. A "Come Home Year." Why not? We've got a lot to be proud of. By God, I'm going to do it.
(The song, "Come Home, Newfoundlanders," plays.)

Come Home Year
Scene 14

(Newfoundland, 1966. Captain Joe is working on the boat when Pat enters. Pat is dressed garrishly with sunglasses and gold chains; completely tasteless.)

CAPTAIN JOE: Well, where can I be takin' you, young...fella?

PAT: Oh, just takin' a little cruise down to Round Harbour, eh?

CAPTAIN JOE: Now, what would somebody like you want to go down there for?

PAT: Just a holiday. I'm from Huntsville, eh? Been in Toronto for five months though, livin' with me sister.

CAPTAIN JOE: Do all of ye up in Toronto dress like that now?

PAT: Oh, yeah, this is the norm. This is the norm, you know. You should see Toronto nowadays, hangin' out on the corner of Yonge and Jarvis. Lookin' up at all the big buildin's, the big cars goin' by...big bucks in Toronto now. Some good to be comin' home though.

CAPTAIN JOE: Another one. Lard God, that's all I been hearin', "Come Home Year." Not that it was a bad idea that Joey had— but where did you say you were from?

PAT: You didn't even recognize me, did you, Captain Joe?
(Pat takes off his sunglasses.)

CAPTAIN JOE: Pat Morgan, son of Eli and Mary Morgan.
(They shake hands.)

PAT: And come home for good.

CAPTAIN JOE: For good? You're as stunned as you ever were. Between you and me, there's more folks gettin' out of here because they can't find a job of work than is comin' back for this Come Home Year business.

PAT: Well, I'm comin' home for good, Captain Joe. Gonna build a house over on Pilley's Point.

CAPTAIN JOE: Lovely spot.

PAT: All kinds of new equipment on order. Sonar, radar, there ya are. I'll be all set, b'y, to make this fishin' work for me. I'll bet you Dad is goin' to be some happy to see me comin' home.

CAPTAIN JOE: I daresay he will. Maybe his luck will change for the better. But, Pat, look, when you sees him first, don't go wearin' that, eh? He's got an awful weak stomach.
(Lights cross fade from Pat and Captain Joe to Joey.)

Churchill Falls Deal
Scene 15

(14 May 1969.)

JOEY: This is a selfish project we are opening today at Churchill Falls. It's entirely, completely, selfish. This is our land. This is our river. This is our waterfall. It's Newfoundland first, Quebec second, the rest of the world last. And if you don't believe me, try me and see. I declare this power project open.

Eli and Mary Leave
Scene 16

(Eli and Mary's house.)

MARY: My God, you should have heard Marg on the phone. She

can't wait until we gets up to Toronto. And then she puts the young Eli on the phone. Four years old and he going like the devil. "We can't wait to see you, Nan. How are you, Nan?" The sweetest little thing. "Tell Granddad to bring us a fish."

ELI: What are you doin' with that wireless?

MARY: I'm bringing it up to Toronto.

ELI: No, you're not. They got electricity up there, they don't need wireless.

MARY: That's an antique. Marg would love to...

ELI: It belongs here. It's stayin' here.

(He throws the radio into the water.)

MARY: What? Are we gonna leave everything belongs to us, are we? What are ya going at the nets now for?

(Mary exits.)

ELI: Would you leave dirty dishes in the sink? You won't be trappin' no more fish now, I don't need you because they don't need me. I spent a lifetime learnin' every inch of this coast. But Joey says what I know is no good to no one. "You gotta go," says he. By God, there's somethin' wrong in that.

(Pat enters.)

PAT: Dad, did I just see you throw a radio in the water?

ELI: Yes.

PAT: What are ya gonna throw in next?

ELI: You.

PAT: I was hopin' maybe you'd change your mind. Stay on with me. Be my junior partner, Morgan and Dad.

ELI: You enjoyed being throwed off that wharf, didn't you?

PAT: Why Toronto?

ELI: Because if I'm bein' drove, I'm bein' drove all the way. Thousands they resettled are on welfare anyway. Well, not me. And if you had any sense you'd be comin' with me.

PAT: All right, all right. We had it all out last night. I'm gonna stay right here and make a go of it.

ELI: Well, as long as you're stayin', the old house will be lived in, anyway.

PAT: Live in that? You nuts? I'm gonna build a nice new split-level with two driveways right over there on Pilley's Point.

ELI: Sure, what's wrong with her? She only needs a coat of paint.

PAT: The only thing holdin' her up is the four hundred coats of paint you got on her.

ELI: We never agreed on anything, did we? All right, b'y, good luck to ya.

(Embraces him.)

CAPTAIN JOE: *(Yells to them from his boat.)* Time to get settled way down below now.

MARY: Now Pat, keep that gate closed. Don't let Joe Driscoll's goat get in and eat up me few flowers.

(Mary and Eli exit.)

PAT: (*Approaching Captain Joe.*) Should be smooth sailin', Captain Joe.

CAPTAIN JOE: I'm glad they took Joey's money for resettling!

PAT: I wish some of that Joey's money would go in to makin' the fishery work.

CAPTAIN JOE: Thought you were goin' to make it work by yerself. So don't go sayin' nothin' bad about Joey.

PAT: I'm not. I wish they'd start thinkin' about us, the ones makin' a livin' in Newfoundland. Spendin' all that money on hospitals, schools and universities. We're supposed to have that. We're a part of Canada. What about puttin' money into the people—just don't make sense—there's gotta be another way.

CAPTAIN JOE: Well if there is another way, Joey'll find it. He found Confederation for us when times were bad.

PAT: Times are bad now and all Joey can do is talk about the things we got. Look around. Mom and Dad leavin'. There's nothin' to show in Round Harbour for Confederation, for anythin'.

CAPTAIN JOE: Times are bad now? Twenty years ago your mother and father would have had to starve to death here. Now they got the choice to go, and get paid for it. No one begged you to come back and complain.

PAT: Yes, Captain Joe, I've been to Canada. I've seen what they got. If we're a part of Canada we should at least have the same things they got. The same chances. The chance to work in your own home.

CAPTAIN JOE: (*He moves away.*) If I didn't know you better I'd say that was anti-Liberal talk.

Joey and John Crosbie
Scene 17

(*St. John's, Newfoundland, 14 May 1968. Joey's office.*)

JOEY: Where's Mr. Crosbie? Where's young Mr. Crosbie? This meeting was supposed to start three minutes ago.

JOHN CROSBIE: Good morning, Mr. Smallwood. How are ya?

JOEY: Wonderful. Disappointed. I'm going to make a great, a great announcement. I've decided to give Mr. Shaheen an extra five million dollars to add to his investment in Newfoundland.

JOHN CROSBIE: An extra five million dollars. Sure we already gave him thirty million dollars without so much as a feasibility study. What are you running here a government or a pawn shop?

JOEY: How dare you attack such a great man? How dare you? A man on a par with Squires and Sir Robert Bond. Would you say the same about them? I have endless respect for the man, endless respect. He has the heart of not two bulls, but the courage and strength of ten bulls.

JOHN CROSBIE: That's a lot of bull.

JOEY: Do you know how long the wharf will be at Come by Chance? Just the wharf alone, from the landwash to the head of the wharf, three quarters of a mile, three quarters of a mile, John.

JOHN CROSBIE: And Shaheen is asking the government to take a mile long walk off that wharf. Listen, are we going to give the province away to every entrepreneur who comes in here with a fistful of dollars? Under your leadership, Mr. Smallwood, this province is going to be bankrupt.

JOEY: That sounds like a campaign speech, John.

JOHN CROSBIE: Not a bad idea.

JOEY: John, I have something for you.

JOHN CROSBIE: I have something for you too, sir. I quit.

(They both pull out documents.)

JOEY: You're fired.

JOHN CROSBIE: I resign.

JOEY: I said it first.

JOHN CROSBIE: No, you didn't.

JOEY: Yes, I did.

JOHN CROSBIE: No, you didn't.

JOEY: Well, this is my office, out you go. Now who's firing who?

(They argue as the lights go out. Music plays.)

Pat at the District Meeting
Scene 18

PAT: All right, b'ys, you all know me, Pat Morgan. Now, I been home for two-and-a-half years. You all know the fishery is only gettin' worse. It's time for a change. There's a leadership convention coming up and that's our chance. Send me in there to support John Crosbie for the leadership of the Liberal Party. We gotta change Joe Smallwood, so send me in to that convention on Crosbie's slate, because John Crosbie is our man. He understands, and with him we'll be able to wipe Smallwood and that whole crowd right out of power.

CAPTAIN JOE: Get down out of there talkin' about Joey like that.

(He hauls him down.)

PAT: Listen, Captain Joe, Smallwood is finished, that whole bunch of bandits are gonna be out in no time at all and we're gonna be puttin' in Crosbie and the younger crowd. You and your kind are finished.

CAPTAIN JOE: Finished are we? Me and my kind? It was me and my kind that kept this place going when we had nothin'. Oh, I'll tell you what we had, we had our name. I'm a Newfoundlander, so I got the right to die before me time. Pride—foolish, foolish, pride. And Joey Smallwood saved us from that and that's somethin' you'll never have to know. So get out of here. Go on!

(Music plays.)

Convention
Scene 19

(The Liberal leadership convention. St. John's, Newfoundland, 1 November 1969.)

JOHN CROSBIE: Talk, talk, talk. I'm not surprised, Mr. Smallwood, you've got to work sixteen hours a day; you spend fifteen talking.

JOEY: John, you're a jackass. You were a jackass to start with, then you stupidly crossed the house, that made you a double jackass. Then you crossed back again, and that made you a triple jackass. You've never made a right decision in your life. You're a jackass.

JOHN CROSBIE: Speaking of animals, if it hadn't been for my father you'd still be a pig farmer, shovelling shit.

JOEY: Your grandfather, Mr. John C. Crosbie, came into St. John's harbour flying the skull and crossbones, and you, Mr. John C. Crosbie, the dead spit of the man, have been flying it ever since.

(Pause.)

JOHN CROSBIE: Do you know what we call you behind your back? The King of Cost Plus and then we laugh. Ha, ha, Smallwood has become a demi-god. He listens to no one but himself. It's time for a new kind of leadership in Newfoundland.

JOEY: Now that is a man, that's a face only a mother could love. Only a very kind mother, and only on the very best of days.

JOHN CROSBIE: It's a sad, sad day when a man stays beyond his time.

JOEY: The people know where my heart is. It's with the people, where it's always been, and the people will decide, and they'll decide at this convention.

(Sounds of the convention. The results of the balloting. Banners fly throughout the audience as the convention tape plays. Announcement of the ballots. The screen and the house lights go up. Joey comes down over a long flight of stairs alone.)

PAT: *(Chanting throughout Smallwood's speech from the audience.)* Sieg Heil, Sieg Heil.

JOEY: *(On microphone.)* I am very thankful and grateful to you. Mr. Hickman has been down to offer me his congratulations. I wonder now will Mr. Crosbie make it unanimous? The Liberal Party is bigger than Mr. Smallwood and Mr. Hickman and Mr. Crosbie put together. I'm waiting for you, John. Where are you, John?

(Crosbie approaches the microphone. The lights go out on the house, and the tape and music stop. Joey and Crosbie slowly shake hands.)

JOEY: Mr. Crosbie, I am going to bury you ten feet under.

(Crosbie exits.)

PAT: Smallwood, you've played God long enough. You killed the fishery and you split our people right down the middle. Well, now your dictatorship is at an end because you're finished. Tonight you're finished, finished.

(The lights go out on Pat.)

JOEY: *(Alone on the stage. Everything has become silent. The banners are gone. He is a solitary figure.)* I've won. The victory is mine. But is it not an empty victory? If all the laws of God and nature and economics and social existence point to the disappearance of something, and something comes along and delays that, is that not an empty victory?

(Music plays.)

Captain Joe and Pat
Scene 20

(On the boat.)

CAPTAIN JOE: A man's got the right to finish his job. Not get booted out like a dog.

PAT: Did my father have a chance to finish his job fishin'?

CAPTAIN JOE: Ah, you're just sore now because Joey won and Crosbie lost, aren't ya?

PAT: He hasn't won it all yet, Captain Joe.

CAPTAIN JOE: He's still Premier.

PAT: He might be your Premier, but he's certainly not mine. And there's a good few more that feels the same way I do about him. There's an election comin' up. It won't be long before we'll be bringin' him down.

CAPTAIN JOE: The ingratitude.

PAT: Can't you see through him?

CAPTAIN JOE: S'pose I'm just an old codger am I?

PAT: S'pose I'm just a young know it all. Can't you just look at things in a new light? That's all I'm doin'.

CAPTAIN JOE: You must be right. I don't think you are, but you might be. *(Lights fade on the stage. Slides of Joey's career are shown as the taped announcement plays.)*

TAPED VOICE: Results of the Provincial Election are now Clear: 1971 will go down in history as the year in which Premier Joey Smallwood finally tasted defeat at the polls. Some observers have remarked that the small margin of defeat for Mr. Smallwood in the popular vote is almost identical to the margin by which he first won victory in the Confederation referendum twenty-three years ago.

(At the end of the taped announcement the lights come up on the stage. The actors have entered in the dark and have dropped their characters. Brian removes his Captain Joe hat and begins to speak as himself.)

BRIAN DOWNEY: Joseph R. Smallwood was the only man...The *only* one who ever...(He shakes his head.) Aww, what's the point?

Half of you wouldn't understand and the other half...
(Present-day Smallwood, sitting in the audience, interrupts. He approaches and climbs up onto the stage. The actors are somewhat taken aback.)

"Joey" and Joey
Photograph by Dick Green

JOEY: *(To the actors.)* I'm not dead yet. I'm not dead yet. I did this and I did that. I made this blunder and I made that blunder. *(To the audience.)* But I don't mind. Because I will be remembered. Others will be remembered by historians but I'll be remembered by the masses, by the ragged-arsed artillery. People will say Peckford, Peckford, what was that? Moores, who was he? A fish merchant? You know, everywhere I go people come up wanting my autograph. They know me as one thing—Joey. Half of them probably don't even know my last name. Vanity. Yes, I have vanity. But how many other men have had a play written about them, in their own land, in their own lifetime, in a theatre that they built? *(To the actors.)* Well is that it?

DAVID ROSS: We'll probably take a bow and go up for a beer, I guess.

JOEY: *(Mocking.)* You're going to take a bow and go up for a beer? You have the gall, the bare-facedness, the audacity to do a play about Newfoundland—about me—and send these good people home without singing so much as one verse of the "Ode to Newfoundland."

DAVID ROSS: Come on. *(Laughing.)* It's a pretty corny ending for a play.

JOEY: I don't think it's corny. *(To the audience.)* Do you? *(Audience applauds. To David.)* You see. They don't think it's corny. I don't think it's corny. And I'm not going to let you go until you do.

DAVID FOX: (*To musicians.*) You want to give us a chord?
EVERYBODY: (*Singing.*) "The Ode to Newfoundland."
> When sun rays crown thy pine-clad hills
> And summer spreads her hand,
> When silvern voices tune thy rills,
> We love thee, smiling land,
> We love thee, we love thee,
> We love thee, smiling land.
>
> When spreads thy cloak of shimmering white
> At winter's stern command,
> Through shortened day and starlit night
> We love thee, frozen land,
> We love thee, we love thee,
> We love thee, frozen land.
>
> When blinding storm-gusts fret thy shore
> And wild waves lash thy strand;
> Though spindrift swirl and tempest roar,
> We love thee, wind-swept land,
> We love thee we love thee,
> We love thee, wind-swept land.
>
> As loved our fathers, so we love;
> Where once they stood, we stand;
> Their prayers we raise to Heaven above,
> God guard thee, Newfoundland,
> God guard thee, God guard thee,
> God guard thee, Newfoundland.

THE END.

Wonderbolt

On Edge

1989

Written by
Beni Malone and **Rick Mercer**

ON EDGE

On Edge was produced by Wonderbolt Productions as a co-production with Resource Centre for the Arts (RCA) Theatre Company at the LSPU Hall, 3-7 May 1989. The play, written by **Beni Malone** and **Rick Mercer** was acted by the following cast:

Beni Malone	Eddie.
Rick Mercer	Tony, Hitman.
Mary Lewis	Harlow, Monroe.
Randy Follett	Lenny, Jailer, Reginald, Waiter, Courier.
Christine Taylor	Violet.
Daniel Lear	L'il Eddie.
Lois Brown	Director.

Additional credits:
Andrew Younghusband performed the telephone voice of Peter and **Jennifer Ross** played Monroe's body double. The "Santa" video, by **Barry Nichols** featured **Lois Brown** as the woman, **Rick Mercer** as Santa, **Daniel Lear** as L'il Eddie and **Chris Paton, Jeffrey Paton** and **Brendon Lelieveld-Amiro** as orphans. Set design was by **Peggy Hogan** and **Barry Nichols**, lighting **Boo Noseworthy**, costumes **Peggy Hogan**; stage management/properties **Barry Nichols** and sound **Derm English**. Photographs are by **Peggy Hogan**.

The production of *On Edge* was assisted by the Canada Council and the Newfoundland and Labrador Arts Council. The play was sponsored by Mobil Oil.

CAST OF CHARACTERS
(In order of appearance.)

TONY — Tony, Eddie's underling, a loquacious would-be womanizer.

LENNY — Tony's cell-mate, musician, a nice guy and the most sensuous sex symbol since Elvis.

EDDIE — Eddie Bossanova, a laconic dangerous crime boss and drug king.

HARLOW — Eddie's wife, a troubled and unhappy woman.

JAILER

VIOLET — Eddie's mistress, a sexy, saucy and smart barkeeper at the Vicious Circle Bar.

HITMAN

MONROE — Monroe Sanzo, Harlow's sister, Eddie's business partner and art gallery manager.

REGINALD — Reginald Wipe, art critic.

PETER — Underworld art dealer.

WAITER — Waiter at the Dying Duck Cafe.

COURIER

L'IL EDDIE — Eddie and Harlow's son.

ON EDGE

ACT 1
Scene 1

The play opens with a series of brief non-verbal vignettes, accompanied with appropriate music. In each scene the characters are preparing to attend an opening at an art gallery:
ONE. A small jail cell, Tony and Lenny are the sole occupants. Tony is smoking a cigarette and Lenny is strumming a guitar showing a to-hell-with-it attitude. Elvis Presley's "Jailhouse Rock" plays.
TWO. Eddie and Harlow Bossanova's penthouse. Eddie is in the den snorting cocaine and operating a remote control to watch a portion of a video over and over again. Harlow is downstairs, she's dressed in black, smoking a cigarette and is viewing slides through a child's Viewmaster. Aria from Madame Butterfly *plays.*
THREE. Jail again. Tony is getting out; his possessions are being returned and Jailer helps him on with his jacket. A definite personality is emerging. "Jailhouse Rock" plays.
FOUR. Violet's bedroom, just behind the bar at the Vicious Circle. Violet is lying on her back in a seductive pose as she adjusts her stockings. Annie Lennox and the Eurhythmics' "I Need a Man" plays.
FIVE. Jail again. Tony adjusts his jacket and preens himself; he looks ready for anything. He flips Jailer a coin. They exit. "Jailhouse Rock" plays.
SIX. Monroe Sanzo's apartment. She paints her toenails while draped across a large swivel chair. She spins around in the chair several times. Linda Ronstadt's "Blue Bayou" plays.
SEVEN. Enter masked Hitman. He picks up a telephone receiver, listens and replaces receiver. He draws and cocks a pistol. Exits. Sinister music plays.
    The play is performed in a combination of film-noir and commedia dell'arte styles. The costumes are varied and colourful. The ultra mod set is constructed on various levels which are interconnected by short stairways and steps. The spaces represent Monroe's art gallery and office, her apartment, the Vicious Circle Bar and Violet's bedroom behind it, Eddie's penthouse, jail, etc.

Scene 2

(Lights come up on centre stage showing Monroe's trendy art gallery. Enter Monroe. She turns on video player connected to a bank of monitors which play a continuous image of a flame. She picks up a tray of hors d'oeuvres. Enter Reginald.)

MONROE: Reginald! So glad you could make it. Reginald, I think you're going to love this show. Scott LaScone is the hottest item on the east coast. The Left-Hand Twister on Christopher Street went wild over him. Everybody in this city wanted his solo show and we got it. Reggie, buckle your boots before you take a look at it. It's simply going to knock you off you feet!

REGINALD: I'm sure it will. As you know I have a penchant for revulsionistic pre-natal post-modern video installations.

MONROE: Of course I know. That's why I invited you.

REGINALD: As a matter of fact, I have a penchant for Scott himself. Is he going to come?

MONROE: Well, it's too soon to say. You know Scott. He could go either way!

REGINALD: Yes I know. But then, so could I.

(Monroe hands trays of hors d'oeuvres to Reginald. She exits. Reginald sets the hors d'oeuvres on top of a video screen and examines them. Re-enter Monroe.)

MONROE: Listen, don't critique the food. I tried to get Natasha to cater, but things are too busy. I had to settle for Ralph, her ex. Well, he is like a bull in a china shop. He simply can't cook, and according to Natasha that's not all he can't do.

(Enter Violet.)

VIOLET: Girl, you really got taste.

MONROE: Yeah, I'm excited about it. Listen, Reginald the reviewer is here. Get him a drink will you before he starts pawing all over the hors d'oeuvres.

VIOLET: Sure.

MONROE: Pour one for yourself too. Be with you in a sec.

(Exit Monroe. Violet pours a drink for herself and Reginald. She passes him his drink which he drinks very quickly.)

VIOLET: Hi. I'm Violet. Just Violet. Very Violet.

REGINALD: Reginald. The reviewer. Just the reviewer.

VIOLET: Yes, I've read your reviews...over and over and over again.

REGINALD: Oh. Do you know if Scott is coming?

VIOLET: Well, uh, this is his exhibit, isn't it? Do you, uh, know if he's from here?

REGINALD: Hmm. I'm not sure where he's from. But I know where he lives.

VIOLET: *(Seeing his empty glass.)* Oh. Would, uh, you like somethin' to drink?

REGINALD: Yes, ah something hot and exotic perhaps.

VIOLET: If you're lucky.
> *(Enter Eddie and Harlow.)*

VIOLET: Hi, Eddie. What're you doin' here?

EDDIE: Checkin' my investments. Shouldn't you be at the Vicious Circle?
> *(Eddie takes drinks from Violet for himself and Harlow.)*

EDDIE: *(Giving Harlow her drink.)* Here, honey. *(Pause.)* Buy something.
> *(Harlow wanders around and moves to image of the flame. She sees Fire. Eternal flame. Blow torch. Startled, she drops her glass. Eddie, Violet and Reginald look at her. Eddie and Harlow exit. Violet and Reginald look at each other and exchange drinks. They move to the video image as if reappraising it. They look at each other and shrug. Reginald begins to scribble his review of Harlow's broken glass. Violet appraises the hors d'oeuvres on the video monitors as if they are part of the art. Reginald picks up Harlow's glass on floor and drops it into a box in the exhibit. He scribbles some more reviewing the mess he's made. Eddie re-enters.)*

VIOLET: *(To Eddie.)* What's wrong with her?

EDDIE: She's not used to crowds. She was overcome. One face too many.

VIOLET: *(Looking around.)* Yeah, well I wasn't expectin' to see you here. I'm just leavin' anyway.
> *(Enter Monroe.)*

MONROE: Hi, Eddie, being a bull in a china shop? Where's my sister? Ain't she coming?

EDDIE: Come and gone. She said to wish you well.

VIOLET: Yeah, well I gotta go too, Monroe. See ya later.
> *(Exit Violet.)*

MONROE: Strange to see you here, Eddie. To what do we owe the pleasure?

EDDIE: I'm in the office.
> *(He crosses to the gallery office area.)*

REGINALD: *(Showing Monroe his notepad.)* I love art that can elicit powerful gut reactions.

MONROE: *(Taking pad.)* Yes.
> *(Monroe bends down to sweep up broken glass using Reginald's notebook. Enter Tony. He walks up behind Monroe as she sweeps up the glass.)*

TONY: Naw, too much like jail, Monroe. Roll over, would ya.

MONROE: *(Rising.)* Oh Tony! *(Kissing him.)* You haven't changed a bit.

TONY: Where's the boss?

MONROE: In the office.

TONY: *(Gesturing toward the office.)* After you.

Scene 3

(Tony and Monroe join Eddie in office area.)

TONY: *(Shaking hands with Eddie.)* Two years, hey boss? Only seems like yesterday. Not really though, boss. *(Pause).* So boss, uh, too bad you never made it out to visit me in prison. But I know what it's like. *(Pause.)* So boss, it, uh, looks like some things have changed around here. Hear you been doin' real well. Ya got no worries now.

(Monroe pops champagne bottle and Tony and Eddie draw
their guns. They realize what's happened and relax.
Monroe laughs.)

TONY: Bit edgy are we? *(Pause.)* So boss, gettin' this gallery was a great front, wha' boss? Not bad, it's pretty shit hot. So's the building. I hear ya own that too. Not bad though, boss. I didn't know you were in this art stuff. It's, uh, not bad. Pretty classy.

(Eddie removes a skull-shaped sculpture from a crate, smashes
it in his hand with a crowbar to reveal a bag a cocaine. He
throws what's left of the sculpture on top of one of the crates.)

MONROE: *(To Tony.)* Check it out.

TONY: So boss, I dig it! This art has what you would call an intrinsic insular inner value. Don't mind if I do up a few steel rails, do ya boss? A couple of freedom lines? It'll give me a real appreciation of the stuff.

(Monroe offers champagne. Tony proceeds to cut the cocaine
putting lines out; he fills the coke spoon he wears on a chain
around his neck. All three inhale the cocaine.)

TONY: Jeeze, boss, my spoon runneth over. *(He picks up rock coke.)* This is the gear—one-hundred-percent primo, uncut, maximo, coco nose candio.

MONROE: So, Tony, are you gonna stick around for the opening? What're your plans?

TONY: I dunno. I was hopin' to get somethin' on the go. I figure Eddie here will have somethin' for me, hey boss? Ya said you'd take care of me, didn't ya boss?

(Eddie glares at him.).

TONY: Uh, sorry, boss, didn't mean to rush ya, boss. I know you're good for it. Don't wanna crowd ya or nutting.

(Tony and Monroe continue to snort cocaine. Eddie stops and
withdraws a glossy brochure from his overcoat. He slaps it
down on the table.)

TONY: *(Picking the brochure up.)* Jeeze, boss, what's that? Wow! It's a series of state-of-the-art, top-of-the-line hydraulic gym machines. What'd ya do, boss...buy the whole system? Jeeze, boss, you're really gonna go ahead with it, eh? You're really gonna close the gallery and open a health spa.

(Monroe sneezes on her coke.)

MONROE: You're doing what?

TONY: He's closin' the gallery, Monroe. The Colombian connection has gone sour. He's cuttin' his losses and coverin' his tracks. (*Tony and Monroe look at the gallery space.*) This time tomorrow, the only thing left of this gallery will be your fond memories.

MONROE: Eddie, you can't do this to me! The exhibition just opened! We're gonna get great reviews. The papers have been advertizing it for two weeks.

TONY: Eddie will buy the art, we'll tell 'em it's sold out.

MONROE: Eddie, look, this gallery is creating real waves. Andre wants me in *Vogue*. We're gonna put this place on the map.

TONY: So what, Monroe?

MONROE: (*To Eddie.*) We're an established gallery now. I've worked too hard. You just can't walk in off the street and shut me down.

TONY: Don't worry. Monroe. Eddie's not cuttin' you out of the picture. You're an integral part of the operation.

MONROE: That's right, Eddie. I *am* an integral part of this operation. In fact, I know this operation inside out.

TONY: Don't worry, Monroe, you'll be there along with *me* the whole way, right boss?

MONROE: Worried about covering your tracks, Eddie? Hmm? Well I got a map of your tracks tattooed on my skull.

EDDIE: What're you sayin' here, Monroe?

MONROE: I think you know what I'm saying!

TONY: Hey! Keep it down, all right. That writer guy still out there? I'll handle him, boss.

(*Tony enters gallery area with Monroe following.*)

TONY: (*Tapping Reginald on the shoulder.*) Hey you! Get out! The gallery's closed.

(*Monroe tries to stop Tony.*)

REGINALD: (*With wine bottle in hand, obviously drunk.*) But sir, you don't understand. I love the work, it's a fabulous exhibit. I'm gonna give it a great review.

TONY: Yeah? Well I'm givin' you the boot.

REGINALD: But sir, I really do love the work.

(*He sits down.*)

TONY: (*Grabbing Reginald and throwing him out.*) Yeah? Well work it up ya! There's the door, buddy.

(*Reginald leaves indignantly. Tony and Monroe cross back to the office space.*)

TONY: I showed him, hey boss?

MONROE: Look, all I'm saying here, Eddie, is the gallery is mine.

TONY: Yours?

MONROE: And I'm gonna need a few weeks to smooth things over with my contacts. It's in everybody's best interests. This is just too quick. It's too suspicious.

TONY: Come on, Monroe. You're way outta line here. Eddie's not tryin' to cut you outta the picture. Just play the game, all right?

MONROE: Tony, will you shut up? Look, Eddie, I never meant nothing just then. Just tell me what's going on. I can't think straight with all of Tony's babbling.

EDDIE: You're a loose cannon.

MONROE: What?

TONY: You heard 'im, Monroe. You're a loose cannon on the deck.

MONROE: Will you shut up? Were you in solitary confinement for the last two years or what?

TONY: And there's no place for loose cannons in the boss's organization, Monroe, 'cause ya know what happens to loose cannons?

MONROE: Shut up!

TONY: They get thrown overboard! And ya know what happens to loose cannons when they get thrown overboard, Monroe? They sink. Glub, glub, glub!

MONROE: Look, Eddie, just tell me what's goin' on. (*Pause.*) Eddie? Eddie, Eddie speak to me.

EDDIE: You're out.

MONROE: Look, I just need a few weeks...

EDDIE: *Right now.*

MONROE: Eddie!

EDDIE: We're closin' it down.

MONROE: Over my dead body.

EDDIE: (*Smiling.*) That can be arranged.
(*Eddie resumes inhaling cocaine.*)

MONROE: You better watch yourself, Eddie, I've got the goods on you. You try to send me down and you're coming with me.

EDDIE: Get out. You're finished.

(*Eddie goes to snort cocaine. Monroe angrily sweeps it onto the floor and exits.*)

TONY: Jeeze, boss, what're ya gonna do about her? Must be that time of the month. Hey boss, you know what women're like. Anyway, I haven't got time to worry about that now, do I boss? We've got a shit load of gym equipment arriving here any minute, gotta figure out where it's all gonna go. This time tomorrow, boss, there's gonna be a spa here. Class, boss, it's gonna be a class place. Definitely. Maybe we can go with a tropicana motif...yeah, with palm trees, masseuses and little straw skirts, with maybe a rococo, romano, greco, deco stuccoed sort of affair. Yeah, that's the ticket.

(*Blackout.*)

Scene 4

(*The Vicious Circle Bar. "I Need A Man" plays. Violet is strategically applying make-up to her face and other parts of her body. Enter Tony and Lenny (carrying guitar), drunk, singing "Tequila." Violet moves behind the bar.*)

TONY & LENNY: (*Singing in unison.*) Na, na, na...tequila.

VIOLET: Hi, boys, welcome to the Vicious Circle. What's your poison?

TONY & LENNY: (*Singing in unison.*) Na, na, na, na, na, na, na, na, na, na, na, tequila.

> (*Violet pours tequilas. Tony and Lenny drink.*)

TONY: Violet honey, pretty quiet night.

> (*Tony taps Lenny.*)

TONY & LENNY: (*Speaking in unison.*) Violet honey, pretty quiet night.

VIOLET: Yeah, 'til you got here, Tony.

TONY & LENNY: (*Together.*) Oooohhhh.

VIOLET: So, uh, Tony...who's your friend here?

TONY: This is my buddy, Lenny, from jail. I just got 'im out.

LENNY: I'm a singer.

> (*Lenny spins with guitar, strikes an Elvis pose.*)

TONY: He's a real Elvis, Violet. He made the jailhouse rock. How 'bout givin' 'im a job?

VIOLET: Things've changed, Tony. I got a juke box now. Less hassle.

TONY: Aw, c'mon, Violet. Ya still got the bandstand.

> (*Tony and Lenny break into "Don't be Cruel," complete with Elvis-like gyrations. Violet is noticing Lenny, obviously sizing him up.*)

VIOLET: All right, all right, all right. (*To Lenny.*) Lenny, how 'bout singin' us a tune?

LENNY: Yes, ma'am.

TONY: He's fabulous, Violet. Wait 'til ya hear this.

> (*Lenny mounts the bandstand and sings "Suspicious Minds." Violet watches intently but Tony keeps trying to break her train of thought.*)

TONY: So, uh, Violet.

> (*Violet, still watching Lenny, does not respond.*)

TONY: Uh, uh, Violet.

> (*Tony takes Violet's hand, kissing it.*)

TONY: Violet.

VIOLET: Yeah, Tony.

TONY: I really missed you while I was in the slammer.

VIOLET: Yeah, what'd you miss, Tony?

TONY: Your eyes, Violet, I missed your eyes. I always loved your eyes.

VIOLET: Tony?

TONY: Yeah?

VIOLET: (*Putting her hand over Tony's eyes.*) What colour are my eyes?

TONY: Why, Violet, they're uh...they're uh...I'm colour-blind, you know that. But love is blind, Violet. And Violet?

VIOLET: Yes.

TONY: I think I love you.

(Tony takes her hand and holds it.)

VIOLET: You what?

TONY: I love you, Violet. Come on. It's been three years. A man got needs you know, Violet.

VIOLET: Yeah? Go haul yourself off in the can, Tony. Take your hand, you might need it.

TONY: Thanks, Violet. I coulda told that to myself. How do you know I never already did? I'm serious here. One more time just for old times sake?

(Violet drops his hand.)

VIOLET: Tony, what old times? I never so much as looked at you in my life.

TONY: But you wanted to, didn't ya? Did I tell ya about the spa? Eddie's givin' me a spa.

VIOLET: Oh yeah, congratulations. *(She looks at Lenny.)* Maybe I could have a singer around here. And I stress *have*.

TONY: It's gonna be called "Tony's Body Tune-Up," Violet. Ever need an oil change, give me a call. My dipstick needs a dip. I got a fuel injector engine and my pistons are in overdrive.

VIOLET: Tony, Tony, Tony, Tony, *Tony*. Tony-o-man. Why don't you have a drink, it's on the house.

(Violet pours a drink down Tony's trousers.)

TONY: *(Trying to get rid of the drink.)* It's gonna have the works, Violet. All new hydraulic Nautilus, sauna, masseuse, the works. And with the view from Monroe's office—that's where I'm gonna put the hot-tub, right where her desk is.

VIOLET: What?

TONY: The view from Monroe's office.

VIOLET: Yeah, what about it?

TONY: That's where the hot-tub's goin'. Pretty classy wha', Violet?

VIOLET: When?

TONY: Tonight. The workmen are over there now. Neat hey? I'm out of prison for ten minutes and I'm the almost owner of a spa. Pretty sharp wha', Violet?

VIOLET: What about the gallery?

TONY: It's closed. It's deceased. Kaputnik. So, how 'bout it, Violet? Ya wanna be my aerobics instructor?

VIOLET: And what's Monroe think of your little spa idea?

TONY: Monroe loves the idea.

VIOLET: Tony?

TONY: Yeah?

VIOLET: I knew you were bullshittin', Tony. I know your whole family and between the *twelve* of you couldn't run a lemonade stand, let alone a spa. And you think you can get me into bed with some two-bit jock-strap fantasy.

TONY: Yeah.

VIOLET: Real romantic, Tony. I see you haven't lost your touch. Now beat it.

TONY: Yeah?
VIOLET: Yeah!
TONY: Yeah?
VIOLET: Yeah!
TONY: ⸱ Well we was just leavin'. See you at the spa, Violet. Come on, Lenny, we're outta here.
VIOLET: Stick around, Lenny. I want to talk to the talent.
TONY: Are you comin' Lenny, or what?
LENNY: I'll catch ya later, Tony. I think I got a booking.
TONY: I thought we were brothers, Len, cell-mates!
VIOLET: Yeah, well me and Lenny are soul-mates now.
(Tony starts to walk toward the bar.)

Photograph by Peggy Hogan

TONY: Yeah?
VIOLET: Yeah.
TONY: Yeah?
VIOLET: Yeah!
TONY: Yeah?
VIOLET: Yeah!
TONY: Well put this on my tab, Violet. *(He takes a bottle of tequila from the bar.)* I'll see you at the spa. I thought we were friends, Len.
(Exit Tony.)
VIOLET: So, uh, Lenny. You think you'd like workin' here singin' and tendin' bar and, uh, what not?
LENNY: Yeah, sure.
VIOLET: You been in prison a few years, huh?
LENNY: Yeah. I hope you don't hold that against me.
VIOLET: No, no. I was just wonderin' if you can, uh, still perform.

LENNY: Huh?

VIOLET: I mean, why don't you come out back and I'll give you a private and personal audition.

LENNY: What about the bar?

VIOLET: It's a slow night, we'll close it down and have our own little happy hour. Here's a buck. There's a machine in the men's can.

LENNY: What do you want—the French Tickler or the Black Stallion?

VIOLET: Surprise me, Lenny.

LENNY: You move pretty fast, Violet.

VIOLET: I'm so full of action my name should be a verb.
(Blackout.)

Scene 5

(Eddie and Harlow's penthouse. Aria from Madame Butterfly *plays. Eddie stands behind Harlow as she sits and listens to the music.)*

EDDIE: You shouldn't let yourself get so upset. God, you're beautiful. So beautiful. So pure. Like fresh fallen snow. Smooth, white, crystal clear. You're like a jewel. The jewel in my crown. Of everything I have you're my most prized possession. You're like an angel. A perfectly chiselled ice angel. A frozen flame. And I'm the moth that just wants to get caught inside your flame and have you melt around me.

HARLOW: I feel like Anna Pavlova dancing the dying swan—not that I ever saw it, but I read about it when I was a child...(*She cries.*) child.

EDDIE: I want to take ya out, hon. Have ya on my arm like the good old times. Remember those great times, honey?

HARLOW: Do you ever feel like you're falling?

EDDIE: What, hon?

HARLOW: Falling. I feel like I'm falling but I never hit. They say that if you hit in your sleep, you die. There was this dead guy on "Oprah" and that's how he died.

EDDIE: What, hon?

HARLOW: Not now, Eddie. I just don't feel like going out tonight.

EDDIE: Tonight? Tonight? It's not just tonight. It's every night, every week, every month since...Well, you know how long it's been. For the past three years. We've got to get back to our lives.

HARLOW: Our lives?

EDDIE: Even now, every night, I still run that scene over and over in my head...like a...a never ending replay. Is there anything I could've done, anything I could've changed. Do you know how much that hurts me? There was nothin', absolutely nothin'—it was God's plan, Harlow.

HARLOW: God is a bastard.

EDDIE: Look, what you want, what you need, what we both need
is a family. We could have a family now, Harlow. If you would just
let us. (*He approaches her seductively.*) We've just got to try,
break the ice, just once. It'll be easier from then on, I promise.
Why don't you just relax. Lie back. I'll do all the work.
(Pause.)
HARLOW: No! It's no good. I can't.
EDDIE: It's all right, hon. It's okay. Take your time. I understand,
I know it's hard. It's good we talked about it. Want some scotch?
Ice maybe? (*She shakes her head.*) The doctor said it was gonna
take time, but I know you're gonna snap outta it. Do you want
your pills. (*He passes them to her.*) Here you go. Now, I'll be back
soon, I've got, ah, a business appointment I forgot all about. I'll
see you soon, I'm late already. I've got to go. I'll see you later.
(Exit Eddie.)
HARLOW: Okay, Eddie, see ya.
(Harlow goes to phone, picks up receiver and dials. Sound of
ringing.)
HARLOW: Hi, Monroe, it's me, Harl...That machine again. (*She
starts again in a message-leaving voice.*) Hi, Monroe, it's me,
Harlow. I'm calling to apologize about today. I hope I didn't cause
any problems. Well, I thought I'd drop over, just for a chat. I'll let
myself in if you're not there and I'll see you when you get back.
Bye.
(Blackout.)

Scene 6

(Violet's Place. "I Need a Man" plays. Sounds of grunting, hot
sex noises, bed squeaking. Lights come up on Eddie and Violet
in bed----Violet reading a magazine---just as Eddie orgasms.)
EDDIE: Ah, ah, ah, ha, ha, ha, Harlow! Ah, ah, ah, ohhh, woaw.
(Violet puts her magazine down. Eddie gets up, buttons his
trousers and leaves without a word. Lenny emerges
from under the bed.)
VIOLET: (*Spitting after Eddie.*) Pig!
LENNY: Who's Harlow?
VIOLET: Shut up, Lenny. Can't you see I'm havin' a crisis?
LENNY: Sorry. Listen, we haven't got to, uh...Well, do you want
some tea?
VIOLET: Yeah, thanks, I'd love some tea.
LENNY: Got any dope around? I'll roll us a spliff.
VIOLET: Yeah, there's some there in the jewellery box.
(Lenny finds a joint and lights it. There is a knock at the door.)
VIOLET: It's him! He's back! Get back under the bed!
LENNY: Listen, if you don't want this guy here, you know, I can...
VIOLET: Shut up and get back under the bed, Lenny, and stay
there.

(The knocking is repeated. Violet gets up, opens door and Tony stumbles in with a half bottle of tequila.)

TONY: Na, na, na, na, na, na, na, na, na...Violet, how come the bar is closed?

VIOLET: Tony, it's not a good time.

TONY: I'm all alone, Violet. The neighborhood's changed. All my friends have moved on.

VIOLET: Tony.

TONY: I found out that Mom's dead.

VIOLET: Tony?

TONY: Yeah?

(She pushes Tony out the door.)

VIOLET: Sober up!

(Violet slams the door crosses back to her bed. From behind the bed Lenny raises his arm, holding up the rolled spliff. Violet takes it, lights it, falls back on the bed where Lenny joins her. He takes the spliff.)

VIOLET: Oh, my Excalibur.

(Violet takes the joint. They both smoke it and start to giggle and laugh. Lenny sings verses from "In the Ghetto" and "Love Me Tender".)

VIOLET: Oh, Lenny.

LENNY: You like that, don't ya?

VIOLET: Don't make me puke.

(Lenny is crest-fallen.)

VIOLET: No, no, really, I love it, sure, uh, you're, uh...so, uh...cute.

(Blackout.)

Scene 7

(Monroe's place. "Blue Bayou" plays. Monroe speaks into the telephone. She's visibly upset, pouring a drink, shaking, etc.)

MONROE: Violet, where are you? God! The bar can't be closed this early.

(Doorbell rings.)

MONROE: Thank God—Violet!

(She slams down phone answers the door. Tony enters, very drunk carrying his bottle of tequila.)

MONROE: Tony! Did Eddie send you here?

TONY: Naw, I'm here on my own, Monroe. I wondered if you want to, uh...(He embraces Monroe and spins her a few times.)...talk turkey. I figured you might need some company.

MONROE: No, I'm fine alone, thank you.

(Monroe tries to push Tony out, unsuccessfully.)

TONY: Got any booze, Monroe? Anything to drunk...er drink?

MONROE: Some coffee maybe.

TONY: Naw. I'm tryin' to cut down. (Holding up his bottle.) Some tequila maybe.

(He hums a line of "Tequila" and takes a swig.)

MONROE: Tony. It's time for you to leave, my friend.

(Monroe tries again to push Tony out, in the process, more or less holding him up.)

TONY: No, no. I gotta talk to you...very important.

MONROE: Oh yeah? What is it?

TONY: It's very important.

MONROE: Okay, what is it?

TONY: Don't take this the wrong way, okay?

MONROE: Okay.

TONY: Ya promise?

MONROE: Yes, Tony, what is it!

TONY: You wanna fuck?

(Monroe drops him to the ground.)

MONROE: Tony, it's time for you to leave.

TONY: No, no, no, seriously, Monroe, Eddie's, uh...

(She steps over Tony to sit down. Tony is momentarily speechless.)

TONY: ...pissed off with you. You said all the wrong things to him.

MONROE: Yeah, I know.

TONY: *(At Monroe's feet.)* I wouldn't want to be in your pants...I mean shoes! *(He begins kissing her feet.)* I'm sorry, Monroe. I didn't want it to end up like this. I woulda been happy just doin' security for ya. I ain't cut out to run no business. That's your department. You're the one with the brains. I hate spas. I love you though. Maybe it could be a...a...an art-spa...or a...gee, I dunno.

MONROE: Tony, are you sure you don't want a coffee?

TONY: Ah jeeze, Monroe. What's with the coffee? All I want is you. Come on, let's get it on one more time, just for old time's sake.

MONROE: Tony, we didn't have any old time's sake.

TONY: Did I tell ya that Mom was dead?

MONROE: Yeah, for nine years now. Come on, Tony, time for you to hit the road.

(She tries to push him out.)

TONY: No, no, no. Come on, Monroe. Let's dance. Let's do some aerobics.

(Tony jumps about, arms flailing, trying aerobic exercises.)

MONROE: Come on, leave!

TONY: One more. Two more.

MONROE: Tony! Leave!

TONY: Come on, Monroe.

(Tony inadvertently hits Monroe on the head, knocking her unconscious. Pause. He looks at Monroe. He looks at his hand. He laughs.)

TONY: Come on, Monroe, get up out of it. Let's go another ten rounds! *(Pause.)* Come on, Monroe, get up. *(Pause. He lifts her and puts her into a swivel chair.)* Get up. That's more like it.

Coffee? No? Jeeze, Monroe, sorry. I'll call back. I better get out of here. I'll check up on ya. You'll be all right. Jeeze, I better leave. Uh, see ya around. See ya at the spa.

(Tony gives the swivel chair a hard turn causing it to spin several times with the unconscious Monroe still in it. He exits.

Photograph by Peggy Hogan

The phone rings four times. Monroe's answering machine responds with a few bars of "Only the Lonely" and Monroe's voice recording, "Hello, you've reached the phone of Monroe Sanzo. Sorry, I'm not able to come to the phone right now, but if you leave a message I will get back to you. During business hours I can be reached at 789-9273. Bye-bye." A curt male voice with British accent leaves message, "Hello, Miss Sanzo. This is Peter. We are anxiously awaiting word pertaining to our pre-arranged shipment of goods. It would be most appropriate to promptly comply with our mutual arrangement. Our investors are losing patience if not concluded on or before schedule. I trust you'll treat this matter with the urgency that it deserves."

The doorbell rings several times, Monroe awakens and makes it to the door. She peeks at her visitor and opens the door. Enter Violet.)

VIOLET: Come on, Monroe.

MONROE: Violet, get in here!

VIOLET: Look, Tony was down at the bar and he was spoutin' some bullshit, so I figured I'd better come up and check it out.

TONY: Yeah. Tony was just here. He practically killed me, he was that drunk.

VIOLET: What!

MONROE: Oh, it was just an accident, don't worry. But, uh, he was talking about the gallery-spa thing. It's true, Eddie wants to close the gallery.

VIOLET: What? Great! When? How could this happen just after the openin'?

MONROE: I dunno, I dunno. He said something about his Colombian connection going sour and having to cover his tracks. He wants out.

VIOLET: So fast? What's goin' on? What are you tryin' to pull, Monroe?

MONROE: Nothing. I'm in this just as deep as you are, deeper even. I pleaded with him to keep it open, but he wouldn't. I even threatened him—big mistake. Tony says he's really mad.

VIOLET: Look. Look. The bar's in my name. Eddie's name is nowhere near it. I have the lease. Isn't that the same deal with the gallery—Eddie's money, your name?

MONROE: I was thinking the *exact* same thing.

MONROE & VIOLET: (*Speaking in unison.*) Fine minds stay aligned.

MONROE: I was just looking for the deed when Tony showed up. God, what a knock he gave me. Uh, they're around here somewhere.
             (*Violet and Monroe start looking for the papers.*)

VIOLET: Yes.

MONROE: Ooh. Sorry, I gotta sit down.
             (*Monroe sits.*)

VIOLET: All right, all right, all right. You find the deeds. They might get us back in the gallery just long enough...But if Eddie finds out about the missin' money, we are really screwed.

MONROE & VIOLET: (*Together.*) Woooooo.

VIOLET: Look. All we gotta do is buy ourselves a little bit of extra time, and then we'll be on easy street. No Eddie, no worries.
             (*They laugh. Monroe gets up.*)

MONROE & VIOLET: (*A cheer-leading chant, with gestures.*) One, two, yea team!
             (*Monroe holds her head and sits down again. Violet looks
                                  worried.*)

VIOLET: God, how could this happen now? You can't stay here, you know that.

MONROE: Okay, where will I go?

VIOLET: Go across town, rent a hotel room under a different name. Get the deeds and we'll meet tomorrow. And don't bring your car, I'll get a rental, all right? Just, uh, hang tight until then, you know? I'll be back, all right?
             (*Blackout.*)

Scene 8

(*The Vicious Circle. Lenny is tending bar. Enter Tony.*)

TONY: Hey Len, see I told ya it'd be no sweat gettin' set up. Violet would do anything for me. She loves me. Where is she anyway?

LENNY: She had to go out.

TONY: Yeah?

LENNY: Yeah...and she left me in charge!

(Lenny gets Tony in a headlock and rubs his head. Lenny lets go and they do a ritual handshake.)

TONY: Great, Len. So we're in charge are we? Don't waste any time, do ya?

LENNY: No, I don't. Listen, ya don't happen to know a Harlow, do ya?

TONY: Yeah, sure, the boss's wife.

LENNY: Who?

TONY: You know, Eddie, the boss. And watch what you say about her now. The boss is quick to take offense.

LENNY: Why's that?

TONY: She a bit, uh (*He makes crazy sign.*) flip-city, wacko, the-lights-are-on-but-no-one's-home, if you know what I mean.

LENNY: No, what do ya mean?

TONY: Well, she freaked out a few years ago, and after that she took the veil.

LENNY: What're ya sayin' there, Ton, she became a nun or some-thin'?

TONY: Sorta. From what I hear, she put on a chastity belt and swallowed the key.

LENNY: What do you mean sorta?

TONY: I mean sorta. Kinda. Somethin' like a nun. Sorta kinda like...

(He trails off.)

LENNY: What?

TONY: She really freaked out. She went into permanent mourn-ing—black veil, Valium, constant tears, vow of silence, the whole bit. She really freaked out.

LENNY: What did she freak out about?

(Pause.)

TONY: Bad vacation.

LENNY: What'd she do? Lose her luggage?

(Pause.)

TONY: No. Her son. See, her and Eddie were on vacation in South America a few years back. She stayed behind one day when they were goin' to the beach. There was a terrible accident. Eddie lost control of the car. The kid was horribly burned to death. Unrec-ognizable. They were devastated. I had to go down and take care of the arrangements. The kid was like bacon. He came back in a box. I tell ya, boy Len, when I think of that cute little kid...char-broiled...chokes me up. (*Tony cries.*) It was just after that that Eddie made his fortune. The money's been rollin' in ever since. Funny, Eddie worked his ass off to make Harlow happy. She hasn't been able to enjoy a penny of it.

LENNY: Why's that, because of the kid?

TONY: Jeeze, Lenny, I never though of that!

(Enter Eddie.)

TONY: Oh, uh, hi boss. This is my buddy Lenny. I was just, uh, tellin' him what a great guy you are.

EDDIE: Yeah, save it, Tony. How's the spa goin'?

TONY: Fantabulous, boss. The Nautilus is gonna be there tomorrow and I hired some men to work all night installin' the sauna. And I'm gonna put the hot-tub right where Monroe's office used to be.

EDDIE: Nice touch, Tony.

TONY: Uh, yeah, boss.

EDDIE: Yeah?

TONY: Speakin' of Monroe...

EDDIE: Yeah, what about her?

TONY: Uh, I uh, I just knocked her out.

EDDIE: Come again, Tony.

TONY: Yeah well, boss, I uh, well, I was havin' a few drinks and, uh, I went over there to talk to her, to straighten a few things out, and, uh, tell her what a great guy you are and all and I, well, she started to bad-mouth ya. So I, uh *(Smacking his fist into his palm.)* clocked her. When I left her she was out like a chunk.

EDDIE: Great, Tony. Real slick. Neanderthal.

TONY: Neander-what, boss?

EDDIE: Forget it, Tony. What time was all this?

TONY: I dunno, boss. About twenty minutes ago. She's probably still out.

EDDIE: Okay, Tony, I got to make a phone call. I'll take care of the damages. Sit tight. I'll handle this end of it.

(Exit Eddie.)

LENNY: You're lucky, Ton. He's gonna handle damages.

TONY: Yeah, if I hadda known that I woulda cleaned the place out. Who knows? Maybe I already did.

LENNY: Why's that? Does she live in one of those posh apartments by the gallery?

TONY: No, b'y, she lives right there on centre stage.

(Enter Eddie, carrying a violin case.)

EDDIE: Okay, Tony, sober up, I got a job for you. *(To Lenny.)* Hey, you!

LENNY: Yeah, Eddie?

EDDIE: Evaporate!

TONY: Beat it!

(Exit Lenny. Eddie places the violin case on the counter.)

EDDIE: Here, I want you to go on a little business trip to Canada. I want you to visit that orphanage again.

(Sinister music plays. Tony opens up the case and removes a video camera.)

TONY: You still into that, boss?

EDDIE: 'Course I am! What do ya think?
(Tony begins panning around with the camera.)
EDDIE: Now look, I got it all arranged with the brothers. Only this time, more action shots. More close-ups.
(Blackout.)

Scene 9

(Monroe's apartment. Enter Harlow.)
HARLOW: Hello? Monroe?
(Harlow investigates the apartment. She picks up a bottle, pours herself a drink and drinks it. She stops at the vanity mirror, looks at herself, examines her face for wrinkles and starts doing a what's-wrong-with-me-and-how-do-I-look head space thing. She picks up a bow and holds it under her neck like a bow tie. She pulls her hair up, like a man, and turns. She speaks in a male voice with a foreign accent.)
Madame, I've come for the rent.
(She turns again to the mirror and places the bow on her head. She speaks like a woman:)
But I have no money for the rent.
(As a man.)
Well, what can we do? You can't pay the rent, no?
(As a woman.)
But I can't...I can't...I can't pay the rent.
(She takes one of Monroe's wigs from the vanity, puts it on and imitates Monroe.)
Scott LaScone is the hottest item on the east coast.
(She hears sounds of break and enter—a smash, the sound of breaking glass, a thump. She runs and hides behind a full-length curtain. Lenny, enters through a window and looks around with a flashlight. He pauses, looks at the flashlight, the ceiling, the flashlight. He realizes the lights are on and turns off the flashlight. He goes to the vanity and picks up Harlow's drink and downs it. He looks about the vanity, opens a jewellery box, takes out a necklace and pockets it. Harlow makes a noise behind the curtain. Lenny is startled, he runs into the closet and hides. Harlow, still wearing wig, comes out from behind her curtain. She sees Lenny disappear into the closet. She picks up a letter opener and begins randomly stabbing into the clothes in the closet.)
HARLOW: *(Screaming.)* What're you doing in there? Get out! I know you're in there.
(She stabs Lenny in the arm. He screams. She screams. He emerges, with the letter opener still stuck in his arm.)
LENNY: You stabbed me, you stupid bitch. I'm bleedin' and you stabbed me.
(Harlow pulls the letter opener out. Lenny winces. She

brandishes it against him. Lenny takes off his shirt and ties it
around his arm.)

HARLOW: Get back. Stay back! Don't you touch me!

LENNY: I'm not gonna touch you. Put down that knife! I'm not gonna hurt you. I'm the one who's bleedin' for Christ's sake. You stabbed me!

HARLOW: What're you doing here? Why did you break in here?
(Monroe's body falls out of the closet. Harlow screams.)

HARLOW: *(Melodramatically.)* Oh, my God! *(She bends down over the body.)* My sister's on the floor. My sister...you killed my sister.
(Harlow beats on Lenny, then sobs and howls over her sister in
an over-the-top melodramatic fashion.)

LENNY: What do ya mean, I killed your sister. I couldn't've killed your sister. I just broke in. You saw me. I wasn't gonna hurt nobody. I'm not even supposed to be here——I got the wrong address. *(Pause as Lenny puts two and two together.)* You were here with the body. You got the knife. How do I know you didn't kill her?

HARLOW: She's my sister! I didn't kill her! She's dead! My sister is...DEAD!
(She sobs hysterically again and throws herself on the body.)

LENNY: Get up off the floor. We can't leave her there. We'll put her in the chair. God, I'm bleedin' to death. Come on, get off the floor and give me a hand. Come on.
(They move Monroe into the chair. Enter Violet. She looks
around but doesn't see the body. She's upset but
keeping her cool.)

VIOLET: *(To Lenny.)* Well. Well, well, well, *you* seem to be gettin' around tonight. *(To Harlow.)* Monroe, your headache all cleared up? Here's the key *(She throws it to the table.)* I'll meet you at the Dyin' Duck Cafe. Early. And don't be late. *(She moves to leave, stopping at the door. She looks at Lenny.)* And Lenny, don't bother comin' into work tomorrow. Like I said——juke boxes are less hassle.
(Exit Violet.)

LENNY: I gotta get outta here.

HARLOW: You're not goin' anywhere.

LENNY: She saw me. She thinks I'm sleepin' with you.

HARLOW: Eugh.

LENNY: *(Indicating Monroe.)* I mean her.

HARLOW: Euggghhh!

LENNY: I gotta get outta here. I gotta get outta here! I can't get involved. I gotta split. You deal with it. She's your sister.

HARLOW: What?

LENNY: I'm sorry. No offense. I'm on parole and if you call the cops, I'll go back to jail. Look, I didn't even do anything. I only broke in by mistake. And ya stabbed me, that's punishment enough.

HARLOW: Don't worry, I'm not gonna call the cops. I'm gonna call my husband Eddie Bossanova, he'll know what to do.

LENNY: Oh Christ, you're Eddie's wife. You're Harlow. Great!

(The phone rings, Harlow reaches to pick it up.)

LENNY: Don't answer that. Just leave it alone and let's get out of here.

(The answering machine answers and Monroe's message plays.)

TONY: *(His voice coming through the phone.)* Hello, Monroe, it's me, Tony. Sorry I was such a jerk, but you know me, uh, that's what I'm like, right? *(He laughs.)* I, uh, I want to talk about Eddie. I was serious. You got him really riled-up, he's out for blood—*yours*. If I were you I'd lay low for a while and stay out of his way, if you know what I mean. *(Tony hangs up.)*

LENNY: So what're ya gonna do now? Call Eddie?

HARLOW: I don't know.

LENNY: And you can't call the cops. They'll nail me and you'll never find out who killed her.

HARLOW: I need time to think. Who could have killed my sister?

LENNY: I know. Let's hide the body and get outta here.

HARLOW: We can't just hide her away. She needs a wake and proper funeral, priest, church, family and...

LENNY: We'll put her on ice. I know a place—she's gonna be fine for a day or two. If nothin' breaks, we'll call the cops then.

HARLOW: Don't worry, Monroe. Everything's gonna be okay. You never looked so peaceful. I'm gonna look after you. I'm gonna find out who killed you. I'm gonna find out who killed Monroe Sanzo.

(Lenny picks up Monroe's body. Harlow picks up Monroe's purse. Blackout.)

ACT 2
Scene 1

(Eddie and Harlow's penthouse early the next morning. Eddie is talking on the phone. Sinister music plays.)

EDDIE: ...neat job? No mess? Good. Good. I'll be in touch.

(Eddie hangs up the phone. Enter Harlow. She makes tea.)

EDDIE: You're up early. How come? *(Pause.)* Why are you up so early? *(Pause.)* Harlow?

HARLOW: No reason.

EDDIE: You were out late last night. Where'd ya go, Harlow?

HARLOW: To Monroe's. I was at Monroe's.

EDDIE: Oh. How was she?

(During Harlow's next speech Eddie is trying not to freak out.)

HARLOW: She wasn't...She wasn't in...at first. I let myself in. I have a key. Monroe came back. We talked. She's fine. You should have seen us, Eddie, two sisters gabbing over coffee...just like old times. We talked about you, Eddie, how important you are to us.

We're closer than ever before, we're almost like the same person.
We even talked about the accident and Monroe cried. God, I love
Monroe. Don't you just love Monroe, Eddie?

EDDIE: Yeah, I love Monroe. Especially the way she is now.
(Harlow pirouettes.)

HARLOW: Eddie, that was a pirouette. Eddie, I'm thinking about
becoming a ballerina. I wonder what Monroe would think about
that? She'd love the idea! Eddie, I'm so alive I'm tingling all over!

EDDIE: Ah, I think it's time for your morning medication, babe.

HARLOW: Eddie, don't call me babe.
(Exit Harlow.)

EDDIE: Gotcha, babe.
*(Exit Eddie. Sinister music plays. Harlow re-enters with
Monroe's purse. She takes Monroe's appointment book
out of it and reads her appointments for the day.)*
Breakfast meeting. Oh, good, there's still time.
(Harlow takes Monroe's black wig from her purse. Blackout.)

Scene 2

*(The meat-locker. Enter Lenny, dragging Monroe's body, now in
a body-bag, in with him. He stops, panting.)*

LENNY: Monroe, God, you're some heavy.
*(He lifts the body-bag up and hangs it on a chain. He takes out
a cigarette and strikes a match on the zipper of the bag. He
lights his cigarette. Blackout.)*

Scene 3

*(The spa. Tony is lying on a bench in the sauna, wearing only a
towel and a walkman. He sings a verse from Ron Hynes's
"Sonny's Dream."*
     *Enter Eddie, wearing a suit. He picks up a ladle of water
and pours it on the hot-rocks of the sauna. He walks around
Tony, whose eyes are closed. Eddie spreads his fingers into a "V"
and slowly brings them down to meet Tony's eyes, which he
pries open with his fingers.)*

TONY: *(Shouting.)* Not bad, hey boss? *(He takes off the headphones.)* It's a big hit in Canada, boss. Here ya go, boss. One
night and one sauna. Don't tell me I'm not a shaker and a mover,
wha' boss? Boss, you're supposed to lose the threads in the sauna,
boss.

EDDIE: Chill out.

TONY: What's wrong, boss? It's Monroe, isn't it. She's gonna cause
you trouble, isn't she? Is she mad about last night?

EDDIE: Nope.

TONY: Oh good! What is it then, boss?

EDDIE: She's dead.

TONY: Who's dead?

EDDIE: Monroe's dead, Tony. You killed her. I went over to clean up your little mess...and she was dead.

TONY: Wha', boss, wha'? I couldn'ta killed Monroe, boss. It was an accident. I didn't mean to kill Monroe, boss. I only wanted to dance! Oh God, what am I gonna do?

EDDIE: Don't worry, Tony, I told you I'd take care of everything. I'll take care of everything. Now it's gonna look like an accident, right Tony? Because it was an accident.

TONY: Yeah right, boss. It was an accident.

EDDIE: Now listen. You're goin' to Canada, same as before. Only you're gonna go earlier and stay longer. Give me a couple of hours to work out a few details. Be here when I get back.

(Exit Eddie. Blackout.)

Scene 4

(The Dying Duck Cafe. Waiter is serving tables and Violet is seated with a glass of wine in front of her, waiting for Monroe. Enter Harlow dressed as Monroe. She sits with Violet.)

HARLOW: Ahhh.

VIOLET: You're late.

HARLOW: I slept in.

VIOLET: It's a wonder you got any sleep at all.

HARLOW: What's that supposed to mean?

VIOLET: Let's just drop it, Monroe. He's not worth it, all right?

HARLOW: So. What did you want to see me about, Violet? *(She speaks to Waiter who brings her a glass of wine.)* Thank you...what a lovely cafe.

(Waiter grunts and leaves.)

VIOLET: Cut the crap, Monroe. Have you been talkin' to Peter?

HARLOW: Ah, no...But, ah, you know how he is.

(Harlow laughs. Violet joins in then stops abruptly.)

VIOLET: No, I don't, Monroe. Enlighten me. He's your contact.

HARLOW: Yes he is. And I'll take care of it.

VIOLET: What are you going to do about Eddie?

HARLOW: Eddie?

(Waiter returns with two menus.)

VIOLET: Yeah, Eddie. Eddie. You know, Eddie, the guy who's gonna take us down unless we get our shit together. Look, Monroe, wake up. I've taken care of my end. My end's holdin' up. Your end is fallin' apart. I wanna know what you're gonna do about the gallery contact, and I wanna know now!

HARLOW: Violet, don't you think you're over-acting a bit?

VIOLET: *(Giving her a look.)* Over-reacting? What have you got to be so calm about? When I left you last night you were in hysterics. And now you're like the ice-lady. What gives, Monroe?

HARLOW: I'm just trying to get a grip on the situation.

VIOLET: Get a grip on the situation? Well, there's not much of a sitch to grip now is there, Monroe? We got no place to make the drop, but that's okay because we got nothin' to drop. We gotta replace Eddie's money, but that's all right, because when Eddie finds out we took it, he's gonna kill us.

HARLOW: Eddie wouldn't do that. He's a businessman. Some businesses lose money.

VIOLET: A million dollars?

HARLOW: A million dollars? That is a lot of money.

VIOLET: Yes, Monroe. That is a lot of money!

HARLOW: But it's business.

VIOLET: But not Eddie's...Too bad Eddie didn't know he's the sole investor. Now he might think we stole that money, Monroe.

HARLOW: What an idiot!

VIOLET: (*She pulls out a gun.*) But *we did*, Monroe...or whoever you are. Start blabbing, babe, or I'm gonna blow your brains all over the bistro. Who are ya? Did Eddie send ya? What did ya do with Monroe? You got three seconds, sister. Sing, or say your prayers. One Mississippi, two Mississippi (*Pause. Harlow opens her purse.*) I said two Mississippi! What're you doing! This is a gun! A gun! G-U-N. Gun! Bang bang! Are you laughing? (*Without looking Violet unintentionally shoots approaching Waiter. Wounded, he retreats. Harlow laughs.*) What are you laughing at?

HARLOW: I'm just getting a tranquillizer out of my purse. (*She removes her sun-glasses.*) It's me, Harlow.
(*Pause.*)

VIOLET: Give me one too.
(*Harlow fishes in her purse for the pills. She gives one to Violet and they both swallow.*)

VIOLET: Thanks.

HARLOW: (*Beginning to sob.*) Monroe is dead.

VIOLET: Oh, my God! Monroe is dead?

HARLOW: Monroe is dead.

VIOLET: Monroe is dead?

HARLOW & VIOLET: (*In unison.*) Monroe is dead!

VIOLET: Oh, my God, it's curtains. Oh, that creep Eddie! Where is she? Where's her body?

HARLOW: Lenny was there by accident. He said he'd help me put it in storage. We were moving the body when you came in last night.

VIOLET: You mean it was you, not...

HARLOW: Yes.

VIOLET: And Lenny wasn't with...

HARLOW: Exactly.

VIOLET: And now she's dead.

HARLOW: Monroe is dead. Somebody killed her. I'm so confused. I didn't want her to die. (*She has an idea.*) You thought I was her last night. If she's still alive maybe I can find out who killed her.

Photograph by Peggy Hogan

VIOLET: By pretending to be Monroe?

HARLOW: Exactly!

VIOLET: Look, sweetheart, take my advice. Go home, take your pills, quit your playactin'. You're in way over your head. You wanna to go around impersonatin' a dead woman, fine, you're gonna end up dead. You wanna run around pretendin' to be Monroe? Monroe's in deep shit. She's not dead for nothin', baby.

HARLOW: Violet?

VIOLET: Yeah?

HARLOW: Don't call me baby.

VIOLET: (*Getting up to leave.*) Your treat. I'm short a million bucks.

> (*Harlow takes out the gun from Violet's purse and points it at Violet.*)

HARLOW: Forget your gun, Annie?

VIOLET: All right, all right, all right. (*She laughs.*) Okay, all right, you got me over a barrel. Look I'd like to walk outta here, I'd like to walk outta here and leave you alone to your theatrics. But, what the hell, I need ya.

> (*Harlow gives the gun back to Violet who replaces it in her purse.*)

VIOLET: Stick with me and I'll tell ya who killed Monroe Sanzo.

HARLOW: Who?

VIOLET: Monroe and I had five million dollars worth of stolen art treasures comin' into the country with one of Eddie's coke shipments.

HARLOW: Coke?

VIOLET: Yeah. That's how your hubby makes his fortune, Harlow.

HARLOW: Get to the point, Violet.

VIOLET: It's not South American artifacts, it's South American cocaine.

HARLOW: Get to the point.

VIOLET: He's a glorified crack-head. Eddie's on par with a street pimp in a pool hall.

HARLOW: Who killed my sister?

VIOLET: Monroe used her art contacts to find a buyer, a very slick and very dangerous patron of the arts. Monroe was supposed to make the drop at the gallery today.

HARLOW: She never told me she had an exciting life. I could just kill her now!

> *(Pause. They both cross themselves and drink.)*

VIOLET: I financed the deal with Eddie's money. I was gonna give it back before he noticed it was missing. But Eddie closed the gallery, so there's no front. Eddie stopped the coke shipment, so there's no art. Eddie killed Monroe so there's no contact.

HARLOW: I don't believe it.

VIOLET: Well then go home, sweetness.

HARLOW: Eddie wouldn't kill my sister. He loves me.

VIOLET: Yeah? Well he screws me--every time you say no. Think about it, Harlow. You say no a lot. You said no last night.

> *(Pause. Harlow goes to slap Violet who catches her hand. They arm-wrestle over the table, grunting as the match goes back and forth. Finally, Harlow wins.)*

HARLOW: Okay. I'll do it.

> *(Sinister music plays.)*

VIOLET: All right, all right, all right. We've got Monroe but we still don't have the gallery. The deed, we need the deed. Monroe said she was gonna look for the deed. Do you know where it is?

HARLOW: Oh, do you mean these things in Monroe's purse?

> *(She takes papers out of her purse and passes them to Violet.)*

VIOLET: *(Looking through the papers.)* All right, all right, all right. It says here that the gallery is in your name—Monroe's name—so we got the gallery.

HARLOW: But we don't have the art.

VIOLET: We'll give 'em fakes. It's only a courier and they won't be checked until they get to Europe.

HARLOW: But if I give them fakes they'll kill me.

VIOLET: Yeah? But you're already dead, Monroe.

> *(They laugh, clink glasses and drink. Pause. They throw the drinks over their shoulders.)*

HARLOW: But what about Monroe?

VIOLET: Look, after the drop you got seven hours to run around and play detective. After that our overseas friends will come lookin' for her. But all they're gonna find is the body. And make sure it's not yours, you'll wanna be around to spend the money, honey.

HARLOW: I don't care about the money.

VIOLET: Yeah, well you better start carin' about it. Monroe did. Now after you make the drop, five million dollars will be transferred to a Swiss bank account. The money will automatically be laundered through two holding companies and then back into two equal separate Swiss accounts—in my name, and yours. Here's your number. Don't lose it. It's worth two-and-half-million dollars. Now we gotta move fast. Listen, we're goin' on a little trip and I'll do all the talkin'. And the Camels? Get rid of 'em. Monroe never smokes Camels.
(They lean forward adlibbing conversation on makeup, etc. Blackout.)

Scene 5

(The spa. Eddie and Tony are going over plans. Tony is dressed but is drying his hair. Sinister music plays.)
EDDIE: You'll be travellin' under the name of Ricardo Vincelli. You'll meet our man at the airport; he'll take care of you. You're gonna be stayin' in a place called the Hillview Terrace. So you know you're gonna be livin' in style.
TONY: Thanks, boss. I won't forget this, boss.
EDDIE: That's right, Tony, you won't forget this.
TONY: What about when I get back, boss?
EDDIE: Back?
TONY: Yeah. When I get back from Canada, boss...
EDDIE: We got plenty of time to think about that, don't we Tony? Just remember—I went out on a limb for you.
(Enter Harlow and Violet. Tony is dumb-struck. Violet pushes past him and he faints. Harlow catches him and lets him slide to the floor.)
EDDIE: *(Surprised.)* Monroe!
VIOLET: Hey, Eddie. My friend here says she doesn't want you in her gallery. She's got an exhibit to run. It's all here in the deed. It's Monroe's gallery to do with as she pleases. Now I suggest that you get out before it pleases her to call the police.
EDDIE: Monroe?
HARLOW: Yeah, Eddie, how's it goin'? *(She offers her hand to shake. Pause. Eddie refuses to shake.)* How's business?
(Violet and Harlow circle Eddie.)
EDDIE: What's goin' on? What's goin' on? Somethin' smells here!
VIOLET: I think it's you, Eddie.
EDDIE: What are you tryin' to pull? No one pulls one over on me, got it? I'm, ah, I'm callin' my lawyer.
(Exit Eddie. Violet and Harlow try to wake Tony.)
VIOLET: Tony. Yo, Tony. Tony. Tony, my man, rise and shine, wakey-wakey, Tony. Tony, cutchy-cutchy-coo. Tony, wake up! Yo, Ton!
HARLOW: Tony.

VIOLET: Yo, Tony. Rise and shine.
HARLOW & VIOLET: Tony!
VIOLET: Ton!
(Tony wakes, sees Monroe and screams. He jumps up. It takes him several moments to phrase a response.)
TONY: I'm not goin' to Canada! I'm not goin' to Canada! I'm *not* goin' to Canada. *(To Harlow.)* What're you doin' here. I thought you were dead. Eddie told me you were dead. Eddie said I killed you by accident. I never killed nobody by accident. I'm not that kinda guy, I shoulda known that. I'm not goin' to Canada. You're not dead, Monroe. That's great! *(He kisses her.)* You're alive. I'm not goin' to Canada, and that's that! Shit! Eddie was gonna set me up for somethin' I never done. That bastard. I'm gonna screw him. I'm gonna screw him over and over and over. He's gonna wish he never heard of Tony Stundasmihola. You're dead meat. I'm dead meat for that matter. You wanna keep the gallery, Monroe? You wanna keep breathin'? You're gonna need a weapon to get Eddie—and I got it. I know somethin' that'll hurt him real bad, to the core. I get you this piece of goods it'll throw him for a loop, Eddie will be in the palm of your hand. I'll be back. I'm not goin' to Canada. I'm not goin' to Canada. I'm not goin' to Canada.
(Exit Tony.)
HARLOW: What was all that about? He said he killed Monroe.
VIOLET: Look, we don't have time for that. They'll be here in less than an hour. We gotta move fast.
(Blackout.)

Scene 6

(Eddie's office. Eddie is talking on the phone.
Sinister music plays.)
EDDIE: She's not dead. You told me she was dead. I want her dead. You keep screwin' up and you're dead, got it? I don't care how ya do it. Use a bullet, use a baseball bat if you want to, it doesn't matter how you kill her any more. Just kill her. I got your blood money right here. *(He picks up a wad of bills.)* But you don't get a sniff of it till I got a stiff on my desk, got it?
(He hangs up and puts the money in his shirt pocket. The phone rings again.)
Yeah. Yeah, this is Eddie. Yeah, the Vicious Circle building, yeah, on fire? What do you mean, it's on fire? Well, put it out! I got enough troubles right now. No, I don't store dynamite on the premises. What the hell kinda question is that? *(He hangs up the phone.)* Dynamite?
(Loud noise from outside. He goes to the window and yells.)
Hey you! Yeah you! Get away from the car! Get away from the car!
(An explosion is heard, the force of which knocks Eddie to the

ground. He gets up, looks out the window.)
My Delorean. (*He pulls out his gun, screaming.*) They blew up my fucking Delorean!
(*Eddie exits, running in a rage. Enter Tony, wearing Rambo-like attire, from a cloud of smoke and dust through the office window. He proceeds to perform a series of chops, kicks, screams and machine-gun blasts à la Rambo. He seizes several video tapes from Eddie's desk. He takes one. He pours Ajax cleanser onto the pile of coke on Eddie's desk, repeats his Rambo performance and exits through the window. Enter Eddie. He slams his gun down and sits at the desk. He notices the missing video tape and freaks out. He snorts some of the adulterated coke. He writhes, screams and sneezes, bleeding from the nose. Blackout.)*

Scene 7

(*The spa now restored as a gallery. The lighting is dim. Harlow and Courier do the deal. She hands him a briefcase; he hands her an envelope. She opens it. They shake hands. Courier exits. Lights come up. Enter Violet from her hiding place.*)

VIOLET: Let me see, let me see. (*She grabs the envelope.*) Harlow. Harlow, we did it. We did it, we did it, baby.
(*Enter Tony, carrying a video tape.*)

TONY: Ya got a VCR? I got the goods.

VIOLET: What took you so long, Tony?

TONY: I had places to go, things to do, cars to blow up, stuff like that. You'll read about it in the papers tomorrow.

VIOLET: This better be good or I'm on a plane for Tahiti tonight.
(*Violet puts the tape in the VCR. It is a recording of Santa, the kid on his lap pulls his beard revealing that Santa is Tony. There is a woman and some kids. It's an innocent Christmas party.*)
Great secret weapon, Tony! I'm glad you're on our side! What's Eddie think—there's a real Santa Claus or something?

TONY: Hang on! Wait! Just look at the screen. See him...the cute kid...the one with the teddy bear? That's the boss's kid. He's alive. That time in South America? The boss was doin' a coke deal and it went bad so he covered his tracks by fakin' his own kid's death and stuffin' the closed coffin fulla coke. What a scam! He made a fortune. He put the kid in an orphanage in Canada; he's been up there ever since. They take good care of 'im up there, lots of kids his own age, lots of fresh air. I took care of the details. I still go up and see 'im when I can. I guess I'm the only daddy he knows. He calls me Uncle Tony.
(*Harlow is breathless.*)
Oh, uh, sorry, Monroe. I forgot he was your nephew...he's fine and everything...there's plenty of fresh air in Canada. I don't think

you could do...

(Violet has been noticing Harlow showing signs of shock.)

VIOLET: Harlow. Your son, your son, he's alive!

TONY: What! What! Harlow! Son! Shit! You're Harlow? Who's Monroe? Where's Monroe?!

VIOLET: She's in a freezer, Ton.

TONY: What do you mean in a freezer?!

VIOLET: She's dead, Tony, she's dead!

TONY: Dead! She's dead! I really killed her. I killed her—the boss was right. Shit! Shit! I just blew up the boss's Delorean. I put Ajax into his coke. He was tellin' me the truth. She's dead.

VIOLET: Tony, shut up. You didn't kill Monroe, Eddie did. He tried to set you up, remember? I was talkin' to her later on that night after you knocked her out, she was fine, all right? Now just shut up. *(She turns to Harlow.)* Harlow...uh...what do you wanna do? It's your move.

HARLOW: *(Taking charge.)* Tony?

TONY: Yeah?

HARLOW: Your tickets to Canada?

TONY: Yeah?

HARLOW: Use 'em. Go to Canada. I want my boy back. *(Exit Tony. Sinister music plays.)* I want my boy back. Violet?

VIOLET: Yeah.

HARLOW: Get ahold of Lenny. He knows where the body is. Go get it and meet me at Eddie's office in an hour.

VIOLET: Eddie's?

HARLOW: It's time we had a little talk. Monroe Sanzo has a few scores to settle.

(Blackout.)

Scene 8

(The meat-locker. Lenny and Violet are passionately embracing and kissing with the body-bag stuck between them.)

VIOLET: I still can't believe it.

LENNY: ...like a nightmare. Tony comes into the bar dressed like Rambo, laughin' and screamin', talkin' about a bomb in a buildin'. I thought he was kiddin'.

VIOLET: Kiss me, it's freezin' here.

LENNY: You don't seem too upset, Violet.

VIOLET: It's a long story. I'll tell you about it over drinks.

LENNY: The bar's blown up!

VIOLET: Yeah, well I know a great bar in Negril.

LENNY: Where?

VIOLET: Jamaica, Lenny. We're goin' on a little holiday to Jamaica.

(They exit. Blackout.)

Scene 9

(Eddie's office. Sinister music plays. Eddie is ranting and frantically searching through a pile of video tapes.)

EDDIE: Where is it? Where is it? It's gone. Kidnapped! They've kidnapped my son!

(Eddie goes to snort some of the coke piled on his table, but checks himself. He picks up an handful and lets it flow through his fingers.)

Bastards! They'll pay—every goddamn one of them. You're all dead! I'll kill ya twenty times over if I have to. (*Screaming.*) Nobody messes with Eddie Bossanova!

(Enter Harlow.)

HARLOW: Hard day at the office, Eddie?

EDDIE: What do you want here, Monroe? Why are ya doin' this to me?

HARLOW: You're doing it to yourself, Eddie. I just came over to watch.

EDDIE: I gave you whatever you needed.

HARLOW: You never gave anyone anything, Eddie, but heart-aches and hard times. You're a vacuum, Eddie, sucking up coke, sucking in people. You're a leach. You set people up and you suck people dry. And then you call them dusty. You did it to Tony. You did it to Violet. You did it to Harlow...(*Eddie tries to reach for his gun but it is missing from his holster*) and you tried to do it to me. But it didn't work. I'm living proof of that.

EDDIE: But not for long, dusty.

HARLOW: You tried to take me down, Eddie, but you couldn't do it. You killed my sister, but you couldn't kill me.

EDDIE: What're you talkin' about. I love Harlow.

HARLOW: You killed Harlow, Eddie—three years ago. You killed Harlow the same day you killed your own son. You bastard!

(Harlow spits on him. Eddie dives for her but she easily steps out of the way. He falls to the floor.

EDDIE: Harlow's alive!

HARLOW: Harlow's dead, Eddie. You killed her once when you took away her son and you killed her again when she found out.

EDDIE: What?

(Lenny and Violet drag the body-bag into the room and drop it on the floor.)

HARLOW: She's dead, Eddie. There she is, Eddie. Was it worth it?

EDDIE: What? Liar! (*He goes to the body-bag, breaks down and hugs it. He sniffles and cries. He opens it, his jaw drops and he moves back in horror. Then he laughs.*) Monroe. It's Monroe! (*Pause while he figures it out. He looks at Harlow.*) Harlow? Honey? Is that you?

HARLOW: Harlow's dead, Eddie. You killed her.

EDDIE: No, no. I love you. I did it all for you, Harlow.

(Sinister music plays. Enter Hitman.)
EDDIE: *(Screaming.)* No! No!
    (Hitman pumps his rifle and aims at Harlow. Eddie jumps
    between them. Hitman fires twice hitting Eddie. He
            falls into Harlow's arms.)
(Dying bloodily.) She's already dead.
    (Hitman fishes the wad of bills out of Eddie's pocket. He exits.)
Ah, ah, ah, ha, ha, ha, Harlow! Ah, ah, ohhh, woaw. I did it all for
you. If I gotta die, I wanna die in your arms.
HARLOW: Eddie?
EDDIE: Yeah, baby.
HARLOW: Drop dead. *(She drops him to the ground. He dies.)* And
don't call me baby. *(Violet embraces Harlow.)* Goodbye, Violet.
VIOLET: Goodbye.
    (Harlow stops briefly at Monroe's body. Exit Harlow. Lenny
    zips the body-bag and carries it off. Violet picks up
            the phone, dials.)
VIOLET: Hello, police? I wanna report a murder. Two murders—
Eddie Bossanova and Monroe Sanzo. I'm an employee, I work in
his bar, the Vicious Circle. Yeah, somebody burnt it down. I came
over to tell Eddie about it but I found him here dead. I don't
know. The place is all torn up. There's drugs everywhere. I didn't
know he was into any of this. I gotta get outta here, man, I gotta
get outta here. They could come back.
    (While Violet has been talking, Lenny has taken the body out of
    the body-bag and set it on the floor next to Eddie. He holds the
    folded body-bag. Violet hangs up the phone. She picks up the
    receiver and dials again.)
VIOLET: Hello, operator? Yeah, overseas to Switzerland—1-853-
979-7800. *(Pause.)* I'm seeking confirmation on account number
1856667028. Yeah. Two-and-a-half-million dollars. Yes, that's
correct. Thank you.
    (Lenny and Violet kiss. Violet goes to Monroe and kisses her on
    the forehead. She looks as if she is about to cry. She realizes
    that there is no longer a Monroe. Lenny takes her gently by the
    arm. Blackout.)

Scene 10

(The airport. Airport sounds, "Now boarding," "Would passen-
ger...," etc. Paul Simon's "Mother and Child Reunion" begins to
play and continues to the end of the play. Enter Harlow, she
looks around anxiously. Enter Tony with L'il Eddie. They spot
Harlow. The boy runs to her. They embrace. Blackout.)

THE END.

Resource Centre for the Arts
(RCA) Theatre Company

Time Before Thought

1991

Collectively written by
Mercedes Barry
Andy Jones
Agnes Walsh

TIME BEFORE THOUGHT

Time Before Thought was first produced by Resource Centre for the Arts (RCA) Theatre Company at the LSPU Hall, 7-17 November 1991. The second production, produced by the Great Canadian Theatre Company, took place at GCTC, Ottawa (13-30 January 1993). The text presented here is a revised version of the Ottawa performance. The first draft of an adaptation for CBC Radio played at the Hall (3-4 June 1994). The radio play version, produced by Glen Tilley, was broadcast nationally by CBC Radio in 1996.

The play, which was written collaboratively by **Mercedes Barry**, **Andy Jones**, and **Agnes Walsh**, was performed by **Mercedes Barry** and **Agnes Walsh** and directed by **Andy Jones**. The actors played the following roles:

Mercedes Barry   Mercedes, Mrs. Laura, Stephen, Bob Dylan, Kate.

Agnes Walsh   Agnes, Aunt Rose, Bob Dylan, Ruth, Bride, Martin.

Additional credits:
Music for both productions was by **Geoff Panting**. The St. John's set was designed by **Don Short** with lighting by **Harold Hiscock**. The Ottawa set was designed by **Elly Cohen** with lighting by **Boo Noseworthy**.

The film sequences featured **Elizabeth Pickard** as Princess Maria, **Paula Nolan** as Princess Joanna, **Mercedes Barry** as Aunt Hortense, **Agnes Walsh** as Aunt Beatrice, **Andy Jones** as King, **Jon Whalen** as Stephen, **Marcel Levandier** as Martin, **Jack Lamphere** as Simon, **Lois Brown** as Ghost Mother/Fairy Godmother, with **Randy Follett**, **Frankie Paul Nolan**, **Torquil Colbo**, **Steve Lush**, **Tim Green**, **Don Ellis**, **Lily Hynes**, **Eli Whalen** and **Elizabeth McMillan**. The film sequences were directed by **Andy Jones**, camera **Justin Hall**, editor **Derek Norman**, sound **Jim Rillie**. Photographs of the 1991 St. John's production of *Time Before Thought* are by **Mary-Lynn Bernard**.

The production of *Time Before Thought* was funded by the Canada Council, the Newfoundland and Labrador Arts Council, Knowing Canada Better and the Government of Newfoundland Cultural Affairs Division. The play was sponsored by Norcen Energy and Superior Propane.

TIME BEFORE THOUGHT

ACT 1

1. Three For Wine
2. Graveyard Truths: Bussey's / Bathtub Reality
3. Aggie in the Sky
4. Agnes' Diary: Tom Bonfiglio
   1. Film Fairy Tale: Once Upon a Time
5. Mercedes' Diary: Baby is Born
6. Agnes' Diary: Mother's Courtship
   2. Film Fairy Tale: Maria Leaves
7. Agnes' Diary: Garden State
8. Howard Johnson's
9. Dylan: (a) Mercedes' Story (b) Agnes' Story
   (c) Mercedes' Story
   3. Film Fairy Tale: Goobdye
10. Ruth Proposes
11. Phone Call from Hell
12. Mom in Merasheen
13. Stephen Update
14. Dylan: (a) Agnes' Version (b) Mercedes' Version

ACT 2

1. Essay on Romance
2. Diary: (a) Birth of a Boy (b) Stephen Update
3. Box Bag Daddy
4. Agnes and Mercedes Arrive in Newfoundland
5. Diary: (a) Ruth Dies / Nail in Bowling Ball
   (b) Mercedes Called (c) Martin Dozen Roses
6. Gun Scene: Full Metal Jacket
7. Fairy Tale: The Promise of Neighbouring Kingdom
8. Barbecue
9. Diary: (a) Joaquim Suggests (b) Leaving Martin
10. Graveyard Truths: Fairy Tale / Tin Table Ending

CAST OF CHARACTERS
(In order of appearance.)

Agnes	Young girl from Placentia who marries American service man/present day Agnes.
Mercedes	Young girl from Placentia who marries American service man/ present day Mercedes.
Ruth	Mercedes' mother-in-law.
Kate	Mercedes' daughter.
Bob	Bob Dylan who is also Bob Noseworthy from Placentia.
Martin	Mercedes' husband.
Stephen	Agnes' husband.

TIME BEFORE THOUGHT

ACT 1
Three for Wine
Scene 1

The set consists of three painted backdrops. The centre panel depicts a fairy tale world with a painted road curving upward into a cloud from behind a table and two chairs at centre stage. The cloud serves as the screen for the film sequences. The side panels depict a Newfoundland outport and New York City. The Newfoundland panel at stage right has a picket fence coming forward from the panel to form a waste area which contains a mattress and other debris to give the effect of a garbage dump. The New York panel at stage left has a concrete ledge which projects onto the stage.

The action takes place both in the United States and in Newfoundland over a time span of some twenty years as the two women relive their childhood in Placentia in the early sixties, their experiences in the United States during the late sixties to mid seventies and their return home to Newfoundland. The main characters are Agnes and Mercedes. Bob is married to Agnes, but is romantically involved with Mercedes. He is both Bob Noseworthy from Placentia and Bob Dylan. His presence is either mimed or is acted by Agnes or Mercedes throughout the play.

The play opens in New York in 1975. Mercedes is sitting at the table. Agnes enters to centre stage and faces the audience.

AGNES: (*To audience.*) I strolled in as casually as I could and eyed the situation. The intimate table set for two, the champagne glasses, the flowers, Mercedes' blush and surprised look. We eyed each other (*They stare at each other.*) but not in the way that women do when they are sharing the same man. Bob and I were still emotionally tied and the three of us knew it. But I also knew there was something going on with Mercedes.

MERCEDES: (*To audience.*) I suggested that I should leave, but she said seeing as how the three of us were involved, why didn't I stay?

AGNES: Mercedes, Mercedes Barry, what now is a better place to live--the city or the country?

MERCEDES: It was a topic from debates we'd had at Sacred Heart High. Bob looked confused.

MERCEDES: Should England join the European Common Market?

AGNES: Should Canada reintroduce the death penalty?

MERCEDES: Is mercy killing beyond the law?

AGNES: Maybe we'll find out tonight, Mercedes.

MERCEDES: (*To audience.*) I admired the way she kept her cool. She poured herself a glass of wine and came and sat next to me.

AGNES: Neither one of us looked at Bob. He paced back and forth for a while (*Both move their heads as if watching him pace.*) then faded into the woodwork as we immediately began talking about growing up and back home. Her mother had died, and so had my father.

MERCEDES: We talked about all the characters we'd known back in Newfoundland and fell easily into our Placentia Bay accents.

AGNES: (*Pointing to Mercedes' shoes.*) What's the difference between your shoes and mine?

MERCEDES: (*Pointing to Agnes' shoes.*) Yours are black and mine are black.

AGNES & MERCEDES: (*Together.*) Right, right, right, right, right.

MERCEDES: (*Tapping on the table.*) What's this?

AGNES: I don't know. What is it?

MERCEDES: Sexual tapping.

AGNES: What?

MERCEDES: Sexual tapping. Remember Mr. Hayward who used to live on the end of our house?

AGNES: Yeah, but, how do you know it was sexual?

MERCEDES: Listen.

(*Taps faster and builds to an orgasmic crescendo.*)

MERCEDES & AGNES: (*Together.*) All right then.

(*Agnes and Mercedes become Aunt Rose and Mrs. Laura commenting on the girls' early life in Newfoundland.*)

AUNT ROSE: There she goes off to marry her Yank. Wonder how long that'll last, now? Her mother must be some glad to see her go. She crucified her poor mother.

MRS. LAURA: Go on, Aunt Rose girl. (*Rises and looks out imaginary window.*) Bride'll be lost without her, say Christ. Sure even after she kicked her out, she came back every other night to put the bread in rise—hm, say Christ.

AUNT ROSE: All her sisters were the same, none of them were any good. Everyone of them got knocked up, and the boys were no better. That crowd from Merasheen, they're all savages. (*To imaginary cat.*) Here, puss, puss, puss.

MRS. LAURA: God have mercy on your soul, Aunt Rose, for saying things like that—hm, say Christ. Look at her getting into the taxi with the baby. Lovely baby, Aunt Rose, big, small though—say Christ. I hope she'll have good luck with her Yank, poor old soul—hm, say Christ.

AUNT ROSE: Goddamn Yanks. Just like the other day that Yank saying "Good evening" to me at ten o'clock in the morning. "Good evening," I said. You know goddamn well it's not evening. Just like the goddamn Yanks, they can't say anything serious. All the girls swarming off to the States after them. Don't know what they're getting into. Shouldn't be allowed. (*Bends over to call cat.*) Drink your milk, that's the good puss.

(Mercedes lies on the mattress. Characters revert to present time.)

MERCEDES: (*To audience.*) Bob got fed up with us after a while and said we were making him sick.

AGNES & MERCEDES: (*Together.*) Fuck off, Bob!

AGNES: That stopped him in his tracks. He pulled up a chair and joined us. And by three in the morning we were laughing and talking like old friends. And Bob's Placentia Bay accent had come back too.

MERCEDES: Are you still writing poetry, Agnes?

AGNES: (*Speaking to audience from in front of New York flat.*) Poetry! It's been kinda hard to write poetry with four kids. But that's bullshit! It wasn't just the kids. Back then when you knew me I was so idealistic. Always going on about gloriously sad matters of the heart, the American Civil Rights movement and so many other things I knew nothing about. But back then poetry had a cause to me. It struck out against the unfairness of it all. Sailor boyfriends were bringing me books of the Beat poets and, although I knew it was too late, I left with Bob wanting to be part of it all. But when I got there, got to New York, I realized I was just a girl from Placentia, and all I knew about America was what I'd read in books, seen on TV and listened to in rhythm and blues on the radio. I didn't fit in there, but I had nothing of back home to identify with either. So I floundered around, aimlessly in search of something that wasn't part of me for years and years. And then the kids with Bob, and Bob's career well, you know how it is, Mercedes.

MERCEDES: Yeah.

AGNES: (*To audience.*) But I used to get a feeling sometimes, when there was a storm off the New Jersey coast, and men had to batten down their yachts, and rain beat down senselessly for hours on end. I used to stand outside the apartment off St Mark's Square, stand outside, and let the rain and wind pelt me and I'd feel like something was letting loose deep inside, like I'd almost remembered something long buried in my heart, and then Bob would come out and lead me back in. There'd be musicians gathered singing songs about some grave social injustice in this country that was now my own, and I'd forget, I'd forget what I'd almost remembered...standing there in the rain.

MERCEDES: (*To audience.*) And then Agnes asked me what I'd been doing and I told her I'd married an American, had two kids, and that now I was trying to figure out what to do with my life. She said her mother had mentioned that I'd gotten divorced.

AGNES: (*To audience.*) I just kept looking at the side of his face in the candle light so clear. I though, my God, he's just a little boy, just little Bobby Noseworthy from Placentia, but still I was angry at him for being a little boy, and I was angry at myself for letting my poetry and my love for the island take a back seat to my love for him. (*She sits at table. Mercedes is still on the mattress.*)

MERCEDES: (*Standing and addressing audience.*) By six in the morning all the barriers were down and there was no question too personal to ask. So I took advantage of the situation and asked Bob the question that had *never* been answered. (*She questions the imaginary Bob and responds to his imagined replies.*) Why did you change your name? (*Pause.*) And why Dylan? What was wrong with the name Bob Noseworthy? (*Pause.*) Oh yeah. I never thought of that.

AGNES: Then Mercedes said something that set us deep in thought. She said,

MERCEDES: Why don't the three of us take the kids and go back home for awhile?

AGNES: Perhaps we could find an old house to rent on the Cape Shore for the summer. (*To Bob.*) I think it would do us good to get out of the States. (*Pause stretches.*) God, Mercedes, it's six-thirty in the morning. I've got to get some sleep.

Photograph by Mary-Lynn Bernard

MERCEDES: I hate going to sleep after I stay up all night. I'm bound to get the Hag.

AGNES: The Hag! God, Mercedes, I haven't thought of the Hag in years.

MERCEDES: You're lucky. I get it all the time.

AGNES: Your grandfather used to get it all the time too, didn't he?

MERCEDES: Gus, yeah, he claimed to have invented the Hag board.

AGNES: The what?

MERCEDES: The Hag board. It was a piece of board with nails sticking up through it. He used to strap it on his chest at night with the sharp ends pointing up. He said it kept the Hag from sitting on his chest and choking him.

AGNES: God, Mercedes, there's so much of that old stuff that I'd forgotten about. I mean, I never talk to old people in this country.

MERCEDES: I've been thinking a lot about Newfoundland lately, it all feels so ancient to me now. We were only youngsters when we left, sixteen years old. What did we know?

AGNES: I knew that I wanted to get out of there. I felt that if I stayed I'd rot, or marry a dentist. So I left, took off for the Big Apple.

(Banjo begins to play Newfoundland music in the background.)

MERCEDES: *(To audience.)* Three days later Agnes and I started our drive across America to Newfoundland.

AGNES: *(To audience.)* Bob, along with our kids and Mercedes', was to join us later, after his tour.

(She moves to sit on fence in front of Newfoundland flat.)

Graveyard Truths
Scene 2

*(Women revert to childhood roles. Agnes is sitting on the fence
and Mercedes on the ground in the "graveyard." Placentia,
Newfoundland in 1961.)*

AGNES: I'm eleven years old, sitting on a fence at the entrance to the graveyard. I thought nobody else went to the graveyard but me. But there she was, strolling up the hill, minding her own business, not knowing I was there. Then she saw me and we smiled at each other and gave each other "the nod" (*A gesture that is both knowing and acknowledging. It is performed by a quick lateral flick of the head, with the eyes never leaving the subject.*) She told me her name was Mercedes. I couldn't believe that I had never seen her before, such a small town and such strangers.

MERCEDES: I'm twelve years old and sitting on the back of the beach, babysitting my older sister. She's not allowed to go out with the Yanks, so I'm sent along when she goes out in the evenings to keep an eye on her. Her and her Yank pay me well to keep quiet. One evening I saw a young girl stroll towards me. At first I thought she was a spirit. Then she told me that her name was Agnes and that she had the same job as I did, keeping her older sister away from the Yanks. I couldn't believe that I had never seen her before, such a small town and such strangers.

AGNES: We didn't feel like telling any lies so we told each other the God's honest truth. She told me she was adopted and that her real parents were exiled Spanish nobility, who kept horses in Virginia. I confessed that my father was a merchant sea captain out of Amsterdam and I was waiting for him to bring me back a beaded jacket from Algiers.

Bussey's / Bathtub Reality

(Placentia, March 1966.)

MERCEDES: Ag, I got a confession to make.

AGNES: What's that?

MERCEDES: Remember those letters that we used to tear up down at Bussey's and put them back together, so that they said something different? Well, my letters weren't from boys. I wrote them myself. Did you?

AGNES: Well, some of them were real, but yeah, I wrote most of them myself. Especially the ones from our sea cadets. But that wasn't really the point. I couldn't wait to rush home after school, tear off my uniform and head down to Bussey's to talk to Bernard and Billy. Then the Yanks'd come in, and we'd look at them and say how cute this and that one was. They had lots of jukebox quarters, they wore white socks and they were impossibly handsome, unbearably polite.

MERCEDES: I can't relax with the Yanks, the way I can with Bernard and 'em, but do you think Bernard could ever say "I love you" to a girl? Pretty well every Yank I've gone out with has said "I love you." Of course, I don't believe it, but it sure is nice to hear.

AGNES: That's a pretty cute Yank you're going out with now.

MERCEDES: Martin, yeah. He keeps saying he wants me to have his baby.

AGNES: Do you think he's just trying to get you to sleep with him? I mean, do you love him?

MERCEDES: I don't know. Do you love Stephen?

AGNES: I don't know but I'm definitely not sleeping with him.
(Agnes walks slowly offstage as if deep in thought.)

MERCEDES: The Yanks seem so foreign to me. Do you think they ever have to deal with bathtub reality?

AGNES: *(As she disappears offstage.)* Bathtub reality? What's bathtub reality?

MERCEDES: The class structure in Placentia for me started in Swan's Lane. The O'Rourkes were at the top. Mrs. O'Rourke was a nurse. They were above us but friendly, especially after Mrs. O'Rourke got caught stealing money down at the hospital. Then there was us, the Barrys. We were baymen, but we were from Merasheen so we were a step up from the Red Island baymen, and everyone knew the Red Island baymen were so low that when they fell from grace, there wasn't even a thud. The Red Island bay boys, they weren't even allowed to use the toilets in school, the nuns were afraid they'd tear them up. Of course, to the townies, we were all stunned baymen.

AGNES: (*Still offstage.*) So what's bathtub reality?

MERCEDES: Remember at the beginning of the school year the teacher would ask who had bathtubs and who didn't, then she'd divide up the class, bathtubs on one side, no bathtubs on the other. I was ten when we got our first bathtub. It was only half a tub really, more like a laundry tub. I told the teacher, but I never got moved to the tub side. In the eyes of the town our crowd never amounted to much. My sisters all got pregnant and had to get married, and the boys were no better. They all got girls pregnant too and here I am, March 1966. (*To audience.*) I'm definitely pregnant. My period is two weeks overdue. I'm never late. I wonder what Martin is going to say. He said he wanted me to have his baby. Why couldn't Martin have married me first? Ah, shag him. I must go see what Agnes is up to!

(*Change of pace. "Sugar Shack" plays briefly on accordion.*)

MERCEDES: (*Calling to Agnes.*) Are you going to the dance on the base tonight?

AGNES: (*She sticks her head out from the wings.*) Yeah, are you? What are you wearing?

MERCEDES: I don't know yet. Probably my red A-line with the suspenders. I'm not going to school this afternoon. I'm going to stay home and wash and set my hair.

AGNES: Not me, girl. I'm just gonna wash me bangs in the glass.

(*Appears again, grabs her bangs and mimes washing them in a glass of water, disappears.*)

Aggie in the Sky
Scene 3

(*Five months have elapsed since the previous scene. Lighting changes indicate this passage of time. Mercedes walks to centre stage.*)

MERCEDES: August 1966. I suppose the whole town knows by now that I won't be marrying Martin. When I told him I was pregnant, he said he wanted to marry me. He went to his commanding officer for permission...he's only nineteen and had to get the okay from the Navy. Like Uncle Sam says, "If the Navy wanted you to have a wife it would have issued you one." His commanding officer said yes, but his mother said no. She said I was probably trying to trick him and that it was someone else's baby. Then she called the base chaplain and he told Martin not to see me again. He still comes up to see me, but I get the feeling he's happy not to be marrying me.

(She moves to sit on concrete ledge. Placentia church bells sound in the distance to indicate that time has passed.)

I'm tired of walking around this town, everyone staring at me, I feel like the town whore. I don't know what I'm going to do. Mom says she doesn't want the baby in over the doorstep. All she calls me is slut or whore, and Dad won't even look at me. They won't give me Welfare 'cause I'm only seventeen. They say I should be living at home. Dad asked me if I wanted to go to the Salvation Army home in St. John's and give the baby up but I can't do that. I'll always be wondering where it is. Oh Jesus, here comes Ag. I haven't seen her in months. I wonder what happened? I heard she left for the States with Stephen to get married. *(Encouraging herself.)* Now, Mercedes, don't get upset if she doesn't stop and speak to you, just nod and say hello.

(Enter Agnes.)

AGNES: Mercedes, how are you?

MERCEDES: Pregnant. How are you, Ag? What happened? I thought you left for the States with Stephen?

AGNES: Oh, I did, girl. Me and Stephen were driving back, but they wouldn't let me through the border without a note from Mom. So I just told him to go on and I came back home.

MERCEDES: Are you going to try to go back or what?

AGNES: Yeah, as soon as Stephen gets settled in, he's going to send me the money, plus I have to get my papers ready. How's Martin?

MERCEDES: Oh, he's around. That's a really nice ring, Ag.

AGNES: Oh, thanks. Stephen and I got engaged on my birthday.

MERCEDES: What happened to the girl he was engaged to in the States?

AGNES: Oh, he broke off with her and she gave back the ring.

MERCEDES: That's not the same ring, is it?

AGNES: Yeah.

MERCEDES: That's supposed to be bad luck.

AGNES: Sure, what odds? It's a nice ring, isn't it? *(Puts out her hand to admire the ring.)* So what do you think you're going to have, a boy or a girl?

MERCEDES: Oh, it's a girl. Aunt Rose did the needle on me. I'm going to call her Kate.

AGNES: Well, girl, good luck with it all. I have to go now. But we should get together sometime before I leave.

MERCEDES: *(Pointing to Agnes' shoes.)* What's the difference between your shoes and mine?

AGNES: *(Pointing to Mercedes' shoes.)* Mine are black and yours are black.

AGNES & MERCEDES: (*Together*) Right, right, right. All right then.

(*Agnes walks away, waving, still looking back, stops after a few steps and faces Mercedes.*)

MERCEDES: Give me a call before you leave. Tell Stephen I said hello. It was good seeing you again, Ag.

AGNES: You too. Take care now.

MERCEDES: See ya.

AGNES: Bye.

MERCEDES: See ya.

AGNES: Bye.

MERCEDES: Why did I get pregnant? It's true what they say. Once you give in to them and have sex they have no respect for you. I should have held out for the engagement ring, like Ag, even if it is secondhand. I wonder if Ag is going to the dance on the base tonight. Martin will probably be there too. He said he had to work, but I don't believe that. Ah, shag him! I think I'll go over and see if Mrs. Bussey needs any potatoes peeled.

(*Lights fade on Mercedes.*)

Agnes' Diary: Tom Bonfiglio
Scene 4

AGNES: (*To audience. She is standing in front of the Newfoundland flat.*) Poor Mercedes. She acts so brave, but she must be scared to death. I know I would be. I'm glad Stephen and I never went all the way. I don't want to have a baby...oh, God...Stephen, what am I going to do? Last month when I was down at Bussey's I met Tom. I went over to the jukebox and pressed "A3," a new song I hadn't heard before. I leaned against the jukebox and heard, "You got a lotta nerve to say you are my friend." I kept listening to the words, the snarling nasal voice and I felt pinned, nailed. I heard another voice behind me, someone saying, "So you like Bob Dylan, do you?" That was Tom, Tom Bonfiglio, and now I see him every evening and most days he's not on duty. He's from New York City and he comes up to my parents' house with bags of books for me to read. Mom and Dad seem to totally accept him. He falls asleep on the couch and picks out of the pot on the stove like a member of the family. He excites me in a way no one has ever done before, challenges me and has taken over my education. But I'm still engaged to Stephen...

(*Agnes sits on mattress.*)

Fairy Tale: Once Upon a Time
Film 1

(*Black leader. Lights fade to half and fade to black by the end of Agnes' first speech. Mercedes is still sitting on ledge of the New*

York flat. Music plays. It has a reverb "in-the-mind" quality at first; volume lessens and music is gone by the time Mercedes speaks. Mercedes and Agnes open large fairy tale books from which they read the following narration.)

MERCEDES: Once upon a time, not in my time or in your time, but in a time long ago, there was a princess who married the prince from someone else's fairy tale and apparently found complete fulfilment in being a generic princess—a "walk on" from the last chapter in the story of some hero-prince.

AGNES: But this is not her story. This is the story of her two younger sisters—the ones that are rarely written about and who were each determined to be in their very own story.

(The narrative goes from being spoken live to voiceover on tape.)

To do this it was imperative for them to leave their homeland. Yet this was very difficult as their father, the King, had, in his sadness at the loss of his eldest daughter, decreed that his two younger daughters were never allowed to leave the kingdom and that if they did they were never allowed back in. *(Pause.)* So the two princesses were *very unhappy* in their homeland. *(Pause.)* They longed to travel to points beyond and exotic, and they longed for love.

(The film begins. It is silent, but accompanied by music and sound effects. The camera moves in on a typical outport bungalow and focuses on the two princesses who are sitting on the front steps. The princesses are wearing tiaras. Princess Maria sighs deeply while Princess Joanna looks sadly off into the distance. Close up on princesses. Camera pans away.)

MERCEDES: They lived in the royal palace with their father, the King, an unaffectionate man to say the least, a bitter man, troubled by the burdens of administering the poorest kingdom in Christendom.

(Suddenly their father, King of Kingdom of Homeland, steps out onto the steps of the house. He is wearing a faded royal robe and rubber boots. The king descends the steps separating the two princesses and walks worriedly down the path.)

Since their mother had died when they were very young they lived under the yoke of their two domineering aunts, Beatrice and Hortense, who worked the girls like drones and who never showed them anything even vaguely resembling affection.

(Maria sighs deeply while Joanna is still looking off into the distance. Aunt Beatrice and Aunt Hortense step out of the house, brooms in hand, sweeping the two princesses off the front step.)

AGNES: Beatrice insisted that dirty clothes be beaten within an inch of their lives. She saw doing laundry as a way of venting a lifetime of frustration and bitterness.

MERCEDES: On the other hand, Hortense's obsession with banishing dirt from the kingdom forever was but another in a life-time list of lost causes and daily drudgeries.

(Scene changes to Princess Joanna scrubbing clothes on a scrubbing board while Hortense shouts over her. Aunt Beatrice looks angrily at Maria who is sweeping.)

This contrasted sharply with the distant memory of their mother, whose warmth and love they remembered in their hearts as the most wonderful part of their lives, and a part they desperately sought to restore. *(Pause.)* But in the meantime every waking moment of their daily lives was controlled by the aunts who drove them to the limits of their endurance. *(Pause.)* Yet at the same time the princesses were expected to sparkle with wit and feminine charm on all state occasions. *(Pause.)* They were also called upon to intervene in local political disputes. *(Brief pause.)* But, ever the diplomats, they remained aloof from the details of negotiation.

(The princesses are sitting on the steps again looking off into the distance, thinking of their mother. A shadowy representation of her comes out of the house and gives them cookies. The scene changes to show the two princesses in the garden pulling weeds and picking flowers. The scene changes to Maria chopping wood. Her aunt Beatrice demonstrates the correct technique by throwing her arms up and down in an exaggerated chopping motion while Maria, who is actually doing the work, looks on for guidance. The scene changes to the Homeland garden party. A raffle wheel is spinning while the two princesses stand beside it chewing gum. Suddenly two men mime a fight. As the princesses, shaded by an umbrella, walk by on a boardwalk with the sea behind them, the men stop fighting, stand up, and bow to them. When Maria and Joanna have passed by, the men resume their former fighting positions. B sits on A's chest and continues to mime punching him. Fade to black.)

AGNES: One day when the two princesses were working in the outdoor accounting chambers...

(Film fades in. Princess Maria and Princess Joanna are seated on rocks on a hillside. There is a filing cabinet behind them and a painting on an easel. The princesses have books in their laps.)

...Aunt Hortense came rushing in to announce that the navy of Neighbouring Kingdom was entering the Capital City port. At first the two princesses were frightened, fearing that the kingdom was under attack, but Aunt Beatrice spoke up and assured them that Neighbouring Kingdom was friendly. *(Pause.)* "Nonetheless," she prophesied. "I feel they will bring great sadness to this family." *(Pause.)* Beatrice tended to see the dark side of things—a court psychiatrist diagnosed her as manic depressive schizophrenic and prescribed Valium—but Beatrice refused insisting she was simply, "in mourning for her life."

(*Little pause.*) She always wore black and she whined a lot. Hence the princesses' nickname for her, "Black Bee." Hortense, by the way, the girls called the "Hornet."

(*Hortense walks angrily towards them and speaks. The princesses look at each other in amazement. Aunt Beatrice is sitting with a book on her lap on a rock covered with a blanket. She waves her hand up and down motioning them to relax and not worry; she appears to be quite dotty. Beatrice sighs deeply and lies back on her blanket with her hands behind her head. She rubs her head as if suffering great pain, her eyes are closed.*)

MERCEDES: Princess Maria was intrigued by the notion of the friendly invasion. She longed to meet the sailors from Neighbouring Kingdom, as she had always been interested in the art of foreign lands. Her first loves were painting and poetry, and she had often begged her father to buy some of the works of foreign painters. But, as she knew deep inside, there was just no money for what her father called frivolities. (*Pause.*) Besides, rumour had it that a lot of these sailors were incredibly cute!

AGNES: Joanna, the older princess, was not immediately as excited at the prospect of meeting these sailors, as she dreaded the inevitable row with her father. If she even spoke to foreigners he flew off the royal handle. But once again the rumoured cuteness of the sailors overcame her reservations. (*Pause.*) And so both princesses longed for the end of the day when they would be relieved of their bureaucratic duties.

(*The two princesses look at each other again. Hortense is speaking angrily, Maria looks sad, she is painting an Andy Warhol style picture of a can of Campbell's Chicken Noodle Soup. The King walks angrily up to her, wearing his crown and kingly robe over his plaid shirt and carrying kingly general ledgers in his hand, he grabs the painting and throws it away in disgust. Maria looks saddened by his act. Joanna continues to write, quill in hand. She is sitting quietly; she looks up——a thought flashes through her mind and a smirk crosses her face. Both princesses appear to be in a better mood. Fade to black. Sound has reverb quality as in opening dialogue. Lights up on Mercedes and Agnes holding their books.*)

MERCEDES: They worked hard until five o'clock. Once home, they had to get the boarder's supper, wash the dishes and sweep the royal dining room. It was nearly eight-thirty before they could sneak out disguised as peasant girls. (It wasn't difficult to find peasant disguises since most of their clothes were on a par with those of lower-middle-peasant-class peasant girls.) And as they approached the harbour they heard the unmistakable strains of dance music. "Who could be dancing on a Wednesday night," they wondered. As they got closer to the ship they saw a huge orchestra on the main deck playing a heavenly waltz, as the conductor waved his baton from a modified crow's nest half way up the main mast.

Sailors from Neighbouring Kingdom swarmed the cafes and bistros of the ancient capital. (*Pause.*) They were animated and happy, they laughed a lot and they were impossibly handsome, unbearably polite.

Photograph by Mary-Lynn Bernard

(Film fades in to show six clean-cut sailors standing casually outside Mullaley's Chicken Bar. Some are sitting, others are standing smoking cigarettes. Maria and Joanna walk up to them. One sailor kisses Maria's hand as she smiles delightedly. Another kisses Joanna's hand. The princesses and their sailors appear happy and interested in each other as they begin to talk.)

AGNES: Yes, there is no doubt that the two princesses were charmed that day. The sailors were the height of politeness. They called the princesses "ma'am" or "miss" and the sauciest term they used was "pretty lady."

(The film fades briefly to black.)

MERCEDES: This contrasted with their experience of their royal boy cousins who tended to be markedly less tender and generally greeted the princesses with phrases like, "Suck dis, luh."

(Film fades in to show five boy cousins leaning against a building, wearing baseball caps and looking generally scruffy. They are smoking cigarettes and grab their genitals in rude gestures at the princesses' approach.)

Each of the young women found a special sailor that day. For Maria it was Stephen, a self-assured handsome poet sailor, who pleased her with his interest in her poetry. Maria was excited and a tiny bit frightened of his bold forays into matters of the human soul. Her skin tingled as she stared at his handsome blue eyes, and when he kissed her she felt a new and delicious vulnerability grow within her.

AGNES: Joanna's love was a beautiful, quiet sailor named Martin, who spoke rarely and succinctly, wasting neither breath nor words. Joanna was unable to kiss him that first day. She knew it would be a while before she could kiss him because as they stood by the wharf he reached out, he held her hand, and she had come frighteningly close to losing her mind.

(Film shows sailors and princesses talking; the princesses continue to chew gum. Maria and Stephen sit by a rusted metal fence and Stephen reads to her. He puts his hand around her shoulder pulling her near him, he kisses her. Joanna is with her sailor named Martin. They are standing and talking. Maria and Stephen are close by, still absorbed in poetry. Joanna and Martin stare at each other. Martin reaches for Joanna's hand and she reaches for his. They hold hands. Fade to black.)

MERCEDES: There is no doubt that the princesses were changed forever that day. Hortense intuited that it had something to do with the sailors, and she made up her mind to spy on the girls. She listened at their door and she heard all—she heard about their joy, their longing, their uncontrollable surrender to the chaos of love. The next day the two princesses disguised themselves once again and went to meet their sailors.

AGNES: And so the world of the princesses had been invaded by the forces of love. *(Pause.)* Early one morning while the palace slept, the princesses ran to meet their sailors.

(Film fades in. Sound of wind in cave, slight echo, etc. Maria and Joanna are running down a path at the side of a cliff, heading toward a cave.)

They climbed over the hills to their favourite childhood playing spot, in a cave near the steep ocean cliffs, where they had arranged the rendezvous. *(Pause.)* As they wandered into the cave a powerful wind suddenly douted their candles. *(Pause.)* Then, as if by magic, the cave was filled with light. The light became brighter and brighter; they looked up, and there was a ghostly form. *(Pause.)* But rather than fear, the princesses felt an inner serenity; then they broke into wide smiles. It was their mother!

MERCEDES: They were unable to embrace her for she was a ghostly presence—yet they felt the inner satisfaction of such an embrace just from being near her. *(Pause.)* It was then that a troubled look came over their mother's face, and in her haunting eyes they saw a vision. *(Pause.)* In the vision they could see the Hornet and the Black Bee approaching the beach below with two royal guards.

(The princesses enter the cave holding candles to find their way

in the dark. Suddenly their candles blow out and a bright light blinds them. They cover their eyes and a woman dressed in a long white gown, her head covered with a veil, appears. She is radiant and smiling; she holds out her arms to them. The princesses walk towards her and see her smile fade and her expression become worried. The ghost of their mother shows them a vision of Beatrice and Hortense below, running toward them on the beach, followed by two guards. The camera lingers on the guards' white spats and black boots. Fade to black.)

AGNES: Wasting no time the princesses ran to the sailors and with tearful embraces told them of their real identities. They urged the young men to run away—but they refused. And so all four of them decided to hide on a nearby island and make plans to escape from the kingdom.

(Film fades in. Maria and Joanna run towards their sailor-loves on the dock. Together they get into a small row boat and the sailors row them towards a nearby island.

MERCEDES: They all knew that this might be their last night together and their hearts ached to breaking with despair and world weariness. *(Long pause.)*

AGNES: Once on the island Joanna and Martin, Maria and Stephen, had a lifetime of soul love and body enjoyment in one night. *(Pause.)* In their innocence they thought this love had made them one with the earth and they would be hidden from the mean laws of men.

(On the island the couples separate. Joanna and Martin kiss in the tall, end-of-summer grass. Stephen and Maria walk to the top of a cliff. The sea is seen behind them. Stephen kisses Maria, they lie on the ground embracing and kissing each other. Joanna and Martin disappear into the long grass in a passionate embrace. Fade to black. End of Film 1.)

MERCEDES: They were wrong. *(Pause.)* And in the morning they were discovered by the King, the aunts, and the palace guards. Their sailors were saved from death by the admiral of their fleet, but were sent from the land forever. Nine months later the Princess Joanna gave birth to a girl child, whom she called Kate.

Mercedes' Diary: Baby is Born
Scene 5

(Mercedes moves to stand in front of New York flat.)

MERCEDES: October 1966. When the baby was a week overdue I went to my sister Mary for advice. She told me to drink castor oil. I put a bottle of it in a glass of Tang. I had a really hard time getting it down. I can still see it cling to the sides of the glass. My cramps started about four in the morning.

Dad took me to the hospital. Martin came up sometime during the day, but I was in so much pain I could hardly talk to him. He didn't stay long. He asked me to call him when the baby comes. They won't give me anything for pain because I'm an unwed mother.

At three-fifteen Sunday morning she's finally born. A beautiful baby girl. I count her fingers and toes and she has enough hair on top of her head to make a curl. Martin had to leave the day I got out of the hospital with Kate. He was being stationed in Virginia. He came up to see us before he left. He held Kate for a long time and promised to send for us as soon as he could. I'm really glad to have Kate, even if I never get married, but I think he loves me and I know that I love him. He had to leave at five in the morning to catch his plane. I stood in the doorway with Kate and watched him go. He looked so handsome in his uniform with his sea-bag over his back. I wonder if I'll ever see him again? I guess there's nothing I can do but wait.

(Lights fade as Mercedes turns to exit stage. Lights up on
Agnes who remains sitting on the mattress.)

Agnes' Diary: Mother's Courtship
Scene 6

AGNES: In 1935 my mother went to work for the local merchant in Placentia. As she was twenty-three years old, the merchant thought it was high time for her to get married. He told her about a man he knew, who worked on the Labrador, and came home every winter to take care of his old aunt. This man, the merchant said, was steady, reliable, would inherit his aunt's house, didn't drink and always paid up his accounts in the fall of the year. He advised my mother to consider the prospect and told her that he would arrange for a meeting. On Saturday night, after the shirts of the eight sons were starched and flat-ironed for the week, he told my mother that Bill Walsh was coming tomorrow after dinner and to put on her good dress. Next day my mother did this and came downstairs at the appointed time to sit on the daybed and wait. Dad came in and took a chair by the door and talked to the merchant about the weather, the price of fish, and working on the Labrador. He never looked at Mom and Mom never spoke to him. Then Bill said good day to the merchant and left. Two weeks later Mom was walking up the road with Harry O'Keefe, and Dad came along, elbowed Harry out of the way, saying, "What are you doing, Harry? She's my woman." Mom figured that was a proposal even though she never got to say yes. When they got to the front gate Dad said, "We'll get married next month." On their wedding night my mother was cleaning up from the wedding supper and she playfully threw a cup towel at my father. He picked it up and said, "We'll have none of that nonsense." When she told me that my heart sank for her, just like I'm sure hers sank that night.

*(Lights fade on Agnes. Mercedes in the black
with fairy tale book.)*

Fairy Tale: Maria Leaves
Film 2

*(Black leader. Lights dim on Agnes and Mercedes holding
books. They exit in black. Music has the reverb quality of Film
1. Voiceover narrative begins.)*

MERCEDES: And so the princesses were near destroyed by the tragic loss of their sailor-loves and the scornful and righteous contempt of the citizens of the kingdom. Joanna's lot was easier to bear because of the love of her little child. Maria on the other hand, spent more and more time alone, writing her poetry, as each day she sank deeper and deeper into depression at the loss of her true love, Stephen.

AGNES: As the royal coffers were now completely empty, Joanna had heavy responsibilities on her young shoulders. So she went to work at the fish plant to support herself, her sister and little Kate.

(Film begins with a close up of Princess Joanna.)

MERCEDES: One day as Joanna returned home to the waiting arms of her daughter, she noticed the depths of Maria's despair, whose childless life had only made her loneliness for Stephen keener. *(Pause.)* Maria then informed Joanna of her hellish intention to commit suicide. *(Pause.)* Joanna tried to dissuade her, but it was to no avail. *(Pause.)* She rushed toward the cliff. *(Pause.)* Split seconds before the deed was done, Joanna pulled her back. *(Pause.)* Though both were relieved to be alive, Joanna saw the lingering sadness in her sister's eyes. *(Pause.)* Suddenly their mother appeared to them again. They looked into her eyes where Maria saw a vision. *(Pause.)*

(Joanna looks pensively around her. She hugs her daughter and smiles. Maria sits and writes, almost in tears. She gets up and tells Joanna she is planning to commit suicide. Maria runs off up the path on the side of the hill with Joanna chasing her. Maria reaches the top of the cliff and Joanna grabs her. The beach is seen far below. The two girls look at each other and behind them a blinding light appears. Still hugging they turn and see that it is their mother in a white dress, her face covered with a veil.)

AGNES: She saw herself in a foreign land where she was being drawn toward a group of homeless people. *(Pause.)* One of them pointed her toward a young man who lay ill on the ground. It was Stephen. *(Pause.)* She ran to him and took his frail body in her life-giving arms. *(Pause.)* And then the vision faded and the sisters fell into a peaceful sleep. *(Pause.)* When they woke up Maria's mission was clear. She must travel to Neighbouring

Kingdom to find her sailor-love. (*Pause.*) And so the princesses bade each other a sad farewell.

(Maria has a vision of herself surrounded by homeless men. One man resembles John Lennon, another Jim Morrison and yet another Bob Dylan. One of them points to a man on the ground. Maria rushes to his side and upon turning his head sees it is Stephen. She touches his face and kisses him. He wakes up and they hold each other. Return to blinding light and their mother. The two princesses awake and find themselves lying on the ground. They rub their eyes and bid each other a sad farewell.)

When Maria got to the top of the hill she looked back at the little kingdom below her where she imagined she could see her sister on her way to the afternoon shift at the fish plant, her niece Kate swinging on her garden swing, and her aunts, Beatrice and Hortense, walking arm in arm on the Palace grounds. She stayed for a long time drinking this scene in for she felt certain she would never return.

(The town of Placentia is seen from the top of Castle Hill. The camera pans slowly from left to right showing the town, its central church, the sea and the surrounding landscape. Fade to black. Music ends quickly as if to mark the end of a segment. After a few beats it starts up again immediately before the following dialogue.)

MERCEDES: It took Maria three days to find her way to a little seaside town at the far edge of the island. (*Film shows Maria carrying a suitcase. It is night.*) She set about finding a boatman who would take her to Neighbouring Kingdom. This proved to be difficult as the seas separating the two countries were fierce and unpredictable. (*Pause.*) There was only one man in the community who had ever ferried people across the sea; his name was Simon, a man who made his living as a sign painter and a house painter. (*Pause.*) Almost from the moment they met, Maria felt a strong, magical attraction to this eccentric boatman.

(Maria walks past a white fence in front of a small white house. Simon emerges from the darkness and in the darkness they meet. He opens the gate, allowing her to pass through. Fade to black.)

The next day they left in a small schooner in which they crossed the stormy gulf between the beautiful Kingdom of Homeland and the large unknown and exciting land of Neighbouring Kingdom. With an aching heart she said farewell to her foggy island and all its many memories. (*Pause.*) The voyage took three days and Maria and Simon told many stories to each other of their respective sides of the island.

(Daylight returns and the two walk towards a schooner. Maria sits in the boat with her suitcase and they set out to sea. Simon hoists the sail and takes the wheel as Maria looks on smiling.

They talk and Maria begins to sketch in her book.)

AGNES: As Maria spoke she drew sketches of the people in her stories and showed them to the painter Simon. The shared stories and drawings made them fall in love, not only with each other, but with the land they had left behind. (*Pause.*)

They soon arrive on the shores of Neighbouring Kingdom. (*Pause.*) Once on the shore they hugged a polite hug...and turned to pursue their separate paths. (*Pause.*) Then Maria stopped, turned back and they hugged again not so politely. But they managed to separate once more, knowing that it must be their last farewell. (*Pause.*) But no! Seized with longing they returned to one another's arms for the least polite hug of all. Oh, how they would like to fulfil their desires. (*Pause.*) They stopped short of becoming lovers, however, as Maria believed it would betray her bond to her own Stephen.

(Near the shore Simon carries Maria and her suitcase through the water to the safety of the beach. She hugs him, turns to leave and moves a few steps off. She stops, looks back, and runs back to hug him, then kisses him. They part again but Maria once again stops and runs back to him. She leaps into his arms, wrapping her legs around his waist, and kisses him passionately for some time. They part once more and Maria picks up her suitcase and walks over the rocky beach.

The Neighbouring Kingdom's flag is seen blowing in the wind, it resembles the American flag but the stars are white hearts in a blue field and the white stripes consist of rows of white snakes against the red background. Agnes enters and stands in front of New York flat. Fade to black. End of Film 2. Mercedes enters in black and lies on mattress.)

MERCEDES: This is not to say that her head hadn't been turned and that she wasn't very confused. They had both believed that it was only possible to be in love with one person at a time. Being in love seemed to fill the soul of the lovers. Did this mean that they had a second soul that filled with the second love? Or did the first soul merely stretch to admit this twin love? It was the stretchability of the human soul that Maria pondered as she walked toward an unknown destiny in Neighbouring Kingdom.

Agnes' Diary: Garden State
Scene 7

(New Jersey, 1967.)

AGNES: New Jersey is called the Garden State. It says so on the licence plates. All I know is that it's hot here, hotter than it ever was back home. Stephen and I are going to get married. He seems the same as he did back home, except here he has friends he went to high school with. One guy, Eddie Haskel, has a girlfriend, Betty Anderson, who Stephen says can stand up for me. I don't know about Betty though. She's so perfect with her long blond hair, pink lipstick, pink fingernail polish, pink toenail polish. I can tell she doesn't really want to have anything to do with me, but she'll be my witness for the chance to dress up. Every boy has his own car here and the girls borrow their parents'. On Friday night everyone goes to the Dutch Hut, a drive-in hamburger place. They rev up their engines and drive up and down the main drag, then circle back to the Dutch Hut. I find this both boring and exciting at the same time.

Stephen's mother calls me to go shopping with her. At first I find it all so exciting, all the big stores and so much stuff so cheap. Back home there was only Noseworthy's and one or two others and the catalogues of course. Then last week I met Stephen's teenage girl cousins at his aunt's cottage on the lake. Since everyone around here is always kissing and hugging, I decided to push myself out of my shyness a bit so I walked up to where they were sunbathing and gave each of them a hug and a big kiss right on the lips. They got flustered and put on their beach robes. At first I thought they were as shy like me, but later Stephen pulled me aside and said, "What were you doing kissing them on the lips like that? Everyone will think you're a lesbian." I almost died, even though I wasn't too sure of what a lesbian was. Five days later Stephen and I get married, and have our honeymoon at the Howard Johnson's Motor Lodge off the Garden State Parkway. (*Light comes up on mattress where Stephen [Mercedes] is lying.*)

Howard Johnson's
Scene 8

(Continuation.)

STEPHEN: (*Played by Mercedes.*) What are you doing, sweetheart? Come on back to bed with me.

AGNES: (*Facing Stephen with her back to audience.*) No.

STEPHEN: What's the matter, hon? You can't sit there all night. Anything wrong?

AGNES: Yeah, everything.

STEPHEN: What do ya mean? Come on over.

AGNES: No, I'm not getting back into that bed with you now or ever.

STEPHEN: Are you upset about earlier? Well, it was your first time, hon. It'll get better.

AGNES: Yeah, right. No thanks.

STEPHEN: Oh, come on, you're just shaken up because it hurt a bit. It always hurts women the first time.

AGNES: Yeah, well why didn't you stop? You knew it was hurting me, goddamn it. Why didn't you just stop?

STEPHEN: Because if I stopped then you'd never get used to it.

Come on, hon, it'll get better.

AGNES: Just go to hell. You don't care about anyone except yourself and getting what you want. You didn't even hear me crying, when I tried to push you away you just kept at it more. So fuck you. I hate your guts and I want out of this shit hole of a marriage.

STEPHEN: If you don't love me, why did you marry me then?

AGNES: No, I don't love you. I don't even like you. God, I'm only sixteen. Maybe I married you to get out of Newfoundland or because I was scared of being here alone.

STEPHEN: You're just confused. Look, I love you. It's just this sex thing, it'll take time. I'll be gentler and you'll get used to it.

AGNES: Stop saying that. I won't get used to it. It hurt, goddamn it. What if I hit you over the head with a baseball bat or stuck a stick up your hole and said you'll get used to it? What would you say?

STEPHEN: But, hon, what could I do?

AGNES: You could have stopped. You could have stopped and just held me and talked about it.

STEPHEN: You could have stopped me...

AGNES: Yeah! With what? A Mack truck?

STEPHEN: Look, it's supposed to hurt and I'm supposed to keep doing it. That's what I've heard, that's what I've read...I'm supposed to keep at it.

AGNES: Yeah, well keep at it on your own or with someone else. (*To audience.*) But of course I didn't say any of that. How could I? Back then young girls might have thought that but they certainly didn't say it. Instead I set the seed in the back of my mind to get independent of this man with whom I've just tied a bond. I look at him and say to myself, "I'm sorry, Stephen, but when you wake up, I'll be the ogre you never dreamed of, for I plan to lay ruin to this marriage while it's only just begun."
(Lights fade.)

Dylan
Scene 9
(a) Mercedes' Story

(Toronto, 1975.)

MERCEDES: (*She moves from mattress to table.*) I first met Dylan in 1975. I'd just gotten divorced and I was living in Toronto. My friend Gord was a dope dealer there and he had unlimited access to all the back stages in the Toronto music scene. The night we went to see Dylan, I knew who he was but hadn't listened to his music much, and I was struck immediately by the power he had when he came on stage.
*(Light comes up behind and Agnes strikes a pose as
Bob Dylan. Fade.)*

After, when we went back to his dressing room, Gord dealt with the manager and Dylan just sat there and he never said a word to anyone. As I was leaving I caught his eye in the mirror and I gave him...the nod!

(Bob [Agnes] is in half light. When Mercedes says "the nod," he whips his sunglasses off, stares intently then freezes. He backs off, thinking, and presents his profile.)

The next day I got a call from his manager, he said that Dylan wanted to meet me, and he asked if I could come over to the Four Seasons Hotel where they were staying. I was really nervous but I agreed to go. When I got there Dylan opened the door and invited me in. He seemed really awkward and shy which put me at ease and then he came and sat next to me.

(Bob pulls up a chair and sits next to Mercedes.)

BOB: I've been haunted all night by that nod you gave me. Could you nod at me again?

MERCEDES: *(Speaking nonchalantly.)* If you want me to.

(She nods at him. He nods at her. These nods are repeated four times. She nods at him and looks away.)

BOB: Where are you from?

MERCEDES: Newfoundland. I'm Mercedes Barry.

(Bob gets nervous and looks away.)

Mercedes: *(To audience.)* He told me he was married and that he had four kids, but his wife couldn't understand his lifestyle, and he couldn't give it up. He said he knew he couldn't live without his music and it was a price he had to pay. We talked and laughed for hours and *(She finishes mysteriously.)* there was something strangely familiar about his sense of humour.

(Lights fade on Mercedes and come up on Agnes who rises from chair and moves to front of Newfoundland flat.)

(b) Agnes' Story

AGNES: I first met Bob when he was five years old. Mrs. Muriel Noseworthy, one of the town grocers, adopted him. He wasn't much to look at really, kinda skinny with fluffy hair and a bowed nose.

(Light up on Mercedes who strikes a Dylan pose. Fade.)

He seemed shy, but later I was to discover that he was moody. We hung around together because he lived so close and our mothers were friends. By the time we got into high school we were talking on the phone a lot. Both of us loved poetry and we used to read our poems to each other.

Before long Bob got himself a guitar and taught himself how to play it, also a harmonica and an accordion. He also took to wearing dark sunglasses a lot, even indoors and when I asked him why the shades in a place where the fog never rolls out, he said...

BOB: *(Played by Mercedes, standing in front of New York flat with her back toward audience putting on sunglasses.)* Mind your own fucking business.

AGNES: He was moodier than ever since he got his guitar. He'd call me up and say...

BOB: What do you think of this? *(Sings.)*
> Let's go to New York City, babe,
> Where the folks are just like us.
> We'll send them all a postcard,
> And say, "Hey, take the bus."
> Well, they've shut down our rail roads,
> And they've taken all our fish,
> But we just hang our heads, babe,
> And say it's only politics.

AGNES: ...accompanying himself with guitar and harmonica. Then he'd say,

BOB: Ya like it or what?

Photograph by Mary-Lynn Bernard

AGNES: Well, Jeeze, I was scared to death to hurt his feelings and I thought, "The poor little fella, he's going through a hard time being adopted and all." So I said, "Yeah, Bob, that was great. Really interesting. Far out." And he'd say...

BOB: *(With hand to groin motion.)* Suck dis, luh!

AGNES: ...and hang up. But a couple of days later he'd call back with another one.

BOB: (*Sings.*)Ya know, our forefathers came here, babe,
  Thinkin' they could make it work.
  But there's so much greed and corruption
  When you're tryin' to make a buck...
  (Bob carries on singing while Agnes speaks, raising
  her voice above his.)

AGNES: He wrote a lot then. Me too. And who wrote the best? Well, time will tell. (*She walks toward bed, sits down and says.*) Anyway, one day after school Bob came over, plunked himself down on the bed and said...
  (Bob goes to mattress and kneels beside her.)

BOB: I'm splittin', babe, I'm gettin' out of here and goin' to New York. You wanna come or wha'?

AGNES: Well, of course I wanted to go. I had no intention of sticking around this one-horse town so I said, "Yeah, Bob, sure." (*Pause.*) Then Bob did something he'd never done before. He leaned across the bed and kissed me full on the lips. (*Pause, Bob kisses her. She responds with a lump-in-throat look.*) We met on a Wednesday morning in front of the court house. All he had with him was his guitar, harmonica, collection of poems and songs and a leather jacket he'd gotten off an American sailor who said it used to belong to James Dean. We hitchhiked across the island. I was excited, but also kind of sad as I looked out the car window at all the little forget-me-nots and yellow mustard flowers alongside the road. I knew this was a farewell to Newfoundland.

(c) Mercedes' Story

(Toronto, 1975.)

MERCEDES: (*Still kneeling on bed, but she is now Mercedes.*) So there I was after four hours, still sitting and talking to Bob Dylan. I had this haunting feeling that I'd known him before. I stayed and had supper with him, and he asked me to go to the concert he was doing that night.
  (Bob, now played by Agnes, leaves the mattress and moves
  downstage.)
I sat front row centre and was again struck by the power he had when he came on stage, and I nearly died when he looked into my eyes and said...
  (Spotlight Bob who strikes a pose, head tilted to the ceiling.)

BOB: (*Played by Agnes.*) I wanna do a song right now, that I wrote on my way here tonight. I don't have to mention any names 'cause she knows who it's for. (*Sings to Mercedes.*)
  Shut the light, pull the shades,
  You don't have to be afraid,
  'Cause I'll be your, your baby, tonight.

MERCEDES: When I got back to his dressing room, Dylan came over, took me in his arms and said...

BOB: I missed you, babe. Please don't leave my side again. Say that tonight you'll be stayin' here with me.

MERCEDES: I said, if you want me to...okay. And when he kissed me, there was enough electricity between us to light up all of Toronto. My knees went weak. (*She bends her knees slightly.*) I spent the next three weeks on the road with him. We talked, drank champagne, ate, and necked. But we never made love because we both felt that if we did we would explode. By the end of the tour Bob became edgy. (*Bob paces wildly. Then sits at table.*) At first I thought it was lover's nuts, then he said he had something to tell me.

BOB: (*Speaking abruptly.*) You remember that nod you gave me? Well, the reason I recognize that nod is because I'm from Newfoundland. I'm Bob Noseworthy.

MERCEDES: Bob Noseworthy? You're not Misery Noseworthy, that weird young fella who used to follow me home from school and give me those strange notes?

(Mercedes joins Bob at table.)

BOB: You never even read my poems, babe. You used to tear 'em up.

MERCEDES: Jesus, Bob, I never understood 'em. Who was Maggie and what did I care whether you worked on her farm or not? Whatever happened to you anyway? I can't remember seeing you after, what was it, grade eight or nine?

BOB: (*The light fades on his face as he speaks.*) I got sent to St. John's. Muriel and Tom threw me out because I kept tryin' to run away. I tried hitchhiking across Newfoundland, but the Mounties picked me up and brought me to Mount Cashel in St. John's. But that's a whole other story.

(Lights fade. Music fades in. Mercedes and Agnes exit in black.)

Fairy Tale: Goobdye
Film 3

(Black leader. Music softly plays in background.)

AGNES: Meanwhile in the realm of Homeland, the King had become impossibly morose in his futile search for schemes to save the country from poverty. He fantasized a socialist model with a capitalist engine, a capitalist model with a socialist heart. He thought of a nation of small businesses, co-ops and cottage industries held together by an imported eastern philosophy. He dreamed of a benevolent fisherman's dictatorship; of a constitutional theocracy, or a confederation of outport states. But no solution seemed to fit the unique problems of this island kingdom.

So one day, using a bunch of skipping stones, he wrote out the following message. "GOOBDYE" which most people figured meant "GOODBYE." He took off his royal robes, laid them on the beach and swam out to Red Island off the coast of Homeland where he stayed and refused to budge.

(Film shows stones on a beach spelling out "GOOBDYE."
Clothes fall to the ground as King walks into the water.
The camera focuses on his feet.)

MERCEDES: His sisters Beatrice and Hortense decoded his cryptic message and immediately swam out to join their distraught brother. Homeland's parliament met and decided to dissolve the kingdom and join up as a provincial appendage to Mainland Kingdom. Since the caplin were just about to roll, Joanna knew that it would be useless to organize any popular resistance. And since she longed to see her sister and her true love Martin again, she took her daughter Kate and fled to Neighbouring Kingdom.

(Beatrice and Hortense see the message and rush into the water. A crown washes up on the shore as the sun sparkles on the sea. Joanna picks up her daughter and we see the hearts and snakes flying in the wind. Music rises to conclusion. Fade. End of Film 3.)

Ruth Proposes
Scene 10

(United States, 1967. Mercedes enters in black and stands in front of New York flat.)

MERCEDES: After Martin left he wrote me long letters every week, and kept asking me to send him a picture of Kate. I finally did and he showed it to his mother. If he hadn't I probably never would have married him, but the picture did the trick, and two weeks later his mother proposed. Before I knew it I was off to America.

(Sound of traffic noises.)

When I got to the States his mother Ruth and his father Joseph met me at the airport. Martin was late getting in from Virginia. When we got to their house I was struck by the abundance of everything, but what impressed me the most was Ruth's pantry off the kitchen. It was twice as big as my room at home and jam-packed with six different brands of every kind of food you could imagine. *(She moves to centre stage.)* I went into the living room to put my bags down and had to go through another room called the TV room to get there. I got lost and had to call out to them to come and find me. Hello, hello, America.

(Atmospheric music plays. Echo effect.)

Phone Call from Hell
Scene 11

RUTH: *(Played by Agnes. Enter Ruth with hands clasped in front of her.)* Hello, dear, we're over here. I can't believe the way you look. We were expecting an Eskimo. That Martin said, "Now don't expect her to do any dishes or any housework, but if you need the outside of the house painted or any ditches dug, she'll do it." He also told us you had to get up every morning and feed the huskies. That kidder! Do you want some spaghetti? Why don't you call your mother and let her know you got here? She'll be worried about you and Kate all night.

MERCEDES: I'll call her later.

RUTH: Well dear, I think you should call her now. Why don't you let me hold the baby and you have some spaghetti?

MERCEDES: No thanks, I ate on the plane.

RUTH: Do they speak a language in New*found*land? Now dear, the relatives will be here tomorrow to meet you and Kate, and we've told them that you and Martin were married last year. We don't want anyone to know that Kate is...(*She mouths the word, "illegitimate."*) Now, call your mother and let her know you got here all right. (*Yells offstage to Joseph, steps forward holding an imaginary phone.*) Here, give me the baby. Joseph, hand her the phone.

MERCEDES: (*Holding imaginary phone to her ear.*) Hello, Mammy, it's me. I just called to tell you I got here all right.

(*Light fades on Ruth, up on Bride.*)

BRIDE: (*Played by Agnes.*) You go fuck yourself, you fucking whore, and don't go calling here again. (*Bride hangs up. Light fades on Bride.*)

MERCEDES: Ah...no, Kate is fine. No, Martin isn't here. His parents picked me up at the airport. Yeah, well I won't keep you, I just called to say I got here. Yeah, I'll write soon, when I get settled in. Yeah, okay, I love you too.

Mom in Merasheen
Scene 12

MERCEDES: (*Walking toward audience.*) My mother was born on Merasheen Island in Placentia Bay. She was a beautiful girl with long, blazing red hair and pale white skin. She loved to dance, and whenever there was a time on the go, she was there. She fell in love with my father in 1931 while she was in service to his family. They had ten kids together and Mom kept us all fed from her vegetable garden. For the most part, Merasheen was a happy community despite the hardships. Then one day the government decided that everyone had to move to the big island, Newfoundland. They gave people a small pittance for their land and moved them all out. Although my family left Merasheen before resettlement, I still remember as a young girl standing on Soldier's Point, watching all the boats loaded down with furniture and people moving in a funeral-like procession across the bay. Some people put their houses afloat and hauled them behind their boats, sometimes without a crack in the plaster and it was a strange sight to see people in their windows having a cup of tea as they floated along.

My mother was forty years old when we left Merasheen and I always thought that that's what made her bitter, but when I look back at her life after that, the ten kids, my father away on the boats most of the year and the stroke she had after my youngest brother was born, I think, who wouldn't be bitter?

When I first met Ruth she seemed like the ideal mother. she was a powerful woman who took total control of me. She wouldn't let me have any friends. I guess I was pleased that she liked me so much and wanted to keep me to herself, but I think she's even jealous of my relationship with Martin. She's always going on to me about sex and says that women are just garbage cans for men. Even though I don't say anything, I don't really feel that way. In fact, I'm starting to fall in love with Martin all over again. Yesterday he wrote me this poem. (*She recites.*)

> Can't they tell it, can't they see
> What's so special 'bout you and me?
> Poor old world can't recognize
> That's love light shinin' in our eyes.
> Well look at us and look again,
> And maybe you'll remember when
> You walked this tall and knew it too,
> And the whole world turned to look at you.

(Lights fade on Mercedes who exits, and come up on Agnes seated at table.)

Stephen Update
Scene 13

(New Jersey, 1968.)

AGNES: July 1968. I love my job in New York City at RCA Recording Studio working as a receptionist. I even go into the city on weekends to visit museums and go to coffee houses. All Stephen does is sit around on the couch, smoke dope, listen to the Beatles, and fantasize about being a disc jockey. Plus criticize me for what I like to do. I'm only eighteen years old. This is the first time I've been out of Newfoundland. Greenwich Village is fifteen minutes away. I refuse to sit here and rot with him, so I leave.

(Lights fade on Agnes sitting at table, arm leaning on inner thigh as if propping herself up.)

Dylan
Scene 14
(a) Agnes' Version

(New York, sixties. Light up on Agnes at table.)

AGNES: So Bob and I left Newfoundland on a Wednesday morning, and got into New York City on Monday at four a.m. and booked a room at the Roxy Hotel on 42nd Street. Bob hit the streets right away looking for work. Within a matter of weeks he was playing in several clubs in the Village. As the months rolled on he was making quite a name for himself. It was at Gerdie's Folk City one night that a young man pulled up a chair at my table and introduced himself as Phil Ochs. We talked and became fast friends. (*Enter Mercedes.*) One evening during intermission Bob came over, elbowed Phil out of the way and said...

BOB: (*Played by Mercedes. Bob walks up to imaginary Phil and gives him an elbow and sits at table.*) What do you think you're doing, Ochs? She's my woman.

AGNES: Phil blushed and I said..."Now wait a minute, Bob. I'm nobody's woman, not even Bob Noseworthy's." This seemed to shock him. I don't know why because all we had ever shared of a intimate nature was one kiss and a flea-ridden Platonic bed at the Roxy. He said...

BOB: Are you deaf, babe? All those songs I've been a singin', they're for you.

AGNES: Boy, his accent sure had changed a lot in a few months. Then he said,

BOB: Let's get married and have four kids.

AGNES: Well, I kinda felt like saying, "Suck dis, luh," but then again, I was kinda lonely sitting there night after night listening to him make a name for himself and I thought if I had four kids at least they could sit with me.

(*She remains at table.*)

(b) Mercedes' Version

(*New York, mid-seventies.*)

MERCEDES: (*She stands, moves her chair downstage centre, sits and addresses audience.*) Bob said after he got sent to Mount Cashel that he kept mostly to himself. He wrote songs and taught himself how to play guitar. One day while he was there a couple from Hibbing, Minnesota, Abraham and Beattie Zimmerman, came to the orphanage to visit. They met Bob, adopted him, and took him back to Hibbing, Minnesota.

(*She moves from the table, takes a chair and moves to centre
stage where she whispers in secretive detective style,
taking the audience into her confidence.*)

But what Bob didn't know was that the woman, Beattie Zimmerman, was in fact the former Beattie Noseworthy from Point Verde, Placentia Bay, and was in fact his real mother. She got shipped out when she was a young girl to New York City where she went to work as a housekeeper for Rabbi Abraham

Zimmerman. Abe fell in love with her and she became pregnant. But he was torn between his love for her and his faith, and he couldn't tell anyone he was in love with a Catholic girl, so he asked her to give the baby up. She called her sister Muriel back in Point Verde and Muriel agreed to raise the child as her own. Now later when Bob got sent to the orphanage, Beattie insisted that her and Abe go back to Newfoundland and take up the responsibility for Bob. Abe agreed and he gave up being a rabbi. The three of them went to live in Hibbing, Minnesota, where Abe's brother had a furniture shop. Bob got along well with Beattie, but Abe never forgave her nor Bob for having to give up his faith.

　　Now, Bob didn't know any of this and when I finished telling him he was shaking. I went over and I took him in my arms. That night was the first time we made love. Our bodies became one and we each felt like we had entered the soul of the other. We both knew that no matter what else happened in our lives, we would always be together.

　　(Mercedes takes her chair back to table and sits.)

　　When we got back to New York we moved into the Chelsea Hotel and we kept mostly to ourselves. The only time we argued was when I talked about going back to Newfoundland. To me it was a place that was sacred and unspoiled. To Bob it was a place for the dead or the dying. He wanted us to go to Malibu and sit in the sun. One night as we were having supper there was a knock on the door. Bob went over and answered it, and I got the shock of my life. It was Agnes Walsh from home.

　　(Agnes leaves table and walks downstage to talk to audience.)

AGNES: I strolled in as casually as I could and eyed the situation. The intimate table set for two, the champagne glasses, the flowers, Mercedes' blush and surprised look.

　　(Mercedes looks at Agnes in amazement.)

MERCEDES: I suggested that maybe I should leave, but she said, seeing as the three of us were involved, why didn't I stay?

　　(Music up and fade. Agnes and Mercedes exit in black.)

ACT II
Essay on Romance
Scene 1

(Newfoundland, 1977. An accordion is playing Dylan's "Just Like a Woman." Agnes and Mercedes enter. Mercedes sits on chair at centre stage, Agnes stands behind chair with arms folded across her chest.)

AGNES: All we wanted was romance but we kept getting love.

MERCEDES: All we wanted was love but we kept getting romance.

AGNES: I wouldn't call it love. Cupid had nothing to do with it. What we wanted was ROMANCE...a long term cultural phenomenon...as opposed to "falling in love," which is short and intense. Although wonderful, love cannot compare to romance.

MERCEDES: But love is forever, that's what love is.

AGNES: (*Pacing back and forth behind Mercedes.*) No, romance is forever. It never dies of reality. It's a crush on someone you've never met. LOVE is when you finally meet him, and as you embrace for the first time, you discover you are standing on a fatal patch of quicksand...you are sinking. Suddenly he's everything in the world. You melt into his arms for these last few intense minutes of your life. There cannot possibly be anyone else. There is no other reality than this wild piece of time with this, the representative of all humanity.

MERCEDES: Sounds like romance to me.

AGNES: No, sadly this is love...for then you discover you are not on quicksand...the ground is quite solid and you have to be to work in fifteen minutes. The quicksand experience, though memorable, is over.

MERCEDES: If it's over, then it wasn't real love.

AGNES: No, *all* love is just about to be over. Only romance is ongoing..."romance," where you are what you are without melting into anyone else, where you look longingly from your escape-safe tower over to him in his equally escape-safe tower. You curl your hair, you wear your best red peddle-pushers. Once a month, your evil keepers let you and him out on chains to dance together for a few minutes in the moonlight. You neck, you talk aimlessly, he calls you, "ma'am," he's from far away, he's a Yank, you're a girl from Placentia.

MERCEDES: Aw, that's no good because you're still an individual, vibrant, healthy, fun-loving...what you want to be is a "couple"...wounded, sick, reclusive, endlessly nuzzling one another in some dark corner of reality while the rest of the world is forced to carry on "discovering."

AGNES: Go on, girl, all that stuff is only to trick babies out of ya. Then when the baby tricking time is over, whether you've had babies or not, mother nature withdraws the feeling and reuses it on some other unsuspecting duo.

(*Agnes walks upstage to centre flat. Mercedes picks up chair and moves to table.*)

Diary
Scene 2
(a) Birth of a Boy

(*United States, 1972.*)

AGNES: But God, Mercedes, he's gorgeous.

MERCEDES: I know. I don't known why I waited so long to have another baby.

AGNES: Well girl, it's a lot easier on you this time.

MERCEDES: It's certainly different—the baby showers, the presents, the anesthetic.

AGNES: Not to mention the husband. What are you going to call him?

MERCEDES: I wanted to call him Jim, after Dad, but Ruth insisted on calling him Martin Junior and, like always, I gave into her.

AGNES: What did Martin have to say about it?

MERCEDES: He wants us to break away from her and move out to the country and try to get out of some kind of rut that we're in, but Ruth won't hear of it. I know I shouldn't let her have so much control over me, but she's such a big part of my life. Even her morals and values have become mine. I don't mind her most times, but since you've been here she's upset with me, 'cause she knows we stay up all night talking and she thinks you're a bad influence on me because you've left Stephen.

AGNES: To me you always seemed so settled here and every time I come to see you there's part of me that envies you, your security and the way you've fit into the American way of life. While here I am kicking around all over the place, trying to fit in with them and their extroverted ways. (*Agnes addresses audience, taking its members into her confidence.*) I can't explain this to Mercedes because we're in such different worlds, but I'm in love too...I'm in love with this wonderful guy, Rick Jones and I'm living with him in Atlanta. But it's 1972 in America, not a time for old fashioned love. No one wants to make a commitment. He has other girlfriends, I have other boyfriends. We're both so careful to make sure the other has enough space to do their own thing. No jealousy or rage allowed. This is unreal, but I fall for it. I long to be emotionally correct.

MERCEDES: Maybe I've fit in too well, Ag. Sometimes I think that if they didn't exist, then I'd just disappear too.

AGNES: Well, you wouldn't disappear, because there would always be me and you staying up all night, and doing all those characters we knew growing up back home...

MERCEDES: (*Mercedes and Agnes point frantically at the other's shoes.*) What's the difference in your shoes and my shoes?

AGNES: Yours are black and mine are black.

MERCEDES & AGNES: (*Together.*) Right, right, right. All right then, girl.

AGNES: But sometimes I want to take you with me, hit the road with you and join a travelling circus or something, but I know it's just a crazy dream, because your life is here and mine seems to be out there somewhere. But do you think this is what you really want?

MERCEDES: It's all I know. I can't imagine leaving Martin and the kids, and Ruth.

(Lights go off Mercedes.)

(b) Stephen Update

(Agnes walks over to Newfoundland flat while delivering her lines.)

AGNES: For me leaving was easy, staying impossible. But then again I didn't have kids. I was foot loose and fancy free, kicking around America at a time when travel was cheap and the country was in turmoil. The Vietnam War was an emotional war on the home front and changed the way I looked at America. Fathers were kicking their sons out of the house for growing their hair or burning their draft cards. I was shocked at how parents could turn against their children.

(Flute music can be faintly heard in the background.)

I had no contact with Stephen after I left. One day his mother called me to tell me Stephen was in an accident and was on a life-support system. She said there was no chance for him and wanted my okay to disconnect the system. We both broke down and cried, but I realized I was crying for her loss and not for mine. He was like a high school sweetheart, and it all seemed so long ago. I told her to disconnect the system and, since we never divorced, I was suddenly a widow.

(Music ends. She sits on the Newfoundland fence. Mercedes leaves the table, moves to New York flat and sits on ledge.)

Box Bag Daddy
Scene 3

(Newfoundland, seventies.)

MERCEDES: Aggie's father is in hospital. Mr. Walsh always seemed so old to me. More like her grandfather than her father. It wasn't his age, it was his ways. That seemed so ancient to me.

AGNES: Yeah, it seemed like Dad could have stepped out of Placentia and into eighteenth-century Ireland and not been out of place.

MERCEDES: He never said much to anyone, did he, and almost nothing to young people. I know that the people we came from are all pretty odd and we accepted it all, but there is one thing I've always wondered about. What was your father doing in that box?

AGNES: I could see where you might think he was a bit eccentric, but the thing is he was a man obsessed with keeping warm. I guess because he was so thin and frail. Although Mom always used to tell me that the doctors used to say he might be thin, but he had the best blood they'd ever seen in a man his age.

MERCEDES: What about the box, Ag?

AGNES: (*To audience.*) But it's true, he used to sit in a cardboard box in the living room. It was a box that our refrigerator came in and he cut the front away. He had a rug on the bottom, set his chair in it, and he'd sit there every evening and watch TV. No one thought it was strange, in fact, his friends who knew how he hated the cold thought it was pretty clever.

MERCEDES: (*Shaking her head imitating Bill's friends.*) Dandy idea you got there, Bill b'y, Bill B'y, Bill b'y.

AGNES: He also used to put his tools in the oven to heat them up before he'd go outside to work. And before he went to bed every night he'd put a paper bag on his head.

MERCEDES: What? Right down over his head?

AGNES: (*She mimes placing a paper bag on her head, pulling it down and folding up the edges.*) No, no, he'd fold up the edges and pull it down over his ears like a cap, claimed it was the best way to keep in the body heat.

MERCEDES: Did he use a new bag every night?

AGNES: No, no, no. He'd wear them for three or four nights or until they wore out. He kept a pile of them in his top dresser drawer.

MERCEDES: Where most guys would keep their ties?

AGNES: Yeah, that's my dad.

(*She lies on mattress. Lights fade.*)

Agnes and Mercedes Arrive in Newfoundland
Scene 4

(*Placentia, seventies.*)

AGNES: At six-thirty in the morning we got our first glimpse of Newfoundland. Those familiar rocks with houses scattered here and there. Mercedes grabbed ahold to my hand and we both started crying.

MERCEDES: We went straight to Agnes' mother's house. Her mother said some fellow Dylan had called and his van had broken down in Edmonston, New Brunswick, and that he and the kids would be a few days late. We were so exhausted from our odyssey across America that we both collapsed on the beds. (*She lies on ledge.*)

AGNES: I was lying on the couch in the living room and Mercedes was in my old bedroom. All I could hear was the blower on the stove and the fridge cutting in and out. I couldn't take my eyes off the fuzzy wallpaper. Mercedes, who do you think sold all this fuzzy wallpaper to the Newfoundlanders?

MERCEDES: I don't know, but they sure made a lot of money. Although I was in Newfoundland I couldn't stop thinking about America, and wondering how I ever got into the habit of letting other people control my life. Is it in the genes I wonder?

AGNES: Jesus, Mercedes, you were sixteen years old. It's in every sixteen-year-old's genes. Anyway, you always talk about Martin's family like they really liked you.

MERCEDES: Well, for a short while they seemed like my dream family. They accepted me, fed me, gave me cigarettes and totally took control. Well, not totally. There was always that internal me that they couldn't crack. Maybe it was that part of me that kept me so unaware of what was going on around me. Like Vietnam, Kent State and what was happening with the blacks...it never even touched me. (*Pause.*) America was not only a time before thought, but a time before feeling. I just went along with whatever was programmed for me to think and feel. But what did I do there for ten years? (*To audience.*) I got up in the morning, took a trank, fed the kids, cleaned the house, talked on the phone, did a bit of shopping, took a trank, made dinner, watched TV, took a trank and went to bed. Some nights when I was watching TV, I'd look at Martin and get a terrified feeling of not knowing who he was. I tried to talk to him about it once and he suggested I get a hobby. That's when I started bowling. I always think of bowling as the start of the breakdown of my marriage. Martin was vicious. He said no decent wife and mother should be allowed to go bowling every Wednesday night with the girls. I think that's when I started to see the injustice of it all.

AGNES: Well, at least the voices of the women's liberation movement were getting through to you.

MERCEDES: I don't known how that could be. My only reading material was Ann Landers and *Reader's Digest*. But I do remember one incident about a mother who went on strike against her family. She sat out on the lawn for three weeks and refused to come in until they recognized her as a human being and helped her around the house. You know what Martin's comment on the matter was?

AGNES: What?

MERCEDES: (*Standing.*) Shoot the bitch!

AGNES: That's America's answer to everything.
(*Lights fade.*)

Diary
Scene 5
(a) Ruth Dies / Nail in Bowling Ball

(*United States, 1974. Light up on Mercedes standing in front of New York flat.*)

MERCEDES: December 6th, 1974. Ruth had been complaining about pains in her chest all day. We'd finished our Christmas shopping and she said she was going out with Joseph to eat. Not long after that I got a call telling me that she'd collapsed on the sidewalk. Martin rushed down and within the hour, he called and told me she was dead. I never even got a chance to say goodbye.

When I was helping Joseph to clear out Ruth's belongings I found Kate's hospital band. Joseph wouldn't let me have it because it said Baby Girl Barry and he said he never wanted Kate to know that she was born without the protection of a marriage certificate.

I can't get over Ruth's death. My whole world has fallen apart. Martin accuses me of being married to her and not to him. I'm not content to stay home any more and I've started going bowling with the girls on Wednesday nights. Martin is vicious and said I wouldn't be going if Ruth were alive.

The other day when I got home from shopping my bowling ball was hanging in the corner where the swag lamp used to hang. Martin had spent hours lightly tapping a four inch nail into it, and he told Kate it was my head. He wouldn't be doing *that* if Ruth were alive.

(Light fades on Mercedes, up on Agnes.)

(b) Mercedes Called

AGNES: Mercedes called me this morning from the hospital. She said Martin had beaten her up badly. I was shocked. I never thought he was violent like that. She told me she's going to sue for a divorce.

(c) Martin Dozen Roses

(Light up on Mercedes.)

MERCEDES: Martin has brought me a dozen red roses. His face is full of remorse and sorrow. I'm really angry at him for doing this to me, but in a way I understand. He's losing control over me. God, Ag, why can't I just stay home and do as he says? He's been good to me; he denies me nothing but my freedom. Lots of women would be happy to have what I've got. I'm scared about getting a divorce. I think I still love him. What should I do, Ag?

AGNES: *(Light goes off Agnes and she moves to Newfoundland flat.)* Leave.

MERCEDES: It's so easy to say to someone who's in an abusive relationship, "You should leave." I've tried leaving Martin many times but I always end up going back. It's the staying away that I find the hardest.

Gun Scene: Full Metal Jacket
Scene 6

(United States, seventies. Agnes takes a book, sits on fence and reads. Mercedes takes a book and sits on the chair at centre stage.)

MERCEDES: Thanks for the supper, Martin. I'll get the dishes done now before I go.

MARTIN: (*Played by Agnes. Reads.*) "Where are you going? I thought you and the kids were going to spend the night? I cooked the goddamn supper for you."

MERCEDES: Martin, I never said I was spending the night. Walt and Carol are picking us up. We're going back to Binghamton with them.

MARTIN: You bitch! Who are you fucking up there?

KATE: (*Played by Mercedes.*) Daddy, please don't start. Mommy, let's go now.

MARTIN: You just shut up, shorty. This is between me and your whore mother. She doesn't care about you or me. Do you, bitch?

MERCEDES: Martin, please. You're scaring the kids. I'm going down to Mrs. Vitalie's and wait.

MARTIN: You're not going anywhere, you fucking bitch. Sit down. (*Reads.*) "He hits her and knocks her down in the chair. Kate is standing by her chair shaking, and the baby is crying in the high chair. She's trying to comfort them."

MERCEDES: (*Reads.*) "Martin has left and gone into the other room. He returns with a gun and an armful of photographs. He dumps the photos in the middle of the table."

MARTIN: Now tell me who you're fucking and I'll take care of him with this little baby right here.

MERCEDES: (*Reads.*) "He puts one bullet in the gun." Martin, please. I'm not seeing anyone. I just don't want to be here. Please don't hurt the kids.

MARTIN: (*Moving to sit on ledge of New York flat.*) You don't want to be here, do you, bitch? You want to go back to your dirty Newfies. Did she tell you about her dirty Newfies, Kate? I took you out of that filth and gave you everything. There's nothing I wouldn't have done for you, honey, and now you've fucked it all up.

MERCEDES: Martin, there's no one else. Please put the gun away. I just don't know what I want. I tried to talk to you about it and you wouldn't listen to me.

MARTIN: (*Reads.*) "He lights a match and holds it to the photos."

KATE: Daddy, don't burn them! Me and the baby are there too!

MARTIN: Talk to your whore mother. If she cares about you, she'll tell the truth, Kate. I'm doing this for her own good. She's got a bit bad and I have to punish her and make her good again. Well, bitch?

MERCEDES: Please don't say those things to her. Let us go, Martin. I'll come back and talk to you.

MARTIN: Lying bitch! (*Reads.*) "He puts the match to the photos and they flame up. The baby is screaming in the high chair. She stands up to get him. Martin grabs for her and knocks the high chair over. She tries to get the baby. Martin pushes her into the breakfast nook. He holds the gun to her head. Kate picks up the baby and is down on her knees begging."

KATE: Daddy, please, don't shoot my mommy. I'll do anything. Please Daddy, don't.

MERCEDES: Martin, if you're going to shoot me for God's sake, get the kids out first. Take them to Mrs. Vitalie's. I won't go anywhere. I'll wait for you.

MARTIN: Now we'll play Russian roulette.

MERCEDES: (*Reads.*) "He pulls the trigger and it's an empty chamber. There's a stunned silence and they look into each other's eyes. Martin begins to sob and buries his face in her lap."

MARTIN: I'm sorry, honey. I love you. I don't want to hurt you. I just want you back. I have nothing without you. I'll change. I'll do anything you want, just don't leave me.

MERCEDES: (*Reads.*) "She strokes his head as he clings to her. She motions to Kate to take the baby and leave. She silently mouths the words 'Mrs. Vitalie.' Kate quietly, but reluctantly leaves with the baby. She keeps stroking Martin's head and looks around at the smouldering photographs, the remains of the chicken dinner, the knocked over high chair and says...It's okay, Martin, I'm sorry too."

MARTIN: (*Reads.*) "She lays down beside him and they cling desperately to each other as the sounds of police sirens gets closer and closer."

MERCEDES: (*Standing and addressing audience.*) Once Martin started using violence, that was the only way he could deal with things. But for eight years there'd been no sign of violence. And it wasn't until I saw the movie *Full Metal Jacket* that I had any true understanding of what happened to Martin as a human being. He was as much a victim as I was. I had him holding loaded guns to my head, but he had a whole nation holding them to his. I still can't forgive him, even though I understand. I'm sure he was, in his own way, trying to save me and make me see the right way, his way, but for the torture he forced on the kids, I have no forgiveness.

Fairy Tale: The Promise of Neighbouring Kingdom
Scene 7

*(Mercedes moves to Newfoundland flat and reads from fairy
tale book. Eerie piano music plays in the background.))*

MERCEDES: The promise of Neighbouring Kingdom could not have turned out to be more empty, the promise of love could not have been less fulfilled. The gods of love had turned out to be worse than blind, random, and uncaring masters of the human heart; they appeared now in Princess Joanna's mind as evil manipulators, driving events towards tragedy, and heartache, to fulfil their perverted desires. Either that or their realm had been usurped by devils of hate, hell cats bent on erasing forever the forces of hope and love from the kingdom of the human heart. *(Music ends. Agnes sits on the chair at centre stage, facing audience directly.)*

Barbecue
Scene 8

(Mercedes lays down the book, walks towards Agnes, and looks off into distance. Slow and melancholy piano music plays in the background.)

MERCEDES: Was there a big barbecue?

AGNES: Yes, there was.

MERCEDES: Were you and I and Martin and Stephen and Ruth and Stephen's grandmother and Kate and Mom there?

AGNES: And Mom and Dad and the princesses and the horseman from Virginia and the merchant sea captain and Bob.

MERCEDES: ...but nobody said a word...

AGNES: No. They talked constantly.

MERCEDES: *(Looking at Agnes.)* What did they say?

AGNES: Well, they all said, "I love you."

MERCEDES: Who to?

AGNES: Everyone to at least someone...

MERCEDES: ...even Mom?

AGNES: Yes, even your mom. She said it to her young self, the long red-haired self in her garden on Merasheen Island.

MERCEDES: Her "inner child?"

AGNES: Her girl on the brink, her girl when adulthood burned with time and hope and possibility.

MERCEDES: A short candle that one. And who did Martin say he loved?

AGNES: Kate...and your boy.

MERCEDES: Why won't he talk to them now?

AGNES: He couldn't say.

MERCEDES: And your Stephen?

AGNES: He said that he had loved me. That he'd adored me once.

MERCEDES: And who did he love now?

AGNES: No one.

MERCEDES: And who did Ruth love?

AGNES: You.

MERCEDES: And who did your mom love?

AGNES: Me.

MERCEDES: So you had Stephen and your mom and I only had Ruth?

AGNES: Up to the barbecue, yes.

MERCEDES: What about Dad?

AGNES: Oh yes, he said he loved you too. And my dad said he loved me too.

MERCEDES: So you're still ahead of me?

AGNES: Up to the barbecue, yes.

MERCEDES: And Bob?

AGNES: Said he loved both of us, absolutely, positively equally. His love was an egg that split off at the moment of conception and identical twinned.

MERCEDES: Fuckin' poets, eh?

AGNES: Yeah. Poetry as laser-powered bullshit...

MERCEDES: ...like when Martin said, "I want you to have my baby." That was the arrow of bullshit that pierced my already weakened heart...

AGNES: ...the more leather-hearted survive those arrows until they get a dentist...

MERCEDES: ...and dentists are able to help everyone. Poets only help their ragtag followers to stumble through the fog.

AGNES: Yeah, and I've had enough poetry and romance to do me a lifetime!

> *(Lights fade on Mercedes who remains on chair. Agnes goes toward Newfoundland flat.)*

Diary
Scene 9
(a) Joaquim Suggests

AGNES: (*To audience.*) Joaquim left this morning. He left again. For the third time he has kissed my tear-stained face and whispered "Breve mente," and again I say "Sim, meu amore." His swollen fisherman's hands cup my face and tilt my chin for our last kiss, and I watch him walk up the gangway for his return voyage to Aveiro. He is unlike the rest, he is singular in his passion, and melancholy, his "saudade," which he explains to me as a longing for something that can never be, but for which you cannot stop the longing. He writes me from Tenerife and tells me about an apartment he has set up in Morocco, and begs me to come to him for the winter. As the cold freezing rain bites my cheek on Water Street, I think of him on the Santo Andre singing the fadoes of Coimbra. I have counted one-hundred-and-seventy-five postcards, twenty telegrams, and a million kisses and caresses. A blue scarf blows blue on the horizon...and yes...I know...longing is the better part of love.

> *(Lights fade on Agnes as she sits on fence. Lights up on Mercedes who is sitting on the chair at centre stage.)*

(b) Leaving Martin

MERCEDES: I've just said goodbye to Martin for what I think is the last time. I'm going back to Newfoundland with the kids for the summer. Martin drove with us as far as the overpass. We both got out of the car to say goodbye. We kissed awkwardly and held onto each other a long time. My heart is broken as I watch him fade in the rear view mirror. We were so much in love once. When do we stop loving each other? When did he stop writing me poetry? When I first got to the States, he was stationed in Virginia and I stayed in Scranton with his parents, and on weekends he'd come home late and climb in my bedroom window. One night he came home, climbed into my window, got down on his knees and asked me to marry him. He had matching gold bands and a tiny silver heart with a diamond in it for me to wear around my neck. Of course I said yes.

Graveyard Truths: Fairy Tale/Tin Table Ending
Scene 10

(Placentia.)

AGNES: I'm forty years old and Joaquim doesn't come here any more, or maybe he never did. *(Pause.)* I thought nobody else still came to the graveyard but me, but there she was, strolling up the hill, minding her own business not knowing I was there. Then she saw me and we smiled at each other and gave each other the nod. *(They both nod.)* I moved over where I was sitting on the fence to make room for her, even though there was miles of it. She looked so foreign, like she belonged to some lost and forgotten Indian band.

MERCEDES: At first I thought she was a spirit and as I got closer I realized it was Ag. I asked her if she wanted to go for a walk in Brulee and she said,

AGNES: All right then, girl. We decided to tell each other the God's honest truth. We admitted that we were in fact princesses who married sailors from Neighbouring Kingdom. We further admitted that things hadn't worked out all that well and we'd decided to return to Homeland.

(Music in the background.)

MERCEDES: As it turned out, we arrived just in time to bid the old King a final farewell. It was during his wake our aunts revealed to us that the King was not in fact our father, but our uncle, and that they were not our aunts, but our mothers. Beatrice the mother of Maria...

AGNES: ...Hortense the mother of Joanna.

MERCEDES: We had both been love children born into a society which strangely considered such children inferior to those born under the dubious protection of a marriage certificate.

AGNES: Those warm memories of our mother were in fact the memories of the younger and less troubled Beatrice and Hortense. The ghost queen who appeared to us was Homeland's official fairy godmother called out of retirement at the request of the King.

MERCEDES: After the old King was laid to rest, we invited the entire town back to a funeral supper where we all sat down to a meal at a tin table. But the tin table bended so our story ended. If the table had been stronger our story would have been longer.

AGNES & MERCEDES: (*Together.*) We wish good luck in the games of love and life to both them and ye.

THE END.

John Taylor

My Three Dads

1992

MY THREE DADS

My Three Dads first played as a Resource Centre for the Arts (RCA) Theatre Company Second Space production at the LSPU Hall, 19-22 March 1992. The play was produced at the Hall as an RCA Theatre Company main stage production (22-26 April 1992). *My Three Dads* has also played Charlottetown (July 1992), Halifax (September 1992), Sechelt, BC (April 1993) and Victoria (September 1993). *My Three Dads* was written and performed by **John Taylor** and the St. John's productions were directed by **Andy Jones**.

The play is a monologue with narrative and reported conversations and was performed by **John Taylor**. There are two other characters: The Beehive Lady was played by **Rebecca Moyes** in the March 1992 production and by **Mary-Lynn Bernard** in April 1992; the Technician in both productions was played by **Geoff Seymour, Jr.** In 1992 lighting was by **Geoff Seymour, Jr.**, sound **Flip Janes**, music **Geoff Panting** and technical direction **Phil Winters**. Illustrations are by **Julian Lawrence**.

The production of *My Three Dads* was funded by the Canada Council, the Newfoundland and Labrador Arts Council and RCA Theatre Company Second Space.

MY THREE DADS

*The stage is set with five chairs: two chairs side by side at centre
stage right, one chair downstage centre, one chair left of upstage
centre and one chair centre stage left.*

*Preset lighting. Middle Eastern music plays as lights fade to
black. Cross fade music to "Popcorn." Beehive Lady enters and sits in
chair stage left. She mimes driving a car in surreal lighting for ten
seconds, then fade. Beehive Lady exits in dark. John enters stage
right carrying a backpack. Music fades as lights come up.*

JOHN: I always knew that there was something weird going on
behind the scenes, the Lady with the Beehive Hairdo just proved
it. I know we all have feelings of abnormality or inadequacy or
something, but at the age of eight I realized that the key to
surviving was to just deal with these feelings and put them
behind you. What happened then? As hard as I tried I couldn't
seem to shake these feelings at all. By age nine I was convinced
that I was not only different but retarded; mildly retarded, but
retarded nonetheless. I carried the burden of being a psychic
medium through my tenth year, at eleven I was definitely dying
of cancer, at twelve I turned to religion which was a total trip in
itself. But at the age of thirteen I realized that I wasn't merely
retarded or psychic, I realized that I was the Antichrist.

(Pause.)

If you're ever going to be different you might as well make it
big. I was going for the big stakes, the whole farm, nothing but
"Lord of Evil" could satisfy my longing to understand why I felt
different. I often look back and ask myself how I could have
believed such a ridiculous thing. Then again, I often get the
feeling that it just might be true.

The whole thing started when my mother asked me to try on
all the shirts in this big pile before she gave them to the
Salvation Army. *(He kneels and takes shirts from backpack.)* It
was a sunny morning and I didn't have anything else to do, so I
brought them all into the bathroom and started trying them on
in the mirror. Every time I put on one of the shirts I liked to

stand in front of the mirror and say something like, "John, cool guy," or "John, rock star extraordinaire." Then I saw "it." A red satin shirt. I thought it was beautiful. This was the time of the Village People and of Donna Summer.

(Donna Summer disco plays.)

In my mind I was stopping a crime in progress. How could my mother ever have thought of throwing this shirt away? It epitomized everything I wanted to be—a disco king. That's the sad thing about my generation, about me. When disco was in I was too young, and by the time I started liking it, everyone else thought that it sucked. Out of context and out of time I was a macho man of the lost generation.

(Disco music quickly fades.)

But that was actually the least of my problems, because as I was standing there in front of the mirror, just like I had done with all the other shirts, these words just popped into my head. A voice just said them, "JOHN, SON OF SATAN."

I couldn't get the cursed shirt off fast enough. I threw it into the corner of the bathroom and stared at it in horror, my brain reeling. I felt like I had just been kicked in the balls / stood up too fast / just woke up, all the while having a really powerful deja-vu. My own heaving breath was the first thing I heard as I ran from Satan's friggin' bathroom.

(He takes refuge behind the centre stage chair.)

My eyes were blinded by tears by the time I reached my bedroom. I threw open the window and thrust out my head and took a deep breath of air. I was a mess. Then again I was trying to deal with my new role as the ultimate evil. Who wouldn't be a little freaked out?

There was this little girl out on the lawn between the apartment buildings I lived in. She was running around on this big field of grass, and I swear the only concrete around was this thin strip of sidewalk way off to her right. As I was watching her it happened again. The voice came back. This time it said "SHE'S

GOING TO FALL DOWN!" Sure enough, the little girl falls. Not on the acres of soft grass around her, no, she does a humungous face plant right on the strip of sidewalk. AHHHHHH! The second sign. I was really losing it. This was too much. My knees gave out and I found myself crumpled and defeated on the bedroom floor. Then this calmness came and I realized that the things that I was considering were ridiculous. So I grabbed my Dataman and headed for the living room.

(Pause.)

Now Dataman looks like a calculator, but it's really one of those cheesy educational toys that tricks you into doing math over the summer holidays. It's filled with hundreds of number games perfectly suited to taking your mind off the fact that you're the Antichrist, so I decided to play "Guess that Number." The object of the game is to guess a secret number between one and one hundred in the least amount of tries. I finally guess sixty six and sure enough, Dataman's final report, his apocalyptic prophecy, his judgement on me tells me that I guessed the secret number in six guesses. Three sixes — six, six, six. I knew the number of the Beast and I knew that this was the third sign. Oh, my God, it was true! It was absolutely, totally true. I was the Antichrist. I couldn't deal with it alone anymore. I had to tell someone. I burst into my sister's room and she sat bolt upright in her bed.

(He runs to sit on chairs stage right and awakes as sister.)

"What's the matter with you John?"

I was crying and hyper ventilating as only a kid can and I said, "I...think...that...I...am...the...mmmmmmm..." She was getting kind of scared now and she wanted to know what I was trying to say. I got a hold of myself long enough to say, "Don't be afraid, okay. I can control it...for now!"

"What the hell are you talking about, John?"

I decided to give it to her. "I'm the Antichrist!"

There was a moment of silence in which I began to regret having told her the truth about my identity.

(He stands.)

What if she lost it all together and stabbed me with seven silver daggers in a cross shape. That would be the only way to stop me. Maybe my death was a small price to pay for the millions of souls that I would undoubtedly possess and devour. Maybe the best thing was for her to just do it.

(He drops to knees.)

"Just kill me now!" I shouted.

A picture of myself with seven stainless-steel nail files sticking out of my chest flashed through my brain causing me to wretch violently. This caused another pregnant pause. It was finally broken by the shrill siren of laughter that came out of my sister.

(He stands.)

"You're serious, I know you are. You're never going to live this one down—ever. Get the tape recorder! Quick! Somebody get the tape recorder. John thinks that he's the Devil, it's really funny."

Then she got serious for a minute. "Look, John, the things that you're talking about don't even exist. The Bible isn't meant to be taken literally, and anyway, do you think that if the Devil was going to come to earth he'd pick your pathetic, scrawny, little body?"

That just made things all the more real. Of course the Devil would want a disguise, and my scrawny body was it. I wasn't even listening to her anymore because all I could think right was that she'd be sorry. Boy, would she be sorry!

(He sits. Pause.)

For a long time after I strove to be pure, to be holy. I was constantly on guard, waging this inner battle between good and evil. I fully believed that I was doing this to save the souls of the human race. I was martyring myself for...like your soul. I really believed that.

I guess it seems kind of silly now. In the nineties, it's okay to be the friggin' Antichrist. But in the early eighties it was definitely out. Heavy Metal was reaching some sort of a peak and I knew enough to realize that being a Satanist, or Satan for that matter, would involve a lot of tacky spandex and even more bad music.

It would be many years and embarrassing situations before the truth reared its ugly head. Who would ever believe that there're any truths to be learned in school? But that's where the fateful moment passed. *(He stands.)* MacDonald Drive Junior High School biology lab. Three seats from the front, next to a reeking bucket of fetal pigs, my life took a drastic turn into a brick wall. A big black ugly brick wall better known to the world of science as genetics.

(He moves behind chair.)

My teacher was at the chalk board drawing diagrams explaining heredity. He was one of those Cro-Magnon men with a chin that jutted out causing his entire face to slope backward at a perfect forty-five degree angle. He employed the all-too-familiar sarcastic teaching method. So there he was with all his angles telling a bunch of uninterested fifteen-year-olds that, "Blue eyes are the recessive gene and brown eyes are the dominant gene." And it's like, "Okay...I believe you." But in his infinite wisdom he thought that it would eradicate all doubt in our minds if we drew these diagrams for our own families. So off we went.

But wait. John's diagram isn't working out. What was wrong? I tried again and again, and still nothing. So I start thinking that maybe the Neanderthal is actually wrong. He

definitely is wrong and I'm going to prove it. So I jumped out of
my seat and proclaimed to the whole class that, "Sir, your
diagrams are so full of shit and I can prove it." About a thousand
veins popped out of his head and he said, "Well, go ahead then,
Mr. Taylor."

Victory welled up in me like puberty as I sauntered up to the
chalk board. In mere moments the very foundations of science
were to come crumbling down. I felt a little scared and for a
moment that Antichrist thing flared up like a mental
hemorrhoid, but I let it go, let it move aside. I drew my diagram
out in huge proportions on the board and started explaining.

"Sir, according to your theory, and a pretty flimsy one at that
(I was being really righteous), two blue-eyed parents cannot give
birth to a brown-eyed baby. But alas, you sorry wretch, I am that
brown-eyed child of those very blue-eyed parents. I am that case,
I am that loophole. You must let the facts speak for themselves. I
stood up on my desk to really drive the last theory crushing
statement. (*He stands on chair.*) You sir, are pathetic, and the
time is right for you to admit that I am right and you are wrong.
So very, very...wrong."

(He steps down off chair.)

I don't know, I think it was his face. He just stood there with
this very nervous smile. In fact the whole class just smiled
nervously. That's when it happened. An entire class of grade
nines at MacDonald Drive Junior High School stared on in
horror as I turned into an Iranian right before their very eyes.

(Middle Eastern music plays, just a quick sting.)

I spent the next year and a half staring into my mother's
eyes making sure that they were in fact blue. Sometimes I had
myself convinced that they were a shade of green but deep down
inside I knew. What I knew was that somewhere in the past
someone had hopped the fence of my gene pool and taken a little
dip. But who? I spent weeks fantasizing about where I had come
from and one of the things that stuck in my mind was something
that my sister used to tease me with when we were younger. I
mean maybe she hadn't been lying when she told me that my
mother had found me in a bus station locker when she was on
vacation in Mexico City. Then there was another possibility that
I came up with on my own. Years ago, before we moved to
Newfoundland we had lived in Houston, Texas. We had these
neighbours called the Louaras. I don't know, maybe I was just
making this up, but every day it grew clearer.

I was playing in the backyard of our house, and the strange
thing was that I was speaking Mexican. I looked up and saw the
smiling face of my grandmother Louara. She was making a
piñata for my third birthday. My sister was there, getting ready
for a date with one of the banditos. Then I saw the hole in the
fence and I crawled through. The house behind me exploded and

I then saw the face of the woman I now know as my mother, and the next thing you know, I'm standing on a gravel road in Badger's Key, Bonavista Bay, with a woman with a two dollar bill in her hand saying, "Oh, Johnny, run up to the shop and get me a drop of Pepsi, will ya?"

Something snapped at that point. Phillipe Louara died and Johnny was born. And so I've remained pretty much to this day. I thought about these theories every day at first, weighing one against the other. Both seemed very real and I never could fully decide. After a while I finally forgot about them all together. Ain't that just the way?

(He walks as if agitated, making a circle.)

It was a Saturday afternoon and I had just returned from free swim at Bannerman Park pool. I was upset, to say the least. If you've ever been to a free swim I'm sure you understand. You see free swim, especially on Saturday, is like taking a dip in the holy Ganges River in India. Every person in the area is crammed into a pool the size of a hot tub. The water is almost approaching the boiling point because of the phenomenal number of children peeing in the pool. If you're lucky you might get to swim a few strokes every now and then. That's just the shallow end.

In the deep end people are dropping out of the sky off the diving boards in rapid fire succession. Every two or three minutes, the lifeguard will haul some poor kid out of the water coughing and crying, screaming that Ricky jumped on his face "on purpose."

There's people in there washing their kid's hair and shit. I wouldn't be surprised to see a line of women doing laundry as the funeral pyre of someone's dead husband raged in the background. To say the least, free swim had me a little on the raw side.

When I walked into the house, my mother was sitting at the table. I sat down and stared at a piece of paper that was lying there. *(He sits.)* It was the plans for some chainsaw-motor-powered skateboard my brother had been talking about building for years. He probably would build it, and then I would undoubtedly test it and end up in the Janeway Children's Hospital again. The last time it was the chainsaw-motor-powered crazy carpet that nearly wrenched my life away from me. This on top of free swim had me close to suicide already, so when my mother began pulling down my sleeves and insisting that I was cold I really had no time for it. I told her that I wasn't cold and rolled my sleeves back up.

"You are cold," She said and rolled them down again.

"I'm not cold!"

"You're cold."

"I am not cold, Mother, and why the hell don't I look like anyone else in this family? Why am I...ethnic?"

Now this wasn't really a coherent statement, but I was upset. This took her for a bit of a loop and there was a long silence before anyone spoke again. I knew I had hit on something *big*. She came towards me with her arms out and I wanted to hug her but instead I shouted. (*He stands and points at mom.*)

"Don't take another step closer to me, stand right there and tell me what the hell is going on."

She started to cry.

"Oh, God, what the hell was going on?" I started to think that I didn't want to know the truth, but it was coming in on me fast.

She said it slowly, "The man that you thought was your father isn't. We were separated before you were born. Your real father is a man—a plastic surgeon that I was seeing—and he's from Iran. The reason I never told you before is because I didn't want to hurt you."

She wasn't crying any more. She looked kind of relieved. For a moment I felt relief too, just for a moment. I knew that what she was saying was true. I knew that she was only trying to protect me by not telling me. She didn't see it as a big deal. I knew that was just the way she was, but I knew that for me it was a big deal.

(Pause.)

I had this image of Iranians built up as people who wore Sergio Valente jeans and carried around semi-automatic rifles. Did you ever tell a "Paki" joke or a "nigger" joke and say, "I'm not prejudiced, it's just a joke." Well, you might be, and for a while I think I was actually prejudiced against myself.

That night a lot of things became crystal clear. I had a dream, but I'll make it quick. I was working at a McDonald's, and a lady came up to the counter with two medium drink cups in her hands and asked me which one was diet. I told her to drink them and see which one made her fat. Then I threw my arms up in the air and told everyone that I was going to buy postage stamps. When I got to the post office I got in the lineup, the place was packed. When I got up to the counter, the man asked me in a thick accent, "'Ow many stamps do you want? Do you want the thirty-six cent or the one dollar or the one cent? What kind of stamp eta la vista a madre quanto cinqo cinqano?"

And right in front of my eyes the man had gone from speaking English to speaking some third-world language. When I turned and looked at the people in the lineup, they were all holding up chickens or selling goats or grinding corn into powder. That's when I felt the hand on my shoulder, and I turned to see the man behind me.

"Father?" I said.

And he said, "Do you feel like peeing in the pool anymore?"

I said I didn't.

And he said, "Now, my boy, you are an adult."

(He looks at the audience as if he's just said the most important thing ever, because, hey, he has!)

When I awoke I was wide awake. I know that the truth had set in. It wasn't as drastic as being the Antichrist or being found in the bus station locker, and I felt like I should be relieved, but it was too real. The whole thing was no longer far away, it was here and I couldn't get away from it. I knew that there was no way in hell that I was ever going to meet my real father. As far as I was concerned he was a pig, and I'd rather shoot myself in the side of the head than sit down and have a conversation with that man.

That day had been really horrible, but it was also really exciting. Everything that had been said had this extra edge of excitement. I didn't feel like waking up in the morning and ignoring it. The next words that even came close to having that edge were spoken by a bleached-blonde woman wearing a blue blazer and pants.

(He picks up backpack.)

"Stand-up, passenger Taylor, please go to gate four."

I was going to meet my real father.

The plan was that I would fly to Montreal with a good friend of mine then get a train to Houston; that's where my father was.

I saved some money and bought the return portion of somebody's train ticket to El Paso, passing through Houston, leaving from Albany, New York. I decided that I was going to hitchhike to Albany to get the train. Actually, my finances decided it for me.

I left Montreal with thirteen dollars and a backpack that was near impossible to carry, with tents and sneakers hanging out the side. I fancied myself as looking like one of those Turkish buses. I walked down to the nearest on-ramp, stuck out my thumb and I was on the road.

I had this stupid haircut. It was supposed to be fashionable, but it made me look like Dorothy Hamill. The first few cars that drove by refused to even look at me, but I put on a hat, I started looking less eager to chop someone's head off with a figure skate, and I got my first ride.

The man's name was Tom. He was part black, part Micmac, part French Canadian, but he told me he felt most comfortable where he was living now, in the Jewish Hispanic quarter in Chicago. Tom was nice enough but he had a chip on his shoulder so big that it dwarfed his head. His mother hated him because he couldn't speak her native tongue or French either, and according to him his father hated him because he couldn't dance or something like that. And apparently the rest of the world hated him for being Jewish and Hispanic. It never occurred to me that Tom might have been a little paranoid, and I chose to ignore the fact that he seemed to be some sort of omen sent to me by God. A fat, greasy, neurotic, paranoid angel of God sent to me to show me that life wasn't so bad after all.

The whole time Tom was laying his life story out to me, he was taking pulls off of a bottle of light brown diet 7-Up. When he finally finished it, the car was doing about fifteen miles an hour and we were swerving all over the road. You'd think that going that slow it wouldn't be too scary, but the cars flying past you at a hundred and ten were like random torpedoes. My life was at the mercy of Tom's drunken whims. I mentioned to him that maybe it would be a good idea if I drove for awhile, but I think that he passed out. He didn't respond anyway. After a while I couldn't take it anymore, and I was just about to tell him that I wanted to get out when he just kind of swerved off the road and the car rolled to a stop. Tom was out cold, so I shut off the engine and climbed out of the car, got my pack out of the back and started walking.

At this point there didn't seem to be any cars on the road, but I had the feeling that I was pretty close to the border. I had a little piece of hash in my pocket, about a gram. A good gram, not the shitty old grams you get around now, so I decided to roll up a big draw before I crossed. The less I had on me when I went through the better. By the time I reached the border I was wasted, and I poked the little piece of hash I had left in the very bottom of my pocket and entered the building.

I love border guards, what an attitude! It's like they're already pissed off at you before you get there. Anyway I laid my backpack down on a chair and walked up to the counter. On the wall behind the guard was a bumper sticker that read, "A good wife is her husband's crown and joy." What the hell was that supposed to mean anyway? And underneath that was another sticker with Huey, Dewey and Louie—or one of them ducks anyway—wearing a camouflage head band and holding a big rifle and it said, "This country wasn't won with a handshake"—just to give you an idea of the mentality.

The guard was pretty cordial and stupid, but everything was

going fine. Then he asked me where I was going. Whenever I cross the border I always feel guilty for some reason, so I lied and said I was going to Vermont.

Then he said, "You're going to check out Vermont?"

I was wasted and really nervous, and I thought he said, "I'm going to check your pockets." So I said, "There's nothing in my pockets." And the little piece of hash seemed to grow about two pounds. Then he said, "What did you say?"

So I said, "No, wait now...ummm, what did you say?"

Then he said, "I said, 'What did you say?'"

"No, before you said 'What did you say?' what did you say?"

"I don't know what I said before, but what I wanted to know is what you said after I said it."

"Said what?"

And this went on and on, and I was getting worried that he might get really mad, but instead he just started laughing and said, "What difference does it make?"

"None," I said.

That's when he asked me to check my pockets.

I took out everything minus the minuscule yet illegal quantity. I dumped all this junk out on the counter.

"You Catholic, son?" he was pointing at my St. Christopher medal.

I lied, "Ummmmm...yeah." I thought that he must be, because of those bumper stickers.

"Good, I thought you might be one of those Jesus freaks."

And I said, "No, I'm Catholic. That's why I carry my St. Christopher medal, patron saint of travellers."

"Don't you know that St. Christopher is defunct? The Pope decided that he didn't exist, boy."

What a crime I didn't know that. So I said, "Yeah, I knew that, it's just that they never got anyone to take his place, so I just go with St. Christopher."

Then he started in..."You see the Pope was right. They don't need a patron saint of travellers. People don't like travellers, transients, loose ends. People like people with roots. If you don't know someone's past and present how are you ever gonna be able to know their future? Too much risk. My daughter on the other hand is the exact opposite. She's off in the woods with any scum that's got the strength to drag themselves into town. Black scum, hippy scum, scum from Europe. She says that it's interesting to meet different people from different places. I say you could be with one of these scum, and he could pull out a knife and try and take your money, and you'd have no choice but to shoot 'em with your gun, and you can bet your bottom dollar I always got my gun. You for or against guns, son?"

I didn't know what to say. I felt like this question could determine whether or not I got across the border, so I said, "Well, this country wasn't won with a handshake, sir."

And he said, "You're very wise."

(Pause.)

Needless to say the prick didn't let me across the border because I only had thirteen dollars and no vehicle, so I found myself walking back in the direction of Tom's car. That's when I got a ride with a Pakistani family on their way to New York City. When we got to the border we didn't even have to go in, they had a drive through service. The woman looked into the car and the man handed her the papers for his family. She inspected them and then looked at me.

"What about your other son, sir?"

The man just laughed, and I got out of the car and showed the woman my ID. I felt like an idiot when I got back into the car. I mean these people had been nice enough to stop and pick me up, and now they'd practically adopted me. We drove about a mile in silence and then I started to laugh and the man said, "Is this true? Am I your father now? Ha, ha, ha."

I didn't find that very funny, since he quite probably could have been for all I knew. So I said, "I don't know. Are you?" This took him by surprise and I felt that I should explain, so I told him my story. I felt good about doing it. I hadn't talked to anyone about it in awhile. They were very interested and wished me the best of luck. The man even ventured to tell me the story of his grandfather who had been a blind Tibetan monk who had fled to Pakistan to escape punishment for having committed some crime. This blind man had travelled hundreds of miles through snow, rivers and forests to end up on the doorstep of this man's forefather in Pakistan. He slept with his grandmother and promptly died the next morning. I wondered if his grandmother was anything like the border guard's daughter, off in the woods with Tibetan scum this time. I also wondered if he was just making the whole thing up.

I told him I thought that his grandmother sounded like a wonderful person. I wanted to say that because his story had made me feel better. Less like a freak in some ways, and exactly like a freak in others.

(Pause.)

I saw them in the distance long before we reached them. At first they looked like Jerry Garcia and Cher, but as we got closer I realized that they were just hitchhikers. My new Pakistani father was slowing down to pick them up too. What was with this man? I figured that he was probably trying to pay off some cosmic debt, but the car was already filled with karma. Before I knew it, their biological son was taken up into the front seat and two leather clads climbed into the back seat, and off we went.

Things changed a lot once they were in the car because they were French. Four months in Montreal and I hadn't learned anything but how to party in French. You know, I learned how to get a light or bum a beer. I never learned how to actually speak to someone. From what I could gather, they were also on their way to New York. At one point I noticed that Cher was gesturing towards me, talking about me to my new father, and then they all started laughing. I tried to smile and be pleasant but I really wanted to know what the hell they were saying. They kept blathering on and on, until finally Cher turned to me and said, "I did see somet'ing like dat on 'Dee Unsolved Mystery,' dee...ahhh, Remy, Qu'est que c'est le blah blah blah blah blah? Ah, dee night before last?"

I smiled at her and said, "What?" I felt like I couldn't even speak English after being quiet for a whole hour.

That's when my new dad said, "Oh, I took the liberty of telling her your story. She was wondering why my son was being so quiet, so I told her what you told me about your father. I hope you don't mind. Anyway she says that she saw a woman on television who was also looking for her father."

Oh great! So I'm not the only one. God, the whole world was looking for their father. I wonder if she tried the south western states? You know Arizona, New Mexico, California? That's where all the ex-military men go when they're put out to pasture. I have this theory that if you're looking for your father—or a father for that matter—just pop down around the holidays when they're feeling lonely, and you're likely to find one. I was living in San Diego for a little while and I swear I met a hundred of them. The Tecelote golf course has more fathers who've taken off on their families than you could hack to pieces with a machete in a week. It seemed like every time I was golfing with my dad—I mean the man who I thought was my dad, but really wasn't, but really was in a way—I'd meet about ten of them, golf club in hand. (*He mimes a golf stance.*)

"Uh-huh, I got me a little family up in Bangor/Halifax/New York/Toronto. I wonder what they're doing now?"

"Probably better off without you, you fucking jerk."

"I never much met the kids, but their mother and I, we have an understanding. She understands that I had to leave. She understands me. God, I love that little lady."

"A good wife is her husband's crown and joy, buddy."

"You know what I admire, son? It's the freedom of the golf ball. One minute it's here. (*He swings.*) Whack! Next minute it's gone."

My Pakistani family dropped me off just outside of Plattsburgh, New York. There was a really nice goodbye and we all wished each other luck. Cher even kissed me on the cheek. I haven't met many men as nice as my Pakistani father.

(*He picks up pack.*)

Plattsburgh, New York, has five exits off the Interstate. Isn't that great? What a silly name for a city, hey? Plattsburgh. It's like somewhere Bugs Bunny took a wrong turn or something.

Anyway, there I was at the first exit, four more to go. I was still feeling pretty good from my last ride. I was feeling pretty normal. I had talked with some people, thought about things. I mean, I was standing on the side of the road, rain falling on my shoes. I kid you not. Bob Dylan or not, it was happening to me. I was feeling so cliché, so typical. For the first time I didn't feel different. Ain't that just the way?

If there's one thing I have faith in this world, it's "The Twilight Zone," and that's when it'll get you too. Just when you think you've got a grasp on reality.

("Popcorn" begins to play.)

The long Chevy pulled up and I peeked in. that's when I saw it. The other reality.

(Enter Beehive Lady. She sits in her chair, driving. Music fades.)

She was about forty, forty-five, with a beehive hairdo that was smooshing itself against the top of the car. She was wearing one of those fake leather, one piece, wet-look motorcycle suits with a big metal loop on the zipper. She sat there smiling, nestled in on the sheepskin seat covers motioning for me to "get in the car."

I opened the door, threw my pack in the back seat and crawled in. *(He sits next to Beehive.)* The only thing that separated me from her was a tiny plastic Fisher Price cassette player playing "Popcorn." You know that song. *(He starts to sing it. Music comes in.)* As the car accelerated forward the little bird mounted on a spring on the dashboard bent forward and took a little drink from the birdbath. Ooooh, I liked that. It was really kind of tense in the car.

JOHN: Exit two. *(Pause.)* So where are you from?
BEEHIVE: Plattsburgh.
JOHN: Oh. *(Pause.)* Exit three. So where are you going?
BEEHIVE: Plattsburgh.
JOHN: Oh. *(Pause.)* Exit four. Which exit?

BEEHIVE: Five.

JOHN: Oh. (*Pause.*) Exit five. Couldn't have come at a better time. Thanks.

And I got out of the car.

("Popcorn" out.)

She drove away. Whoa. That was just enough of a shifting of the brain for me to remember I didn't really know where I was going, or why, or who I was. I kinda thought that meeting my father would explain all these things. I kinda thought that it might even explain her. That's why when that psychopathic looking fellow pulled up in the jeep, I jumped right in without thinking twice. (*He hurries to sit in chair centre stage.*) "Oh God, oh God, oh God, thank you, thank you, thank you." I promptly began sucking up to him. I was so grateful you'd think he performed triple bypass surgery on me. Then he said the strangest thing. He said, "You don't see many hitchhikers around these days. There's been a lot of murders." That's exactly the way he said it too. Practiced, refined, knowing. I knew right away that he had said it many times before, "Murders." For a minute I thought I heard that music from *Psycho.* I looked over my shoulder and saw that the back of the jeep was filled with axes. I'm serious. Like I was sure that it was over. I was dead. He was going to perform that triple bypass after all. He chuckled a little at first. "Those are my tools of work," he acknowledged the axes. I saw Albany rise in the distance, reach its peak and start to sink.

"Look," I said, "There's Albany. Why don't I just get out here?"

Then he said, "The funny thing about the Albany train station is that it's not in Albany, as such. It's in a small town just outside Albany called Redslayer." Or Deer Slayer or something like that.

"Yeah, right buddy. Look it's not the dying I got a problem with, it's the mind games I hate. Either kill me now or let me out of this jeep."

So he stopped the jeep, I got out. As he was driving away I read the writing on the door. It said, "ALBANY MUNICIPAL FIRE DEPARTMENT." Oooops. I guess I didn't really know what was going on again. I ended up walking seven miles because, you see, the funny thing about the Albany train station is that it's not in Albany, as such. It's in a small town just outside of Albany called Redslayer.

(He takes the centre chair turning the two stage right chairs toward it to form train seating.)

I spent all of my money the first half an hour I was on the train. It wasn't really my fault. I ordered a rum and coke. I didn't know it was going to cost six dollars and fifty cents. I had already ordered the drink and I didn't want to look like a bum, so I just paid. I really can't explain why I bought the second one. The only way I could get something to eat on the train was to wait in the bar car till they put out the free chips at happy hour. Sour cream and onion. After two days of eating sour cream and onion chips and not having any toothpaste to brush your teeth with, you've reached the bottom. It may not seem that bad to you now—just try it some time. Not to mention the dirty looks that everyone was giving me simply because of the peanut incident with that old man. So I wanted the whole basket for myself. "Screw off, old man, you've got a pension coming in."

At one point these two German girls lost their wallet with all their money in it. They were crying and acting so foreign, that everyone immediately became so concerned. We were all "bar car people" because it was the only place on the train where you were allowed to smoke. So we had grown quite close to each other over the past few hours together. That's why I was so surprised when Doris from Newport stood up and said, "John from Canada probably took that." But Steve from Ohio and Roz from Jersey came to my defense and said that we were all smokers in the bar car and a non-smoker most definitely stole it while the movie was playing. Everyone bought that right away. We had a vendetta against the non-smokers.

Then the most wonderful thing happened. Fat men from Texas and old ladies from Arizona began donating large sums of money to help out the German girls. I was amazed. The girls were so happy, they didn't know what was goin' on. But just as the money was about to be given to them in a little presentation, some of the Amway convention people had worked out, the news came that the wallet had been found. As quick as the money had appeared, it disappeared, back into the bulging pocketbooks and wallets, and everything returned to normal. I thought about saying, "My wallet was stolen too." But then I thought—nahhhh. That'd never work. Not after that peanut incident anyway.

After everything had settled down, I did take the time to lean close to Doris from Newport and breathe on her. (*He leans into Doris and gives her a healthy dose of deadly vapour.*) The waft of sour cream and onion hit her so hard, it made her head spin. Don't fuck with me, lady. Nearly friggin' killed her.
(*He picks up backpack and exits train while "Duelling Banjos" plays.*)
I got off the train in Houston at approximately ten-fifteen pm. I thought that I'd just sleep in the station that night and get my sister in California to wire me some money in the morning. Then there came an announcement. "Boom...attention, Amtrak passengers. The station will be closing in ten minutes. The station will be closing in ten minutes. Boom."

The station, as they called it, was no bigger than an elevator, and I immediately located and locked in on the woman with the public address system in her hand. I rushed toward her and I think she thought that I was going to stab her or something.

"Excuse me," I said, "what did you just say?"

She repeated the announcement. "The station will be closing in ten minutes."

I was taken aback I must admit. I wasn't expecting to hear that same famous public address voice. I felt like I was speaking to a celebrity or something.

I said, "That's okay that the station is closing, but I'm going to be able to sleep here tonight, aren't I?"

"No," she said and turned and walked away. Then she turned and added, as an afterthought. "And I wouldn't sleep outside the station either, you know."

(He makes cutting gesture across throat.)

I was frantic, I was losing it, I was on the edge, I was going to die, so I called my mom. To say goodbye, I guess. I was determined not to stress her out. I just wanted to talk to her one last time. I was independent and ready to deal with the consequences of my actions. That's why when I heard her voice on the other end of the line...I started freaking out and saying that I didn't have any money and that the station was closing and I was going to die...die...die! What a thing to do to someone you love, hey? Call them from hundreds of miles away in the middle of the night and say, "I'm not dead yet...but I probably will be very soon." I'm still really embarrassed about that.

Then she said, "Oh, calm down now, John, and we'll figure something out." And, bang! I was okay all of a sudden.

She gave me the name of a friend of hers from, like fifteen years before, and told me that if that didn't work out then I could just go stay at the YMCA and tell them that I'd pay in the morning.

Then I called my sister and asked her to wire me fifty dollars. Then I bummed a quarter off the security guard when he came by to kick me out and called my mom's friend Thelma.

(He sits.)

The only memory I have of Thelma is this one time when I was a baby. It's more like a picture than a memory. She didn't see me sitting in this chair and sat on me by mistake. I can just remember the seam of a pair of polyester pants straining as the light from the television was suddenly eclipsed. This is what was going through my mind as I heard the voice on the other end of the line.

"Hello."

"Hi. This is John Taylor." There was a long pause during which I remembered that the pants she was wearing were lime green.

"I'm Mrs. Taylor's son...your friend-from-fifteen-years-ago's son." God, I hope she remembered me. I mean I remember her——in a way, at least. The pause went on.

Then all of a sudden she snapped, "John-John?"

I was overjoyed. "Yes-yes, it is John-John."

Thank God she remembered. You see that's what everyone used to call me as a child. John-John. It was all coming back to me now. I could hear her in the background going, "John-John, John-John. Oh, my God, it's John-John. Martin, wake up it's John-John." Martin, however, didn't seem to be impressed by the fact that John-John was in town. Thelma came back to the phone. "John-John, where are you?"

"I'm at the train station, and it's closing."

"Martin, John-John's at the train station, get up, Martin, we have to go get the boy."

Then I heard Martin say, "It's ten-thirty at night, Thelma." Then Thelma said, "What is the matter with you Martin?" And her hand went over the phone.

It's like, "Yeah—what the hell is the matter with you, Martin. Don't you know John-John is in town."

She came back on the phone. "John-John," I could tell she was getting some kind of charge out of saying that name over and over again, "Do you have any money?"

I didn't want to say no, because who wants to take a broke person into their home, and I didn't want to say yes because I didn't. So I said, "Yeah," leaving it up to her to read the pain in my voice.

"Then you check yourself into the nearest YMCA and call us back with that number. And, John-John, don't you go walking around down there at night, ya hear? You get yourself a taxi cab."

I wanted to scream, "With what? I don't have any money! Couldn't you read my mind?" Maybe she couldn't, so I said, "Unhh, okay." If she didn't know I was lying after that, she was never going to.

"All right then, I'll see you tomorrow, John-John. Bye." Click.
(He places chair next to downstage centre chair to form cab.)

And with that plan B kicked in. There were these two cab drivers outside who were waiting around for...me, I guess. There was no one else left now. I walked out the door which clicked locked behind me. They were staring at me, me at them. We were sizing each other up. They were probably wondering what I was going to say, 'cause I know that I was. That's when it was my turn to click for a change. I opened my mouth and the shit just started pouring out.

"I lost my wallet on the train. It was stolen on the train...I am from Germany." I only added that part, "I am from Germany," because my accent sucked so bad I couldn't take the chance of them figuring it out by themselves. I must say I was great. I copied the pain and anguish of the two German girls to a tee. Everything from their facial expressions to the nervous stance that people have when they've been ripped off.

One of the taxi drivers said, "Germany? I was stationed in Germany for years. What part you from, boy?"

My mind went blank and my palms started sweating. Out of all the cities in Germany I knew, for some reason I still shouted out, "Plattsburgh."

They looked at me, "Plattsburgh? Shit."

Before they could say anything else I said, "Look I'm lying. But I'm lying because I really need to get to the YMCA alive. I don't have any money and I'm not used to all the dying and stuff you have down here. Really I'm from Newfoundland." I may as well have said Never Never Land. At least they would have heard of that before. I guess it was interesting enough for them to offer me a ride anyway. We climbed into the cab all three of us because the cabbies ride two to a cab at night.

(Taking his pack, he sits in cab.)

The place was a friggin' war zone in my eyes. They asked me where I was going and I said the Y.

"Which one?"

"What do you mean, 'Which one?'"

"Well there's the gay Y, the straight Y, the black Y, the white Y, the Y for Hispanics, the Episcopalian Y, the Baptist Y. Then you can do combinations like the Catholic black Y for gays. We'll just take you to the Louisiana Street Y."

"What's that?" I asked.

"That's the Y for people who don't know their ass from their armpit." That sounded like the right one for me.

(Pause.)

As we cruised along the empty streets I got a chance to look around at the place where I was born. A few gunshots sounded in the distance, and I caught a glimpse of someone go down in the blue neon light that spilt from a gun and guitar shop on Ohio Street. The sounds of sirens wailed around us as I sat bolt upright. I didn't want to miss one minute of my surroundings. This was my homecoming, and as hard as I tried to make it seem romantic, I knew that it sucked. Somewhere in this city my father was getting ready to go to sleep with absolutely no idea that John-John was in town. That struck me as truly bizarre.

They let me off at the Y and I buzzed in past the three security gates to the counter. I looked at the big black woman through a thick layer of glass and simply said, "My mother said I could stay here tonight and pay in the morning." That's what I said too.

She had definitely never heard that one before, I could tell. She stared at me for a while, then her face broke out into a smile and she buzzed me in through the fourth and final gate.

(He drops pack.)

I awoke in the morning to the sound of the telephone. I picked it up and someone said, "John-John Taylor? There's someone down here to see you."

When I got down to the lobby it was pretty weird, because I had no idea what Thelma looked like. I just stood there waiting for someone to recognize me. There were a few people hanging around, but no one that I could recognize. Then I saw it. A woman was bent over tying her shoe and she was wearing lime green polyester pants. I recognized her butt immediately.

"Thelma?"

"John-John!"

And that was that. We drove out to her house and I re-met everyone that I had known as a baby and they all called me John-John. John-John went swimming in the pool, John-John went for a drive through his old neighbourhood, John-John got a shower and got ready to go to his appointment at the plastic surgeon's office.

(Pause.)

As Thelma was driving me out to my father's office, she began telling me about him. How she had seen him at the supermarket about three weeks ago, or at the movies last year, and stuff like that. This was really freaking me out. I started to realize that I wasn't on a soap opera or something like that. You know, I kind of had this image of me striding into the office past the secretary as she pushed frantically on the PA button.

"Dr. Winthrop...Dr. Winthrop...it's your son...he's returned." And then a door would fly open and my father would step out and embrace me in the fatherly way, and say, "My son!" But only I'd know that he meant more—so much, much more.

Yeah, anyway...There I was outside the office door looking pretty strung out. I pushed open the door and stepped into the waiting room. *(The remains of the train now become the waiting room.)* There were a few women sitting there who immediately looked up in horror as I entered. One of them was wearing a fur coat—I couldn't believe it! It was like two hundred degrees outside that day, like we were living on the sun and this bimbo has on a fur coat. So there they sat. An army of oil tycoon wives with faces that were painted on and finger nails that looked more like butter knives.

An army of rich Texas bitches just sitting there flipping through pamphlets filled with pages and pages of eyes, ears and noses, lips and stomachs that my father could sew on to you, if you had the cash. There were things like the "Liz Taylor 912031" which was about the cutest nose this side of El Paso. The secretary was hardly excited to see me. She stood up in shock. I admit I wasn't looking my best, but I made my way towards her. (*He circles anxiously around the chairs.*) My feet sank in the high pile of the carpet, and I started to feel like I was in one of those dreams where something's chasing you but you can't run because the floor is a big marshmallow. I finally made it to the desk and there were tears welling up in my eyes. I guess this sort of softened her up a bit 'cause she smiled.

"Don't worry," she said, "we can fix that."

"Fix what? " I said.

"Your nose."

Bitch!

We filled out the form that was required of all first-time patients and I couldn't help but laugh as we did it. Especially the part where I told her I didn't have any insurance.

"What? No insurance?"

"Don't worry about it," I said, "I'll be dealing in cash only today."

(*He sits. Pause.*)

All eyes in the room were on me, which was really bizarre because there were only two kinds—two sets of Bo Derek's and three Christie Brinkley's. They watched me as I walked back to take a seat, and began flipping through a copy of "Let your lips do the talking." In just a few moments I had the whole room wondering if they should sneer at me because I was a bum, or kiss my ass because I was the richest eccentric in this here town. I wasn't even thinking anymore. I was actually looking at the lips trying to decide which ones I might wear. I just didn't want to think about where I was. I think maybe I should have. I heard the secretary talking to "the Doctor" in the hallway and then she called two names. I was early, and I've never been early for anything in my life. The one thing I was sure of was that I was not going to get nervous and blow this thing, even though I had no idea what I was going to say. Then the secretary smiled at me and told me to go into the office.

(He walks slowly as if reluctant.)

I walked into an empty office and sat down in a chair and began waiting again. My father's out moving around in the hallway going from room to room dealing with patients. I felt like one of those spring snakes in a fake peanut can. It was a beautiful hot day outside with a warm breeze blowing and my brain felt like it was on morphine...fighting with itself to play the situation through once more before it happened. Too late, the door swung open and he stepped in.

"Hello, can I help you?" were the first words I ever heard my father say. Not unlike the first words I heard a McDonald's employee say. I said, "You may think that I'm here because of my nose." What a stupid thing to say, I can't believe I said that stupid a thing.

"Well, why are you here then?"

So I asked him if he remembered my mother. He thought for a second and said, "Yes."

So I decided to give it to him. "I'm your son."

He turned away from me for a moment, and when he turned back, he had gathered this unbelievable composure out of nowhere. Everything he said from that point was very measured out and calculated. Almost as if he had consulted a tiny lawyer that he kept inside his head. *(He moves apprehensively.)*

"There's some debate as to whether or not I'm your father." We just stared at each other...I saw parts of my face in his. I think that he saw the same thing.

He said, "So you're my son."

And I said, "Yes."

"So, what do you want from me?"

"I don't know exactly, I'm not here to mess up anyone's life if that's what you think." I started to cry for a second and apologized by saying, "I'm sorry, but it's just that this is a strange thing to be dealing with."

"Yes, it's quite a surprise for me too. How did you find out that I was here?"

"My mother gave me your name and I called the hospital where you worked together, back then. They told me that you had a private office now, so I called the operator and got the number and made an appointment. That's how I ended up here."

"I see. Well this is quite a shock. You have to understand that...well, you lived in Houston for a while, yes? And then you moved and, well, I...I have a wife now and...she would never understand this. I'm a Zoroastrianist. That's my religion, and divorce and scandal like that aren't acceptable. You can't expect me to...I don't know how this will affect my family."

(He moves toward audience.)

I didn't like the way things were going. They were summing themselves up too quickly. I was searching my entire self trying to think of something wonderful to say. Something to make things last longer so we could get to know each other. Something that would make him like me. I really wanted him to like me. It's so weird. I didn't even know this man, and for some reason, some biological need, I wanted him to like me. And from as well as he could get to know me in that short period of time, I don't think that he did.

I decided to ask him a practical question. "Is there any history of heart disease in our family?"

"No."

"Do I have any relatives?"

He told me that my grandfather had been dead for years and that my grandmother had been very sick and died last year.

"How about children? Do you have any children?"

"I have two children."

I asked if I could meet them. *(He appears hopeful.)*

"No, I don't think that would be possible. They're only eleven and thirteen years old and I don't know how they would take this. It's just out of the question."

"Do you have any pictures of them that I could see?"

"I don't think that would be a good idea either. And please don't try to get in touch with them. That would be doing more harm than good. Basically, I don't want my family to know about you."

That was heavy. Then he said, "Well, is there anything else you can think of that I might be able to do for you?"

"Do you want me to just go away? Like I said, I'm not here to mess up your life or your family. I can just walk away."

He didn't seem to even hear me.

"Well then, if there's nothing...you may as well think of your father as dead."

As I was leaving he said maybe I could drop him a letter sometime. At the office.

And I said, "Yeah, that'd be great."

(Pause.)

You may as well think of your father as dead. You may as well think of your father as dead. At least it was final. I mean the man was pronounced dead by a doctor. He made an attempt to explain a few things, but my mind had wandered out the window. I stared at the buildings and the roads. I just wanted to be out there again. Free from all this.

Shortly after I left the office I got on a bus and headed downtown. I picked up the fifty dollars my sister had wired me. As I was walking out of the Western Union Office I saw one of those guys. One of those "hey-lady dudes" I like to call them. You know the ones.

(Funky sort of inner-city groove music plays.)

"Hey, lady! Hey, lady! Just stop for a minute, I just want to talk to you for a minute. See, what I do is help people. That's what I do, I help people, see. Like if you was hungry...like you like McDonald's? I show you where there be a nice McDonald's just down the road. Or if you like Mexican food, I show you...I'll walk with you to that place, and you give me two dollars or something. See, that's what I want, two dollars. 'Cause you know I got to go see my parole officer on the other side of town and if I don't get there I'm gonna be in trouble."

(Music quickly fades.)

And these guys aren't stupid. They'll give you the spiel till you break down and give them the money. I'm like a freak magnet when it come to these guys. They can see me coming for miles, like I got a big neon sign on my head saying, "Take my money!"

As I was standing there trying to figure out where to go, this finger nail filled with white powder is shoved up underneath my nose.

"You want to buy some crank, man? Just try it, man."

It was the hey-lady dude. I couldn't believe it. I led him over to the corner of the building away from the crowd and said, "Listen, man, I don't want to buy any crack."

See, I thought that he said "crack." Then I started lecturing him about the evils of crack and how it could mess up a brother's mind. Between listening to my Public Enemy CD and watching Detroit news, I thought that I was an expert in the field.

"No, no, no. This ain't crack, man, it's crank."

So I said, "What's crank?"

Then he looked at me like I was from another planet (which I was) and said, "Where you from, brother?"

(He moves nervously to sit.)

I proceeded to tell him where I was from, why I was here, how much money I had been wired, like an idiot.

There was this donut shop across the street, and I was thinking that if I could only get in there, I could buy myself a cup of coffee and figure out a way to get out of this hell hole. While I'm thinking this, this other guy comes up and hauls out this big wad of cash from his pocket and gives me ten dollars.

"I want you to read this sign, man."

This guy was offering me ten dollars to read a sign. So I said, "Okay, what sign do you want me to read?"

"It's over there."

So we follow this guy over to this overpass, and there's people there laying around moaning and groaning with big beards and shopping carts, talking to nothing in particular.

Then out of nowhere, this third guy shows up and starts

calling the guy with the wad of cash a stupid nigger. And the hey-lady dude starts telling me not to mind them stupid niggers. There were niggers calling niggers, "niggers," and I was having trouble trying to figure out who was the stupid nigger here, and I was starting to get the feeling that it was definitely me. So when the hey-lady dude said, "Let's split." I was with him.

We ran down the street and around a corner. We stopped out of breath, laughing. He gave me the whole, "Yo brother! What's your name?" handshake thing. He told me that his name was Mark. I even felt like I had made a friend or something. But as I was walking away he said, "So you gonna buy some of this stuff from me, or what?"

I told him that I didn't have any money, but he told me that I did, and exactly how much. I didn't want to buy anything from him, and I didn't want to give him any money either, so I got that little piece of hash out of my backpack and gave it to him. I was thinking that it would be a nice enough gesture to buy me time to get away from the whole situation.

"Look, you just keep that for yourself and I'm gonna take off, okay?"

I turned to walk away and I felt the pull on my backpack, I was being hauled back. When I turned I saw the knife in his hand and I heard him say, "Give me the money."

It was like a distant dream, my brain was just saying, "I don't care anymore." I said, "I can't give you this money," as I was reaching for the money to give him—I'm not that stunned. Then a blue van pulled up and a car screeched around the corner. A bunch of guys jumped out and grabbed the hey-lady dude and myself and threw us down on the ground, shouting, "Don't make a move!" They had guns pointed at the back of our heads.

Needless to say, I lost it, I had reached my daily excitement quota somewhere back at Thelma's house. Lying there on the sidewalk, my life story spewed out in one big torrential vomit that formed the most elaborate pity-me story you've ever heard. The whole thing built itself up slowly and ended climatically with me screaming, "I just wanted to meet my father!"

You don't know the meaning of the word embarrassment. You don't know what an arsehole is. I'm an arsehole, 'cause when I looked up there was nobody around me anymore. They were all up the road a ways dealing with the hey-lady dude. So I stood up really fast, hoping that no one had noticed; you know, trying not to prolong the humiliation. I had filled that quota for today too.

But of course there was a cop sitting in his car alone eating a boston cream and laughing at me. I walked over to the window. He said, "Was all that stuff you just said real. I mean was it the truth?"

What a jerk! I said, "So listen, what do I do now? You got to help me."

He told me that they could only hold the hey-lady dude for another five minutes since the crank wasn't real and the knife wasn't big enough. He suggested that I get out of there as fast as I could and not show my face around there again. I immediately turned and started to run away. As I was leaving all I could hear was the hey-lady dude saying, "That motherfucker just gave me that piece of hash."

(Pause.)

When I finally got back to the YMCA I crawled into my bed full of cockroaches and proceeded to have a breakdown or something. As I was taking off my jeans I reached into my pocket and pulled out the ten dollar bill that buddy had given me to read the sign. Oh, my God! I had actually made ten dollars off my mugging. That was the only thing that kept me from going completely insane. That was the most exciting day of my life.

Later on that evening my father called me at the Y. I picked up the phone.

"Hello."

"Hello, John."

"Yes, yes, this is John." I just wasn't expecting him to call.

"I just wanted to speak with you again, because, today in the office when you came in, I was very surprised. Now that I've had a chance to think about it, I wanted to check with you once more to see if there was anything you needed. When are you leaving?"

"Actually, I had planned to hitchhike to California, where my sister is, but I had a horrible experience today after I left your office. I was mugged, basically." I told him the whole ordeal of the afternoon. "Now I just want to get out of here as soon as possible. I hate to ask you this but I feel like I have no other choice. Could I borrow some money or something to get a plane to California?"

"Yes, yes, I think that would be possible. When do you plan to leave?"

"Tomorrow afternoon, if I can."

"I will bring the money down to you tomorrow morning."

So I was going to get another chance to see my father.

The next morning the shit was frightened out of me by the buzzer on the phone. Of course, I had slept in, so I jumped up and got dressed and washed my face and stuff, trying to get a clear head.

When I got down to the lobby I saw him. He looked anxious standing there. He was slightly abrupt which made me anxious too. He said, "Good morning."

And I said, "Good morning."

I asked him if he wanted to go somewhere to get some breakfast—a great idea I had come up with the night before, but he said, "No, I have to be getting to the office." Strike one million. I realized that we weren't going to be pals.

"I brought the money." He handed it to me rolled up. I didn't even look at it then. I just put it in my pocket.

"You don't know how much I appreciate this."

When I looked at it later it was more than enough. I have to admit, I felt kind of humiliated.

Then he said, "Well, I better be going."

And I said, "I'm glad that I met you."

He held out his hand to me and I took it. Then he asked me the only question about myself that he ever asked.

"Are you a good boy?" I didn't really understand what the question was supposed to mean.

I just said, "I uh...suppose. I guess...yes."

And then he left. He turned and walked away. I didn't stay and watch him cross the lobby and go out the door. I didn't watch him till he was a tiny speck on the horizon.

(He walks close to audience.)

Why didn't I? Why didn't I answer the question "Are you a good boy?" differently? Why didn't I take the moment to use honesty and say, "Yes I'm a good person, I have a few faults like anyone, but I'm basically good. I might be someone you would want to get to know." Why didn't I push harder?

I find it strange that the Pakistani man who picked me up hitchhiking could treat me kinder and act more like a father, even though it was only a joke, than my real father. And the man who I thought was my father, the father of all my brothers and sister, always treated me equally. But the man who actually fathered me treated me more like I had just sold him a car. What the hell does it mean to be a father anyway?

I mean, right now it seems like I'll never be able to forget about the things that have happened. I think about them everyday, almost once an hour. Like if I'm not thinking about anything specific, my mind will wander back to it. But soon something will come along that will take my attention away from it.

(Enter Beehive Lady. John looks at her in confusion as if she's screwed her cue. She is wearing the short bolero and gauze pants of a harem dancer. "Popcorn" begins to play.)

JOHN: Umm...something else will come along to create a diversion. It uhh...it uhhh...*(He calls to sound technician at back of house.)* Line?

TECH: It doesn't have to be something monumental.

("Popcorn" cross fades into Middle Eastern belly-dancing music and Beehive is belly dancing around stage stealing attention.)

JOHN: Oh right. It doesn't have to be something monumental. It uhh...It uh...Shit! I lost it! It's gone.

TECH: Just try and keep it going.

JOHN: It doesn't have to...it uh...I'm gonna start again, okay? I'm gonna start again.

(John goes and gets backpack. Music becomes louder. Lights

are trippy. Beehive dances wildly. John produces a Persian carpet and a hookah pipe from the backpack. He clears away the chairs from centre stage and they sit smoking the hookah as Middle Eastern music fades away and lights dim on the tableau.)

THE END.

Innuinuit Theatre Company
and
Nalujuk Players

Braindead

1993

Written collectively by

Pauline Angnatok	Julius Barbour
Mary Dicker	Olivia Edmunds
Barbara Flowers	Jenny Holwell
Andrew Karpik	Bernice Lucy
Catherine Mitsuk	Susan Nochasak
Wayne Piercy	Connie Pijogge
Molly Shiwak	Beverly Tuglavina

Paulette Winters

Under the direction of
Bill Wheaton and **Norma Denney**

BRAINDEAD

Braindead was performed in Nain, Labrador on the weekend of 9 April 1993 and in Hopedale during the second week of May 1993. The play was also performed at the eighteenth Labrador Creative Arts Festival in Goose Bay, 24 November 1993. "Scene 3" which had been performed in Nain and Hopedale was omitted in Goose Bay and "Scene 5" was written and performed in its place. The text presented here contains both these scenes. Members of Innuinuit Theatre Company in Nain and members of Nalujuk Players in Hopedale collaborated on the play.

Braindead was directed by **Bill Wheaton** of Innuinuit Theatre Company and **Norma Denney** of Nalujuk Players. The play was written collectively by the directors and members of the cast who played the following roles:

From Innuinuit Theatre, Nain:

Pauline Angnatok	Pauline
Julius Barbour	Julius
Mary Dicker	Mary
Olivia Edmunds	Olivia
Jenny Holwell	Jenny
Andrew Karpik	Junior
Molly Shiwak	Authority/Teacher
Paulette Winters	Paulette, Angie

From Nalujuk Players, Hopedale:

Barbara Flowers	Mother
Bernice Lucy	Bernice
Catherine Mitsuk	Kathy
Susan Nochasak	Susan
Wayne Piercy	Wayne, Bobby
Connie Pijogge	Connie
Beverly Tuglavina	Beverly

Additional Credits:
Producer **Bill Wheaton**. Illustrations for the play are by **Bill Wheaton**.
Development of the script was funded by the Labrador Inuit Health Commission.

CAST OF CHARACTERS
(In order of appearance.)

AUTHORITY	Counsellor in rehabilitation centre, narrator, teacher in final scene.
JULIUS	Problem student, joke teller.
SUSAN	Street kid, orphan.
MARY	Epileptic, novice sniffer.
JENNY	Bored sniffer, friend of Paulette.
PAULETTE	Bored sniffer, friend of Jenny.
WAYNE	Screwed up kid from welfare home, grade eight education, Beverly's boyfriend.
BEVERLY	Fifteen-years-old, pregnant with Wayne's child.
PAULINE	Novice sniffer, from unhappy home.
JUNIOR	Experienced sniffer, friend of Olivia.
OLIVIA	Experienced sniffer, friend of Junior.
ANGIE	Pauline's sister, not a sniffer.
BERNICE	Sniffer from middle-class home, pressured by parents' expectations.
BOBBY	Kid who sniffs to belong, wants to feel popular.
CONNIE	Friend of Kathy, not a sniffer.
KATHY	Bobby's younger sister, not a sniffer.
MOTHER	Bobby and Kathy's mother.

BRAINDEAD

Scene 1

The set is divided into a rehabilitation centre for young native offenders and the village in which their experiences occurred. There is a card table surrounded by chairs at stage right where the young offenders in the rehab centre are playing cards, an area at centre stage where gas sniffing scenes occur, and chairs to represent the school at stage left. There is also one stool at stage left and one at stage right which are used by the authority figure, Authority, who directs the other characters and narrates the action of the play. The action begins with the stage dark except for a spotlight on Authority.

AUTHORITY: Good evening, ladies and gentlemen, members of the audience, welcome to our play. "Braindead" addresses the issue of inhalant abuse in the north, and has violent scenes, accompanied by abusive language. This play may not be suitable for young children.
(She claps her hands twice. A chant begins from the entrance to the theatre. The chanting actors march down aisles and onto stage.)

CAST: Braindead!
Braindead!
Toxins! Gas!
Braindead!
Braindead!
Sniffing glue!
Braindead!
Braindead!
(Actors stop and point at audience.)
It'll get you!
I'm lost!
I'm lost!
I'm lost!
(Actors put hands on head and stagger about stage.)
I'm braind-e-e-a-a-d!

(Actors separate to positions. Authority goes to stool at stage left. Pauline, Julius, Susan, Bernice, Wayne, and Mary go to card table. Jenny and Paulette go to centre stage. Card game begins, cards are shuffled, dealt and played. There is ad lib between the players: crude language, teasing, pushing, sexual innuendoes. Julius interrupts with a joke.)

JULIUS: Hey! Hey, you guys! Wanna hear a joke? Wait a minute! Wait a minute! What's green and wrinkled?

SUSAN: A dollar bill!

JULIUS: Na, boy! Your face! Ha! Ha!
    (Card players react boisterously.)

AUTHORITY: (Stands up and walks towards card table.) Stop! Stop! Be quiet! Listen up, boy! You! *(Points at Mary.)* You! Stand up! Come here and tell these people who you are!

MARY: *(Stands up and walks to front of stage.)* All right! I'll tell you who I am. My name is Mary, and this is my story.
    (Lights fade on card game, and come up on Jenny and Paulette.)

JENNY: Man, oh man! Isn't it boring? What can I do? *(She sits down, takes out a cigarette, and flicks a lighter.)* This smells kinda good. Maybe we should get stoned. My folks won't mind, they'll be out drinkin' brew all weekend anyways! Yeah! What the hell? Let's get stoned! Nothin' else to do! Okay, Paulette?

PAULETTE: Yeah, sure! Boring old weekend anyway. What are we going to get stoned on, Jen?

JENNY: Lighter fluid, boy! I got some somewhere!

PAULETTE: Get some bags then!
    (Jenny gets a couple of white plastic bags and puts lighter fluid in them. They both get "right to it." Paulette tries the first couple of "hoots"...coughs...gets used to it. Both girls stagger aimlessly about.)

PAULETTE: Smells like yeast!

JENNY: Nah, boy, smells like gas! What's the matter with your nose?

PAULETTE: Smells like toe-jam!

JENNY: Well, you feel somethin' yet? You're takin' awful long gettin' off.

PAULETTE: (*Shrieks.*) Look! Over there! The purple snowman is comin'!

JENNY: Ah! You're seein' things. There's no such thing as a purple snowman!
(She sniffs some more and starts to laugh. Mary enters.)

MARY: What are you guys doing?

PAULETTE: Waiting for Santa to come! We're sniffin', boy! What do you think?

JENNY: Do you want to try?

MARY: (*Backing away from her in fear.*) No! No, I can't!

JENNY: (*Coming at her with a bag.*) Come on! Come on! Have some fun, boy! Life is for livin'!

MARY: I'm afraid! I'm an epileptic! I get fits! Sometimes I think I'm going to die!

JENNY: Come on! Live life for once! You're goin' to feel like you're on top of the world. You'll forget about all those old fits soon enough.
(She straightens out her arms to the side at shoulder level and staggers around.)

MARY: (*Takes the bag, sits and begins to sniff.*) I'll try a bit, I suppose.

JENNY: Good stuff, hey?

MARY: Holy shoot! I'm starting to hear things.

JENNY: What did I tell you? It's good stuff, eh? Leaves you with bad breath, but a good cheap high! Have another hoot, boy. There's lots more where this came from! (*Jenny and Paulette are staggering, disoriented.*) Light up a smoke, I suppose.

MARY: (*She jumps up, frightened and bawling.*) No! No! You're going to blow us up!

PAULETTE: Bite her head off, boy!

JENNY: Nothin' goin' to happen!

MARY: (*Collapsing to her seat, screaming.*) No! No! They're all laughing at me! They hate me! I'm ugly! I'm ugly! They're always laughing at me!

JENNY: (*Reaches out and tries to grab her.*) Hey! Hey! Calm down!

MARY: (*Paranoid, still screaming. She pushes Jenny away.*) Don't touch me! She's always trying to touch me! She's always getting at me!

JENNY: Jesus!
(Mary falls to floor and starts to convulse. She has an epileptic seizure.)

JENNY: Let's get the hell out of here!
(Jenny and Paulette exit quickly. Mary lies still. Four figures walk on stage and slowly carry her off. Authority walks to front of stage.)

AUTHORITY: Well, that's Mary's story. Fortunately, she survived but she was in a coma for three days. When she got better, she was sent here for therapy, and is also learning how to cope with her epilepsy. It's not easy for Mary, because the other kids make fun of her, but she's learning to like herself a little more.

(Lights fade and come up on card game.)

Scene 2

(Card game continues: ad lib between players, crude language, teasing, pushing, sexual innuendoes. Julius interrupts with another joke.)

JULIUS: What's green and hangs from trees? Hey, you guys! Be quiet a bit! Shut up! Thanks. Now where was I? Oh, yeah, what's green and hangs from trees?

PAULINE: Your head, stupid!

JULIUS: Nah! Giraffe snot.

(Card players react boisterously. Authority figure appears.)

AUTHORITY: Silence! Stop what you're doing! You there! (*She points at Susan.*) Come here and tell everyone who you are!

(Susan stands up and walks to front of stage.)

SUSAN: Sure! I'll tell you who I am! I'm Susan! Do you wanna hear my story?

(Lights fade as Susan crosses stage. Lights come up on Susan sitting and holding a bag of gas. She sniffs and begins to cough.)

This isn't so bad. What's all the fuss about anyways? I've been sniffing for months, and it hasn't hurt me yet, at least, I don't think it has. It's the same thing as breathing. Everyone breathes or else you die. This is no different, you're just breathing in smelly, fantasy-filled air. (*She rises and begins to dance in a disoriented manner.*) Yeah, that's it, smelly, fantasy-filled air, like helium. (*Laughs.*) I should sniff more often and become a comedian like Eddie Murphy, and make millions. (*Laughs again and collapses to her seat. She continues to sniff and to cough.*)

Sure, last week I was at my hangout, and a social worker comes up to me and asks me why I'm not at school. Then she asks me if I want to go to a shelter. Goodness, don't they ever get tired of this guardian angel stuff? Every week there's someone new offering us food and free advice, which I might add, we don't want...and religion, "Change your ways or burn in hell for eternity." (*She stands up angrily.*) Why don't they try their speeches on someone who really cares? When I was about to leave, she asked me if I was afraid of her. Can you believe it? Afraid of her? You got to be kidding! After she shut her big mouth, I told her, "Why should I come with you? I've heard everything you have to say before!" Then she started calling me a "smart assed little girl." That no-gooder busybody. She doesn't know anything about me, and she certainly don't know anything about what goes on down here.

Down here, it's the law of the jungle. If you're smart and fast, you live. If you're slow and dumb, you die. It's survival of the fittest, and there's no place here for people like them. People on the streets got enough problems as it is, they don't need someone coming down here reminding them of what they are, and who they can be. They're alone and afraid, and have no place to go.

They've been kicked out of their homes and forced to live this way. Do you think we want to live like this? Do you think we enjoy fighting for a place to sleep and eat, and running from some guy who wants to beat the crap out of you for taking his last cigarette butt? Well the answer is "NO"! It stinks! It's cold, and lonely, and cruel. Then people like them wonder why we sniff. Wake up and face reality! This isn't the promised land!

You all find it so easy to pass judgement on us because of who we are, and how we look. No wonder we sniff, and can't quit. You all don't make it any easier. The way I'm going, I don't think I'll ever give it up.

(Susan stands and pushes her chair aside in frustration. Lights fade on her as she crosses back to card game and resumes her seat. Lights up on card players.)

Eventually I came here for treatment. It's hard for me because I don't want to return to the streets, and I have no home to go to. My parents died in a fire...but I'm trying...I'm really trying. If other people can beat the habit of sniffing, I can too! (*She turns to her fellow players.*) Let's play cards, boy!

(Card game continues in boisterous manner. Julius interrupts with another joke.)

JULIUS: Wait a minute! Wait a minute! I've got another joke. Okay...what do whales and the Montreal Canadiens have in common? Okay! Okay! I'm gonna tell ya. Both get confused when surrounded by ice. Ha! Ha!

(Card players boo Julius's joke. Authority walks around card table and stops behind Wayne.)

AUTHORITY: Hey buddy, I want you to come with me and tell your story to these people.

Scene 3

(Authority and Wayne walk to front of stage.)

WAYNE: Do you really want me to tell everyone what happened?

AUTHORITY: Yes I do. Don't be afraid.

WAYNE: Me! Afraid! Huh! All right, my name is Wayne and this is what happened to me.

(Lights fade as Wayne crosses stage. Lights up on Wayne and Beverly.)

WAYNE: Oh, good! You're back! (*He kisses her.*) What did they say? Are you pregnant?

BEVERLY: Yes!

WAYNE: (*Becoming angry, his voice grows louder.*) Oh shoot, man! What are we gonna do? You can't be pregnant! I don't need this!

BEVERLY: You! You don't need it! What about me? I'm fifteen years old. Do I look like I need a baby?

WAYNE: I thought you were on the pill. What happened?

BEVERLY: You happened, that's what! The pill isn't foolproof, you know, and it certainly didn't help that you weren't wearing a condom. I can hear you now, (*She imitates him.*) "Ah, don't worry. You won't get pregnant. Besides, it's so much better without a rubber!"

WAYNE: Don't go blaming me. I shouldn't be the one to get the rubbers all the time. You have to do your part too!

BEVERLY: Well, it's too late now! The damage is done, and I'm left with a baby that I have to raise.

WAYNE: What? You're gonna have it? You can't do that!

BEVERLY: Oh yes, I'm gonna have it, and you're gonna help me raise it!

WAYNE: Hey, no way! I ain't gonna be no daddy. Forget it! You're going to get an abortion and forget it ever happened.

BEVERLY: (*Pointing at him.*) You're the one who got me into this mess and you're going to be the one to help me through it. What do you think my parents will do when I tell them I'm pregnant? They'll kick me out!

WAYNE: Tell them when they're both drunk. They'll never know the difference, and when you start to show, just tell them you're putting on weight!

(Laughing uncontrollably, he tries to pat her belly.
She pushes his hand away.)

BEVERLY: This is one big joke to you, isn't it? Well you wait until this baby is born, and then you'll really laugh. The feedings, changing diapers, getting sick, crying...you're really gonna have fun.

WAYNE: There's no way I'm going to do all that. You're gonna get rid of the kid and get both of us out of this mess.

BEVERLY: The more I listen to you, the more I want to have this baby, even if it's to get back at you. It's about time guys like you owned up to some responsibility. I'm not doing this all alone. You're half responsible for this baby too, you know.

WAYNE: If you think I'm gonna give you money to raise a baby, then you're wrong! Where am I going to get money? I don't have a job!

BEVERLY: Well then, get one!

WAYNE: Where? Don't you listen to the news? There's no jobs anywhere! What do you expect me to do, haul a job out of thin air?

BEVERLY: All I know is that I'm having this baby and you're going to help me one way or the other, even if I have to drag you into court to get the money.

WAYNE: Ah, I'm getting out of here. You're just talking crap. Look, talk to me again when you're calmed down. You'll see then that an abortion is the best answer for all of us. If you want to talk later, I'll be at Joe's.

(He turns to leave.)

BEVERLY: Oh, yeah! Joe! Wonderful Joe! What are you gonna do over there, discuss current events in the news?

WAYNE: Hey, you leave Joe out of this! He's my friend! I can talk with him! He understands me!

BEVERLY: Oh yeah! He knows you all right! He knows how stupid you are, and how easy it is for him to get you to sniff. God! Don't you realize that he's not your friend? He's your enemy. He's going to kill you if you're not careful.

WAYNE: You don't know what you're talking about. You're just mad because I got you pregnant, and you're saying this to make me feel guilty. Well it's not going to work! You can't stop me from going to Joe's house!

BEVERLY: Fine! Go then! You're just going to go out to your father's shed and sniff your brains out. But when you come back, I'll still be here, and the baby too. You can't escape your problems that easily, and if you think you can, you're just fooling yourself.

(Beverly pushes Wayne away and exits.)

WAYNE: *(Yelling after her.)* Hey! Wait a minute! Come back here! I'm not finished with you! *(He realizes she's not coming back.)* Stupid girl! What does she know? Can you imagine me as a father? Forget it. I'm too young. I've got things to do, places to go, people to see. Some day, when I'm fifty maybe, but not now. My life is screwed up enough now as it is. I don't need no kid to complicate matters. Oh yeah, so what if I sniff! I ain't hurting nobody. It's my escape from reality. You're all there thinking, "What a cop out"...right? Well, it ain't no cop out. If you had my life you'd be looking for some way out too. How would you like to have an old man who beats you if you look at him the wrong way, or a mother who's so high on nerve pills she can't tell fantasy from reality? Not exactly the perfect family, huh? Don't people understand? Just look at me! I'm from a welfare home, with only a grade eight education. What chance do I have out there?

(Authority enters and walks to front of stage. Wayne returns to card game.)

AUTHORITY: Well, Wayne never did go to Joe's house. He began to think about Beverly and the baby, and went to a drug and alcohol worker for help. They sent him here for treatment. Here he is—I hope he can learn to help himself.

(Lights fade on Authority and up on continuing card game. Julius interrupts game with another joke.)

JULIUS: You guys wanna hear another joke, eh? I know you do! I know you do! Okay, here goes...what's black and white and red all over?

WAYNE: Your eyeballs.

JULIUS: No stupid, a newspaper. (*Laughs.*)

(Card players shout and stomp their feet. Authority interrupts game.)

AUTHORITY: Stop this foolishness at once! Be quiet every one of you! (*She points at Pauline.*) You over there, come here and tell these people who you are!

Scene 4

(Pauline walks to centre stage. Lights fade out on card game, up on Pauline.)

PAULINE: My name is Pauline. I'm not proud of what happened, but I'll tell you anyways.

(Lights fade on Pauline, lights up on Junior and Olivia, sniffing.)

JUNIOR: This is great, man! Hey, Olivia, how you feelin'? I feel great.

OLIVIA: Yeah, man, this is great! I feel like I'm floatin' on cloud nine!

JUNIOR: Hey, there's someone comin'! Quick! Hide the stuff!

OLIVIA: Huh! Yeah! Give me the stuff!

JUNIOR: It's only two kids. Hey, you! Come over here!

(Pauline enters with Angie.)

PAULINE: What do you want?

OLIVIA: What are you kids doin' out so late?

PAULINE: It's none of your business!

OLIVIA: Oh, big time, eh? Hey, kid, want to have a real good time without leavin' the ground?

ANGIE: No! Leave us alone! Come on, let's get out of here!

PAULINE: Wait, Angie. Hey, how can we have a good time, and with what?

OLIVIA: You kids want to sniff, or what? Gas or glue?

JUNIOR: It makes you feel great!

OLIVIA: Come on, kids, you're a bunch of chickens! (*She clucks.*) Nothin' but sissies!

PAULINE: I'm no chicken!

JUNIOR: (*Offering the bag.*) Well here, try some!

ANGIE: (*Grabbing Pauline.*) No! Don't try any of it!

OLIVIA: Leave her alone!

JUNIOR: You try it, you chicken!

ANGIE: No way, buddy! I'm getting out of here! Are you coming, Pauline?

PAULINE: Leave me alone. I'm staying here. (*She sniffs some gas.*) Oh yeah! This feels great!

ANGIE: Well you can stay if you want, but I'm leaving. I don't want to be any part of this crap!

OLIVIA: Chicken! Mommy's baby! Go back to where you came from, you sissy!

PAULINE: (*Still sniffing.*) Oh man, this is awesome! I've never felt like this before!

OLIVIA: Oh man, this is only the beginnin'. We can really make you fly!

JUNIOR: Hey, kid, we're gettin' out of here. You wanna come or wha'?

(Pauline lies on the ground and laughs continuously.)

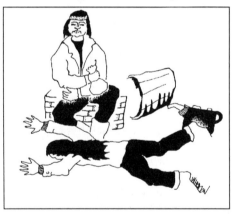

OLIVIA: Do you think she'll be okay? It's her first time tryin' the stuff.

JUNIOR: Yeah, she'll be fine. Let her stay here and enjoy the pleasure of being high, besides, the poor kid looks like she could use a lift.

(Olivia and Junior leave and Pauline is left alone, still sniffing gas. She suddenly realizes that she is all alone and starts to think about her father who beats her mother. Then she begins to act strangely, talking to herself.)

PAULINE: Yeah, man, this is heaven! This is all I need! Who cares about my old man. Damn him! (*She shouts.*) I hate you, you old drunk! He doesn't care about me! Nobody does! My mother is afraid of my father, and they're always fighting. They wouldn't notice if I never came home again. I know what I'll do, I'll sniff until I get so high, I'll never come down!

(She begins to sniff more heavily than before, then blacks out and falls to the ground. At that moment, Angie walks on stage.)

ANGIE: Oh God! I wonder where she is? Damn! I knew I shouldn't have left her alone. If something happens to her, I'll never forgive myself. *(Calling.)* Where are you? Pauline! Pauline! *(She sees Pauline.)* Hey! Wait a minute, there's someone over there. Hey, buddy, wake up! I'm looking for my sister. Have you seen her? She's about fifteen years old. *(She bends over and rolls figure over.)* Pauline! Pauline! It's you! Wake up! Damn! What have they done to you? *(She holds Pauline in arms and begins to cry.)* Oh please, God, don't let my sister die. Pauline, please wake up! You can't leave me alone! Not now!

(Authority hears Angie crying and goes over to her.)

ANGIE: *(Looking up at Authority.)* Please help my sister. She won't wake up!

AUTHORITY: What happened to her?

ANGIE: She was sniffing. I think she had too much!

AUTHORITY: Sniffing? With who?

ANGIE: I don't know. There were two people who had some gasoline and they made Pauline sniff it, but I left to get some help. Is she gonna be all right? Is she gonna die?

AUTHORITY: *(Kneeling down and checking Pauline.)* I think she'll make it. She's still breathing, but she needs to get to the hospital right away. I'll help you!

ANGIE: Thanks. I'm glad you came along. I don't know what would have happened if you hadn't come.

AUTHORITY: *(Standing up and facing audience.)* What happened here was real. We got Pauline to the hospital, and she lived. But what would have happened if she hadn't been found? Dead! Dead as a doornail!

(Lights fade out on scene and up on card game.)

Scene 5

JULIUS: Hey! What about you? How'd you get here?

BERNICE: Same way you did. I sniffed my way here.

WAYNE: You've been here a long time. Ever since I've been here.

BERNICE: Yeah! Eight months and nine days.

JULIUS: So? What did you do?

BERNICE: Just like you, I sniffed. I sniffed a lot. Every chance I got. I sniffed before school, after school and even in school. Oh yeah, once I even did it in the bathroom at school. Everybody thought I was so cool. What a joke! You see, I'm not like you guys.

I'm not even like those other kids who came here a few months ago. I didn't want to die. I'm not from a broken home. You see, people out there have this idea of what a sniffer is, you know, because of the other kids. People think we're useless trouble-makers from broken homes.

JULIUS: What?

BERNICE: Come on! Wake up, you saw the news. We're all sup-posed to be poor, on welfare with no parents. Look! (*Getting up and pointing to the audience.*) See those people! Some of them think that because we have native blood in our veins, we got gasoline running through them too!

WAYNE: So, what makes you so different? What's your story?

BERNICE: I didn't come from a broken welfare home. Daddy works with Hydro and Mummy works with the Labrador Inuit Association. They've been married for years. I got an older sister and two younger brothers. Up until the time I started sniffing I was a straight A student, the top of my class. I got every award for good grades you could imagine.

JULIUS: So, what happened?

BERNICE: Those good grades didn't come easy. I was under a lot of pressure, from my teachers and especially my family. Every time when I came home from school my father would ask me what I learned, and look at my scribblers. Mommy would say how proud she was that I was going to be the first one in the family to go to university. Then Daddy would say how happy he was that I didn't turn out like the other kids, and that I was his favourite. He was really glad that I wasn't like my older sister.

WAYNE: What did your sister do?

BERNICE: She got pregnant when she was fifteen. Mummy and Daddy don't talk about her very much. Mummy told me that when Daddy found out she was pregnant, he hit her, and took his gun to kill her boyfriend. He didn't do it, Mummy stopped him. Daddy sent my sister away to live with Grandma because she brought shame to our family. That was eight years ago, Daddy hasn't spoken to her since.

JULIUS: Hard old man!

BERNICE: When I came along he made sure things would be different. He said an education would give me a good life and respect. He bragged to his friends about me all the time. How good I was! How smart I was! I had no choice. I couldn't let him down. I couldn't disappoint him. Then one night I was out with my friends. One of them had a bag of gas. They teased me and I gave in. Just like that, I was hooked. You know what it's like. That high was so good. I found my way to escape the pressure and it was great!

JULIUS: How'd your parents find out?

BERNICE: Daddy caught me stealing gas from his boat.

WAYNE: What did he do?

BERNICE: He just stared at me. I'll never forget that look on his face. He was so disappointed. Later that night when I went home, my mother and I had a fight. It was awful. She said she loved me and blamed herself for my sniffing. We cried a lot. I told her it wasn't her fault, after that I went to bed. While I was walking up the stairs, I heard something that really scared me—my father was crying. It wasn't too long after that I came here.

JULIUS: Have you talked to your family since you been here?

BERNICE: Just my mother. My daddy is still having problems with all of this.

WAYNE: Was he the one who made you come here?

BERNICE: No! I made me come here. When I heard my father crying, I realized how much pain I had caused. I wasn't only hurting myself, but the people who loved me. You know, that's the great thing about his place, they teach you how to look at yourself, and work out your problems. They really show you there's a way out of this mess.

JULIUS: What are you going to do about your family?

BERNICE: I'll let you know when they take me home tomorrow.
(Card game continues.)

Scene 6

(Authority interrupts game.)

AUTHORITY: *(Points at Bobby)* Well, I see that there's someone else here who has a story to tell. You, come over here and meet these people!
(Bobby walks to front of stage. Lights fade out on Bobby and card game and up on two girls sitting on chairs. They have a radio and mime listening to music on it.)

CONNIE: Good old song, eh?

KATHY: Yeah, but sometimes they sing about ol' weird stuff.

CONNIE: What do you mean?

KATHY: You know, like when they sing about death and hell. That's scary ol' stuff.

CONNIE: I don't like it either. Sometimes when my brother listens to it, he turns it up real loud, then Mommy bawls at him to turn it down. *(They both laugh.)* I guess your mommy is bawling all the time.

KATHY: What?

CONNIE: You know, Bobby listens to it all the time.

KATHY: Not all the time, just sometimes. So what if Mommy bawls? Every mommy does that!

CONNIE: Well, I heard that only sniffers listen to that music.

KATHY: Are you saying that we're sniffers?

CONNIE: No, silly, but that's what they say at school.

KATHY: Who says that?

CONNIE: Margaret and Johnny.

KATHY: Ahh! You can't believe them. They're just saying that because they don't want other people to know they're sniffers.

CONNIE: Well, that's not all I heard.

KATHY: Oh yeah, what else did you hear?

CONNIE: Somebody told me that they saw Bobby down on the old dock sniffing with David in grade twelve.

KATHY: When?

CONNIE: Saturday night.

KATHY: Oh no, he wasn't!

CONNIE: That's what I heard.

KATHY: Well you heard wrong. He doesn't sniff!

CONNIE: So how come he was suspended from school for acting funny in Mr. Butler's class last week?

KATHY: He wasn't suspended, Mommy kept him home from school because he had the flu. Why are you asking so many questions? It's none of your business!

CONNIE: I just asked because you're my friend and I don't want people saying bad things about you.

KATHY: I wish people wouldn't talk. It's not my fault he sniffs. I can't help it.

CONNIE: I know it's not your fault. People at school like to spread rumours.

KATHY: I'd like to spread my hands over their faces.

CONNIE: You might help some people.

(Both laugh.)

KATHY: He makes me mad when he does it.

CONNIE: Why do you think he's at it?

KATHY: Because he wants to be like the popular crowd. Real tough and a big man!

CONNIE: What does your mommy say to him?

KATHY: She gets mad and cries a lot. She said if he doesn't stop it she's going to call social services and get him sent out for help.

CONNIE: Maybe she should do it. It helped those other kids.

KATHY: He says he only done it once. But he's lying, crazy ol' boy.

CONNIE: The crowd he hangs around with are at it all the time.

KATHY: Shhh! I think he's coming. Don't say anything.

(Enter Bobby.)

BOBBY: Well, if it isn't my baby sister and her little friend. What ya doin'...playin' dollies?

KATHY: No, listening to music.

BOBBY: Yeah, the best music. I knew you would start to think like me.

KATHY: Oh no, I won't! I don't ever want to be like you!

BOBBY: Why not? I'm popular, everybody likes me. I've got lots of friends.

CONNIE: You got the wrong kind of friends.

BOBBY: Ahhh! What do you know, silly girl? Play with your dollies and mind your own business.

KATHY: She's right! You should stop hanging around with them, or you'll get in trouble.

BOBBY: What do you know, baby?

KATHY: I know plenty. I know that you been hanging around with a bunch of sniffers, and you've been sniffing too. Everybody in school knows. They've been talking and whispering and laughing at me because I've got a brother who's a walking gas station.

BOBBY: You better shut up or I'll...

KATHY: You'll what? You'll hit me? Sure, big man, go ahead and hit your baby sister. Beat me up to prove to your friends how tough you are.

BOBBY: Shut up, you!

KATHY: Just look at yourself! A real hero! It's no trouble to tell you've been sniffing again. We could smell it as soon as you came through the front door.

BOBBY: Leave me alone!

KATHY: Hey, Connie! You know something? Maybe it's a good thing he sniffs.

CONNIE: What!

KATHY: Yeah, I bet he's sniffed so much gas already we could put him in the front yard, poke a hole in him and pump gas!

BOBBY: Now you're really going to get it!

KATHY: No! Mommy!

(Bobby runs towards Kathy. He tries to grab her, when their mother enters.)

MOTHER: What's going on in here?

KATHY: He tried to beat me up!

MOTHER: Bobby, why?

BOBBY: She was teasin' me!

MOTHER: That's enough you two. I can't take it anymore. Connie, I think maybe you should leave now.

CONNIE: Kathy, I'll call you later, okay?

KATHY: Sure, talk to you later.

(Connie exits.)

MOTHER: I don't know how much more of this I can take. This has got to stop.

KATHY: If he'd stop sniffing we wouldn't have a problem.

BOBBY: Ahh...Be quiet!

MOTHER: Kathy, please be quiet. It doesn't help that you're yelling and teasing.

BOBBY: Yeah!

MOTHER: And you, Bobby, you're a different story.

KATHY: What are you gonna do? Kick him out? You should, Mom! The ol' butt head.

MOTHER: Kathy, stop it! You're no help. Now go to your room!

KATHY: But, Mom!

MOTHER: Now, Kathy! Go!

(Kathy exits.)

BOBBY: So, are you gonna kick me out?

MOTHER: Bobby, I have to do something, and soon. Otherwise you're going to destroy yourself and your family.

BOBBY: Ah, come on, it's not that bad!

MOTHER: Yes, it is that bad, Bobby. I don't know what to do anymore. You're always out late, I don't know where you are, the school is always calling about your behaviour, and your grades are bad. When you do come home, you and your sister are always fighting. Bobby, we used to be so close! What happened?

BOBBY: I'm not a baby anymore! Don't treat me like one!

MOTHER: I just want you to tell me why you're doing it.

BOBBY: Because everyone else is buggin' me. They call me a wimp and a sissy, so I give in and do it. It's no big deal!

MOTHER: It is a big deal! You're slowly killing yourself. Don't you realize those kids are not your friends?

BOBBY: They are my friends! I hang around with them and they treat me like I belong. We go places, and do things.

MOTHER: Well it's stopping here and now. From now on you are not allowed to hang around with those kids anymore, and there'll be no more going out on school nights!

BOBBY: You can't do that!

MOTHER: Yes, I can!

BOBBY: No way, I'll leave this house!

MOTHER: Oh, you'll leave all right. First thing tomorrow morning, you and I are going down to Social Services to make arrangements for you to get into a treatment program, and that's final! I'm not going to take one more minute of this. It's about time you faced your problems.

BOBBY: Mom! No! Please, I'll stop.

MOTHER: No. I've heard it all before. You're going!

*(Mother leaves stage. Lights fade out and Bobby returns
to card game. Spotlight rises on Authority.)*

AUTHORITY: Bobby left home all right. His mother took him to Social Services the next day, and a week later he ended up here. His mother told him not to come back until he got his act together. We hope he gets all the help he needs.

*(Spotlight goes out. Lights up on card game. Card game
continues, everyone laughing and joking. Julius
interrupts with joke.)*

Scene 7

JULIUS: Hey! I thought of another joke. Come on, you guys! Shut up and Listen! Why did the chicken cross the road?

SUSAN: To get to the other side.

JULIUS: Wrong again, stupid, because it was stuck to Wayne's ass! Ha! Ha!

SUSAN: Sick joke!

> *(Authority interrupts card game.)*

AUTHORITY: *(She points at Julius.)* You there, the one telling the jokes, come over here!

JULIUS: Who me?

AUTHORITY: Yes you! Come here and tell everybody out there who you are!

JULIUS: *(Walks to front of stage.)* All right! I will! My name is Julius, and this is my story if you really want to hear it.

> *(Lights fade. Other characters get up from card game and carry their chairs across stage to set up classroom. Bell rings and lights come up on class. The students are talking together.)*

SUSAN: Gee, not much people in class today.

BEVERLY: God, ugly ol' flu! I'm starting to get it. Guess I won't come to class tomorrow.

PAULINE: *(Pantomimes opening window.)* Guess I'll open the window and let some fresh air in. Hey, everybody, look! There's ol' Julius, stoned again.

> *(Everybody crowds at window. Julius staggers around sniffing a bag of gas. Students yell and jeer at him. Authority enters and assumes teacher's role.)*

TEACHER: Please return to your seats! Sit down!

> *(Julius stumbles in.)*

JULIUS: Hi, Teach!

TEACHER: Julius, you're late again. This is the fourth time this week. I have no choice. You have a detention.

JULIUS: Okay, Teach!

> *(Julius trips and slowly sits down, nodding off to sleep. Class giggles.)*

TEACHER: *(Passing out papers.)* Well I'm really disappointed. This is the test you did in social studies last week, and most of you failed. I don't think you studied very hard. You know these results are going to lower your report card marks. The subject we're going to study today is Africa—the tribes, music, climate...Julius! Pay attention! What did I just tell the class?

JULIUS: *(Confused, wakes up.)* Where the hell am I? *(Goes to sleep again.)*

TEACHER: *(To class.)* Calm down. Take it easy. *(She hands Julius his paper.)* Julius!

> *(He balls paper up and throws away. She doesn't see his action as she addresses the class.)*

The rest of you, you're reading page one-hundred-and-twenty. I have to go down to the office and make some photocopies. I'll be back in a few minutes. Behave yourselves and do your work.

> *(Teacher exits. Julius goes back to sleep. Pauline gets up and walks over to him. She starts pulling his hair and making fun of him.)*

PAULINE: Long hair, boy. Looks like a girl! Anybody got any

scissors? I think I'm gonna cut it!
> *(Mary jumps up and goes over to Pauline.)*

MARY: Leave him alone. He doesn't do anything to you!

PAULINE: *(Pushing Mary.)* Oh yeah! Is he your boyfriend or something?

MARY: *(Shoving Pauline. The girls start to fight.)* Bitch!

JULIUS: *(Waking up, disturbed, angry. He gets up and violently grabs girls.)* Stop it! Always fightin'! Always fightin'! Are you crazy, or what?
> *(Rest of class starts to laugh and hoot.)*

JULIUS: *(Losing temper. He kicks over chairs, grabs one and raises it over his head, threatening classmates.)* Assholes! I'll give you somethin' to look at! Good look or wha'! Bunch of assholes!
> *(Teacher enters.)*

TEACHER: Julius, stop! Enough! Put that chair down.
> *(She takes Julius' arm and leads him to front of stage.)*

TEACHER: Come on, Julius.

JULIUS: Damn! Damn! I wish I had my life to live over again.

TEACHER: You can! You can! Hey, look where you are! You're on stage! This is only a play.

JULIUS: *(Shaking his head, he looks around. Recognition appears on his face.)* Hey! I forgot where I was! You mean I'm not brain-dead?

TEACHER: No, you're not!

JULIUS: Hey! Everybody! We're not braindead!
> *(All the cast and crew move out on the stage, slowly moving down-stage, chanting.)*

CAST: We're not braindead!
>   We're not braindead!
>   We're not braindead!
>> *(They shout.)*
>   We're a-l-i-i-v-v-e
>> *(They line up and face audience.)*
>   Thank you for coming to our play!

THE END.

Musical Scores

They Club Seals, Don't They?

1. A Sealer's Reply To His Wife
   Poem by Samuel Solomon, Music by Terry Rielly
   Lyrics supplied by Mrs. Dorothy Cook

2. That's What He Does
   Lyrics and Music by Glen Tilley

3. The Seasons Song
   Lyrics and Music by Glen Tilley

4. Punk Rock Song
   Lyrics by David Ross, Glen Tilley, Terry Rielly
   Music by Terry Rielly

5. Standard of Living Song
   Lyrics by Chris Brookes, Glen Tilley, Terry Rielly, David Ross
   Music by Glen Tilley and Terry Rielly

Transcription by Charlie Barfoot

Notation edited by Wayne Warren

Score published and produced by Sandy Morris

A Sealer's Reply To His Wife

Poem by Samuel Solomon
Lyrics supplied by Mrs. Dorothy Cook Music by Terry Rielly

Now that March month has come,

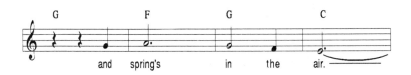

and spring's in the air.

the old seals are swim - ming

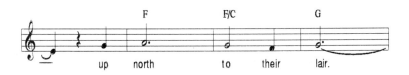

up north to their lair.

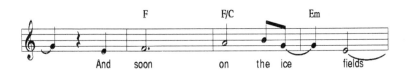

And soon on the ice fields

their young will be strown

A Sealer's Reply To His Wife

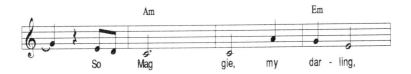

So Mag - gie, my dar - ling,

i must leave _____ you a - lone.

My berth

to the ice, I can -

not turn down. _____ I must

join the o - ther sea - lers, _____ and go

A Sealer's Reply To His Wife

into town ———————— to sign

on a sea - ler ———————— to the ice

fields that go. ——————— So Mag -

gie, my dar - ling, I must leave

you a - lone

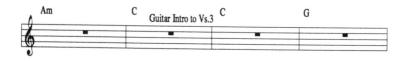

A Sealer's Reply To His Wife

We will soon reach the ice,

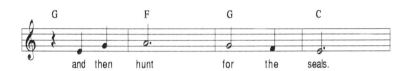

and then hunt for the seals.

I will jump from my ship

as she shi - vers, and she reels

Copy - ing the ice - pans

with my com - rades and so ———

A Sealer's Reply To His Wife

Mag - gie, my dar - ling,

I must leave you a - lone.

The call

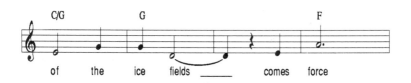

of the ice fields _____ comes force

ful and clear. _____ It makes

me feel rest - less _____ at this

A Sealer's Reply To His Wife

time   of   year. _____   But   when

I'm   too   o - ld _____ to the   ice,

to   be   goin'   then   Mag -

gie,   my   dar - ling,   I'll   not   leave

you   a -   - lone.

That's What He Does

Lyrics and Music by Glen Tilley

There's a

man   on   the   west coast.   He takes his

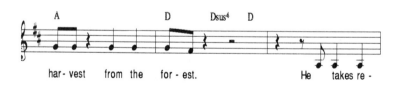

har-vest   from the   for - est.   He   takes re -

spon - sa-bil- i - ty   for what he's   done.

And he   be - li - eves   the trees will

That's What He Does

grow a - gain.   He's a   log - ger,

that's wh - at he   does.

There's   a

The man on the prairie,
He takes his harvest from the wheat fields,
With a little luck he'll reap the seed he's sown,
And he believes the wheat will grow again,
He's a farmer, that's what he does.

There's a man in north Ontario,
He takes his harvest from the trap line,
A native skill he learned when he was young,
And he believes the animals will come again,
He's a trapper, that's what he does.

And there's a man living by the sea,
He takes his harvest from the ice–fields,
He takes responsibility for what he's done,
And he believes the swiles will come again,
He's a sealer, that's what he does.

The Seasons Song (Late In The Spring)

Lyrics and Music by Glen Tilley

Late In The Spring

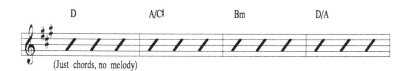

(Just chords, no melody)

Late in the spring when the

ice flows are mel - ting. The

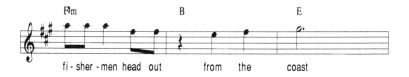

fi - sher - men head out from the coast

Late In The Spring

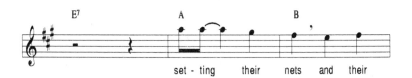

set - ting their nets and their

traps for the sum - mer. Liv - ing a

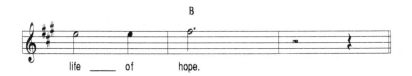

life _____ of hope.

Some years are good ones, the fish, they are

run - nin', and bad years can break a man's

soul. _____ Some boats come back

Late In The Spring

with   fish   to   the   gun - nels.

Some   boats   nev - er   come   home. _____

(Guitars)

Late In The Spring

Late in the fall when the sea - son is

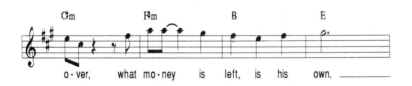

o - ver, what mo - ney is left, is his own. ____

He won - ders if it   will last him till

Late In The Spring

swi - lin', when it's time to go out on the flows. _____

Some years are good ones. Some years are

bad ones. No mat - ter which way it

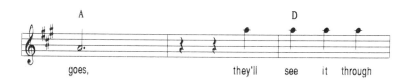

goes, they'll see it through

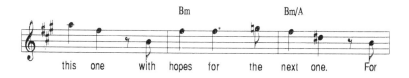

this one with hopes for the next one. For

this is his life and his home.

Punk Rock Song

Lyrics by David Ross, Glen Tilley, Terry Rielly
Music by Terry Rielly

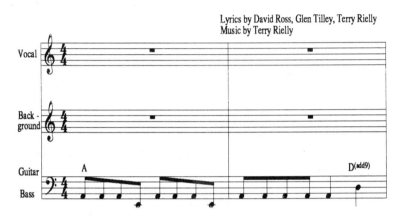

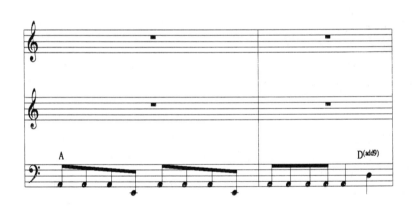

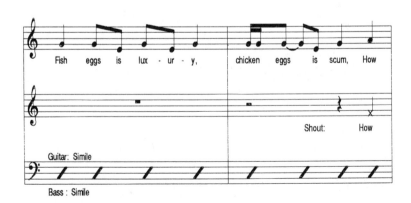

Punk Rock Song

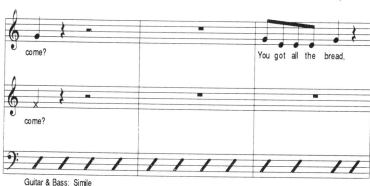

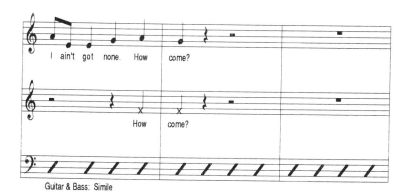

Punk Rock Song

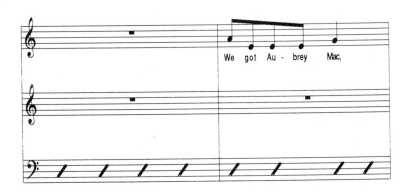

We got Au - brey Mac,

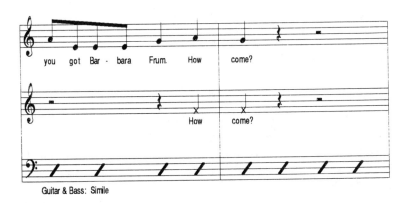

you got Bar - bara Frum. How come?

How come?

Guitar & Bass: Simile

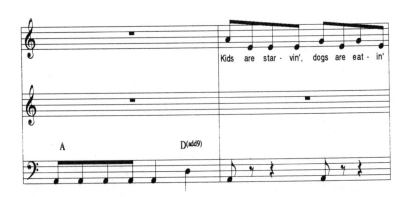

Kids are star - vin', dogs are eat - in'

Punk Rock Song

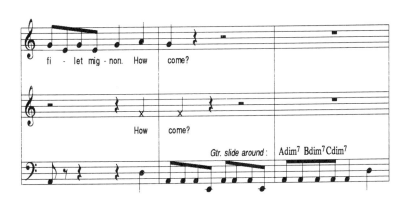

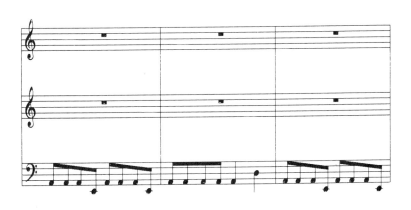

Punk Rock Song

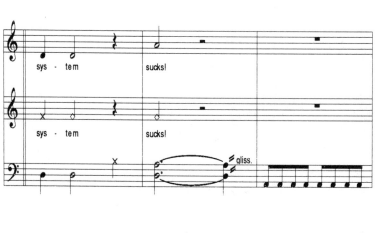

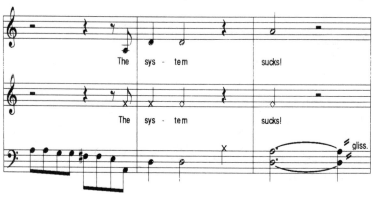

Punk Rock Song

Punk Rock Song

Qua - dra - phon - ic ster- e - o

ster - e -

chan - nel co - man - der co - lour T. - V.

o

T. - V.

And your re - frid - ger - a - tor, ba - by, Is

Punk Rock Song

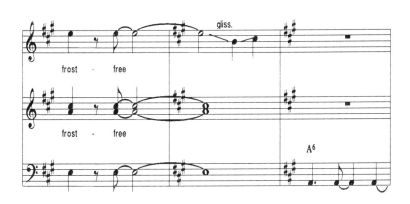

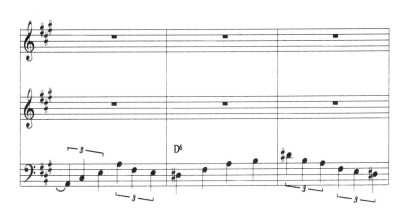

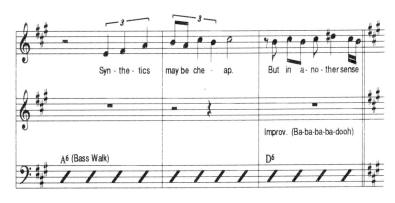

Punk Rock Song

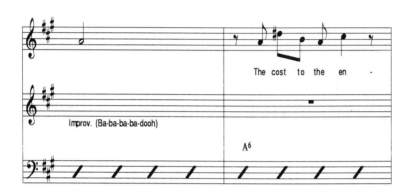

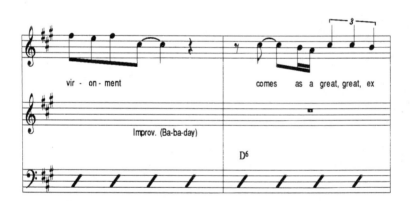

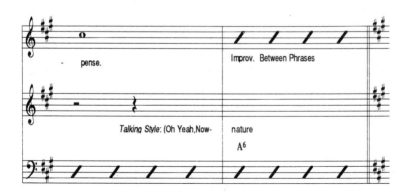

Punk Rock Song

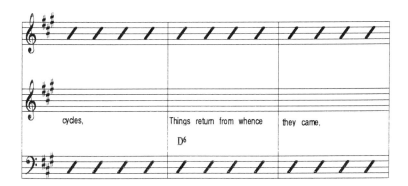

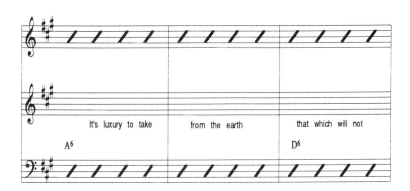

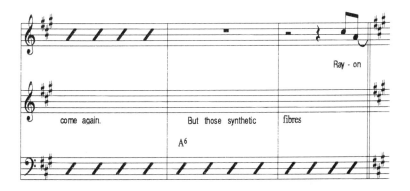

Punk Rock Song

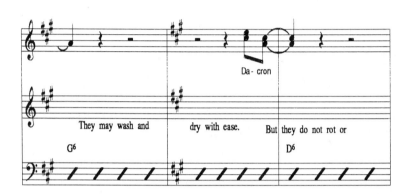

Punk Rock Song

Stars in the Sky Morning

Punk Rock Song

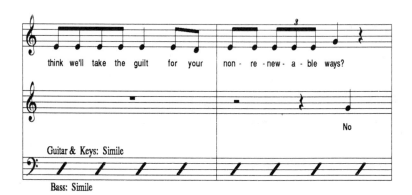

think we'll take the guilt for your non - re - new - a - ble ways?

No

Guitar & Keys: Simile

Bass: Simile

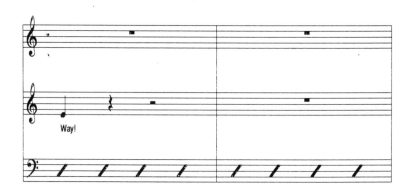

Way!

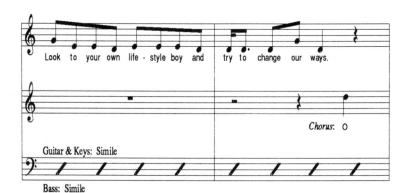

Look to your own life - style boy and try to change our ways.

Chorus: O

Guitar & Keys: Simile

Bass: Simile

Punk Rock Song

Punk Rock Song

Standard of Living Song

Lyrics by Chris Brookes, Glen Tilley, Terry Rielly, David Ross
Music by Glen Tilley and Terry Rielly

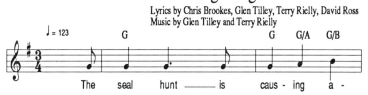

The seal hunt ——— is caus - ing a -

lot of up - set. And how ——— am

I ——— to feel, _____ when

I ——— am told, it's a ter - ri - ble

thing. This kil - ling of the ——

seals. _____

Standard of Living Song

They say it is right to be

sav - in' the seals But ex - am - ine the faults.

For you say how you feel ____ so -

lu - tions are sim - ple. When you don't pay the cost,

but it's some - bod - y's live - ly - hood

you're wri - ting off. Who pays the

Standard of Living Song

price,   do you   know   who   pays.   For your

comf - 'ter - ble   cu - shions   and   af - flu - ent

ways.   Who   pays   the   pi - per   that's

sing - ing   your   song.   Who   owns   the

hog   that   your   liv - in'   high   on.

You   see

Standard of Living Song

a - ni - mals killed, we say we can't

stand, but we're ea - tin' pork - chops all

o - ver this land. It's ea - sy to

judge when we're one step re - moved, and we

don't have to walk in a - no - ther man's

shoes. Who pays the price? Do you

Standard of Living Song

know   who   pays,   for your   comf - 'ter - ble

cu - shions,   and   af - flu - ent   ways.

Who   pays   the   pi - per   that's   sing - ing   your

song.   Who owns   the   hog   that you're

liv - in'   high   on.

Jaxxmas

1. The Buckaroo Song
   Words and Music by Sheila's Brush

2. The Portugese Waltz
   Traditional
   From the collection of Art Stoyles

Transcription by Geoff Panting

Score published and produced by Sandy Morris

The Buckaroo Song

The Buckaroo Song

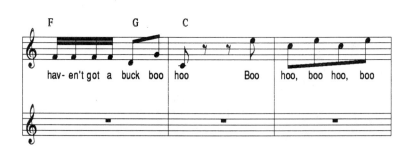

The Buckaroo Song

The Buckaroo Song

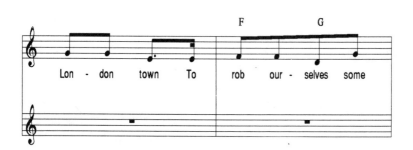

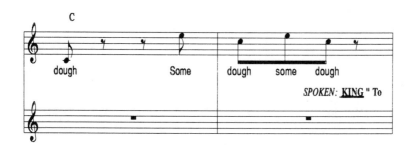

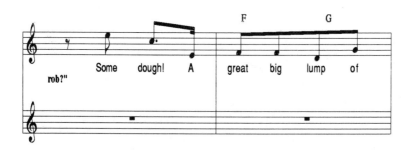

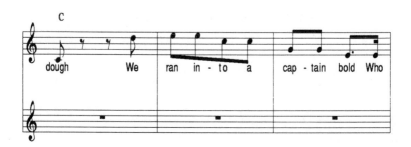

The Buckaroo Song

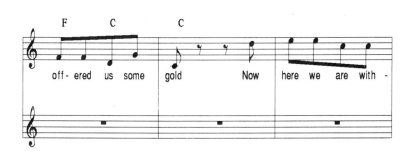

The Buckaroo Song

The Buckaroo Song

Portugese Waltz

Traditional
From the collection of Art Stoyles

Portugese Waltz

Portugese Waltz

Portugese Waltz

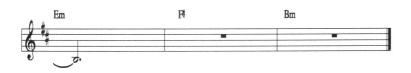

Terras de Bacalhau

1. Overture/ The Portugese Waltzes
   Traditional
   From the collecton of Art Stoyles

2. Crossing The Sea
   Traditional
   Adapted and arranged by Jim Payne

3. Only A Fisherman
   Lyrics by Greg Thomey and Jim Payne
   Music by Jim Payne

4. Go To Sea No More
   Traditional
   Adapted and arranged by Jim Payne

5. Blood Is Thicker Than Water
   Lyrics by cast
   Music by Jim Payne

6. San Joao
   Traditional Portugese folk song
   Adapted and arranged by John Koop

7. Quando os Outros te Batem
   Traditional Portugese folk song
   Adapted and arranged by Jim Payne

8. Soup of Sorrow
   Lyrics by Greg Thomey and Jim Payne
   Music by Jim Payne

9. Saltwater Charly
   Lyrics by Janis Spence and Jim Payne
   Music by Jim Payne

10. O Mar Enrola na Areia
    Traditional Portugese folk song
    Adapted and arranged by Jim Payne

Transcription by Jim Payne

Notation edited by Wayne Warren

Additional transcription by Wayne Warren

Score published and produced by Sandy Morris

Overture
(Portugese Waltzes)

Traditional
From the collection of Art Stoyles

Stars in the Sky Morning

Overture

Overture

Overture

Crossing The Sea

Traditional
Adapted and arranged by Jim Payne

Stars in the Sky Morning

Crossing The Sea

Only A Fisherman

Lyrics by Greg Thomey and Jim Payne
Music by Jim Payne

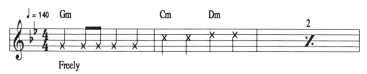

I'm on - ly a fi - sher - man, ___ and I ___ do ___

what ev - er I can, don't like to

take from my bro - thers and sis - ters, Who are ___

just as poor as I am. Yeah, _____ when mo - ther

Stars in the Sky Morning

Only A Fisherman

Por - tu - gal was a great power,

We left our home - land to die by the hour,

In some for - eign land,

we'd take what we can, Leave no - thing for the

peo - ple. We in - curred the wrath of

Jah, When we plun - dered E - thi - o - pi - a, ___

Only A Fisherman

Bul - lets flew a - gainst the wall,

We marched in and took it __ all, But Jah said co -

lo - ni - al - is - m must fall.

I'm on - ly a fi - sher - man, and I do

what - ev - er I can, Don't like to

take from my brothers and sis - ters, Who are ____

Only A Fisherman

just   as   poor   as   I   am.   Yeah,   I'm

on - ly   a   fi - sher - man,   I   take   my   liv - ing   from the sea,

We _____ catch the fish,   one   man   chop   their

head off,   then in - side   what you got,   split   the back - bone,

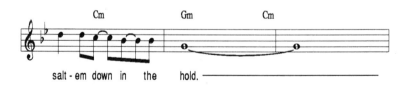

salt - em down in   the   hold.

In   In -   di - a,   in

Only A Fisherman

Gui - ne- a   Ca - bo Ver - de

We   were   mas - ters   there   and   we   were

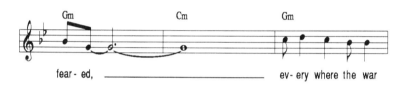

fear - ed,   ev- ery   where the war

plan   was   tried,   but   like   Mo - zam - bique,   the

peo- ple's   spir - it   nev - er   died,   'cause they

cried   out,   they said no,   no

Stars in the Sky Morning

Only A Fisherman

no   to   your   pri - sons,

no,   no,   no   to ex - ploi - ta - tion, ————

no   more   will I   be your   slave,

no more go   to ear - ly grave, said no,   no no

no,   to op - pres - sion.

Only A Fisherman

We finally left Angola alone.
Now they are masters of their own home.
Much to the dictator's dismay,
The people's revolution had its day.

VERSE

There's still bad blood in Brazil.
People there have had their fill.
Still many tears, still much pain,
People there are still in chains.
Workin', workin', workin' for the rich man.

1st. CHORUS

Portugal was fascisto for years,
People shed their tears for freedom,
For a better way, they had their say,
Like Mozambique, like Angola, they cried out.

CHORUS

They said, "No, no, no, no, to your prisons."
They said, "No, no, no, no, to exploitation."
They said, "No more I'll be your black slave.
No more go to early grave.
They said, "No, no, no, to oppression."

Go To Sea No More

Traditional
Adapted and arranged by Jim Payne

Well they shipped me a - board of a

fish - ing barque bound for North At - lan - tic

seas,   Where cold winds blow through

ice and snow and Ja - mai - can rum would

freeze,   And worse to tell we'd a

hard wea - ther spell,   I thought I was gone for

Go To Sea No More

sure. A man must be blind to

make up his mind, to go to sea once

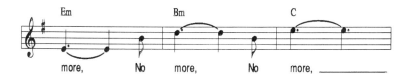

more, No more, No more, _____

Go to sea no more. A

man must be blind to make up his mind, to

go to sea once more.

Go To Sea No More

Some days, boys, we got lots of fish,
More days, boys, we got none.
With haulin' nets and settin' trawls
From four o' clock in the morn,
And then you see the night come on,
And your back is getting sore,
'Tis then you wish that you were dead
And could go to sea no more.

Chorus: No more, me boys, no more, go to sea no more,
'Tis then you wish that you were dead
And could go to sea no more,

So come all you hard living sailor men
And listen to me song,
When you come off of that long sea trip,
I'll have you not go wrong.
Take my advice drink no strong drink,
Don't go sleeping with no whore,
Get married instead, spend all night in bed,
And go to sea no more.

Chorus: No more, no more, go to sea no more,
Get married instead, spend all night in bed,
And go to sea no more.

Blood Is Thicker Than Water

Lyrics by Cast
Music by Jim Payne

Verse

Ma - ma   said   Dad - dy   was   a   sail - or.

From   some - where   a - cross   the deep blue

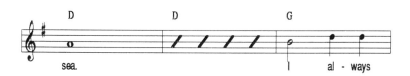

sea.   I   al - ways

Blood Is Thicker Than Water

longed to see my Dad - dy, _____ I

won - der if Dad- dy longed for me. _____

Chorus

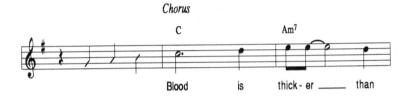

Blood is thick- er _____ than

wa - ter, _____ That's what my

Ma - ma said to me,

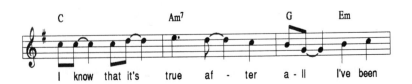

I know that it's true af - ter a - ll I've been

Blood Is Thicker Than Water

through,   Cause Ma- ma nev - er   lied _____ to

me._____

At fifteen I was hitting all the nightspots,
Looking for a daddy in each man,
And then one night alone down at the Stardust,
A young boy gently offered me his hand.

"Pareces uma flora de Portugal,"
His big brown eyes begged me to understand,
And when he asked to sit down at my table,
I knew I'd met a different kind of man.

We strolled down the steps to the Concorde,
And danced 'til 'bout a quarter after three,
He said I'm leavin' in the morning,
So won't you please spend the night with me.

We took a taxi to the south side,
I could see the tears in his eyes,
And as that ship sailed slowly through the Narrows,
I knew our love would never die.

For fifty days and fifty lonely nights,
I dreamed about my dark–haired sailor boy,
Then one sunny day in mid–October,
The sea returned to me my only joy.

CHORUS

Blood Is Thicker Than Water

I couldn't wait to take him home to Momma,
Up over Barter's Hill we both ran,
Momma stood there speechless staring at him,
She wanted me to name that sailor man.

"Miguel Manuel Aveiro is his name, Mom"
A troubled look crept into her bright eyes
"Daughter, there is something I must tell you,
That you should know about your sailor boy."

Chorus: "Blood is thicker than water,"
That's what my momma said to me,
And I know that it's true after all I been through,
'Cause Momma never lied to me.

SPOKEN
"That boy is your own half–brother,"
Were the very words my momma spoke to me,
No wonder that you both love each other,
But married you and him can never be.

Momma said Daddy was a sailor,
From somewhere across the deep blue sea,
I never knew a thing about my daddy,
But now I know he was a Portugee.

Chorus: "Blood is thicker than water,"
That's what my momma said to me,
And I know that it's true after all I been through,
'Cause Momma never lied to me.
And I know that it's true after all I been through,
'Cause Momma never lied to me.

San Joao

Traditional Portugese Folk Song
Adapted and arranged by John Koop

Foi no por - to de Saint John's, Que

con - he - ci u - ma me - ni - na, _____

Que se cha - ma - va An - drei - a, _____

Que se tour - na - va _____ coi - sa fi -

na, _____ En - tao eu dis - se

An - drei - a quer - i - da, E - u te quer o a -

San Joao

Quando os Outros te Batem

Traditional Portugese Folk Song
Adapted by Jim Payne

Guitar Intro.

Se bem que nao me

vis - ta fos-tem-bor - a _____ E_

tu - do que in - ter-san - te me es que coeu _____

Com mui-to eo me-o gri - to des-te a-

gor - a _____ Quan-do os out-ros

te ba - tem bei-jo tao. _____

Quando os Outros te Batem

Se bem que as minhas modicoes fugiste
Por ti hei–de dar tudo que ile moeu
Com muito eo meo grito de agora deste
Quandos os outros te batem beijo tao.

Mas ha de viro dia que eu saudade
Que lembra que em porti je se perdeu
O fado quando triste qui averdade
Quandos os outros te batem beijo tao.

Soup of Sorrow

Lyrics by Greg Thomey and Jim Payne
Music by Jim Payne

(Guitar Intro.)

I'm a

lost man, I'm a dead man drift- in in the fog, with the

soup of sor - row cour - sing through my

ve - ins, Bound to the banks,

Bound to the sea, I'm bound to this cold and mis- er -

Soup of Sorrow

y. _____ I'm a

lean man, I'm a strong man, haul - in in the nets, with the

soup of sor - row cour - sing through my

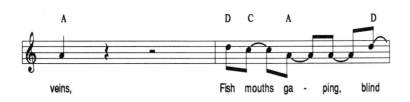

veins, Fish mouths ga - ping, blind

eyes star - ing, the vir - gin rocks are sing - ing in my

brains. _____ All night long, dream

Soup of Sorrow

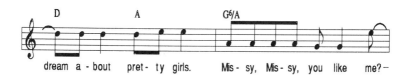

dream a - bout pret - ty girls. Mis - sy, Mis - sy, you like me? —

I love you! (Guitar Melody)

I'm a

work- er, I'm a do - er, fil - lin' up the hold, with the

soup of sor - row cours - ing through my veins,

Soup of Sorrow

Day in, day out, it nev - er ends. —

Split me, gut me, 'fore I go in -

sane.

All night long, All night long,

All night long, All night long,

All night long, dream a - bout pret - ty girls.

Soup of Sorrow

I'm a ladies' man, a gentleman, I want my share of loving
With the soup of sorrow coursing through my veins,
But my hands are rough, skin cracked and raw,
It's freezing and my hands will never thaw.

I'm a killer, I'm a hunter, like my father long ago
With the soup of sorrow coursing through his veins,
The codfish moan, down in the hold,
My father's sins are floating in my soup bowl.
All night long, I dream about pretty girls,
Missy, missy, you like me? I love you!

Soup of Sorrow

I'm a worker, I'm a doer, I'm filling up the hold,
With the soup of sorrow coursing through my veins,
Day in, day out, it never fills,
Split me, gut me, 'fore I go insane.

All night long, all night long,
All night long, all night long,
All night long I dream about pretty girls,
All night long I dream about pretty girls,
All night long I dream about pretty girls,
Missy, missy, You like me? I love you!

I'm a dead man, I'm a lost man, I'll never make it home,
'Cause the soup of sorrow is a curse from God,
We eat it now, they ate it then,
We'll never end the search for this goddamn cod.
All night long, I dream about pretty girls,
Missy, missy, you like me? I love you!

Saltwater Charly

Lyrics by Janis Spence and Jim Payne
Music by Jim Payne

She was   on – ly   a   salt – wa – ter

Char – ly,   But   a   queen   to   the

Saltwater Charly

Por - - tu - guese. _____ In a

dress of chif- fon_____ and a glass of John

Bar - ley, She dreamt of a life_____ of

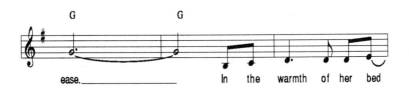

ease._____ In the warmth of her bed

in the dark of night, _____ she'd hold –

them and kiss them and cry. _____

Saltwater Charly

Car - los   Man - uel,   Fran -

ces - co Mi - guel,   I   need   you,   don't   leave

me,   I'll   die._____   I'll   mar - ry   Mi -

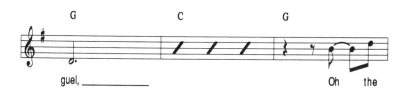

guel,_____   Oh   the

lies   that he'd   tell,_____   as   he   held -

me   and called   me   his   own,_____   He

Saltwater Charly

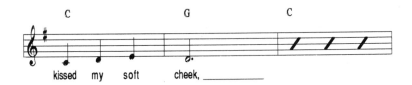

kissed　　my　　soft　　cheek, _____

Oh　　the　　words　　he would　　speak, _____

Mi　　a - mor - e,　　Mi　　a - mor - e ——

he'd　　　　moan.

Saltwater Charly

She was only a finger pier girl,
But a lady to the boys at the bar,
With a twirl and a turn, she'd dance and she'd yearn,
For her sailor to take her afar.

I'll marry Luis, oh, the sweet dreams of peace,
As he gently caressed my brown hair,
My gown is all ready, is your arm steady?
His answer dispelled my despair.

When the piers of the harbour are empty,
No velvet-eyed boys at the Dust,
She'd squat down to Cross's, forgetting her losses
With men who knew nothing but lust.

I'll marry José, he'll take me away,
To Coimbra, Lisboa, Oporto,
And the scent of red roses, sand warm 'neath my feet,
We'll drift till the red sun sinks low.

She was only a Saltwater Charly,
But a queen to the Portuguese,
In a dress of chiffon and a glass of John Barley,
She dreamt of a life of ease.

O Mar Enrola na Areia

Traditional Portugese Folk Song
Adapted and arranged by Jim Payne

O mar en - ro - la na a - re - ia, ____

Nin - guem sa - be o que ele diz, ____

Bate na a - re - ia des - mai - a,

Por - que se sen - te fe - li - z. ____

O mar tam - bem e ca - sa - do

ai   O mar tam - bem   fil - hin -

O Mar Enrola na Areia

os E ca - sa - do com a -

rei - a ai Os fil - hos sao os peix - hin - os

VERSE
O mar também é casado, ai,
O mar também tem mulher
É casado com a areia, ai
Bate nela quando quere.
O mar enrola na areia
Ninguém sabe o que ele diz
Bate na areia e desmaia
Porque se sente feliz.

Makin' Time With The Yanks

1. Makin' Time With The Yanks
   Words and Music by Brian Downey

2. You Never Said Wait For Me
   Words by Jane Dingle
   Music by Paul Steffler

3. Operator
   Words and Music by Paul Steffler

4. Temptation
   Words by Jane Dingle
   Music by Paul Steffler

5. Finale
   Words by Janis Spence
   Music by Paul Steffler

Score published and produced by Sandy Morris

Makin Time With The Yanks

Boogie Swing

Words and Music by Brian Downey

(Lights up)

(Upper harmony optional)

Ho - ly moth - er church says don't dance in Lent

Makin' Time With The Yanks

That's the kind of rule that's meant to be bent the

Yanks got the moo-lah that's got to be spent

State - side is gone but this burg is sent Mak - in'

Makin' Time With The Yanks

Makin' Time With The Yanks

Makin' Time With The Yanks

Makin' Time With The Yanks

Makin' Time With The Yanks

Makin' time with the Yanks,
I'm glad they're here.
Makin' time with the Yanks,
Year after year.
Makin' time with the Yanks,
A ninety-nine year lease.
Are there more? Will they come?
Will their jeeps need more grease?

You Never Said Wait For Me

Music Paul Steffler
Words Jane Dingle

You Never Said Wait For Me

Stars in the Sky Morning

You Never Said Wait For Me

die ____ The clock on the

wall will tick off the hours 'til you're

safe in my arms a gain

You Never Said Wait For Me

Stars in the Sky Morning

You Never Said Wait For Me

You Never Said Wait For Me

You never said, "Wait for me,"
As you climbed on that midnight train.
How I hoped, how I prayed, that you'd come home to me
To a cottage in a country lane.
Oh, darling, it's hard to stay home alone,
Waiting till God knows when,
So write me a letter and send all your love,
'Cause this town is crawling with men.

Operator

Words and Music by Paul Steffler

Lines are bus - y the wires are crossed All the lights are flash - ing and my

Operator

mem - 'ry is lost The calls just keep on com - ing and my

arms are get- ting weak I've said so man - y "Bus - y sirs!" that

I can hard - ly speak It's a bat - tle that is nev - er won

Operator

I'll be so hap-py when the shift is done

1.-3.

Fade under patter

Operator

Operator, please hang on,
I know you must be lonely working midnight to dawn,
Your "number please" is charming,
And I love your sweet "Hello,"
But I've had enough long distance, let's get on with the show.
Operator, put me on your line,
And we could have a real fine time.

Sorry, soldier, I can't quite hear,
My supervisor's standing with her face in my ear,
I know you need assistance but you'll just have to wait,
So call again tomorrow and we'll fix up a date,
Sorry, soldier, gotta end this call,
But tomorrow night we'll have a ball.

Temptation

Music Paul Steffler
Words Jane Dingle

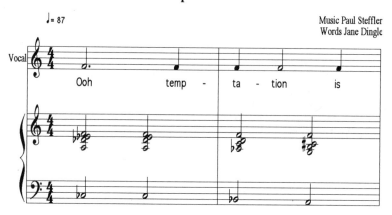

Ooh   temp - ta - tion   is

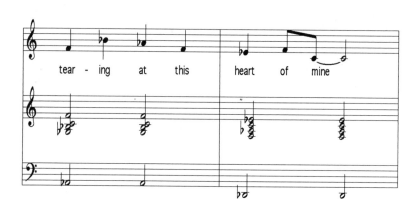

tear - ing   at   this   heart   of   mine

Can't you hear   me   cry - ing   in   the

Temptation

Temptation

How can I keep wait- ing when I long to have you home Babe to

Temptation

Temptation

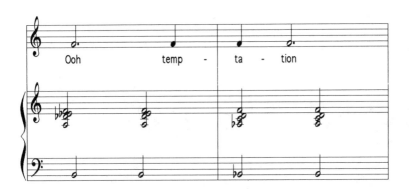

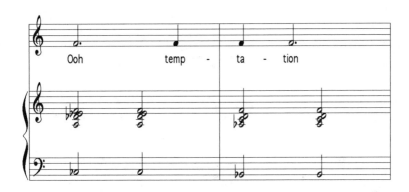

Temptation

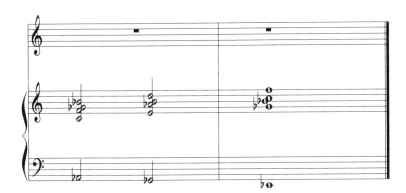

Finale

Finale

When pop was beer and

stock - ings on - ly paint - ed lines on

shape - ly legs of work - ing girls who

Finale

Finale

Finale

Finale

Stars in the Sky Morning

Finale

Finale

Coda

Oh yes weren't we the luck - i -est peo - ple in

all the whole wide world

Girl 2:
Those days are only memories,
Sad sweet strains of song.
Sisters married stateside, we didn't hear 'fore long
From Pennsylvania, Akron, Dallas or Tucson.

Boy 2:
Those faces now are fading,
Only snapshots to recall
Those boys and girls whose bright brave smiles
Said live and fight, no backward glance,
They'll say we had a ball.